BLUE GUIDE

LOMBARDY, MILAN & THE ITALIAN LAKES

ALTA MACADAM
& ANNABEL BARBER

SOMERSET • LONDON

CONTENTS

MAPS & PLANS

First edition 2019

Published by Blue Guides Limited, a Somerset Books Company
Winchester House, Deane Gate Avenue, Taunton, Somerset TA1 2UH
www.blueguides.com
'Blue Guide' is a registered trademark.

ISBN 978–1–905131–83–9

A CIP catalogue record of this book is available from the British Library.

Distributed in the United States of America by
W.W. Norton & Company, Inc.
500 Fifth Avenue, New York, NY 10110.

The authors and publisher have made reasonable efforts to ensure the accuracy
of all the information in *Blue Guide Lombardy*; however, they can accept no responsibility
for any loss, injury or inconvenience sustained by any traveller as a result of
information or advice contained in the guide.

Statement of editorial independence: Blue Guides, their authors and editors,
are prohibited from accepting any payment from any restaurant, hotel, gallery
or other establishment for its inclusion in this guide, or for a more favourable
mention than would otherwise have been made.

Your views on this book would be much appreciated. We welcome not only specific
comments, suggestions or corrections, but any more general views you may have: how
this book enhanced your visit, how it could have been more helpful. Blue Guides authors
and editorial and production team work hard to bring you what we hope are the best-
researched and best-presented cultural guide books in the English language. Please
write to us by email (editorial@blueguides.com), via the comments page on our website
(*blueguides.com*) or at the address given above. We will be happy to acknowledge useful
contributions in the next edition, and to offer a free copy of one of our titles.

Cover: Colleoni Chapel, Bergamo, by Michael Mansell & Gabriella Juhász © Blue Guides.
Frontispiece: The Iron Crown of Lombardy.
© Museo e Tesoro del Duomo di Monza/photo Raffaello Brà.

Maps: Dimap Bt. and Blue Guides
Floor plans: Imre Bába
Architectural line drawings: Michael Mansell RIBA & Gabriella Juhász
All maps, plans and drawings © Blue Guides.
Photographs by James Howells (pp. 205, 207, 286, 296, 317, 319);
© Museo e Tesoro del Duomo di Monza/photo Raffaello Brà (p. 131); © Museo e Tesoro del
Duomo di Monza/photo Piero Pozzi (p. 127). All other photographs © Blue Guides.

All material prepared for press by Anikó Kuzmich.

Every effort has been made to contact the copyright owners of material reproduced in this
guide. We would be pleased to hear from any copyright owners we have been unable to reach.

Alta Macadam would like to thank the official tourist offices of Lombardy,
who were ready to give assistance (Alessandra Pitocchi in Bergamo was especially kind).
Peter Assmann and James Bradburne, directors of (respectively) Palazzo Ducale in Mantua
and the Brera in Milan, went out of their way to be helpful. Particular thanks also to
Stella Romoli for her advice on where to eat in Milan, to Sasha Slater for her contribution
on fashion, and to Giovanni Colacicchi for his insight on literary subjects.
Grateful thanks from Annabel Barber to the staff of the Museo del Duomo in Monza,
as well as to Paola Pugsley for contributions to the Brescia chapter;
and to Emma Kenedi and Dr Walther Scholl for their help in decoding medieval Latin.

Printed in Hungary by Dürer Nyomda Kft., Gyula.

Alta Macadam has been a writer of Blue Guides since 1970 and some 50 titles have come out under her authorship since then. She lives in Florence with her husband, the painter Francesco Colacicchi. As author of the Blue Guides to Rome, Venice, Florence, Venice and the Veneto, Emilia Romagna, Friuli-Venezia Giulia, Central Italy, Tuscany and Umbria, she travels every year to revise new editions of the books. She returns to visit all the places described, as she has learnt that nothing can be taken for granted between one edition and the next, and every time she gains new inspiration from seeing and studying the wonderful patrimony of Italy. She also enjoys writing regularly for the Blue Guide website. In the past she has worked for the Photo Library of Alinari and for Harvard University's Villa I Tatti, and is at present external consultant for New York University at the Photo Archive of Villa La Pietra in Florence.

Annabel Barber is the series editor of the Blue Guides. She is the author of *Blue Guide Budapest* (where she lives and works) and also author and co-author of a number of Blue Guide titles on Rome.

Introduction &
History of Lombardy

Lombardy, with Milan as its capital, has played an important part in the making of Italy. The region includes areas of remarkable diversity, extending as it does from the summits of the central Alps to the low-lying, fertile plain of the Po river. Lombardy takes its name from the Lombards (or Langobards, so named from their long beards), a Germanic tribe who arrived in Italy, via modern-day Hungary, in the 6th century. Over the centuries they adopted the Latin language and the Roman Catholic religion and established their capital at Pavia.

Apart from the great city of Milan, Lombardy has many other towns and cities of beauty and interest: Brescia, Bergamo, Cremona and Mantua being just some of the many. It is also home to Italy's great lakes: Lake Como, Lake Maggiore (which it shares with the region of Piedmont) and Lake Garda (shared with the Veneto).

HISTORY OF LOMBARDY

In 1611, an English traveller, Thomas Coryate, climbed up the tower of the great Gothic cathedral in Milan and surveyed the land around him. 'The territory of Lombardy, which I contemplated round about from this tower, was so pleasant an object to mine eyes, being replenished with such unspeakable variety of all things, both from profit and pleasure, that it seemeth to me to be the very Elysian fields...' Lombardy, with the River Po flowing through it, is the richest region of Italy and this fact has conditioned its history. Its fertility was always the focus of attention, often from outsiders, whether they were lured across the Alps, whether they captured it from the south or, in the case of the Spanish and Austrians, whether they ruled it as a dependent kingdom. Its capital, Milan, came to see itself as the 'moral' capital of Italy, upright and hardworking in comparison with decadent Rome to the south—and to this day, Milan remains a centre of entrepreneurial initiative and achievement. Recently it has also been a magnet for Italy's foreign-born population.

The Po Valley is a natural depression in the earth's surface. Many thousands of years ago, it was filled with water from the Adriatic. Now dry, it is nevertheless well irrigated by the streams and rivers flowing down from the Alps. Evidence of human habitation can be found from nearly 800,000 years ago but the first named peoples of the central valley are Celtic, notably the Insubres, who had moved over the Alps by 400 BC. Inevitably they later came up against the expanding power of Rome. Rome was determined to control northern Italy after Hannibal had invaded from Spain and found many Celts ready to join him. By 194 BC the Insubres were subdued and the region was incorporated into the emerging Roman empire as Cisalpine Gaul (the part of Gaul south of the Alps). All its inhabitants were given Roman citizenship in 49 BC and the province was formally transferred (from Gaul) into Roman Italy in 42 BC. Its capital was Mediolanum, 'the middle of the plain', the modern Milan, strategically placed between the Alpine passes and the river Po. The Celts had seen its importance as a settlement and the Romans made it the capital of the region.

With the region now totally secure, its prosperity was assured. The river Po always offered a thoroughfare from west to east and a large network of roads (the Via Postumia and Via Æmilia) accompanied it and connected the region with Rome along the Via Flaminia. The land was drained, large quantities of grain were produced, and in the foothills of the Alps there was excellent grazing for sheep. The lakes of Como and Garda became favourite resorts of the leisured classes—we have a fine description of his two villas on the shores of lake Como by Pliny the Younger, who was born there.

By the 3rd century AD, all this prosperity was threatened as barbarian tribes sent raiding parties across the Alps. In 286 the emperor Diocletian made Mediolanum one of the four new capitals of the Empire, one from which the northern borders could be defended more effectively than from Rome. Fragments still exist of the new city walls that enclosed some 100 hectares. Mediolanum went on to play a prominent part in early Christian history. In AD 313, the emperor Constantine issued the Edict of Milan, which gave toleration to all religions including, for the first time, Christianity. In 374, a formidable new bishop, Ambrose, was appointed and over the next 23 years he championed the Nicene Trinity as orthodox Christian doctrine, at a time when furious debates still raged about the nature of Christ. Ambrose's body still lies in the basilica of Sant'Ambrogio, alongside two earlier martyrs, Protase and Gervase. Among Ambrose's many converts was Augustine, the city orator and later the most prominent theologian in western Christianity. Indeed, Ambrose's influence pervades the city so powerfully that his feast day, 7th December, is still the opening date of the opera season. The archbishops of Milan remained strong figures, in effect ruling the city as late as 1100 and earning the city the title of 'the Second Rome'.

After the fall of the Western Empire (476), there was a brief period of stability in the area under the Ostrogothic ruler Theodoric, who administered his kingdom through Roman civil servants, but by the middle of the 6th century there was total collapse. Only recently a fabulous cache of Roman gold coins was found, concealed from the chaos, at a building site in Como. Into the vacuum a new people moved across the Alps from territory they had occupied in what is now Hungary. These people were the Lombards, and the region still bears their name today. At first they were disorganised, but gradually emerged as a society headed by dukes, over 30 of them, who held the most important centres. Milan fell to them in 569. Other Lombard strongholds were Brescia and Bergamo but eventually, as their society was consolidated, Pavia, closer to the Po river, became their capital. The Lombards were Christians, eventually adapting their faith to the orthodox Christianity of the popes, and their organisation of the land included large estates and monasteries, which brought the Po Valley back into order. Well-built churches in Brescia (San Salvatore) and Bergamo show that building skills survived. Yet despite a number of strong individual kings (notably Liutprand, r. 712–44), the power of the local dukes was retained, which made the kingdom vulnerable to Charlemagne when he invaded northern Italy in 773 at the behest of a pope (Hadrian I) who feared further Lombard expansion. Pavia fell in 774 and Charlemagne seized the Iron Crown of Lombardy (still preserved at Monza; *see p. 130*). In 800 he was crowned in Rome as the first Holy Roman Emperor, and his successors claimed suzerainty over the former Lombard possessions, a claim that was to frustrate the politics of the area for centuries.

From 1100 the region started to recover its wealth and although the cities—Milan, Cremona, Como, Pavia and Brescia—began to assert their independence from the emperors, this largely led to infighting for control of territory. This disunity left them open to exploitation when Como invited emperor Frederick Barbarossa to side with the city against its enemies. Frederick embarked on a series of invasions lasting over 20 years (1154–76) before a 'Lombard League' of leading cities decisively defeated him at Legnano, close to Milan. The Peace of Constance (1183) recognised the freedom of the Lombard cities, even though technically they remained feudal subjects of the emperors. Freedom, however, did not necessarily mean peace. For the next 350 years the cities of Lombardy were consumed by their own factional struggles, between Guelphs (supporters of the pope) and Ghibellines (supporters of the emperors), between rival families and with each other. Most cities developed commune governments, in which there was (limited) public participation under ruling magistrates. These governments were often unstable and—once again—vulnerable to takeover by ambitious outsiders. Yet the region's trading networks spread wide: Lombard Street in the City of London is a reminder of land granted to Lombard goldsmiths in the 13th century.

In Milan, the leading family was the Ghibelline Visconti, following a successful seizure of power from the commune government by Ottone Visconti (the city's archbishop) in 1277. The family enjoyed the patronage of the emperors and it was Gian Galeazzo Visconti (r. 1385–1402) who bought the title Duke of Milan (they had formerly been mere lords) from the emperor–elect Wenceslaus IV in 1395. Duke Gian Galeazzo was an efficient administrator, a great collector of manuscripts, a builder (of the wonderful Gothic cathedral of Milan and a massive castle at Pavia to house his collections) and a generous patron. The great Charterhouse (Certosa) of Pavia was his foundation (1396) and he is buried here as he intended. He was also hugely ambitious and hungry for territory, extending his duchy across much of the Po Valley, even attacking Florence. It was just as he was about to seize that city that he died, on campaign, in 1402.

Gian Galeazzo had two sons and it was the second, Filippo Maria, who took over Pavia (1402) and then the whole duchy in 1412. After the loss of territory to Venice (Bergamo in 1428) and Filippo's failure to produce a male heir, the duchy passed, in 1447, to his son-in-law Francesco Sforza. The Sforza made Milan into a truly Renaissance city. It was Francesco's second son, Ludovico (known as Il Moro), who usurped the duchy from his young nephew and created a stable regime, balancing Milan's old enemies, Florence and Venice, against each other and arranging marital alliances with other cities. Leonardo da Vinci came to work at his court (creating his famous *Last Supper* and constructing irrigation canals to sustain rice growing) and the architect Bramante started his career here (the beautiful San Satiro) before he went to Rome to rebuild St Peter's. Meanwhile, the consolidation of the Lombard economy was ensured through a system of canals (the Navigli), constructed by the Visconti and Sforza, that linked Milan directly to the Po and to Lake Como. Transportation costs fell dramatically and the city grew fast. By the late 15th century it had spread well beyond its medieval walls and while it never had the attractions of Florence, Rome or Venice, Milan was recognised as one of the great cities of Europe, drawing in wool and grain from the countryside and manufacturing silks and armour.

The usurper Ludovico finally managed to get the emperor Maximilian to recognise him as duke (1494) but he relied too heavily on the French king Charles VIII for support against his Italian enemies, so encouraging Charles to invade Italy. This brought a long period of unrest for the peninsula. Charles was succeeded by Louis XII, who not only wished to possess Milan but pressed a claim to it through his grandmother, a Visconti. In the ensuing power struggles it was the Spanish Habsburgs who seized the Duchy, after the defeat of the next French king, François I, at the Battle of Pavia in 1525 and the death of the last Sforza in 1535.

The Spanish were to rule Lombardy as part of their territories for nearly 200 years. Lombardy was strategically important as it helped protect Spanish possessions in southern Italy and was to provide a vital thoroughfare for troops and supplies after the revolt of the Spanish Netherlands in 1567. In order to achieve continuity, the Spanish maintained Lombardy's status as a duchy (albeit with the Spanish king as its distant duke) and kept much of the Sforza bureaucracy in place. The Sforza castle was also incorporated into the regime as the Spanish military headquarters under its commander, the *castellano*. New walls, completed in 1560, confirmed Milan as a fortress city, vital for Spain's European security. After 1557, every governor of Lombardy and every *castellano* was a Spaniard.

Milan had a traumatic history after 1525, the year of a plague that killed thousands of its inhabitants, perhaps half the population. Years of famine and outbursts of plague well into the 17th century meant that the city never had a stable population and in fact it stagnated under Spanish rule. The countryside, with its underlying fertility, appears to have been more productive but with the global economy shifting from Italy to the Atlantic seaboard, and with Spain herself in decline after 1600, there was no impetus for growth. Instead the Duchy played on its history as a centre of Catholic orthodoxy, something the Spanish were only too keen to exploit.

The key figure of this period, one who would rival the 4th-century Ambrose in his impact, was Carlo Borromeo, appointed archbishop in 1565 (ending an 80-year hiatus of absentee primates). Borromeo came from a prosperous banking family whose estates were, and still are, around Lake Maggiore and on its islands. The young Carlo had been secretary to the pope during the Counter-Reformation Council of Trent (1545–63) and he returned to Milan to ruthlessly enforce its decrees. It was said that he recreated, in ecclesiastical dress, the hierarchy and bureaucracy of the Sforza state, as a mechanism through which the Church could impose reform. Monasteries were cleared out, religious orders such as the Umiliati were dissolved and their assets seized, and parish priests were issued detailed instructions, even covering such minutiae as how they should organise the space in their churches. City entertainments were banned (leading to tensions with municipal governors, who understood their propaganda potential) and devotional images became a feature of every street. Soon the archdiocese of Milan had become a model for Catholic reforms. The *Acta Ecclesia Mediolanensis*, Borromeo's handbook of good practice, spread across Catholic Europe and later penetrated the United States as the model to be followed. While many opposed the rigid authoritarianism, Borromeo nevertheless earned himself enormous respect by staying in the city and ministering to the sick when plague broke out in 1576. He died in 1584 and canonisation was soon underway, sanctioned by the pope (Paul V) in 1610. Carlo's cousin Federico Borromeo, bishop from 1595 until his death in the terrible plague year of 1631, attempted to carry on his predecessor's legacy but is chiefly remembered for his cultural projects, above all the Pinacoteca Ambrosiana, a public picture gallery with a library open to all scholars. This was also the period when two of Italy's great skills, music making and craftsmanship, united in Cremona to make it the leading centre of string instruments. The culmination came with Antonio Stradivari (1644–1737), whose name is synonymous with excellence in violin making to this day.

The plague of 1630–1 killed not only Federico but 64 of the city's 70 parish priests. A harrowing account of the devastation is to be found in the most famous of Italy's novels, *I promessi sposi* (*The Betrothed*), published in 1827 by a celebrated son of Milan and Lake Como, Alessandro Manzoni. Set during the years of Spanish rule, it tells the story of Renzo and Lucia, separated but then finally reunited in the turmoil of the times. By now the Spanish monarchy was aware that Lombardy was crucial to maintaining its strategic position and it reached out to local aristocratic families and representatives of the towns, offering honours and patronage in return for loyalty to the regime. These relationships intensified when war with France (and even a destructive invasion in 1655 that reached the walls of Milan) led to new demands for funds from the Duchy by a weakening Spain. Part of this need was met by the sale of titles (3,000 ducats to become a count and 4,000 for a marquisate, according to the 1648 price list). A brilliant politician, Bartolomeo Arese (1590–1674), from a Milanese patrician family, successfully created a ruling network of Spanish and Lombard noble families, bankers and landowners who pledged loans to the government in return for political influence. Arese is said to have made himself as powerful as the governor. At any rate, he created a situation whereby court life became based in the palaces of the aristocracy, just at a time when the hopelessly weak Madrid government of Charles II was about to expire. Charles' death in 1700, without heirs, led to the War of the Spanish Succession, and Lombardy was among the prizes.

The winners were to be the Austrian branch of the Habsburgs, who were granted Lombardy in 1713 by the terms of the Treaty of Utrecht. Austrian rule—though much chafed against later—was not without its benefits in the 18th century. The enlightened rule of Empress Maria Theresa (1748–80) saw the Milanese aristocracy pushed aside (to their bitter resentment), the government reorganised and a programme of agricultural reform put in place. Tolls were lowered and the guilds, seen as hindrances to free trade, were abolished. The most successful industry was silk. In 1751, a total of 186,000 librae (1 libra of silk is 76kg) were exported from Austrian Lombardy, rising to 500,000 librae in 1778, making silk the leading commodity in the financial budget, overtaking grain. Education was reformed by the expulsion of the Jesuits and a new focus on training loyal officials. The University of Pavia, until the 19th century, the only university in the Duchy, was reorganised. Among its graduates was the philosopher and criminologist Cesare Beccaria, a leading figure of the Enlightenment who advocated more tolerant prison regimes and the abolition of the death penalty. One of Milan's great cultural institutions, the La Scala opera house, held its inaugural performance in 1778.

But Austrian rule was doomed to be overthrown. The easy victories of Napoleon in northern Italy in 1796 saw Milan made capital, first of the Cisalpine Republic and then of the kingdom of (northern) Italy. Napoleon crowned himself king with the Iron Crown of Lombardy in the duomo of Milan in 1805. His reforms, which included the suppression of many religious orders and confiscation of their assets, were primarily focused on raising money and troops, an increasingly heavy burden on Lombardy. Yet by ruling over the whole peninsula, Napoleon sowed the seeds of possibility for a united Italy. And though following his defeat, the Congress of Vienna of 1815 restored Lombardy to Austria along with Venice and the Veneto, those seeds had not fallen on stony ground.

While Austrian rule continued to be relatively efficient, the ideals of a united Italy, stimulated by the upheavals of Napoleonic rule, were reviving. There was now a well-educated class of young Italians who began to resent being controlled by Vienna. Instead, these young liberals pinned their hopes on Piedmont, the only independent Italian state. As revolutions swept Europe in 1848, the uprising in Milan, the *Cinque Giornate* or Five Days, saw the complete expulsion of the Austrians. It was only an interlude. The defeat of the Piedmontese army in the following year by the Austrian general Radetzky heralded another decade of Austrian rule, only brought to an end in 1859 with the defeat of the Austrians by the Piedmontese and French at the battles of Magenta and then Solferino. The horrific suffering of the latter battle led the Swiss Jean-Henri Dunant to found the Red Cross (*see p. 329*). Following the ousting of the Austrians, Lombardy was united with Piedmont and then made part of the Kingdom of Italy in 1861. By 1870, Rome had been wrested from papal control and was once again the capital of the peninsula.

The unification of Italy led to new possibilities for Milan, which was already the centre of a rail network. Tunnels through the passes of St Gotthard (1882) and Simplon (1906) opened up the routes to the north. The large agricultural estates in the Po Valley also gave the region immense advantages over the undeveloped south, advantages that have lasted to this day. Industrialisation soon began. The first of the great international exhibitions was held in 1871. One of the world's great rubber companies, Pirelli was founded in Milan in 1872. Alfa Romeo was founded in 1910. Textiles remained the largest industry, second to engineering works and electrical goods, produced in factories that could rely on hydroelectric power driven by the good flow of water from the Alps. There was a slow consolidation of firms into larger units, with new labour pouring in from the countryside, so that Milan developed an organised working class with trade unions under a Chamber of Labour.

Overall, however, the region remained miserably poor, unable to compete successfully in world markets. In the countryside, the traditional industry of silk cultivation, which had continued to be dominant through the 19th century, maintaining its position as the most important in Europe, declined dramatically (it finally collapsed completely in the crash of 1929). Rural Lombardy in 1898 is brilliantly evoked in Ermanno Olmi's haunting film *The Tree of the Wooden Clogs* (1978), which features a backdrop of the Milan riots in May of that year, when high bread prices and a growing working class led to a massacre that may have taken 400 lives. The assassination of King Umberto I in Monza in 1900 was said to have come in retaliation.

After the carnage and frustrations of the First World War, it was in Milan that Benito Mussolini founded the *Fasci di Combattimento*, the Fascist movement, in 1919. A deadly attack on the Socialist magazine *Avanti* in Milan in the same year marked the beginning of social breakdown: soon Lombardy and the Po Valley was prey to roving Fascist gangs smashing up Socialist gatherings. Inspiration came from the flamboyant and unscrupulous writer Gabriele d'Annunzio, who brooded from his residential estate at Lake Garda, the Vittoriale degli Italiani, 'Shrine of Italian Victories', from 1922 to his death in 1938. It was from Milan that Mussolini launched his march on Rome in October 1922, a push which saw the Fascists bullying their way into power. By 1925, Italy was a dictatorship and Fascism's birth in Milan was not forgotten. The massive new station, Milano Centrale, which opened in 1931, remains as a symbol of its impact. The Fascist era consolidated Lombardy as the centre of 'modern' industry, of engineering, steelmaking, chemicals and hydroelectricity. As international order broke down in the 1930s, a conference on Isola Bella (on Lake Maggiore) in 1935 briefly united Italy, France and Britain against the rising power of Germany. It was all in vain, however, as Mussolini allied himself with Hitler and led an unprepared Italy into war again.

Lombardy also bore witness to the endgame of Fascism. Air raids in April 1943 destroyed much of the centre of Milan, including La Scala (soon restored, with the ageing Arturo Toscanini, who had been principal conductor in 1898, taking the baton for the reopening). With the surrender of Italy in September 1943, the Germans set up the Republic of Salò, a town on Lake Garda, from where a subdued Mussolini still claimed control of Italy. Milan now became the city of resistance, liberating itself from Fascist and German control. As the war ended in April 1945, Mussolini and his mistress, Carla Petacci, were hunted down and hanged near Lake Como, their bodies then displayed in Piazzale Loreto in Milan.

By 1950, however, an economic miracle was underway in northern Italy, with Milan and Turin the leading cities drawing in thousands of workers from the impoverished south. Milan's population grew by 400,000 between 1950 and 1965, most of them now spreading to industrial suburbs outside the city core. A famous, if controversial, film of 1960, Luchino Visconti's *Rocco and his Brothers*, catches the mood of the period as a family of southerners struggle to adapt to their new life. Famous firms showed off their prominence through architecture (the Pirelli and Olivetti buildings). Yet the boom brought conflict. In 1968 Milan was one of the centres of the radical student movement that swept Europe. In 1969, a bomb planted by a far-right terrorist group killed 18 and injured 88. And eventually the boom slackened and the factories began to close. The turning point was January 1996, when the last of the Falck steelworks, founded in 1906 in the suburb of Sesto San Giovanni and still employing 10,000 workers in the 1950s, closed down, leaving a city full of social unrest and apparently without purpose. Yet remarkably, Milan reinvented itself. Banking, advertising, publishing (Mondadori), the Borsa Italiana (Stock Exchange) and above all the fashion industry, took the place of the vanished industrial works. Milan is the home of Armani, Versace, Dolce & Gabbana and Missoni, as well as to a world-famous annual fashion show.

Politically, northern Italy was a stronghold of the Christian Democrats after the Second World War but power gradually shifted to a moderate Socialist party that drew support from the large workers' movements of Milan. The Communist party, Partito Comunista Italiano or PCI, also built on its foundations in the resistance to Fascism. In Milan's city elections between 1975 and 1990, it was the largest single party among the many that competed. The dark side of the boom was revealed in 1992, when the arrest of a Socialist official for taking bribes in the city led to the uncovering of massive corruption in public contracts, the Tangentopoli, 'the City of Bribes' scandal, from which most political parties had benefited. It spread from Milan throughout Italy, destroying the political system. From the resulting vacuum, Umberto Bossi's Lega Nord, the 'Northern League', emerged to reassert the region's traditional identity. Drawing on support in large part (though not exclusively) from rural areas, its aim was to achieve greater autonomy for the north within Italy by stressing the traditional values of hard work (compared to the decadent south) and family life. Lega Nord joined the Forza Italia of Silvio Berlusconi, himself Milanese by birth, in coalition, for the first time in 1994. Berlusconi had come to prominence through a number of things: his construction projects in the city, his brilliant control of the media and, from 1986, his ownership of the football team AC Milan. Despite many internal divisions and changes of leadership, Lega Nord remains strong, winning 28 percent of the vote in Lombardy in the election of 2018. Paradoxically perhaps Lega Nord drew heavily on the traditional supporters of the left, who were increasingly concerned with immigration. Immigrants have been hugely attracted to northern Italy because of the economic opportunities there and (in 2011 figures) make up over ten percent of the population, compared to less than three percent in the south.

For the modern visitor, Lombardy is a region of contrasts. There is the bustling modern city of Milan, still the innovative capital of Italy despite wartime destruction and a continuous rush of rebuilding which makes it less immediately pleasant to visit than smaller centres such as Bergamo or Cremona, where medieval cores remain intact. As for landscapes, there are the Alps, the fertile plains and—perhaps the most famous attractions for the visitor—the lakes: Garda, Maggiore and Como. Agriculture continues to flourish. Rice, first cultivated in the 15th century, is still grown today, as is grain and maize, and there are fruit trees and vineyards in the foothills of the Alps. There is also, of course, a rich cultural heritage, which is explored more fully in the succeeding chapters of this guide.

by Charles Freeman

TRE TORRI
Arata Isozaki's Allianz tower reflected in Zaha Hadid's Generali building.

Milan

Milan is the second largest city in Italy and the principal commercial and industrial centre of the country. It is a dynamic, forward-looking city and at the same time a place of enormous historical and artistic interest, with magnificent art collections, the renowned La Scala opera house, a remarkable cathedral, and churches holding important artworks, including Leonardo da Vinci's famous *Last Supper*.

Busy and stimulating, Milan offers a good quality of life and today is enjoying a period of success. It is at the forefront of contemporary innovation in Italian art and sculpture and new urban spaces have been created at the foot of tall towers designed by some of the world's most famous architects. The city's great museums (and in particular the innovations in museum culture at the Brera) reflect the atmosphere of modernity in their presentation. The transport system works well and is easy to use. All in all, Milan is a fun and rewarding place to visit. Partly this is thanks to a well-run municipal council; many also see it as a direct result of the success of the World Expo which was held here in 2015. There is no denying that the rest of Italy is at present looking to this great Lombard city for inspiration and as a model for the future. Changes are occurring continuously and our text can naturally only reflect the situation as we found it at the time of writing.

It is possible to spend many days exploring Milan. If your time is limited, we have listed a few of the highlights on pp. 22–23.

HISTORY OF MILAN

Milan has long been an important place. The city's ancient predecessor, Mediolanum (middle of the plain), was a Celtic settlement which came under Roman control in 222 BC. Occupying a key position on trade routes between Rome and northern Europe, by the 4th century AD it had a population of nearly 100,000 and rivalled Rome in importance. It was by an edict made here, in 313, that Constantine the Great officially recognised the Christian religion, and in the years that followed, the city became a major centre of that faith. Foremost among the influential Church fathers who lived and worked here was the great bishop of Milan, St Ambrose (340–97), the friend and mentor of St Augustine.

Though devastated by the barbarian invasions, Milan survived to become a typical Italian city-state, governed by an assembly of free citizens who cast off their feudal obligations and advanced one of Europe's early claims to self-determination. In an attempt to crush Milan's independent spirit, the Holy Roman Emperor Frederick Barbarossa sacked the city in 1158 and 1162, but was beaten at Legnano in 1176 by the survivors and their allies, who came together to form the Lega Lombarda (Lombard League). In recent years, the name and example of this medieval alliance have been taken up by a separatist political movement, now known simply as the 'Lega'.

In the late Middle Ages Milan was ruled by a succession of powerful families, including the Torriani, who took control of the city around 1260. They were overthrown in 1277 by the Visconti, who held power until 1447. The city enjoyed a period of particular splendour under Gian Galeazzo Visconti (1385–1402), who founded what is still the city's most impressive monument, the Duomo (cathedral), in 1386. After a republican interlude of three years, Francesco Sforza, the famous mercenary general and defender of Milan against Venice, who had married Bianca, daughter of the last Visconti, proclaimed himself duke. He was succeeded by his son Galeazzo Maria, and then by his infant grandson Gian Galeazzo, under the regency of his mother. The infant duke's power was usurped by his uncle Ludovico il Moro, who, despite a low opinion of rule by law, was a great patron of the arts and under whose rule the city flourished.

A succession of invasions, which would bring Milan under foreign rule for nearly four centuries, began in 1494 with the expedition of Charles VIII of France. Between 1499 and 1535 the dukedom was contested by the French and the Spanish, and under the Spanish emperor Charles V, Milan became capital of a province of the Holy Roman Empire. In 1713 the city passed to Austria under the terms of the Treaty of Utrecht, which marked the end of the War of the Spanish Succession. In 1796 it was seized by Napoleon, who three years later made it the capital of his Cisalpine Republic and, after a brief occupation by the Austrians and Russians, capital of the Italian Republic (1802) and of the Kingdom of Italy (1805). After the fall of Napoleon (1814), the Austrians returned but the Milanese tenaciously opposed this renewed imposition of foreign control. After three decades of passive resistance, the populace rose up in the rebellion known as the *Cinque Giornate* (18th–22nd March 1848). When the troops of Vittorio Emanuele II and Napoleon III defeated the Austrian forces at the Battle of Magenta in 1859, the city declared its allegiance to the nascent Kingdom of Italy.

With the industrial development of the city at the end of the 19th century, Milan expanded to absorb a huge influx of immigrant workers from all over Italy. The International Exposition held in the city in 1906 symbolised the city's achievements and its international role as a rich industrial city (Rome was where 'Italy talked', whereas Milan was where 'things got done'). The city was bombed 15 times in the Second World War: the worst air raids were in August 1943, when a great part of the city centre burned for several days. The years of reconstruction were followed by a period of economic boom when sprawling new suburbs were built.

Milan today, fast-paced, dynamic and cosmopolitan, stands firmly at the leading edge of new trends in Italy.

MILAN ART AND ARCHITECTURE

Milan is primarily an architect's city, where ideas are transposed with singular grace and skill from the two-dimensional surface of the drawing table to the three-dimensional volume of real space. Here you can trace the history of Italian architecture from antiquity right up to the present day. All periods are represented, from the very old to the very new. The years of Austrian rule have also left their mark: Milan has the appearance of an Italian town, yet with an unmistakable admixture of Vienna.

Romanesque to Art Nouveau

In the early Middle Ages, Milan's church builders gave rise to a style now known as the Lombard Romanesque. Its distinctive characteristic is a mixture of early medieval architectural devices from the West, such as round arches and cylindrical columns, with elements inherited from the Byzantine tradition, such as the extended forecourt or narthex. The most important example is the magnificent basilica of Sant'Ambrogio, which also has the typically distinctive type of façade with a kind of tented roofline, extending laterally over both aisles (*see p. 71*). Milan's Duomo is one of the most striking Gothic buildings in the world. Its flamboyant tracery rivals the best examples of the genre in France and northern Europe.

The wealthy and cultured court of the Sforza (14th–15th centuries) attracted many great Renaissance artists, including the architects Filarete, Michelozzo and Bramante, the sculptor Amadeo, and the painters Foppa and Bergognone. Bergognone (active 1480–1522) is an important exponent of the native Milanese style, a style he clung to despite the artistic revolution that took place around him. For Milanese art was completely transformed by the arrival from Tuscany in 1483 of Leonardo da Vinci. This great artist, and the city he adopted, became the centre of an artistic and humanistic flowering that continued until the fall of Ludovico il Moro in 1499. Leonardo's pupils Bernardino Luini and Gaudenzio Ferrari (*see p. 138*) formed schools of their own. The sculptors Bambaia and Cristoforo Solari also felt his influence.

Towards the end of the 16th century, Camillo and Giulio Cesare Procaccini introduced a new, Baroque style of painting from Bologna, and Galeazzo Alessi imported Baroque ideas from Rome into architecture. Milan's most important Baroque architect is Francesco Maria Richini. The Neoclassical buildings of Luigi Cagnola and Luigi Canonica (both born in 1762) reflect the tastes of the Napoleonic period.

The turn of the 20th century saw the emergence of a distinctive Art Nouveau style, called Liberty after the London shop that played so large a part in its dissemination. The area around Porta Venezia has some good examples (*see p. 107*).

Early twentieth-century trends

In the early 20th century, bustling, industrial Milan was one of the centres of Futurism, Italy's great contribution to the Modern movement, which hailed the new world of mechanical forces and denounced all attachment to the past. 'A roaring motorcar, its hood adorned with pipes like serpents with explosive breath...is more beautiful than the Winged Victory of Samothrace', declared Futurist theorist Filippo Tommaso Marinetti (who launched the Futurist movement from offices in this city; *see p. 101*). The original members of the movement were the painters Umberto Boccioni, Carlo Carrà, Luigi Russolo, Giacomo Balla and Gino Severini, and the architect Antonio Sant'Elia. They were later joined by many others. The Futurists aspired to bring art into closer contact with life, which they conceived as governed by force and movement. The Futurist doctrine of simultaneity, by which movement was to be rendered in art by the simultaneous presentation of successive instants of form in motion, was similar to the Cubist notion of the simultaneous presentation of views of a single object from multiple angles; but the Futurist idea differed from the more exclusively visual simultaneity of Cubism: the Futurists spoke of the simultaneity of plastic states of the soul in artistic creation. They were the first to advocate a new conception of picture space whereby the observer would be situated at the centre.

The most important artistic event of the 1920s in Italy was the formation, again in Milan, of the group that exhibited together in 1924 under the name Novecento. Coined by the theoretician of the movement, Margherita Sarfatti, the name means 'nine hundred', a reference to the new century. The leading figure of the Novecento, the painter Carrà (a former Futurist), called for a return to a quieter figurative style based on traditional values. But to find a common denominator for all the artists associated with the Novecento is difficult. Even Sarfatti was vague in describing the movement's goals. She cited 'clarity of form and dignity of conception, nothing magical, nothing eccentric, an increasing closure toward the arbitrary and the obscure'. Thus one finds in the Novecento movement such painters as Mario Sironi, who captured the movement of modernity with expressionistic force, as well as subtly melancholy artists such as Pietro Marussig. The movement was much loved by the Fascists because of its emphasis on tradition and national identity.

The architecture of the 1920s developed in two distinct directions. The Modernist movement gave rise to the functionalist trend known as Rationalism, which made an appeal to ideals of logic and order but claimed also a definitive break with the past. The protagonists of the movement were Giuseppe Pagano and Giuseppe Terragni (who worked mainly in Como), but many other architects—including Giò Ponti and Ignazio Gardella in Milan—expressed Rationalist ideals in their buildings and objects. Though initially apolitical, the movement later won the support of the Fascist regime, at the point when it had achieved full power and was needful of a cultural trademark.

In reaction to this, conservative architects of the period proposed yet another return to Classical models. A new traditionalist orientation, again called Novecento to underscore its bonds with the conservative trend in painting, developed throughout Italy and particularly in Milan, where growth was most rapid and where the Neoclassical tradition of the early 19th century offered inspiration and continuity with the past. The leading figure of architectural Novecento was Marcello Piacentini, promoter of a supposedly balanced and dignified, spiritual and expressive Classicism.

Post-war Milan

After the Second World War, Milan became the undisputed centre of contemporary culture in Italy, asserting its primacy in painting, sculpture and architecture as well as in industrial design and fashion. The painter Lucio Fontana, as well as the precursor of Conceptual Art, Piero Manzoni, both lived and worked here.

The first clearly identifiable architectural style of the post-war period was Neorealism. This trend, like Neorealism in Italian cinema, arose in reaction to Fascist triumphalism, to which it opposed simpler, more organic forms. It clearly reflected the desire, of a generation of architects compromised by association with the regime, to atone for past sins; but it was also brought about by the arrival in Italy of ideas originating in the United States and northern Europe and expressed in the work of figures such as Frank Lloyd Wright and Alvar Aalto.

By the early '50s, Italy was well on the way to attaining the status of a modern industrial democracy. Here, as elsewhere in Europe and in North America, the dominant architectural trend became the International Style, a functionalist re-reading of the teachings of the great masters of the Modern movement that advocated the adoption of common standards in all buildings, regardless of location. Giò Ponti and Pier Luigi Nervi's Pirelli Building is a good example of the International Style. In more recent times this trend has been followed, in Milan as elsewhere, by a Postmodern reaction, embodied in a new eclecticism combining Classical elements (such as arches and columns) with forms derived from vernacular architecture. This is reflected in many Milanese interiors—shops, cafés, hotels and restaurants.

The 1950s marked the beginning of Italy's economic miracle: living standards increased enormously, creating demand for high-quality consumer goods. Industry responded by increasing production and by involving some of the country's great creative talents in product design, giving rise to that distinctive look for which Italian products are famous. Today the creations of Milanese designers grace homes and workplaces throughout the developed world.

For the developments in the city's architecture in the 21st century, see p. 107.

MILAN HIGHLIGHTS

Top sights

The sights on every visitor's itinerary will be the **Duomo and its roof terraces** (*p. 28*), **Leonardo da Vinci's *Last Supper*** (*p. 66*) and the **Brera picture gallery** (*p. 45*). The Duomo attracts millions of visitors a year and there is always a queue to get in. Leonardo's *Last Supper* is the only place in Milan which must be booked in advance. The Brera Pinacoteca is one of the great art galleries of Italy. Naturally enough, no visitor will want to miss these sights (the Brera is the least crowded of the three). Aside from these, though, there are exquisite works of art and wonderful buildings of all eras all over the rest of the city, where you will quite often have churches and museums almost to yourself.

Art galleries

Duke Ludovico Sforza (Il Moro) enticed Leonardo da Vinci to Milan in 1482/3 and his influence on the Lombard painters of his time (Bernardino Luini, Ambrogio de Predis, Giovanni Antonio Boltraffio among them), often grouped together as the 'Leonardeschi', can clearly be seen in their work. There is plenty of it in the picture galleries here, notably the Brera; but also the **Pinacoteca Ambrosiana** (*p. 75*), where you can also see the only portrait by Leonardo still in Italy; and the **Museo Poldi Pezzoli** (*p. 41*), which has an exquisite private collection with some masterpieces by Leonardo's pupils as well as by other great artists of the 15th century, including Bellini and Mantegna. For 19th and 20th-century art, there is the **Galleria d'Arte Moderna** (*p. 105*), the **Gallerie d'Italia** (*p. 38*) and, the most important collection of 20th-century art, the **Museo del Novecento** (*p. 35*). **Fondazione Prada**'s collection of contemporary art is on show in its white 'Torre', designed by Rem Koolhaas (*p. 112*).

Museums

The huge **Castello Sforzesco** (*p. 57*) houses collections of painting, sculpture and decorative arts, including Michelangelo's *Rondanini Pietà*. The **Museo Nazionale della Scienza** (*p. 74*) is an excellent Science Museum and the **Natural History Museum** (*p. 104*) is the most important in Italy. The **Archaeological Museum** (*p. 83*) has a well-displayed collection of Greek, Etruscan and Roman material relating to Milan and Lombardy. The history of opera at **La Scala** (*p. 38*) is well documented in its museum, from which you can visit the famous theatre when not in use. Milan also has a clutch of interesting house-museums, whose contents reflect certain periods in the life of the city as well as the taste and personalities of their former owners. They include the **Museo Bagatti Valsecchi** (*p. 44*); the **Villa Necchi Campiglio** (*p. 102*) and the **Casa Museo Boschi di Stefano** (*p. 103*).

Churches

The great Lombard basilica of **Sant'Ambrogio** (*p. 69*), founded by St Ambrose, is one of the finest churches in Milan, particularly important for its place in Church history. Two of the three other churches known to have been founded by St Ambrose survive: **San Nazaro** (*p. 97*) and **San Simpliciano** (*p. 57*). The atmospheric **San Lorenzo Maggiore** (*p. 85*) has a beautiful 5th-century mosaic-clad chapel. Attached to the basilica of **Sant'Eustorgio** (*p. 88*) is the Portinari Chapel, with wonderful Renaissance frescoes by Vincenzo Foppa, amongst the great masterpieces in the city. Some of the best early 16th-century paintings and frescoes can be seen in the chapter house of **Santa Maria della Passione** (*p. 100*; by Bergognone) and in **San Maurizio al Monastero Maggiore** (*p. 82*; by Bernardino Luini).

Architecture

The great architect Donato Bramante was called to Milan in 1478 by Duke Ludovico il Moro and his extraordinarily innovative architecture can be seen in the churches of **Santa Maria delle Grazie** (*p. 65*) and **Santa Maria presso San Satiro** (*p. 80*). Civic architecture of all periods can be found in Milan: one of the most imposing examples is the early 15th-century **Ca' Grande** (*p. 98*) by Filarete (with later additions), the seat of the University. At the turn of the 20th century, Milan was known for its **Art Nouveau**, or Liberty-style buildings, of which Casa Galimberti is a good example. There is some fine architecture of the 1930s too (for where to find examples of 20th-century architecture, see pp. 107 and 109), but today it is contemporary architecture which draws the most attention. To see it, go to **Piazza Gae Aulenti** and the Porta Nuova district, as well as the area known as **CityLife** (*p. 108*).

Fashion

Characteristic of the traditional elegance of Milan are the streets around the Brera, the 'Design District' or '**Fashion Quadrilateral**' (*p. 43*), and the **Galleria Vittorio Emanuele II** (*p. 37*), the glass-roofed arcade which leads out of Piazza Duomo. Contemporary design is showcased in the **Tortona Design District** (*map p. 110*). The **Navigli** area (*p. 94*), where some of Milan's old transport canals survive, has a bustling atmosphere all of its own, with numerous places to eat.

Food and drink

Milan is home to Campari and to the *costoletta alla milanese* (breaded veal schnitzel). In recent years, international cuisine has become very popular and fashionable here and you will see plenty of sushi restaurants. A selection of places to eat and drink is given at the end of the chapter (*p. 117ff*).

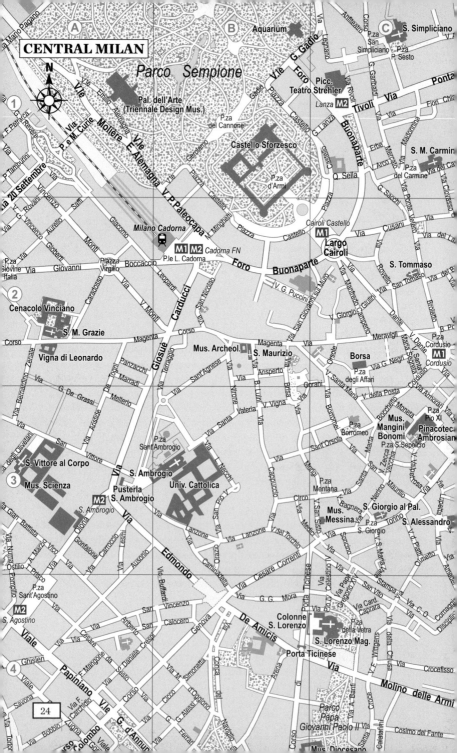

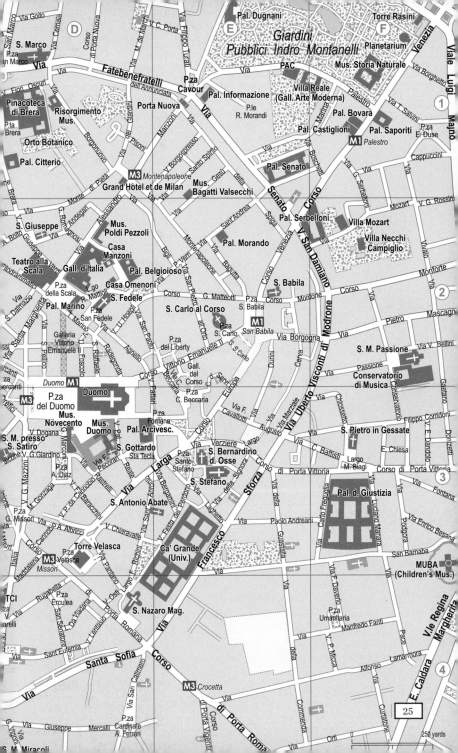

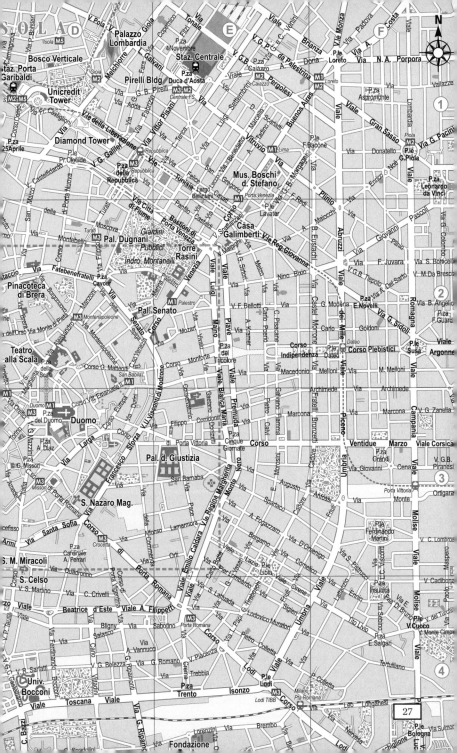

THE DUOMO

Map p. 25, D3. Piazza del Duomo. The interior, roof terraces and archaeological area beneath the nave are all open 8am–7pm. The Museo del Duomo is open 10am–6pm but closed on Wed. T: 02 7202 3375, duomomilano.it. The standard ticket includes admission to the archaeological area, Museo del Duomo and church of San Gottardo. There is a separate ticket for the roof terraces. The Duomo Pass ticket gives access to all these areas (one for the roof terraces by lift, and another, less expensive, for the roof terraces on foot). All tickets allow access within 72hrs after you validate them for the first time.

Ticket offices. *There is a large ticket office (and information office) opposite the right flank of the Duomo, efficiently run but usually crowded. There is another ticket office (usually less crowded and not well signed) at the Museo del Duomo. Over six million people visit the Duomo every year: to save time, it is a good idea to buy your ticket online (booking.duomomilano.it), although there is a booking fee and the ticket does not give you a timed entrance. On arrival you have to exchange your vouchers for a ticket at the priority desk (and you still have to join the queue to gain entrance). The Duomo tends to be particularly crowded at weekends and on Mondays, when museums are closed.*

Entrances. *The duomo itself is entered from the main west front. There are two separate entrances for the roof terraces, outside the north and south transepts, both with lifts and stairs.*

Dress. *You are not allowed into the Duomo in shorts or with bare shoulders: cloaks are on sale at the Ticket Office.*

Services. *Mass is held every day (at 7, 8, 8.30, 9.30, 11, 12 and 5.30), on weekdays in the Cappella Feriali behind the organ and in the central nave on Sat–Sun.*

Milan's magnificent late-Gothic Duomo is the second largest church in Italy, after St Peter's in Rome. It is the only Gothic cathedral in the country, the exterior decorated with some 2,000 sculptures and with a forest of pinnacles and spires around the tower over the crossing supported by numerous flying buttresses. Extraordinary gargoyles, leafy crockets and finials and figured corbels appear everywhere on the gables and canopies, and the tracery is magnificently intricate. The façade, which was added in the 16th century, is also basically Gothic in inspiration though with the addition of Renaissance windows. The building was particularly admired in the Romantic age, but is still today Milan's most famous monument and the most visited. The Milanese consider its piazza the centre of their city and it is always crowded.

Building history

The cathedral was begun in 1386 under Gian Galeazzo Visconti, who presented it with a marble quarry at Candoglia (which still belongs to the cathedral chapter and is used for its maintenance today). The design is attributed to a group of Lombard masters, apparently assisted by French, German and Flemish craftsmen. At the beginning of the 15th century, Filippino degli Organi from Modena was appointed master mason and documents name his successors as Giovanni Solari and his son Guiniforte. The

DUOMO: WEST FAÇADE

first well-known name to be connected with the building work is Guiniforte's son-in-law Giovanni Antonio Amadeo (*see p. 163*), who at the beginning of the 16th century designed the lantern over the transepts and the tallest spire. Under Sforza rule the dome was completed.

In 1567 Pellegrino Tibaldi was appointed architect by Charles Borromeo under whom, as Bishop of Milan, the Duomo was dedicated. Tibaldi designed the façade but more work was carried out on it in the following century by Francesco Maria Richini and Carlo Buzzi. The three large upper windows which revert to the Gothic style were added in 1805 by order of Napoleon, just in time for him to crown himself King of Italy here. The façade has numerous reliefs and a series of caryatids, 19th-century statues, and 17th-century high reliefs above the portals.

The central bronze doors are by Lodovico Pogliaghi (1906), those on the extreme left by Arrigo Minerbi (1948) and the last doors on the right by Luciano Minguzzi (1965). The exterior of the apse is particularly splendid, with three huge windows made in 1402 by Filippino degli Organi.

There is a good view of the exterior from the courtyard of Palazzo Reale and another from the Museo del Novecento, but it is from the roof terraces that the intricacy of the carving on the exterior can be appreciated to the full.

The 'Veneranda Fabbrica del Duomo' still looks after the cathedral and is responsible for the conservation of its numerous delicate sculptural works, some of which have had to be replaced (but are preserved in the Museo del Duomo).

SOME CELEBRATED REACTIONS

*How glorious that Cathedral is! worthy almost of standing face to face with the snow
Alps; and itself a sort of snow dream by an artist architect, taken asleep in a glacier!*
Elizabeth Barrett Browning, letter, 1851

*The cathedral is an awful failure. Outside the design is monstrous and inartistic. The
over-elaborated details stuck high up where no one can see them; everything is vile in it;
it is, however, imposing and gigantic as a failure, through its great size and elaborate
execution.*
Oscar Wilde, letter to his mother, 25th June 1875

... the beautiful city with its dominant frost-crystalline duomo...
John Ruskin, *Praeterita*, 1885–9

THE INTERIOR

The huge cruciform interior, with double-aisled nave, single-aisled transepts and a pentagonal apse, has a soaring vault supported by a forest of 52 tall columns, most of which bear circles of figures in canopied niches instead of capitals. The plain stone of the building provides a contrast to the beautiful bright pink, white and black marble pavement by Tibaldi. The splendid effect is heightened by the stained-glass windows, which are the most important feature of the interior (as in numerous other Gothic cathedrals, especially in France).

The windows: Although the windows have been reworked, renewed and restored over the centuries, it is worth taking time to study them as they include some especially good glass from the 15th and 16th centuries (at which date windows were usually designed by painters). The **windows in the south aisle** are amongst the earliest: the first, with stories of St John the Evangelist **(A)**, was made by Cristoforo de' Mottis in 1478; the second, third and fourth, with stories from the Old Testament, date from the 16th century; the fifth, with stories from the New Testament, was made by some of the most important 15th-century Lombard masters of this art, including Niccolò da Varallo, who

also produced the next (sixth) window with stories from the life of St Eligius **(B)**. The seventh window was the last to be made for the church (in 1988).

The eight **windows in the tiburio**, which crowns the crossing, were commissioned in 1964 to commemorate the Second Vatican Council. However, they are some 60m from the pavement and almost impossible to see.

The first window in the **south transept**, with stories of St James the Greater **(C)**, dates from 1565 (by Corrado de' Mocchis from Cologne). The other windows here were made in 1842 by Giovanni Battista Bertini. In the window above the side door, the stories of St Catherine of Alexandria **(D)**

THE DUOMO

A   St John the Evangelist window
B   St Eligius window
C   St James the Greater window
D   St Catherine of Alexandria window
E   St Martin of Tours window
F   East window
G   St John Damascene window
H   St Charles Borromeo window
I   St Catherine of Siena window
J   Apostles window
K   St Ambrose window

a   Sarcophagus of Archbishop Aribert
b   Tomb of Ottone Visconti
c   Tomb of Marco Carelli
d   Monument to Giovanni Vimercati
e   Monument to Gian Giacomo Medici
f   San Giovanni Buono altar
g   *Presentation of the Virgin* by Bambaia
h   *St Bartholomew*
i   South sacristy door
j   Statue of Pope Martin V
k   Monument to Cardinal Caracciolo
l   Trivulzio candelabrum
m   Federico Barocci: altarpiece of St Ambrose
n   Arcimboldi tomb
o   Reliefs of Apostles
p   Font

F   Entrance to crypt

Presbytery

Tiburio

Entrance to archaeological area

are dated 1556. The next window dates from a few decades later and illustrates the life of St Martin of Tours **(E)** (incorporating prophets by Michelino da Besozzo, c. 1420).

In the ambulatory the huge **east window (F)**, with its splendid Gothic tracery, has scenes of the Apocalypse partly dating from the 15th century and partly from the 1830s by Giovanni Battista Bertini (in the lower registers). The glass in the two majestic windows flanking it was entirely remade by Bertini.

In the **north transept**, the first window, illustrating the life of St John Damascene **(G)** was made by Niccolò da Varallo in 1480. The window next to it (1910) celebrates the life of St Charles Borromeo **(H)** and the three windows in the centre were made in the 1840s by Bertini. The next window, with stories of Joachim and Anne and from the life of St Catherine of Siena **(I)**, dates from the 16th century and is by Corrado de' Mocchis, who was also responsible for the adjoining window with its monumental figures of the Apostles **(J)**.

The window at the top of the **north aisle**, with scenes from the life of St Ambrose **(K)**, dates from the end of the 19th century, and the seventh window was made in the mid-17th century; the sixth and fifth in the 16th century. The fourth window is by Corrado de' Mocchis. The third and first windows date from 1947, and the second is made up of panels from various epochs.

South aisle: At the beginning of the south aisle is the plain granite **sarcophagus of Archbishop Aribert (a)** (d. 1045). **Archbishop Ottone Visconti** (d. 1295), who took Milan from the Torriani, is buried in the red-marble sarcophagus on pillars **(b)**, his effigy sunk into the lid guarded by the four symbols of the Evangelists while the front is used for a long celebratory inscription. The **tomb of Marco Carelli (c)**, a rich merchant who was an important benefactor of the church, is by the master mason Filippino degli Organi (1406), and has good statuettes in canopied niches. Beyond a relief with a design for a new façade (never used) by Giuseppe Brentano (1886), is a small **monument to Canon Giovanni Vimercati (d)**, another benefactor of the church (d. 1548), which was made by one of the best sculptors at work in Milan at this time, Bambaia.

South transept: Here is the **monument to Gian Giacomo Medici (e)** (d. 1555; no relation to the Florentine Medici), ruthless *condottiere* and elder brother of Pius IV, who commissioned the commemorative bronze statues from Leone Leoni. In the manner of Michelangelo, they depict the deceased flanked by Strength and Constancy. In the transept apse an elaborate **altar (f)** was set up in 1763 with numerous sculptures in memory of San Giovanni Buono, a 7th-century Bishop of Milan known for his 'goodness'. Another altar has a marble **relief by Bambaia (g)** of the *Presentation of the Virgin* (1543). The anatomical **statue of St Bartholomew (h)** flayed (and draped in his own skin) was made in 1562.

Crossing and east end: On the pendentives of the **tiburio**—the great lantern over the crossing (the four piers had to be reinforced in 1984 and it was restored in 2018)—are medallions with 15th-century busts of the Doctors of the Church.

The **presbytery**, with its large bronze ciborium, was designed by Pellegrino Tibaldi in 1567. There are two organs (the earliest one by Gian Giacomo Antegnati, 1577). From 1484–1522 the Duomo's famous choir school was directed by Franchino Gaffurio, thought to have been the sitter for Leonardo's portrait in the Ambrosiana (*see p. 79*).

Together with Galeazzo Alessi, Tibaldi also decorated the **crypt** with stucco reliefs. The **chapel**, designed by Francesco Maria Richini in 1606, contains the richly-robed body of St Charles Borromeo (*see p. 201*). Visitors process around the coffin along a narrow corridor lined with silk.

Tibaldi also designed the beautiful 16th-century **marble screen** which curves round the ambulatory to separate it from the choir. It has relief panels and caryatids and lovely carving above. The **carved decoration above the south sacristy door (i)** dates from the late 14th century and is the earliest carving in the interior. Beyond (high up) is a portrait statue of **Pope Martin V (j)**, a very good example of Lombard Gothic sculpture, made a few years after the pope consecrated the high altar in 1418. In great contrast, since it is made of incongruous black marble, is the **monument to Cardinal Caracciolo (k)** (d. 1538) with statues by Bambaia. Here, at the east end of the church, has been placed a scale copy made in gilded bronze in 2015 of the colossal statue of the Madonna (over 4m high, but known as the *Madonnina*) which was placed on the summit of the Duomo in 1774. The ancient Crucifix here, with Byzantine elements, is 'dressed' in a red robe.

North transept and aisle: In the middle of the north transept (normally cordoned off for worshippers) is the **Trivulzio candelabrum (l)**, a seven-branched bronze candlestick nearly 5m high, of French or German workmanship (13th or 14th century).

In the north aisle is one of the very few paintings in the Duomo: the altarpiece of ***St Ambrose Forcing the Emperor Theodosius to Penitence (m)**, by Federico Barocci. In the third bay, the **tomb of three archbishops of the Arcimboldi family (n)** is attributed to Galeazzo Alessi; and in the second bay are late 12th-century **marble reliefs of apostles (o)**. Opposite is the **font (p)**, a porphyry bath thought to date from Roman times, covered with a canopy by Tibaldi.

THE *QUADRONI DI SAN CARLO*

An interesting series of 52 paintings illustrating the life and miracles of St Charles Borromeo (*see p. 201*) is hung in a double row between the nave and transept pillars for a few months in winter every year (usually from Oct until after Christmas). Known as the *Quadroni di San Carlo*, they were commissioned in 1602 by Cardinal Federico Borromeo to honour the memory of his cousin St Charles. Above are hung scenes from the saint's life (1602–4) and below, scenes of his miracles (1609–10): the best ones are by Il Cerano and Giulio Cesare Procaccini (there are others by Morazzone and Fiammenghino). The last eight were painted in 1660–1740 to complete the series, which survives intact.

THE ARCHAEOLOGICAL AREA WITH THE BAPTISTERY
Open at the same time as the Duomo and with the same ticket. Entrance at the west end.
Excavations underneath the Duomo have revealed the remains of the earliest basilica on this site, **Santa Tecla**, dating from the 4th century. In front of its west end stood the **baptistery of San Giovanni alle Fonti**, built by St Ambrose. It is here that he baptised St Augustine in 387 and its visible remains are a moving sight. Its octagonal plan can clearly be seen, with fragments of its opus sectile marble decoration and traces of medieval frescoes.

Traces of the church of **Santa Maria Maggiore**, consecrated in 836 by Bishop Angilbert and which survived until the 15th century as the 'winter' cathedral, have also been found, along with an adjacent cemetery and funerary chapel.

On a lower level you can see remains of 1st-century BC **Roman baths**. In display cases there are 5th-century mosaic tesserae and other finds.

THE ROOF TERRACES

The entrances to the roof (open all year round, except when it snows) are outside the north or south transepts. You need to buy a separate ticket at one of the two offices, and specify if you wish to climb up the stairs (158 steps) or take the lift (more expensive).

The ascent to the roof is highly recommended: not only does it enable you to see the exterior sculptural decoration up close but it also provides wonderful views over the city—and on clear days as far as the Alps. The walkway goes round the entire east end, up and down a short flight of steps at the transepts, and then along the outside of the nave at the level of the Gothic windows. At the west end, some 70 steps continue up to the roof of the nave where you can walk right along its spine to see the lantern of the crossing and the tallest spires. The Carelli Spire, the oldest of the Duomo's pinnacles, is at the angle facing Corso Vittorio Emanuele. The tallest building on the skyline (looking directly north) is the Unicredit Tower (2011; at the time of writing the tallest building in Italy), with its glass stalagmite that echoes the Duomo's pinnacles. It is sometimes possible to ascend another staircase, in the northeast turret, to the topmost gallery at the base of the central spire, surmounted by the *Madonnina* (108m from the ground), a statue of gilded copper, nearly 4m high. From this height there is a magnificent view of the city, the Lombard plain, the Alps (with the prominent peaks of the Matterhorn, Monte Rosa, the two Grigne and Monte Resegone) and the Apennines.

MUSEO DEL DUOMO

Map p. 25, D3. Piazza del Duomo 12. Open 10–6 except Wed. Tickets for the Duomo and the 'Duomo Pass' (see p. 28) include admission. T: 02 7202 2656, duomomilano.it.

Milan's cathedral square is characteristic of the bustling atmosphere of the city. It opens out in front of the former **Palazzo Reale**. Standing on the site of the 13th-century Town Hall, it was rebuilt in Neoclassical style in 1772–8 for the Austrian grand dukes by Giuseppe Piermarini (altered again in the 19th century, and restored after bomb damage in 1943). It is now used as Milan's premier exhibition space (it usually hosts two or three exhibitions at a time) and in one wing is the Grande Museo del Duomo. Behind the palace there is a pleasant tiny garden provided with one or two wooden benches where you can sit and rest and under the portico is the equally pleasant **Café San Giacomo**. The Museo del Duomo includes the Treasury formerly displayed in the Duomo itself. Labelling is good and also in English. Highlights are described here.

The first room has the **masterpieces from the Treasury**: there are three precious diptychs: one of 'five parts' made in the 4th or 5th century; one in bone made in the 5th century in Rome; and a Byzantine ivory of the late 10th or early 11th century. Also in ivory is the chalice ('of the liberal arts') which was given its stem in the 16th century, and the situla dating from the 10th century. The Evangelistary cover decorated with enamels, jewels and silver c. 1026 belonged to Archbishop Aribert, who is buried in the Duomo, and the very unusual Crucifix (displayed on the wall) is also known to have been made for the Archbishop (the Cross itself is of embossed and gilded copper: note the symbols of the sun and the moon at the top). The Cross of Chiaravalle, decorated with jewels, dates from the late 13th century (until 1797 it was in the possession of Chiaravalle Abbey; *see p. 138*). The Lombard altar statues in gilded copper, of the Madonna and Child with two angels, are from the 14th century.

One room is entirely filled with a **model of the Duomo**, which was begun during work on the building in 1519 and to which parts were added right up until 1891. It is on a scale of 1:22. Beyond a 16th-century mitre embroidered with humming birds is an early 15th-century processional panel painting by Michelino da Besozzo. Among the paxes is one which belonged to Pius IV.

Sculpture from the exterior of the Duomo includes an early 15th-century spire statue of St George by Giorgio Solari; saints, apostles and prophets; and a pair of lovely seraphim with folded wings from the exterior of the central apse window, dating from around the same time. A huge keystone in gilded copper with the head of God the Father comes from the apse conch. There is also a display of twelve of the extraordinary late 14th-century zoömorphic gargoyles. The statuettes made for the capitals in the 14th or early 15th century, all in Candoglia marble, are particularly lovely. Galeazzo Maria Sforza was also immortalised in stone in around 1480. There is a circular display of fragments of (mostly) 16th-century **stained glass from the windows**.

From a corridor you are signposted out to a little courtyard where you can see the pretty brick campanile of **San Gottardo in Corte**, the chapel of Palazzo Reale. Dating from the 1330s, it is attributed to Francesco Pecorari of Cremona. The Neoclassical interior of San Gottardo, with stuccoes by Giocondo Albertolli, contains the tomb of Azzone Visconti by Giovanni di Balduccio (unfortunately rather high up), and very worn frescoes of figures at the foot of a Crucifixion scene showing the influence of Giotto (who is known to have been in the city in 1335).

Back in the museum, the **paintings** include the *Infant Christ among the Doctors*, an early work by Jacopo Tintoretto, and tempera monochromes by Il Cerano displayed with terracotta models from the same period. The good collection of **tapestries** includes some from Brussels and others made in Mantua. The 18th-century '*Madonnina*' (*see p. 33*) is documented with a model for its head, in walnut, by Giuseppe Antegnati and its original metal core. The models for the 20th-century doors are also on display.

MUSEO DEL NOVECENTO

Map p. 25, D3. Palazzo dell'Arengario. Entrance at Via Marconi 1. Open Mon 2.30–7.30, Tues, Wed, Fri, Sun 9.30–7.30, Thur and Sat 9.30am–10.30pm. T: 02 8844 4061, museodelnovecento.org. Restaurant (Giacomo all'Arengario) on the top floor. Part of the important group of 20th-century paintings which belong to the city are now exhibited at the Casa Museo Boschi di Stefano; see p. 103

The Arengario, beside Palazzo Reale, is an interesting building designed in 1939–56 by a group of architects including Giovanni Muzio and Piero Portaluppi, with reliefs by Arturo Martini. It now houses the city's museum of 20th-century art. The building has been very well adapted to display the excellent collection, donated to the city over time by Milanese collectors. The entrance is up a bright white circular ramp, reminiscent of the Guggenheim Museum in New York, although there is only one painting displayed on the way up: **Giuseppe Pellizza da Volpedo's** *Il Quarto Stato*. Painted in 1901, it was originally entitled *The Advance of the Workers [Movement]* but was renamed *Il Quarto Stato* (*The Fourth Estate*) from a phrase in a Socialist journal of the time. It symbolically suggests that nothing can arrest the progress of the workers' movement in a democratic revolution. The painting was largely ignored at the time but the memorable crowd of protesters, seen from the front approaching the viewer, became famous much later in the 20th century, as a manifesto of humanitarian socialism.

At the top of the ramp, escalators and lifts connect the various levels. On Level 1, a small room illustrates the **international avant-garde**, with just two works, one by Picasso and the other by Matisse (*Odalisque*, 1925), both from the Jucker collection. The long hall with columns is dedicated to the **Futurist movement** and in particular to **Umberto Boccioni**, who is represented by numerous works including *Elasticity* (1912) and his masterpiece of sculpture *Unique Forms of Continuity in Space* (1913). Other sculptures show the dynamism of the human body. The movement is explained also through photographs and publications, and with paintings by Giacomo Balla, Gino Severini, Carlo Carrà, and small works by Ardengo Soffici and Mario Sironi. The small room at the end is dedicated to Giorgio Morandi. The loggia above has good works from the 1920s and 1930s by Giorgio de Chirico (*The Prodigal Son, Gladiators, Isa in a Black Dress*).

On Level 2 is a room with works in clay, bronze and stone by **Arturo Martini**, including the bronze bust of a boy (1921) and the memorable *Thirst in Stone* (1934). The section on the Italian **Novecento** has good paintings from the 1920s by Mario Sironi (*Melancholy*), Carlo Carrà (*Summer*), Virgilio Guidi (*The Visit*) and Felice Casorati (*La Toilette*), and later works by De Pisis, Scipione and Fausto Melotti. Three rooms are dedicated to the sculptor **Marino Marini**. Abstract art is hung in the end room.

Level 3 continues the chronological order with works by Kounellis (1967) and Capogrossi, and examples of Conceptual Art (Piero Manzoni's canister of 'Artist's Shit'). At the very top, the room decorated by Lucio Fontana has a wonderful view of the Duomo.

PALAZZO ARCIVESCOVILE AND PIAZZA FONTANA

Palazzo Arcivescovile (*map p. 25, D3–E3*), the Archbishop's Palace, was built by Pellegrino Tibaldi when he was in charge of the Duomo (around 1570), although the façade on **Piazza Fontana** (approached by Via Cardinale Martini) is by Giuseppe Piermarini (1784–1801). Here in 1969 a terrorist bomb killed 16 people (and wounded 88). Today there is a commemorative stone on the grass to Giuseppe Pinelli ('anarchist railway worker'), who died under interrogation in the police headquarters here in the same year (the subject of a play, *Death of an Anarchist*, by Dario Fo). The year 1969 marked the beginning of a disquieting period in 20th-century Italian history, which lasted for almost two decades. Terrorist organisations including the *Brigate Rosse* ('Red Brigades') and *Prima Linea* ('Front Line') organised bombings and gun attacks throughout Italy, but especially in the north. A total of 370 people died (270 of them civilians) and more than 1,000 were wounded. Despite numerous arrests, the authors of many of the massacres have never been identified. A small fountain, one of the few to be found in Milan and after which the square is named, provides a little cheer.

Just off the west side of Piazza del Duomo is the peaceful and ancient **Piazza Mercanti** (*map p. 25, D2–D3*), with a well and the Gothic Loggia degli Osii (1316) as well as the Baroque Palazzo delle Scuole Palatine (1645). Here too is the rear wall (with a remarkable equestrian relief of 1233) of Palazzo della Ragione, built in 1228–33, although the upper storey was added in 1771. There are remains of 13th-century frescoes inside.

GALLERIA VITTORIO EMANUELE II

The north side of Piazza del Duomo is connected with Piazza della Scala by this colossal glass-roofed shopping arcade (*map p. 25, D2*), named after Italy's first king, whose **equestrian statue** in the centre of Piazza del Duomo is the most noted work by Ercole Rosa (1896). The Galleria is always busy with Milanese as well as visitors. It was built in 1865 by Giuseppe Mengoni, who fell from the top and was killed a few days before the inauguration ceremony in 1878. Mengoni's design combines a severely Classical style with a remarkable sensitivity for new materials such as iron. The gallery was part of a grandiose project to renovate Piazza del Duomo, and its success led to the construction of numerous imitations in other Italian cities, notably the Galleria Mazzini in Genoa, the Galleria Principe in Naples and the Galleria Sciarra in Rome. Today it is still considered one of the 'sights' of the city, with crowded cafés and restaurants as well as flagship stores of some of the most famous fashion houses. In the central area of the arcade, opposite the restaurant and café **Cracco** with its two neon eyes (*see p. 118*), is Fondazione Prada's **Osservatorio**, dedicated to exhibitions of photography (*open weekdays except Tues 2–8; weekends 11–8; take the lift to the fifth floor; same ticket valid for the Fondazione Prada, see p. 112; fondazioneprada.org*). The exhibition space overlooks the Galleria's magnificent cast-iron and glass roof. Below, on the first floor, the old-established *pasticceria* **Marchesi** (*open daily 7.30am–9pm*) has pleasant premises with windows overlooking the inside of the Galleria.

PIAZZA DELLA SCALA

In the centre of Piazza della Scala (*map p. 25, D2*), which takes its name from the celebrated opera house, is a **monument to Leonardo da Vinci**, surrounded by figures of his pupils, Giovanni Antonio Boltraffio, Cesare da Sesto and Marco d'Oggiono, and the mysterious Andrea Salaino. Set up in 1872 by Pietro Magni, who had studied at the Brera Academy, it is surrounded today by creamy yellow Susan Daniel roses, donated to the city in 2006 by the great soprano who performed at La Scala and after whom the rose is named.

LA SCALA AND THE MUSEO TEATRALE ALLA SCALA

The **Teatro alla Scala** (*map p. 25, D2; open 9-5.30; T: 02 8879 7473, teatroallascala. org*) is Italy's most famous opera house, with an internationally acclaimed orchestra. It was begun in 1776, for Empress Maria Theresa of Austria, after the destruction by fire in the same year of the Regio Ducale Teatro. Standing on the site of the church of Santa Maria della Scala, the architect was Giuseppe Piermarini. It opened in 1778 with *Europa Riconosciuta* by Antonio Salieri and Mattia Verazi. Works by Rossini, Donizetti, Bellini, Verdi and Puccini were first performed here. From the beginning of the 20th century its reputation was upheld by the figure of Toscanini (who led the orchestra again in 1946, when the building reopened after war damage). In 2004 it was given an extension by Mario Botta, to provide rehearsal rooms and changing rooms.

Tickets give admission to the opera house itself, which you visit first from one of the boxes (unless rehearsals are in progress) and then to its museum, the delightful little **Museo Teatrale alla Scala** (*museoscala.org*), which first opened in 1913. There are mementoes, curios and musical instruments, including a 17th-century spinet from Naples and a Steinway piano that belonged to Franz Liszt. The *prime donne* of 19th-century opera are recorded as well as the composers Rossini, Bellini and Donizetti. There are also exhibits connected to Verdi (his *Nabucco* was first performed at La Scala to great acclaim in 1842) and Puccini (who wrote *Madama Butterfly* for La Scala). There are also sound recordings of memorable performances (the voice of Maria Callas can be heard).

PALAZZO MARINO AND PIAZZA SAN FEDELE

Palazzo Marino, the Town Hall (Municipio), stands opposite La Scala: its façade was completed by Luca Beltrami (1892) but the earlier front on **Piazza San Fedele** is by Galeazzo Alessi (1558), who also designed the splendid Mannerist courtyard. Also on Piazza San Fedele is a statue of the novelist Alessandro Manzoni (*see below*) by Francesco Barzaghi (1883) and the **church of San Fedele**, begun by Pellegrino Tibaldi (1569) for St Charles Borromeo and completed by Martino Bassi and Francesco Maria Richini. You can see another Baroque church by Richini, **San Giuseppe** (1607–30, considered his masterpiece), in a little piazza on Via Verdi behind La Scala. Here a showy aediculed façade with lateral volutes disguises an interior of pleasantly unexpected grace and simplicity.

GALLERIE D'ITALIA

Map p. 25, D2. Piazza della Scala 6. Open Tues–Sun 9.30-7.30, late opening until 10.30 on Thur. T: 800 167619, gallerieditalia.com.

Housed in a building built in 1906–11 by Luca Beltrami for the headquarters of the Banca Commerciale Italiana, and today owned by Intesa SanPaolo, the Gallerie are used to exhibit the bank's collection of 19th and 20th-century art as well as for temporary exhibitions. Displays are arranged in the old banking hall, which retains the cashiers' cubicles, as well as the strong-vaults. The **20th-century collection** includes works by Giorgio De Chirico, Lucio Fontana, Piero Manzoni, Alberto Burri, Renato Guttuso and Enrico Baj.

The **19th-century collection** is arranged in two adjoining palaces, Palazzo Anguissola Antona Traversi, dating from 1778 (it preserves some of its interior decorations from that time), and Palazzo Brentani. Both buildings were modified by Luigi Canonica around 1829. Highlights of the large collection are a series of 13 bas-reliefs by Canova and four Romantic historical paintings by Francesco Hayez. The upper floor is dedicated to the Risorgimento period, with works by Domenico and Gerolamo Induno and numerous views of Milan (the Duomo, the Navigli). The last section has important works by the Futurist painter Umberto Boccioni.

You can go out to the peaceful little **sculpture garden** (overlooked by Manzoni's house; *see below*), which has works by Giò Pomodoro and Hans Arp.

VIA ALESSANDRO MANZONI & THE 'FASHION QUADRILATERAL'

The fashionable Via Alessandro Manzoni (*map p. 25, D2–E1*) leads northeast from Piazza della Scala. At no. 29, the **Grand Hotel et de Milan** (founded in 1865), still one of the most elegant hotels in the city, is where Giuseppe Verdi died in 1901. The first turning on the right is Via Morone, a delightful narrow winding street, characteristic of 19th-century Milan (the barber's shop Colla has been here since 1904). At no. 1 is the **Casa di Alessandro Manzoni** (*open daily except Sat, Mon and holidays 9.30–12 & 2–4; casadelmanzoni.it*), where Italy's most famous 19th-century novelist lived from 1814 until his death.

ALESSANDRO MANZONI

Alessandro Manzoni, Romantic nationalistic poet, essayist and playwright, is by universal agreement Italy's greatest novelist thanks to his only novel, *I promessi sposi* (*The Betrothed*). Born in 1785 in Lombardy, his mother was Giulia Beccaria, eldest daughter of Cesare Beccaria, philosopher of the Enlightenment and criminologist, jurist and politician, who in his *On Crimes and Punishments* (1764) had argued against torture and the death penalty. Giulia married Pietro Manzoni in 1782, though Alessandro's true father is thought to have been Pietro's brother Giovanni Verri. After Giulia and Pietro separated, Manzoni was brought up at boarding school; later he spent a few years in Paris, where his mother had moved with her new companion, and there he came into contact with Enlightenment ideas. When he returned to Milan he married Enrichetta Blondel (a Calvinist with whom he had ten children) and lived in the city for the rest of his life. However, Enrichetta died in 1833 and only two of their children outlived Alessandro. He made a second marriage in 1837, to the cultivated Teresa Borri, widow of Count Stefano Decio Stampa. His most creative phase was between 1812 and 1827, during which he wrote patriotic and religious poems and plays and worked on various drafts of his celebrated novel. In 1860, at the height of his fame, he was made Honorary Senator of the Kingdom of Sardinia (which a year later was to merge into the newly born Kingdom of Italy). He died in 1873.

Casa degli Omenoni.

The definitive version of *I promessi sposi* came out in 1840, its language and style improved after a sojourn in Florence where, as Manzoni famously claimed, he had gone to 'rinse his clothes in the Arno'. With its remarkable opening description of Lake Como, which has been hammered into generations of Italian schoolchildren, it is Manzoni's *magnum opus*, a work which brought the spoken language of the lower, middle and upper classes into the literary sphere. The novel describes the troubled romance between Renzo and Lucia, star-crossed lovers who fall foul of the evil Don Rodrigo (the story is set during the 17th-century Spanish domination of Italy but this is a thinly-veiled allegory of the political tensions between northern Italy and Austria in Manzoni's own day). When Rodrigo has Lucia kidnapped, she prefers to take a vow of chastity rather than ending up in his bed. *I promessi sposi* is a witty, psychologically refined and exciting historical novel (partly inspired by Walter Scott's *Ivanhoe*, which Manzoni admired) and it captures many perennial vices and virtues of the Italian people: excessive bureaucracy, a tendency to turn mobsters into martyrs, a keen sense of one's own limitations and, above all, generosity of heart.

The simple apartment on the *piano nobile* has been kept much as it was in Manzoni's day (it was carefully restored in 2017) and portraits of the novelist and his relations have been hung on the walls (the most celebrated portrait of Manzoni is the one by Francesco Hayez, for which the novelist sat in 1841, the year after the publication of *I promessi sposi*, and which the painter donated to the Brera; *see p. 54*). Manzoni's study is on the ground floor off the little cobbled courtyard. Mementoes include his cloak, top hat and umbrella. Manzoni entertained Balzac in this house in 1837. Stendhal, 17 years older than Balzac, complained that when he was in Milan he had only been able to see from afar the great man he so much admired.

In 1941 the house was donated to the city of Milan and it is also now the seat of the Centro Nazionale Studi Manzoniani, instituted in 1937 (it is in the process of publishing Manzoni's complete works, a total of some 36 volumes).

At the bottom of Via Morone, in Piazza Belgioioso, is the huge **Palazzo Belgioioso**, (*map p. 25, D2*), one of Milan's most important Neoclassical buildings (by Giuseppe Piermarini, 1772–81). The **Casa degli Omenoni**, in the street of the same name (derived from the caryatids on the building's façade), was the residence and studio of the sculptor Leone Leoni from 1565 until his death in 1592. Vasari described it as one of the most eccentric houses he had seen in the city.

MUSEO POLDI PEZZOLI

Map p. 25, D2. Via Manzoni 12. Open daily except Tues 10–6. T: 02 796334, museopoldipezzoli.it.

This museum, once the private residence of Gian Giacomo Poldi Pezzoli, was bequeathed by him, with his art collection, to the city in 1879, and opened to the public in 1881. Together with the Wallace Collection in London and the Musée Jacquemart-

André in Paris, it is considered the most important private collection in Europe. It reflects the very special Milanese tradition of collectors who have left their property to the city. In this case the benefactor also had the vision to recommend that his collection should continue to be augmented, and numerous other donations have indeed been made over the decades. In order to fit these in, a next-door apartment was acquired in 2017. It has been connected directly to the building and is now the place where the most recent donations are exhibited. The museum possesses a few choice paintings by some of the most famous Italian artists at work in the 15th century and it also excels in the decorative arts.

Entrance hall and first floor
The entrance hall contains a portrait of Poldi Pezzoli by Francesco Hayez. Around a Baroque fountain winds a pretty elliptical staircase, with landscapes by Alessandro Magnasco. On the first floor to the left are the three little Lombard rooms, which have an excellent collection of works by 15th-century Lombard painters.

Lombard rooms: In the first room are lovely small Madonnas and a portrait of Giovanni Francesco Brivio in profile, all by **Vincenzo Foppa**, father of the Lombard school. His pupil Bergognone is also represented here. In the second room are works by the **Leonardeschi**, so called since they often copied Leonardo's works and sometimes seem to have actually worked with him. These include a *Madonna and Child with a Lamb* by Cesare da Sesto; works by Andrea Solario (*Rest on the Flight into Egypt*) and Giovanni Antonio Boltraffio (his *Virgin and Child* dated 1490 is thought to have been based on a drawing by Leonardo). Another pupil of Leonardo, Bernardino Luini, is also well represented here. The room of foreign artists has Flemish works and a portrait of Martin Luther and his wife by the German painter Lucas Cranach the Elder (with the intervention of his workshop), and a tiny *St John the Baptist* and the *Virgin*, autograph works by him.

Golden Room: Beyond the **Room of Stuccoes**, with porcelain from Meissen, Doccia and Capodimonte and a bronze bust of Bishop Ulpiano Volpi by Alessandro Algardi, the Salone Dorato, or **Golden Room** is hung with the masterpieces of the collection, by some of the most important Italian artists of the 15th century. The attribution of the famous **portrait of a lady in profile**, the symbol of the museum, is still disputed between the brothers Antonio and Piero del Pollaiolo. The *Madonna and Child* is a superb work by **Botticelli**, who also painted the *Deposition* here. The *St Nicholas of Tolentino* by **Piero della Francesca** is in poor condition. The great Veneto painters **Giovanni Bellini** and **Mantegna** are also present (the former with a *Christ in Pietà* and the latter with a portrait of an old man in profile and a *Madonna and Child*). Also on display here is an interesting *Madonna of Humility* by the Tuscan painter Zanobi Strozzi and a 15th-century Brussels tapestry.

Visconti Venosta room: There is a lovely little *Madonna and Child* by Neroccio di Bartolomeo de' Landi. The scene of St Hugh of Lincoln exorcising a possessed man, by Gherardo Starnina, is particularly interesting for its subject matter. The *Virgin and Child* is by Bergognone and the portrait of a cardinal (c. 1490, thought to be Ascanio Maria Sforza) is by an anonymous Lombard painter. The processional Cross (painted on both sides) is almost certainly by Raphael (c. 1500).

The rooms beyond have a collection of **antique clocks and scientific instruments** donated in 1973 by Bruno Falck. In the new wing, **recent donations** are arranged (including more precious clocks, antiquities and porcelain).

Further rooms: In the **Black Room** are works by Sassoferrato, Bergognone and Justus Sustermans (*Portrait of Cardinal Carlo de' Medici*). The marble sculpture of a girl in prayer (entitled *Trust in God*) is by the 19th-century artist Lorenzo Bartolini. The **Murano Glass Room** also has a small self-portrait (in the company of friends) by Hayez. The neo-Gothic **Fumoir** has a bust of Rosa Trivulzio Poldi Pezzoli by Bartolini. The **Perugino Room** is named after the small work by the Umbrian artist displayed here. There are also works here by Mariotto Albertinelli, Andrea Previtali (note the *memento mori* painted on the back of the *Portrait of a Man*) and Cima da Conegliano (*Triumph of Bacchus and Ariadne*). The later Venetian school is represented with small paintings of saints by Giovanni Battista Tiepolo and views and capriccios by Francesco Guardi and Canaletto. The ancient jewellery and goldsmiths' work, together with medieval religious bronzes and Limoges enamels, are displayed in the **Sala degli Ori**. Don't miss Palma il Vecchio's *Portrait of a Courtesan* (a beautiful Venetian lady with her hair down). The **Trivulzio Room** has a painting by Alessandro Magnasco and a collection of timepieces, sundials and meridians which belonged to the architect Piero Portaluppi (d. 1967).

Ground floor

On the ground floor the **Armoury**, with 15th-century arms and 16th-century Gonzaga armour, was given a superb new arrangement and a barrel vault in 2000 by Arnaldo Pomodoro. Another room here exhibits a splendid large **Persian carpet** with hunting scenes, signed and dated 1542–3, and there are two rooms with study collections of velvet and lace.

THE 'FASHION QUADRILATERAL'

Via Manzoni continues up to the crossroads with Via Montenapoleone, considered the most famous street in the city and the western perimeter of the so-called 'Fashion Quadrilateral'. The most elegant stores are located here, in a small area bounded by Via Montenapoleone, Via Spiga (which is totally pedestrian), Via Sant'Andrea and Via Santo Spirito. The important fashion houses have their flagship stores here and the streets are usually filled with elegant shoppers carrying their purchases in branded bags. **Cova** in Via Montenapoleone (*see p. 122*) is a celebrated café.

Palazzo Morando on Via Sant'Andrea is an 18th-century palace with a large collection of paintings, sculpture, drawings and prints depicting the changing face of Milan from the mid-17th century onwards (*Via Sant'Andrea 6; open Tues–Sun 9-1 & 2-5.30, T: 02 8844 6056, costumemodeaimagine.mi.it*). There are paintings of the Duomo, the Navigli, and church interiors. Some of the rooms have Egyptian antiquities, Maggiolini furniture and 18th-century frescoed ceilings.

SOME TOP NAMES IN ITALIAN FASHION

Born in Piacenza in 1934, Giorgio Armani began his career as a window-dresser at the Rinascente department store. In 1975, the brand name Giorgio Armani was launched for ready-to-wear fashion. In 1981 the first Emporio Armani opened in Milan. Today, the 83-year-old master of understatement still dominates the Italian fashion scene, projecting his vision of cool minimalism. Armani has also designed the costumes for numerous important films over the years, and his brand name is now attached to other products such as perfume, eye-wear and watches. The Armani Concept Store is on Via Alessandro Manzoni and the Armani Silos opened in 2015 (*see p. 110*).

The exuberant duo Dolce & Gabbana are as beguiling as ever with their richly patterned dresses. They make great use of internet influencers to promote their brand through a vision of the Italian good life. Gucci is also currently riding high, with theatrical shows and a doctrine of gender-fluid dressing. Another famous Italian fashion house, Prada, has turned its attention to culture (*see p. 112*).

MUSEO BAGATTI VALSECCHI

Map p. 25, E1. Via Gesù 5. Open Tues–Sun 1–5.30. T: 02 7600 6132, museobagattivalsecchi. org. There is a restaurant and café (Il Salumaio di Montenapoleone) in the courtyard, with tables outside.

With its dark interior crowded with furniture and artworks, this remarkable private house museum succeeds in avoiding a faded atmosphere and instead invites the visitor to explore its nooks and crannies leaving you full of admiration for the way it has been conceived from the outset as a habitable museum.

The mansion was built by the brothers Fausto and Giuseppe Bagatti Valsecchi in 1876–87, in the style of the Lombard Renaissance, and furnished by them with 16th-century works of art (or excellent 19th-century imitations by Lombard craftsmen, commissioned to fit the rooms). It was the family home up until 1974, when the Bagatti Valsecchi established a foundation and sold the building to the regional government. Its main façade is in Via Santo Spirito (opposite another fine palace in red brick, also built by the brothers in 1895 in 15th-century style). The palace and its contents represent an extremely interesting and well-preserved example of the eclectic taste of 19th-century collectors. It was opened to the public in 1994 and is still carefully looked after by volunteer custodians. There are handsheets in each room, also in English.

The two brothers lived in separate apartments in the palace, on either side of the drawing room, gallery of arms and dining room, which they shared. The rooms are richly decorated with carved ceilings, fireplaces, doorways and wall hangings, and filled with a miscellany of furniture and works of art.

The main staircase leads up to a landing, off which is a vestibule where a marble portal carved in 1884 in Renaissance style gives access to the Sala dell'Affresco, named after the fresco here by Antonio Boselli (1496). The Sala Bevilacqua takes its name from a very unusual 'painting' in various materials by Ambrogio Bevilacqua (late 15th century). Beyond the panelled library, with a collection of 17th-century sundials, is Fausto's bedroom, with an intricately carved 16th-century bed and two paintings, once part of the same polyptych, by Giampietrino (the frame was designed for it by the Bagatti). Beyond the dressing room and bathroom, with ingenious plumbing masked by Renaissance carvings, is the tall Galleria della Cupola, interesting for its architecture and containing a collection of ceramics. A little side room has photos and a home-movie showing four generations of the family (their keepsakes are housed in the drawers you can open here).

The three rooms of Giuseppe's apartment have a magnificent old stove, a late 15th-century Venetian painting of the Blessed Lorenzo Giustiniani, a painting attributed to Giovanni Bellini, and an early 17th-century Sicilian bed. The largest room in the house is the drawing room, with a 19th-century fireplace (made up of 16th-century fragments) and red wall hangings. The long Galleria delle Armi was created to display the collection of 16th- and 17th-century armour. The dining room has a pair of sideboards, one 16th century and the other a 19th-century copy. The walls are covered with 16th-century tapestries. The cupboards contain 16th-century Murano glass and Faenza ceramics. Beyond the study, a staircase leads down to the Via Santo Spirito entrance.

PINACOTECA DI BRERA

Map p. 25, D1. Open Tues–Sun 8.30–7. pinacotecabrera.org. Excellent shop in the courtyard. The exit takes you through the pleasant café.

Brera is traditionally the artists' quarter of Milan and its great Pinacoteca is one of the most famous art galleries in Italy. It contains the finest extant collection of Northern Italian painting from the 13th–20th centuries and has for long been a centre of the arts and sciences in Lombardy.

THE BUILDING

The building, which comprises the Pinacoteca, Accademia di Belle Arti and Biblioteca Nazionale Braidense, stands on the site of the medieval church of Santa Maria di Brera. There was a Jesuit college here from 1572–1773 and in 1627–8 the Jesuits had Francesco Maria Richini, the most important architect then at work in Milan, rebuild it for them. One of its most successful features is his monumental Cortile d'Onore. The building was finished in the 1770s and '80s by Giuseppe Piermarini (architect of La Scala), who added the main portal. Piermarini also designed the Biblioteca Nazionale

Braidense for its founder, Maria Theresa of Austria, who also founded the Accademia di Belle Arti here (now one of the most prestigious in Italy) and began the collection of paintings for the Pinacoteca.

Richini's great **Baroque Cortile d'Onore** provides a grand entrance to both the Pinacoteca and the Accademia. In the centre is a heroic nude statue in bronze of Napoleon by Antonio Canova (1809; the marble version is in Apsley House, London). He holds a 'Victory', a copy of the original, which was stolen in 1978.

The **ticket office** is in the hall at the top of the monumental stairway. On the left-hand stairs is a statue of Cesare Beccaria (1735–94), shown leaning on the book he wrote denouncing capital punishment and torture (he was the grandfather of the novelist Alessandro Manzoni; *see p. 39*). Immediately in front of you as you enter the ticket hall, through a glass door, you can see Piermarini's **Biblioteca Braidense** (*see above*). It contains some 40,000 precious volumes dating from the 16th–18th centuries.

THE PINACOTECA

Founded in the 18th century as part of the Accademia di Belle Arti, the gallery was enlarged through acquisitions and with works from Lombard and Venetian churches, many of them confiscated by Napoleon during his conquest of Italy. It was Napoleon who officially opened the gallery in 1809. The architect Piero Portaluppi carried out work here from 1919 onwards and in 1950 collaborated with Ettore Modigliani on a new arrangement. The Brera has been an independent institution since 2014.

The collection is extremely well displayed: the arrangement proceeds chronologically from the 13th century onwards and is organised by schools. The labels beneath each work are exceptionally useful, putting them in context and pointing out their significance. Plenty of comfortable places to sit are provided. The room numbers given here correspond to those in situ. Floor plans are also available at the front desks. There is wall text on how to explore the collection, which quotes the credo of Franco Russoli, director in the 1970s: 'A museum is a place for participation.'

Room IA: This room was designed to contain the little frescoed private chapel of the Oratorio Porro at Mocchirolo when it was donated to the Pinacoteca in 1949. The frescoes with St Catherine and St Ambrose may be by the hand of Giovanni da Milano, or more probably an artist influenced by him.

Rooms II–IV (early works): The earliest works in the gallery are hung here, against red walls. Room II has a panel painting of *Christ Enthroned with Four Angels in Adoration* by **Giovanni da Milano**. This work (c. 1360) was part of an altarpiece and although damaged it shows the painter's great skill and sensitivity. Giovanni Baronzio, a painter from Rimini and Giovanni's contemporary, painted the three panels with scenes from the life of St Columba, and the earlier panel of St Veranus with six stories from his life is attributed to a painter from Pisa who was at work in the late 13th century known from this painting as the Master of San Verano.

Beyond Room III, with more 14th-century paintings, Room IV introduces the **International Gothic** period. The small *Adoration of the*

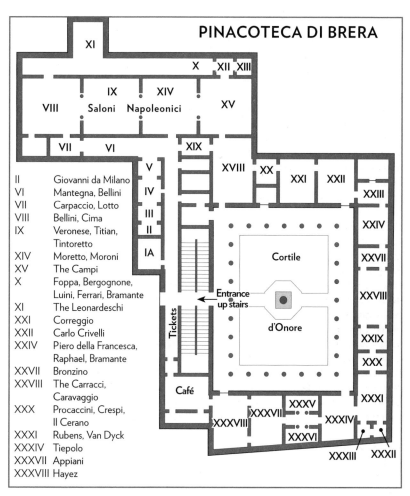

PINACOTECA DI BRERA

II	Giovanni da Milano
VI	Mantegna, Bellini
VII	Carpaccio, Lotto
VIII	Bellini, Cima
IX	Veronese, Titian, Tintoretto
XIV	Moretto, Moroni
XV	The Campi
X	Foppa, Bergognone, Luini, Ferrari, Bramante
XI	The Leonardeschi
XXI	Correggio
XXII	Carlo Crivelli
XXIV	Piero della Francesca, Raphael, Bramante
XXVII	Bronzino
XXVIII	The Carracci, Caravaggio
XXX	Procaccini, Crespi, Il Cerano
XXXI	Rubens, Van Dyck
XXXIV	Tiepolo
XXXVII	Appiani
XXXVIII	Hayez

Magi is a charming work by Stefano da Verona and there is a small fragment of a *Madonna and Child* beautifully painted by Jacopo Bellini (father of Giovanni). The *Praglia Polyptych* is by two Venetian painters who almost always worked together, Antonio Vivarini and Giovanni d'Alemagna. The small *Annunciation* is a rare work by a contemporary Spanish painter, Pere Serra.

Rooms V–VII (Venice): This group of rooms, with blue walls, illustrates the great 15th-century Venetian school. As an introduction, Room V has works by painters who worked mostly in central Italy: the two sides of a processional painting by **Luca Signorelli** are of particular interest for the figure studies in the *Flagellation* scene. The *Pietà* is by the Spanish painter Pedro Berruguete, who worked in Umbria, and there is a predella panel by **Benozzo Gozzoli** illustrating a *Miracle of St Dominic*, with splendid crimson details.

The first part of a long gallery (VI) has famous masterpieces by Mantegna and Giovanni Bellini. **Mantegna's *Polyptych of St Luke the Evangelist***, painted in 1453, shows the genial saint writing at a lectern (supported by a coloured-marble column) with a few medlars scattered on the ground around his sandalled feet. This large altarpiece includes a *Pietà* above, neatly fitted into the frame, and eight compartments with figures of saints. The same artist's well-known ***Lamentation over the Dead Christ***, with its memorable foreshortened figure, is necessarily less bright since it is painted in tempera on canvas. It reveals Mantegna's fascination with perspective and illusionism, which had an important influence on later artists including Correggio and Raphael. This painting was still in his studio in Mantua when he died there in 1506 (*see p. 372*). Also displayed here is a *Pietà* by Mantegna's contemporary (and brother-in-law) **Giovanni Bellini**, one of his most moving works. Bellini's *Greek Madonna* (with the standing, mournful Child) is displayed next to Mantegna's *Madonna of the Cherubim* (once attributed to Bellini). Both are particularly memorable. The *St Sebastian* by the much less well-known painter Liberale da Verona has been hung here not only because of its extraordinary background recalling Venice, but also to show the high quality of works being produced all over the Veneto at this time.

At the far end of this hall (Room VII) are large works by **Vittore Carpaccio**, well-known for his charming painting cycles made for the Venetian *scuole*. Most of these are still in Venice but three are preserved here: two from the Scuola degli Albanesi and one, of particular interest, showing *St Stephen Disputing with the Doctors* from the Scuola di Santo Stefano (1514). Giovanni Bellini's wonderful *Madonna and Child* in a landscape dominates the end of the room: dated 1510 it is one of his last works. Three scenes of *St Jerome in the Desert*, one of the most popular subjects for artists at this time, are exhibited together. **Lorenzo Lotto** is represented by a little-known small work showing the *Assumption of the Virgin* (its witty details are explained on the label).

Saloni Napoleonici (Lombardy and the Veneto): This enfilade of four grand rooms (VIII, IX, XIV and XV), divided by Neoclassical columns and lit by skylights, and with a central marble version of Canova's courtyard statue of Napoleon, was built to exhibit paintings which joined the collection between 1809 and 1812, following the suppression of churches and convents in northern Italy by order of Napoleon. Today they provide space for the largest works in the collection by painters from Lombardy and the Veneto who were at work in the 15th and 16th centuries.

Room VIII has **Gentile and Giovanni Bellini**'s *St Mark Preaching in Alexandria* (the two brothers make a feature of the white cloaks and head-dresses of the seated veiled ladies as well as the white turbans and black berets of the male Muslim and Christian onlookers). It was painted for the Scuola Grande di San Marco in Venice. **Cima da Conegliano** is represented with three of his characteristically large altarpieces and there is a *Crucifixion* by Michele da Verona.

Room IX is devoted to large paintings by **Veronese, Tintoretto and Titian**, the chief Venetian painters of the 16th century: *Agony in the Garden*, a huge, incident-rich *Supper in the House of Simon*, the *Baptism and Temptation of Christ*, a *Last Supper* and *St Anthony Abbot with Sts Cornelius and Cyprian* by Veronese; *Saints Beneath the Cross* and *The Finding of the Body of St Mark at Alexandria* by Tintoretto (the latter a magnificent work with a dream-like atmosphere).

Titian's *Penitent St Jerome* was restored in 2017. Signed 'Ticianus F' on the stone in the foreground, it was painted on board between 1556 and 1561 for the burial chapel of Heinrich Helman, a German merchant resident in Venice (the chapel has been destroyed). The numerous details are symbols of qualities associated with the saint (the lizard = temptation and the snail = patience and resistance).

Room XIV has large **16th-century Venetian paintings**, showing how strongly they influenced some of the **Lombard painters** whose works have been hung here. The huge *Adoration of the Magi* (in the presence of St Helen) is by Palma il Vecchio, painted in 1522, just six years before his death. This painter, though born in Lombardy (*see p. 281*), belonged to the Venetian school (today most of his works are widely dispersed outside Italy). Callisto Piazza (from Lodi) and **Moretto**, Brescia's most famous painter (*see p. 302*), are both well represented. Paris Bordone, who looked closely at Titian's works, painted the *Baptism of Christ*. The *Assumption of the Virgin* is by **Giovanni Battista Moroni**

(*see p. 269*), one of the most interesting painters of this group: the misty landscape makes the crowd of disciples all the more striking. Giovan Girolamo Savoldo's Pesaro altarpiece, with the *Madonna in Glory*, includes a view of the Fondamente Nuove in Venice.

Room XV displays a remarkable *Crucifixion* by Bramantino. There are also Cremonese works here by the **Campi family** (*see p. 402*). Giulio Campi chose religious subjects. Those by his brother Vincenzo provide quite another atmosphere: they include genre scenes of fishmongers and poultry sellers. The colourful *Martyrdom of St Catherine of Alexandria* is by **Gaudenzio Ferrari**.

Rooms X–XIII (Lombard school):

The long corridor **(Room X)** beyond the Saloni Napoleonici exhibits Lombard works. The *Presentation in the Temple* by **Vincenzo Foppa** (*see p. 91*) is exhibited close to three small but important works by his disciple **Bergognone** (*Adoration of the Shepherds*, *Madonna and Child with St Catherine of Siena and a Carthusian Monk* (note their remarkable grey-toned faces) and the *Madonna 'della Vela'*. The two detached frescoes by Foppa from the church of Santa Maria di Brera almost seem to have been painted in honour of the great architect and painter **Bramante**, who had just arrived in Milan and who painted the 'Men at Arms' frescoes for the house of Gasparo Visconti.

Other works include an *Adoration of the Magi* and *Stories of Sts Joachim and Anne* by Gaudenzio Ferrari (both with delightful small dogs) and some very odd detached frescoes by Bernardino Luini (the air-borne corpse of St Catherine held up by angels, and nymphs bathing).

His *Madonna del Roseto*, on the other hand, prominently displayed at the end of the room, is one of his best works.

Room XI: This room, off the long corridor, is devoted to the **Leonardeschi painters** of Lombardy.

THE LEONARDESCHI

Since Leonardo da Vinci spent many years in Milan (*see p. 66*), it is natural that a school of painters (now known as the 'Leonardeschi') should have grown up around him. They included Ambrogio de Predis and Giovanni Antonio Boltraffio, considered the great painter's pupils and closest followers. Other artists who show a direct influence are Cesare da Sesto, Giampietrino (Giovan Pietro Rizzoli), Andrea Solario, Marco d'Oggiono and Bernardino Luini. Francesco Napoletano (Francesco Galli) is also thought to have worked closely in the wake of Leonardo when he was in Milan in the last decade of the 15th century. Aside from the Brera, the Ambrosiana is a good place to see the work of some of these painters (*see p. 76*). The Museo Poldi Pezzoli also has a room dedicated to them (*see p. 42*) and Cesare da Sesto's *Polyptych of St Roch* (1523) is in the Castello Sforzesco.

These artists are interesting also because some of their subjects probably record ideas for compositions devised by Leonardo himself: a *Madonna* in the Poldi Pezzoli by Boltraffio, for example, is thought to have been painted directly on a design by the master. Ambrogio de Predis is known to have been closely in contact with Leonardo and he made a fine copy of the famous *Virgin of the Rocks* (of the version owned by the National Gallery, London), which Leonardo painted while in Milan. A copy of Leonardo's Milan *Last Supper* was made in 1612–16 by order of Cardinal Borromeo by Andrea Bianchi (known as Il Vespino) and this can still be seen in the Ambrosiana, together with some of his other works which imitate the master.

Bernardino Luini, although usually included in this group, stands somewhat on his own as he seems to have been inspired more by Bramantino and Bergognone. His beautiful paintings and frescoes can be seen here at the Brera, at the Ambrosiana, in San Maurizio (and other churches in the city) as well as in Saronno.

Portraits by the Leonardeschi include three of young men: two by Boltraffio, and another, of a man in a black hat, by Andrea Solario, all very fine works. On the end wall, the *Polyptych of Santa Maria delle Grazie* is by Vincenzo Foppa, with a lovely central panel of the Madonna (and among the saints, the artist's namesake St Vincent in a particularly splendid dalmatic). The *Annunciation* by Bernardino Zenale has a very original composition. Another typically original work is the fragment of a *Holy Family* by Bramantino: the Madonna wears a turban and the stocky Child has his arms stuck up in the air (it is a figure which could almost have been painted by Picasso). The *Three Archangels Defeating the Devil* is a superb work by Marco d'Oggiono.

The so-called **Pala Sforzesca** (1495) by a master known from this work as the Maestro della Pala Sforzesca (but otherwise unidentified) also demonstrates the difficulty a court artist had at this time in assimilating the influence of Leonardo with the figurative tradition of Lombardy.

This is a work well-known because it commemorates Ludovico il Moro (*see p. 167*), who with his wife Beatrice d'Este and two small children (one of them still swaddled) is portrayed together with the Madonna and Child and four huge, rather looming Doctors of the Church.

Room XII has two small Madonnas by Giampietrino; a self-portrait by Giovanni Paolo Lomazzo (a little-known painter born in Milan in 1538); a small *St Francis of Assisi* by Bernardino Lanino (set in a lovely wood) and an altarpiece by Gerolamo Giovenone.

Room XIII, the **Cappella di San Giuseppe** from the church of Santa Maria della Pace in Milan, has been reconstructed with its fresco cycle illustrating stories from the lives of St Joachim and St Anne and the Virgin and Joseph by **Bernardino Luini** and assistants. They were detached and transferred to canvas and brought to the Brera in stages, between 1805 and 1875, so it has been difficult to reconstruct their original arrangement. The story of the life of Virgin and Joseph reflects the new devotional imagery promoted by the Franciscans (the iconography is based on the *Apocalypsis Nova,* written by the Blessed Amedeo Mendez da Silva). The stylistic influence of Bramantino is evident.

Room XVIII is a restoration laboratory with glass walls so visitors can see work in progress.

Room XIX has superb **portraits** by Tintoretto, Palma il Giovane, Lorenzo Lotto, Titian and Giovanni Battista Moroni (the splendid likeness of

Antonio Navagero with an unforgettable scarlet codpiece, 1565). There is also a self-portrait by Sofonisba Anguissola.

Room XX: In this small room dedicated to **central Italian painting** of the 15th and 16th centuries are two panels of saints by Francesco del Cossa; *Adoration of the Magi* by Lorenzo Costa il Vecchio; the severed *Head of St John the Baptist* by Giovanni Francesco Maineri; a *Madonna and Child* by Boccaccio Boccaccino and *Portrait of a Man* by Filippo Mazzola (clearly influenced by the Flemish school).

Room XXI (Ferrara and Emilian school): Ercole de' Roberti's *Virgin Enthroned* has an unusual composition with a throne mounted on a very tall dais. There are two small Nativity scenes by Correggio; panels of saints by Dosso Dossi; *Lamentation over the Dead Christ* by Garofalo; *Annunciation* by Il Francia; and *Portrait of a Friar* by Girolamo Mazzola Bedoli.

Room XXII has a group of stunning works by **Carlo Crivelli**, including two triptychs from Camerino in the Marche region. The *Madonna of the Candle* (from the slender taper at the foot of the steps before the throne) is considered one of his most important works to have remained in Italy. Both triptychs have typical Crivellian symbolic fruits (they could not have been painted better, even by Mantegna): the *San Domenico Triptych* includes a particularly memorable broad bean pod.

Room XXIII is used for storage (through the glass walls visitors can see the way the deposits are arranged).

Room XXIV has just three masterpieces, two of them world-famous. The **Montefeltro Altarpiece** by Piero della Francesca (1465–70) is justly acclaimed as perhaps the most beautiful of his paintings and is his last known work (the only other work by him in Lombardy is *St Nicholas of Tolentino* at the Museo Poldi Pezzoli).

The other celebrated work here is **Raphael's *Marriage of the Virgin*** (1504), his best-known work in Lombardy—though not the only one: his huge cartoon for a fresco in the Vatican is preserved in the Ambrosiana in Milan, and there are also works by him in Brescia and Bergamo.

The third work, **Donato Bramante's *Christ at the Column*** (1487–90), is the only known panel painting of a sacred subject by this artist, who was also a great Renaissance architect (*see p. 80*). Christ is shown tied up waiting to be thrashed, and his hauntingly beautiful visage is painted in starkly grey tones. The work was painted for the Abbey of Chiaravalle (*see p. 138*) c. 1490 and its attribution was disputed for centuries between Bramante and his pupil Bramantino.

Room XXVII (Mannerism): The display includes **Bronzino's** famous portrait of Andrea Doria in the guise of Neptune. The *Martyrdom of St Vitalis* is by Federico Barocci.

Room XXVIII: 'Between Naturalism and Classicism': Here are paintings by Ludovico and Annibale Carracci, Guercino and Guido Reni. But the most interesting work here is by **Caravaggio**, the very beautiful *Supper at Emmaus*, painted in 1606 (his virtuosity marked by the figure of the disciple in the foreground, who is in total shadow).

Room XXIX (Rome and Naples): Paintings by Orazio Gentileschi, Salvator Rosa, Mattia Preti, Jusepe de Ribera and Caracciolo.

Room XXX (17th-century Lombardy): The display includes Giulio Cesare Procaccini (*St Charles Borromeo in Glory*; another version can be seen in the church of San Tommaso on Via Broletto; *map p. 24, C2*), Il Cerano and Daniele Crespi (*Last Supper*, influenced by Gaudenzio Ferrari's *Last Supper* in Santa Maria della Passione; *see p. 100*).

Room XXXI (Italy and Flanders): Notable Flemish works are **Rubens'** *Last Supper* and the *Madonna and Child with St Anthony of Padua* by **Van Dyck**.

Rooms XXXII–XXXIII: Portraits by a number of 17th-century artists, including Annibale Carracci (a self-portrait) and Bernardo Strozzi, and four 17th-century still lifes.

Room XXXIV: This large room houses a huge painting from the Carmine in Venice by **Giovanni Battista Tiepolo** and an *Ecce Homo* by Luca Giordano.

Rooms XXXV and XXXVI: These two rooms, separated by pretty Neoclassical columns, have 17th-century genre scenes by Pietro Longhi; Venetian views by **Canaletto and Guardi**; landscapes by Bellotto; and *Rebecca at the Well* by Giambattista Piazzetta. On the other side are mostly Lombard portraits and still-lifes, including a good portrait of his father by Gian Pietro Ligari.

PIERO DELLA FRANCESCA'S MONTEFELTRO ALTARPIECE

This beautiful painting was originally made for San Bernardino degli Zoccolanti, a little country church near Urbino. With its solemn figures and rather grim Child asleep on the Madonna's lap, it has an extraordinary, other-worldly atmosphere. The donor is the armoured gentleman praying in the foreground—Federico da Montefeltro, a famed mercenary general who eventually became one of the most powerful political and cultural figures of the Renaissance. The painting may have been a memorial to Battista Sforza, his wife, who died in childbirth. It has been dated between 1472 and 1474 and its clear, crisp presentation of forms in space was widely imitated in monumental devotional paintings in northern Italian and Venetian art. Scholars have long debated the significance of the 'egg' hanging from the ceiling. Some suggest that it is not an egg at all: Marian literature is replete with images of Mary as an oyster and Jesus as her pearl (and the egg—or pearl—does after all dangle from a shell-shaped niche). Nevertheless, there is a convention of the egg as a symbol of the Virgin Birth. The belief that ostriches left their eggs to be hatched by the sun led to comparisons with the sun and the Son. As the great medieval philosopher and theologian Albertus Magnus (guide and mentor of Thomas Aquinas) wrote: 'If the sun can hatch the eggs of the ostrich, why cannot a virgin conceive with the aid of the true Sun?'

RAPHAEL'S *MARRIAGE OF THE VIRGIN*

Perugino, Pinturicchio and Raphael form the 'Umbrian School' of Renaissance painting. But long before they were an art-historical category, these three artists were close friends, Pinturicchio and Raphael having been Perugino's most distinguished students. The *Marriage of the Virgin* is Raphael's first major painting and both its composition and its palette recall Perugino's *Giving of the Keys to St Peter* (1481) in the Sistine Chapel in Rome—which also features a dense group of foreground figures and an idealised architectural setting. Originally painted for a church in Città di Castello, the *Marriage of the Virgin* entered the Brera in 1806 as a donation by Eugène de Beauharnais. It has a totally different atmosphere from the Piero della Francesca, being almost a conversation piece, with people in memorable headgear strolling about in the background and one of the Virgin's rejected young suitors rather stealing the show by leaning forward to break his rod, which has failed to flower, across his knee. This work typifies the way that everything appears more natural in Raphael, the figures freer and more animated, the setting less rigid and formal. Giorgio Vasari attempted to describe what, in modern marketing language, we might call the Raphael Difference. 'The liberality with which Heaven now and again unites in one person the inexhaustible riches of its treasures and all those graces and rare gifts which are usually shared among many over a long period, is seen in Raphael. Those who possess such gifts as |he| are not mere men, but rather mortal gods'.

Rooms XXXVII and XXXVIII (19th century): The gallery's holdings of this period are small but they nicely fill these two rooms. There are Neoclassical paintings by Andrea Appiani and a particularly good collection of works by **Francesco Hayez**. His most famous painting here is the Romantic *Il Bacio*

(*The Kiss*), of 1859. On either side of it hang works by Gerolamo Induno with a related theme. *A Great Sacrifice* (1860) shows a mother kissing her soldier son goodbye. *Doleful Premonition* (1862) shows a young girl in her bedroom (which has a print of *The Kiss* on the wall) contemplating a portrait of her sweetheart who is away fighting in the War of Independence. Portraits by Hayez include the novelist Alessandro Manzoni, who sat for the artist in 1841 (and donated the portrait to the Pinacoteca in 1874) and Manzoni's second wife Teresa Borri Stampa (an earlier likeness of her, as a young widow, also by Hayez, hangs here too).

PALAZZO CITTERIO

The radical (and controversial) restoration of the 18th-century Palazzo Citterio (*Via Brera 12–14*) has finally been completed and the building is to provide space for the Brera's collection of 20th-century art, which includes a number of self-portraits by Umberto Boccioni. The Jesi collection of Italian and European art from 1910–50, which will form the nucleus of the works to be displayed, was donated by Maria Jesi in 1976, two years after the death of her husband Emilio, with whom she had formed the collection. It has paintings and sculpture by Futurist, Cubist and Metaphysical artists (Medardo Rosso, Amedeo Modigliani, Carlo Carrà, Arturo Martini, Marino Marini, Giorgio Morandi, De Pisis and Mario Sironi).

THE BOTANICAL GARDENS AND MUSEO ASTRONOMICO

Close to the Brera, hemmed in by surrounding buildings, is the small and charming **Orto Botanico** (*entrance at Via Brera 28 or Via Fratelli Gabba 10; open Mon–Sat 10–6, in winter 9.30–4.30; T: 02 5031 4680, brera.unimi.it*). Founded at the end of the 18th century by the Jesuits, it is now maintained by Milan University and has well-labelled themed plots. The **Museo Astronomico** (*also entered from Via Brera 28; open weekdays 9–4.30*) was created in 1760, also by the Jesuits, and is the city's oldest observatory (it is also now run by the University). There is a gallery of historic astronomical instruments and there are guided tours (usually at 2pm) to the Schiaparelli dome (5th floor, reached by stairs).

THE BRERA DISTRICT

The 'Design District' around the Brera is famous for its boutiques, galleries, concept stores, old-established cafés and grand restaurants. It is particularly busy during Milan's annual Fashion and Design weeks.

The bronze statue in the little Piazzetta Brera commemorates the painter Francesco Hayez, director of the Brera in the 19th century. On the corner of Via Fiori Chiari, directly opposite the Pinacoteca, the delightfully old-fashioned Bar Brera does good business, along with other bistros, cafés and tearooms in Via Brera. It is worth exploring Via Fiori Chiari, Via Fori Oscuri and Via Madonnina, nicely paved pedestrian precincts. The Bar Jamaica (*Via Brera 32*), where the 20th-century Italian poets Quasimodo and Ungaretti were habitués, was much frequented in the 1960s but

VIA MADONNINA

it is now considered somewhat *passé* by the Milanese themselves: it has pictures of the food outside. There are a number of non-Italian places to eat in this district, reflecting the present fashion for international food.

SANTA MARIA DEL CARMINE AND SAN TOMMASO

The 15th-century church of **Santa Maria del Carmine** (*map p. 24, C1*), with a façade completed in 1879, has a good Baroque chapel decorated by Camillo Procaccini. **San Tommaso** on Via Broletto (*map p. 24, C2*), with an early 19th-century Ionic portico, has a pretty mosaic pavement running all the way up the nave, with Christian symbols (peacock, pelican, dove) and the Four Rivers of Paradise. On the north side is an altarpiece of *St Charles Borromeo in Glory* by Giulio Cesare Procaccini (another version of the same work hangs in the Brera).

VIA BORGONUOVO

The narrow Via Borgonuovo (*map p. 25, D1*) is lined by a series of fine town houses with interesting courtyards and gardens. Huge 19th-century palaces, often now divided up into numerous apartments around their interior courtyards, are a characteristic of Milan. One of the grandest of these, at no. 11, is now home to the Armani fashion house (*see p. 44*). The building opposite (no. 14–16), with its roof garden, was restored after war damage by the Studio BBPR. The **Civico Museo del Risorgimento** (*Via Borgonuovo 23; open Tues–Sun 9–1 & 2–5.30; T: 02 8846 4176, civicheraccoltestoriche. mi.it*) occupies Palazzo Moriggia, rebuilt in the 18th century by Giuseppe Piermarini. It includes material dating from the arrival of Napoleon in Lombardy in 1796 up to the taking of Rome in 1870. There is a good library.

SAN MARCO

Preceded by a pleasant cobbled court, the church of San Marco (*map p. 25, D1*) dates from 1254 but has a mock-Gothic façade of 1873. Its doorway and three statuettes from the 14th century are the only medieval elements. Verdi's *Requiem* received its first performance here. In the Baroque interior, the exceptionally long nave has numerous paintings from the 16th and 17th centuries and interesting tombs. The first south chapel was entirely decorated with frescoes on the vault and walls (1571) by Giovanni Paolo Lomazzo, who also provided the altarpiece. At the end of the aisle is a painting of *St Jerome* by Legnanino, who also painted the altarpiece at the end of the north aisle of *St Jerome Translating the Holy Scriptures* (it is beside a charming little Baby Jesus, a fully dressed doll, highly venerated). In the north transept, the Cappella del Crocifisso was also decorated in the 17th century and has a copy of Caravaggio's *Deposition* in the Vatican Pinacoteca. In the south transept is a 14th-century fresco fragment of the *Crucifixion and Saints* and tombs including that of the Blessed Lanfranco da Settala (d. 1264), ascribed to Giovanni di Balduccio. The presbytery has a vault and apse frescoed in the early 17th century by the little-known Bartolomeo Roverio (Il Genovesino), who also carried out the two paintings in the choir, where there are more paintings from the same period by Camillo Procaccini and Il Cerano. The altar dates from 1816 (by Giocondo Albertolli). The organ was made by the Antegnati in the late 16th century.

CORSO GARIBALDI AND SAN SIMPLICIANO

Corso Garibaldi (*map p. 24, C1*) runs through Milan's theatreland. The red-brick **Piccolo Teatro Strehler** was founded by the great director Giorgio Strehler in 1947 and rebuilt by Marco Zanuso in 1996. It is still one of Milan's most important theatres for prose performances and there are a number of theatre workshops in the area, including the Piccolo Teatro Studio Melato. On the other side of Corso Garibaldi is the church of **San Simpliciano**. During the Middle Ages, Milan's northern districts grew up around this early Christian basilica, traditionally founded by St Ambrose himself in the 4th century and dedicated to the Virgin Martyrs. It was later dedicated to Ambrose's successor in the episcopal chair. Despite alterations of the 12th century, it survives largely in its original form. Today it stands in a peaceful little close and is much visited by worshippers. In the restored Romanesque apse (unfortunately masked by the towering Neoclassical altar with its domed temple) is one of the most important frescoes by Bergognone, the *Coronation of the Virgin* (c. 1508), crowded with angels and saints: women on one side and men on the other.

CASTELLO SFORZESCO

Map p. 24, B1. Piazza Castello. The castle is home to various important museums (see below). Its courtyards are open as a public park 7am–7.30pm.

Foro Buonaparte, Largo Cairoli and Piazza Castello were all designed in 1884 as a huge hemicycle in front of the magnificent Castello Sforzesco and are still a pleasant pedestrian precinct, with an abundant fountain and a monument to Garibaldi (Ettore Ximenes, 1895). The castle was built for Francesco Sforza in 1451–66 on the site of a 14th-century Visconti stronghold. It was intended as an ornament to the city rather than as a defence against the people. Ludovico Sforza carried out more work on it towards the end of the 15th century. After a long period of use as a barracks, it was restored by Luca Beltrami (1893–1904). Badly damaged by bombing in 1943 (when two-thirds of the archives and many other treasures were lost), it was again carefully restored and now contains important art collections and cultural institutions.

The fortress is square in plan. The central gatehouse, the **Filarete Tower**, was destroyed by an explosion of powder in 1521 and rebuilt by Beltrami following the supposed design of the original. This provides the main entrance to the castle. Beyond it is the huge **Cortile delle Armi**, the main courtyard, a particularly pleasant wide-open space where people come to stroll (it has entrances on two other sides and also provides an approach to the public gardens of the Parco Sempione behind the castle).

Almost in the centre of the far side is the 15th-century **Torre di Bona di Savoia**, beyond which to the left is the **Rocchetta**, which served as a keep. It has an enclosed courtyard, cobbled and arcaded, in the design of which both Filarete and Bramante had a hand. On the right is the **Corte Ducale**, once the residential part of the castle, which also has a charming courtyard, with a rectangular pool designed in 1954.

MUSEI DI CASTELLO SFORZESCO

Open Tues–Sun 9–5.30. T: 02 8846 3700, milanocastello.it. There are two ticket offices (see plan). A single ticket serves for all the museums so keep it handy to show at the entrances to the various collections.

The museums include collections of sculpture, paintings, furniture, musical instruments, decorative arts, archaeological finds and Egyptian artefacts. They are so extensive that it is not really possible to do them justice in a single visit.

MICHELANGELO'S *RONDANINI PIETÀ*

The most famous work in the Castello, Michelangelo's *Rondanini Pietà*, is exhibited on its own in Cortile delle Armi, in a separate building which was used as a military hospital when Milan was under Spanish rule (there are remains of frescoes on the vault). The display, especially successful in the dramatic approach and the lighting, was designed in 2015 by Michele De Lucchi. This moving but pathetic sculpture, with its dramatically bent curved figures of the Madonna and Christ, is Michelangelo's last work. The sculptor worked on it at intervals during the last nine years of his life, and up to six days before his death, but he clearly left it unfinished. For this work, according to Vasari, Michelangelo re-used a block of marble in which he had already roughed out another *Pietà*, to a different design and on a smaller scale.

The provenance of the work is somewhat mysterious. Although a sculpture of a *Pietà* is recorded on Michelangelo's death in his studio in Rome, almost nothing more was heard of it until this was purchased (it is not known where or when) by the Rondanini family, who displayed it in the courtyard of their Rome palace. It was purchased by the *comune* of Milan in 1952.

Although today acclaimed as the most important work in the city's collections, some scholars of Michelangelo see it as merely a last attempt by the great sculptor, in extreme old age, to come to terms with a block of stone and feel that it can in no way be considered on a level with his great (and also famously 'unfinished') masterpieces.

The bronze head of Michelangelo, one of several versions of the famous portrait by his great friend Daniele da Volterra (1564), is also displayed here. Daniele was with the artist at his death. The celebratory bronze medal is a version of one by Leone Leoni which was sent to the artist in 1561, just three years before he died.

In the tiny side rooms are the bases formerly used to support the *Pietà* (the current simple grey base is undoubtedly the most appropriate), including an ancient Roman altar which was in the Rondanini collection. The quiet of the room is disturbed by noise from Milan's metro (but this does not, unfortunately, manage to drown out the piped music).

MUSEO D'ARTE ANTICA (SCULPTURE MUSEUM)

Corte Ducale, ground floor. Entrance through the Portale della Pusterla dei Fabbri (one of the oldest city gates in the medieval walls, moved here in 1954).

The arrangement of these superb works from the medieval period to the 16th century,

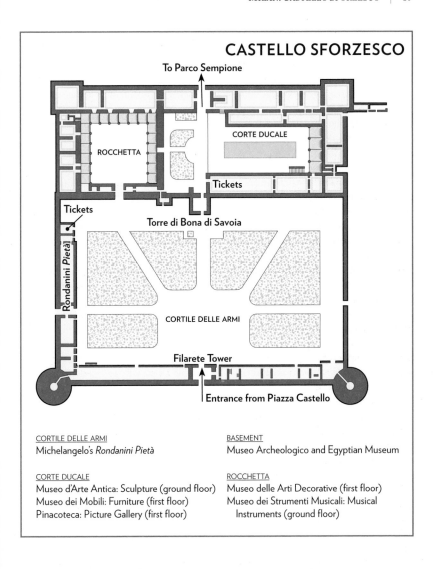

CASTELLO SFORZESCO

To Parco Sempione

CORTE DUCALE

Tickets

ROCCHETTA

Tickets

Torre di Bona di Savoia

Rondanini Pietà

CORTILE DELLE ARMI

Filarete Tower

Entrance from Piazza Castello

CORTILE DELLE ARMI
Michelangelo's *Rondanini Pietà*

CORTE DUCALE
Museo d'Arte Antica: Sculpture (ground floor)
Museo dei Mobili: Furniture (first floor)
Pinacoteca: Picture Gallery (first floor)

BASEMENT
Museo Archeologico and Egyptian Museum

ROCCHETTA
Museo delle Arti Decorative (first floor)
Museo dei Strumenti Musicali: Musical
  Instruments (ground floor)

---

dates from 1954, and is the creation of the architects Lodovico Barbiano di Belgiojoso, Enrico Peressutti and Ernesto N. Rogers (members of the Milanese studio known as BBPR). The display, revolutionary for its time, remains as it was on an open plan and is one of the most successful museum designs in Italy, in no way dated. The stone and wood supports succeed in creating a delightful interplay between the sculptures and the visitor. The labelling is good (with hand-sheets usually available in each room), so only a few of the works are mentioned here. The first rooms overlook the courtyard.

Rooms I–IV: Early Christian and Gothic sculpture. Highlights include fragments from ancient churches and other Byzantine and Romanesque remains, including a 6th-century marble portrait head supposedly a likeness of the Empress Theodora; Visconti tombs by Bonino da Campione (1363), notably the equestrian monument of Bernabò Visconti, his masterpiece; remains of the façade of Santa Maria di Brera and statues from the east gate of the city, by Giovanni di Balduccio; a 14th-century pavement tomb with an effigy thought to be that of Bona of Savoy, second wife of Galeazzo Maria Sforza; and a sepulchral monument of the Rusca family by a late 14th-century Lombard master. The vault of Room IV is frescoed with the arms of Philip II of Spain and his consort Mary Tudor, from the period of Spanish rule.

Rooms VI–VII: Beyond a small chapel with 14th-century Venetian sculpture are works from the periods of the *comune* and Spanish rule. Room VI contains 12th-century reliefs from the old Porta Romana, showing the triumph of the Milanese over Barbarossa (1176). Room VII, with frescoed escutcheons of the Dukes of Milan, is hung with 17th-century Brussels tapestries. Here is displayed the Gonfalon of Milan, designed by Giuseppe Meda (1566).

Room VIII (Sala delle Asse): This room, in one of the towers, was closed for restoration at the time of writing (*see saladelleassecastello.it*). It has remarkable frescoed decoration in the vault, designed in 1498 by Leonardo da Vinci for Ludovico Sforza. When the Duke set about rebuilding Castello Sforzesco, he gave Leonardo a studio

here so that he could paint the vault of the Sala delle Asse with its symbolic emblem of the mulberry tree (a pun on Il Moro's nickname) and a golden rope weaving in and out of its foliage which opens up in the centre of the ceiling to reveal the coat of arms of Ludovico and his wife Beatrice d'Este in the 'sky'. In the 18th century the frescoes were covered over with a layer of plaster. The vault was then virtually repainted at the beginning of the 20th century(so the results of the present restoration are eagerly awaited). The ilex branches and leaves are used in a complicated architectural structure in which the form of the octagon recurs. On the far wall are two fascinating fragments of monochrome tempera decoration by the hand of Leonardo, depicting tree trunks with branches and roots growing out of cracks in stratified rock formations.

Rooms IX–X: Off the Sala delle Asse, these two small rooms over the moat have Sforza portraits attributed to Bernardino Luini and his circle; reliefs by Bambaia; and an oval low relief carved on both faces by Pierino da Vinci.

Room XI (Sala dei Ducali): This vaulted chamber is decorated with coats of arms showing the ancestry of Galeazzo Maria Sforza. It contains a panel in very low relief by Agostino di Duccio from the Tempio Malatestiano at Rimini, and 15th-century sculptures.

Room XII: This, the former chapel, has lovely frescoes by Bonifacio Bembo and assistants (1473). The seated statue of the *Madonna and Child* is a Lombard work of the late 15th century, and the standing *Madonna* is by Pietro Solari.

The beautiful small painting of the *Madonna and Child* shows the influence of Leonardo and his *Virgin of the Rocks*. The work of Francesco Galli, it includes an accurate view of the Castello Sforzesco. Outside you can see the Renaissance 'Portico of the Elephant', named after a faded fresco.

Room XIII (Sala delle Colombine):

The red-and-gold fresco decorations have the arms of Bona of Savoy and sculpture by Giovanni Antonio Amadeo and Cristoforo Mantegazza.

Room XIV (Sala Verde): This long room is divided by Renaissance doorways salvaged from Milanese palaces: that from the Banco Mediceo (1455) is by Michelozzo. Displayed here are tombs, armorial sculptures and a fine collection of armour.

Room XV (Sala degli Scarlioni):

Displayed here is the effigy of Gaston de Foix, who died in battle in 1512 at Ravenna. The tomb of the young hero was commissioned by François I of France. Exquisite delicate reliefs from it (1525), masterpieces by Bambaia, are also on display.

You are now directed out to a wooden bridge above the Corte Ducale across a subterranean court with a 16th-century fountain. Stairs lead up to the first floor.

MUSEO DEI MOBILI FURNITURE MUSEUM

Corte Ducale first floor.

Rooms XVI–XIX have a splendid collection of furniture. Remains of the Visconti-Sforza treasury are also exhibited here, and a very precious crystal goblet made in Murano for the Gonzaga at the end of the 15th century. Marriage chests with painted fronts, a carved table top and caskets also all date from the 15th century. An entire *Camera Picta* was rescued from the fortress of Roccabianca near Parma and reconstructed here: the frescoes illustrate the story of Griselda (from Boccaccio) and are in grisaille except for the green background and some red details on the horses. The enchanting scenes were painted by an unknown Lombard artist in the 15th century, clearly influenced by Niccolò da Varallo. On the vault are the signs of the Zodiac, the constellations and the planets.

Another room has sculptures with religious subjects (including a 13th-century figure of Christ from a *Deposition* made in Umbria) and a Flemish tapestry of the *Raising of Lazarus*. A 'chamber of marvels' or *Wunderkammer* has been reconstructed with curiosities, bizarre objects (including a clockwork devil), scientific instruments as well as the chests and cabinets in which they were kept in the 17th century. The Baroque period is illustrated with carvings and furniture including console tables. Milanese interiors from the 17th and 18th centuries are recorded with wallpaper, paintings, furniture and Meissen porcelain. There is also a section on design which includes a circular chair by the cabinet-maker Carlo Bugatti, made in 1902, and pieces from the exhibitions held between 1890 and 1940 (with porcelain which Giò Ponti made for the Richard-Ginori manufactory in the 1920s). The last section has furniture produced by Memphis to designs by Ettore Sottsass in the 1970s and 1980s.

There is a selection of small 17th-century Flemish and Dutch paintings (including a monochrome sketch by Rubens) from the Belgioioso collection.

PINACOTECA
Corte Ducale first floor.
Rooms XX–XXVI contain the Castello's huge collection of Italian paintings, with Lombard painters well represented. The works date from the 13th–18th centuries. Highlights are given below.

Room XX: Late Gothic and quattrocento painting is exhibited in this corner tower, including the Torchiara Polyptych, signed and dated 1462, the only known work by Benedetto Bembo, brother of Bonifacio.

Room XXI: Here are Lombard Renaissance works, with Vincenzo Foppa particularly well represented with panels (a small *Madonna and Child with an Angel*, known as the *'Madonna del Libro'* and dating from around 1475, and a large *Martyrdom of St Sebastian*) and frescoes. A *Madonna and Child* by Marco d'Oggiono clearly shows the influence of Leonardo. The *Portrait of a Lady* painted by Andrea Solario around 1507 reflects aspects of Raphael's works. On the end wall the huge detached fresco lunette of *Hercules and Atlas* is by Bernardino Luini (1515).

Room XXIII: This room, in the Torre di Filarete, has twelve paintings from the Trivulzio collection: a lovely *Madonna and Child* (by Giovanni Bellini, although probably painted with the intervention of assistants) displayed next to another painting of the same subject by Bartolomeo Montagna; a large *Madonna and Child* signed and dated 1497 (on the book held by the angel at the bottom) by Andrea Mantegna; and the *Madonna of Humility with Angels and Saints* by Filippo Lippi (the attribution of this rather odd lunette with Carmelite saints is not accepted by all scholars).

Room XXIV: Correggio and Lombard Mannerism are illustrated here and there is also a splendid portrait of Lorenzo Lenzi by Bronzino, showing the influence of Pontormo.

Room XXV: The memorable portrait of an unknown youth is a small work by Lorenzo Lotto (1520s) and one of the masterpieces of the collection. Also here are Venetian works (portrait of a Humanist, dressed in a toga, by the workshop of Giovanni Bellini). There are works by Giovanni Cariani, Romanino and Moretto da Brescia, all of the same generation, born at the end of the 15th century; and others dating from the 16th century by Giovanni Battista Moroni and Jacopo Bassano (as well as the great Venetian painters of that century, Titian and Tintoretto).

Room XXV: This huge room is crowded with later Lombard paintings (including works by Fra' Galgario, Giacomo Ceruti and Daniele Crespi). At the end are two large ideal scenes of Venice painted around 1735 by Canaletto, and landscapes by Bernardo Bellotto, as well as three small Venetian capriccios by Francesco Guardi.

You are now directed out to a terrace and up some steps to enter the Rocchetta.

MUSEO DELLE ARTI DECORATIVE
Rocchetta first floor.

This museum includes an important collection of ceramics, with medieval and Renaissance pottery (16th-century historiated ceramics from Urbino and Casteldurante, and lustreware from Deruta), as well as Meissen figurines and porcelain. It also has a geometric compass designed by Galileo in 1606; small Renaissance bronzes (including a group by or after Giambologna) and medieval ivories with a series of plaques carved in the late 6th or early 7th century and thought to have been part of an episcopal throne. A reliquary chest here, made in Lombardy, is dated around 1000.

From here you go down steps to the floor below and the Museum of Musical Instruments.

MUSEO DEI STRUMENTI MUSICALI AND SALA DELLA BALLA
Rocchetta ground floor.

The **Museum of Musical Instruments** is a large collection, founded in 1881 and later increased by donations. It has stringed instruments including violas and violins from the 17th-century and mandolins from the 18th century. The keyboard instruments include a clavichord of 1503; double virginals by Ioannes Ruckers of Antwerp (c. 1600, with a painted case); spinets, including one played by the 14-year-old Mozart; and a fortepiano by Muzio Clementi. There is an outstanding group of wind instruments. A recording studio has been reconstructed with the equipment used by the Italian Radio and Television National Network (the RAI) in 1955 (in use until 1983).

More musical instruments are displayed in the huge aisled **Sala della Balla**, erroneously identified at the end of the 19th century as a ballroom and ball court. It is now known that in fact it was used as a grain store, but nevertheless it has retained its name. It was restored in the 1960s by the architectural studio BBPR. It is hung with tapestries of the Months from designs by Bramantino. The tapestries were commissioned after the expulsion of the Sforza by the French marshal Gian Giacomo Trivulzio, and were woven in Vigevano between 1504 and 1509.

A touch screen enables you to 'read' the **Trivulzio Codex**, one of Leonardo da Vinci's fascinating notebooks preserved here.

MUSEO ARCHEOLOGICO
Corte Ducale basement.

The **Prehistory Collection** has material from Lombardy dating from the late Bronze Age to the Roman period. The Golasecca culture (*see p. 213*) is particularly well represented.

The **Egyptian section** (*closed at the time of writing*) has a small collection of objects dating from the Old Kingdom to the age of Ptolemy, illustrating the funerary cult of ancient Egypt, with sarcophagi, mummies, canopic vases and papyrus Books of the Dead. There are also household and personal objects, jewellery, funerary masks and stelae.

SPECIALISED LIBRARIES AND CULTURAL INSTITUTIONS
Castello Sforzesco contains numerous precious collections and study centres. These include the important collection of prints and maps named after Achille Bertarelli (1863–1938), who donated the first part of the collection to Milan in 1925; the Archivio Storico Civico; the renowned Biblioteca Trivulziana with codices, manuscripts (including a series relating to Dante's *Divine Comedy*) and incunabula (its most famous possession, Leonardo's Trivulzio Codex, can today be seen in digitised form; *see above*); the Archivio Fotografico; the Archaeology and Numismatics library, founded in 1808; the Art History library; the Vinciana collections with material related to Leonardo da Vinci; and CASVA, a centre for the study of the visual arts.

PARCO SEMPIONE

On the far side of Castello Sforzesco is Parco Sempione (*map p. 24, A1–B1*), a public park of 47 hectares laid out in 1893 on the site of a ducal hunting chase. It is the largest public park in central Milan, with magnificent trees. It has a track for runners over 3km long and is equipped with enclosed areas where dogs are allowed to run free. It was the site of the World Exhibition in 1906, dedicated to the theme of transport and celebrating the Simplon tunnel under the Alps, which had just made possible the first direct rail link between Milan and Paris. The only building which survives from that time is the Art Nouveau **Aquarium** (*open Tues–Sun 9–1 & 2–5.30; acquariocivicomilano.eu*), which has delightful 'aquatic' decorations on the exterior and is considered one of the most important buildings of the Liberty style in Italy. Today it contains marine and freshwater fish, important study collections, and a marine biology station. The **Arena**, built by Luigi Canonica in 1806–7 for public spectacles, is now used for sporting events. The equestrian monument to Napoleon III is by Francesco Barzaghi (1881). At the far end of the park is the **Arco della Pace** (*map p. 26, C2*), a triumphal arch built by Luigi Cagnola in 1807–38 and modelled on the Arch of Septimius Severus in Rome. It was begun in honour of Napoleon but was dedicated to Peace by Ferdinand I of Austria on its completion. It marks the beginning of the Corso Sempione, part of the 182km-long historic Simplon Road, constructed by order of Napoleon from Geneva to Sesto Calende across the Simplon Pass (1800–5).

PALAZZO DELL'ARTE (TRIENNALE DESIGN MUSEUM)
On the west side of Parco Sempione is the Palazzo dell'Arte, now usually known as the Triennale Design Museum (*map p. 24, A1; Viale Emilio Alemagna 6; open Tues–Sun 10.30–8.30; T: 02 724341, triennale.org*). Built in brick and clinker in 1931–3 by Giovanni Muzio, its tall entrance arch stretches right up to the roof. It was commissioned to house the Triennale exhibitions of decorative arts and design when they moved here from Monza (*see p. 135*) and its architecture influenced the succeeding generation of Milanese architects. The garden façade is even more interesting and in the garden (*closed in winter*) there is a fountain with a painted sculpture by Giorgio de Chirico (1973). Close by you can see the high tower (110m), made of aluminium, by Giò Ponti and others, erected at the same time.

The interior has been much altered. In 1994, Gae Aulenti designed a gallery for exhibitions and in 2007 Michele De Lucchi provided additional exhibition space above (approached by a flying bridge made of bamboo). One original element is the mosaic by Achille Funi at the foot of the stairs (1933). There is a pleasant café and a restaurant on the roof terrace (*open noon–midnight; T: 02 3664 4340*), from where there is a splendid view of the city skyline, with the towers around Piazza Gae Aulenti, the tower which houses the Lombard regional offices, the Pirelli Building and the Diamond Tower.

The closest metro station to this side of the park is Piazzale Cadorna, where the railway station has recently been spruced up in red and green with two amusing knot sculptures outside in green, red and yellow. A good place for a snack is Binario II (Patti), just outside the station at Via Paleocapa 1.

OLD CHINATOWN AND THE CIMITERO MONUMENTALE

North of Parco Sempione, the district centred on Via Paolo Sarpi and Via Canonica (*map p. 26, C1*), which used to be known as **Chinatown**, is now an up-and-coming part of Isola. For years this was an off-limits area but it is now a popular district, with numerous good restaurants (*some of them listed on p. 121*) and crowded with young Milanese, who also choose to come here to shop (house prices have soared). The nearest metro stations are Garibaldi and Monumentale. The district has a very distinct atmosphere, with almost all the signs in Chinese: the influx of Chinese immigrants began in the 1920s and reached its peak in the 1990s.

Those interested in 19th-century architecture and sculpture will want to visit the **Cimitero Monumentale** (*map p. 26, C1; Metro 5 to Monumentale*), designed by Carlo Maciachini in 1863–6. The central pantheon, or *famedio*, contains the tombs of Alessandro Manzoni, Italy's most famous novelist of the 19th century, and Carlo Cattaneo (1801–69), patriot and scientific writer. A former electricity station near here is to be turned into an 'Innovation Design District'.

SANTA MARIA DELLE GRAZIE
& THE CENACOLO VINCIANO

Map p. 24, A2. Corso Magenta. Open 7.30–12.30 & 2.30–7, Sun and holidays 7.30–1 & 3–8. NB: This is still a Dominican religious house. Fourteen friars live here and hold their services in the choir, so it is only officially open to visitors from 10–12.55 & 3–5.55 and on Sun from 3.30–5.55 (otherwise a good time to see it is between 7.30 and 8.30 in the morning). There are coin-operated lights for the east end and for the side chapels.

A church of brick and terracotta with a very beautiful exterior, Santa Maria delle Grazie was erected in 1466 to the design of Guiniforte Solari, who also worked on the Duomo. In 1492 Ludovico il Moro (*see p. 167*) chose the church as his prospective burial place and, deciding that it was not grand enough, ordered that it be rebuilt with a new choir and domed crossing (where his tomb was to be installed). He called in the great architect Donato Bramante (*see p. 80*), who had already worked for him on Santa Maria presso San Satiro. Giovanni Antonio Amadeo was put in charge of the actual building work (having already proved his worth at the Veneranda Fabbrica del Duomo). While work was in progress, Leonardo was painting in the refectory, where the Dominicans had commissioned him to paint a *Last Supper* in 1492. It is known that the erudite prior at the time, Vincenzo Bandello, was a close friend (and advisor on theological issues) of Ludovico il Moro, who was a generous patron of the friary. When the Duke decided to rebuild its church in the same year, Leonardo must also have been in touch with Bramante, his elder by a few years, since it was Bramante's plan that was chosen. It is extraordinary to think that these two great men may well have walked together in the vineyard, a few hundred metres away from the friary, which the Duke gave to Leonardo in 1498 (*see p. 68*). The presence of both Leonardo and Bramante in Milan meant that Ludovico's court was particularly admired and the arts flourished under his rule. Things came to an abrupt end in 1499, when King Louis XII of France, a great-grandson of Gian Galeazzo Visconti, claimed the dukedom and installed himself in Castello Sforzesco. Leonardo decided to return to Florence and Bramante to Rome. Ludovico il Moro was taken prisoner (he died in France in 1508).

LEONARDO IN MILAN

Leonardo arrived in Milan from Florence in the year 1482 or 1483, offering his services to Ludovico Sforza, il Moro (*see p. 167*), who had been in contact with the Medici ruler of Florence, Lorenzo the Magnificent. Ludovico's original commission for Leonardo was a huge and incredibly heavy equestrian monument to commemorate the founder of the Sforza dynasty, the *condottiere* Francesco Sforza (who had ruled Milan from 1450 to 1466), a project which had already been mooted by Ludovico's predecessors. In fact, this over-ambitious plan came to nothing (only a clay model was produced, which was destroyed by French troops a few decades later). Leonardo did not lose time in recommending himself to Il Moro, not only as a sculptor but also as an engineer. While in Milan, he also painted a portrait of Ludovico's mistress, Cecilia Gallerani (known as the *Lady with an Ermine*, this masterpiece is now in Krakow), and produced his famous *Virgin of the Rocks* (now in the Louvre) for the confraternity of a church which no longer exists. The wonderful *Portrait of a Musician*, which he also produced in this period, is preserved in the Ambrosiana (*see p. 79*).

THE CENACOLO VINCIANO
(LEONARDO DA VINCI'S *LAST SUPPER*)

Map p. 24, A2. Piazza Santa Maria delle Grazie 2. Open Tues–Sun 8.15–6.45. Admission only by advance booking at cenacolovinciano.net or T: 02 9280 0360. You are asked to pick up your ticket at least 10mins before your timed entrance, from the ticket office outside the church of Santa Maria delle Grazie. In order to protect the painting from atmospheric pollution, visitors (only 30 or 40 at a time) go through a series of glass 'cubicles' equipped with air-filtering systems, from which there is a good view of the main cloister with its palm trees as well as the exterior of Santa Maria delle Grazie. You are only allowed 15mins in the refectory.

In the *cenacolo* (refectory) of the Dominican convent of Santa Maria delle Grazie is the world-famous *Last Supper* by Leonardo da Vinci, painted in 1494–7. It survived WWII, even though the vault and right wall of the refectory were destroyed by a bomb in 1943 and had to be entirely rebuilt. This extraordinary painting, which was to have a lasting effect on generations of painters, depicts the dramatic moment when Christ announces, at supper with his Disciples, that he is to be betrayed by one of them. The monumental Classical figures of the Disciples are shown in perfect perspective in a stark room, an extension of the refectory itself. The light enters through the real windows on the left and the painted windows in the background which look out over a landscape, and the wonderful colours culminate in the blue and red robe of Christ. On the side walls, Leonardo painted tapestries decorated with bunches of flowers. One of the most memorable figures is St Philip, who seems to be asking if he is the one who will betray Christ and his face is lit up by an extraordinary light. The hands of the Disciples are particularly striking. Fascinating details of the objects on the table have recently been revealed, including the pink, blue and red of the Disciples' robes reflected in the pewter plates and the glass carafes. The tablecloth still has creases showing how it was folded up and is knotted at one end so that it fits the table. Above are lunettes with garlands of fruit and flowers around the coats of arms of the Sforza family. There is no evidence that Leonardo made use of a cartoon while working on this masterpiece.

NOTES ON LEONARDO'S TECHNIQUE

The *Last Supper* is painted with a technique peculiar to Leonardo, in tempera with the addition of later oil varnishes, on a prepared surface in two layers on the plastered wall. It is therefore not a fresco. In fresco-painting, pigments are dissolved in water and then painted onto a surface primed with fresh lime plaster. If the climate is dry, true frescoes will retain their brightness for an exceptionally long time. In Leonardo's work, errors in the preparation of the plaster, together with the dampness of the wall, have caused great damage to the painted surface, which had already considerably deteriorated by the beginning of the 16th century. The *Last Supper* has been restored repeatedly and was twice repainted (in oils) in the 18th century. Careful work (begun in 1978 and completed in 1999) was carried out to eliminate the false restorations of the past and to expose the original work of Leonardo as far as possible.

Giovanni Donato Montorfano was chosen by the friars (with the encouragement of the Sforza duke) to work with Leonardo on the decoration of their refectory. Although nowhere near Leonardo's stature as an artist, the fine remnant of his large *Crucifixion*, on the wall opposite the *Last Supper*, is nevertheless a vindication of the lasting quality of true fresco-painting. At the bottom of the fresco, at either side, are the kneeling figures, now nearly effaced, of Ludovico il Moro and his wife Beatrice d'Este and their two children, added in tempera and oil by Leonardo before 1498.

THE CHURCH OF SANTA MARIA DELLE GRAZIE

Between the aisle chapels are frescoed tondi of Dominican saints attributed to Bernardino Butinone (1480s). The nave vault and aisles have pretty frescoed decoration carried out at the same time (restored in 1937). Highlights are as follows:

South aisle: The first chapel has 15th-century detached frescoes and a Della Torre funerary monument (1483). The walls and vault of the fourth chapel are decorated by Gaudenzio Ferrari (1542). The fifth chapel has terracotta angels on the walls in low relief covered with white stucco (late 16th century). In the last chapel, beneath a pretty vault painted in the 16th century by Ottavio Semino, is an altarpiece of *St John the Baptist* by Marco d'Oggiono, a pupil of Leonardo's.

North aisle: At the top (east) end of the north aisle is the elaborate entrance (with 17th-century stuccoes and a dark lunette painting by Cerano) to the chapel of the Madonna delle Grazie (*reserved for prayer*), containing a highly venerated 15th-century painting of the Madonna beneath a vault with restored 15th-century frescoes. The sixth chapel has a small *Holy Family with St Catherine* by Paris Bordone, and in the fifth chapel is a good copy of Titian's *Martyrdom of St Peter of Verona* (Titian painted a *Crowning with Thorns* for the church but it was taken to the Louvre in 1797). The first chapel has an altarpiece of the *Madonna with Two Saints* by Niccolò da Cremona (1520) and 20th-century works in bronze and terracotta by Francesco Messina. The lunette frescoes are by Giovanni Donato Montorfano, the artist chosen to work with Leonardo on the refectory (*see above*).

East end: At the uncluttered east end, the lovely light Tribuna or domed crossing, designed by Bramante, has very unusual bright graffiti decoration, with pronounced colouring in pink and dark grey against a white ground, also carried on into the choir (where the stalls date from 1470 and 1510). The decoration has geometric patterns except for the four roundels with Doctors of the Church, each supported by three angels in relief, and the lower walls are left bare. This space, with the dome lit by small round windows, is extraordinarily pleasing.

Chiostrino: The small cloister, also thought to have been designed by Bramante, is planted with a delightful little garden with four dwarf magnolias and a fountain decorated with bronze frogs. From here you can study Bramante's very beautiful exterior of the church, with its terracotta decoration against the white plaster. His other work on the church was on the old sacristy (unfortunately usually kept locked.)

LA VIGNA DI LEONARDO

Map p. 24, A2. Corso Magenta 65. Open daily 9–6. Visits every half-hour on the half-hour (you are lent an audio-guide). To book, vignadileonardo.com, T: 02 481 6150. There is a café at the entrance.

Across the road from Santa Maria delle Grazie is the Casa degli Atellani, on the site of a vineyard which belonged to Ludovico il Moro and which he is known to have given to Leonardo in 1499, after the completion of the *Last Supper*. Since 2015 the house and garden have been open to the public, and the vineyard replanted.

The 15th-century house was restored in antique style in 1921, for the senator Ettore Conti, by the well-known Milanese architect Piero Portaluppi (and reconstructed by him after damage in WWII). Beyond two little old-fashioned courtyards (which Portaluppi united), you enter the house with its four furnished rooms, one of which has portraits of the Sforza in roundels frescoed by Bernardino Luini. Conti's study is entirely panelled, and Portaluppi's more characteristic Art Deco style can be seen in some of the details. At the end of the garden (you are asked to keep off the grass) you can walk in the little vineyard of Leonardo, which has recently been replanted in a sunken plot. We know that the French confiscated the vineyard when they took over the government of the city (after Leonardo had left), but in 1507 the artist managed to get it back and it is mentioned in his will of 1519. The original grape variety was re-introduced by Luca Beltrami in 1920, only to be lost again in an Allied bombing raid in 1943. After a careful dig in this century, it was once again identified as Malvasia di Candia Aromatica and replanted. It seems to have taken well: it is likely that this was the very fruit that Leonardo enjoyed.

To walk from here to the church of Sant'Ambrogio, go along Corso Magenta past the beautiful exterior of Santa Maria delle Grazie. Take the first right, Via De Togni, a street typical of the residential area of Sant'Ambrogio, with stately old flats, many in period-revival buildings with shady gardens, and then left along Via San Vittore.

SANT'AMBROGIO

At the end of Via San Vittore is the **Pusterla di Sant'Ambrogio** (*map p. 24, A3*), a gate in the medieval city walls (with three statues of bishops, including St Ambrose), reconstructed in 1939, which leads into the pedestrian precinct close to the renowned **Università Cattolica**, founded in 1921. The University occupies the former monastery of Sant'Ambrogio, which includes two important cloisters designed by Bramante. The Ionic one was finished by Cristoforo Solari in 1513 and the Doric one in 1620–30. Here, on Piazza Sant'Ambrogio, you will find the venerable basilica of Sant'Ambrogio.

THE BASILICA OF SANT'AMBROGIO

Map p. 24, A3–B3. Open 7.30–12.30 & 2.30–7, Sun 7.30–1 & 3–8pm. basilicasantambrogio. it. There is a small fee to visit the Treasury and the exquisite little Cappella di San Vittore in Ciel d'Oro with its mosaics (which is only open 9.30–11.45 & 2.30–6). Some of the chapels have coin-operated lights. Mass at 11am on Sun from Oct–June is in Latin, in the ancient Ambrosian chant.

This, the most interesting church in Milan, was the prototype of the Lombard basilica. Built in 379–86 beside a Christian cemetery, it was enlarged in the 9th century and again after 1080. It was founded by St Ambrose (Ambrogio in Italian), Bishop of Milan.

ST AMBROSE

Milan has always been proud of it bishop and patron saint. A friend and mentor of St Augustine, whom he converted to Christianity (remains of the baptistery where the baptism took place can today be seen beneath the Duomo), Ambrose was born in Gaul, the son of an imperial official, c. 339. He likewise embarked on a career in the imperial administration but in 374 was popularly proclaimed Bishop of Milan. He promptly received baptism, assumed the role, and had four basilicas built on the outskirts of the city, which at the time was the administrative capital of the Empire. He dedicated this church to the Holy Martyrs, but after his death, he naturally became its titular saint and it has been the basilica of Sant'Ambrogio ever since. The other basilicas he dedicated to the Apostles (now San Nazaro; *see p. 97*), the Virgin Martyrs (later dedicated to Ambrose's successor as bishop, San Simpliciano; *see p. 57*) and to the Prophets (no trace of this basilica remains). He was famous in his lifetime for his fervent defence of Christianity against Imperial interference and he had to deal with three emperors in succession (as well as their funerals). These were the young emperor Gratian, who was assassinated in 383, Valentinian II (only a boy, so his mother Justina, an Arian, acted as regent), and Theodosius I, who in 392 united the empires of East and West and was the last emperor to rule over both. It was Theodosius who established orthodox Christianity according to the terms of the Nicene Creed and much of Ambrose's life was taken up with resistance to Arianism. Although extremely learned and staunch in his support for orthodoxy, he is always also remembered as a particularly generous person. Today he is considered one of the four great Latin Fathers and a Doctor of the Church. He was a contemporary of St Jerome, another Doctor of the Church. There are two portraits of Ambrose, evidently made before his death in 397, which can still be seen in Milan. One is here in Sant'Ambrogio in mosaic, and the other is a stucco roundel (now in the Museo Diocesano). The Feast of St Ambrose, celebrated on 7th December, is an important annual event in the city and celebrations normally last four days. He is buried in the crypt of the basilica that bears his name.

The present building is the result of numerous careful restorations and the dating of its various parts is still uncertain. After a radical restoration in the 19th century, it had to be repaired again after serious War damage in 1943.

The memorable solemn **atrium** or forecourt in front of the church, on an early Christian plan, was probably built in 1088–99 but was reconstructed in 1150. The columns have very interesting carved capitals, sculpted by Lombard stonemasons, with both geometric and figurative designs, including a quaint *Daniel in the Lions' Den*. The austere **façade** consists of a five-bayed narthex below, with five arches above, gradated to fit the gable and with decorative arcading. There are two square bell-towers: the monks' campanile dates from the 9th century; the higher canons'

SANT'AMBROGIO
View of the atrium and the two bell-towers.

campanile is an elegant Lombard tower of 1128–44 (even though the top storey was turned into a loggia in 1889). The great *doorway* (now protected by glass) has wood imposts made up of fragments from the 8th and 10th centuries (heavily restored in the 18th century); the bronze doors date from the 11th–12th centuries. Note the large bull and pig (?) clinging onto one of the columns.

INTERIOR OF SANT'AMBROGIO

The beautiful low rib-vaulted nave is divided from the aisles by wide arcades supported by massive pillars beneath a matroneum. There are no transepts, and beyond the tower over the crossing, with its lovely ciborium protecting the high altar, are three deep apses, the central one raised above the crypt. The architecture has a striking simplicity except for the column capitals which, like those in the atrium outside, were sculpted in the 11th and 12th centuries with delightful figures, vegetation and animals.

North side: The **first chapel** in the north (left-hand) aisle has a good (detached) fresco of the *Risen Christ* (with very unusual iconography) by Bergognone. Diagonally opposite in the nave is a free-standing **granite column topped by a graceful serpent**, which is traditionally held to represent the serpent of brass that Moses had made in the desert (*Numbers 21*): it probably dates from the Byzantine period and is thought to have been here since the 11th century. It remains one of the most astonishing works to be seen in a church. The **pulpit** is a superb Romanesque monument. It was saved after the vault collapsed in 1196 and at once reconstituted from the beautiful fragments carved in the 11th and early 12th centuries. The reliefs include a banqueting scene. The angel and eagle (with a very long neck, like a goose), in embossed and gilded copper, date from the late 7th century. The pulpit is raised up on ancient columns so that, rather bizarrely, it encloses a huge Palaeochristian (4th century) sarcophagus of Roman craftsmanship, which in turn has carvings on all four sides, including a quadriga, rows of Romans, Christ seated between the twelve Apostles, the Sacrifice of Isaac and Noah's Ark, as well as a tondo with the portraits of the affectionate husband and wife who must have commissioned the carvings for their tomb.

Sanctuary: Under the sanctuary dome (which was rebuilt in the 13th century and restored in the 19th) is the tall **ciborium**, thought to date from the 9th century, although the column shafts are probably survivals from the time of St Ambrose. The four sides of the baldacchino are decorated with reliefs in coloured stucco in the Byzantine style (mid-10th century). They represent (on the side facing the nave) Christ enthroned between the two figures of Peter and Paul, bent in deeply reverent obeisance. This iconography is repeated on the other three sides with pairs of figures flanking a central one (on the side facing the apse, the main figure is St Ambrose).

The **Carolingian altar** has a magnificent and justly celebrated casing presented in 835 by Archbishop Angilbert II. Made of gold and silver plates sculptured in relief, with cloisonné enamel and gems, it is partly the work of a certain Vuolvinius, and represents scenes from the lives of Christ and St Ambrose (unfortunately it is difficult to appreciate the workmanship at a distance). It is for this altar that Antonio Parma of Saronno designed his special protective strongbox (*see p. 138*).

The **apse mosaic**, of uncertain date but possibly not earlier than the 13th century, was reset in the 18th century and then restored after the Second World War. It shows Christ Pantocrator and saints and archangels, with scenes (framed by two pairs of palm trees) from the life of St Ambrose. The 9th-century marble **bishop's throne** survives beneath it.

South side: At the top end of the south aisle, beyond a fine 18th-century wrought-iron screen, is the entrance (*for opening times, see above*) to the Treasury and Sacello di San Vittore in Ciel d'Oro.

The **Sacello di San Vittore in Ciel d'Oro**, a little Palaeochristian sepulchral chapel built in a Christian cemetery in the 4th century and thus pre-dating the basilica, has a fabulous golden mosaic dome (the 'Ciel d'Oro') with a bust of St Victor in the centre, and six figures of saints, all provided with their names, against a blue ground. The **likeness of St Ambrose** is thought to be a portrait from life of the great bishop. The chapel has survived a restoration in the 19th century and near destruction in WWII. A 9th-century marble transenna serves as the altar. The chapel's tiny crypt also survives but is unfortunately not open.

The **Treasury**, with a charming old-fashioned arrangement, has a silver urn dated 1449 and various liturgical objects (the basilica's most precious possessions are exhibited in the Museo Diocesano; see p. 92). The 6th-century relief of a lamb against a damaged instarsia ground is from the apse of the original basilica.

Also opening off the south aisle is the main basilica **crypt**. Here can be seen the skeletal figures, fully robed and stretched out side by side of St Ambrose (in white) between St Gervase and St Protase. St Ambrose had discovered the relics of these two saints and raised their status to protomartyrs of the city. The shrine dates from 1897 and the rest of the crypt was decorated in the 19th century.

Closing the south aisle is a modern altar fashioned from a **6th-century sarcophagus** recording two martyrs called Nabor and Felix who were beheaded in Milan in the 3rd century.

The south chapels: The frescoes in the **Cappella di San Giorgio**, illustrating the legend of St George, are by Bernardino Lanino, who also painted the delightful decoration on the intrados of the entrance arch, with putti amongst the dense green leaves of pear trees. The

Cappella del Sacro Cuore (*reserved for prayer*) has a statue of Christ over the altar by Lodovico Pogliaghi.

The **Cappella di Santa Marcellina**, designed in 1812 by Luigi Cagnola, commemorates Marcellina, sister of St Ambrose. Her relics were found in the church in 1722. The **Cappella dei Santi Bartolomeo e Satiro** preserves relics of St Ambrose's brother Satyrus. It has an altarpiece attributed to Gaudenzio Ferrari and two detached frescoes by Tiepolo (difficult to see as the gate is kept locked; Tiepolo's vault fresco of the *Glory of St Bernard* in one of the sacristies was destroyed by a bomb in 1943).

The **side entrance vestibule** has a painting by Camillo Procaccini of *St Ambrose Preventing the Emperor Theodosius from Entering the Basilica.* This alludes to the famous stand-off between emperor and prelate after Theodosius had allowed a massacre of citizens in Thessalonica. St Ambrose refused to allow Theodosius to attend Mass until he had performed public penance (which he duly did). The fresco of the *Deposition* opposite is attributed to Giovanni Battista della Cerva (1546) and the other frescoes to the workshop of Bernardino Luini and Gaudenzio Ferrari.

A bookshop has been set up in the **monks' bell-tower**, which has fragments of frescoes and two dizzyingly tall, slender ladders.

The canonry: From the north aisle, a door leads into the Portico della Canonica, commissioned from Bramante by Ludovico il Moro just before he fell from power at the hands of the French in 1499. It was never finished, as in the same year the architect fled to

Rome (where he took up work for the pope on St Peter's). Only the colonnade next to the church was completed (four of the columns imitate tree trunks or clubs of Hercules) and it had to be reconstructed after WWII. A second side was added in 1955. The complex now houses the precious archive and Chapter Library (*open to scholars*), which includes 9th-century codices and a choir book with a depiction of the coronation of Gian Galeazzo Visconti in Sant'Ambrogio in 1395.

SAN VITTORE AL CORPO

A short distance from the old Gate of Sant'Ambrogio, on Via San Vittore (with its castellated building of 1910 by Adolfo Coppedè), is a little piazza with the church of San Vittore al Corpo (*map p. 24, A3*), in part by Galeazzo Alessi. The 17th-century façade is plain except for the heads of four fat cherubs. The church's name (lit. 'at the body') is thought to come from the fact it was on the site of a burial ground, or that it contained the body of St Victor the Moor from Mauritania in North Africa, martyred in Milan in 303. The interior is particularly interesting for its 16th-century works. The barrel vault is decorated with gilded stucco and small paintings by Camillo Procaccini and the cupola is also delightfully frescoed by Moncalvo and Daniele Crespi, with angels playing musical instruments. Crespi also produced the three paintings in the fourth north chapel. The south transept has more works by Procaccini. The little-known painter Giovanni Ambrogio Figino decorated the north transept. There is an altarpiece of the *Blessed Bernardo Tolomei* by Pompeo Batoni (1745) in the third north chapel, where there are also paintings by Batoni's contemporary Pierre Subleyras. The beautifully carved choir stalls date from around 1583.

The huge ex-convent of the church is now occupied by the Science Museum.

MUSEO DELLA SCIENZA

Map p. 24, A3. Via San Vittore 21. Open Tues–Fri 9–5, Sat–Sun and holidays 9.30–6.30. T: 02 485551, museoscienza.org. A useful map is available and pamphlets are given to young 'explorers', indicating the sections which they are likely to find the most fun (there are special 'tinkering zones'). You need to book at the ticket office to visit the inside of the submarine. Volunteer guides are usually available. The museum is almost always filled with groups of school children. It is extremely well labelled, also in English.

Housed in an old Olivetan convent (1507), the Museo Nazionale della Scienza e della Tecnologia Leonardo da Vinci is arranged on three floors around two beautiful cloisters and in two huge pavilions. The museum was first opened in 1953 and was for long famous above all for its models of the inventions of Leonardo da Vinci, but it is now one of the most up-to-date and largest museums of its kind in Europe. The declared aim is 'to help people develop an interest in technology, share our passion for science, and support the discovery of a fascinating past.' It is naturally therefore in permanent evolution.

Near the entrance, you pass a robot which interacts with you. Beyond are sections on Nutrition and Particle Physics. On the upper floor are the two long galleries, stretching the entire length of the two cloisters, dedicated to Leonardo da Vinci, with fascinating models which reproduce his drawings (displayed on the wall beside them) of machines and apparatus. The Sala delle Colonne, the former conventual library, is only open for events. At the end there is a small room which preserves goldsmiths' work and precious stones. On this floor there is also a collection of musical instruments (and the reconstruction of a lute-makers' workshop), an exhibition on radio and telecommunications and three unique motor cars.

On the lower floor are displays dedicated to energy systems, steel, aluminium, copper, rubber and plastic, and there are exhibits on industrial plants and the petrochemical industries.

An external pavilion, in the form of a 19th-century railway station, contains railway locomotives and rolling stock, including *Bayard*, one of Stephenson's engines supplied from Newcastle for the Naples–Portici line in 1843. Another huge external pavilion illustrates air and sea transport on three (open-plan) floors, with a splendid display of aeroplanes, along with relics of aeronautical and maritime history, including a naval training ship and models of ships made in 1922.

The submarine outside the railway pavilion (*book your visit at the ticket office*) was declared obsolete in 1997, marking the end of the Cold War.

You are asked to leave the museum through the bookshop beyond the second pavilion, which brings you out onto Via Olona (close to the Sant'Ambrogio metro station).

PINACOTECA AMBROSIANA

Map p. 24, C3. Piazza Pio XI 2. Open Tues–Sun 10–5.30. T: 02 806921, ambrosiana.it. Leonardo da Vinci's famous portrait is exhibited in the last room, from which you enter a hall of the Library, where drawings by him are on view. The exit and bookshop are here.

The Palazzo dell'Ambrosiana contains the famous Library and Pinacoteca founded by Cardinal Federico Borromeo at the beginning of the 17th century. The palace was begun for the Cardinal by Lelio Buzzi in 1603–9 and later enlarged.

The Pinacoteca contains a superb collection of paintings. The core of the collection is a donation that was assembled by the Cardinal and bequeathed to an art academy founded here in 1621 under the direction of Giovanni Battista Crespi, known as Il Cerano. Cartoons by Pellegrino Tibaldi for the stained-glass windows of the Duomo and by Giulio Romano for the fresco of the *Battle of the Milvian Bridge* (in the Vatican), still in the collection, attest to the educational as well as the artistic value that artists' preparatory drawings held for Borromeo and his academy. The same teaching role was assigned to the many copies of paintings commissioned by the Cardinal, such as the copy by Vespino of Leonardo's *Last Supper* (in the last room). The original donation comprised 250 paintings, including originals and about 30 copies. Now there are more than 1,500 works on panel, canvas and other supports.

The Pinacoteca is arranged in 24 rooms on the first and second floors. The collection is arranged chronologically, though an effort has been made to set apart Federico Borromeo's original collection, mostly reassembled in the first rooms. The atmosphere is slightly dowdy and labelling is kept to a minimum.

Entrance hall and stairs: On the walls are **16th-century plaster casts** from Trajan's Column, the *Laocoön* and Michelangelo's *Vatican Pietà*, made by the sculptor Leone Leoni and later used in the art academy here.

Gallery: In the Gallery at the top of the stairs you immediately come to the heart of **Federico Borromeo's collection**, with two of the most precious paintings: Bernardino Luini's *Holy Family with St Anne and the Young St John*, from a cartoon by Leonardo, and Titian's *Adoration of the Magi* (painted, with assistants, for Henri II and Diane de Poitiers in 1560, and still in its original frame: the grey horse is the protagonist of the scene). Also by Titian is a portrait of an old man in armour, thought to be the artist's father (Gregorio Vecellio, captain of the Centuria di Pieve). There is a *Holy Family* by Veronese. Other works by Luini include *Christ Blessing*.

Right of the Gallery: The two rooms here display 15th–16th-century paintings not part of the collection of Federico Borromeo. In the larger room is Botticelli's charming, light-filled tondo of the *Madonna del Padiglione*. The Child is learning to walk, held up by an angel, and beyond the red folds of the tent (*padiglione*) there is an exquisitely painted landscape. Two panels with

saints are good works by Bernardino Zenale. The great *Sacra Conversazione* by Bergognone is a splendid example of the Lombard quattrocento.

In the adjoining room, among the **paintings by the Leonardeschi**— Giampietrino, Marco d'Oggiono, Bernardino Luini—are three intriguing works by Bramantino: the symbol-laden *Adoration of the Child*; the fresco for the church of San Sepolcro showing *Christ in Pietà* (witnessed by an extraordinarily expressive St John); and the disquieting altarpiece with the *Madonna Enthroned between Sts Michael and Ambrose*, with at their feet the bodies of a toad and an Arian, symbols of the Devil and of heresy which they both respectively extirpated (with skilful foreshortening they are shown lying away from the viewer). Note also the austere buildings in the background. In the central glass cases are amusing ex-voto panels from the 19th and early 20th centuries, including one giving thanks for a young man's survival of an explosion and another showing a woman hit by a tram.

Raphael's cartoon for *The School of Athens*: The only remaining cartoon of this famous Vatican fresco cycle was purchased by Cardinal Borromeo in 1626. It is the largest known Renaissance drawing (285 by 804cm). The figure of Heraclitus is missing from the cartoon: the Greek philosopher was in fact added

PINACOTECA AMBROSIANA
Ex-voto panel giving thanks to the Virgin for saving the life of a woman hit by a tram.

by Raphael in the final fresco, using Michelangelo's features. Restoration began *in situ* on this incredibly precious work in 2014. A new exhibition setting has been designed for it by Stefano Boeri.

Flemish and German works: Only two of the four allegories of the elements painted by Jan Brueghel for the Cardinal and removed by Napoleon in 1796 were returned here. These are *Water* and the enigmatic *Fire*, a rather fiendish forge full of tiny pieces of goldsmith's work. Brueghel also painted the life-sized vase of flowers with jewels, coins, shells and a butterfly, one of the finer examples of this kind of still life, as well as the little painting on copper of a *Mouse with Roses*. Both works are allegories of transience and corruption. The other

Flemish painter whose work Cardinal Borromeo supported is Paul Bril, here represented by a number of meticulously detailed religious landscapes.

In an adjoining room is an important group of 16th-century Flemish and German paintings from the De Pecis collection, including more works by Jan Brueghel (*Paradise* and *Original Sin*).

In the corridor are reliefs by Bambaia from the unfinished tomb of Gaston de Foix (*see p. 61*).

The Galbiati Wing: Steps lead down to these old-fashioned rooms, named after Giovanni Galbiati, who redecorated them in 1928 when they were acquired by the Ambrosiana. They include the Sala della Medusa and Sala delle Colonne, and at this time too the Basilica of San Sepolcro was incorporated into the building. The rooms are used to display the collection of *objets d'art*, including an octagonal casket with bone plaquettes by the Embriachi (15th century) with scenes from the story of Pyramus and Thisbe, and a curious profane **reliquary with a lock of Lucrezia Borgia's hair** (Byron famously obtained a few strands of it when he visited Milan and enclosed them in a letter to Augusta Leigh). In another room is the Sinigallia collection of miniature portraits on porcelain, ivory and copper.

There are also more **15th- and 16th-century Lombard paintings**, including works by Leonardo's followers Giampietrino and Antonio Solario (*Head of the Baptist*).

Off the courtyard in the Sala dell'Esedra (the exedra itself was decorated in 1930 with a mosaic reproducing the miniature made by Simone Martini for Petrarch's personal copy of Virgil, preserved here in the library) are works by **painters from Bergamo and Brescia**. Moretto's dramatic *Martyrdom of St Peter of Verona*, in which the martyr writes on the ground, in his own blood, *Credo* ('I believe'), and Giovanni Battista Moroni's remarkable full-length portrait of Michel de l'Hopital, French ambassador to the Council of Trent, are perhaps the most striking.

Upper floors: Stairs lead up through the exedra to the Sala Nicolò da Bologna, named after the 14th-century miniaturist from whom the reliefs of Sciences and Virtue in the squat lunettes were derived in the 19th century. Here and in the next room are **16th-century**

Flemish and 17th-century Italian paintings, including Guido Reni's *Penitent Magdalene* and Giuseppe Vermiglio's *Judith with the Head of Holofernes* and *Jael and Sisera*. Plenty of room is given to the Lombard seicento, represented mainly by religious paintings by Giulio Cesare Procaccini, Morazzone, Francesco Cairo, Nuvolone and Daniele Crespi.

Among the paintings that mark the passage from the 17th to the 18th century in the various Italian schools are the *Portrait of a Young Man*, seemingly caught by surprise, by Fra' Galgario. The pastoral genre is represented by *Rebecca Going to the Well* by the Genoese artist Giovan Francesco Castiglione.

A room with huge windows overlooking a courtyard displays **19th-century works from the De Pecis collection**, given to the Ambrosiana in 1827 and including miniatures on ivory by Giambattista Gigola depicting historic and literary scenes; small gilt bronzes and marble self-portraits of the Neoclassical sculptors Antonio Canova and Bertel Thorvaldsen (one of the bronzes reproduces Thorvaldsen's marble monument to Appiani which is in the Brera café). The stiff official portrait of Leopold II of Habsburg Lorraine is by Anton Raphael Mengs.

In the last room are Andrea Appiani's portraits of Napoleon (c. 1805) and of the French dancer Carolina Pitrot; and Francesco Hayez's *Mary Magdalene*, as well as a watercolour study for *The Kiss* (*see p. 54*).

The Leonardo Room: Stairs take you down to the **Oratory of the Santa Corona**, which still has its fresco of the

Crowning with Thorns by Bernardino Luini and collaborators (1521–2). The highlight is the ***Portrait of a Musician*** by Leonardo da Vinci, a masterpiece of psychological insight and the only portrait by the master still in Italy. The subject is thought to be Franchino Gaffurio, Maestro di Cappella of Milan Cathedral. It is painted in oil on panel and has recently been recognised as a work from the Borromeo collection. It dates from 1484 or 1485.

Also here is a **portrait of a young lady in profile**, which was listed by Borromeo in his donation in 1618 as 'a portrait of a duchess of Milan by the hand of Leonardo'. But the attribution of this charming work, portraying a slightly chubby girl in a splendid head-dress and wearing pearls (once thought to be a portrait of Beatrice d'Este, great patroness of the arts and wife of Ludovico il Moro), is still discussed. In the past it has been attributed to Lorenzo Costa and Giovanni Ambrogio de Predis, as well as to Leonardo, but most recently it has been ascribed to an unknown Bolognese painter.

The copy of Leonardo's *Last Supper* was made in 1612–16 by order of Cardinal Borromeo by Andrea Bianchi (Il Vespino). Vespino also painted the *Madonna and St Anne with the Young St John*, and the good copy of Leonardo's *Madonna of the Rocks*, both hung here (and both from the Borromeo Collection). The *Mocking of Christ* is by Giampietrino. *Christ as Salvator Mundi* is by Leonardo's pupil Salaì (Gian

Giacomo Caprotti). It is thought to be a copy of a work by the master which, after restoration, appeared on the art market in 2018 and fetched the highest price ever paid for a work of art (USD 450 million). The purchaser is unknown but the work is apparently to be exhibited in the Louvre Abu Dhabi.

The Library: From here you enter the **Sala Federiciana**, a hall of the famous Ambrosiana Library, also founded by Cardinal Borromeo at the beginning of the 17th century. It has some 750,000 volumes including 3,000 incunabula and 35,000 MSS. Among the most precious works are Arabic and Syriac manuscripts; a *Divine Comedy* (1353); Petrarch's *Virgil* illuminated by Simone Martini; a printed *Virgil* (Venice, 1470); and a *Boccaccio* (1471). Part of one of its most important treasures, **Leonardo's Codex Atlanticus**, is exhibited here. This collection of drawings on scientific and artistic subjects, covering 1,119 pages, was formerly bound in twelve heavy volumes which threatened their conservation; they have now been unbound and mounted separately. This also means they can be exhibited on a rotating basis.

Caravaggio's Basket of Fruit is also displayed here. That Cardinal Borromeo was aware of the value of this extraordinary still life is clear from his complaint that there was no other work beautiful enough to place beside it: he would undoubtedly have approved of its new location.

On the right side of the Ambrosiana is the **Museo Mangini Bonomi** (*Via dell'Ambrosiana 20; map p. 24, C3; open Mon and Thur 3–7, Wed 3–5; T. 02 8645 1455, museomanginibonomi.it*). From 1978 this was the home of Emilio Carlo Mangini, a compulsive collector who at his death in 2002 left the house and its contents to a foundation in his name. It has a charming little courtyard and in underground rooms with brick vaulting are a collection of arms, while on the upper floor are clocks, toys, porcelain, walking sticks: collections of just about everything.

VIA TORINO

SANTA MARIA PRESSO SAN SATIRO

The church (*map p. 25, D3; open 7.30am–5.30 or 6.30pm*) contains magnificent work by the great architect Donato Bramante. The T-shaped interior, by a clever perspective device of ***trompe l'oeil*** and the skilful use of stucco, is given the appearance of a Greek cross; the rear wall is actually almost flat. On the high altar is a 13th-century votive fresco. The **coffered dome** was the first to be built since ancient times, and Bramante's architecture is clearly influenced by Alberti. At the beginning of the south side, by the side door, the eight-sided **sacristy** (transformed into a baptistery in the 19th century) is a beautiful Renaissance work also designed by Bramante, with terracotta decoration by Agostino de Fondulis.

Off the north transept is the **Sacello di San Satiro** (*coin-operated light*). Dedicated to Satyrus, brother of St Ambrose, it dates from the time of Archbishop Ansperto (868–81) but altered during the Renaissance with an attractive plan and large capitals. The terracotta group of the *Lamentation* is by Fondulis.

> ### DONATO BRAMANTE
>
> Though Bramante, born near Urbino in 1444, began his career as a painter, it is as an architect that he first made his name in Milan, where he arrived in 1478. Santa Maria presso San Satiro was the first building he designed in the city for Duke Ludovico Sforza (Il Moro) and later his patron called him to erect a new church of Santa Maria delle Grazie. The illusionistic perspective he created at Santa Maria presso San Satiro, and the new forms of architecture he introduced, were quickly copied in the backgrounds of numerous altarpieces in Lombardy. Remains of the series of frescoes of Warriors, and his painting of *Christ at the Column*, all executed when he was in Milan, can be seen at the Brera. When Il Moro fell from power in 1500, Bramante left for Rome where, under the patronage of Pope Julius II, he produced buildings which secured his reputation as an architect of comparable genius to those of Classical times. He died in Rome in 1514.

SANT'ALESSANDRO

Approached off Via Torino by Via Lupetta is **Sant'Alessandro** (*map p. 24, C3; Mon–Fri 7–12 & 4–7, Sat, Sun, holidays and Aug 9.30–12 & 4.15–7*), the best Baroque church in the city, with elaborately carved confessionals (some, facing the high altar, inlaid with *pietre dure*), an elaborate Rococo high altar of *pietre dure*, inlaid gems and gilt bronze, and a pulpit dating from 1741, just as highly decorated. Many of the altarpieces are by Camillo Procaccini (notably the *Nativity* in the chapel at the end of the south aisle) and

SANTA MARIA PRESSO SAN SATIRO
The dome of Bramante's octagonal sacristy.

there are frescoes by Moncalvo and an altarpiece by Daniele Crespi (*Assumption*, third south). The choir was decorated by Federico Bianchi and Filippo Abbiati. Opposite the church, at Piazza Sant'Alessandro 6, is **Palazzo Trivulzio** (1707–13), attributed to Giovanni Ruggeri and now used by the University. It contains, in its courtyard, a doorway from a destroyed house attributed to Bramante. Piazza Sant'Alessandro is a secluded spot, with a pleasant café and wine bar.

Back on Via Torino, on the north side of the street, is the round **San Sebastiano**, dating from 1577. Further west is **San Giorgio al Palazzo**, with a chapel decorated by Bernardino Luini.

CORSO MAGENTA

Milan's Stock Exchange, the **Borsa** (*map p. 24, C2*), faces Piazza Affari which, with the neighbouring Piazza Edison, was designed in the early 20th century as the main business district connected to **Piazza Cordusio**, laid out in 1889–1901. This piazza, with its busy metro station, is at the centre of a pedestrian route between the Duomo and Castello Sforzesco. The huge, handsome old Post Office building is now home (since

SAN MAURIZIO
Alessandro Bentivoglio with Sts Stephen, Benedict and John the Baptist, by Bernardino Luini.
The aged St Benedict is thought to be a self-portrait of the artist.

2018) to Italy's first ever Starbucks, which dubs itself a roastery and has a cocktail and cold-brew coffee bar on the first floor. Flying in the face of Italian tradition, the price for coffee taken standing up at the counter or sitting down at a table is the same.

On Corso Magenta, to the west, is the church of **San Maurizio**. It and the adjoining **Museo Archeologico** are both part of the complex of the former Monastero Maggiore, a Benedictine convent which was suppressed in 1798. It in turn stood on the site of the circus of Roman Mediolanum, whose long axis extended along what is now Via Luini and Via Cappuccio. San Maurizio's bell-tower was once a tower of the circus. Church and museum are linked, so you can choose which to visit first.

SAN MAURIZIO

The convent church of San Maurizio al Monastero Maggiore (*map p. 24, B2; open Tues–Sun 9.30–5.30*) was begun in 1503, perhaps by Gian Giacomo Dolcebuono. It has a façade of 1574–81. The interior is frescoed on every inch of the surface and is divided by a wall into two parts, with a window grille in the central section, since the convent was of a closed order and the nuns participated in the services unseen by the laity. The frescoes, recently restored, were commissioned by Alessandro Bentivoglio and his wife Ippolita Sforza, whose daughter Bianca took the veil here in 1522. Alessandro came under the protection of the Sforza when he and Ippolita arrived in the town from Bologna, where the pope's troops had expelled the ruler, his father Giovanni II.

The **first part of the church**, designed for lay worshippers, has chapels below and a graceful loggia above. The most interesting frescoes are those by Bernardino Luini on the dividing wall, carried out at the end of his life (he died in 1532). These are the best frescoes to have survived by him *in situ*. In the lunette to the left of the altar, his patron Bentivoglio is shown kneeling in front of St Benedict (thought to be the artist's self-portrait) accompanied by Sts Stephen and John the Baptist. In the right-hand lunette, Ippolita Sforza kneels accompanied by St Scholastica and Sts Catherine of Alexandria and Agnes. In the two panels below are four female saints, possibly subtle portraits of some of the couple's entourage. Two of the scenes above the altar are also by Luini: that on the left with the *Martyrdom of St Maurice* and that on the right with the *Martyrdom of St Sigismund*. The central panel of the *Assumption* dates from the early 16th century and is by Bernardino Ferrari. The altarpiece itself is by Antonio Campi (1578).

The chapels to left and right of the altar are dedicated to the Bentivoglio. Bernardino's sons Aurelio, Giovan Pietro and Evangelista Luini continued work on the frescoes in these and other side chapels from 1550 onwards. Bernardino Luini also frescoed the Chapel of St Catherine on the south side in 1530, with *Christ at the Column* and scenes from the life of St Catherine. The chapel next to it was frescoed by Callisto and Fulvio Piazza (1555), who also painted the altarpiece of the *Deposition*.

The architecture of the **nuns' choir** repeats that of the church but it has more side chapels, with a loggia above, and in the centre are the nuns' stalls. The organ, built by Gian Giacomo Antegnati in 1557, is the oldest in Milan. Here you can see Bernardino Luini's frescoes on the other side of the dividing wall. The lunettes illustrate the Passion and Resurrection of Christ, with four beautiful female saints. The low vault here is also frescoed, with angels in a starry sky, God the Father in the centre and the Evangelists in the angles. The lunettes in the side chapels, lit by circular windows, have more frescoes of saints, thought to be the earliest part of the decoration to have been carried out here. They are attributed to Giovanni Antonio Boltraffio or Bernardino Zenale. High up in the loggia are frescoed medallions, also thought to be by Boltraffio. At the back, behind the stalls, the chapel on the left has a charming fresco by Aurelio Luini of the animals entering the Ark. Two unicorns are among the procession.

You can usually leave the church by the door which connects it to the rest of the convent, to visit the Archaeological Museum. If closed, there is another entrance to the museum on Corso Magenta.

CIVICO MUSEO ARCHEOLOGICO

Map p. 24, B2. Corso Magenta 15. Open Tues–Sun 9–5.30. T: 02 8844 5208, museoarcheologicomilano.it.

The museum has a very good collection of Greek, Etruscan and Roman material relating to the history of Milan and Lombardy. The displays are well arranged and fully labelled, also in English.

MUSEO ARCHEOLOGICO

The 4th-century silver Parabiago patera, a ritual platter probably dating from around the reign of Julian the Apostate, which saw a resurgence of pagan religious observance. It shows the triumph of Cybele and Attis, in a chariot drawn by lions, with three Corybantes dancing around them. Oceanus, Tellus (the Earth) and the Four Seasons are below, and to the right is Aion, borne by Atlas and sourrounded by the firmament.

Ground floor and basement

Beyond the ticket office there is an interesting wood model of Milan in Roman times. The silver **Parabiago patera**, with Attis and Cybele and other fine embossed figures, is an exceptional Roman work of the late 4th century AD. The highlight of the ground-floor exhibits is the famous **Coppa Trivulzio**. Dating from the early 4th century AD, it is an intricately worked cage cup, in white, yellow and blue glass, with the inscription *bibe vivas multis annis* (drink and live for many years) in appliqué letters of turquoise glass. It was found in a sarcophagus near Novara in 1675 and was acquired by Abbot Carlo Trivulzio in 1777. A (damaged) small silver bowl has delightful engravings and reliefs of a fisherman with his basket and his catch of fish all around the rim.

In the basement are **mosaic pavements** and exhibits of **Roman glass**. A well-preserved head of Alexander Severus (3rd century AD) is displayed near the toppled base of a stretch of Roman wall, part of the defences which crossed this area of the city. A separate section displays **Gandhara sculpture**, which was being produced in India in the late Roman period.

Buildings off the garden

The cloisters display **Roman funerary monuments**. The itinerary takes you across a footbridge into the Torre di Ansperto or **Polygonal Tower** (polygonal on the outside and circular within). It was built by the Romans in their walls in the 3rd century AD (and is the only tower which remains today from the Roman defences of the town). The frescoes in it were painted in the 13th century when it was used as a chapel.

The footbridge continues to a modern building with a display on several floors. The ground floor has **finds from Caesarea in the Holy Land** (south of Haifa in Israel). The digs, made by an Italian archaeological expedition in the 1960s, found Roman glass, gold jewellery, and (in the theatre) a headless statuette of a nymph (from the time of Hadrian).

The chronological archaeological display continues on the three floors above. At the top is the **Greek section**, where the oldest exhibit is preserved: a remarkable female figurine with her arms crossed, made in reddish marble and dated between 2400 and 2100 BC. The impressive collection here includes black- and red-figure vases from 500 BC and a terracotta of the enthroned Demeter with a dove on her lap, which may date from the same century. Also here are charming terracotta animals and masks, gold jewellery and bronze helmets. A bell krater has two scenes of actors giving a performance. The second floor has **Etruscan material** from the Villanovan period and finds from Cerveteri in Lazio. A small room here explains the history of the convent: two of its towers can be seen from the terrace and windows.

The first floor illustrates the **early Middle Ages and the Lombard period**, with 6th–7th-century jewellery and bronzes, and objects which illustrate life in 5th- and 6th-century Milan. From here you can follow a walkway into the upper part of the polygonal tower.

SAN LORENZO MAGGIORE

Map p. 24, C4. Corso di Porta Ticinese 39. Tram 3 from Duomo. Open 8–6.30, weekends 9–7.

In the southern part of the old city centre is one of the most conspicuous reminders of Roman Milan: the **Colonne di San Lorenzo**, a colonnade of 16 Corinthian columns which in the 4th century were part of a portico. Today they stand in majestic isolation between a narrow road and a spacious paved precinct, with two trees and low benches in front of the **basilica of San Lorenzo Maggiore**, in effect forming a forecourt for the church. The bronze copy of an ancient statue of Constantine (set up here by order of Mussolini) is a reminder that it was this emperor who through his Edict of Milan in AD 313 gave freedom of worship to Christians. The two soberly handsome symmetrical buildings of the canonry on either side of the church date from 1625.

The church was founded in the same 4th century that the Romans built their portico. It was rebuilt after the collapse of the vault in 1103, and again in 1574–88 by Martino Bassi, though he preserved its original form (the ungainly façade was added in 1894).

The old campanile and ancient exterior can be seen from the park behind. As you walk around the basilica's north flank, be sure to admire the **street art murals** on the wall that bends round into Via Pio IV. The scenes provide a pictorial history of Milan and were commissioned by the church itself—partly as a way of combating graffiti. San Lorenzo is a very popular nightlife spot and the park behind the church and forecourt in front attract large numbers of revellers.

Interior of San Lorenzo

The huge interior has an unexpected circular plan and its 12th-century architecture is of great interest. The ancient grey stone masonry (reused from a Roman building) supports a dome, surrounded by an ambulatory beneath a gallery.

(A) Chapel of St Aquilinus: The highlight of the visit to San Lorenzo is this chapel (*ticket required; under restoration at the time of writing*), with remains of mosaics dating from 410. Look left as you go in to see a fine 12th-century **fresco of the *Deposition* (a)**. The doorway takes you into a wide **atrium**, where there are scanty fragments of mosaic against a lovely blue ground. It is thought that the original decorative programme would have illustrated the heavenly Jerusalem: all that survives is the **head of Judah (b)** and, in a rectangle beside it, a scene with his daughter-in-law Tamar; the heads of three patriarchs and the feet of three Apostles. In two showcases are mosaic tesserae and marble fragments salvaged from the original decoration and a delightful **late 15th-century painted panel** showing a procession from this very chapel bringing the sacraments to the house of a sick man, with a long Latin text painted beneath it explaining the ancient origins of this brotherhood who performed the last rites. An early 14th-century **fresco of the *Crucifixion* (c)** survives on the wall.

The chapel proper is entered between huge **door jambs** made up from nine separate fragments of Roman carved friezes of the 1st century AD, carefully fitted together in the 5th century so that you can't easily make out the

joins. Medieval chroniclers record the splendour of this domed octagonal chapel, once entirely decorated with mosaics and precious marbles. Two lovely 5th-century **mosaic lunettes** survive. One shows a very young Christ with the Apostles, with two pools of water in the grass at their feet. The other (less well preserved) has an idyllic scene with shepherds in a flowery meadow with waterfalls, and here you can see a fragment of the original sinopia for the mosaic, with the drawing of two horses from a quadriga which may have shown Elijah in his chariot of fire or perhaps Christ as the sun-god. Fragments of very early fresco decoration have been found in the matroneum above. The huge **sarcophagus** in Greek marble was made in the 3rd century, but adapted in the following century for a Christian burial, probably in Ravenna. Beneath a pretty stuccoed and painted 17th-century vault (by Carlo Urbino), the **relics of St Aquilinus** (said to have been born in Würzburg and martyred in Milan while visiting the tomb of St Ambrose) are preserved in a Baroque urn made of silver and rock crystal in the same century. Behind the altar you can go down to see the remains of the chapel foundations, made up of huge blocks of masonry clearly from a Roman building (they were 'rearranged' here in 1913).

As you leave the chapel, don't miss the

SAN LORENZO MAGGIORE

A Chapel of St Aquilinus
   a *Deposition* fresco
   b *Head of Judah* mosaic
   c *Crucifixion* fresco
B Chapel of St John the
   Baptist
C Chapel of the Holy Family
   d Corinthian capital
   e Horse relief
   f *Madonna* fresco
   g 15th-century tomb
D Cittadini Chapel
E Chapel of St Hippolytus
F Chapel of St Sixtus
   h *Last Supper* fresco,
      terracotta *Pietà*,
      statue of John XXIII

lunette of the *Pietà* above the portal, attributed to Bergognone.

(B) Chapel of St John the Baptist: The altarpiece of the *Baptism of Christ* is by Aurelio Luini, son of the more famous Bernardino.

(C) Chapel of the Holy Family: The chapel has a copy of Daniele Crespi's *St Charles Borromeo at Supper* (*see p. 100*). Opposite the entrance, the pier has a Roman Corinthian capital **(d)**

incorporated into it, used as a base for an engaged column. On the free-standing column to the left is a relief of a horse **(e)**. On the pilaster to the right are frescoes in the Byzantine style **(f)** of the *Madonna and Child Blessing*, near a 15th-century tomb **(g)** with a fresco of the *Madonna and Child with Saints* (and two male donors).

(D) Cittadini Chapel: The circular apse has remains of frescoes with, at the bottom, a frieze of elephants and ostriches and what appears to be a *St George and the Dragon*.

(E) Chapel of St Hippolytus: To be admired here (seen through the glass door) are the ancient African marble columns.

(F) Chapel of St Sixtus: Octagonal in form and dating from the 6th century, the vault was frescoed in the 17th century with a crowded scene of Christ and a medley of saints. Outside it **(h)** is a **fresco of the *Last Supper*** dating from the early 16th century and in front of it a polychrome **terracotta *Pietà*** of 1775. The statue of the portly **Pope John XXIII** records the greatly-loved pontiff, always known simply as 'Papa Giovanni', who was born in Lombardy and who died in 1963 (he was canonised in 2014).

AROUND PORTA TICINESE

The arches of the **medieval Porta Ticinese** (c. 1330; with a tabernacle by the workshop of Giovanni di Balduccio) stand astride the Corso di Porta Ticinese (*map p. 24, B4*), which ends at the busy crossroads known as the Carrobbio, which was the Roman and early medieval centre of the city. On Via San Sisto is the **Francesco Messina Museum** (*open Tues–Sun 9–5.30; T: 02 8645 3005*), arranged in the sculptor's former studio with drawings and examples of his work.

At the time of writing major excavation works were in progress outside San Lorenzo for Milan's Metro 4. When completed, **Parco Papa Giovanni Paolo II**, named after Pope John Paul II (formerly called the Parco delle Basiliche), will be reopened. It links San Lorenzo with the area's other great medieval church, Sant'Eustorgio, the bell-tower of which dominates the view from here since it is the tallest in the city.

SANT'EUSTORGIO

Map p. 26, C4. Tram 3 from Duomo. Although the west door closes at noon, the church can be visited throughout the day from the cloisters and Museo Diocesano. The church's most important chapel, the Cappella Portinari, is also entered from the cloisters.

There are benches and a drinking fountain in this peaceful corner of town. Emergency, an Italian humanitarian NGO founded in 1994, has its headquarters here. It provides free medical and surgical care for victims of war and deprivation.

The exterior of Sant'Eustorgio, dedicated to Eustorgius, ninth bishop of Milan, is impressive. The façade, with four relief panels of the Evangelists, was well reconstructed in 1865 in neo-Lombard Romanesque style. Beside the left-hand door is a 16th-century open-air pulpit (protecting the relief of St John's eagle). On the south side (right; seen from Via Santa Croce) is a series of fine chapels. The apse is Romanesque and the towering campanile dates from 1297–1309. At the east end is the Renaissance Portinari Chapel (visited as part of the museum; *see below*).

The long, low interior, with aisles and apse, is typical of old Lombard basilicas and is very dark. An important series of **chapels on the south side** was added from the 13th–16th centuries: the first chapel (*light on right*) dates from 1484 and has good sculptural detail in its Renaissance interior. It contains the beautiful tomb of Giovanni Brivio, with carving by Benedetto Briosco (1486), and an altarpiece by Bergognone, made up of seven paintings (no longer in their frame) including a lovely central *Madonna and Child*. The second chapel has a Gothic tomb of the Torelli family, thought to be by Jacopino da Tradate, who was also at work in the Duomo in the first decades of the 15th century. The fourth chapel has damaged frescoes of the Evangelists in the vault dating from the 1330, and on the walls an interesting fresco of the *Triumph of St Thomas* dating from later in the same century. Also here is the tomb of Stefano Visconti (d. 1327) and his wife Valentina, attributed to Bonino da Campione (formerly thought to be the work of Giovanni di Balduccio). The fifth chapel has an altarpiece of the *Vision of St Francis* by Il Cerano. The two tombs in the sixth chapel date from the 15th century, one with the deceased shown holding a large rosary, and the other supported by two lions with a relief of the *Adoration of the Magi* instead of an effigy. The seventh chapel has vault frescoes of Dominican saints and symbols of the Evangelists attributed to Michelino da Besozzo (c. 1440).

In the south transept is the **Chapel of the Magi**. Legend relates that the church's titular saint, Eustorgius, 4th-century archbishop of the city (some decades earlier than St Ambrose), was given the relics of the Magi when he visited Constantinople. He is said to have dragged them back with him in the colossal Roman sarcophagus which is still here but now empty: almost a chapel in itself it has an air of memorable antiquity. The relics were seized in 1164 and taken to Cologne, but some were returned in 1903 and are preserved in a niche above the altar (which has reliefs carved in 1347). Eustorgius was apparently martyred because of his fierce defence of Arianism.

On the **high altar**, behind splendid silver reliquary busts, is a finely carved dossal, and above in the nave hangs a painted Crucifix. Both date from the 14th century. Beneath the raised apse you can visit the **confessio**, with its nine slender monolithic columns (above early Christian foundations).

MUSEO DI SANT'EUSTORGIO

Map p. 26, C3–C4. Piazza Sant'Eustorgio 3. Open Mon–Fri 7.30–12 & 3.30–6.30, Sat, Sun and holidays 8.40–1 & 3.30–6.30. T: 02 8940 2671, santeustorgio.it. The ticket includes entrance to the Portinari Chapel and the Palaeochristian cemetery. You can also get a combined ticket with the Museo Diocesano. NB: The Museo Diocesano is closed on Mon.

The Dominican friary of Sant'Eustorgio was in use from the 13th century up until the end of the 18th, and its two cloisters were restored at the end of the last century by the BBPR studio of architects. Beyond the ticket office, follow the first cloister walk and continue straight on through the exhibition rooms (you can visit them all on the way back) to the Portinari Chapel (Cappella Portinari), behind the church sanctuary.

SANT'EUSTORGIO
Head of Prudence, one of the Virtues on the tomb of
St Peter Martyr by Giovanni di Balduccio (1339).
She has three faces, keeping watch in every direction).

The Portinari Chapel

This beautiful Renaissance chapel was commissioned by the Florentine merchant Pigello Portinari in 1462–8, inspired by the Old Sacristy of San Lorenzo in Florence, which Brunelleschi had built for the Medici. Portinari was the Milan agent for the Medici bank and wished to be buried here. The chapel **frescoes by Vincenzo Foppa** are the most important Renaissance fresco cycle in the city. In the rainbow-coloured vault are roundels with the four Doctors of the Church, and around the drum of the dome is a graceful choir of angels in coloured stucco, with festoons on a golden string. In the lunettes are an *Annunciation* and scenes from the life of St Peter Martyr, including the miracle he performed while preaching to a large crowd on a stifling hot day when he conjured up a big black cloud to rain down on them (Portinari himself is portrayed on the left as one of the listeners, seated with his back to us and dressed in green, ready to receive a good soaking). The other miracle in this lunette illustrates the saint banishing a heretic who had convinced some of the faithful to worship a false Madonna: she and the Child are shown with the horns of the devil. Portinari is also present here, in profile next to his brother Tommaso, in red on the other side of a column (Tommaso was the Medici agent in Bruges around this time).

> ## VINCENZO FOPPA
>
> Vincenzo Foppa (1425–1515) was fundamental to the development of painting in Lombardy, combining archaistic elements with the new Renaissance style from central Italy. A characteristic of his figure studies are the silvery grey tones, sometimes bordering on monochrome. Other works by him to be seen in Milan are in the Brera, the Castello Sforzesco and the Museo Poldi Pezzoli. In the Accademia Carrara in Bergamo can be seen one of his greatest works (just restored), the *Three Crucifixes*, signed and dated 1456. Foppa was originally from Brescia and spent the end of his life, from 1489 onwards, in that city, where some of his paintings can be seen in the Pinacoteca Tosio Martinengo. He also worked in Pavia, where there is a good painting by him in the Musei Civici. He was clearly influenced by Flemish painting as well as by Jacopo and Giovanni Bellini and the architect and painter Donato Bramante. His closest follower was Bergognone but Romanino and Moretto, also natives of Brescia, were later to look carefully at his painting technique.

In the centre of the chapel is the elaborate **tomb of St Peter Martyr**, borne by eight female figures of the Virtues and extremely well preserved. Peter, a Dominican friar here, was a fierce inquisitor of heretics, being a converted Cathar himself. He was ambushed and murdered by brigands on his way from Como to Milan in 1252 (and as a symbol of this violent death, is characteristically represented in art with a knife in his head). The tomb, commissioned by the Dominican brothers, is signed and dated by Giovanni di Balduccio (1339) and is his masterpiece. It was moved here in 1875. In Carrara marble, it has a tabernacle with the *Madonna between Sts Dominic and Peter Martyr* and relief panels showing St Peter Martyr's miracles (preventing a shipwreck, conjuring up a thunderstorm), his funeral and his canonisation. On the left end is his murder and on the right end the translation of his corpse.

On the wall behind the altar is a **gold-ground panel** of c. 1460 attributed to Benedetto Bembo and showing St Peter Martyr venerated by Pigello Portinari, who kneels before him.

Sacristy, Treasury and Palaeochristian Cemetery

On leaving the Portinari Chapel, retrace your steps through the **Cappella di San Paolo**, with frescoes in its shallow dome and a 16th-century panel painting by the little-known Cristoforo Bossi of the ambush and murder of St Peter Martyr (he is shown writing the word *Credo*, 'I believe', in his own blood). Beyond it is the **Treasury**, housed in the old sacristy of 1565, with reliquaries and other precious artefacts carefully stored in cupboards. The next room is the **Chapter House**, its vault supported on two columns. The paintings include a *Beheading of St John the Baptist* by Carlo, Giulio Cesare and Camillo Procaccini and a copy of the central section of Gaudenzio Ferrari's *Martyrdom of St Catherine* in the Brera. There is also a late 13th-century polychrome statue of St Eugene, with staring eyes.

Outside the Chapter House, steps lead down to the **Palaeochristian cemetery**, a 5th-century burial site where St Eustorgius is said to be buried amidst simple rectangular tombs, some with tile roofs. The amphorae were used for the burial of children. Funerary epigraphs are also preserved here, including a fine fragment of a well-dressed young man with his arms raised in prayer. The earliest inscription (of AD 377) commemorates a certain Victurinus, an exorcist.

In the second cloister is the entrance to the Museo Diocesano.

MUSEO DIOCESANO

Map p. 24, C4. Piazza Sant'Eustorgio. Open Tues–Sun 10–6. Combined ticket with the Museo di Sant'Eustorgio. T: 02 8942 0019, museodiocesano.it. Exhibitions are frequently held here.

The museum documents the importance of Christianity in the Diocese of Milan from the time of St Ambrose (334–97) to the present. The diocese covers an area which includes the present provinces of Milan, Varese and Lecco and part of the province of Como. Since 2016 the museum has been named after Carlo Maria Martini, Archbishop of Milan from 1980–2002. Appointed cardinal in 1983, he was one of the most distinguished and admired churchmen of the 20th century (he died in 2012). The arrangement, which is somewhat confusing, is subject to change.

Ground floor: The visit begins with works relating to St Ambrose. Most interesting, for historical as well as aesthetic reasons, are the large 10th-century stucco tondo with the bust of St Ambrose (probably based on a portrait from life) and the fragments of the wooden main door of the basilica of Sant'Ambrogio, which date from the 4th or 5th century. Objects from the basilica treasury include a 12th-century Cross; a sweet 13th-century Eucharistic dove made in Limoges; and the early 15th-century Reliquary of the Innocents.

Other works exhibited here include a 4th-century silver reliquary casket; a large lunette fresco by Michelino da Besozzo showing a crowded cavalcade of the Magi, including camels and horses; a Lombard wood Crucifix (14th–15th century); and a marble *Madonna and Child* by Tommaso Rodari.

Upper floor: In the first small room the collection of Federico Visconti (1617–93) is represented by three works, including Cerano's jewel-like little panel painting of *St Charles Borromeo in Glory*. Visconti collected about 40 paintings and drawings by contemporary Lombard artists. A later collection made by Cardinal Giuseppe Pozzobonelli (1696–1783) of artists at work during his lifetime has Arcadian subjects: mainly landscapes, often without figures.

The 172 paintings and drawings that made up the private collection of Cardinal Cesare Monti (1593–1650) adorned the archbishop's palace until 1811, when Andrea Appiani transferred a selection to the Pinacoteca di Brera. The cardinal's tastes, perfectly aligned with the spirit of the Counter-Reformation, were oriented toward the 16th-century Venetian school, the early 17th-century Lombard painters and the Emilian school. Among the best works are: Bernardino Lanino, *Salvator Mundi*; Cerano, *Fall of St Paul*; Morazzone, *Jacob and the Angel*; Tintoretto *Christ and the Adultress*; Guido Reni, *St Joseph with the Christ Child*; and Giulio Cesare Procaccini, *Pietà*.

Benedetto Erba Odescalchi (1679–1740), appointed Archbishop of Milan in 1712, gave the diocese a series of 41 portraits of Milanese bishop-saints in 1737. Highlights are two works by an anonymous 18th-century Lombard painter: *St Barnabas* and *St Castritian*. There is a large exhibition of drawings from the 15th century onwards from the collection of Antonio Sozzani (1918–2007). Three works left to the diocese by Gualtiero Schubert (1915–90) include a 13th century reliquary Cross from northern Europe and two panels of an *Annunciation* by Starnina. The collection of gold-ground paintings donated by Alberto Crespi has many works by the Tuscan and Venetian schools, including Sano di Pietro, Agnolo Gaddi, Bernardo Daddi (*St Cecilia*) and Starnina (*Madonna of Humility*).

The Caterina Marcenaro (1906–76) collection of wood sculptures from the 15th century onwards includes works from Lombardy, the Veneto and Florence.

Basement and route to the exit: Here are arranged Lombard goldsmiths' work, Crosses, liturgical objects and choir books. You are then directed back to the ground floor, where a cycle of 26 canvases is displayed in one hall. Commissioned from the most important painters in Milan in the late 17th century, by the Arciconfraternità del Santissimo Sacramento, they are dedicated to miracles of the Eucharist and to St Catherine, the lay brotherhood's patron. They used to be hung in the aisles of the Duomo during the feast of Corpus Domini. There is also a room dedicated to ceramics and plaster models by Lucio Fontana (d. 1968).

THE NAVIGLI

In the centre of the huge **Piazza XXIV Maggio** (*map p. 26, C4*) stands the handsome **Neoclassical Porta Ticinese**, an Ionic gateway by Luigi Cagnola (1801–14). It marks the point where the dead straight Roman road from Pavia (the ancient Ticinum) entered Milan. That road, outside the gate, is now called Corso San Gottardo.

Stretching away to the west is the **Darsena**, once the port of Milan. It was connected to an extensive system of rivers and canals (*navigli*), particularly busy in the 19th and early 20th centuries. Today this area is named after them and is known simply as the Navigli. When canal traffic declined, it became a neglected part of the city but was rejuvenated at the end of the 20th century, when many of the characteristic little canal-side houses and courtyards were restored and numerous architects' and designers' studios opened here, as well as a selection of good restaurants. In those early days it was much frequented by the Milanese but in this age of mass tourism, the Navigli area has been discovered and is crowded with visitors, meaning that its atmosphere has somewhat changed. The neighbourhood is very lively at night. Some of the more 'genuine' places to eat are listed on p. 120.

THE CANALS OF MILAN

Since Milan has no river, it was for centuries made navigable by a system of canals which met at a circular port, the Darsena (on the site of the present Via Conca dei Navigli). The water in the two main canals flows in opposite directions: the Naviglio Grande, most important and oldest canal, once linked the Darsena to the River Ticino, 50km away. It was begun in the 12th century and was navigable as far as Milan by the 13th century. It used to carry commodities to and from the city, and there was a regular passenger service along it from the beginning of the 19th century. The nearby Naviglio Pavese was begun by Gian Galeazzo Visconti in the 14th century as an irrigation canal from Milan to Pavia, which also lies on the Ticino river. It became navigable in 1819, when it was provided with a series of locks. The tow-paths or *alzaia* provided space for horses to pull the barges upstream. At the time of writing there was a project ('Via d'Acqua') to open up more canals to the north of the city, including the Naviglio della Martesana (dating from 1460, which passes through Gorgonzola and connects Milan with the Adda river) and the Canale Villoresi (which flows through Monza, also into the Adda), and to provide cycle paths along their banks.

The former Darsena has a wide esplanade with numerous stone benches where people come to relax and catch the sun. A new Mercato Comunale has been built here. The Naviglio Pavese has narrow lanes on both sides but the prettier of the Navigli is undoubtedly the **Naviglio Grande**, with houses often with courtyards lining both sides and the tow-paths recently re-cobbled and totally closed to traffic (except for deliveries at certain hours of the day). It is crowded on sunny days even in the depths of winter, when some of the tables of the almost continuous line of restaurants, cafés and pizzerias are put outside. Old stone and iron bridges at the ends of Via Corsico

TOURING CLUB ITALIANO
Detail of the statue of Luigi Bertarelli, compiler of the first edition of *Blue Guide Northern Italy*.

(where Libraccio is a well-known shop for second-hand or out-of-print books) and Via Casale cross to the other side. Both these side streets lead to Porta Genova station, which has a metro station which serves the up-and-coming area around MUDEC and the Armani Silos (*both described on p. 110*).

Just south of Porta Ludovica (*map p. 27, D4*) is the **Università Commerciale Luigi Bocconi**, Italy's leading economics university, which opened a new building on Via Röntgen in 2008, designed by Grafton Architects (who also curated the Venice Architecture Biennale in 2018). The original university buildings (1938–41) are by Giuseppe Pagano. Luigi Einaudi, second President of the Italian Republic (elected in 1955), was a professor here.

CORSO ITALIA & SANTA MARIA DEI MIRACOLI

TOURING CLUB ITALIANO
The headquarters of the TCI (*map p. 25, D4*) have has always been at Corso Italia 10, in a building of 1915. In the foyer there is a statue of the Touring Club's founder, Luigi Vittorio Bertarelli, dating from 1927. This was the same year that the first edition of *Blue Guide Northern Italy (from the Alps to Rome)* came out under his name, edited by Findlay Muirhead and published in London by Macmillan and in Paris by Librairie

Hachette. Bertarelli's involvement was explained in the preface: 'The present volume is based (by arrangement) on the comprehensive and authoritative Italian guides of the Italian Touring Club, and has been mainly written by Signor L.V. Bertarelli, late President of the Club, whose own intimate knowledge of Italy has thus been supplemented by the resources of a great organisation'. This *Blue Guide Lombardy, Milan and the Italian Lakes* is a descendant of that early volume. Touring Club Italiano is still famous for the production of excellent maps and guides, and volunteer members of the society act as custodians for various monuments in Milan and Lombardy.

SANTA MARIA DEI MIRACOLI

Also known as Santa Maria presso San Celso, the sanctuary complex of Santa Maria dei Miracoli and San Celso (*map p. 27, D3; Corso Italia 37; closed Thur; tram 15 from Duomo*) is protected from the busy Corso Italia by a railing giving onto a little garden in front of the Romanesque church of **San Celso** (*kept closed*), founded in the 10th century. The present façade is by Luigi Canonica (1854). To the left of it, doors lead into a wide paved forecourt designed by Cesare Cesariano (a pupil of Bramante) in front of the church of **Santa Maria dei Miracoli**. Its façade, rather over-elaborate with its engaged columns, vases, obelisks and angels blowing trumpets into the sky, was designed in 1572 by Galeazzo Alessi and Martino Bassi. The best of the numerous statues and reliefs are by Stoldo Lorenzi and Annibale Fontana.

Interior of Santa Maria dei Miracoli

The interior has a particularly beautiful floral pavement in orange and black inlay against a white ground by Martino Bassi. The little cross vaults in the side aisles are decorated with pretty stuccoes and fresco by Cerano, Camillo Procaccini and others. In the south aisle (third bay) is a painting by Giulio Cesare Procaccini (*Martyrdom of Sts Nazarius and Celsus*), surrounded by frescoed putti. The next chapel has an altarpiece of the *Holy Family*, complete with a predella and a lunette, by Paris Bordone. The crossing has good sculptures by Annibale Fontana (who is buried here, as well as Cerano) and by Stoldo Lorenzi. The frescoes below the dome were added in 1795 by Andrea Appiani (although the drum was already decorated with the twelve Apostles in niches in terracotta by Agostino de' Fondulis). The black-columned altar of the Madonna here, dating from 1588, is by Martino Bassi; beneath the altar table you can see the miraculous image of the Madonna in honour of which the church was erected. The statue of the Madonna is by Annibale Fontana, considered his masterpiece (he also made the beautiful candelabra).

The vaults in the ambulatory behind the choir (the high altar is an early 19th-century work by Luigi Canonica) are beautifully decorated by the Campi, Callisto Piazza, Moretto and Carlo Urbino. Moretto painted the first altarpiece (going round from the left) of the *Conversion of St Paul* (featuring his horse). Further round, the *Baptism of Christ* is by Gaudenzio Ferrari, with pretty flowers in the foreground. Annibale Fontana's original statue of the Virgin from the façade stands opposite (replaced *in situ* by a copy). The other ambulatory altarpieces are by Carlo Urbino and Antonio Campi. Unfortunately the choir stalls, with very fine intarsia work, are difficult to see.

In the north aisle, the first altarpiece is a beautiful *Madonna with Saints* by Bergognone. The second chapel has a 14th-century fresco attributed to Michelino da Besozzo, the third a *Martyrdom of St Catherine* by Il Cerano and the fourth a *Pietà* by Giulio Cesare Procaccini. In the fifth chapel, with its altarpiece by Camillo Procaccini, is a 4th-century sarcophagus carved with Christian scenes once used for the relics of the titular saint, Celsus (he now lies beneath the main altar). Here is another altarpiece by Camillo Procaccini.

SAN NAZARO MAGGIORE

Map p. 25, D4. Corso di Porta Romana. Open 7–12 & 3.30–7. Museo Lapidario and excavations beneath the church only open 3.30–5.45.

The easternmost of the four churches founded by St Ambrose, the Basilica dei Santi Apostoli e San Nazaro Maggiore, was dedicated to the Apostles in 386, making it the earliest church in the city. Ten years later, Ambrose found the relics of St Nazarus outside the walls and translated them here. They were reburied beneath the high altar by Charles Borromeo in 1579.

The entrance to the church, on the busy Corso di Porta Romana, gives no sense of the antiquity of this basilica, which had to be reconstructed after a devastating fire in 1075, was altered around 1578, and restored in the 20th century after war damage.

You enter through the elegant hexagonal **Trivulzio Chapel**, begun in 1512 by Bramantino and continued by Cristoforo Lombardi. The uniform family tombs are in niches high up on the walls.

The main body of the interior preserves in part the **cruciform plan** of the early Christian church (and some of its masonry), the first time this plan, based on the church of the Holy Apostles in Constantinople, was used in a church in the West. The architecture of the crossing is particularly fine. All the same, today the building has a distinctly modern feel. In the **nave** are paintings by Camillo Procaccini and Daniele Crespi, and on the right, a lovely small *Madonna and Child with the Young St John* (and a lamb) by Bernardino Luini. In the **south transept** is a *Last Supper* by Bernardino Lanino, and in the floor in front of it a (barely legible) Palaeochristian tomb slab of an Egyptian doctor called Dioscorus with the funerary epitaph in Greek. In the **sanctuary** is the reconstructed dedication stone (with two original fragments), and off the south side the little 10th-century **Chapel of St Linus** (over-restored in 1948), founded by Bishop Ardericus as his burial place. In the **north transept** you can see the reconstructed funerary epitaph of Bishop Glycerius (435); a small painting of the *Pietà* by Bernardino Luini; and a carved wood Gothic tabernacle with the *Nativity* (*light on right*), made by an artist from Cologne in the 16th century and very well preserved. Luini also frescoed a wall of the **Chapel of St Catherine**, approached off this transept, with the saint's martyrdom and four scenes from her life and a lunette with God the Father above.

The **Lapidarium** (*for admission, see above*) is housed in the old Romanesque sacristy to the left of the high altar. It contains Palaeochristian epigraphs, funerary inscriptions, and an early medieval stylised Crucifix. Also here are finds from the tomb of Bishop Ardericus (10th century), including two rings and fragments of his pastoral staff (ringed with red seals and looking rather like Havana cigars). The ferrule is inscribed in Latin, 'In times of anger, remember to be merciful'.

The **excavations beneath the church** (entrance off the south transept) have revealed part of the walls from the Ambrosian period and Roman finds including pagan altars, roof tiles, bricks and amphorae. The five large sarcophagi were reused in the foundations of the Chapel of St Linus. You can go out into the old **cemetery** around the church, where there are some surviving sarcophagi clustering against the walls.

TORRE VELASCA

Close by on Piazza Velasca (*map p. 25, D3*) is the Torre Velasca, an important building typical of the architecture of the 1950s. It takes the form of a curious skyscraper with its upper floors protruding above the lower ones—today it has a distinctly out-of-date air, though it was designed by the prestigious studio of architects known as Studio BBPR.

Beyond the basilica is the splendid **Ca' Grande**, a huge building used by the University in an area always busy with students.

CA' GRANDE

The former Ospedale Maggiore, known as the Ca' Grande, is the headquarters of the University of Milan (*map p. 25, E3*). Founded in 1924, it occupied the Città degli Studi, laid out in 1927 on the eastern outskirts of the city, until it was moved here in 1958.

This remarkable building, still one of the largest in the centre of the city, was built to house a hospital founded by Francesco Sforza in 1456. The architect was Filarete, who completed the **right-hand wing** (towards the church of San Nazaro), where the terracotta decorations with numerous busts in roundels are thought to have been designed by Guiniforte Solari, who continued the building work after 1465. The hospital had two matching wings, one for men and one for women. The incredibly long façade has a raised portico. More work was undertaken in the 17th century by Francesco Maria Richini and others, and the left-hand end, in Neoclassical style, dates from 1797–1804.

The decoration of the façade becomes more elaborate around the central 17th-century portal. Here you can enter the huge **central courtyard**, a superb work with a double loggia and beautifully carved friezes and tondi. It extends around a lawn with low box hedges and is very well kept (and sometimes used for outdoor exhibitions). Designed by Filarete but completed by Richini, it separated the men's and the women's wings and incorporates a church. The hospital closed down in 1939 and the buildings were badly damaged in WWII but have been very well restored.

The little garden in front of the entrance is named after the journalist Camilla

Cederna (1911–97). It is surrounded by rows and rows of stands for bicycles and scooters and the area has lots of cafés and bistros.

THREE LITTLE CHURCHES

North of Ca' Grande, in a secluded little piazza, stands the church of **Santo Stefano** (*map p. 25, E3*), which has a Trivulzio chapel built in the late 16th century at the end of the south aisle. Caravaggio was christened here on 30th September 1571 and outside, on 26th December 1476, Galeazzo Maria Sforza was assassinated. Next to it is **San Bernardino delle Osse**. In the atrium there is a sign to the 'Ossario', a small chapel with its walls entirely decorated with bones and row upon row of skulls. The *Glory of Angels* on the circular ceiling, as well as the four pendentives, were frescoed by Sebastiano Ricci. The chapel had a separate entrance in the alley here.

Further southwest, in the street of the same name, is the church of **Sant'Antonio Abate**, from 1582 but preserving a 12th-century campanile. Inside are good 17th-century stalls and next door (at no. 5) you can see its charming early 16th-century cloister.

ON & AROUND CORSO DI PORTA VITTORIA

Corso di Porta Vittoria leads east from the centre to the **Palazzo di Giustizia**, designed by Marcello Piacentini in 1932–40 and which stands opposite the church of San Pietro in Gessate.

SAN PIETRO IN GESSATE

This Gothic church (*map p. 25, F3*) was built around 1475 and most of the works it contains date from that century. On the wall at the end of the south aisle is a very damaged detached fresco of the *Funeral of St Martin* by Bergognone. Opposite (in the north transept), the Cappella Grifo has interesting remains of frescoes depicting the life of St Ambrose signed by Bernardino Butinone and Bernardino Zenale. The best-preserved part is the vault, which has delightful angels (1489–93). The tomb of Ambrogio Grifo, who was the Sforzas' doctor and who died in 1493, has an unusual effigy in pink and white marble (now protected by glass) and two portrait medallions above. It is the work of Benedetto Briosco. Next to this chapel is the little 13th-century Chapel of St Benedict, with painted angels in the vault by Agostino de' Mottis and a highly venerated popular statue of the Madonna. In the fourth north chapel is a painting of the Madonna with the (standing) Child attributed to Aurelio Luini. In the third chapel is a polyptych by Giovanni Donato Montorfano, who also carried out the frescoes here in 1480. The second chapel was frescoed around the same time, again by Montorfano, together with Agostino de Mottis.

Behind the church, follow Via Corridoni to Via Conservatorio, where the Music Conservatory occupies a cobbled forecourt next to the church of Santa Maria della Passione.

SANTA MARIA DELLA PASSIONE
Detail of Daniele Crespi's *St Charles Borromeo at Supper.*

SANTA MARIA DELLA PASSIONE

This huge church (*map p. 25, F2. Via Bellini 2; open 7–12, Sun 9–12.15 & 3–6.15*), founded c. 1485, has an octagonal dome by Cristoforo Lombardi (1530–50) and a façade by Giuseppe Rusnati (1692).

Inside, in the nave, is hung a fine series of portraits of popes and monks (in matching frames), some by Daniele Crespi. The vault is frescoed by Martino Bassi. The chapels in the south aisle have Lombard frescoes and altarpieces of the 16th–17th centuries.

In the crossing, beneath the fine domed octagon, is another series of paintings (in their original frames) of the Passion, one by Daniele Crespi. On either side of the altar, the two magnificent **organs** by the Antegnati family preserve their painted doors: those on the left (1613) by Crespi, and those on right (1558) by Carlo Urbino. Under the right-hand organ is the funerary monument of the founder of the church, Archbishop Daniele Birago, by Andrea Fusina (1495). The beautiful choir stalls are attributed to Cristoforo Solari.

In the south transept is an altarpiece of the *Deposition*, complete with predella, by Bernardino Luini. In the north transept, the *Last Supper* is one of Gaudenzio Ferrari's last works (1546), but it still shows the influence of Bramantino in the architectural setting (an idea which was imitated, together with the vertical format, by Daniele Crespi in his *Last Supper* in the Brera). It was finished by Giovanni Battista della

Cerva. The *Crucifixion* on the wall is by Giulio Campi. The chapels in the north aisle have more 16th–17th-century works, including a painting of *Christ Among the Doctors* by an unknown Lombard painter.

Daniele Crespi's most famous painting here is his **St Charles Borromeo at Supper** (1628), in the first north chapel. A perfect example of how his work reflected the devotional world of the Counter-Reformation, it has none of the sumptuous, stagey sensuality of the Baroque; instead it is notable for an austere—but sympathetic— naturalism, showing the saint as a middle-aged balding cleric, eating alone in a sparsely furnished room, his repast mere bread and water, with tears in his eyes as he studies his Bible.

Beyond the old sacristy is the **chapter house** (*admission on request*), beautifully decorated c. 1510 by Bergognone. The splendid and unusual cycle of paintings of Christ and the Apostles (eight of them in pairs and four on their own) are all depicted under a wooden loggia open to the sky. The painting of Christ is particularly beautiful, with scenes of his miracles in the background. Opposite, the frescoes of saints and Doctors of the Church are also by Bergognone and at the top of the walls are lunettes with portraits of the popes. The ceiling decoration has a pretty pattern.

Also in this area of the town is the Rotonda di Via Besana, now the **Museo dei Bambini** (MUBA; *map p. 25, F3; Via Besana 12, T: 02 4398 0402; for information, see muba.it*), which organises exhibitions and activities for children.

CORSO VITTORIO EMANUELE II & CORSO VENEZIA

Behind the Duomo begins **Corso Vittorio Emanuele II** (*map p. 25, E2*), a pedestrian street with numerous shops and shopping arcades as well as theatres and hotels. To the left, off Via San Paolo, is **Piazza del Liberty**, where Milan's Apple Store opened in 2018 in a former cinema. The piazza, with its water features, was redesigned by Norman Foster for the occasion. Further up the Corso, you pass the columned portico of the round church of **San Carlo al Corso** (1839–47), modelled on the Pantheon in Rome. **San Babila** is a busy crossroads (at the time of writing, large-scale building work was in progress here for Metro line 4, scheduled to open in 2022). A 17th-century column bearing the Lion of St Mark stands outside the little red-brick 12th-century church of San Babila, over-restored at the end of the 19th century.

From here, the busy **Corso Venezia** leads north, lined with grand mansions. At no. 11 (north side) is a former seminary with a monumental gateway with huge caryatids (1564). Opposite at no. 10 is the Casa Fontana, now Silvestri, with interesting terracotta work of c. 1475. Further up on the left, on the corner of Via Senato, no. 21 has a **plaque commemorating Filippo Tommaso Marinetti**, who in 1905 founded the journal *Poesia* here. In 1910 it published the first *Manifesto dei pittori futuristi*, which launched the Futurist movement. (Take a detour down Via Senato to see **Palazzo del Senato** at no. 10, a good Baroque building of 1627 by Francesco Maria Richini which now houses the State Archives.) On the corner of Corso Venezia opposite the Marinetti building is the Neoclassical **Palazzo Serbelloni** (no. 16) by Simone Cantoni (1793), which occupies a deep block stretching all the way to Via Mozart, parallel to Corso Venezia. Soon after it was built, Napoleon stayed here and in the 19th century, Metternich.

Another detour off Corso Venezia, down Via Damiano and then left into Via Mozart, takes you past **Villa Mozart** (*Via Mozart 9*), a small two-storey *villino* built by Piero Portaluppi in 1927–30 for Alberto Zanoletti. It is sometimes open for exhibitions. Opposite is the garden entrance to Villa Necchi Campiglio, Portaluppi's best-known residential building in Milan (*see below*). Further down Via Mozart, on the corner of Via Melegari, is **Palazzo Fidia**, built by Aldo Andreani in 1926–30, as was the building on the corner of Via Serbelloni and Via Maffei (note the **bronze ear by Aldolfo Wildt** which listens for the doorbell at Via Serbelloni 10). The visitor entrance to the Villa Necchi Campiglio is at the junction of Via Serbelloni with Via Mozart.

TWO HOUSE MUSEUMS

These two house museums, Villa Necchi Campiglio and the Casa Museo Boschi di Stefano, are fairly close together in the northeastern part of the city and both reflect the taste of their Milanese occupants in the 1930s. Both were also designed by the Milanese architect Piero Portaluppi. Having said that, they are very different since one is a luxurious villa and the other an apartment; but for those interested in this period of architecture and Italian art of the Novecento, they are both well worth a visit. They were first opened to the public in the first years of this century.

VILLA NECCHI CAMPIGLIO

Map p. 25, F2. Via Mozart 12–14. Open Wed–Fri 10–6, when it is shown only by guided tour (c. 1hr). Also open for non-guided visits Sat–Sun 10–6. T: 02 7634 0121, fainecchi@ fondoambiente.it, villanecchicampiglio.it. Restaurant in the garden.

Entered through the porter's lodge and hidden beyond its little garden, the house was designed by Piero Portaluppi in 1932–5 for the sisters Nedda and Gigina Necchi and Gigina's husband Angelo Campiglio. Portaluppi's characteristic wood floors and ceilings and light fixtures survive intact, with much use of marble and bronze in a broadly Art Deco style. It still has some of the furnishings the architect made for it, and he also equipped it with a lift and an up-to-date kitchen and pantries. The furnishings were modified after WWII by Tomaso Buzzi to provide the family with a cosier environment. The paintings were sold before the property was donated to the FAI (Fondo Ambiente Italiano) in 2001 and have been replaced by 20th-century paintings and sculpture, mostly from private Milanese collections and including works by some of the most important exponents of the art of the time: Arturo Martini, Giorgio Morandi, Felice Casorati, Achille Funi, Piero Marussig, Giorgio de Chirico, Gino Severini, Alberto Savinio, Filippo de Pisis and Mario Sironi. In 2017 the Guido Sforni collection of 20th-century graphic art was donated.

Portaluppi also built the tennis court and swimming pool in the garden, rare luxuries for the time.

VIA SERBELLONI
Bronze ear by Adolfo Wildt.

CASA MUSEO BOSCHI DI STEFANO

Map p. 27, E1. Via G. Jan 15. T: 02 8846 3736, fondazioneboschidistefano.it. Open Tues–Sun 10–6. Outside Porta Venezia, off Corso Buenos Aires, it is just a few steps from the Lima station of Metro line 1. There are good places to eat in the vicinity.

This apartment block was built by Piero Portaluppi in 1929–31: the protruding terraces on the corner of the building allowed for exceptionally light bow windows. The pleasant ten-room apartment on the second floor, with its ample windows and glass doors, parquet floors and Murano glass lights, was the residence of Antonio Boschi (1896–1988) and Marieda Di Stefano (1901–1968). It still has its period furniture (some of it by Portaluppi himself) and the choice collection of paintings by Italian artists of the Novecento which the couple acquired (although some had already been purchased by Marieda's father, Francesco Di Stefano). The artists, many of whom became their friends, include Carlo Carrà, Felice Casorati, Virgilio Guidi, Achille Funi, Piero Marussig, Ardengo Soffici, Aligi Sassu, Renato Guttuso, Giorgio Morandi, Filippo de Pisis, Massimo Campigli and Alberto Savinio. The works by Giorgio de Chirico are particularly interesting. There are small sculptures by Lucio Fontana, Marino Marini and Giacomo Manzù. All the paintings in the dining room are by Mario Sironi, who also designed the furniture (the three terracotta statuettes are by Arturo Martini).

The apartment and the large collection were donated to the Comune of Milan in 1973 by Antonio Boschi (some of the works from his collection are also now exhibited in the Museo del Novecento; *see p. 35*).

THE NORTHERN SECTION OF CORSO VENEZIA

Back on Corso Venezia (Fratelli Freni, at no. 43, is a good Sicilian *pasticceria*), you can't miss **Palazzo Castiglioni** (no. 47), dating from 1900–4 and considered Milan's most conspicuous interpretation of the Art Nouveau or Liberty style. It is heavily decorated with playful stonework and elaborate iron bars in the circular ground floor windows.

The architect was Giuseppe Sommaruga. There are more impressive mansions dating from the 18th and early 19th centuries further up the Corso, including **Palazzo Bovara** (no. 51), built in 1787; it became the French Embassy ten years later. The plaque records that Stendhal was billeted as a soldier here from June–October 1800, a period he recalls fondly in his Journal as '*l'aurore de ma vie*'. You can sometimes catch a glimpse of its courtyard, with statues on the garden wall beyond. On the opposite side of the road is the particularly handsome Neoclassical **Palazzo Saporiti** (no. 40), built in 1812 with a carved classical frieze behind its Ionic columns and ten statues on the roof. It was designed by Giovanni Perego, who worked at La Scala as a set designer.

GIARDINI PUBBLICI INDRO MONTANELLI

These public gardens on Corso Venezia (*map p. 25, E1–F1*) were named after the Milanese journalist and historian Indro Montanelli in 2002, the year after his death. They were laid out in 1786 by Giuseppe Piermarini and have fine trees. Very well kept, they are dog-friendly and have drinking fountains for runners. The **Museo di Storia Naturale** (*map p. 25, F1, Corso Venezia 55; open Tues–Sun 9–5.30; T: 02 8846 3337, comune.milano.it/museostorianaturale*), founded in 1838, is housed in an amusing building of 1893 designed by Giovanni Ceruti. The style is neo-Romanesque, with elaborate terracotta decoration and good wrought-iron work. It had to be restored after serious damage in WWII. The Natural History collection is the most important of its kind in Italy. The mineral collection includes the largest sulphur crystal in the world and a topaz weighing 40kg. The extensive zoological section contains reptiles, giant dinosaurs, etc. It has a good library and study collections. Also in this part of the gardens, the Neoclassical **Planetarium**, on an octagonal plan, is one of the best-known works by Piero Portaluppi. It was financed by Ulrico Hoepli, the Swiss publisher (d. 1935) and inaugurated by Mussolini in 1930 (apparently to keep up with Germany, since this was a time when almost every city in that country was being provided with a planetarium).

In a peaceful corner at the other side of the park, behind a single-jet fountain, is the handsome 18th-century façade of **Palazzo Dugnani**. Two of its greenhouses are now used as a biolaboratory by the Natural History Museum. Inside are frescoes by Giovanni Battista Tiepolo (1731), but it is not at present open to the public.

At the corner of the park closest to the Piazza Cavour gate is a **sculpture group by Harry Rosenthal** of the Four Horsemen of the Apocalypse with a (riderless) white Horse of Peace grazing on the grass, installed here in 1973. In a marble enclosure is a statue of Montanelli, appropriately seated on a pile of newspapers and bent over his Olivetti typewriter (the bronze portrait is by Vito Tongiani).

PIAZZA CAVOUR AND VIA PALESTRO

Piazza Cavour (*map p. 25, E1*), with its trams, buses and motorbikes, is typical of the busy atmosphere of the city. The traffic passes through the **Archi di Porta Nuova**, one of the old gates reconstructed in 1171, with 14th-century sculptures of the town's patron saints by a follower of Giovanni di Balduccio (today replaced by copies) and, on the inner face, Roman tomb effigies below a votive tabernacle to the Madonna and Child. The monument to the great statesman Count Camillo Cavour stands provocatively close to the newly-named **Palazzo dell'Informazione**, which was built by Giovanni Muzio in true Fascist style in 1938–42 as the Palazzo dei Giornali for the regime's propaganda newspaper *Il Popolo d'Italia*, which had been founded by Mussolini in 1914. The marble reliefs were designed by Mario Sironi, who also made a mosaic for the interior. It is now a grand office block. The Milanese atmosphere of this spot is underlined by the efficient, pleasant café (Swiss Corner), where you can sit (for no extra cost) and enjoy the scene, and drink a good coffee.

On **Via Palestro**, which borders the southern side of the Giardini Pubblici, is Villa Belgioioso or **Villa Reale**, built by Leopold Pollack for the influential Belgioioso family in 1790. It was once occupied by the Regent Eugène de Beauharnais and by Field Marshal Radetzky, who died here in 1858. It now houses the Galleria d'Arte Moderna (*see below*). A plaque commemorates four firemen and a street vendor who lost their lives here in a Mafia bomb attack in 1993. The bomb destroyed the **Padiglione d'Arte Contemporanea (PAC)**, which had been built by Ignazio Gardella in 1954 on the site of the stables of the Villa Reale. It was reconstructed by Gardella himself (with the help of his son Jacopo) and is open for exhibitions (*pacmilano.it*).

GALLERIA D'ARTE MODERNA

Map p. 25, E1–F1. Via Palestro 16. Open Tues–Sun 9–5.30. T: 02 8844 5947, gam-milano. com. Café with seats outside in good weather (open until midnight).

The Galleria d'Arte Moderna or GAM, in Villa Reale, has been home to the city's modern art collection since 1921. It is well arranged and beautifully looked after.

Ground and first floors: In the atrium and corridor are Neoclassical sculptures in keeping with the period of the palace. On the grand staircase are marble portraits of the two great Neoclassical artists Antonio Canova and Andrea Appiani. The rooms on the first floor are dedicated to the late 18th and early 19th centuries, beginning with Canova and Appiani. One of the best rooms to have survived in the villa (Room XVII) still has its ceiling fresco of *Parnassus* by Appiani (1811). Works by Francesco Hayez are hung in Room V and his splendid portraits (including one of several he painted of the great novelist Manzoni) in Room XII. Other artists worth looking out for are Domenico Morelli (Room XIV), Vincenzo Cabianca (Room XVI), the brothers Domenico and Gerolamo Induno (Room XIX), the portrait painter Il Piccio (Room XX) and Tranquillo Cremona (Room XXI). Room XXII records some of the Italian painters who went to work in Paris (Giuseppe de Nittis, Giovanni Boldini) and there is a sculpture here by Rodin and wax models by Vincenzo Gemito. Room XXIII has works by Giovanni Segantini and Room XXVII is dedicated to the sculptor Medardo Rosso, with a particularly representative group of his works in terracotta, plaster, bronze and wax, left to the city by his son Francesco in 1953.

CASA GALIMBERTI
Detail of the ceramic tiling on the façade showing Bacchic revellers.

Second floor: The arrangement here was designed for the Carlo Grassi collection by Ignazio Gardella, the best-known architect of his time. It is approached by his interesting white marble and iron staircase with its ingenious banister (covered in dark green velvet). His well-designed supports, lighting and wooden stools have been preserved and still provide an excellent exhibition space. Grassi's huge collection was left to the city in 1956. On the staircase and in the first rooms his eclectic taste is recorded in a few works which one does not expect in a gallery of modern art: gold-ground paintings, Oriental art, rugs (including a prayer rug from Turkey), genre scenes by Pietro Longhi, a portrait of an old lady by Gerrit Dou.

From Room III onwards the works from the 19th and early 20th centuries are displayed. Here is a beautiful small landscape by Corot (*Le coup de vent*) dating from around 1865 beside a small pastoral scene by Jean-François Millet painted around ten years earlier, together with works by Vincenzo Cabianca and Giovanni Fattori. In Room IV are paintings by Giuseppe de Nittis and Domenico Morelli. Beyond a room dedicated to Armando Spadini, the collection of graphic art is displayed (especially Corot and Toulouse-Lautrec). Room VIII is dedicated to the Impressionists and post-Impressionists (including one painting each by Edouard Manet and Van Gogh). Room IX has works by the Italian Futurists (Umberto Boccioni, Giacomo Balla).

Rooms X and XI are dedicated to the Giuseppe Vismara Collection of 20th-century art donated to the gallery in 1975. Formed in the first part of the 20th century, with the help of the art dealer Gino Ghiringhelli, it shows the interest Vismara shared with Grassi in the painters of the Italian Novecento (Giorgio Morandi, Filippo de Pisis) as well as in the graphic art of the time.

The **Parco Villa Comunale** (*open 9–dusk*) was laid out in 1790 *all'inglese* around the Villa Reale, the first parkland garden to be introduced in the city. It is now an attractive public park reserved for children up to the age of 12 (who are allowed to accompany grown-ups) but not to dogs nor to over-12s who are unaccompanied.

OUTSIDE PORTA VENEZIA

The area just outside Porta Venezia has plenty of good places to eat (*see p. 119*). It is also rich in examples of Liberty (Art Nouveau) architecture. A supreme example can be seen in Via Malpighi (*map p. 27, E2*), the **Casa Galimberti** at no. 3, with its colourful tiles of neo-Bacchic revellers. Dating from 1905, it is the work of Giovanni Battista Bossi. The wooden shutters at no. 7 (corner of Via Sirtori) and the stucco excrudescences at no. 12 (corner of Via Melzo) are also good examples of the period.

MODERN & CONTEMPORARY MILAN

No visitor to Milan will be unaware of the new high-rise buildings which have been constructed in the last decade or so. The panorama from the roof of the Duomo now takes in some of them, and from outside the entrance to the refectory that houses Leonardo's *Last Supper*, the view down the street frames a mighty skyscraper. Contemporary Milan is a hive of activity, with numerous cultural events organised both in conjunction with and independently of the celebrated shows of fashion and design: the city has gained a reputation as one of the best places to come to discover what is new in the air.

At the time of writing, development was happening so fast that public transport links had not been able to keep pace. The **Fondazione Prada**, **MUDEC** and the **Pirelli HangarBicocca**, all outside the centre, are examples of this. Other areas, such as **Piazza Gae Aulenti** and **CityLife**, are easy to get to and very lively. During all this building activity, special care is being given to the areas at the foot of the tallest towers to create public spaces and gardens (rather than roads). In 2017 the Museo di Arte Urbana Aumentata (**MAUA**), dedicated to Milan's street art (over 200 murals), was set up, with an app (Bepart; *see also streetartfactory.eu/maua*).

The nearest metro stations are provided for all the places described below, but some of them are still not served directly by public transport. Tram no. 33 from Lambrate to Piazzale Lagosta passes some of the newest areas of the city.

CITYLIFE

Map p. 26, A1. Tre Torri (Metro 5) or Amendola (Metro 1). Open daily 6am–1am.

This bold experiment at changing the face of the city spreads over a vast open space formerly occupied by the Fiera di Milano trade fair site, now planted with trees, lawns and grassy banks, and refreshed by fountains. The main approach is from the south, where Piazzale Giulio Cesare, with its 19th-century residential buildings forming a broken crescent and with pyramids and pine cones decorating its old-fashioned fountain, have been left as they were to give an axis for the new area as well as to provide a feeling of continuity with the old city.

The planned centrepiece of CityLife is the **Tre Torri** (Three Towers), designed by three star architects as if in dialogue with each other. Only two of them had been completed at the time of writing. One of them, by Zaha Hadid, for the Generali insurance company, suggests an undulating rather than a simply vertical movement. Taller still (50 floors) is Arata Isozaki's tower for the Allianz group, bulging at the seams like a pile of gigantic pillows and supported by four gilded beams planted in the ground. The third tower, by Daniel Libeskind, was expected to be completed by 2020.

On various levels, the buildings and porticoes beneath the towers provide space for shops, food halls, cinemas, car parks and a metro station. The aim has been to create a new urban centre; however, there are fears that it might be used more as a shopping mall. The name adopted by the development, CityLife Shopping District (*citylifeshoppingdistrict.it*), perhaps portends what its principal identity will become. The Trussardi Foundation runs the sculpture park here (*fondazionenicolatrussardi. com*). In the surrounding area the same trio of architects has provided bright white housing for those who can afford it.

THE PORTA NUOVA DISTRICT

Map p. 27, D1. Porta Garibaldi (Metro 2 and 5).

North of the centre, between Stazione Centrale and Stazione Porta Garibaldi, is an area of striking new development. Formerly called Isola since it was 'isolated' from the rest of the city by a network of railway lines and a canal, it is now usually known as Porta Nuova (it lies outside the gate of that name in the old city walls) and is home to some monuments of contemporary architecture, described below.

PIAZZA GAE AULENTI AND ITS ENVIRONS

Porta Garibaldi station has been modernised as an approach to a new piazza named after Gae Aulenti, the architect and designer, and inaugurated in 2012, the year she died. From outside the station, escalators and a circular lift ascend to the round piazza, raised a few metres above ground and just 100m in diameter, with stone benches curving round a pool with interactive water jets. The buildings which encircle the piazza include César Pelli's **Unicredit Tower** (2011), whose spire pays tribute to the pinnacles of the Duomo. At 231m, it is the highest building in Italy at the time of writing and for many the most beautiful of the country's new clutch of skyscrapers. The double porticoes which encircle the piazza are at first sight rather less handsome (but once you know that their photovoltaic panels supply all the electricity needed for the buildings above them, they take on a greater attraction). Below the piazza is the so-called Porta Nuova Food District, with cafés, eateries, fast food outlets and a supermarket.

North of Piazza Gae Aulenti, between Via Confalonieri and Via De Castillia, is the **Bosco Verticale** (Vertical Forest), two towers designed in 2015 by the Milan-born architect Stefano Boeri as residential and office space. Their balconies, constructed at irregular intervals, are entirely covered with plants, shrubs and trees (forming a 'forest' of some 2 hectares). Boeri, who teaches at the Politecnico in Milan, has extrapolated the 19th–20th century idea of the garden city into a programme of urban forestation. The **Biblioteca degli Alberi** ('Tree Library'), an eco-sustainable urban park, is still being planted. In total there is a plan to plant some three million trees in Milan and its hinterland before 2030. At the time of writing yet more building was in progress between Piazza Gae Aulenti and the **Palazzo Lombardia** (or Palazzo della Regione) tower, seat of Lombardy's regional government, built in 2010 and emblazoned with Lombardy's logo, the four-lobed 'Camunian rose', based on a commonly-occurring device in the region's prehistoric rock carvings (*see p. 320*).

South of Porta Garibaldi station is the **Fondazione Giangiacomo Feltrinelli** (*entrance at Viale Pasubio 5; open Mon–Fri 9.30–5.30; fondazionefeltrinelli.it*), the well-known publishing house founded in 1955 by Giangiacomo Feltrinelli, lifelong champion of the workers' movement and first publisher of *Dr Zhivago* in the West. The new building by Herzog & de Meuron (who designed London's Tate Modern), inaugurated in 2016, has a huge bookshop and library.

To the east, in Piazza San Gioachimo, rises the irregularly-shaped **Diamond Tower** (Torre Diamante), built entirely of steel in 2012 by Kohn Pederson. It is one of the most conspicuous high-rise buildings in the city.

STAZIONE CENTRALE AND ENVIRONS

Close to Porta Nuova is the vast **Stazione Centrale** (*map p. 27, E1*), the largest railway station in Italy, designed in an eclectic post-Art Nouveau style by Ulisse Stacchini and built in 1925–31. It has been described as a Train Cathedral and has recently been equipped with escalator ramps. There are shops and cafés here open 24hrs a day.

In the piazza outside is the **Pirelli Building** (127m), built in reinforced concrete in 1955–9 by Giò Ponti and Pier Luigi Nervi and long considered the best modern building in the city (until 2010 it was also the highest). Built on the site of the first Pirelli factory and formerly the seat of the Lombard regional government, it was empty at the time of writing and awaiting a new role.

Via Pisani leads directly from Stazione Centrale toward the city centre. The huge **Piazza della Repubblica** (*map p. 27, D1*) has more skyscrapers, including, at no. 27, the first to be built in the city (1936, by Mario Baciocchi), marble-clad on the lower storeys and brick above. The Torre Breda opposite was built in 1955, designed by Luigi Mattioni. The largest and most expensive hotels have always been here.

Via Turati continues towards the centre past the **Palazzi Montecatini**, built in 1926–36 by Giò Ponti and others, which stand at the junction with Via della Moscova, facing the Novecento-style apartment house known as **Ca' Brutta** (1923) by Giovanni Muzio.

At the edge of the Giardini Pubblici (*see p. 104*), on the street called Bastioni di Porta Venezia, is another tower by Giò Ponti (1932–5, with Emilio Lancia), the handsome **Torre Rasini**, with the Palazzo Rasini adjoining it, built as part of the same project.

THE TORTONA DESIGN DISTRICT

Map p. 26, B4. Porta Genova (Metro 2), from where it is a walk of 20mins. Free entrance to the permanent collection; ticket for exhibitions. There is a renowned restaurant on the third floor (Enrico Bartolini; T: 02 8429 3701, enricobartolini.net) and a bistro café on the ground floor.

The approach on foot is along Via Tortona. At the point where it crosses Via Bergognone, there is a roundabout called Largo delle Culture. Here a huge building of mirror-glass has been erected by Deloitte, self-styled as an 'innovation workshop' (it has to be said that some Milanese are beginning to feel that this entire area is perhaps over-hyped and directed more to visitors than to the needs of the city itself). At Via Bergognone 40 (left), the **Armani Silos**, designed by Tadao Ando, opened in 2015 (*open Wed–Sun 11am–7pm; T: 02 9163 0010, armanisilos.com*). The famous maison also holds fashion shows here (*for more on Giorgio Armani, see p. 44*).

From Largo delle Culture the huge old factory building of the Ansaldo works, which has a flying bridge across the road, is conspicuous. The first entrance leads into an area called **Base Milano** (with an entrance on Via Bergognone), a support base for events and an 'innovation centre'.

The second entrance, many metres further on, opens onto **MUDEC** (Museo delle Culture). The new building, in the courtyard of the old factory, was designed by David Chipperfield. It has become one of Milan's most important exhibition venues. On the first floor there is also a permanent exhibition of the collection of the scientist Manfredo Settala (1600–88), on loan from the Ambrosiana. This is a *Wunderkammer* or cabinet of curiosities, including scientific instruments, *objets d'art*, a crocodile and a clockwork devil.

Part of this huge industrial area is also used by the Teatro alla Scala for laboratories and set design workshops (*to book a visit, T: 02 4335 3521, teatroallascala.org*).

THE PORTA ROMANA DISTRICT
AND FONDAZIONE PRADA

The huge area around Porta Romana railway station, well to the south of the city centre, is being developed as a business district ('Symbiosis'). The well-known Prada

PORTA VENEZIA
Torre Rasini (1932–5). Detail of the façade.

fashion house led the way in 2000 by creating an arts institute and exhibition space here; its Fondazione has become one of the most visited sights in the city.

FONDAZIONE PRADA

Map p. 27, E4. Largo Isarco 2. Metro 3 to Lodi TIBB, from where it is a walk of 20mins. Open Fri–Sun 9am–10pm, Mon and Wed–Thur 9am–8pm. Closed Tues. T: 02 5666 2611 or 02 5666 2612, fondazioneprada.org. Entrance is free for under 18s and over 65s. As well as the exhibition venue there is a café and restaurant and a 'Haunted House' (timed entry tickets available when you buy your entrance ticket; no advance or online booking). This is one of the most crowded places in the city at weekends.

The Accademia dei Bambini organises activities for children at weekends 11–5 (book in advance, fondazioneprada.org/accademia-dei-bambini or T: 02 5666 2644). The cinema has an interesting programme of films (buy your ticket online or in the hour before the film starts; T: 02 5666 2674, info.cinema@fondazioneprada.org).

On your way to or from Fondazione Prada, if you feel like a good plate of pasta, call in at Pastamadre (Via Bernardino Corio 8, pastamadremilano.it), on a short road off Corso Lodi (near Porta Romana).

Prada, which under the direction of Miuccia Prada championed 'ugly' fashion with its clumpy shoes and utilitarian fabrics, has shifted its attention to art and is now as influential as a collector and curator of contemporary art shows (here and in Venice) as it is as an arbiter of cutting-edge style. Rem Koolhaas was chosen to design the Milan site: his 60m white **'Torre'** (with a bite out of it) is now the most conspicuous building on the approach from the metro station. Opened in 2018, six of its nine floors, all with different floor-plans, some trapezoidal, and with various exposures to the light, exhibit Prada's permanent collection of contemporary art (works dating from 1960–2016 by Carla Accardi, Jeff Koons, Damien Hirst and others). The sixth-floor restaurant (Torre) has furnishings from a New York restaurant of the 1950s (plus ceramics by Lucio Fontana). There is a roof bar on the panoramic terrace. Although there is a lift in the external pylon, the visitor is directed to the stairs in order to get the full flavour of this 'Ideal Museum'.

At the foot of the tower are the exhibition halls, some of them in the renovated buildings of a 1910 distillery and others in two other new buildings (the Podium and Cinema), with various (imposed) entrances and exits. The 'many spatial variables' give an air of (deliberate?) confusion and there is no covered access between one building and another. In addition, there is a cumbersome feel to the heavy solid steel doors (even to the bathrooms) and there are lots of stairs (and no escalators). The **Haunted House**, otherwise known as the Casa d'Oro (the English name is notoriously difficult for Italians to pronounce, and the exterior is covered with gold leaf), is arranged on various floors, with installations by Robert Gober (1954), and Louise Bourgeois *(for admission, see above)*.

The **Bar Luce**, designed by Wes Anderson, is a café in one of the buildings at the entrance to the area. Anderson's intent was to recreate the atmosphere of a typical Milanese café of the 1950s and 1960s, recalling the film sets of the time which also inspired him in his own films.

CHIESA ROSSA

The Chiesa Rossa, the parish church of Santa Maria Annunziata in Chiesa Rossa (*Via Neera 24; open 4–7; Metro 2 to Abbiategrasso, the end of the line though beyond the city tariff zone*), built by Giovanni Muzio in 1930, was given a site-specific installation by Fondazione Prada in 1997. Entitled *Untitled*, it is based on a display of coloured lights by the Minimalist artist Dan Lavin. The church is also used as an exhibition space.

Also in 2018, Fondazione Prada opened the **Osservatorio** in Galleria Vittorio Emanuele II (*see p. 37; it can be visited with the same ticket, valid 7 days*).

NOLO

Loreto (Metro 1 and 2). Map p. 27, F1.

The name NoLo is an acronym for 'North of Loreto'. Although Piazzale Loreto is now just a busy road junction, it remains a haunting name to Italians. It is here that a group of 15 partisans were shot in 1944 and hung up by their feet. In an act of reprisal, Mussolini's body was brought here after his execution by partisans a few months later, together with those of his mistress and other Fascist loyalists. The bodies were subjected to enraged beatings by the crowd.

Today, to catch a feel for the direction the city is taking, it is worth visiting this up-and-coming district. The Naviglio della Martesana (or Naviglio Piccolo), the waterway which formerly connected the port of Milan to the River Adda, now has a cycle lane along its length for some 30km (there are plans to reopen the entire canal as far as the Darsena; *map p. 26, C4*). The main street of NoLo is Viale Monza, once the main road to Monza and lined with buildings of the 1920s and '30s. The district becomes particularly alive during the Fuori Salone events, which run in conjunction with the Salone del Mobile trade fair.

PIRELLI HANGARBICOCCA

Via Chiesa 2. Bicocca (Metro 5). Open Thur–Sun 10–10. T: 02 6611 1573, hangarbicocca. org. Iuta Bistrot inside.

In the northern suburbs, an industrial plant once used by the Pirelli factory is now a venue for modern art exhibitions. Outside is *La sequenza*, a gigantic sculpture by Fausto Melotti. In 1999 the University of Milano-Bicocca was established near here (part of the city's Università degli Studi), but the attempt to make this a residential area by moving student housing here seems not to have worked; the district still feels very isolated.

The **Museo Interattivo del Cinema** (an interactive cinema museum), at Viale Fulvio Testi 121, can also be reached on Metro 5 (Bignami Parco Nord stop).

PRACTICAL INFORMATION

GETTING AROUND

• **By air:** Milan is served by two airports: Malpensa, 45km northwest, for most international and domestic flights, and Linate, 7km east, for a few international and domestic flights and the shuttle to Rome (*sea-aeroportimilano.it*). Milan is also served by the airport of Orio al Serio-Bergamo, 45km northeast (*orioaeroporto.it*).

Transport to Linate: Bus 73 runs to Linate from Via Gonzaga (Duomo; *map p. 25, D3*) about every 10mins (*see atm. it*); from Stazione Centrale (Piazza Luigi di Savoia), autostradale bus (*autostradale.it*).

Transport to Malpensa: Express train from Stazione Centrale in 50mins (*malpensaexpress.it*), with stops at the stations of Cadorna and Porta Garibaldi. Airport buses from Piazza IV Novembre, outside Stazione Centrale, take about 1hr (*see malpensashuttle.com*). At the time of writing, the fixed taxi fare from Malpensa to any location in Milan was €95.

Transport to Orio al Serio: Bus from Stazione Centrale (Piazza Luigi di Savoia) in c. 1hr (*orioshuttle.com*).

• **By rail:** Milan has several railway stations and before you make any journey, you need to check which one your train will leave from. The largest is Centrale (*map p. 27, E1*). All main services of the state railways, Trenitalia (*trenitalia.com*) and Italo (*italotreno. it*) leave from here, as well as some Trenord services and some trains for Malpensa airport. Cadorna (*map p. 25,*

B2) is the main station for Trenord services (*schedules and info at trenord.it*) and trains for Malpensa also leave from here. Information about railway links to destinations outside Milan is given in the relevant chapters of this guide.

There is a **left luggage** facility at Stazione Centrale, open daily 6am–11pm in the Galleria Commerciale (*see milanocentrale.it*). There is also an app (BagBnB) which (for a small fee) helps you find a place to leave your bags.

• **By public transport:** The transport system, run by ATM (*atm.it/en*), is efficient and easy to use. There is an app which can be downloaded. Information offices (with a map of the system) are located in Piazza Duomo metro station and at Centrale railway station.

Tickets (which can be used on buses, trams, the metro and suburban trains within city limits) are valid for 1hr 15mins (flat rate fare), although it is usually best to buy a 24hr or 48hr ticket or a 'carnet' of 10 journeys. There are automatic ticket machines in metro stations, and tickets are sold at newsstands, tobacconists and ATM offices. Before travelling, you must validate your ticket at the turnstiles at the entrance of the metro stations and on board trams and buses. Tickets cannot be bought on board.

The metro runs from 5.40am to half past midnight. At night and in the very early morning, bus services replace some of the metro routes (*giromilano. atm.it*).

There is a lost and found on office at Via Friuli 30 (*map p. 27, E4; open Mon–Fri 8.30–4; T: 02 8845 3900*).

Metro: The Milan metro system is efficient and easy to use. Stations are not too far underground and trains are frequent. The metro lines are as follows:

1 (red) from Sesto railway station in the north to Bisceglie or Rho Fieramilano in the west. The central section stations are Lima, Porta Venezia, Palestro, San Babila, Duomo, Cordusio, Cairoli (for Castello Sforzesco) and Cadorna (for Cadorna railway station and Parco Sempione).

2 (green) from Gessate and Cologno Nord in the north to Assago Milanofiori Forum or Piazza Abbiategrasso in the south. The central section links the railway stations of Lambrate, Centrale, Garibaldi, Cadorna and (by way of Sant'Ambrogio) Porta Genova.

3 (yellow) from Comasina in the north to San Donato in the east. Its central stations are Centrale, Repubblica, Turati, Monte Napoleone, Duomo and Missori, and it continues along Corso di Porta Romana to Lodi TIBB (for the Fondazione Prada).

4 (under construction at the time of writing). It will have central stations at Sant'Ambrogio and San Babila. It is expected to be functional by 2022.

5 (purple) from Bignami Parco Nord in the north to San Siro in the west. Its modern, driverless trains link Tre Torri (in the centre of the new urban area of CityLife), Porta Garibaldi, Isola and Bicocca (for the Cinema Museum).

Trams: For the visitor, a ride on one of Milan's famous trams is a delightful experience, even if they are not the fastest way of getting you to your destination. There are numerous lines which run sedately about the city. Some of the rolling stock is modern, some somewhat retro, and other tramcars are beautifully vintage, made of wood with gleaming brass fittings. Their rumbling noise and the clank of their bells are a memorable characteristic of the city. You will even sometimes see a party in progress on board (they can be hired for the purpose). A few of the most useful tram lines are as follows:

1 Piazza Repubblica—Via Manzoni—Piazza Scala—Cordusio (for the Duomo)—Via Cusani (for the Castello Sforzesco)

3 Duomo—Via Torino—Colonne di San Lorenzo—Sant'Eustorgio—Piazza XXIV Maggio (for the Navigli).

24 Via Mazzini—Corso Magenta (Santa Maria delle Grazie, for Leonardo's *Last Supper*).

33 From Lambrate to Piazzale Lagosta. It is a good way to take in some of Milan's contemporary architecture.

There are also numerous **bus lines** and **suburban rail links**, all well mapped on the Milan transport website (*atm.it/en*), where you can use the journey planner and download the app.

• **By taxi:** Various companies run taxi services, and as in the rest of Italy there are no cruising cabs. *T: 02 7777; 02 5353 (etaxy.it); 02 8585 (028585.it).*

• **By car:** There are car parks by the underground stations of Pagano (M1) Lambrate (M2), Rogoredo (M3) and Romolo (M2). Some are free and some fee-paying (*see atm.it*).

In Milan you can park for free only in the white-line spaces; in the blue-line spaces you pay according to the area of the city. Area C is subject to a congestion charge (*Mon–Fri 7.30am–7.30pm; Thur 7.30am–6pm*). *comune.milano.it.*

• **By bicycle:** Bicycles can be hired by the hour, day or week. You will need a credit card (electric bikes also available). *bikemi.com.*

INFORMATION OFFICES

There was only one Tourist Information Office at the time of writing: InfoMilano, in Galleria Vittorio Emanuele II at the Piazza Scala end (*map p. 25, D2; turismo.milano.it, T: 02 8845 5555*). The website is to become *yesmilano.it.*

WHERE TO STAY

There are naturally numerous hotels in Milan, but it is still difficult to find a room when big international fairs are in progress. Although many visitors may prefer to rent rooms or flats through the usual channels on the internet, below is a brief selection of hotels to suit all moods and budgets.

€€€ **Grand Hotel et de Milan**. This has been considered the city's finest hotel for over 130 years, occupying a patrician palace within easy walking distance of the Duomo. *Via Alessandro Manzoni 29. T: 02 723141, grandhoteletdemilan.it. Map p. 25, D2.*

€€€ **Park Hyatt Milano**. On a side road just north of Piazza del Duomo. With luxury suites, a spa, cocktail bars and a celebrated restaurant called Vun, run by chef Andrea Aprea (*ristorante-vun.it*). *Via Tommaso Grossi 1. T: 02 8821 1234, hyatt.com. Map p. 25, D2.*

€€€ **Principe di Savoia**. This huge luxury hotel has been famous since the 1920s and is still popular with Americans. In the vast square midway between Stazione Centrale and the historic city centre. *Piazza della Repubblica 17. T: 02 62301, dorchestercollection.com. Map p. 27, D1.*

€€ **Manzoni**. Quiet and comfortable, this is a good all-around choice in the heart of the Fashion Quadrilateral. *Via Santo Spirito 20. T: 02 7600 5700, hotelmanzoni.com. Map p. 25, E1.*

€€ **Alle Meraviglie**. With just five individually decorated rooms on the first floor of an 18th-century town house between the Duomo and the Castello Sforzesco. Breakfast is served in your room. *Via San Tomaso 6. T: 02 805 1023, allemeraviglie.it. Map p. 24, C2.*

€€ **Antica Locanda Leonardo**. A pleasant, quiet, family-managed boutique hotel in a 19th-century town house, a stone's throw from Leonardo's *Last Supper*. *Corso Magenta 78. T: 02 4801 4197, anticalocandaleonardo.com. Map p. 24, A2.*

€€ **Fenice**. Well-run, reliable three-star hotel (the rates can be advantageous if you book in advance for a minimum stay of 2 nights). Friendly staff, clean and functional rooms. In an area with numerous good places to eat and with good transport links. *Corso Buenos Aires*

2. *T: 02 2952 5541, hotelfenice.it. Map p. 27, E2.*

€ **Antica Locanda Solferino**. With just 11 rooms, this is an old-fashioned hotel which has a faithful clientèle. Off Via San Marco, which leads south to the Brera gallery. *Via Castelfidardo 2. T: 02 657 0129, anticalocandasolferino. it. Map p. 27, D1.*

€ **Residence San Vittore 49**. Run by a cooperative of enterprising young Milanese, six single rooms and one double room were opened in 2017 on the attic floor (lit only by sky-lights, but which can be opened). All with good modern bathrooms and kitchen facilities. Spotlessly clean but unfortunately lacking in good sound-proofing. You are given your own keys. There is a courtyard where you can sit, and a small garden. Half of the building is occupied by the nuns of the Compagnia di Sant' Orsola. Close to Sant' Ambrogio and its metro station, and even closer to Conciliazione metro station. Shops and supermarkets close by. A good choice if you are on a budget and on your own. *Via San Vittore 49. T: 02 9287 1158, residencesanvittore49.com. Map p. 26, B3.*

WHERE TO EAT

Milan is full of places to eat of all kinds and in all price ranges. It is a city with a wide range of cuisines to choose from, from across the globe as well as from all over Italy. In a single block chosen at random near Porta Venezia, for example, there is a Roman, a Tuscan, a Venetian and a Sicilian restaurant. Having no single dominant tradition, but an identity which is instead derived from all the peoples who have gravitated here, Milan is, in culinary terms, much more national capital and world metropolis than Rome.

Places to eat that were particularly popular at the time of writing, and in convenient central positions, have been listed below by area. Some are restaurants true and proper while others are bistro-type cafés where the Milanese come for an aperitif and snack, but which always have enough on offer to take the place of a traditional full meal. You will often see places labelled 'bistrot', usually denoting an informal place to eat, sometimes the simpler offshoot of a smart restaurant. There is very often not much difference in the offering between a place calling itself a *trattoria* and another branded a café. Milan is a busy city and it is always best to book. The most usual closing day is Sunday. A useful website to find places to eat is *conoscounposto.com*.

LUXURY-CLASS RESTAURANTS

Milan has numerous Michelin-starred restaurants, their famous chefs constantly contriving ever more outlandish and original dishes, as much designed to startle the eye as to jolt the palate into newness of life. Amongst the most fêted are:

€€€ **Sadler** (*Via Cardinale Ascanio Sforza 77, T: 02 5810 4451, sadler.it, open evenings only, closed Sun; map p. 26, C4*), along the Naviglio Pavese, and €€€ **Il**

Luogo di Aimo e Nadia (*Via Privata Riamondo Montecuccoli 6, T: 02 416886, aimoenadia.com; closed midday Sat and all day Sun; beyond map p. 26, A3*), a long way west of the centre.

Another *haute cuisine* restaurant, which moved in 2018 to the heart of town, is €€€ **Cracco in Galleria** (*Galleria Vittorio Emanuele II, T: 02 876774, ristorantecracco.it; closed Sun; map p. 25, D2*). It has neon eyes over its entrance and inside, the 19th-century décor is complemented by tiles designed by Giò Ponti and a mosaic pavement by Richard Ginori, as well as site-specific contemporary installations. The restaurant is on the upper floors, and there is also a café and *pasticceria*. Carlo Cracco is arguably the most famous chef in Italy today.

€€€ **Boeucc** in Palazzo Belgioioso, is a traditional, ceremonious, expensive, silver service establishment. Closed all day Sat and Sun lunch (*Piazza Belgioioso 2; T: 02 7602 0224, boeucc.it; map p. 25, D2*).

MEDIUM-PRICED RESTAURANTS AND BARS

PIAZZA DEL DUOMO DISTRICT
(*M1 and M3 Duomo*)

€€ **Camparino in Galleria**. Historic cocktail bar dating from the beginning of the 20th century. It takes its name from the famous mixer drink Campari (the family by the same name lived here in the 19th century and ran a bar). This is still a typical relic of old-world Milan in the heart of the city, well worth a visit for an aperitif. The Campari soda is served very cold, very fizzy and without ice. *Corner of Piazza del Duomo and the Galleria Vittorio Emanuele II. T: 02 8646 4435, camparino.it. Map p. 25, D2.*

€€ **Chiostro del Piccolo Teatro**. Attached to one of Milan's most important theatres, in the beautiful 15th-century cloister of Palazzo Carmagnola, this is a good place to come for a light lunch or aperitif. The café is approached from the corner of Via Rovello. In the Chiostro Nina Vinchi there is a bookshop and place for literary encounters and book presentations. Convenient before or after a visit to the Castello Sforzesco. *Via Dante 10. T: 02 7233 3505, piccoloteatro.org. Map p. 24, C2.*

€€ **Signorvino**. Italian wine specialists where you can buy wine or order it with a meal, or taste it as an aperitif with tapas etc. *Piazza Duomo, corner of Corso Vittorio Emanuele II. T: 02 8909 2539, signorvino.com. Map p. 25, D2.* There is another branch near the Castello Sforzesco (*Via Dante 15, T: 02 8909 5369; map p. 24, C2*).

€€ **Bar/Ristorante 5 Vie**. Tucked away amongst 20th-century buildings (approached from Piazza Cordusio), this is an extremely simple *trattoria* with no pretensions whatsoever, frequented by Milanese office workers. Certainly not the place to come for chic atmosphere, but probably the cheapest good meal to be found in this area. *Via del Bollo 8 (corner of Via Bocchetto). T: 02 8646 2500. Map p. 24, C3.*

€€ **Pizzeria Gino Sorbillo Lievito Madre al Duomo**. If you feel like a pizza after a visit to the Duomo, this is the place to come, just a short way along Corso Vittorio Emanuele II (and very close to the San Babila metro station). First opened in Naples, Sorbillo has made a name for itself in producing excellent Neapolitan pizzas and there is now also a branch in New York. *Largo*

Corsia dei Servi 11. T: 02 4537 5930, sorbillo.it/gino-sorbillo-lievito-madre-al-duomo. Map p. 25, E2.

€€ **Principe**. Friendly bar on the peaceful Piazza Sant'Alessandro, a stone's throw from the hurly burly of Via Torino. Good drinks and snacks, popular with a local after-work crowd. *Piazza Sant'Alessandro. Map p. 24, C3.*

€€ **Vino Vino**. Wine bar right next door to the Bar Principe. Low key and relaxed, a good place to sample fine wine. *Piazza Sant'Alessandro. Map p. 24, C3.*

BRERA DISTRICT (*M3 Turati*)

This district has numerous restaurants in the higher price range, including sushi bars. There are also plenty of cafés and bars. A little further afield, popular with locals at lunchtime, is:

€€ **Fioraio Bianchi Caffè**. Self-styled a 'flower laboratory', you eat in a bower of flowers. Short but interesting lunch and dinner menu. The front part operates as a simple café where you can come just for an espresso. Closed Sun. *Via Montebello 7. T: 02 2901 4390, fioraiobianchicaffe.it. Map p. 27, D2.*

PORTA VENEZIA (*M1 Porta Venezia*)

€€€ **Joia**. Michelin-starred vegetarian restaurant. Pietro Leemann has his own philosophy about food (you can read all about it on the website). Many of the dishes are also vegan and gluten free. Near Piazza della Repubblica. Closed Sun. *Via Panfilo Castaldi 18. T: 02 2952 2124, joia.it. Map p. 27, E2.*

€€ **Eppol**. Open all day from 7.30 am to 1 am. In a short street just outside Porta Venezia. A place to come for a good

snack during the day, and popular in the evenings when it becomes a fashionable place for a drink before dinner or a cocktail afterwards (usually very crowded so booking advisable). Bistro-style food also served. It has a few tables outside. *Via Malpighi 7. T: 02 3679 8290, eppolmilano.com. Map p. 27, E2.*

€€ **Gesto**. You can have a good reasonably priced dinner (with small very imaginative dishes), or an aperitif with tapas. It has become a fashionable place, so booking advised. Evenings only. *Via G. Sirtori 15. T: 02 201 006, gestofailtuo.it. Map p. 27, E2.*

€€ **Il Gottino**. Popular wine bar overlooking the church of San Carlo al Lazzaretto. Tables spill out into the small square. The church was built by Pellegrino Tibaldi in 1585, at the behest of Carlo Borromeo, on the site of an earlier church in Milan's old quarantine station. *Largo Bellintani. Map p. 27, E1.*

€€ **Lùbar**. In part of the Villa Reale (seat of the Galleria d'Arte Moderna), including its winter garden and courtyard. Opposite the public gardens. You can come here to have an excellent snack; a drink or fruit juice concoction; or to enjoy a longer lunch or dinner (try the *scutedde* as a starter). Closed Mon. *Via Palestro 16. T: 02 8352 7769, lubar.it. Map p. 25, F1.*

€€ **Nun**. In a small pedestrian street right beside Porta Venezia Metro station. Dubbed the 'kebab revolution', this serves Middle Eastern food for vegetarians using good local produce. An excellent place to come for a quick meal or a take-away. Closed Mon. *Via Spallanzani 36. T: 02 9163 7315, nunmilano.com. Map p. 27, E2.*

€€ **San Pietro Café**. Enoteca-bistro with good food and wines and ample outdoor seating on street terraces front and back. Friendly service, lively atmosphere. The house Gavi is excellent. *Corso Buenos Aires 6/Via Spallanzani. T: 02 7862 2210, sanpietrocafe.com. Map p. 27, E2.*

€–€€ **Swiss Corner**. Very pleasant café with modern décor and plenty of places to sit. Frequented by business people for breakfast or a light lunch. Extremely efficient and with a typically streamlined Milanese atmosphere. *Via Palestro 2/Piazza Cavour. T: 02 7632 0360, swisscornermilano.it. Map p. 25, E1.*

€€ **Wang Jiao**. One of the best places in Milan for Chinese cuisine (with three other branches in the city). Simple minimalist décor. Closed Mon. *Via F. Casati 7. T: 02 261 3224 or 02 8940 2858, wangjiaomilano.com. Map p. 27, E1.*

€€ **Warsà**. Opened some decades ago, this serves Eritrean dishes which you eat with your hands. It was one of the first to be opened in this area, where there are now many other African restaurants. Closed Wed. *Via Melzo 16. T: 02 201 673, ristorantewarsa.com. Map p. 27, E2.*

€–€€ **Enoteca con Cucina**. Wine bar which also offers a short menu of well-chosen dishes. Friendly, knowledgeable staff, good atmosphere. A relaxed place for a simple supper. Closed Sun. *Viale Piave 19 (between Via De Bernardi and Via Morelli).* €€ **Piccola Cucina** next door at no. 17 is also a charming restaurant (also closed Sun). Evenings only. *piccolacucina.it. Map p. 27, E2.*

NAVIGLI AND VIA TORTONA
(*M2 Porta Genova*)

€–€€ **Al Fresco**. Frequented by Milanese office workers at lunch, with a large garden. Limited choice on the daily menu but all good variants of Italian cuisine. Brunch on Sat–Sun 9–11. You can also come here just for an aperitif, Thur–Sat 7.30pm–10pm. Close to MUDEC. Closed Mon. *Via Savona 50. T: 02 4953 3630, alfrescomilano.it. Map p. 26, B4.*

€–€€ **Berberé**. Opened by two Calabrian brothers, this has become one of the most popular places to have a good pizza in Milan. Organic ingredients are used for the traditional types of pizza, which are produced with special care. There is another branch at Via Sebenico 21 (*T: 02 367 07820*). *Via Vigevano 8. T: 02 367 58428, berberepizza.it. Map p. 26, C4.*

€–€€ **Il Brutto Anatroccolo**. A typical Milanese place to eat. Some come here for a quick meal on the hop. Off the Naviglio Pavese. *Via Evangelista Torricelli 3. T: 02 832 3333. Map p. 26, C4.*

€–€€ **Del Binari**. This has ample seating with summer houses amidst traces of the old rail tracks (hence its name). It is redolent of old Milan, and even its website is delightfully old fashioned. There is a popular court for bowls beside it. You can have an 'elevenses' or light lunch here (the dinner menu is more expensive). On the same street as MUDEC. *Via Tortona 2. T: 02 839 5095, osteriadelbinari.com. Map p. 26, B4.*

€ **Empire**. If for any reason you find yourself at Porta Genova station with time on your hands, this is a very good place for coffee, cake, fruit salad and other simple bites. *Via Vigevano 43. Map p. 26, C4.*

€–€€ **MAG Cafè**. One of the many places to eat along the Naviglio Grande, this is a very small old-fashioned

cocktail bar with wood furnishings (from a pharmacy in Argentina), and tables outside on the canal. It functions as a bar and a place for a snack or light lunch until 5.30pm, when it turns into an excellent cocktail bar. *Ripa di Porta Ticinese 43. T: 02 4548 9460, magcafemilano.myadj.it. Map p. 26, B4.*
€€ **Temakinho**. A Japanese-Brazilian restaurant (Brazil has one of the largest Japanese colonies in the world), extremely popular so best to book. An interesting mixture of these two cultures and their food, well worth a try. You can also come here just for a cocktail. *Ripa di Porta Ticinese 37. T: 02 835 6134, temakinho.com. Map p. 26, B4.*

ISOLA AND CHINATOWN
(M2 and M5 Garibaldi)

€€ **10 Corso Como**. In a secluded courtyard near Piazza Gae Aulenti, this is a concept store with restaurant and café on several levels, a conservatory and roof garden. Run by the Sozzani family, well-known for their avant-garde gallery. They have opened branches in Beijing and New York. You can choose between the snacks (*piattelli*) or a full-course meal. Restaurant and café open daily 10.30am–1am. Gallery and bookshop open 10.30–7.30. *Corso Como 10. T: 02 2901 3581, 10corsocomo.com. Map p. 27, D1.*
€–€€ **Anche Ristorante**. Try the *cotoletta sbagliata* (the 'Milanese veal cutlet gone wrong'), which has the addition of pistachio and lime. There is a bar and bakery attached. Very reasonable prices. Near the Bosco Verticale towers. *Via Carmagnola 5. T: 331 822 4002, anche.it. Map p. 27, D1.*
€ **Circolo degli ex Combattenti e**

Reduci. Very simple place in a men's club built for soldiers returning from the First World War. The old-fashioned atmosphere is complemented by the presence of a billiard table and mementoes of military campaigns. There is a little garden shaded with wisteria. Basic Italian fare and a rough-and-ready atmosphere—if you want a change from Milanese chic and elegance. Closed Mon. *Via Alessandro Volta 23. T: 02 657 5872. Map p. 26, C1.*
€ **Otto**. Popular for its delicious and original snacks. When you order an aperitif you are given a special menu so you can choose which *tagliere* you would like to accompany it. More substantial snacks are the *quadrOtti*, a thick slice of good bread with an excellent topping. Brunch served at the weekends. *Via Paolo Sarpi 8. T: 02 8341 7249, sarpiotto. com. Map p. 26, C1.*
€ **La Ravioleria**. Excellent Chinese ravioli with organic ingredients, made by a young Chinese-Milanese. Little more than a hole in a wall but very well run. *Via Paolo Sarpi 25. T: 331 887 0596. Map p. 26, C1.*
€€ **Trattoria Ottimofiore**. Well-known Sicilian restaurant. Closed Sun and Mon lunch. *Via Bramante 26. T: 02 331 01224, latrattoriaottimofiore.it. Map p. 26, C1.*

NEAR PORTA ROMANA
(M3 Porta Romana)

€€ **Lacerba**. A restaurant named after a Futurist journal founded in 1913, and specialising in fish. Attached to Quisibeve, open from 6pm, a place for a good cocktail. Closed Sun. *Via Orti 4. T: 02 545 5475, lacerba.it. Map p. 25, F4.*
Trattoria del Pescatore. This has been known for many decades as a place to

come for good fish served in a traditional Milanese ambience. Closed Sun. *Via Atto Vannucci 5. T: 02 5832 0452, trattoriadelpescatore.it. Map p. 27, D4.*

IN MUSEUMS AND EXHIBITION SPACES

At **MUDEC**, there is the Enrico Bartolini restaurant (*enricobartolini. net; T: 02 8429 3701*) on the upper floor and a bistro-café on the ground floor. The **Triennale Design Museum** has a restaurant on the upper floor and a pleasant café overlooking the gardens. In the **Museo del Novecento** is the rather grand Giacomo all'Arengario restaurant (*giacomoarengario.com*). **Fondazione Prada** has a restaurant in the tower and the popular Bar Luce at the entrance. The **Galleria d'Arte Moderna** has a place to eat (*described above*) in the courtyard, independent of the museum. The Iuta Bistrot is a well-known place in the **Pirelli HangarBicocca**. The **Museo Bagatti Valsecchi** has the Salumaio di Montenapoleone in its peaceful courtyard (closed Sun; *ilsalumaiodimontenapolone.it*). There are also good cafés at the **Brera** and at the **Fondazione Feltrinelli**.

CONFECTIONERS, *PASTICCERIE* AND DELICATESSENS

Marchesi is one of the best-known *pasticcerie* in Milan, in operation since 1824 and now owned by the Prada fashion house. It has three branches: the one at Via Montenapoleone 9 (*map p. 25, E2*) has been newly refurbished, while the smaller café at Via Santa Maria alla Porta 11 (corner of Via Meravigli; *map p. 24, C2*) still has its old décor, with a marble bar and wood furnishings. The café on the first floor of the Osservatorio Prada overlooking the Galleria Vittorio Emanuele II is in the higher price range.

Cova (*Via Montenapoleone 8; map p. 25, E2*) has been in business since 1817, when it was founded by Antonio Cova in Via Manzoni. Claiming to serve the best *cappuccino* in Milan, it became very well-known: famous clients included Verdi, Puccini, Eleonora Duse, Maria Callas, Luchino Visconti, Ernest Hemingway (who mentions it in *A Farewell to Arms*). Since 2013 it has been owned by Louis Vuitton and has some 30 branches all over the world.

An excellent old-fashioned café and *pasticceria* is **Biffi** (*Corso Magenta 87, corner of Viale di Porta Vercelliana; map p. 26, B3*), handy for a coffee and cake after visiting Leonardo's *Last Supper*.

There are myriad fancy food shops all over the centre of town where you can buy an excellent picnic. **Peck** (*Via Spadari 9; peck.it; map p. 24, C3*), close to the Ambrosiana, has been the city's most famous delicatessen for many decades, with a wide selection of cheeses and cold meats and a well-stocked wine cellar.

MUSEUMS AND GALLERIES

Milan has few signs to its museums and monuments, but it is customary to hang three flags over the doorways, which makes their street-facing entrances easy to spot. Generally speaking there are good labels also in English, and audio-guides and apps are often available. Despite this, we still describe many museums in some detail, so that you can prepare before your visit and be sure not to miss the most important works. Many of the smaller museums are kept open by volunteers (often members of the Touring Club Italiano; *see p. 95*).

The Cenacolo Vinciano (Leonardo da Vinci's *Last Supper*) is the only place in Milan which you cannot visit without booking in advance.

The Duomo is the most-visited monument in the city and there is usually a queue outside, even for those who have purchased their ticket online.

Opening times

Times given in the text should be taken as guidelines only and should always be checked prior to a visit (official websites and telephone numbers have been given where possible). Most museums and galleries are closed on Mon, with the notable exceptions of the Museo del Duomo, the Museo Poldi Pezzoli and the Museo Teatrale alla Scala. There is free entrance on the first Sun of the month to many museums (notably the Brera, Leonardo's *Last Supper*, Castello Sforzesco and the Museo del Novecento). The Castello Sforzesco is free on Tues after 2pm and every day from 4.30 (the last hour). Admission charges vary from around €5–€10.

Visitor cards

There are several of these. The annual visitor card gives free entrance to museums, villas and temporary exhibitions in Milan and the rest of Lombardy. It can be purchased online at *abbonamentomusei.it* or directly at some of the museums. Rates vary but it is worth buying if you intend to stay in Milan and/or other towns in Lombardy for more than a day or so. A three-day pass for Milan's Musei Civici is worth purchasing if you intend to visit the Castello Sforzesco, Museo del Novecento, Museo Archeologico, GAM and MUDEC. There is a Casemuseocard, valid one year, which allows one free entrance to the Museo Poldi Pezzoli, Museo Bagatti Valsecchi, Villa Necchi Campiglio and Casa Boschi di Stefano, good value if you intend to visit more than two of these. There is a weekend every year (usually in May) when places not usually open to the public can be seen (*openhousemilano.it*).

Exhibitions

Milan has numerous exhibition spaces, the most important of which is Palazzo Reale in Piazza del Duomo, where multiple shows are usually in progress simultaneously. Exhibitions are also held in the Gallerie d'Italia. Exhibitions of modern and contemporary art (as well as design) are held at MUDEC, the Pirelli HangarBicocca, the Triennale Design Museum, the PAC, the Fabbrica del Vapore and numerous other venues all over the city.

OPERA, CONCERTS AND THE THEATRE

Listings are carried in *Hello Milano!*, published free every month. It is available at most hotels or from the Tourist Information office. **Tickets** can be purchased at the

Feltrinelli and Mondadori bookshops in the centre of Milan, or online at *ticketone.it* and *vivaticket.it*.

The **opera season** at La Scala opens on 7 Dec; ballet and concerts run Sept–Nov. Milan's **symphony orchestra and choir** hold concerts at the Auditorium di Milano, Largo G. Mahler (*map p. 26, C4*). Classical music concerts also take place at the Conservatorio Giuseppe Verdi and at the Teatro Dal Verme.

Throughout the year (except July and Aug) **organ concerts** (Cantantibus Organis) are held in churches, including San Maurizio, Sant'Alessandro, Santa Maria della Passione and San Simpliciano. These usually take place in the late afternoon around 5pm. Information from *ilcantodiorfeo.it* or *lacappellamusicale.com*.

Jazz and blues at The Blue Note, Spirit de Milan, Circolo Masada, Santeria Social Club. **Prose performances** at the Piccolo Teatro Strehler (*map p. 24, C1*); Teatro Franco Parenti and Teatro Filodrammatici. Other theatres include Teatro Nuovo, Teatro MTM Litta, Teatro Verdi, Teatro della Luna. **Experimental theatre** at Teatro Elfo Puccini, and Teatro dell'Arte at the Palazzo del Triennale. Other old-established **popular theatres** include the Teatro Manzoni (*Via Manzoni 42*); Carcano (*Corso di Porta Romana 66*) and Nazionale (*Piazzale Piemonte*).

TRADE FAIRS

Milan is famous for its annual trade fairs. In the weeks when they are held, the city can become extremely crowded and the atmosphere is electric. The most popular include Milan Design Week (in April), Fashion Week, the Triennale, the Salone del Mobile, Artigiano in Fiera. For information, see *fieramilano.it* and *cameramoda.it*. The main trade fairs are held at Fieramilano at **Rho** (at the end of metro M1, outside the city tariff zone) and are usually open to the public on certain days. At the same time numerous '*Fuori Salone*' events take place in other parts of town. **Fieramilanocity**, on the site of the former Alfa Romeo works, just northwest of CityLife (M5 to Portello), is used for other annual fairs, including Miart, an international fair of modern and contemporary art which takes place in April.

FESTIVALS AND EVENTS

Milan's patron saint St Ambrose is fêted on 7 Dec with a holiday which normally lasts four days and during which the street fair **Oh Bei Oh Bei** is held near the Castello Sforzesco. **Stramilano**, a marathon race starting in Piazza Duomo in which some 50,000 people take part, is held in March or April. The tourist board's free monthly booklet *Hello Milano!* has a summary of what's on.

SHOPPING

The area northeast of the Duomo, around Via Montenapoleone, is Milan's famous **Fashion Quadrilateral** (or Brera Design District), bounded by Via Montenapoleone, Via Manzoni, Via della Spiga and Corso Venezia (*map p. 25, E2*). The great designers have their showrooms here and on the smaller Via S. Andrea, Via Gesù, Via Borgospesso, Via Santo Spirito. Important jewellery shops, and design and furnishing showrooms, as well as antique shops can also be found here. This district is one of the most elegant parts of the city, with fine 19th-century townhouses.

East of the Duomo, **Corso Vittorio Emanuele** (*map p. 25, E2*), is Milan's high street: now a pedestrian precinct, it is a popular meeting place for residents as well as visitors, with cafés and tables outside.

The area around **Porta Venezia** (*map p. 27, E1*) is less chic than the Fashion Quadrilateral, but good if you're on a limited budget—and it has the lovely old hat shop Mutinelli, in business since 1888 on the corner of Corso Buenos Aires and Via Lazzaro Palazzi. The area south of the Duomo and around the **Navigli** (*map p. 26, B4–C4*) hosts Milan's trendiest shops.

A very different kind of shopping is offered by Milan's many **markets**. The **Fiera di Senigallia**, a large flea market, is held all day long on Sat along the Naviglio Grande between Via Paoli and Via Lombardini (*map p. 26, B4*). Antiques and bric-à-brac are sold on the last Sun of the month, from the stalls which stretch for some two kilometres along the Naviglio Grande.

The largest and most interesting other **street markets** are held in Viale Papiniano (Tues morning and Sat; *map p. 24, A4*), Via P. Calvi (Thur morning; *map p. 27, E3*) and Via G.B. Fauchè (Tues morning and Sat; *map p. 26, B1*).

MILAN WITH CHILDREN

Children are bound to have a good time in Milan. A ride on a tram is always fun, and the walkway across the roof of the cathedral is memorable.Children are provided with their own place to explore at the Triennale Design Museum (*p. 64*) and special events are put on for them at weekends at the Accademia dei Bambini at the Fondazione Prada. In the new area of CityLife, totally devoid of traffic, children can run free and play on the grass. The Science Museum is also geared very much to children: pamphlets are provided for young 'explorers' and there are 'tinkering zones' where they can work and play. At the Brera there are special labels provided for families and all sorts of incentives for the young to make the most of their visit. The area of the Navigli, where the canals are bordered by quays, is a good place to take children. In the courtyard of the Castello Sforzesco, the Sforzinda organises childrens' activities. The parks of the Sempione and the Giardini Pubblici are well-kept and very pleasant, and the Parco Villa Comunale next to the Galleria d'Arte Moderna is reserved for children up to the age of 12 (*p. 107*). There is even a dedicated Children's Museum (*p. 101*).

Around Milan

The immediate hinterland of Milan has several towns worth exploring. **Desio** (about 16km north of the city; *Atlas B, B1*) was the birthplace, in 1857, of Achille Ratti (Pope Pius XI; r. 1922–39). His reign saw the Concordat with the Italian government (1929) in which the Vatican State became independent and exempt from Fascist law. The pope's comment that Mussolini was 'the man whom Providence has sent us' has been used to demonstrate that he was not forceful enough in his rejection of Fascism, although in 1937 he apparently wrote a denunciation of Nazism and on Hitler's visit to Rome in 1938 he was absent in Castel Gandolfo. His encyclical against Fascism and Nazism was never issued as his Secretary of State Cardinal Pacelli (his successor in the papal chair as Pius XII) apparently advised against it. Pius XI died in 1939, just before the outbreak of the Second World War.

Agliate (*Atlas D, B4*) has a remarkable 10th–11th-century church and baptistery traditionally thought to have been founded in 881 by Ansperto, Bishop of Milan. Restored by Luca Beltrami in 1895, they contain remains of 10th-century frescoes.

East of Milan is **Gorgonzola** (*Atlas B, C1*), on the Naviglio della Martesana canal. Its centre is mainly modern and though the town gave its name to the famous penicillin-rich cheese, there is scant evidence of a dairy industry here today. The headquarters of the consortium in charge of preserving the Gorgonzola name is in fact now in Novara, in Piedmont. In Roman times there was a station for changing horses here. As the Roman Empire disintegrated, the early Christian church on this site was sacked by the Huns. The present church dates from the early 19th century.

The two towns in the immediate purlieux of Milan most rewarding for the visitor are **Monza** (where the duomo houses the ancient Iron Crown of Lombardy in a lovely 15th-century frescoed chapel, and where you can also visit a former royal palace of the Savoy kings) and **Saronno**, with its beautiful paintings by Bernardino Luini and Gaudenzio Ferrari in its sanctuary church and a small museum of industrial heritage. Both are described in detail in this chapter, along with the **abbey of Chiaravalle** on Milan's southern outskirts.

MONZA
Detail of the frescoes in the Chapel of Queen Theodolinda, by the workshop of the Zavattari (c. 1445). Theodolinda is shown offering a goblet of wine to her future husband, Authari, King of the Lombards.

MONZA

Monza (*Atlas B, C1*) is officially the third largest town in Lombardy (pop. 123,000) after Milan and Brescia. Despite being backed by a hinterland of straggling suburbs, its old centre nevertheless remains intact and is a pleasant and surprisingly peaceful place to visit. It is so close to Milan that it can be reached in less than 20mins by frequent trains. Monza cathedral (only 10mins' walk from the station) is closely associated with the Lombard queen Theodolinda (*see below*), and the recently-restored chapel with scenes from her life, as well as the treasures she donated (preserved in the Duomo Museum), are well worth any trouble it may take to see. The magnificent 18th-century Villa Reale, in its huge walled park, is also of great interest.

HISTORY OF MONZA

Situated on the Lambro river, Monza was the Roman *Modicia*, traces of which have been found. During the Lombard rule of Italy (*see p. 156*), it was where Queen Theodolinda lived. Throughout its history, the town has enjoyed periods of great prosperity and—in the early 17th century—a certain notoriety, occasioned by the 'Monaca di Monza' ('the Nun of Monza'). Marianna de Leyra, a Spanish noblewoman born in 1575 into a well-known feudal family, had an affair with Count Paolo Osio (and several children by him) after she had taken the veil as Suor Virginia in a convent here. She was condemned to be immured in a tiny room but was released after 14 years and survived to a ripe old age. Her story inspired Alessandro Manzoni in his famous novel *I promessi sposi*, and the scandal still provided inspiration in the 20th century: no fewer than three films have been made (in 1947, 1962 and 1969), all entitled *La Monaca di Monza*. (The convent was demolished in 1840 when Via Vittorio Emanuele was laid out.)

In the 18th century the huge Villa Reale was built here as the residence of Ferdinand, the Habsburg governor of Lombardy. Monza remained an agricultural town until the second half of the 19th century, when rapid industrial development led to its being dubbed the 'Manchester of Italy' (it was known for its felt hats and cheap carpets). In 1840 the railway line to Milan's Porta Garibaldi station was inaugurated, the second line to be opened in Italy.

Monza occupied the international news headlines in 1900, when the King of Italy, Umberto I, was shot dead just outside the gates of the Villa Reale on 29th July by an anarchist named Gaetano Bresci.

Since 1922 the town's name has been familiar to motor-racing enthusiasts: Monza's famous racetrack occupies the northern part of the Villa Reale park. In 2004 it became the capital of a new province (Monza and Brianza) and is thus no longer considered an appendage of Milan. Today the area is known for its mechanical and electronic engineering works.

Turn right when you leave the railway station and walk straight ahead. You soon reach a triangular crossroads, **Largo Mazzini**, where the buildings all date from the second decade of the 20th century: one has elaborate caryatids and reliefs; another, a former linen manufactory, is now a department store; yet another was originally built as a garage. From here the pleasant, pedestrianised **Via Italia**, with central flower-beds, leads directly to the old town. At the point where the street widens, after you pass the handsome 14th-century brick and terracotta façade of Santa Maria in Strada, you can diverge left into **Piazza Trento e Trieste** (formerly Piazza del Mercato), where the vast War Memorial must be one of the largest in all Italy. It was designed by a local architect, Enrico Pancera, in 1932 (and was thankfully his only public commission; he specialised in cemetery chapels). The huge Neoclassical building here now houses a school and a library, and Palazzo Comunale dates from 1932.

Via Italia ends in **Piazza Roma** with the Arangario, the arcaded, brick Town Hall dating from the late 13th or early 14th century, with a battlemented tower and a balcony for public announcements at one end. The main streets of the old town all converge here. Via Vittorio Emanuele, laid out in 1847, leads directly to the **River Lambro**, where the Roman bridge was replaced in 1842 by the Ponte dei Leoni (the parallel Via Lambro is much prettier). The short Via Napoleone leads into **Piazza Duomo**.

THE MUSEUM AND TREASURY OF THE DUOMO

Open Tues–Sun 9–4; closed Mon. Entrance below the duomo cloister. Good labelling, also in English. To see the Chapel of Theodolinda and the Iron Crown, which are in the duomo, you must take a guided tour offered by the museum. This should be booked in advance on T: 039 326383 or museoduomomonza.it. Guided visits every half hour Tues–Sat 9–6, Sun 2–6. Closed Mon.

THE CHAPEL OF QUEEN THEODOLINDA AND THE IRON CROWN

The guided tour takes you into the duomo, which is visited above all for this chapel, painted all over (an area of some 500m square) in late Gothic style with 45 delightful scenes telling the story of Queen Theodolinda's life (*see p. 130*), based on the *Historia Langobardorum* by Paul the Deacon. These scenes are also exceptional since they are not of sacred subjects but appear in the chapel of a church. They are dated 1444 and signed (collectively) by the Zavattari, whose most important work this is. There is an overall sweetness in these scenes and their courtly flavour recalls works by Pisanello. Some of the faces are skilled likenesses: this is undoubtedly the most important pictorial cycle of early 15th-century Milanese painting to have survived. The technique used was very unusual and not true fresco: on the gold ground made of paste-print covered with gold leaf, lime whitewash was applied and then tempera or oil was used by the painters (the preparatory under-drawing, on the other hand, was carried out in true fresco). The glorification of a queen who ruled wisely for 25 years in the 6th century was interpreted at the time as a tribute to Bianca Maria (an illegitimate Visconti), who was married to Francesco Sforza, Duke of Milan. She, like Theodolinda, was widowed early and so acted as regent for her son (Galeazzo Maria

Sforza, born in 1444). The entire cycle takes as its theme the conferring of legitimacy on a ruler through the female line. The vault was completed some 15 years earlier, by another, unknown, painter.

QUEEN THEODOLINDA

Theodolinda, daughter of a certain Garibaldo, Duke of Bavaria, became queen on her marriage to the Lombard king Authari in 589. She was a very cultivated lady and around 595, after Gregory the Great had converted her and her subjects from Arianism to Catholicism, she dedicated a chapel to St John the Baptist next to the royal palace in Monza.

On the death of Authari, Theodolinda selected Agilulf as her second consort. He succeeded to the throne of Lombardy and was converted to Christianity by his bride. On the birth of the couple's son, Adaloald, in 602, Agilulf renounced Arianism for Catholicism and had his son similarly baptised. Agilulf died in 616 and Theodolinda became regent. Her rule was marked by peace and the steady spread of Christianity, as recorded by the 45 splendid painted scenes in her burial chapel. The treasures she offered to the duomo are preserved in the museum. They include the charming group of a hen and chicks which has always been recognised as a uniquely interesting work of art. Centuries later (in 1872), George Meredith dedicated a poem to her ('The Song of Theodolinda'), based on the legend of her connection to the famous Iron Crown of Lombardy (*see below*).

THE IRON CROWN OF LOMBARDY

Monza is where this famous symbol of majesty has always been preserved. It takes its name from the tradition that it incorporates one of the nails used during the Crucifixion. It is thus a reliquary as well as a crown. It dates from the Lombard period and is made of hinged gem-studded gold plaquettes strengthened from behind by a fillet that has recently been recognised as being of silver not iron. Charlemagne was allegedly crowned King of the Lombards with it in 774 and it was used in many subsequent coronations. Those for which there is firm documentary evidence are the coronation of Frederick Barbarossa (1158), the Holy Roman Emperor Charles V (in 1530; the crown was carried to Bologna for the event) and Ferdinand I, Emperor of Austria (1838). The crown was profaned by Napoleon in 1805 in the Duomo of Milan, when he snatched it from the pope's hands and put it on his own head declaring that God (rather than the pope) had given it to him, so no one else should touch it.

Today the coronet is carefully preserved in a strong-box inside Beltrami's purpose-built altar. It is processed through the streets of town on the 3rd Sunday in September, since its cult (established by Charles Borromeo in 1576) has been recognised by the Church. Because of tensions between the Vatican and the Kingdom of Italy, no member of the Savoy royal house was ever crowned King of Italy with the Iron Crown.

The pictorial decoration was exquisitely restored in 2008–14 (with the participation of the World Monuments Fund) and given an excellent lighting system in 2015 (invented *ad hoc* and now known as the 'Monza method').

MONZA

Theodolinda's Hen and Seven Chicks. The chicks' eyes are of sapphire while the hen's are of garnet. The gem in her left eye contains the incised image of a Roman soldier.

The sarcophagus in which Theodolinda was re-buried in 1308, raised on four short columns, stands in the chapel against the east wall, and in the centre is a neo-Gothic altar created by Luca Beltrami in 1891. It also serves as a reliquary because it is where the Iron Crown is kept and shown—theatrically, as the lights dim—at the end of the visit.

THE DUOMO MUSEUM

After seeing the Chapel of Theodolinda, you can visit the rest of the duomo (*see p. 133*) and also the beautifully arranged rooms of the duomo museum, one of the most important museums in all Europe for its early medieval treasures. Highlights are:

Treasures associated with Queen Theodolinda: Displayed together in a circular area are the personal relics given to the church by Theodolinda and her second husband, as well as the liturgical furnishings she donated. Each treasure is carefully labelled 'donated by Theodolinda'. Her **hen and seven chicks**, pecking at grains of corn on a circular gilded base, was found in her tomb in the Middle Ages. Thought to date from the end of the 6th or beginning of the 7th century

and possibly from the Middle East, it is made of silver on a wooden core. The ensemble was once thought to represent Lombardy and its seven provinces.

The Evangelistary book cover with a dedicatory inscription, decorated with cameos, also belonged to Theodolinda. The small Cross which belonged to her son was donated to the duomo by Gregory the Great. Theodolinda's votive crown is also preserved here and the Cross made for her first husband. There is also a silver and ivory comb which bears her name, though it was made in the 9th or 10th century.

Treasures associated with Berengar of Friuli: The treasury was augmented by Berengar of Friuli, who came to stay in Monza in the early 10th century after he had been crowned emperor at Pavia in 888. His are the splendid ivory diptych of David and Gregory (6th–9th century) and a 6th-century ivory showing a poet with his muse. The large **Stilicho diptych**, named after a Vandal general who was appointed Roman consul in AD 400 and which shows him with his wife and son, is another early Christian masterpiece. Berengar also donated the large reliquary Cross which was made for him, as well as the reliquary with the supposed tooth of St John the Baptist, also made in his lifetime.

Treasures of the Visconti era: Beyond a display of rare **Palaeochristian fabrics**, including silk embroideries, there are very fine works made in Lombardy in 1300–1447, the period when the Visconti family ruled the region. Imaginatively displayed are **relief sculptures by Matteo da Campione** probably intended for the façade of the duomo: note the fascinating monsters and a 'dancing satyr' dressed in a cloak with a large hood and wide sleeves. The huge **silver chalice** (1396–1402) bears the insignia of Gian Galeazzo Visconti on one of the enamels on its base and is considered one of the most important pieces of late Gothic goldsmiths' work in Europe. The exquisite silver statuette of St John the Baptist dates from c. 1425. The rapier belonged to the natural son of Barnabò Visconti, Estorre, born in 1356. A detached fresco of the *Crucifixion with*

Angels, decorated with gilding, attributed to Michelino da Besozzo and dated 1417, hangs beside a very unusual large detached fresco with rows and rows of figures, difficult to interpret.

Treasures of the Sforza era: The section devoted to the subsequent period when the Sforza family ruled from Milan (1450–1535) has a quaint ancona painted with numerous scenes from the life of the Virgin as well as the splendid statue made from gilded copper of St John the Baptist, removed from the façade of the duomo (and replaced *in situ* by a copy). The silver Cross, decorated on both sides with reliefs, which used to hang over the silver altar in the duomo, is also displayed here.

Other exhibits: Another part of the museum has **works from other churches in Monza:** four paintings by a certain Stefano de' Fedeli, all on a gold ground; and five polychrome statues from a *Crucifixion* scene. There is also a collection of 26 glass phials which lit the martyrs' tombs in the catacombs in Rome (5th–6th centuries), as well as some phials made of an alloy of lead and iron to contain oil from sanctuaries in the Holy Land. The two huge 16th-century tapestries were made in Milan. Other exhibits include the 'hat box' used for transporting the Iron Crown; the original 15th-century stained-glass rose window from the duomo façade (replaced in the 19th century) and a *millefleurs* tapestry with St John the Baptist (Flemish, c. 1520). There is also a lithograph showing Napoleon wearing the Iron Crown. Modern religious art includes a ceramic Crucifix by Lucio Fontana (1953).

THE DUOMO

NB: The duomo closes between 12 and 4.

A chapel dedicated to St John the Baptist on this site, founded by Queen Theodolinda c. 595, was subsequently enlarged and then reconstructed in 1300 (and reconsecrated in 1346). The parti-coloured marble facade (1370–96) is the work of Matteo da Campione, although it was restored by Luca Beltrami in the 19th century. The lunette over the entrance portal, carved sometime before 1346, shows Theodolinda presenting objects from her treasury to the titular saint, John the Baptist: her hen and chicks (*see above*) are very conspicuous. The brick campanile was completed in 1606 by Pellegrino Tibaldi.

The interior is heavily decorated, frescoed all over as if in *horror vacui*. The east end was enlarged in the late 16th century at the wish of Carlo Borromeo. The main thing to see here is the Chapel of Theodolinda (*book visit at the museum; see above*), but there are other treasures too. **Sculptures by Matteo da Campione** include a former pulpit now used as the organ gallery in the nave and (outside the Chapel of Theodolinda) a relief of an imperial coronation (*illustrated below*): the archpriest of Monza crowns the emperor with the Iron Crown in the presence of the 'Electors Palatine' and a group of noble citizens. Matteo died while at work in the duomo in 1396 and is buried here.

MATTEO AND BONINO DA CAMPIONE

Matteo and Bonino, who died within a year of each other in 1396 and 1397, were members of a family of sculptors originally from Campione on Lake Lugano, but who worked all over northern Italy from the 12th century onwards and were particularly favoured by the Visconti. Called collectively 'Campionese artists', their work can still be seen today on the façades and interiors of churches of the region, including Pavia and Crema, but also as far away as Parma and Modena. Some scholars suggest that they were influenced

by the Pisan Giovanni di Balduccio. Matteo produced his best work for the Duomo of Monza, where he is buried. He was the first medieval sculptor to be identified by name in this region, but we know little about him other than the fact that on his tomb he is called '*grande e devoto architetto*'. He was the most skilled of the family, as both architect and sculptor, and as such, even though quite elderly, was called to Milan in 1388 (together with Bonino) to advise the Veneranda Fabbrica on the work in progress on the Duomo. There are sculptures by Bonino in Milan's church of Sant'Eustorgio, and a signed work by him in the Duomo Vecchio of Brescia.

In the sanctuary is an exquisite silver-gilt **altar-frontal** by the Milanese goldsmith Borgino dal Pozzo, dating from the 1350s, with scenes from the life of St John the Baptist. Behind it is the Neoclassical high altar by Andrea Appiani (1792). The **silver Cross** hanging above the sanctuary steps is a copy of the original now in the museum.

To the right of the sanctuary, the south wall is covered by a huge ***Tree of Life*** by Arcimboldo (1556), where the Cross of Christ is shown as also representing the Rod of Jesse. Beneath the nave in the north aisle can be seen **early Christian tomb cavities**.

MUSEI CIVICI

Entrance at Via Teodolinda 4. Open Wed–Sun 10–1 & 3–6. T: 039 384837 or 039 230 7126, museicivicimonza.it.

Very close to the duomo is the Casa degli Umiliati, restored in 2014 as the new seat of the civic museums, which were founded in 1935. The display is well-labelled, also in English, and provided with touch screens. Its earliest possession, donated to the town in 1874, is a 1st-century AD Roman altar with an inscription recording the town's Roman name, Modicia. The museum also has good works by local painters active in the second half of the 19th century, little-known outside Monza (including Eugenio Sperafico, 1856–1919). The cartoons by Mosè Bianchi, the most famous native artist, were made for the decorations he carried out for the Saletta Reale, the royal waiting room at the railway station (it survives, on Platform 1, and can sometimes by seen on request; *amicimuseimonza.it*). Portraits include a work attributed to Francesco Hayez (1882) and there are landscapes by the local painter Pompeo Mariani. The sculptures by Arturo Martini and Marino Marini date from the 1920s, when they were teachers at the school for artisans in Villa Reale.

THE REGGIA DI MONZA (VILLA REALE)

Open Tues–Sun 10–7. Tours of the Royal Apartments every half-hour (you are lent an audio guide). T: 039 578 3427, reggiadimonza.it, villarealedimonza.it. Reached on foot in 15mins from the duomo by Via Carlo Alberto and Piazza Citterio, where you can take either Viale Margherita di Savoia or the Passeggiata Eugenio de Beauharnais through a park. In all the Reggia has twelve entrances around its huge perimeter wall. Those to the north are reserved for the race track (monzanet.it, tempiodellavelocita.it) and golf course. There is a café and restaurant in the villa.

On the northern outskirts of the old city is the huge Reggia with the Villa Reale and its gardens, surrounded by a vast park. The Habsburg empress Maria Theresa of Austria (widow of the Holy Roman Emperor Francis I of Lorraine) commissioned Giuseppe Piermarini in 1777 to build it as a summer residence for her son the Archduke Ferdinand, governor of Lombardy and Duke of Modena. Piermarini had completed La Scala in Milan for the empress only the previous year, and he here produced, in just three years, one of the most impressive Neoclassical buildings in Italy. It takes its inspiration from Versailles, the Reggia di Caserta near Naples and the palace of Schönbrunn in Vienna. The gardens were laid out in 1778–83. The park dates from the Napoleonic era, when it was used as a hunting chase and served as productive farmland: it was walled in 1805 and seems to have been modelled on the park of Fontainbleau.

The Reggia was later used by the Savoy royal family and in particular Umberto I and his wife Margherita. The cultivated queen, the first of united Italy (since Vittorio Emanuele II's wife had died in 1855), was very popular and the numerous floral decorations in stone and iron to be seen here and in other buildings of the town (some of them on Viale Brianza), featuring the daisy (marguerite), are a tribute to her. The '*stile margherita*' became a local style of Art Nouveau or Art Deco in the first three decades of the 20th century (back in vogue since the 1970s). It was while staying here in 1900 that Umberto I was assassinated. The Savoy family thereafter never returned to their residences in Lombardy and in 1919 the palace and park were presented to the state by Umberto's son King Vittorio Emanuele III. In the 1920s, the villa was used as an applied arts institute (ISIA). Marino Marini and Arturo Martini both taught here. The Design Biennale was held in Monza from 1923 to 1930 before moving to Milan, where it became the famous Triennale. For decades after its removal, the villa was abandoned and ownership was contested between the state and municipal governments of Milan and Monza, and there was even an attempt to enlarge the motor-racing circuit. A first phase of restoration was finally completed in 2014.

THE VILLA

From the **ballroom** on the *piano nobile*, the windows look down a long avenue of trees directly towards Milan. In the opposite direction lies Maria Theresa's capital city of Vienna, with Budapest beyond it. The villa is alleged to have some 740 rooms; you can visit the empty **State Rooms** (to the left of the ballroom) on your own. They were decorated under the direction of Giacomo Albertolli, who designed the ceiling stuccoes. To the right are the **Royal Apartments**, which can only be visited on a guided tour (*see above*). They are the only area still furnished and in part preserve the appearance they had under the Savoy rulers, in particular Umberto I, although most of the contents were moved out of the building after the king's assassination (and are now in Palazzo del Quirinale in Rome). The rooms are of some interest for their intarsia, for the up-to-date plumbing in the bathrooms, for some of the wallpaper, and the Vietri tiles. The shelves in the library now have Meissen porcelain in place of books.

The second floor is used for exhibitions. In the attic on the third floor (from where on a clear day the Alps are visible from the windows), beneath the open rafters, an excellent **Museum of Design** was opened in 2014 to designs by Michele De Lucchi. The fascinating exhibits present the excellence of Italian design from 1945 to the present.

The villa **gardens** (40 hectares), were designed as English parkland by Piermarini's pupil Luigi Canonica. Beside the rose garden is the Serrone, or orangery, designed by Piermarini and connected to the villa by the Rotunda, a *Kaffeehaus* with delightful frescoes (1789) by Andrea Appiani. The Court Theatre, by Canonica, dates from 1806. Canonica also designed the villa's chapel, with stuccoes by Albertolli.

THE PARK (REGGIA)

NB: Bikes can be hired at Porta Monza on Viale Cavriga.
The huge park (which still requires restoration work), with fine trees, is traversed

by the Lambro river. It was created in 1805–10 for Napoleon by Luigi Canonica and Luigi Villoresi. Covering an area of some 734 hectares, it is still enclosed by Napoleon's wall, 3m high, and with a perimeter of 14km it represents the largest enclosed park in Europe. It has numerous old farmhouses and mills on the river. There is also a riding stables and stud farm.

Behind the villa and to the north is a lake with the neo-Gothic Torretta with a belvedere by Canonica near a little garden temple. Beyond some farmhouses, further north just across Viale Cavriga, which traverses the park from Porta Monza on its western edge to Porta Villasanta on the east, is the Cascina Frutteto, surrounded by orchards and now the seat of a highly-regarded Agricultural School. Close by is the Centro RAI (a radio station), an interesting building designed by Giò Ponti in 1950.

The northern part of the park acquired its motor-racing circuit in 1922. It became the famous Autodromo of Milan and venue of the Grand Prix races (now Formula 1: Gran Premio) in September. It has a 10km circuit. In 1928 an 18-hole golf course was laid out beside it (the club house dates from 1958). On Viale Vedano the Fagianaia Reale (no. 7), a farm building used for raising pheasants, built in 1838, was turned into the Golf Club Milano in 1928–30 by Piero Portaluppi (it is now a restaurant).

THE CAPPELLA ESPIATORIA

Located just outside the park (*reached from the entrance on Viale Margherita di Savoia: take Viale Cesare Battista, which leads to Via Dante, and then turn right into Via Matteo Campione*), this expiatory chapel was erected by Vittorio Emanuele III on the exact spot where his father Umberto I was assassinated in his carriage on 29th July 1900. The deed was done by Gaetano Bresci, born in 1869 in Tuscany, who had emigrated to America and joined an anarchist movement. He returned to Italy with the express intention of killing the king (two earlier attempts on Umberto's life had been made by anarchists in 1878 and 1897). The chapel was designed in 1910 by Giuseppe Sacconi, architect of the huge Vittoriano monument in Rome (and it is as odd and ungainly as that building). It takes the form of a huge stele and is decorated with two alabaster crosses as well as mosaics and bronzes by Lodovico Pogliaghi. Inside is a crypt, where every year on 29th July a commemorative service is held. Umberto is buried in the Pantheon in Rome, as is his queen, Margherita, who outlived him by 26 years.

SARONNO

North of Milan is Saronno (*Atlas B, B1*), once an industrial town with factories producing—among other things—textiles, radios, steel wheels, safes and macaroons, the famous *amaretti*, as well as Di Saronno almond liqueur. It is surrounded by a flat plain with small fields and low-rise buildings and, on a clear day, a magnificent alpine backdrop. The trains into Milan from Malpensa airport stop in Saronno and it is also on the suburban railway line. It is very easily reached from the city.

SARONNO
Detail of Andrea da Milano's *Last Supper* in the Santuario della Madonna dei Miracoli.

SANTUARIO DELLA MADONNA DEI MIRACOLI

From Saronno railway station, an underpass takes you into the west part of town, where the pleasant, cobbled Via Santuario leads to the sanctuary church of the Vergine dei Miracoli (*open 6.30–12 & 4–7, almost continuously in use for Mass on Sun morning; santuariodisaronno.it*). Built to house a supposedly miraculous image of the Madonna, it was begun in 1498, perhaps by Giovanni Antonio Amadeo, who designed the cupola in 1505. It was enlarged after 1556 by Vincenzo Seregni. The façade, with its slightly strangely-proportioned sculptures, is by Pellegrino Tibaldi (1596). The interior is encrusted with stucco and richly decorated. In the dome over the crossing is a beautiful fresco by Gaudenzio Ferrari, usually considered his masterpiece, showing a concert of angels, all singing or playing different musical instruments, with a painted stucco God the Father in the centre and, in the drum, a stucco *Assumption of the Virgin*, surrounded by statues of prophets in niches. In the transept chapels are remarkable groups of lifesize polychrome wood figures representing the *Deposition* (south) and *Last Supper* (north) by a certain Andrea da Milano (c. 1528–31), a woodcarver at work here at the same time as Luini. The *Last Supper* group is interesting for being inspired by Leonardo's famous fresco in Milan, of which it is a three-dimensional version. Both chapels have wrought-iron railings decorated with marble sculptures presented on pedestals. The paintings of the *Kiss of Judas* and *Prayer in the Garden*, on the side walls of the chapel with the Last Supper group, are by Camillo Procaccini and there are angels in the vault by Luini.

The sanctuary walls have lovely paintings by Bernardino Luini (1525 and 1531): *Marriage of the Virgin* and *Presentation in the Temple* on the left and *Jesus Among the Doctors* and *Adoration of the Magi* on the right, admired by Stendhal in his diary.

GAUDENZIO FERRARI

Although Ferrari (c. 1470–1546), painter, sculptor and architect, was the greatest artist of the Piedmontese school, he is barely known outside Piedmont and Lombardy, perhaps because he never left the region throughout his long life (with the exception of one possible visit to the Rhineland). He was born in Piedmont and learned his art under old-fashioned masters who preserved their archaic styles against the encroaching rationalist spirit of the Renaissance. However, it is probable that he also undertook some training in Milan, for he learnt much from the works of Vincenzo Foppa and often collaborated with Bernardino Luini. In turn, he influenced other artists, including Daniele Crespi. Ferrari's patrons included the Trivulzio family, though most of his output was undertaken for churches and monasteries. His love of a crowded, theatrical scene, his realism and use of bright colours won him great popularity and he was much admired in his lifetime. His work can be seen all over Lombardy: here in Saronno, as well as in Milan (Sant'Ambrogio, Santa Maria delle Grazie, Santa Maria dei Miracoli, the Brera) and in the area around Lake Maggiore and Como. He must have been a dog lover: a little mongrel terrier, always a different type and in a different pose, typically appears in the bottom right of his devotional scenes.

CENTRAL SARONNO

On the other (east) side of the railway line, Viale Rimembranza runs parallel to the tracks. Off it, Via Griffante (left) leads to the entrance to **M.I.L.S.** (Museo delle Industrie e del Lavoro del Saronnese; *open Thur 9–11pm, Sat 3–6, Sun 9–12 & 3–5 or 6; museomils.it*), staffed by volunteers and with free entry. Housed in an old railway shed, it documents the history of Saronno's industries, including the famous liqueur and macaroons by Lazzaroni, safes by Parma (including a dismantlable strongbox designed to protect the high altar of Sant'Ambrogio in Milan) and steel wheels by Gianetti. Most of the factories have now closed but Gianetti still exists, though no longer in Saronno.

The collection of ceramics amassed by Giuseppe Gianetti can be seen at the **Museo della Ceramica** (*Via Carcano 9, open Tues–Thur 3–6, Sat 3–7, museogianetti.it*), in a villa of 1936 that belonged to Gianetti's sisters-in-law. It features Asian and Meissen porcelain and Italian and European majolica.

The main street of Saronno, **Corso Italia**, arcaded on one side and with lively local bars, leads past the church of San Francesco (whose adjoining ex-conventual buildings became the home of the Lazzaroni family, manufacturers of the liqueur and *biscotti*) to the spacious Piazza Libertà, closed by the façade of the church of SS. Pietro e Paolo.

CHIARAVALLE

On Milan's southern outskirts stands the beautiful Cistercian monastery of Chiaravalle (*Atlas B, C2*), the tall, tiered bell-tower of its church reaching high into the sky from the flat landscape around it. Chiaravalle was founded in 1135 by St Bernard of Clairvaux (who gave it the same name as his own monastery in northern France), after

CHIARAVALLE

CHIARAVALLE
Detail of the main church doors.

he had come to Milan to help settle a succession dispute between Pope Innocent II and his rival, the antipope Anacletus II. The monastery was in the news in 2014 when a scandal broke concerning sexual exploitation of novices and the needy. Today there are 15 monks here.

The monastic complex comprises the church itself (*open Tues–Sat 9–12 & 2.30–5.30, Sun 2.30–5.30*), a beer garden serving Trappist beers, a shop selling monastic products and a restored mill, making use of the swift-flowing streams in the vicinity. The monastery stands on originally swampy ground. According to Jacobus de Voragine in the *Legenda Aurea*, St Bernard was once called upon to intervene when a great plague of flies descended on a monastery he had founded. He promptly excommunicated the insects and they all fell dead. Sadly, he has not done likewise to the mosquitoes of Chiaravalle.

The church is large and sombre, with a tall nave and clerestory separated from the aisles by huge, elephantine cylindrical columns bearing painted decoration of Cistercian saints and abbots. The choir stalls are heavy and finely carved, with a cornice supported by putto-atlantes. There is a *Madonna and Child* by Bernardino Luini in the south transept.

PRACTICAL INFORMATION

GETTING AROUND

• **By rail:** Rail links are excellent in this part of Lombardy. Trains run by the state railway Trenitalia or by Trenord link Milan with all its suburbs and there are frequent services. Trains for **Monza** leave from Porta Garibaldi station (*map p. 27, D1*); journey time is 10–15mins. For **Saronno**, trains leave from Cadorna (journey time c. 20mins) or Centrale (journey time c. 30mins). The suburban railway network also links Milan with Monza (S7, S8, S9 and S11) and Saronno (S1 and S3). The hubs for the suburban trains are Porta Garibaldi or Porta Venezia. **Gorgonzola** is accessible by metro M2 (green). Note that it is beyond the urban tariff zone; you will need an extra ticket. **Desio** can be reached by trains from Porta Garibaldi (journey time c. 30mins). The nearest station for **Agliate** is Carate-Calò on the Lecco line (c. 50mins from Porta Garibaldi).
• **By bus:** To get to **Chiaravalle** from Milan, take bus 140 (two stops) from Rogoredo railway station (the bus stop is just outside the railway station) or bus 77 from Lodi, on Metro M3 (*map p. 27, E4*).

INFORMATION OFFICES

Monza Infopoint Monza Stazione, Via Caduti del Lavoro (in front of the railway station) or Infopoint Monza Carducci, Piazza Carducci (*beneath the Palazzo Comunale; marketingterritoriale@comune.monza.it, T: 039 237 2352*).

WHERE TO EAT

MONZA
€€ **Moderno**. Formerly just a *pasticceria*, now also a restaurant. The cakes are still excellent and you can also eat a simple, classic meal here. Very well placed just behind the Arangario. *Piazza Roma 2. T: 039 322167.*
SARONNO
For coffee and a snack there is the very pleasant **Il Chiostro ArtCaffè** on Via Santuario, close to the sanctuary church and, in the centre of town, the **Café Noir** bar and *enoteca* on the main Corso Italia.

LOCAL SPECIALITIES

Saronno's almond liqueur is still popular in the UK and US but is difficult to find in Saronno itself. However, Lazzaroni is still in business and still based in Saronno. They make almond *biscotti*, amaretto liqueur and sambuca, mainly for export (you can buy their products at Malpensa airport, for example).

FESTIVALS AND EVENTS

The main events of the year in **Monza** are the festivals celebrating St John the Baptist, around his feast day on 24th June and culminating in a fireworks display at Villa Reale. In September the town fills up for the Formula 1 motor race and, on the 3rd Sun of the month, the Iron Crown is solemnly processed around town.

LODI, DUOMO
Figure of Eve (12th century)
beside the west doorway.

Lodi & the Lodigiano

Lodi (*Atlas B, C3–D3*), 31km southeast of Milan, is an important provincial capital and a very pleasant place to visit. Lying on the River Adda, it has a prosperous atmosphere, being a centre for agriculture and dairy produce. It also offers a clutch of fine churches, an interesting family of local Renaissance painters, a long history and some fine buildings with exterior terracotta mouldings. The fertile and well-irrigated countryside in which it sits is known as the Lodigiano.

HISTORY OF LODI

An ancient town of the Insubrians, Lodi was Romanised as *Laus Pompeia* and became a *municipium* in 49 BC. The original settlement, on the site of today's Lodi Vecchio (*see p. 149*), was destroyed in 1111 by the Milanese. In 1158, following a petition by the citizens, the town was refounded by Frederick Barbarossa on the low hill where it stands today, about 7km further east. In the later Middle Ages, Lodi followed the fortunes of so many other towns in Lombardy, coming first under Visconti rule and then under the Sforza. The Peace of Lodi, aimed at fixing the boundaries of Milanese and Venetian territory, was signed here in 1454. The local Piazza family of painters were active here in the 16th century, and works by Alberto, Martino, Callisto and Scipione Piazza are preserved in churches in the town and province. Lodi was known for its ceramics in the 17th and 18th centuries (examples can be seen in the museum). One of Napoleon's early victories was claimed here in 1796, when at the Battle of Lodi, which was fought on the bridge over the River Adda, his forces defeated the Austrians. The Banca Popolare di Lodi, founded in 1864, was the first co-operative bank in Italy. Today Lodi is home to an important agricultural research institute and is also the headquarters of the IT firm Zucchetti.

LODI HIGHLIGHTS

The centre of town is the wide **Piazza della Vittoria** (*map 3; see below*), lined with pavement cafés and overlooked by the fine duomo.

The beautiful **church of the Incoronata** (*map 1; p. 146*), a tiny little jewel casket, has four lovely panel paintings by Bergognone as well as works by the Piazza family of local artists.

Lodi is an agricultural town, particularly famous for its **cheese**. You will find *raspadüra* (flakes of Grana Padano) on many restaurant menus.

AROUND PIAZZA DELLA VITTORIA

The spacious, arcaded Piazza della Vittoria, in the heart of the old centre of town (*map 3*), is pleasingly surrounded by façades of differing ages and styles. Here, for instance, is the 18th-century façade of the **Broletto** (Town Hall), and next to it the **duomo**, with a 12th-century façade including a fine portal bearing the carved figures of Adam and Eve on the door jambs, attributed to sculptors from Piacenza. In the gable above the rose window is a statue (a copy, the original is preserved inside the church) of the patron saint and first bishop, Bassianus (San Bassiano; d. 409). It was in this church, in 1413, that the antipope John XXIII convoked the Council of Constance, at which the Holy Roman Emperor Sigismund of Luxembourg and others would meet to heal the Western Schism and to try Jan Hus for heresy.

Interior of the duomo

The interior was well restored in the 1960s in the Romanesque style and it has a fine, solemn atmosphere. In the **baptistery chapel** (first south) is a triptych of the *Assumption of the Virgin* by Alberto and Martino Piazza and a polyptych with the *Massacre of the Innocents* by Callisto Piazza, all members of Lodi's family of 15th–16th-century painters.

In the nave, on a pillar on the north side, is the original 13th-century **gilt statue of St Bassianus** that once stood on the façade.

In the raised choir, set into modern stalls (1965), is a set of exquisite **intarsia panels** by Fra' Giovanni da Verona (c. 1523). Particularly lovely are the scenes of ideal Renaissance cities. The Baroque altar here (1694) has angels in the manner of Bernini. The **apse mosaic** of the *Virgin with Sts Albert of Lodi and Bassianus* is by Aligi Sassu.

Above the entrance to the 12th-century **crypt** is a Romanesque relief of the *Last Supper*. The crypt contains the body of St Bassianus, housed inside a mid-19th-century altar. The original sarcophagus, with a false bottom to foil tomb robbers, is to the right. To the left in a small apsidal recess is a wooden *Deposition* group by a local 16th-century sculptor. The altar here has relics of Albert of Lodi, the 12th-century

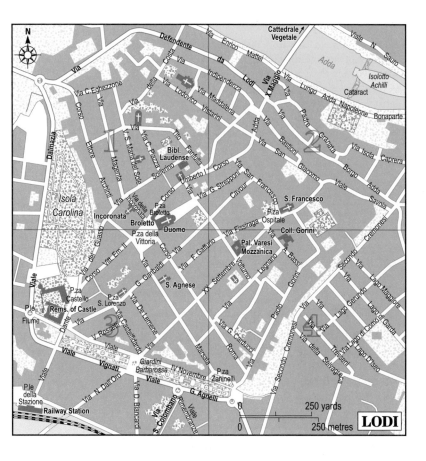

bishop under whom this church was founded as the successor to Bassianus' cathedral in Lodi Vecchio.

The third south chapel has a *Madonna of the Snow* by Giulio Cesare Procaccini (right wall). The door in this aisle leads out, past a very ruined but vivid fresco of the *Last Judgement*, to the Museo Diocesano. The door in the north aisle leads into Piazza Broletto.

PIAZZA BROLETTO AND PIAZZA MERCATO

Piazza Broletto (*map 1*), on the north side of the duomo, has a few trinket stalls built up against the duomo wall. Opposite are remains of the 13th-century part of the Broletto and, in the centre of the square, the **former cathedral font**, in pink Verona marble, now used as a fountain (it is inhabited by goldfish). From here a passageway leads into Piazza Mercato (markets on Tues, Thur, Sat and Sun), with the Bishop's Palace and good views of the duomo's apse.

THE INCORONATA

Via dell'Incoronata leads from Piazza della Vittoria to the inconspicuous entrance to the church of the Incoronata (*map 1*), behind an iron railing of 1699 with worn lettering reading: *Assumpta est Maria in Coeli*. The church (*open Mon 9–11.20, Tues–Fri 9–11.20 & 3.30–6, Sat–Sun 9–11.20 & 3–6*) was built in 1488–93 by Giovanni Battagio and Gian Giacomo Dolcebuono (who may also have designed the great portal of the Certosa di Pavia; *see p. 165*). The centrally planned octagonal interior is totally covered with 16th-century paintings, frescoes, and gilded decoration, mainly by the Piazza and their *bottega*. In the first chapel on the right, the altarpiece of the *Conversion of St Paul*, a late work (1552) by Callisto, is flanked by four exquisite **panels by Bergognone** (1497–1500): *Annunciation, Visitation, Adoration of the Magi* and *Presentation in the Temple*. The last scene is shown as taking place in this very church., with onlookers in the upper gallery and the Christ Child clutching at his mother's cloak for reassurance. The chapels on either side of the main altar also have altarpieces by Callisto (with the intervention of his son Fulvio) and his brother Scipione. In the last chapel is the **Berinzaghi polyptych** (1515–16), a fine solo work by Alberto Piazza in its original frame, with the donor on the left. The original 16th-century organ survives. The charming frescoed decoration on the pilasters, etc., is also by Scipione Piazza. Under the singers' gallery is a lovely late 15th-century Lombard *Madonna and Child* by Giovanni della Chiesa.

SANT'AGNESE

Via Marsala leads south out of Piazza della Vittoria. **Sant'Agnese** (*map 3; opened by volunteers of the Touring Club Italiano Sat 9.30–12.30 & 3.30–6 and Sun 11.30–12.30 & 33.30–6; touringclub.it/i-luoghi-aperti-per-voi*) is a 15th-century church with terracotta decoration on the façade and a polyptych by Alberto Piazza.

PIAZZA OSPITALE

Corso Umberto I (*map 1*), lined with shops and cafés, leads out of Piazza della Vittoria past the **Biblioteca Laudense**, in the Baroque former Oratory of San Filippo Neri at no. 76. Around the corner in Via Fanfulla is the **Museo Civico** (*closed at the time of writing while it was in the process of moving here*), with a collection of local ceramics, including works with floral decorations in the 'Vecchia Lodi' style produced by the Ferretti family in the late 18th century. There is also an archaeological section and an art gallery with an *Adoration of the Magi*, the only signed and dated work by Scipione Piazza (1562). The **courtyard of the Caffè Letterario** on Via Fanfulla preserves lapidary fragments with inscriptions in Hebrew (the Vitali family of bankers and pawnbrokers was active in Lodi and escaped persecution and banishment) and a fragment of a battle scene depicting the Napoleonic victory at Lodi in 1796. The scene once formed part of a monument commemorating the battle which was destroyed by the Austrians after the fall of Napoleon.

Further down Corso Umberto I, opposite nos 23–39 (note the moulded design of artichokes and the wrought-iron hemp leaves), Via San Francesco leads to **Piazza**

LODI, INCORONATA
Detail of Bergognone's *Presentation in the Temple*.

Ospitale. Here you will find the 13th-century church of **San Francesco** (*map 2; opening hours vary, typically morning and late afternoon*). Its interesting façade has a central rose window and lateral two-light lancets open onto the sky, since the aisles are much lower than the façade. The interior has numerous 14th–15th-century frescoes, the most interesting on the nave pillars, in the third chapel on the south, and in the aisles and south transept. Also on the square is a **statue of Paolo Gorini** (1899), a vulcanologist and student of anatomy who lends his name to the museum in the Ospedale Maggiore hospital building opposite. On the sandstone plinth of the statue you will see reliefs of mummified corpses in rock-cut tombs. Gorini developed an embalming technique of his own and a human hand preserved according to these methods is shown in the museum, the **Collezione Anatomica Paolo Gorini** (*entrance on Via Bassi 1; open Wed 10–12, Sat 9.30–12.30, Sun 2.30–4.30*).

PALAZZO VARESI MOZZANICA

Via XX Settembre leads west out of Piazza Ospitale past the fine 15th-century **Palazzo Varesi Mozzanica** (no. 51; *map 4*), with moulded terracotta decoration around its Gothic arched windows and a Renaissance frieze with mythological scenes and a fine carved doorway with four busts, two male (sporting close-fitting caps) and two female (in elaborate hair nets). It is a good example of secular architecture of the period.

PIAZZA CASTELLO

Piazza Castello (*map 3*), in what would have been the southwest corner of the walled city, contains the foundations of **Lodi's castle**, built by Bernabò Visconti in the later 14th century and subsequently endowed with a cylindrical tower by Francesco Sforza, who strengthened Lodi's defences after the 1454 Peace of Lodi had brought Venice's *terraferma* holdings right up to the Adda river. Little remains of the castle (the tower you see today is a reconstruction) except for the platform on which it stood, surrounded by a deep moat and now occupied by the stoutly fenced Police Station. The wide cobbled piazza has a statue of Vittorio Emanuele II and the entrance to the **Isola Carolina** public park (signalled by a statue of a girl with a skipping rope). Below street level, Lodi is honeycombed with tunnels, part of the old medieval system of defences. Tours can be arranged with Lodi Murata (you will find them on Facebook).

ACROSS THE ADDA

Via Lungo Adda Napoleone Bonaparte (*map 2*) commemorates Napoleon, who won a victory over the Austrians at the Battle of Lodi, fought at the bridge here in 1796. The bridge leads across the Adda, which here flows wide and shallow, divided by a tiny island and rippling over a cataract. On the river bank to the left is the **Cattedrale Vegetale**, a living artwork by Giuliano Mauri (1938–2007) consisting of tall, rough-hewn poles of chestnut wood arranged in groups and aligned in rows, mimicking the columns of a cathedral nave. Slender curving branches have been lashed to the top of the poles to create the arches of a Gothic vault. Each of the groups of poles encloses an

LODI, VIA FANFULLA
Fragment of a Neoclassical monument commemorating
Napoleon's victory at the Battle of Lodi in 1796.

oak sapling: the idea is that by the time the poles and branches have rotted and fallen to dust, the oaks will have grown tall and interlaced overhead, forming a green cathedral.

THE LODIGIANO

The Lodigiano, or territory of Lodi, was commercially well placed but nevertheless an unhealthy, marshy area before the local monastic communities constructed canals, notably the Muzza, in 1220. In the well-irrigated countryside there are numerous dairy farms producing cheese (Lodi claims that Grana Padano was first made here, a claim also made by Codogno). Near the River Adda, which borders the eastern side of the province, there are good cycling routes (*information from the Tourist Office*).

LODI VECCHIO
Lodi Vecchio, 7km west of Lodi (*Atlas B, C3*), was the Roman *Laus Pompeia*, a constant rival of Milan until its total destruction by that city in 1111. Only the **Basilica dei XII**

Apostoli was left standing—and it stands to this day, in an isolated position southeast of the centre, surrounded by neatly clipped hedges and shaded by tall poplars (*open Sat–Sun after 4pm*). Founded by Bishop Bassianus in 387, its fine exterior was rebuilt in Gothic style in the early 14th century. The façade is similar to that of San Francesco in Lodi, with two-light lancets on either side giving onto the open sky. High above the rose window is a ceramic statue of St Bassianus. The interior is interesting for its early 14th-century frescoed decoration (restored in the early 1960s) in the nave vaults and apse, with colourful geometric designs and flowers, and including one bay with very unusual rustic scenes of four carts drawn by oxen (the frescoes were financed by a local farming corporation in 1323), and Christ Pantocrator in the apse. Votive frescoes include a scene of St Eligius blessing a horse. At the end of the north aisle (high up) is a relief with bulls and a man on a horse dated 1323. The 11th-century capitals are also interesting, and in the south aisle is a series of 17th-century paintings.

The site of Roman Laus Pompeia was identified in 1987 by aerial photography. Finds yielded by excavations can be seen at the **Museo Laus Pompeia**, housed in a fine old brick granary which stands amid modern residential housing on the site of the Roman forum (*Vicolo Corte Bassa 14; open by appointment; lauspompeiamuseo.it*). It takes about 10mins to walk between the museum and the basilica.

ELSEWHERE AROUND LODI

Sant'Angelo Lodigiano to the southwest (on the Pavia road; *Atlas B, C3*) has a restored castle, Castello Bolognini, originally of the 13th century but which was transformed into a summer residence in the late 14th by the wife of Bernabò Visconti. It is mainly used as a venue for weddings and events but is open to the public on certain days or by appointment (*castellobolognini.it*). **Codogno** (*Atlas B, D3*), south of Lodi, is an agricultural centre (it disputes with Lodi the invention of Grana Padano cheese). In its 16th-century church of San Biagio are two paintings by Callisto Piazza (*Assumption* and *St John the Baptist*, both of 1533) and a *Madonna and Child between St Francis and Charles Borromeo* by Daniele Crespi (c. 1620).

At **Ospedaletto Lodigiano** (*Atlas B, D3*), west of Codogno, the parish church of SS. Pietro e Paolo (on Piazza Roma, beside the Monastero dei Gerolamini) has paintings by the Leonardesque artist Giampietrino. The main panel shows the *Madonna Enthroned between Sts Jerome and John the Baptist*. It originally formed a triptych with the *St Peter* and *St Paul* now in the sanctuary.

East of Lodi is **Abbadia Cerreto** (*Atlas B, D3*), where there is a Cistercian Lombard church built in the 12th century, with a charming exterior and, inside, an altarpiece of the *Madonna and Saints* by Callisto Piazza (c. 1541).

PRACTICAL INFORMATION

GETTING AROUND

• **By rail: Lodi** is linked to Milan by suburban train S1 from Porta Garibaldi or Porta Venezia and by regional trains from Milan Centrale roughly hourly throughout the day (more frequent at rush hours). Travel time is c. 45mins. For **Codogno**, there are regular trains from Milan Rogoredo. Journey time c. 35mins. There are some direct trains to **Ospedaletto Lodigiano** from Pavia (journey time c. 1hr). From Milan Rogoredo for Ospedaletto, you have to change at Casalpusterlengo.

• **By bus:** Local buses from Lodi serving the Lodigiano are run by Line (*for timetables, see www.lineservizi. it*). For **Lodi Vecchio**, bus 3 (the Lodi–Castiraga Vidargo line) from Lodi bus terminus, in front of the railway station. Journey time c. 15mins. Bus 13 serves **Ospedaletto** and **Codogno**. For **Sant'Angelo Lodigiano**, take bus Q40 operated by Star Lodi (*starlodi.it*). Star Lodi also have a service to **Abbadia Cerreto** (bus K402).

INFORMATION OFFICES

Lodi Pro Loco office at Piazza Broletto 4, behind the duomo. *T: 0371 421391, www.apt.lodi.it.*

WHERE TO STAY

LODI
€€ Concorde Lodi Centro. If you want to spend some time exploring the area, this simple three-star hotel, in a bright pink streamlined building of the 1930s, is simple, basic and comfortable. Right opposite Lodi railway station. *Piazzale Stazione 2. T: 0371.421322, hotel-concorde.it. Map 3.*

WHERE TO EAT

LODI
Piazza della Vittoria (*map 3*) has a number of bars and cafés, for example **Bar Lodi,** on the right as you face the duomo, where you can also get a simple meal. The **Caffè Letterario** on Via Fanfulla (*map 1*) has a very pleasant courtyard. **La Piazzetta** on the peaceful Piazza San Lorenzo (*map 3*), serves coffee, drinks and snacks. The cheerful, friendly café/bar at **Viale Dante 22** (*map 3*) does an excellent lunch menu. To try *raspadüra* and other local dishes, go to €–€€ **Osteria del Mercato**, which leads out of Piazza Mercato right behind the Duomo (*Via Giuseppina Strepponi 3; T: 0371 190 5279, osteriadelmercato.it; closed Tues; map 2*).

LOCAL SPECIALITIES

Lodi is proud of its cheeses: mascarpone, Quartirolo (a soft cheese) and Grana Padano (a kind of unmatured parmesan which it claims to have invented and which is served grated in voile-thin slices, known as *raspadüra*, which you eat with your fingers as an *hors d'oeuvre*).

FESTIVALS AND EVENTS

Lodi Festival of San Bassiano (patron saint), 19 Jan.

PAVIA, SAN TEODORO
Detail of Bernardino Lanzani's 1522 fresco of Pavia.

Pavia & its Province

Pavia (*Atlas B, B3*), a city of cobbled streets and squares, is an old provincial capital of Roman origin on the River Ticino. Today it has an air of civic pride and faded splendour: with its vestiges of medieval towers, a number of fine palaces and medieval churches, it is an excellent place to come for a flavour of old Lombardy. There are interesting art collections here and the venerable university, which received support from the Visconti as soon as they took control of Pavia in the mid-14th century, is still one of the most important in Italy and naturally contributes to the town's lively atmosphere. The beautiful 15th–16th-century Certosa di Pavia, a few kilometres north of town, preserves beautiful works of art as well as the tomb of the great Sforza duke Ludovico il Moro.

HISTORY OF PAVIA

The Roman *Ticinum* was founded on this site c. 220 BC. Pavia was the capital of the Ostrogoths under Theodoric, but is particularly famous for the subsequent period, when for two centuries from 572 it was capital of the kingdom of the Lombards (*see p. 156*). The church of San Michele hosted the coronations of Charlemagne (774), Berengar, the first King of Italy (888), Berengar II (950) and Frederick Barbarossa (1155).

The *comune* of Pavia took the Ghibelline side against Milan and Lodi and afterwards passed to the Counts of Monferrato. In 1359, after a long siege, it was finally conquered by the Visconti of Milan. On 24th February 1525 the famous Battle of Pavia was fought here, in which the French king François I was defeated by the joint forces of Spain and the Holy Roman Empire under Charles V, who deployed a new weapon—the cannon—against the old-fashioned crossbow. The beginning of Habsburg power and influence in Italy dates from this battle. King

Francis wrote to his mother: '*Madame, tout est perdu hors l'honneur*' (All save our honour is lost). He was imprisoned in the castle of Belgioioso, east of Pavia, and at Pizzighettone, an old town on the Adda towards Cremona. He was ultimately taken to Madrid and surrendered French claims to Italy the following year. The ramparts which still surround part of Pavia were built by the Spanish in the 17th century. Pavia was the birthplace of Lanfranc (1005–89), the first Norman archbishop of Canterbury. Its university, founded in 1361, is one of the oldest in Europe and until the 19th century was the only university in the old Duchy of Milan.

PAVIA HIGHLIGHTS

The huge and rambling **Castello Visconteo** (*map 2; p. 158*) contains the civic museums. There are some masterpieces in the picture gallery and an interesting archaeological collection.

The church of **San Pietro in Ciel d'Oro** (*map 1; p. 161*) contains a magnificent tomb housing the relics of St Augustine as well as a casket with the remains of Boethius, author of *The Consolation of Philosophy*, who was cruelly executed here. **San Michele Maggiore** (*map 4; p. 156*), a very fine church, was the scene of Charlemagne's coronation as King of the Lombards.

The River Ticino is crossed by a picturesque covered bridge, the **Ponte Coperto** (*map 3; p. 156*).

PIAZZA VITTORIA AND THE DUOMO

Pavia's two main streets, Strada Nuova and Corso Cavour/Corso Mazzini, vestiges of the old ground plan of Ticinum, intersect in true Roman style at the delightful cobbled **Piazza Vittoria** (or Piazza Grande; *map 1*). The square is flanked on its two long sides by the arcades of a medley of pretty houses, and has a number of cafés where students congregate in the evenings. A shopping mall operates here, underground. At one end of the piazza, where the dome of the cathedral is conspicuous, rises the **Broletto**, the 12th-century Town Hall (restored in the 19th century), with a double loggia of 1563. In an upper window, behind glass, is a statue made in 1604 and known as the *Madonna di Piazza*.

A lane leads past all that remains of the Romanesque **Torre Civica** (it collapsed without warning in 1989, killing four people and wounding 15) to the **Duomo** (*map 3*). Its design is a modification by Bramante (with, possibly, also the intervention of Leonardo da Vinci) of an older building begun in 1488. The immense cupola, the third largest in Italy, was not added until 1884–5, and the façade was completed in 1933. The rest of the exterior remains unfinished, with only small sections of marble cladding.

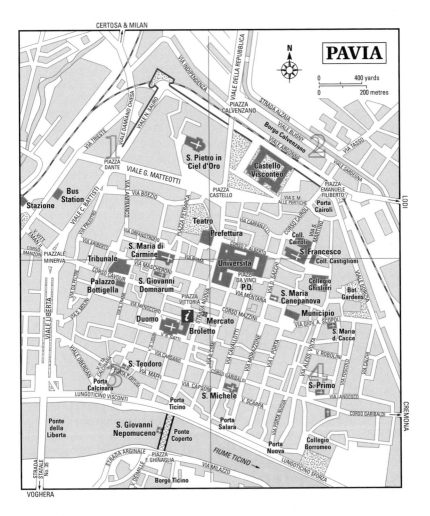

The impressive light, centrally-planned, interior has a very pronounced cornice above the capitals. On the west wall are paintings by Il Cerano and his pupil Daniele Crespi. In the south transept is the tomb and reliquary casket of St Syrus (San Siro), 4th-century bishop of Pavia and its patron saint.

Several porticoed palaces line **Piazza del Duomo**, where a market sets up stalls on Saturday. A gilded bronze ancient Roman statue, thought to represent Septimius Severus and known as the *Regisole*, stood here from the 11th century onwards and became an emblem of the town until its destruction in 1796 by zealous Jacobins, who considered it a symbol of tyranny. Francesco Messina provided a new statue in 1937: a horse and rider with face upturned to salute the sun.

THE LOMBARDS IN PAVIA

Originally a Germanic people from beyond the borders of the Roman Empire, the Lombards, or 'long-bearded barbarians', arrived in the former Roman province of Pannonia (a region of present-day Hungary) in c. 510. There their leader Audoin was victorious over the Gepids. In 568 they moved westwards into Italy, gradually conquering the northern and central parts of the peninsula and establishing a kingdom. Pavia became their capital in 572 and remained so for two centuries. The Lombards originally practised Arian Christianity, until their king Authari married Theodolinda of Bavaria (*see p. 130*) in 589, after which their rule saw the spread of orthodox Catholicism. Lombard power reached its apogee under Liutprand (712–44). His reign has been recognised as the most important period for the arts and by this time too it has been estimated that the Lombards inhabited some two-thirds of Italian territory, with important enclaves of power in the south also. Liutprand is buried in Pavia, in the church of San Pietro in Ciel d'Oro.

Lombard rule was characterised by the fragmentation of power into various dukedoms: apart from Pavia, the most important were Spoleto (in modern Umbria), Cividale (in Friuli) and Benevento (in Campania). When Charlemagne arrived with the Franks, he defeated the Lombards heavily at Mortara (*see p. 181*) and then took Pavia in 774. He crowned himself 'King of the Lombards' and the Italian peninsula and the powers around the Mediterranean began to lose their individual importance as the Holy Roman Empire became established.

SAN TEODORO AND THE PONTE COPERTO

Via dei Liguri leads downhill out of Piazza del Duomo to Via Maffi. To the right (west) is the 12th-century church of **San Teodoro** (*map 3; open daily 8–7*), with an octagonal cupola-tower and 16th-century lantern. Inside, the 15th–16th-century frescoes include a large *St Anthony Abbot* on the west wall (*light switch by a column near the side entrance door*) with, behind him, a remarkable view of Pavia with its numerous towers. Dated 1522, it is by Bernardino Lanzani, a painter known almost exclusively for his works in Pavia. In the raised sanctuary, the scenes with the lives of St Theodore (north side) and the triptych of the *Ascension with Sts Syrus and Augustine* are also attributed to him. A short, broad crypt lies beneath the sanctuary.

South of the church, Via Porta Pertusi curves southwards to the picturesque **Ponte Coperto**, a covered bridge across the Ticino. The original bridge, built in 1351–4 on Roman foundations and roofed in 1583, collapsed in 1947 after bomb damage. When the Ticino is exceptionally low, three stone piles of the Roman and medieval bridge are exposed. The present bridge, a few metres further east, is to a different design, as is the central shrine, which replaces the 18th-century bridge-chapel. It is dedicated to St John of Nepomuk, patron saint of water crossings.

SAN MICHELE MAGGIORE

The church of San Michele Maggiore (*map 4*), the finest in Pavia, with an octagonal cupola and facing a pretty square, was consecrated in 1155. The elaborately ornamented front has profusely decorated triple portals and sculptured friezes, but

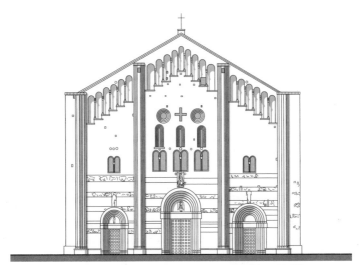

SAN MICHELE MAGGIORE

the sandstone in which they are carved has been almost totally worn away, despite repeated programmes of restoration. The lower part of the campanile, decorated with terracotta tiles, dates from c. 1000.

The interior is similar to that of San Pietro in Ciel d'Oro (*see p. 161*). Charlemagne was crowned King of the Lombards here in 774, after his defeat of the last Lombard king, Desiderius. There is fine sculptural detail, particularly on the capitals of the crypt. Also in the crypt is the tomb of the local notary Martino Salimbeni (d. 1463), by the school of Giovanni Antonio Amadeo. At the end of the north aisle is a superb 12th-century Crucifix, covered in silver leaf. The raised chancel (*ask the custodian to let you in*) preserves a section of late 10th-century mosaic pavement, with personifications of the months and the figure of a king (personifying the year itself) at the centre. Below is part of what would have been a circular labyrinth with depictions of constellations.

THE UNIVERSITY

On Piazza Leonardo da Vinci (*map 4*), three ancient **tower-houses** survive, built by the noble families of Pavia (the town was once called the 'city of a hundred towers' and some 80 of them survived up to the 19th century). Under cover are remains of the 12th-century **crypt of Sant'Eusebio** (*open by appointment at the Castello Visconteo; T: 0382 399770, museicivici.pavia.it*), with restored early 13th-century frescoes.

The **University of Pavia** is one of the oldest in Europe, the successor to the ancient Studium, a School of Law. The Studium was given university status in 1361 by Galeazzo II Visconti. In 1997 its various colleges were united into the Istituto Universitario di Studi Superiori (IUSS). By 2018 it had reached such high standing that it joined the Scuola Normale and Scuola di Sant'Anna of Pisa in a federation of universities of excellence, considered the most prestigious in the country. It is known for its faculties of Law and Medicine. The buildings of 1533 were extended by Giuseppe Piermarini in 1771–9 and by Leopold Pollack in 1783–95. The Aula Magna was begun in 1827.

Off Corso Carlo Alberto and the Strada Nuova are numerous attractive courtyards, all of which are open to the public. From the one with a war memorial you enter the **Museo per la Storia dell'Università di Pavia** (*Strada Nuova 65; open Mon 2–5, Wed and Fri 9–12, T: 0382 984709, ppp.unipv.it/museo/museo/htm*), with interesting collections relating to the history of medicine and physics in an old-fashioned arrangement (the display-cases survive from the 18th century). The collections include mementoes of the most distinguished alumni, including Alessandro Volta (*see p. 221*), whose statue is in the central courtyard. The Teatro Fisico and the anatomical theatre were both designed by Leopold Pollack (1787). The anatomical theatre is named after Antonio Scarpa (1752–1832), a brilliant but famously irascible surgeon, founder of the School of Anatomy at Pavia. As the father of orthopaedic science, he has bequeathed his name to no fewer than ten medical terms, including Scarpa's Shoe, a device for correcting club foot. He was much admired by Napoleon, who made him a present of surgical instruments in silver with ivory handles. Scarpa was less beloved by students and colleagues: after his death his body was decapitated in a revenge attack by one of his housemen.

Strada Nuova continues north past the Teatro Fraschini, built in 1771–3 by Antonio Bibiena, to the Castello Visconteo.

CASTELLO VISCONTEO (MUSEI CIVICI)

Map 2. Open Tues–Fri 2.30–6, Sat–Sun 11–7. museicivici.pavia.it. Some of the collections are only open by appointment. For up-to-date information, T: 0382 399770 or email prenotazioni@comune.pv.it.

The great fortress palace known as the Castello Visconteo, surrounded by public gardens, is still approached over its drawbridge. The interior houses the extensive collections of art and antiquities of the Musei Civici.

The castle was begun in 1360 by Galeazzo II Visconti, a year after the family conquered Pavia for Milan. It was completed by 1365 and it became Galeazzo's residence, where he kept his important collections of art as well as a library of precious volumes. It served as a splendid setting for the life of the Visconti court.

Galeazzo also laid out a huge park (with a perimeter wall of some 22km), which extended all the way north from the castle as far as the Certosa di Pavia (which became the ducal mausoleum). The park (which no longer exists) had farms, woods, areas for wild animals and various buildings, so was not only used as a hunting chase. The famous Battle of Pavia (*see p. 153*) took place in the park in 1525; two years later, in revenge for their defeat, the French destroyed the northern wing of the castle and two of its corner turrets, and today the ruins remain as the French left them: the vast courtyard (through which you enter the castle) lacks its fourth side. In fact the grass gives it a rather scruffy appearance, although the brick architecture is superb, still with its handsome porticoes on three sides and a loggia above. The various sections of the civic museums are signposted here.

PAVIA, CASTELLO VISCONTEO
The donor Bianca Visconti in Vincenzo Foppa's *Madonna Enthroned with Saints*.

First floor (Pinacoteca)

The gallery of paintings is on the first floor (it is worth taking the 'panoramic' lift on the far side of the courtyard). The nucleus of the collection was formed by Luigi Malaspina di Sannazzaro (1754–1835) and is an interesting example of a private collection of this time. Other paintings came from churches in Pavia. The arrangement is chronological and by school. There are also detached 15th-century frescoes from buildings in Pavia by local painters and a few remains of the original wall decorations. Highlights are mentioned below.

In the first room: *Madonna and Child with Sts Francis and Clare* by Gentile da Fabriano, painted for a convent in Pavia; *The Redeemer* (the Veronica) by Giambono; *St Augustine Enthroned* by Jacobello di Bonomo, painted for the church of San Pietro in Ciel d'Oro; *Adoration of the Child* by Ambrogio Bevilacqua (sometimes called Liberale). The two paintings on canvas of the *Adoration of the Magi* and *Expulsion of the Merchants from the Temple* are interesting works by an unknown Lombard painter dating from the late 15th century.

The *Portrait of a Man* is usually considered an autograph work by Antonello da Messina and dated 1465/70. The panel is badly damaged by a crack between the nose and lips of this unknown sitter, with his well-trimmed fringe and slightly ironic expression, and has suffered from repeated restorations. Originally from Sicily, Antonello was clearly influenced by the Flemish school and is known to have worked also in Venice, where he met Giovanni Bellini. So this portrait is fittingly displayed next to a superb *Madonna and Child* signed by Giovanni Bellini, probably painted some ten years earlier, and another lovely *Madonna and Child* by the Flemish master Hugo van der Goes.

The small Room 2 has a beautiful *Madonna Enthroned with Saints* (1480s), with the donors Giovanni Matteo Bottigella and his wife Bianca Visconti, by Vincenzo Foppa (*see p 91*), one of the masterpieces of the collection. The painting by his pupil Bergognone of *Christ Carrying the Cross* shows a procession of Carthusian monks in front of the Certosa di Pavia with the façade still under construction, c. 1494.

Room 3 has works by Venetian painters (notably Giovanni Mansueti and Cima da Conegliano) and Lombard and Flemish paintings. The corner room (frescoed in the 15th century) has a remarkable wood model of the Duomo of Pavia, constructed in 1497 by Gian Pietro Fugazza. A very rare survival, this scale model would have been used during construction work.

In the huge last gallery, 17th- and 18th-century works are exhibited. Highlights include a large *Adoration of the Magi* by Camillo Procaccini; two landscapes with animals by the German painter known as Rosa da Tivoli; a detailed (imagined) scene of the famous Battle of Pavia; *capricci*; and works by Pompeo Batoni. In the showcases are ceramics produced locally and glass.

Ground floor (archaeological collections)

Traces of the original decoration remain in the ground-floor rooms, notably the frescoed Visconti emblem of a snake swallowing a child. Exhibits begin with the Egyptian, Greek and Roman eras (and there is some particularly fine Roman glass and gold jewellery). The Lombard period is well documented with more jewellery, highly decorated buckles, armour, and a fascinating 'camp' saddle in gilded bronze, found in the bed of the Ticino river (only the leather seat has been restored), which could be folded up for easy transport (or erected in a hurry, as the situation in battle required). There are also plutei carved with Christian symbols, one in marble with peacocks and another with dragons, dating from the 8th century. The fascinating small bronze statuette of a soldier dates from the 8th or 9th century.

The Romanesque period (12th century) is well illustrated with remains of mosaic pavements and sculptural fragments salvaged from churches and palaces in Pavia, and a wall decoration in glazed tiles of Islamic inspiration. The church of Sant'Agata al Monte, demolished in 1907, is recorded in a fresco which was detached from its apse in the year it was destroyed and taken to Paris and then ended up in Philadelphia, from where it was returned in 1991.

The famous 15th-century **Library**, put together by the Sforza in the southwest tower of the castle, had already been dispersed by 1499 but the holdings have been reconstructed digitally from other libraries and the database can be consulted today in its historic seat.

Second floor

The **Risorgimento Museum**, founded in 1885, has a room dedicated to the famous Cairoli family, who came from Pavia: Benedetto (1825–89) was known for his anti-Austrian activities and his three younger brothers all predeceased him as volunteers in Garibaldi's army. Garibaldi's visits to the town are also recorded.

The **Gipsoteca** has plaster casts of famous antique sculptures and a small room displays a Neoclassical frieze by Bertel Thorvaldsen. A separate gallery houses **19th-century painting** and illustrates the history of the Accademia of Pavia (opened in 1840). Painters represented include Francesco Hayez and Federico Zandomeneghi.

SAN PIETRO IN CIEL D'ORO

The Lombard church of San Pietro in Ciel d'Oro (*map Pavia 1; open 7–12 & 3–7*), consecrated in 1132, stands on a quiet little triangular green shaded by some venerable trees. The church's name ('with a golden sky') probably comes from its vault, which was formerly gilded. The church is mentioned by Dante in his *Paradiso* (*X: 128*) as the place where the mortal remains of Boethius (who was executed here; *see below*) find eternal peace. The passage is quoted on a modern plaque on the façade. The single portal is asymmetrically placed, and the buttress on the right is made broader than that on the left in order to contain a stairway. The relics of St Augustine are held here and there is still an adjoining convent of Augustinian friars. A notice in the church encourages visitors to consult their website (*www.augustinus.it*). The portal has a curious relief in the tympanum of an Archangel flanked by two kneeling figures and good carving below on the arch.

Steps descend to the ancient Romanesque interior, restored in 1875–99, where the engaged columns and pilasters have 'bestiary' capitals and others carved with foliage. Above the high altar (installed here in the 20th century) rises the **Arca di Sant'Agostino**, a masterpiece of Italian sculpture. Executed c. 1362 by Campionese masters (*see p. 422*), it was made to house the relics of St Augustine (d. 430), removed from Carthage for safekeeping to Sardinia and from there brought to Pavia by the Lombard king Liutprand in 724 (the silver casket made for the relics at that time is preserved in the altar beneath the Arca). The Arca has a galaxy of statuettes and bas-reliefs illustrating the story of the saint and charming angels holding a winding cloth surround the effigy. Even though you can also view it from the sanctuary, it is still difficult to see the details.

There are remains of the **12th-century mosaic pavement** in the chapel at the top of the south aisle, including a depiction of *St George and the Dragon*. The pavement in the nave is in the rippling brown-and-cream toffee-coloured tile so characteristic of Lombardy.

Set into the base of the pilaster to the right of the right-hand entrance to the crypt is a **plaque commemorating Liutprand**, who is buried here: *Hic Iacent Ossa Regis*

Liutprandi (Here lie the bones of King Liutprand). In the centre of the crypt are remains of a **stone sarcophagus**, its lid incised with the figure of St Augustine. The altar in the crypt (reconstructed at the end of the 19th century) contains a casket with the **remains of Boethius** (476–524), the Roman poet and statesman clubbed to death in Pavia by order of the Ostrogothic king Theodoric, on charges of treason. He wrote *The Consolation of Philosophy* while in prison awaiting execution. Boethius (Anicius Manlius Severinus Boethius) is venerated in Pavia as San Severino Boezio.

The **sacristy** (off the north aisle) has a pretty vault with grotesques, dating from 1561.

THE EAST AND SOUTH OF TOWN

In the eastern part of the town is the church of **San Francesco Grande** (*map 2*), a late Romanesque edifice (1238–98) with a restored Gothic façade. A bronze statue of Pope St Pius V by Francesco Nuvolone (1692) faces the Collegio Ghislieri, which the pontiff founded in 1567, a year after becoming pope (he had taught Theology in Pavia for 16 years). With a beautiful courtyard, this is part of Pavia University. The square is closed by the façade of **San Francesco di Paola**, beyond which are the **Botanical Gardens** (*open weekdays 9–12.30 & 2.30–5; T: 0382 984848*).

The church of **Santa Maria Canepanova** (*map 4*), at the corner of Via Sacchi and Via Negri, is a graceful octagonal building begun by Giovanni Antonio Amadeo in 1507, probably to a design by Bramante. It has a pretty little cloister. Further south on Via Scopoli (near the corner of Via Volta) is **Santa Maria delle Cacce** (*closed at the time of writing*), rebuilt in 1629, with frescoes of the life of St Theodoric—not to be confused with Theodoric the nemesis of Boethius. St Theodoric was a French monk (known in France as St Thierry), who earned his fame in Pavia by curing King Theodoric of an eye complaint.

In the south of the town, near Corso Garibaldi, is the much altered Lombard church of **San Primo**. Further south, reached by Via San Giovanni, is the **Collegio Borromeo**, founded in 1562 by St Charles Borromeo (*see p. 201*) and built in 1564–88, largely by Pellegrino Tibaldi. Leopold Pollack's river façade was added in 1808–20. This is also part of Pavia University.

In the southern suburb across the river, Borgo Ticino (which has a pleasant river front; *map 3*), is the 12th-century church of **Santa Maria in Betlem**, with a façade decorated with faïence plaques and a plain Romanesque interior. Its name ('in Bethlehem') derives from its proximity to a hospice for pilgrims to the Holy Land.

THE WEST OF TOWN

To the west of Piazza della Vittoria, on Via Mascheroni, is the 11th-century Lombard campanile of **San Giovanni Domnarum** (*map 3*). The church is entered off a courtyard from the street. The crypt and its frescoes go back to the 11th century. Almost diagonally opposite the church entrance opens the peaceful cobbled **Piazza del Carmine**, with restaurants, and Palazzo Orlandi with a 15th-century courtyard. Here is the fine brick church of **Santa Maria del Carmine**, begun in 1373. It has an attractive façade added in 1490 adorned with three terracotta reliefs and a splendid rose window. The white and pink interior has soaring Gothic rib vaulting. The high altar dates from the 18th century and later. There are 15th-century votive frescoes on the columns at the east end and in the north transept an altarpiece by Bernardino Lanzani (1515) of the *Madonna and Child with Saints* and scenes from the life of the Virgin in the predella. The Sacristy, which has an elaborate stucco entrance, has a charming lavabo by Giovanni Antonio Amadeo.

Corso Cavour is distinguished by the 15th-century Torre Bottigella (no. 17) and, opposite the Tribunale (Palazzo della Giustizia), the Bramantesque **Palazzo Bottigella** (no. 30), with pretty terracotta decorations. The best-known member of this notable Pavese family was Giovanni Matteo Bottigella, humanist, patron of the arts and adviser to the Visconti. He commissioned the altarpiece by Foppa now in the Castello Visconteo (*see p. 159*).

Piazzale Minerva (*map 3–4*) is dominated by a monumental statue of a fully-armed Minerva. It is the work of Francesco Messina (1938), a well-known sculptor who was Director of the Accademia di Brera in Milan and who had been commissioned to make a replacement for the *Regisole* statue outside the duomo the previous year. The Minerva, in true Fascist style and overpowering in size (although the authorities had the sculptor cover her bare breasts), commemorates Ottorino Rossi (1877–1936), a famous neurologist and rector of Pavia University.

SAN LANFRANCO

Corso Manzoni leads west from Piazzale Minerva. Beyond the railway station (5mins) is the church of **San Salvatore**, reconstructed in 1467–1511 with frescoes by Bernardino Lanzani. A further 20-min walk along a busy road, past the cemetery and tennis club (or take bus 4 from the railway station) brings you to **San Lanfranco**, a 13th-century building containing the beautiful tomb (by Amadeo, 1498) of St Lanfranco. Bishop Lanfranco Beccari (1124–98) was a ferocious defender of ecclesiastical power in the face of growing civic authority. Weary of the fight, he at last retired to the monastery here. Frescoes in the church record his struggles, explicitly likening him to the martyred Thomas Becket (a companion fresco shows the latter's murder). The other famous Lanfranco of Pavia was a monk in France before being appointed Archbishop of Canterbury in 1072. He assiduously assisted William the Conqueror in replacing Saxon officials with Norman ones in England, died in 1089 and is buried at Canterbury. One of the cloisters retains some terracotta decoration by Amadeo.

GIOVANNI ANTONIO AMADEO

Born in Pavia, Amadeo (c. 1447–1522) was the most important sculptor and architect at work in Lombardy in the second half of the 15th century. He dedicated many years to the Certosa di Pavia, and he was also appointed architect of the Duomo of Milan in 1481. While in Milan in the same decade he was commissioned to work with Bramante's designs on Santa Maria delle Grazie. One of his more eccentric works is the Cappella Colleoni in Bergamo, where he also sculpted the delicate monument to Colleoni's daughter Medea. He carved an exquisite marble high relief of St Himerius which can be seen, along with other signed panels, in the cathedral of Cremona.

THE CERTOSA DI PAVIA

Atlas B, B3. Open Oct–March Tues–Sat 9–11.30 & 2.30–4, Sun and religious festivals
9–11.30 & 2.30–5; April Tues–Sun and religious festivals 9–11.30 & 2.30–5.30; May–
Sept Tues–Sun and religious festivals 9–11.30 & 2.30–6. www.certosadipavia.com.
The Certosa is served by trains and buses. Bus no. 175 run every 30mins from the bus
station in Pavia. From the Certosa bus stop it is about 20mins' walk to the monastery.
Trains from Pavia or Milan (including the S13 suburban line) also run regularly. From
the railway station, there is also a walk of c. 20mins, around the perimeter wall of the
Certosa (follow the brown signs). If you come by road, glance out of the window from time
to time: you will notice that the Milan road from Pavia is skirted by the Naviglio di Pavia,
an irrigation and transport canal begun by Galeazzo Visconti, lined with abandoned
locks and lock-houses.

The Certosa di Pavia, a Carthusian monastery now occupied and maintained by
Cistercians, was founded by Gian Galeazzo Visconti in 1396 as a family mausoleum.
Its construction was entrusted to the Lombard masons of Milan cathedral and the
builders of the castle of Pavia. The monastery proper was finished in 1452 and the
church in 1472, under the Sforzas. The façade was completed in the 16th century.
Today just ten Cistercian monks occupy the Certosa.

From the entrance, a vestibule with frescoed saints by Bernardino Luini leads
through to the great garden-court in front of the church. On the left are the old
pharmacy and food and wine stores; on the right the prior's quarters and the so-called
Palazzo Ducale, rebuilt by Francesco Maria Richini (1620–5) to house distinguished
visitors and now containing a museum and shop (*described below*).

THE MONASTERY CHURCH

The sculptural and polychrome marble decoration of the west front of the church,
of almost superabundant richness, marks the height of the artistic achievement of
the quattrocento in Lombardy; it was begun in 1473 and worked on up to 1499 by
Cristoforo and Antonio Mantegazza and Giovanni Antonio Amadeo. In the 16th
century, Cristoforo Lombardi continued the upper part in simplified form, but it was
never completed. The attribution of the various parts is still under discussion.

At the base of the façade is a running series of medallions of Roman emperors
and heroes, including Hercules strangling the serpents and the She-wolf suckling
Romulus and Remus. Above are statues and reliefs of prophets, apostles and saints by
the Mantegazza alternating with scenes from the life of Christ by Amadeo. On each
side are two very rich windows by Amadeo. The upper part, by Cristoforo Lombardo
(1540–60), is decorated with 70 statues by 16th-century Lombard masters.

The great portal was probably designed by Gian Cristoforo Romano (though also
attributed to Gian Giacomo Dolcebuono and Amadeo) and executed by Benedetto
Briosco, the sculptor also of the small bas-reliefs of the life of the Virgin and of the four
large reliefs. Right: the *Foundation of the Carthusian Order* (1084) and *Gian Galeazzo*

CERTOSA DI PAVIA
Gian Galeazzo Visconti laying the first stone.
Relief by Benedetto Briosco.

CERTOSA DI PAVIA
The main façade of the church.

Visconti Laying the First Stone of the Certosa (27th August 1396); and left: *Translation to the Certosa of the Body of Gian Galeazzo* (1st March 1474) and *Consecration of the Church* (3rd May 1497).

The church nave

The interior is purely Gothic in plan, but with the introduction of Renaissance decorative motifs. The chapels opening off the aisle were expensively redecorated and provided with handsome Baroque grilles in the 17th–18th centuries, and only traces remain of their original frescoes and glass. As the grilles are kept locked, the works of art in the chapels are difficult to see. The letters GRA.CAR, painted, carved, incised or embossed, recur frequently throughout the building. They stand for *Gratiarum Carthusia* (Charterhouse of the Graces; the church is dedicated to the Madonna delle Grazie).

The church is a good place to admire work by Bergognone (*see p. 168*). The altarpiece of the second south chapel incorporates panels by him and Macrino d'Alba. In the fourth chapel is a *Crucifixion* by Bergognone, and in the fifth chapel an altarpiece of St Syrus, first bishop of Pavia (he is buried in the duomo there), also by Bergognone.

The altarpiece in the second north chapel is made up from a painting representing God the Father by Perugino, flanked by Doctors of the Church by Bergognone, and—below—17th-century copies of panels by Perugino (1499), now in the National Gallery, London. Look up above this chapel, in the nave, to see a *trompe l'oeil* of a Carthusian monk peering out from the biforium. In the fourth chapel is an excellent carved altar frontal of the *Massacre of the Innocents* by Dionigi Bussola. The altarpiece in the sixth chapel, of *St Ambrose and Saints*, is by Bergognone (1492). Opposite, on the wall of the south aisle, is another amusing *trompe l'oeil* depiction of a Carthusian brother peeping out from a window casement.

At the top of the nave is an elaborate iron gate, which is kept locked until the custodian opens it to admit the next group to the guided part of the visit.

North transept

In the centre of the north transept is the **tomb of Ludovico il Moro and Beatrice d'Este**, with beautiful effigies by Cristoforo Solari, the clothing and eyelashes carefully rendered and Beatrice's clumpy shoes sticking out from beneath her gown (a patten said to have belonged to her can be seen at Vigevano; *see p. 177*). Beatrice was lively and cultivated, just 15 when she married Il Moro and not quite 22 when she died, in childbirth. It is said that she had been dancing in her apartments the night before. For Il Moro—if Ariosto is to be trusted—her death was a heavy blow: *Beatrice bea (vivendo) il suo consorte, e lo lascia infelice alla sua morte* (Beatrice blessed her husband when alive, and left him desolate at her demise). The tomb was begun by Solari in the same year that Beatrice died (1497) and was originally in the church of Santa Maria delle Grazie in Milan. It was brought here in 1564.

DUKE LUDOVICO SFORZA, IL MORO

In 1476 Galeazzo Maria Sforza was assassinated outside the church of Santo Stefano in Milan, leaving his seven-year-old son Gian Galeazzo as heir to the dukedom. The boy's uncle, Ludovico il Moro, managed to step in and gain control as regent for his brother's son. In 1491 he made a prestigious marriage to Beatrice d'Este, sister of Isabella d'Este, Marchioness of Mantua. When Gian Galeazzo died, in his mid-20s in 1494, Ludovico was ready to take over the rule of the city and in the following year managed to engineer an investiture by the Holy Roman Emperor, Maximilian. Beatrice died in 1497. Ludovico—though he had always kept mistresses—never remarried and went on to become an enlightened ruler of Milan. As a wealthy patron of the arts, he also called on Leonardo da Vinci and Bramante to help decorate the city and funded the building of the Castello Sforzesco (where he had Leonardo decorate the vault of the Sala delle Asse) and numerous churches: Santa Maria presso San Celso, Santa Maria presso San Satiro, and above all, Santa Maria delle Grazie, where Bramante worked on the church while Leonardo painted his *Last Supper* for the convent. Ludovico also commissioned works of art for Pavia and Cremona, as well as for his birthplace, Vigevano.

Ludovico's power came to an end with the coronation of King Louis XII in France in 1498. Louis, like Ludovico, was also a great-grandson of Gian Galeazzo Visconti and thus had an equal claim to the Duchy of Milan, a claim which he was eager to press. French troops invaded the city the following year and occupied the Castello Sforzesco. Ludovico died a prisoner in France in 1508, but his remains were returned to Lombardy to lie beside those of his bride.

There transept apses have beautiful frescoes by Bergognone, notable for their use of a particularly beautiful pale lapis blue. Here in the north apse is the *Coronation of the Virgin*, with the kneeling figures of Francesco Sforza and Ludovico il Moro. The two frescoed angels on either side of the window above are attributed to Bramante. The *Ecce Homo* over the narrow door facing the effigy of Beatrice d'Este is also by Bergognone. A pretty door by Amadeo, with profile-portraits of the Dukes of Milan above the lintel, leads into the old sacristy, a vaulted space containing fine 17th-century presses and panelling. The remarkable ivory altarpiece, with nearly 100 statuettes, attributed to Baldassare degli Embriachi, was made in the early 15th century.

BERGOGNONE

The Lombard artist Ambrogio da Fossano (c. 1455–1523) is always known as Bergognone. Many of his paintings are to be found in the Certosa di Pavia, where he was at work from 1488 until 1494. He was a painter in fresco as well as in oil, and he used both media to decorate the chapter house of Santa Maria della Passione in Milan, where he can be seen at his best. Other works by him in Milan can be seen at the Ambrosiana and in the church of San Simpliciano. A very pious man, he is considered the most important follower of Vincenzo Foppa, but he was also influenced by the Flemish school and later by Leonardo and Bramante (who were both in Milan at the same time). Other places in Lombardy where Bergognone is well represented include Bergamo (the Accademia Carrara as well as the church of Santo Spirito) and Lodi, where four very beautiful panels survive in the church of the Incoronata.

Choir

The choir contains carved and inlaid stalls (1498), frescoes by Daniele Crespi (1629), and a sumptuous late 16th-century altar.

South transept

The fresco over the narrow west door here, depicting the Madonna, is also by Bergognone. The fresco in the apse depicts Gian Galeazzo Visconti, with his children, presenting a model of the church to the Virgin (higher up are two angels, again attributed to Bramante). The altarpiece is a *Madonna Enthroned with St Charles and St Bruno* by Cerano. Gian Galeazzo appears again in a carved bust over the door to the right of the altar (by the Mantegazza), which leads to the cloister. Opposite is his tomb, by Gian Cristoforo Romano (1493–7; the *Madonna* surmounting it is by Benedetto Briosco, the sarcophagus by Galeazzo Alessi, the figures of *Fame* and *Victory* at either end by Bernardino da Novate).

A door by Amadeo matching that in the north transept, this time with medallions of the Duchesses of Milan, leads into the lavatorium, which contains a well-carved lavabo by Alberto Maffiolo of Carrara, and, on the left, a charming fresco of the *Madonna* by Bernardino Luini.

THE MONASTERY

The south transept doorway by the Mantegazza leads into the **Small Cloister**, with a garden, and embellished by terracotta decorations in the Cremonese style by Rinaldo de Stauris (1465). The beautiful little doorway into the church, with a Madonna, is by Amadeo (1466). Off this cloister is the **New Sacristy** (*only open for services*), with an altarpiece of the *Assumption* by Andrea Solari (completed by Bernardino Campi) and 16th-century illuminated choirbooks. The **Refectory** has ceiling frescoes by Bergognone and his brother Bernardino, a reader's pulpit (the Carthusians are a solitude-seeking and contemplative order and would have eaten their meals in silence while listening to Holy Scripture), and a little fresco of the *Madonna* by the Zavattari or Bergognone (1450).

A passage leads from the Small Cloister into the arcaded **Great Cloister**, with more terracotta decoration by De Stauris (1478). Above the porticoes on three sides you can make out 23 monks' cells, each with its chimney. Entered by a decorative doorway, they have two rooms, with a bedroom and loggia above and a little garden below. All are identical except for one, which is a double cell.

THE MUSEUM AND SHOP

The **museum in the Palazzo Ducale**, on the garden-court in front of the church, has two frescoed rooms by Fiammenghino and Giovanni Battista Pozzo (attributed). The paintings include works by Bartolomeo Montagna, Bergognone, Bernardino Luini, Giuseppe Vermiglio and Vincenzo and Bernardino Campi. The portrait of Pope Paul V is a copy by Gerolamo Ciocca of a work by Caravaggio. There are also sculptures by Bambaia, the Mantegazza and Cristoforo Solari. A gallery of plaster casts occupies the ground floor, where the surviving items from the tomb of Gian Galeazzo Visconti—a sword, a dagger and a pair of golden spurs—are also preserved.

Opposite the entrance to the museum is the **shop**, which sells the products of cloistered industry: liqueurs, beers and curative teas, as well as souvenir guides and postcards. The products are sold by the monks, who are silent.

THE PROVINCE OF PAVIA

The province of Pavia abounds in interesting sights, but in all seasons except summer the roads are subject to heavy fog, so cautious driving is necessary. The southern part of the province of Pavia, beyond the Po, is known as the Oltrepò Pavese. It is well known for its wines, both still and sparkling, vinified from noble French varieties (Pinot Noir, Chardonnay) as well as from Barbera and Cortese.

VOGHERA

An old town with sprawling modern outskirts, Voghera (*map p. 470, B4*) is an important railway junction and centre of light industry with a handsome old centre and a wide, cobbled cathedral square. East of the centre, below street level (in Via del Tempio Sacrario), is the **Chiesa Rossa**, a tiny little Lombard chapel with blind dwarf arcades, today dedicated to the Italian cavalry. Legend attributes its foundation to King Liutprand (8th century). The **Museo Storico** (*open Tues, Wed, Fri 3–5.30; museostoricogbeccari.it*) and **Museo Scienze Naturali** (*open Tues–Fri 9.15–12, Tues, Thur, Fri also afternoons 2–5; museoscienzevog.it*) in an old cavalry barracks on Via Gramsci, have natural history collections and mementoes of war from the Napoleonic era to the present, including the Beretta pistol with which Mussolini was allegedly shot near Lake Como in 1945. At the railway station is the **Museo Ferroviario Enrico Pessina** (*open Sat mornings*), which will delight train enthusiasts. Voghera also has a Visconti castle and the vestiges of piers of a Roman bridge across the Staffora torrent.

THE VALLE STAFFORA

Heading south from Voghera, the SP461 ascends the Valle Staffora passing **Salice Terme** (*map p. 470, B4*), a little spa with sulphurous waters (*termedisalice.it*). Further up the valley is the **Abbazia di Sant'Alberto di Butrio**, founded in the 11th century, suppressed in 1800 and now once again a place of prayer and pilgrimage. Tall tales cling to a certain tomb, said to be that of Edward II of England, who was not murdered with a red hot poker in Berkeley Castle after all, but escaped here. The road continues through **Varzi** (*map p. 470, C4*), noted for its salami, and up over the Passo del Penice (1149m). Here you can visit the **Giardino Alpino di Pietra Corva** (950m; *open May–Sept Tues–Sun 10–6*), a little botanical garden planted in 1967.

EAST OF VOGHERA

At **Montebello della Battaglia** (*map p. 470, B4*), a monument in the form of a little Doric temple (you can see it from the SP10 on the way to Casteggio) marks the site of two battles: a victory of Napoleonic troops over the Austrians in 1800, and a Franco-Piedmontese success in May 1859, during the second Italian War of Independence. A short way further east is **Casteggio**, where the Museo Storico Archeologico dell'Oltrepò Pavese (*open Mon–Wed 9.30–12.30, Thur 9.30–12.30 & 1.30–5.30, 1st Sun of the month 2.30–5.30; museocasteggio.it*) has displays covering prehistoric times to the Middle Ages, including some material from the Roman *Clastidium*.

PRACTICAL INFORMATION

GETTING AROUND

• **By rail: Pavia** is easily reached from Milan by regular trains from Centrale station. Journey time is 25–35mins. The suburban railway S13 (from Porta Venezia and Porta Garibaldi) also goes to Pavia (journey time is slightly longer), also stopping at the **Certosa di Pavia** en route (journey time from Milan is c. 40mins, in the other direction, from Pavia, 5mins). The Certosa station is c. 20mins' walk from the monastery.
• **By bus:** Local buses are operated by PMT (*www.pmtsrl.it*). Service no.175 links Pavia and Milan, stopping at the Certosa en route (20mins' walk from the bus stop).

INFORMATION OFFICES

Pavia IAT on Piazza della Vittoria (in Palazzo del Broletto). *T: 0382 079943, turismo@comune.pv.it.*

WHERE TO STAY

PAVIA

€€ **Moderno**. Convenient central location, in an old Liberty building, completely gutted and turned into a rather heavy-handed but comfortable enough hotel. *Viale Vittorio Emanuele 41. T: 0382 303401, www.hotelmoderno. it. Map 1.*

WHERE TO EAT

PAVIA

€€ **Osteria della Madonna da Peo**. Traditional *osteria* popular with locals. Booking advised. Dinner only Tues–Fri. Lunch and dinner Sat–Sun. Closed Mon. *Via dei Liguri 28, T: 0382 302833, osteriadellamadonna.it. Map 3.*

€€ **Antica Osteria del Previ**. Acclaimed place in a courtyard overlooking the Ticino. Closed all day Tues and Sun evening. *Via Milazzo 65. T: 0382 26203, anticaosteriadelprevi. com. Map 4.*

€–€€ **Osteria alle Carceri**. Tucked away behind Corso Cavour, a nice little place offering local cooking and, at lunchtime, simple dishes of the day with a glass of wine. Closed Sun. *Via Fratelli Marozzi 7, T: 0382-301443, www. osteriaallecarceri.it. Map 3.*

€–€€ **Locanda del Carmine**. On the attractive, peaceful Piazza del Carmine. Does a weekday lunch menu. Closed Sat lunch and all day Sun. *Piazza del Carmine 7/a. T: 0382 29647, locandadelcarmine.com. Map 1.*

€ **Hostaria Il Cupolone**. Checked tablecloths, lively atmosphere, friendly service and typical hearty Lombard fare. Overlooks the mighty dome of the cathedral, hence the name. Closed Mon lunch and Tues. *Via Cardinal Riboldi 2. T: 0382 303519, hostariailcupolone.it. Map 3.*

CERTOSA DI PAVIA

The **Bar Bella Vita** just outside the railway station is a simple place for a drink and a basic snack. Close to the Certosa itself, up the narrow lane that leads left as you leave the precinct, is the **Bar Milano**, down at heel and rather fly-blown, but fine for coffee and a brioche. Further on up the same lane on the other side is the €€€ **Vecchia Pavia al Mulino**, a Michelin-starred restaurant for fine dining. Closed Sun evening and Mon. *Via al Monumento 5. T: 0382 925894, vecchiapaviaalmulino.it.*

LOCAL SPECIALITIES

In Pavia, **Vigoni** (*Corso Strada Nuova 110; map 3*), founded in 1878, in a premises with fine Art Nouveau shop fittings, still makes excellent cakes. The light, sugar-dusted sponge cake known as Torta Paradiso (or Tùrta Vigon in dialect) was invented here. You can order it by the slice, either at the counter to take away or to sit and enjoy with a coffee at a table in the adjoining café section.

The Ticino Valley & the Lomellina

W est of Milan, the landscape is flat and agricultural, with fields criss-crossed by waterways: the Ticino river, the Naviglio Grande former transport canal and numerous smaller irrigation channels all make their tranquil way through the countryside. The Naviglio Grande runs from Milan as far as Abbiategrasso, where it bends north. Close to this stretch are a few fine villas, survivors of the many handsome country houses built by wealthy trading families. Beyond the Ticino is the historic town of Vigevano, birthplace of Ludovico il Moro, and, in the area known as the Lomellina, is Mortara, an old halting place on the Via Francigena pilgrimage route. All three towns have attractive historic centres: Vigevano is especially important for its castle and museums. Also included in this chapter is Magenta, east of the Ticino, scene of a pivotal battle between Italian and Austrian forces in 1859. The preferred means of getting around in all these towns of the Lombard plain is by bicycle.

ABBIATEGRASSO

Just 16km from Milan, Abbiategrasso (*Atlas B, A2*) is an interesting small town, well worth a detour, and all the pleasanter for being completely off the usual tourist itinerary. Its name is thought to derive from the Latin personal name Habiatus and '*grasso*', referring to the fat of the land, in other words the district's prosperity. The town grew up around an old castle of the Visconti, remains of which still stand. Viewed on a map, the outline of the old fortified core is still clearly visible. The grassy glacis is preserved on two and a half sides; the castle ruins stand in a vestigial moat.

VIGEVANO
The Strada Coperta.

ABBIATEGRASSO
Piazza Marconi.

SIGHTS IN THE TOWN CENTRE

The **Castello Visconteo**, built in the 13th–14th centuries, was converted from military to domestic use around 1400. Today there is access to the castle courtyard, which has traces of frescoes commissioned in 1438 by Filippo Maria, the last of the Visconti, with much use of his motto: *À bon droit*. Filippo died in 1447 and the Duchy of Milan passed to Francesco Sforza, founder of the new dynasty with his wife, Bianca Maria Visconti. She bore him nine children, among them Galeazzo Maria Sforza, who founded the convent of the Annunziata here. (Galeazzo Maria proved a cruel and unpopular ruler; he was assassinated in 1476.) Also in the castle courtyard is a fragment of Roman milestone, found at Robecca sul Naviglio and set up here. The castle is home to the local library and to the Tourist Information Office.

A short walk west of the castle is the triangular **Piazza Marconi**, with the Town Hall and attractive arcaded buildings housing cafés and bars. Opening off it is Via Borsani, with two churches. On the left is Richini's sober Baroque façade of **San Bernardino**, and opposite it, the much more ancient **Santa Maria Nuova** (1365). The entrance is just round the corner, across a wide arcaded atrium with terracotta roundels of saints and a huge porch borne on two tiers of paired columns. Until recently attributed to

Bramante, it was built in 1601 to protect the fresco of the *Madonna and Child*, which is by the school of the Zavattari. In the interior, on the north side, is the altarpiece of the *Madonna dei Cordiglieri* by Il Cerano (1594).

OUTSIDE THE CENTRE

North of the centre is the stark pinkish-white façade of the **former convent of the Annunziata**, founded by Galeazzo Maria Sforza after the birth of his son Gian Galeazzo, here in Abbiategrasso, in 1469. Gian Galeazzo succeeded his father as duke aged just seven, allowing his uncle, the celebrated Ludovico il Moro (*see p. 167*), to assume power as regent. Restored in 2007, the Annunziata is now used for conferences and events.

Across the railway line, leading east in a straight line, is the busy **Viale Mazzini**, which follows the course of a former shipping canal. Fine houses once lined its banks (some of these remain, though much altered and rather shabby), as well as the little votive church of **San Rocco**, built in 1631 after an outbreak of plague. Just before the flyover where Viale Mazzini joins the main SS494, turn right down Via Tenca. This takes you to a towpath along the **Naviglio di Bereguardo**, which leads through an area once filled with huge farms that supplied Milan. Follow the canal to the left and curve back towards the flyover, which carries the road across the junction of Naviglio di Bereguardo with the **Naviglio Grande**. Here, on the left, is the church of **Sant'Antonio Abate**. In the chapel on the south side is an *Assumption* by Camillo Procaccini. On the north side, left of the chancel arch, crowned with slightly oversized crowns, is a venerated 13th-century statue of the *Madonna and Child* by a Campionese sculptor. This district of town is known as Castelletto. On the Naviglio Grande is the **Palazzo Cittadini Stampa** (*usually open at weekends and for events*), a good example of the type of handsome villa that was built along the transport canals by prosperous Lombard families. The interior has 17th-century frescoes.

VIGEVANO

Situated close to the south bank of the Ticino, Vigevano (*Atlas B, A2–A3*) is an ancient town which grew to prominence in the 14th century under the Visconti. Ludovico il Moro and Francesco II Sforza were born here. It was famous for the manufacture of shoes from the end of the 19th century until well into the 20th, and the modern city expanded rapidly in the 1950s.

EXPLORING VIGEVANO

If you arrive by train, walk straight up Via Cairoli and follow the brown signs. These bring you to a tall **gateway in the walls** with a huge Visconti device on the inner side facing Via XX Settembre. The house at Via XX Settembre 30 has a plaque commemorating the birth here, in 1859, of the actress Eleonora Duse. The street

VIGEVANO
Detail of the sgraffito decoration on Piazza Ducale.

opens onto the chief beauty of Vigevano, its lovely main square, **Piazza Ducale**, one of the great achievements of Italian Renaissance town planning. In 1492–4 buildings were demolished to create space for the square by order of Ludovico il Moro. It is surrounded on three sides by uniform graceful arcades: grey columns with simple foliate capitals and above them an unbroken red and yellow sgraffito façade with busts of heroic figures, heraldic devices, floral patterns, paired centaurs and other fantastic beasts. Its classical design may owe something to Bramante (or even Leonardo da Vinci). The fourth side was closed in 1680 when the curved scenographic façade of the duomo was added to give the cathedral prominence. At the opposite end, another Baroque element, a statue of St John of Nepomuk, was erected by the Austrians.

CASTELLO VISCONTEO SFORZESCO

A tall Lombard tower, probably redesigned by Bramante and always referred to as the **Bramante Tower** (*it can be climbed, tickets from the Infopoint under the tower itself*), belongs to the huge Castello Visconteo Sforzesco (*open Tues–Sun 8.30–1.30, Sat and holidays guided visits at 2.30 and 6.30; closed mid-Dec–mid-Jan*). The castle, on the site of a former fortress, was begun by Luchino Visconti in the mid-14th century. On a raised site, its was formerly connected to the piazza by a monumental entrance (destroyed) beneath the tower. Enlarged and embellished by his successors, it was transformed by Ludovico il Moro (with the help of Bramante) into a very grand ducal palace, built around an expansive central courtyard (today partly used as an open-air cinema in summer). It has remarkable **columned stables** (to the right as you enter from the Bramante Tower) and the beautiful airy **Loggia delle Dame** (to the left). The loggia overlooks the former Corte delle Dame, where Il Moro's wife, Beatrice d'Este, once had her apartments. From here you can enter the extraordinary **Strada Coperta**, a raised covered way which Luchino Visconti built to connect his new residence with the old castle, the Rocca Vecchia. It takes the form of a wide, brick-vaulted roadway on two levels. The lower level (*open 9–5 or 6*) takes you back into the gateway in the town walls.

There are several museums housed inside the castle precinct, all signposted.

Leonardiana: This ambitious museum (*open Tues–Sun 10.30–6.30, T: 0381 630310, leonardiana.it*) aims to display copies of all the known works of Leonardo da Vinci: codices, notebooks, sketches of inventions, sculpture, painting and the famous *Last Supper*. Particular attention is paid to the great polymath's activities in Lombardy (in the field of engineering as well as the fine arts) and there are some good copies of his works. It is particularly interesting to compare the two versions of the *Madonna of the Rocks* (now held by the Louvre and the National Gallery, London). There is also a detailed section on his proposed equestrian monument to Francesco Sforza. When Leonardo arrived in Milan from Florence, bringing with him the gift of a silver lyre shaped like a horse's head, an instrument of his own design, to be presented to Ludovico Il Moro, he had already been commissioned by Ludovico to produce the equestrian monument to the founder of the dynasty. Sadly, it was never carried out (*see p. 66*).

Pinacoteca Civica (*open Tues–Fri 2–5.30, Sat, Sun and holidays 10–6; free*). The collection is formed around a core of donations by the local artist Casimiro Ottone (d. 1942), who restored the sgraffito decoration in Piazza Ducale. A great many of the works are by Ottone himself, from all stages of his *oeuvre*. There are some good early paintings by Bernardino Ferrari.

Museo Internazionale della Calzatura, or MIC (*open Tues–Fri 2–5.30, Sat, Sun and holidays 10–6; museocalzaturavigevano.it; free*). This International Shoe Museum presents examples through the ages from this great industry of Vigevano. A patten said to have belonged to Beatrice d'Este, wife of Ludovico il Moro, is one of the star exhibits. Others are a mauve fishskin sandal of 1930 and the scarlet papal pumps of St John Paul II. The display goes right up to the present, with modern bling by Giuseppe Zanotti and Alexander McQueen.

Museo Archeologico (*open Tues–Sat 8.30–1.30*). The collection of artefacts from Vigevano and the surrounding Lomellina region, covering the age of the Celtic migrations, the Roman period, late antiquity and the early Middle Ages, is displayed partly in the Castello's magnificent 15th-century stable block. A new exhibition space was opened in 2018. There is some particularly lovely coloured glassware.

THE DUOMO

The duomo's curved façade, its most memorable feature, was designed by the Spanish-born theologian and mathematician Juan Caramuel y Lobkowitz. Caramuel died in Vigevano in 1682, just a couple of years after the completion of his grand work.

The interior of the cathedral (1532–1612; *closed in the middle of the day*) is interesting for its paintings by the 16th-century Lombard school. On the left wall of the Chapel of St Charles Borromeo, right of the crossing, is a lovely altarpiece attributed to Bernardino Ferrari, of *St Thomas Becket with St Helen and St Agatha* (1510). The predella includes a scene of St Thomas's murder though it is shown taking place in the open air, not in Canterbury cathedral. The third north chapel has another work by Ferrari (also 1510), a polyptych with a central *Madonna and Child*, a *Pietà* above, and *Sts Dominic, James, Christopher and Francis* surrounding. The predella has scenes from the life of St James. The duomo also has a notable treasury containing some fine tapestries.

MUSEO DELL'IMPRENDITORIA VIGEVANESE

This museum of Vigevano's industrial heritage is housed in Palazzo Merula, on a street a short way north of Piazza Ducale (*Via Merula 40; open April–Oct Sun 3–6, at other times by appointment; T: 0381 692303; free*). The building, once home to a former convent of Dominican nuns, later became an orphanage and now houses the local history archive as well as the small museum. Old shoemaking machines are arranged in the cloister, together with large painted wooden statues of Sts Crispin and Crispinian, patron saints of cobblers. The exhibition rooms are on the upper floor (you go upstairs past faded frescoes, including an *Annunciation*). There are displays on the model farm of Sforzesca (*see below*) as well as on Vigevano's two most important historic industries, silk weaving and shoemaking.

Just two kilometres southeast of Vigevano, along Corso Pavia, is the large, walled, four-square **Sforzesca**, a model farm designed by Guglielmo da Camino for Ludovico il Moro in 1486. The duke experimented with sheep-breeding here as well as with the cultivation of silkworms. Today it is in a very dilapidated condition.

THE LOMELLINA

The western part of Pavia province, between the Ticino, Sesia and Po rivers, is known as the Lomellina. Rice has been grown here for many years: the first grain was apparently planted by Gian Galeazzo Sforza in 1482. The ancient capital of the region is **Lomello** (*map p. 470, B3*), interesting for its medieval monuments, including Santa Maria Maggiore (11th century) and its baptistery (5th century; upper part rebuilt in the 8th century). The chief town of the Lomellina today, however, is **Mortara**, which offers a fine cathedral, an ancient pilgrimage church set amid paddy fields on the outskirts, and notable culinary delicacies.

MORTARA
Homage to mothers and working women (1939).

MORTARA

Mortara (*Atlas B, A3*) is a sleepy place today, immersed in mists rising off the Ticino, surrounded by fields and canals, with here and there a regimented stand of poplar trees and all the roadside verges overgrown with wild hops and evening primrose. In the Middle Ages it was significant as a halting place on the Via Francigena pilgrim route to Rome. Much later, in 1849, it was the scene of an Austrian victory in the first War of Italian Independence. Today there is no trace of this sanguinary past. The presiding atmosphere is one of peace. And butcher's shops and delicatessens all over town sell the local goose salami as well as *ravioli al brasato* (stuffed with beef ragout). If you arrive in or leave Mortara by train, be sure to notice the brick Rationalist building just outside the railway station (Piazza Marconi 2). Designed in 1939 by Cesare Perelli, it has a large frieze by Eros Pellini: *La madre di famiglia e la donna che lavora*. The main sights of Mortara are as follows.

SAN LORENZO
The principal church is this basilica, dedicated to St Lawrence, which stands in a square facing the back of the Municipio (Town Hall). The wide brick façade, in the Lombard Gothic style, was built between 1375 and 1380, with a rose window, lateral lancets and

MORTARA

The Baptism of Christ, signed 14th-century fresco in the church of Sant'Albino:
'Johanes de Midiolano me pinxit' (Giovanni of Milan painted me).

a central portal richly decorated with terracotta frames. On the slender piers flanking the main door and the wider pier closest to the street are faded frescoes of Amicus and Amelius, paladins of Charlemagne, and Albinus his confessor (*see Sant'Albino, below*). In the interior, the wide nave is separated from the aisles by composite brick columns. The first north chapel (the baptistery) has a copy of Paris Bordone's *Baptism of Christ*, now in the Brera in Milan. In the centre of the aisle is a chapel with a very fine 15th-century altar of the *Nativity*, in carved, painted and gilded limewood, by the local master Lorenzo da Mortara. At the end of the same aisle is the Chapel of the Sacred

Heart with an altarpiece by Pogliaghi. On the south side is a *Madonna and Child with Sts Sebastian and Roch* (1527) by Gerolamo Giovenone. The Chapel of the Rosary has a large altarpiece with a central panel by Bernardino Lanino, signed and dated 1578. In the Cappella Ambrosiana, also on the south side, is a *Crucifixion* by Il Cerano (1610).

In the shallow sanctuary is a venerated 16th-century wooden statue of St Lawrence. Above the high altar rises a baldacchino with interior decoration in charming mock-Palaeochristian style, reminiscent of the mosaics of Ravenna.

SANTA CROCE

Placed slantwise facing a crossroads, this is a church of ancient foundation though rebuilt by Pellegrino Tibaldi in the late 16th century. In the south aisle is an altarpiece of the *Adoration of the Magi*, signed and dated by Bernardino Lanino (1553). On the pilaster between the first and second north chapels is a Carrara marble impression of a foot, said to be that of Christ—a very dubious relic.

SANT'ALBINO

To get to the pilgrimage church of Sant'Albino, once the chief place of worship in Mortara, follow the main street (Corso Cavour) out of town and, at the roundabout, follow the brown 'Via Francigena' signs. The road soon becomes narrow and peaceful, taking you past a derelict factory building and between rice paddies. Across the main SP494, you will see the slim bell-tower of Sant'Albino rising in front of you. If the church is locked, ring for admittance at the adjoining custodian's house.

The origins of the church go back to the 4th century but it has been altered and restructured many times since then. The bell-tower was knocked to the ground by Milanese troops in 1253 and completely rebuilt. The most famous legend concerning the church goes back to the year 773, when Charlemagne fought his great battle against the Lombards under Desiderius near this spot. Two of his paladins, Amicus and Amelius, were killed in the fighting and were buried here. In 801 a monk by the name of Albinus, Charlemagne's confessor, founded a church and monastery here, which survived until its suppression by Napoleon. Today the old conventual buildings belong to the town of Mortara.

The interior of the simple little church is notable for the remains of frescoes (restored in 2000) on the right-hand wall of the sanctuary. They are the work of a certain Giovanni from Milan and are dated to 1410. They show *St Anthony Abbot*, the *Baptism of Christ* and the *Madonna Enthroned with Sts Albinus, Augustine and James*. The fresco of St Lawrence in the lower register is by a later, unknown hand. Also on the right wall of the sanctuary, on some of the bricks, are scratched dates left by pilgrims in the 11th–14th centuries.

Protected by bars in a niche in the right-hand wall of the nave is a small urn containing human remains discovered here in 1928. The results of forensic tests and carbon dating carried out in 1999 suggest that the bones may indeed be about the right age to be those of Charlemagne's two paladins.

MAGENTA

Magenta (*Atlas B, A2*) is an old-fashioned town with a single long main street, pedestrianised in its central section and lined with shops and a few cafés. The main church is the enormous **San Martino**, its exterior decorated with mock Renaissance carvings and white marble roundels of saints. It was begun in 1893 and consecrated ten years later.

In a park very close to the railway station are **monuments to the Battle of Magenta**. On a tall plinth by Luca Beltrami stands a heroic statue of General MacMahon, who led the combined forces of France and Sardinia to victory here over the Austrians, commanded by Ferenc Gyulay, on 4th June 1859, paving the way for the capture of Milan for Italy. Napoleon III, whose forces were in alliance with Vittorio Emanuele, made MacMahon Marshal of France and Duke of Magenta on the very night of the victory. The statue is by Luigi Secchi. Behind it is a tall obelisk, inside which (*no entry*) is an ossuary crypt containing the bones of over 4,000 soldiers, from both sides of the conflict.

In 1860, a London manufacturer of synthetic dyes Simpson, Maule and Nicholson, patented the name 'roseine' for a reddish-purple colorant. The same colour, obtained by a different process, had been patented in France as fuchsine the year before. The name was soon changed to magenta. The battle had so captured the public imagination that it was felt a dye bearing its name would be sure to be popular.

PRACTICAL INFORMATION

GETTING AROUND

• **By rail:** For **Abbiategrasso**, **Vigevano** and **Mortara**, trains from Milan leave from Porta Genova (*map p. 26, B4*; Metro 2). Some trains also leave from San Cristoforo (M2 to Romolo and then the S9, or tram 14 from Duomo and other central stations), but it is a much less pleasant place to wait for a train. Journey time to Abbiategrasso is just under 25mins, to Vigevano c. 30mins and to Mortara 45mins.

Magenta is easily reached from Milan by trains on the line to Novara, which leave from Stazione Centrale. Journey time c. 22mins.

INFORMATION OFFICES

Abbiategrasso Infopoint in the Castello Visconteo entranceway. **Vigevano** Infopoint in the Castello Visconteo Sforzesco gatehouse.

WHERE TO STAY

ABBIATEGRASSO
€ **Nuovo Albergo Italia**. Old hotel behind the Castello Visconteo. Fully

renovated in a plain and spartan style. Basic, clean and comfortable; no frills. *Piazza Castello 31. T: 02 9496 5228, nuovoalbergoitalia.it.*

VIGEVANO

€ **Locanda San Bernardo**. Simple guesthouse decorated with charm, just a few steps from the centre of town. *Corso Novara 2. T: 0381 691035, locandasanbernardo.it.*

WHERE TO EAT

ABBIATEGRASSO

€–€€ **Croce di Malta**. Traditional *trattoria* right beside the Castello Visconteo. Cosy indoor eating in winter, outside in the piazza in summer. *Osso bucco* (*oss bus*) with risotto is the house speciality. Good value lunch menu on weekdays. Closed Wed lunch. *Piazza Castello 24. T: 02 946 9210, trattoriacrocedimalta.it.*

€€ **Taverna del Torchio**. Restaurant opened in 2018 in a lofty space with a fine old wine press (*torchio*). Elegant without being stiff. Atmospheric and central. *Via Misericordia 7/9. T: 02 946 5122.*

€ **Besuschio**. A *pasticceria* and bar under the arcades on Piazza Marconi. Good for drinks, cakes and snacks..

MORTARA

€ **Il Cuuc**. Restaurant in the Albergo San Michele, close to the railway station but still very central. A good place to come to try the local goose salami, risotto and other specialities. Closed Sun eve and Mon. *Corso Garibaldi 20. T: 0384 99106.*

For drinks, try **Il Baretto**, a good wine bar (*Corso Garibaldi 126*). And should you happen to find yourself with time on your hands at the railway station, there is a surprisingly good café there, **Le Rotaie**.

VIGEVANO

There are plenty of places for drinks, snacks and full meals, with choice of sun or shade depending on the time of day, on **Piazza Ducale**.

LOCAL SPECIALITIES

Mortara is in the heart of the rice-growing Lomellina, which makes it a good place to try risotto. The local speciality is the *salame d'oca*, salami made from goose meat.

In **Vigevano** they make lemon-flavoured biscuits called Bramantini, each one stamped with an image of the Bramante Tower. The signature pastry of Pasticceria Dante (*Via Dante Alighieri 6*) is the Dolceriso del Moro, a cake with a soft centre made of rice flour, almonds and pine nuts flavoured with rosewater and candied citron. Tradition asserts that it was invented by Beatrice d'Este, wife of Ludovico il Moro, in 1491.

FESTIVALS AND EVENTS

Every year on the Sun closest to 4th June, **Magenta** re-enacts its historic battle in full period dress. In **Mortara**, a festival dedicated to the celebrated goose salami is held in late Sept (*sagradelsalamedoca.it*). **Vigevano** holds a historic pageant, with games, feasting and costumes, twice a year, in May and Oct (*paliodivigevano.it*).

Varese & Environs

Varese is a pleasant, industrious town, worth visiting for its museum and its Sacro Monte, which has beautiful 17th-century chapels. There are various places of interest nearby, notably Castiglione Olona with its Renaissance works of art and frescoes by Masolino; and Castelseprio, south of Castiglione, which is one of the most important Lombard sites in Italy. There are a number of villas in the province with fine gardens open to the public. These include the Villa Della Porta Bozzolo at Casalzuigno, Villa Cicogna Mozzoni at Bisuschio, and the Palazzo Estense in Varese itself.

VARESE

A flourishing industrial town of about 80,000 inhabitants, with a busy, civic air, Varese (*Atlas D, A3*) has a few attractive streets of old houses with fine courtyards. After the opening of the state and Nord Milano railway lines to Milan (only 50km away) in 1865 and 1886, many Milanese built their summer homes in the environs, and some Art Nouveau villas also survive.

THE CITY CENTRE

To get to the centre from Varese Nord station, walk west in a straight line up Via Como, past the large **Post Office**, a striking building in crimson brick with four huge columns surmounted by giant allegorical figures (Angiolo Mazzoni, 1933). Cross Via Cavour, and beyond the next crossroads, a narrow alley brings you out into the rather stark **Piazza San Vittore** with its church of the same name, built in 1580–1625, probably to designs by Pellegrino Tibaldi. It has a Neoclassical façade by Vienna-born architect Leopold Pollack. In the interior are some good paintings by Morazzone (first and third north altars) and Il Cerano (first south; the memorable *Mass of St Gregory*, 1615–17), and a magnificent 17th-century carved wooden pulpit, choir gallery and organ loft. The baptistery behind (opened by volunteers from Italia Nostra; *at the time of writing, Wed and Fri 4–6, 2nd Sun of the month 3.30–5.30; for updates and to book an alternative time, see italianostravarese.org*) dates from the 12th century. It has an interesting plan and 14th-century Lombard frescoes on the right wall. The unfinished 13th-century font has been raised to reveal the earlier 8th-century total-immersion font.

Separated from Piazza Vittore by a War Memorial arcade is **Piazza del Podestà** with the Palazzo del Pretorio, which until the 18th century was the seat of the city government. A bell tolled from its roof to summon the people to assemblies and signal the time to close hostelries and extinguish fires. It is now cloaked in an 18th-century façade. From here, the attractive **Corso Matteotti**, arcaded on both sides with shops and a tea room (Zamberletti at no. 20), leads to **Piazza Monte Grappa**, laid out in 1927–35 following Varese's nomination as capital of the province and surrounded by interesting examples of Fascist-era architecture, including a tall clock tower (with public toilets in its base). Via Marcobi and Via Sacco lead to the huge, monumental **Palazzo Estense** (now the Town Hall), built by Giuseppe Bianchi in 1766–71 for Francesco III d'Este, Duke of Modena, as the seat of his imperial court. Called by Stendhal the Versailles of Milan, it is one of the best palaces of its period in Italy. The gardens behind it are open to the public. They were laid out in 1837, in imitation of the imperial gardens of Schönbrunn in Vienna (after Duke Francesco's death, his dukedom passed to the crown of Austria). Paths lead up past a fountain to terraces with a good view of the Alps, and a little children's playground in a wood.

VILLA MIRABELLO (MUSEI CIVICI)

On the hill above Palazzo Estense is the 18th–19th-century Villa Mirabello, built in an eccentric *cottage orné* style with a tall turret, surrounded by a garden laid out in the English manner but not terribly well kept. The view from the edge of the garden is, as the name suggests, fine, looking out across the rooftops to Lago di Varese. The villa houses the Musei Civici (*open Tues–Sun 9.30–12.30 & 2–6; cspa-va.it*), with prehistoric and Roman material (including a fine 1st-century bronze stamnos from Bruzzano Milanese), medieval material, and, displayed in a room of its own, the mummy of a small boy who died of pneumonia between 1594 and 1646. There are tomb finds from the Iron Age Golasecca culture (black glazed pottery with incised geometric designs and grave goods from a warrior tomb at Sesto Calende, including remains of a chariot and horse harness) and detailed displays on the lake-dwelling people of Lago di Varese (including pretty glass beads known as *perle delle palafitte*, with decorative spiral inlay). One of the highlights is the Coppa Cagnola, a delicate 4th-century Roman 'cage cup' of reticulated glass. A final section looks at Varese during the Risorgimento. Printed exhortations to the people of Lombardy from Garibaldi and Vittorio Emanuele II are on display, couched in rousing language. At the time of writing there were plans to open a display here of works by Renato Guttuso, the Sicilian-born Socialist Realist artist who is an honorary citizen of Varese and who lived and worked for some years at Velate, at the foot of the Sacro Monte hill.

The museum has a sister museum, the Museo Preistorico at Biandronno (*see p. 188*).

NORTH OF THE CENTRE

On a low hill is the residential district of Biumo Superiore. Here is the 18th-century **Villa Panza**, which was donated to the FAI (Fondo per l'Ambiente Italiano) in 1996 by Giuseppe Panza, together with over 100 works from his collection of 20th-century American art (most of which was sold, and partially donated, to the Museum of Contemporary Art in Los Angeles and the Guggenheim Museum of New York). The villa (*open Tues–Sun 10–6; fondoambiente.it*) also contains furniture and African and pre-Columbian sculpture, and is surrounded by a park.

On the western outskirts of Varese is the **Castello di Masnago** (*Via Cola di Rienzo 2; open Tues–Sun 9.30–12.30 & 2–6*), a 15th-century building which incorporates a 12th-century tower. It is adorned with 15th-century frescoes of court life, in the International Gothic style. The painting collection contains works by Camillo Procaccini, Francesco Hayez and Giacomo Balla. There is also a small museum of contemporary art. The park is open to the public daily.

THE SACRO MONTE

Varese's 'Holy Mountain', a UNESCO World Heritage site, rises on the northern outskirts of the town. It is one of numerous shrines in Piedmont and Lombardy bearing the same name: all were erected during the Counter-Reformation (*see p. 209*). In this Varese version, the pretty chapels lining a broad winding path some 2km long up the steep incline, were designed to be seen by pilgrims on their way up the hill (a walk of c. 40mins, though longer if you linger to look at the chapels).

The Sacro Monte can be reached from the centre of Varese either by car or by bus. The road climbs up through the residential district of Sant'Ambrogio, with numerous handsome villas and their gardens, to end in a broad piazza with the tunnel of the funicular railway and a pleasant café/restaurant. The funicular (*combined bus and funicular tickets available*) operates daily in high season and at weekends at other times of year (*see varesesimuove.it*). The path to the first chapel (**Prima Cappella**) begins behind the restaurant, briefly becoming a tarmac road and then, at an archway, turning to cobbles. The archway marks the beginning of the ascent up the cobbled Via delle Cappelle. The Latin inscription reads: 'Come unto me all ye that desire me.'

The chapels, each of different design, are all works by the local architect Giuseppe Bernasconi, from 1604 onwards. They are all kept locked but you can see the interiors (*push-button lights*) through the windows. They contain lifesize terracotta groups representing the Mysteries of the Rosary, divided into their three categories, Joyful, Sorrowful and Glorious, each heralded by a monumental archway with a fountain (*the water in at least two of these is not drinkable; on hot days, bring your own supply*). Outside the third chapel, the **Chapel of the Nativity**, is a 20th-century fresco by Renato Guttuso, depicting the *Flight into Egypt*.

SANTA MARIA DEL MONTE

At the top of the Sacro Monte is the small village of Santa Maria del Monte (880m) with a few tall houses huddled around a sanctuary church. The views (on a clear day) are stunning, taking in Como with the mountains beyond and the plain towards Milan, and in the opposite direction the Lago di Varese. Immediately on the left as you arrive in the village is the **Museo Pogliaghi** (*closed at the time of writing; T: 3288 377206, casamuseopogliaghi.it*), surrounded by a garden, in the villa that belonged to the sculptor Lodovico Pogliaghi (1857–1950). It contains his eclectic collection of works of art, archaeological material, and some of his own sculptures, including the model for the bronze doors of the duomo of Milan.

The **sanctuary church** is approached either from the north side, across a terrace with fine views and a bronze monument to Pope Paul VI (1984), or from the main west entrance, which also opens off a terrace commanding views of five lakes: Lago di Varese in the foreground, Comabbio beyond it, Biandronno and Monate to the right, and further right again, the tip of Lake Maggiore. The church dates originally from 1472. On the high altar (1662) is a venerated 14th-century image of the Madonna.

Waymarked roads and paths continue from Santa Maria del Monte to the **Campo dei Fiori nature reserve**. Monte delle Tre Croci (1033m) offers a wonderful view (and an observatory). Here in 1908–12, Giuseppe Sommaruga built a huge hotel, restaurant and funicular station, all fine Art Nouveau buildings that have been abandoned for half a century.

LAGO DI VARESE

West of Varese is the Lago di Varese, 8.5km long, a lake admired for its scenery by the English painter and nonsense poet Edward Lear. From **Biandronno** you can take a boat to the little **Isolino Virginia**, an island donated to the town of Varese by Marquis Gianfelice Ponti in 1962 (it is named Virginia after his grandmother). Here is the Museo Preistorico (*open March–Oct Sat, Sun and holidays 2–6*), which contains an exhibition relating to the Neolithic-to-Bronze Age lake dwellings here, built out on stilts over the water, the oldest such dwellings known.

At **Gavirate**, at the north end of the lake, is a pipe museum (*open on request*), with some 20,000 pipes from all over the world and of all periods. There is also a collection of painted ceramics with a pipe and tobacco theme. At **Voltorre**, now contiguous with Gavirate, there is an interesting Romanesque Benedictine cloister, of brick, which is used for art exhibitions.

CASTIGLIONE OLONA

Castiglione Olona (*Atlas D, A4*) is south of Varese, just west of the SS233. The old medieval nucleus was practically rebuilt, in the style of a Renaissance ideal city, by Cardinal Branda Castiglioni (1350–1443) when he returned from a stay in Florence, bringing with him Masolino da Panicale, who produced superb frescoes which still survive here. The buildings that the cardinal commissioned for his native town include the fine Collegiata on the hilltop as well as palaces and civic institutions. Today the huddling centre is an extraordinary ensemble of narrow cobbled streets and tall

SACRO MONTE OF VARESE
The Flight into Egypt by Renato Guttuso (detail), outside the Chapel of the Nativity.

houses with fine arched doorways giving on to wide courtyards, still with a markedly old-fashioned atmosphere. Approaching from the Venegono Superiore side, you descend from modern Castiglione into the old town through the Porta di Levante. On the other side of town, the road descends steeply to the rushing Olona river, spanned by a medieval arched bridge.

The main square, Piazza Garibaldi, has two bars, a church, the entrance to the cardinal's palace (now a museum) and an excellent second-hand bookshop, La bottega delle idee.

MUSEO CIVICO BRANDA CASTIGLIONI
Open Oct–March Tues–Sat 9–12 & 3–6, Sun 3–6; April–Sept Tues–Sat 9–12 & 3–6, Sun and holidays 10.30–12.30 & 3–6.

This large town palace which the cardinal embellished and where he died is now a museum. The little courtyard through which it is entered has an interesting exterior. From the room now used as the ticket office, stairs lead both up to the *piano nobile*, where the main rooms are to be seen, and down to the **Chapel of St Martin**, which has frescoes by the great Sienese artist Vecchietta, painted in the 1430s. You enter the chapel through what was once the sanctuary, with God the Father depicted in the vault. In the next room, in a niche, is a *Man of Sorrows/Crucifixion* and opposite it, a scene showing a procession of bishops and monks with, on the right, a portrait of Eugene IV, who was pope at the time that this chapel was decorated. On the wall to the right of this is a procession of female saints shown coming out of a city gateway, led by St Ursula with a pennant of the Resurrection and with St Lucy bringing up the rear, bearing her own eyes (her attribute) on a dish. The Evangelists with their symbols occupy the vault.

The upper floor is approached via a mezzanine **loggia** (glassed in in the 19th century) with a wooden coffered ceiling and faint traces of a fresco cycle by Paolo Schiavo. Low down on one wall, below a very ruined shape thought to have been a likeness of Sigismund of Luxembourg in the guise of Liberality (*for more on Sigismund, see opposite*) is a frescoed still life with jars, attributed to Vecchietta, interesting as an early example of a depiction of objects in their own right.

The **main hall** has a Renaissance fireplace with Baroque stucco decoration on the walls, above family portraits (including one of Branda Castiglioni). The **bedchamber** (furnished as such, although it is more likely to have been used as a reception room) has very unusual allegorical frescoes; dated 1423, showing ten trees against a vermilion ground and white putti picking all sorts of fruit: coconuts, pomegranates, apples. Playful though their gestures are intended to be, they have sinisterly adult faces. Off this opens the so-called **study**, with a fresco of c. 1435 attributed to Masolino showing a strange landscape of isolated rocky outcrops, like whipped meringues, topped by towery cities and with two other walled cities in the valley. This bizarre topography is said to be inspired by the countryside round the Hungarian city of Veszprém (Castiglioni had been sent to Hungary as papal legate by the antipope John XXIII; *for more, see opposite*). In the corner by the window are two frescoed busts (one of them effaced), interpreted as Justice embracing Peace.

Inquire at the Museo Civico Branda Castiglioni to visit the other museum in the lower town, **MAP** (Museo Arte Plastica; *combined ticket available*), a collection of art from the 1970s displayed in a 14th-century palace opening off a ramshackle courtyard. Artists represented include Giacomo Balla and Man Ray.

CHIESA DI VILLA

Opposite the palace, preceded by a garden courtyard, is the Chiesa di Villa, with an unusual dome, built and decorated in 1431–44 by local masons and sculptors in a centrally planned style, in imitation of the church of the Holy Sepulchre. It has a handsome exterior, and two colossal carved saints (St Anthony Abbot and St Christopher) flank the fine portal. In the lovely, simple interior, which owes much to the Florentine style of Brunelleschi, are six stone and terracotta statues high up on corbels (including, on either side of the triumphal arch, a polychrome *Annunciatory Angel* and *Virgin Annunciate* that have been attributed to Vecchietta). In the apse is a small fresco of the *Resurrection* and a delightful frescoed frieze of red, yellow and white flowers on *trompe l'oeil* drapery. Beneath the altar is a 15th-century stone statue of the *Dead Christ*.

BRANDA CASTIGLIONI

Lawyer, humanist, patron of the arts, papal diplomat and friend, confidant and advisor to Sigismund of Luxembourg, future Holy Roman Emperor, this remarkable man was born in Milan in 1350. He studied civil and canon law and renounced a princely lifestyle in favour of service to the Church. By Boniface IX he was nominated papal legate on successive missions to Germany, Flanders and Hungary, and so began a distinguished career. He took part in several ecclesiastical councils aimed at healing the papal schism. In 1410 he was sent on another mission to Hungary by the antipope John XXIII, who created him cardinal in the following year, attached to the church of San Clemente in Rome. In 1411 he was made Count of Veszprém by Sigismund (King of Hungary since 1387), and from then until 1424 administrated the bishopric of the Hungarian city of Veszprém. In 1413 he was a delegate at the Council of Constance, convoked in Lodi, at which King Sigismund was also present. The papal schism was finally brought to an end in 1417 with the election of Pope Martin V, who sent Castiglioni to Bohemia to extirpate the heresy of Jan Hus. It was at this time too (1421) that Castiglioni announced his intention to rebuild and beautify Castiglione Olona. The Collegiata was consecrated there in 1425, the same year that Castiglioni met Masolino, who was at work in Hungary together with a number of Florentines in the wake of the *condottiere* Pippo Spano, who was in King Sigismund's service. In 1431, Pope Martin V was succeeded by Eugene IV, whom Castiglioni supported in his efforts to reconcile the churches of East and West at the Council of Florence, successor to the Council of Basel convoked by his predecessor. Castiglioni died in his palace in Castiglione Olona in 1443.

THE COLLEGIATA

A cobbled lane leads uphill past the 19th-century Town Hall, which incorporates a school building founded by the cardinal in 1423 to teach grammar and music. Above the door is a bust of the cardinal dating from 1503, and on the left is a fresco from the early 15th century. The courtyard dates from the 18th century. Opposite the entrance façade is a pretty wall fountain.

The road continues up to the top of the hill, where the Collegiata was built in 1422–5, replacing a feudal castle. It stands on a broad forecourt above the Olona river. Surmounting the west portal is a lunette of 1428, in local Malnate grey sandstone, showing the Madonna with Branda Castiglioni kneeling at her feet, accompanied by St Ambrose and St Clement (titular saint of the church in Rome to which Castiglioni was attached as cardinal), as well as the titular saints of the Collegiata, Stephen (with a stone) and Lawrence (with his gridiron).

The ticket office for the Collegiata and baptistery is at the end of the forecourt (*open Oct–March Tues–Sat 9.30–12.30 & 2.30–5.30, Sun and holidays 10–1 & 3–6; April–Sept Tues–Sun 10–1 & 3–6; 1st Sun of month 10–6, museocollegiata.it*). The Collegiata is entered through a side door (with a lunette of the *Man of Sorrows*), to which you are shown after buying your ticket. The well-proportioned and luminous interior, with beautiful flooring and rippling brown and caramel brick, has Gothic Revival decoration in the aisles. In the sanctuary is the tomb (1443) of Branda Castiglioni, with

CASTIGLIONE OLONA
Detail of Masolino's fresco cycle in the Baptistery: *Beheading of the Baptist.*

his effigy supported by four statues of the Virtues. On the apse vault are six frescoed scenes from the life of the Virgin, cleverly tapered to fit the narrow vault segments. They are as follows: *Annunciation to the Shepherds, Annunciation, Coronation of the Virgin, Presentation in the Temple, Adoration of the Magi, Assumption* and are signed by Masolino (under the figure of Joseph in the first scene: '*Masolinus de Florentia pinsit*'). In the lunettes below and above the windows are scenes from the lives of St Stephen and St Lawrence by Paolo Schiavo and Vecchietta. The 15th-century bronze candelabrum showing St George and the Dragon was made in Flanders.

THE BAPTISTERY AND MUSEUM

In a former tower of the feudal castle, at the end of the cobbled yard furthest from the Collegiata's north entrance, is the baptistery, formerly the family chapel before the Collegiata was built. It is a beautiful little building dating from 1435 (with a

CASTIGLIONE OLONA
Detail of Masolino's fresco cycle in the Baptistery: *Salome presents the Head of the Baptist to Herodias.*

modern floor). It is adorned with frescoes of the life of St John the Baptist, Masolino's masterpiece, executed in 1435. We see the Baptist in prison, with the black-clad hired assassin preparing to do the deed, and the *Banquet of Herod* set in a long loggia, with the seated Herodias, serene and dispassionate, receiving the Baptist's golden-bearded head on the far right. In the sanctuary is the *Baptism of Christ*, with a splendid group of robing and disrobing figures on the right and the river disappearing into the distance. In the vault of the sanctuary is *God the Father* and on the soffit of the arch, angels and Doctors of the Church. In the main vault are the symbols of the Evangelists: the scheme chosen for the vault decoration is the same as that of the chapel in Palazzo Branda Castiglioni. The other frescoes (including a view of Rome on the entrance wall) are damaged. The font is a 15th-century Venetian work.

Between the Collegiata and the baptistery, an enfilade of rooms serves as a museum with a miscellany of objects that have survived from the rich treasury (pillaged over the centuries) that the cardinal donated to the church. They include monstrances and other liturgical objects, beautiful illuminated manuscript antiphonals with notation for Ambrosian chant, a wooden *Ecce Homo* by a 16th-century Lombard sculptor and two Florentine paintings, a section of a polyptych showing the *Annunciation* by Apollonio di Giovanni (1415–c. 1465) c. 1440 and a gold-ground *Crucifixion* by Neri di Bicci (c. 1465).

CASTELSEPRIO

South of Castiglione, on a plateau in a wood above the Olona valley, is the extensive archaeological area of Castelseprio (*generally open Tues–Sun until dusk, but check on www.unescovarese.com/castelseprio*). On the site of a late Bronze Age settlement, it includes the ruins of the late Roman castrum of *Sibrium*, occupied throughout the Lombard period (AD 568–771). A fortified *borgo* grew up around the camp, but this was destroyed by Milan in 1287. The site is well labelled and includes the remains of two churches, an octagonal baptistery, defensive walls, towers, medieval houses, and cisterns and wells. The most important church, **Santa Maria Foris Portas**, is a short distance away from the castrum. It has a remarkable plan with lateral apses and windows in the corners of the nave. The building dates from somewhere between the 7th and 9th centuries; it was restored and partly reconstructed in the 1940s, when the frescoes were discovered, and remains of its black-and-white marble floor survive. In the apse are extraordinary mural paintings with scenes from the apocryphal Gospels illustrating the infancy of Christ, including the *Nativity* with the reclining figure of the Madonna, and the *Journey to Bethlehem* (with a graceful donkey). They are in an Oriental (Alexandrian) style and are thought to date from the 8th century.

Part of the camp of *Sibrium* extended across the Olona to the site later occupied by the **Monastero di Torba** (*open March–Sept Wed–Sun 10–6, Oct–Feb Wed–Sun 10–5, last entry 1hr before closing*), which is reached by a path through woods (c. 200m) or—much longer—by a (signposted) road from Gornate Olona. Part of the ruined defensive walls have been exposed and the massive corner tower survives, both dating from the 5th century. A Benedictine nunnery was established here in the late Lombard period (8th century) and the conventual buildings were occupied up until 1480. In a pretty position at the foot of a wooded hill, they were donated to the FAI (Fondo per l'Ambiente Italiano) in 1976. The early medieval church has an 8th-century crypt and a 13th-century apse. Opposite is a 15th-century farmhouse built above the ancient defensive walls, which incorporates the refectory, a splendid old room with a fireplace. The corner tower, on 5th–6th-century foundations, was also occupied by the nuns in the 8th century. Steps lead up past an oven, which may date from the 12th century, to the first floor of the tower and a room used as a burial place (with an 8th-century fresco of a nun named Aliberga). The room above functioned as an oratory, and it contains fascinating Carolingian (late 8th-century) frescoes of female saints and nuns (uncovered in the 20th century).

THE VALGANNA & VALCUVIA

The SS233 leads north from Varese through the Valganna, the narrow valley of the Olona, passing the little Laghetto di Ganna on the left. At the roundabout just beyond it, turn left for the **Badia di San Gemolo**, an abbey founded in 1095. It has a 12th-century church and a five-sided cloister.

Further north up the SS233 is the **Lago di Ghirla** (*Atlas D, A3*), with a bathing lido and hiking path on its west bank. At the tip of the lake, the Lugano road branches right and descends to Ponte Tresa on the frontier with Switzerland. Diverging left from Lake Ghirla, you come to **Cunardo**, known since Roman times for the production of ceramics. Just outside town on the road to Luino, on the left in Località Fornaci, are the old 18th-century pottery kilns of Ceramiche Ibis, with their conspicuous stubby chimneys. Examples of the traditional 18th-century blue-and-white ware can be seen in the Museo Poldi Pezzoli in Milan.

West of Cunardo is the Valcuvia, with hills of chestnut woods and an open landscape extending towards Lake Maggiore. At **Casalzuigno** (*Atlas D, A3*), signposted off the SS394 to the right, is the splendid Villa Della Porta Bozzolo (*open March–Sept Wed–Sun 10–6, Oct–Nov Wed–Sun 10–5; fondoambiente.it*). The villa dates from the 16th century, when it was in the centre of the huge estate purchased by the Della Porta family, and silkworms were bred in the farm buildings. Additions were made to the house in the 18th century by Gian Angelo III Della Porta, and the fine garden was laid out in the French style on the hillside. It was given to the FAI by the Bozzolo family in 1989. Beyond the parterre are four stone terraces with balustrades and statues. A cypress avenue climbs the wooded hillside behind. There is another little garden to the right of the parterre on a line with the façade of the villa, approached by a gate with statues of the Four Seasons and with an avenue of oak trees leading to a little Rococo frescoed garden house. The villa preserves elaborate frescoes by Pietro Antonio Magatti (1687–1768).

Before the turning to the villa a narrow road winds up from Casalzuigno, through a series of seemingly never-ending hairpin bends, to **Arcumeggia**, a tiny hamlet in the hills. It advertises itself as '*La galleria all'aperto dell'affresco*', open-air fresco gallery, because in 1956 the village was chosen as an artists' summer retreat and the exteriors of many of the houses have been frescoed by painters including Achille Funi and Aligi Sassu.

EASTWARDS TO LAKE LUGANO

The SS344 leads northeast from Varese, passing **Bisuschio** (*Atlas D, A3*), where the 16th-century Villa Cicogna Mozzoni, frescoed by the school of the Campi brothers and with 17th- and 18th-century furnishings, stands surrounded by a classical Renaissance garden and fine park. Today it is used mainly for weddings and as an events venue but is also open for guided tours (*April–Oct Sun and holidays 9.30–12 & 2.30–7; villacicognamozzoni.it*).

Porto Ceresio is situated at the foot of high mountains on a wide bend in Lake Lugano (270m, 52km square), a little more than half of which belongs to Switzerland; only the northeast arm and the southwest shore between Ponte Tresa and Porto Ceresio belong to Italy. There are regular boat services between all the main places along the shore.

Campione d'Italia (*Atlas D, A3*), an enclave (or more properly, an exclave) within the Swiss canton of Ticino, also belongs to Italy. Officially it uses Swiss currency but euros are also accepted. Your mobile phone might default to Swisscom (watch out for roaming charges). Campione was historically noted for its sculptors and architects; in the 13th and 14th centuries, stonemasons such as Anselmo da Campione and Bonino da Campione (*see p. 133*) made a name for themselves and for their home town. 'Campionese' is the generic term used to describe such artists from the Lugano, Como and Swiss border area. More recently, however, the village was famous for its casino, occupying a huge lakefront building by Mario Botta (2007). The Casinò, the largest in Europe, first began spinning its roulette tables in 1917, when it was set up as a way of inveigling secrets out of diplomats during WWI. In 2018 it was declared bankrupt and permanent closure was threatened, risking the loss of almost 500 jobs and raising questions about the future of the exclave, which has long been financially dependent on Casinò revenue.

PRACTICAL INFORMATION

GETTING AROUND

• **By road:** This is Milan's industrial hinterland, and traffic can be quite intense on local roads. The 233 from Milan, the shortest route in terms of distance, can also be the longest in terms of time, due to heavy local traffic: it's better to take the A8.

• **By rail: Varese** has a direct rail link to Malpensa airport (journey time c. 45mins). There is a frequent commuter service from Milan to Varese in just over 1hr, the suburban S5 train from Porta Venezia, and there are also regular Trenord services. The two train stations (one for the state railways and one for the Nord–Milano line) are only a few metres apart, a short walk from the town centre.

For **Castiglione Olona**, take a train from Milan Cadorna to Venegono Superiore (journey time c. 45mins). The old Renaissance town is 20–30mins' walk west from the station, westwards through pleasant countryside.

• **By bus:** Varese's bus station is behind Varese Nord railway station. Bus C goes every 20mins from Varese to the **Sacro Monte** (stop at the bottom of the hill, outside the funicular station). There are bus stops in the centre of town (Piazza Monte Grappa) and at the bus station. Bus tickets from the ticket office at the bus station or from coin-operated machines on the bus. The ticket is also valid on the funicular. Bus A goes to Biumo Superiore.

To get to **Castelseprio** by bus from Varese, take line N27 from the bus station. Services are infrequent, however.

Country buses run by CTPI (*www. ctpi.it*) link Varese to other towns in the province, and Lake Maggiore and Como.

INFORMATION OFFICES

Varese Piazza Monte Grappa. Closed Sun.

WHERE TO STAY

VARESE
€ **Hotel di Varese**. Small hotel in a completely modernised Liberty building. *Via Como 12. T: 0332 237559, hoteldivarese.it.*

VARESE SACRO MONTE
€€ **Colonne**. Cosy (8 rooms), with great views of the valley and a restaurant with summer seating outside. *Via Fincarà 37. T: 0332 244633, hotelcolonne.com.*

WHERE TO EAT

CASTIGLIONE OLONA
€€ **Osteria degli Artisti**. Fine-dining restaurant with a good wine list in the heart of the old Renaissance town. Only open for lunch on Sun. On Tues–Sat, dinner only. *Via Roma 40. T: 0331 859021, www.losteriadegliartisti.it.* If you visit Castiglione during the week and need some sustenance, there are two bars in the old town's main square: the Al Bistrot 'bar-paninoteca' and the Old Inn 'pub' and pizzeria.

VARESE
€€ **Osteria di Piazza Litta**. Seasonal fresh ingredients, menu changes monthly. Close to Villa Panza. Closed Mon, Sat lunch and Sun evening. *Piazza Litta 4. T: 0332 289167, osteriadipiazzalitta.it.*
In the Villa Panza is the €€ **Ristorante Luce** (*T: 0332 242199*). The bar in the **Villa Mirabello** (closed Mon) does *piadine* with a variety of fillings, simple meals and drinks. Pleasant terrace on the gardens.

VARESE (SACRO MONTE)
At the bottom of the hill before you begin the climb, is € **Linea Ottantotto**, a café and pizzeria: very pleasant either before or after tackling the Holy Mountain (*Piazza Montanari/Via Guido da Velate, T: 0332 150 6322*). At the top of the hill, in Santa Maria del Monte, the € **Ristorante Montorfano** (*Via del Santuario 74, T: 0332 227027*) has an outdoor terrace with a stunning mountain and lake panorama (as well as good food).

FESTIVALS AND EVENTS

Falò di Sant'Antonio, festival in honour of Varese's patron saint, culminating in a huge bonfire (the *falò*), 16–17 Jan. The **Varese Gospel Festival**, which has been going for some 20 years, takes place in July (*varesegospel.it*). The *Estate Varesina* is Varese's summer festival, with open-air cinema, theatre, music and other events.

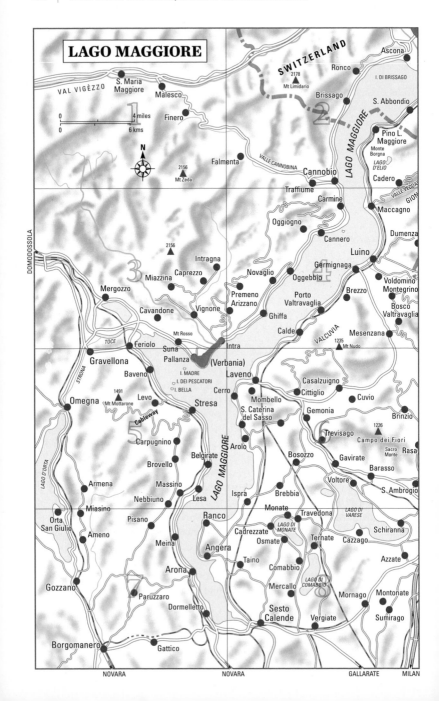

Lake Maggiore

S urrounded by snow-capped mountains, Lake Maggiore (*map p. 470, B2*; 121km square), dividing Lombardy from Piedmont, is the second largest lake in Italy after Lake Garda. The north end (about one-fifth of its area) is in Switzerland.

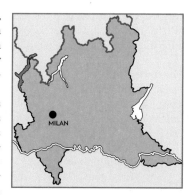

Lake Maggiore became well known as a resort in the 19th century, visited for its romantic scenery and good climate. The lake's other name is Verbano, from the Latin *Lacus Verbanus*, derived from the vervain (*verbena*) that grows on its shores. The Borromeo family have been substantial landowners here since the 15th century: St Charles Borromeo was born here.

LAKE MAGGIORE HIGHLIGHTS

Arona (*map 7; p. 200*) birthplace of St Charles Borromeo, is a pretty town with an altarpiece by Gaudenzio Ferrari in its main church. **Angera** (*map 7; p. 212*), on the opposite bank, preserves its Borromeo castle.

The central part of the lake, around **Stresa** (*map 5; p. 201*), is particularly lovely. From the top of the Mottarone cable car there are stunning mountain views.

The islands (*map 5; p. 202*), especially **Isola Bella** and **Isola dei Pescatori**, make an excellent day trip.

There is a beautiful woodland walk to the Sacro Monte of **Ghiffa** (*map 4; p. 207*) and a dramatic small gorge just behind **Cannobio** (*map 2; p. 210*).

The finest garden on the lake is at **Villa Taranto** in Verbania (*map 5; p. 206*).

Luino (*map 4; p. 211*) is famous for its weekly Wednesday market.

THE PIEDMONT SHORE

ARONA

Arona (*map 7*) is an ancient town looking across the lake to Angera. It came under Visconti rule in 1277 and was a fief of the Borromeo from 1439 to 1797. At the north end of town is the **Parco della Rocca**, where a Borromeo fortress once stood on the high cliff, the companion to the surviving fortress of Angera. Between them they controlled access to the lake. It was in the Arona fortress that St Charles Borromeo was born in 1538. It was destroyed by Napoleonic troops in 1800. From the little park on the waterfront, near the ferry landing, there are excellent views of Angera and its castle.

The town centre
Parallel to the waterfront is Via Cavour, the shopping street, and above that (access along narrow lanes) opens the cobbled Piazza San Graziano. Here, in a wing of the former covered market hall, is **Archeo Museo**, a small archaeology museum (*Piazza San Graziano 34; open Tues 10–12, Sat–Sun 3.30–6.30; T: 0322 48294, archeomuseo.it*). Its collection, which covers the lower part of Lake Maggiore, includes material from the Golasecca culture (*see p. 213*).

From Piazza San Graziano a stepped street leads up past the yellow and white church of the **Santi Martiri** (*often closed*), which has an altarpiece by Bergognone. It was here that St Charles Borromeo celebrated his last Mass. Above it, in Piazza de Filippi (turn right) is the **Collegiata**, the main church of Arona, dedicated to the Virgin of the Nativity (Santa Maria Nascente). The lunette over the main door has a charming 15th-century relief of the Holy Family. At the head of the north aisle is a beautiful early polyptych (1511) by Gaudenzio Ferrari, showing the influence of Perugino. The central scene shows the *Nativity* (with a particularly beautiful lute-playing angel). In the panel above is God the Father and in the predella, Christ and the Apostles. The kneeling figure on the right is thought to be Veronica Borromeo, grandmother of St Charles Borromeo. Six canvases by Morazzone showing scenes from the life of the Virgin are displayed in three of the side chapels (dark and difficult to see): *Visitation* and *Nativity* in the first chapel on the left; *Marriage of the Virgin* and *Annunciation* in the second; and the *Adoration of the Magi* and *Adoration of the Shepherds* in the second right. St Charles Borromeo was baptised here in 1538.

Via Cavour leads into the attractive, arcaded **Piazza del Popolo**, with restaurants and cafés and more splendid views of Angera, where the church of Santa Maria di Loreto (1592), with a fine façade approached by a double stairway, is attributed to Pellegrino Tibaldi (although this has been disputed). The interior contains a replica of the Holy House of Loreto. The former Palazzo di Giustizia on the piazza (also known as the Broletto) dates from the 15th century. It has brick arcades borne on stone pillars and (damaged) terracotta busts of members of the Visconti family, under whom it was built.

The Colosso di San Carlo Borromeo

To the north of Arona, on Via Verbano above the main lakeside road, stands the **Colosso di San Carlo Borromeo**, a colossal copper statue of Arona's most famous son (*open mid-March–mid-Oct daily; mid-Oct–Dec weekends only, closed Jan–Feb; for updates, see statuasancarlo.it*). Standing 23m high, on a pedestal 12m tall, it was commissioned from Giovanni Battista Crespi (Il Cerano) by a relative of the saint and completed in 1697. Popularly called *San Carlone*, it is second in size only to the Statue of Liberty in New York. It can be climbed by steps and an internal stair; there are lookout holes in his ears, eyes, nose and shoulders.

ST CHARLES BORROMEO

Charles Borromeo (1538–84) was born in the castle of Arona and from an early age was destined for the Church. He studied Law and Theology at the University of Pavia and after that was summoned to Rome by his uncle Pius IV, who sped him on in his career, creating him Cardinal in 1560 and Archbishop of Milan in 1564. Charles Borromeo was one of the leading lights of the Counter-Reformation, in 1562 spurring on his uncle to re-convoke the Council of Trent, which had broken up in disarray a decade previously. Many reforms to religious orders, the clergy and the liturgy were introduced by Borromeo. He also inaugurated a sweeping programme of rebuilding and extending churches, employing a coterie of favourite architects (notably Pellegrino Tibaldi) and painters. He was ruthless in his persecution of Protestants, notably in the Valtellina. However, during an outbreak of plague in 1576 he did much for the poor and destitute, selling goods and property and turning his money over to charitable causes, an action which made him greatly loved. Miracles were attributed to him and he was beatified in 1602, just 18 years after his death. Canonisation followed in 1610. His body lies, magnificently robed, in the crypt of the Duomo of Milan.

STRESA

Stresa (*map 5*), nestled in a charming position on the south shore of the Gulf of Pallanza, is mentioned in the Middle Ages as Strixia ('small strip of land'). In the 15th century it was transformed from a small fishing village to a seat of the powerful Visconti and, later, Borromeo families. It became fashionable as a resort in the mid-19th century (Stendhal, Charles Dickens and Lord Byron stayed here).

The Stresa waterfront

South of the ferry landing is **Villa Pallavicino**, built in 1855 for Queen Margherita and King Umberto I, with a small formal garden at the front of the house. It is surrounded by a fine wooded park (*open March–Oct daily 9–6; last entry 4.30; parcopallavicino.it*) planted with palms, magnolias and cedars and with a zoological garden.

Further along the lakefront are Stresa's grand hotels, the Regina Palace, which opened in 1908, and the huge, monumental **Hotel des Iles Borromées**, which has had many famous guests since it opened in 1863. Frederick Henry in Hemingway's *A Farewell to Arms* also stayed here.

ABOVE STRESA: MOTTARONE

Above Stresa is **Monte Mottarone** (1491m). It can be reached by road, but also by cableway, directly from the Stresa waterfront. The Funivia del Mottarone (*stresamottarone.it*) replaces a funicular inaugurated in 1911. The cable cars stop at Alpino (803m), from where you can walk to the Giardino Alpinia (605m), a botanical garden founded in 1933, with some 544 species of Alpine plants (*open April–mid-Oct Tues–Sun 9–6*). Here a private toll road, owned by the Borromeo since 1623 (9km; always open), continues through the meadows, woods and summer pastures of the Parco del Mottarone. To continue up the mountain, change cable cars at Alpino to continue the ascent (*if you have bought a ticket all the way to the top, there will be no wait; the next cable car leaves immediately*). The end stop is at 1385m, from where a chair lift (included in the price) takes you to the summit (where there is the Alpyland bobsleigh piste). Alternatively you can walk up the mountain road, past the little chapel of the Madonna of the Snow. The Albergo Eden offers refreshments (there is an outdoor terrace where you can sit overlooking the lake far below). The summit of Mt Mottarone commands truly breathtaking views of the whole chain of the Alps from Monte Viso in the west to the Ortles and Adamello in the east, and the Monte Rosa group especially conspicuous to the northwest. Below, on a clear day you can make out seven lakes and the wide Po Valley. Even on hazy days the prospect is majestic, with layer upon layer of peaks and arêtes revealed to your view.

BAVENO

Baveno (*map 5*), a short way further up the lake from Stresa, is in a fine position on the south shore of the Gulf of Pallanza, opposite the Isole Borromee and with fine views of the Isola dei Pescatori. Above the waterfront is a pretty little cobbled square, **Piazza della Chiesa**, on which are grouped the church and its baptistery, and an arcade with painted Stations of the Cross. The church, dedicated to Sts Gervase and Protase, has a fine Romanesque portal and bell-tower. The **baptistery** is entered under a Renaissance porch, though its internal structure is much older. The interior is frescoed with scenes from the life of St John the Baptist, with God the Father, the Evangelists and Doctors of the Church in the dome. Also on the square (*Piazza della Chiesa 8*) is an exhibition room entitled **Granum**, a small museum of the pink granite which is quarried here. Behind Baveno to the northwest rises Monte Camoscio (890m), with large quarries, a defining aspect of Baveno from a distance. As you return from the church square to the waterfront, note the **sculpture of a quarryman**, shown seated and chipping at a lump of rock.

THE ISOLE BORROMEE

This group of beautiful little islands (*map 5*) is named after the Italian Borromeo family, who still own the Isola Madre, Isola Bella and Isola San Giovanni. There are regular daily boat services for Isola Bella, Isola dei Pescatori and Isola Madre from Stresa, Baveno, Pallanza and Intra.

ISOLA BELLA

This is the most famous of the islands. It was just a barren rock with a small church and a few cottages before it was almost totally occupied by a huge palace with terraced gardens built in 1631–71 by Angelo Crivelli for Count Carlo III Borromeo, in honour of his wife, Isabella d'Adda, from whom it takes its name. The island measures just 320m by 180m, and there is a tiny hamlet by the pier outside the garden gates: no longer a true hamlet, its winding narrow streets are now filled with restaurants, cafés and gift shops (the Borromeo have their own line of products). A combined ticket gives admission to the palace and gardens (*open late March–late Oct daily 9–5.30; T: 0323 30556, isoleborromee.it*).

The palace

To the left of the pier is the vast grey **palace**, entered from an open courtyard with four palm trees and tiny cobbles. On the right of the courtyard is the chapel, which contains three family tombs (seen through a grille) with elaborate carvings by sculptors including Benedetto Briosco and Bambaia, brought from demolished churches in Milan. On the left of the courtyard is the entrance to the palace. Twenty-five rooms on the *piano nobile*, decorated with Murano chandeliers and Venetian mosaic floors, can be visited (the three floors above are the private apartments of the Borromeo family). The English historian Edward Gibbon stayed here as a guest of the Borromeo in 1764.

The octagonal blue-and-white **Sala dei Concerti** was built in 1948–51 in Baroque style following the original plans. There is a view of the Isola dei Pescatori and (*right*) the Isola Madre. The **Sala di Musica** has musical instruments, two Florentine cabinets in ebony and semi-precious stones (17th–18th centuries), and paintings by Jacopo Bassano and Tempesta. In 1935 a conference took place here between Mussolini and the French and British governments in an attempt to guarantee the peace of Europe. Napoleon and Josephine stayed in the next room in 1797. The **library** preserves, besides its books, some paintings by Carlevaris. Another room has paintings by Luca Giordano, and beyond a room with views of the Borromeo properties, by Zuccarelli, is the ballroom.

Stairs lead down to the **grottoes** built on the lake in the 18th century. Beyond a room with 18th–20th-century puppets (once used in puppet shows held in the 'amphitheatre' in the garden) are six grottoes encrusted with shells, pebbles, marble, etc. Displayed here are statues by Gaetano Matteo Monti and the remains of an ancient boat found in the lake off Angera. A spiral staircase in an old tower that predates the palace leads up to a short corridor of mirrors and from there to the **anticamera**, with a ceiling tondo attributed to Giovanni Battista Tiepolo and two paintings by Daniele Crespi. Beyond the chapel of St Charles Borromeo is the **gallery of tapestries**, with a splendid collection of 16th-century Flemish tapestries commissioned by St Charles Borromeo. The painting of *St Jerome* is by Moretto.

The gardens

The famous gardens, inhabited by white peacocks, are composed of terraces built out into the lake (an extraordinary sight from the water). Soil for the plants had to be brought from the mainland. A double staircase leads up onto a terrace with a huge camphor tree, camellias, bamboos, breadfruit, sugar cane, tapioca and tea and coffee plants. Beyond is the 'amphitheatre', an elaborate Baroque construction with statues, niches, pinnacles and stairs, crowned by a unicorn (the family emblem). The terrace at the top looks straight to Stresa, and below is the Italianate garden with box hedges and yew, and ten terraces planted with roses, oleanders and pomegranates descending to the lake. Other parts of the garden are laid out in the English style, with beds of tulips and forget-me-nots in spring and geraniums in summer. Below the terraces are rhododendrons and orange trees (protected in winter). The azaleas are at their best during April and May. The second exit leads out of the gardens through the delightful old-fashioned greenhouse.

Between Isola Bella and Isola dei Pescatori is a tiny islet, **Isolotto della Malghera**, inhabited by cormorants in winter.

ISOLA DEI PESCATORI

The Isola dei Pescatori, also known as Isola Superiore, is not owned by the Borromeo and is on regular ferry routes all year round. Once home to a pretty little fishing village, it has now been given over almost exclusively to tourism. Nevertheless, with its church tower and cluster of houses, it is an extremely picturesque sight, especially when seen from the water, or from Baveno, with snow-capped mountains behind. There are souvenir shops here, as well as restaurants and places to stay. The island makes a good place for a boat trip, stopping for lunch before catching the ferry back—or on, to the next destination.

ISOLA MADRE

The Isola Madre, nearer to Pallanza than to Stresa, is entirely occupied by a Borromeo villa and **botanical garden** (*open late March–end Oct daily 9–5.30; T: 0323 30556, isoleborromee.it*). It has one restaurant. The landscaped gardens, at their best in April, are laid out in the English manner and were replanted in the 1950s by the botanist Henry Cocker. The particularly mild climate allows a great number of exotic and tropical plants to flourish here. Viale Africa, with the warmest exposure, is lined with a variety of plants, including citrus fruits. The camellia terrace has numerous species of camellia and mimosa. Beyond a wisteria-covered arboured walk is the Mediterranean garden and a rock garden. The cylindrical tower was once used as an ice house; beyond it are ferns. From the little port with its boathouse (and an 18th-century boat suspended from the roof) is a view of Pallanza. Nearby is the oldest camellia on the island (thought to be some 150 years old). On a lawn is a group of taxodium trees, with their roots sticking up above ground—an odd sight; there are more of them on the tip of Isola Bella, facing Isola dei Pescatori—and beyond are banks of azaleas, rhododendrons, camphor trees and ancient magnolias. Beside steps up to the villa, by a remarkable Kashmir cypress—said to be 200 years old—is an aviary with parrots that nest in the cedar of Lebanon here. Near the villa are ornamental banana trees and the Art Nouveau family chapel. The terrace by the villa is planted with tall palm trees,

LAKE MAGGIORE
Isola dei Pescatori.

including a majestic Chilean palm, planted in 1858, which bears miniature edible coconuts. The steps nearby are covered with a trellis of kiwi fruit.

The 18th-century **villa** is also open to the public. It contains 17th- and 18th-century furnishings from Borromeo properties and servants' livery, as well as a collection of porcelain, puppets and dolls (19th-century French and German) and paintings by Pitocchetto. The little theatre dates from 1778.

VERBANIA

Sprawling Verbania (*map 5–3*), across the lake from Baveno and Stresa, is the largest town on Lake Maggiore. It takes its name from the alternative name of the lake, Verbano, and is in fact an amalgamation of two settlements, Pallanza and Intra. It can be reached by boat from Stresa and Baveno and has boat connections to the islands.

PALLANZA

Pallanza occupies the promontory of the Punta della Castagnola, on the slopes of Monte Rosso (697m). The western part of it is known as Suna. Pallanza's waterfront is in a charming position in full view of the Isole Borromee, facing west, which makes it a good place to come in the later part of the day. It has a mild climate which makes the flora particularly luxuriant; the lakefront is planted with magnolias.

The main waterfront square is **Piazza Garibaldi**. In the park here is a WWI monument of a widow holding her child and offering a rose in memory of her fallen husband. It is the work of Paolo Troubetzkoy (*see below*). Beyond it, right on the water, is Marcello Piacentini's mausoleum of Marshal Cadorna (1850–1928), Italian Chief of Staff during the first 30 months of the First World War and a native of Pallanza.

Next to the Town Hall, Via Ruga leads inland (and uphill) to the **Museo del Paesaggio** in the Baroque Palazzo Viani-Dugnani (*Via Ruga 44; T: 0323 502254, museodelpaesaggio.it*), founded in 1914 and containing a beautifully displayed collection of sculptures and plaster models by Paolo Troubetzkoy. Troubetzkoy was born in Intra and spent his summers here in Pallanza, on the bay of Suna. There is also a room with sculptures by Arturo Martini. Upstairs is the collection of paintings, including some by Sophie Browne (*see below*) and by Mario Tozzi, whose frescoes can be seen in the church of Santa Lucia in Suna.

At the end of Piazza Garibaldi, where the street becomes Corso Zanitello, a street and steps lead up to the church of **San Leonardo** (16th century; modernised in the 19th century), the tall tower of which was completed by Pellegrino Tibaldi in 1589.

On the Punta della Castagnola headland

From the Pallanza waterfront a road curves round the Punta della Castagnola. It is one-way for cars coming in the other direction, but there is a pedestrian and bicycle lane (bikes can be hired outside the ferry landing stage). There are views from here of the **Isolino di San Giovanni** (*no public access*). The villa on the island was once the summer home of Toscanini. The **Villa Giulia** (1882; signposted) or Kursaal, built in 1847 for Bernardino Branca (who invented the Fernet Branca liqueur) has fine gardens, open to the public.

The **Hotel Majestic** opened in 1870. Around the headland is the **Villa San Remigio**, built in 1903 and still privately owned (but available for rent; *villasanremigio.it*). The formal gardens, when they were laid out in 1905 by Sophie Browne, an Irish painter, and her husband, the marquess Silvio della Valle di Casanova, were among the best in northern Italy, with topiary terraces, fountains, and statues by Orazio Marinali, who produced much of the statuary for the Palladian villas near Vicenza.

Next to Villa San Remigio is the 19th-century **Villa Taranto**, with famous botanical gardens (*open mid-March–end Oct; T: 0323 404555, villataranto.it*)—the villa has a landing stage served by regular boat services. The huge estate was bought in 1930 by the Scotsman Captain Neil McEacharn (1884–1964), ex-army officer, botanist and heir to a considerable fortune, which he poured into creating these gardens. Together with head gardener Henry Cocker, he created a garden with an outstanding collection of exotic plants from all over the world, which he later donated to the Italian state. The plants include magnolias (at their best at the beginning of April), superb camellias (which flower in April), rhododendrons (which flower May–June), azaleas and paulownias (best in May). The herbaceous borders and dahlias (over 300 varieties) are at their best in July and August. Birches, maples and conifers distinguish the woodlands. There is a very pleasant café and bar beside a shallow pool. Here too is McEacharn's mausoleum, where his tomb-chest is surrounded by beautiful stained-glass windows of flowers of all seasons. There is no access to the villa itself, which has been much altered and now houses local government offices.

Off the main road across the promontory between Pallanza and Intra, on Viale Giuseppe Azari, is the fine church of the **Madonna di Campagna**, consecrated in

PALLANZA
From the Troubetzkoy collection in the Museo del Paesaggio.

1547. Its exterior is remarkable for the fine octagonal arcaded lantern drum. Inside are 16th-century decorations (notably works attributed to Carlo Urbino, Aurelio Luini and Gerolamo Lanino).

Where the main road meets the water again, this time facing the Lombard side of the lake, is a public park and sandy beach with the attractive **Villa Maioni**, now the public library. Next to it is the **Il Maggiore** concert hall and events space (Salvador Pérez Arroyo, 2016), with its billowing zinc roofs. The café here has lovely views across the lake to the cable car going vertically up the Sasso del Ferro.

Above Verbania is the **Parco Nazionale della Val Grande**, a protected mountainous area with fine walks.

GHIFFA

The lake reaches its greatest depth (372m) just off Ghiffa (*map 4*). From the waterfront in the town centre, between the Town Hall (Municipio) and the ferry landing, Via Marconi leads to a series of winding lanes which turn into a cobbled track through chestnut woods up to the Sacro Monte della Santissima Trinità di Ghiffa (30mins). The journey can also be accomplished by car up Via Santissima Trinità.

GHIFFA, SACRO MONTE
Baptism of Christ (1659).

THE SACRO MONTE

The Sacro Monte complex consists of the main sanctuary chapel, three further chapels and a portico with the Via Crucis. The **Sanctuary** stands on the site of the original Romanesque oratory. Work began on enlarging it in 1605. Its portico faces the **Chapel of the Coronation of the Virgin** (1647), an octagon with a rectangular apse. The interior is whitewashed, with a terracotta group of the *Coronation of the Virgin* and terracotta prophets and saints.

Behind the Sanctuary is the **Chapel of St John the Baptist** (1659), octagonal in three tiers. You can process around it and, through a barred window, see the dramatic statue group of St John baptising Christ in the River Jordan. Symbolically, the chapel is built above a water cistern.

The chapel of the Coronation and of the Baptism are linked by the **Porticato della Via Crucis**, made up of 14 arches on stone columns, with scenes from Christ's Passion in moulded and painted terracotta with frescoed backgrounds. It was added in 1752.

The third chapel, the **Chapel of Abraham**, is a bit further away from the others (*signed*). It takes the form of a Greek Cross with a small rectangular portico (1701–3). Within, a sculptural group represents three angels appearing to Abraham, a scene which is interpreted as foreshadowing the Holy Trinity.

The Sacro Monte enjoys spectacular views of the lake and the Lombard Alps. A trail leads into the adjacent forest preserve, deciduous woodland with a prevalence of chestnut accompanied by maple, ash, alder and birch, as well as exotic species such as white pine. Adjacent to the Porticato is an attractive restaurant.

THE SACRI MONTI

The *Sacri Monti* ('Holy Mountains') of Piedmont and Lombardy, groupings of 16th–17th-century chapels and shrines, were conceived as bastions of the Counter-Reformation strategically located at the border between the Roman Catholic Mediterranean and the lands of Calvin and Zwingli beyond the Alps. In 2003, UNESCO added the Sacri Monti to its World Heritage List. There are nine Sacri Monti in the Piedmont and Lombardy regions. Three are described in this guide: the one here at Ghiffa and those of Varese (*see p. 187*) and Ossuccio (*see p. 228*). Each one consists of a succession of chapels containing religious tableaux, taking the visitor on a spiritual journey (always with the symbolism of the arduous uphill climb). They encourage meditation and prayer, partly also because they surrounded by nature and beautifully integrated into the landscape. There is always some kind of welcome refreshment at the top.

CANNOBIO

Cannobio (*map 2*), at the windy top end of the lake, has ancient origins and preserves some medieval buildings. Its stone-paved waterfront promenade (Via Magistris), lined with attractive colourful houses, their ground floors occupied by shops and restaurants, is extremely pleasant. In high season a boat leaves from here for the Wednesday market at Luino. At the end of Via Magistris, just behind the waterfront, is

CANNOBIO

Gaudenzio Ferrari's *Way to Calvary* in the Santuario della Pietà.
This crowded composition, characteristic of Ferrari's later work, includes the addition
of a small dog in the foreground, another Ferrari hallmark.

the **Santuario della Pietà** (reconstructed in 1583–1601), with a fine altarpiece of the *Way to Calvary* by Gaudenzio Ferrari.

The old kernel of town further inland, around Via Giovanola, has the high bell-tower and stout stone building of the old Palazzo della Ragione, known as **Il Parasio**, a 13th-century building with 17th-century alterations.

ORRIDO DI SANT'ANNA

Inland from Cannobio is the Val Cannobina, with a romantic gorge called the Orrido di Sant'Anna. (*Follow signs to Traffiume and then to Orrido.*) The road leads past waterfalls to a car park beside a miniature hump-backed bridge and the oratory of the Madonna of Loreto and St Anne, with a roof made of large stone slabs (*piode*). Here at this beautiful spot, the gorge, with a stream at the bottom, slices through the rock, passing through a wide cavern to form a pool and cataracts. There is a very pleasant restaurant overlooking it.

THE LOMBARD SHORE

LUINO AND LAVENO

Luino (*map 4*), a small industrial town and historically a railway frontier station, is the most important centre on the Lombard side of the lake. The main road along the spacious waterfront is Viale Dante, with the **Palazzo Comunale** (Town Hall) in an eclectic building, part of a never-completed 18th-century *palazzo* originally by Felice Soave. The **statue of Garibaldi** just beyond the roundabout, the first to be erected in Italy, in 1867, commemorates his attempt, on 14th August 1848, to renew the struggle against Austria with around 1,000 men, after the armistice that followed the defeat of Custozza. Further south along the waterfront, opposite the lakeside park, is the church of the **Madonna del Carmine**, with frescoes of 1544 by pupils of Bernardino Luini. Interesting frescoes tentatively attributed to him (they are also attributed to a follower of Bramantino), which include an *Adoration of the Magi*, can be seen in the cemetery church of **San Pietro in Campagna**, east of the centre up Via Bernardino Luini and then Viale della Rimembranza.

From the boat landing stage heading north, you come to a little enclosed harbour for fishing and pleasure boats, protected by a statue of the Virgin known as the *Madonnina*. A **market** has been held in the town on Wednesdays since 1541, centred on Piazza della Libertà in front of the ferry dock. In summer it is a great visitor attraction.

Between Luino and Laveno is **Caldè**, interesting when seen from the water for its row of disused lime kilns, now decorated with colourful murals by street artists.

LAVENO MOMBELLO AND THE SASSO DEL FERRO

Laveno Mombello (*map 6*) commands a fine position, with good views of the Punta della Castagnola and the Isola Madre in the distance. Its port serves the car ferry to Intra. A monument in the piazza by the waterside commemorates the *garibaldini* who fell in an attempt to capture the town from the Austrians in 1859. The former Austrian fort, on Laveno's northern headland, Punta San Michele, is now a sailing school.

A cableway leads from Laveno Mombello to the top of the **Sasso del Ferro** (1062m). There are magnificent views from the top (*funiviedellagomaggiore.it*).

This are was once noted for its ceramics and in the next town as you go south, **Cerro**, there is fine a **ceramics museum, MIDeC** (Museo Internazionale del Design Ceramico) in the 16th century Palazzo Perabò (*midec.org*).

Further south, you come to the solitary convent of **Santa Caterina del Sasso** (*reached in 10mins by a steep path that descends from the main road, or by boat from Laveno or Stresa in high season*). It was founded in the 13th century and reinhabited by Dominicans in 1986 (*open March–Oct daily 9.30–12 & 2–5 or 3–6, Nov–Feb weekends and holidays; santacaterinadelsasso.com*). It is spectacularly built into a sheer rock face directly above the lake (there is an 18m drop to the water). The picturesque

ANGERA
View of the Rocca Borromeo.

Romanesque buildings, particularly attractive when seen from the water, were restored in 1624 and have a good view of the Gulf of Pallanza and the Isole Borromee. They contain 15th- and 16th-century frescoes and a 17th-century *Last Supper*.

ANGERA

Angera (*map 7*) has a handsome, harmonious and spacious waterfront lined with horse chestnuts. Above it stands the **Rocca Borromeo** (*open March–Oct daily 9–5.30; isoleborromee.it*), formerly a castle of the Visconti. The medieval fortress was enlarged and embellished over the years to become a 15th-century ducal residence, passing to the Borromeo in 1449. It is still owned by them. The fine gateway leads into a charming courtyard with a pergola open to the south end of the lake. The Sala di Giustizia and Sala di Cerimonia have interesting Gothic secular frescoes commissioned by Giovanni Visconti, Bishop of Milan, with signs of the Zodiac. Episodes from the battles of Archbishop Ottone Visconti (buried in the Duomo in Milan; *see p. 32*) are also recorded. There is also a collection of majolica, a doll and toy museum and a re-created medieval garden.

SESTO CALENDE

The Simplon road from Geneva to Milan, constructed by Napoleon in 1800–5, skirts the lake's southern tip at Sesto Calende (*map 8*). The town is said to derive its name from its market day in Roman times—the sixth day before the Calends. This part of the lake is very built up with a lot of light industry: historically it has always been a populous site. Just south of Sesto, on the Ticino, is Golasecca, which gives its name to an important prehistoric culture. Sesto Calende's **Museo Civico** (*Piazza Mazzini 1; open Mon–Thur 9–12 & 2.30–4.30, Sun 3–6; July–Aug Mon, Wed, Fri 9–12.30, Tues, Thur 9–12 & 2.30–5, Sun 10–12; T: 0331 928160, www.comune.sesto-calende.va.it*) houses archaeological finds from tombs of the period (800–350 BC). The Golasecca culture, known from its burial sites in this area of Italy, used an alphabet known as Lepontic and buried their dead in black pottery vessels with incised decoration. Their civilisation spanned the Bronze and Iron Ages and numerous metal artefacts—tools, weapons, ornaments—have been found.

PRACTICAL INFORMATION

INFORMATION OFFICES

Arona. On the waterfront (Piazza Duca d'Aosta).
Luino. On Viale Dante (the waterfront road) just north of the ferry landing, opposite the *Madonnina* statue.

GETTING AROUND

• **By rail:** EuroCity services from Milan Centrale to Geneva, Bern and Basel pass through Stresa (55mins). There are also a direct regional services from Milan Centrale to Arona (55mins), Stresa (1hr 8mins) and Verbania-Pallanza (1hr 15mins). Some trains also leave from Porta Garibaldi in Milan, taking a little longer. Services operated by Trenord link Milan Cadorna with Laveno Mombello (90mins). To get to Luino from Milan, you normally have to change. Trains between Luino and Laveno Mombello take c. 15mins, and 25mins between Laveno Mombello and Angera.
• **By bus:** Buses run by VCO Trasporti (*www.vcotrasporti.it*) link Verbania,

Ghiffa and Cannobio on the Piedmont side. Services linking Sesto Calende, Arona, Stresa, Baveno and Verbania are operated by SAF (*safduemila.com*).
• **By boat:** For information about ferry routes and timetables, visit Navigazione Laghi (*www.navigazionelaghi.it*). Routes tend to be organised in three separate clusters: Arona and Angera; the central lake (Stresa, Baveno and the islands); and Cannobio and the north. A car ferry links Laveno Mombello and Intra. A number of other companies also run ferry services. Their booking offices are by the waterside in all the main ports. These can be particularly useful out of season, when the Navigazione Laghi ferries (known as 'ferries of the line') are running to sparser timetables. The local custom is to dock the boats by nudging the prows right up against the slipway. **Private boats** can be hired from a number of companies. A reliable one, in Verbania (very close to the Il Maggiore events space), is Rent Boat Lago Maggiore (Nautica Bego; *Via dalla Chiesa 6, rentboatlagomaggiore.com*).

WHERE TO STAY

CANNOBIO

€€ **Pironi**. Cosy, individually furnished rooms in a 15th-century building in the heart of the old town. A charming place. *Via Marconi 35. T: 0323 70624.*

€€ **Villa Belvedere**. Comfortable, slightly folksy décor in a pretty yellow villa, set back from the water in a quiet position. Garden and pool. *Via Casali Cuserina 2. T: 0323 70159, villabelvederehotel.it.*

STRESA

€€€ **Grand Hotel Des Iles Borromées & Spa**. Magnificent grand hotel, once a favourite resort of the European nobility. In 1870, Alexandra, Grand Duchess of All Russia, etched her name on a window with a diamond. In 1884, the agreement to build the Simplon Tunnel was signed here. Hemingway writes of it in *A Farewell to Arms*. It still meets the highest standards of luxury accommodation. *Lungolago Umberto I 67. T: 0323 938938, www.borromees.com.*

ISOLA DEI PESCATORI

€€ **Verbano**. Charming small hotel. Past guests include Toscanini, Hemingway, George Bernard Shaw, Alessandro Manzoni and Gabriele d'Annunzio. Rooms are warm and comfortable. Lakeside restaurant. *Via Ugo Ara 2. T: 0323 30408, hotelverbano.it.*

VERBANIA

€€€ **Grand Hotel Majestic**. Large luxury hotel with its own restaurant in a renovated *Belle Epoque* building. *Via Vittorio Veneto 32. T: 0323 509 711, grandhotelmajestic.it.*

€€ **Il Chiostro**. Hotel based in a beautiful 16th-century monastery. *Via Fratelli Cervi 14. T: 0323 404077, chiostrovb.it.*

WHERE TO EAT

ARONA

€€€ **Taverna del Pittore**. Pleasant fish restaurant with an open veranda on the lake, now also with a *bistrot prêt à manger*, offering a limited gourmet menu, and a *carpacceria*, both inexpensive (€). Closed Mon. *Piazza del Popolo 39. T: 0322 243366, ristorantetavernadelpittore.it.*

CANNOBIO

€€ **Grotto Sant'Anna**. At the Orrido di Sant'Anna, just behind the church. Excellent restaurant with good food and wine and an idyllic atmosphere. In fine weather you can eat outside at stone tables placed overlooking the gorge and its stream far below. Closed Mon. *Via Sant'Anna 30. T: 0323 70682, ristorantegrotto@gmail.com.*

GHIFFA

€–€€ **La Trinità**. The restaurant at the Sacro Monte is very pleasant, with stone tables and benches outside under the trees in fine weather and cosy seating indoors. Sometimes closed on weekdays in low season (phone to check). *Via Santissima Trinità. T: 032 308 6330, ristorantelatrinita.it.*

ISOLA DEI PESCATORI

€–€€ **Trattoria Imbarcadero**. There are plenty of places to eat on the island but this is perhaps the best, in business since 1899, right beside the landing stage. There are tables right out on the water in fine weather. Excellent unfussy food, good wine and friendly service. *T: 0323 30329, imbarcaderoisolapescatori.it.*

RANCO

€€€ **Il Sole di Ranco**. Acclaimed restaurant famous for its lake fish and seafood, as well as for the views. For foodies, it will merit a special trip to

Ranco (*map 7*). Closed midday Mon
and all day Tues. They also have very
comfortable rooms. *Piazza Venezia 5. T:
0331 976507, ilsolediranco.it.*

STRESA

€€ **Il Ristorante Piemontese**.
Restaurant in a 17th-century townhouse
with private garden. It is known for its
fine regional cuisine—Piedmontese, as
the name suggests. There is a lovely little
courtyard with a pergola for summer
dining. Closed Mon. *Via Mazzini 25. T:
0323 30235.*

€–€€ **Il Vicoletto**. Cosy, friendly
and popular. Refined food and a wide
selection of wines. A gourmet choice.
Closed Thur. *Vicolo del Pocivo 3. T: 0323
932102.*

€ **Caffè Torino**. On the main square, just
inland from the waterfront. Bustling,
busy and friendly, serving very simple
food and pizza. Stays open year-round.
Piazza Cadorna 23. T: 0323 30652.

€ **Paulon di Vino Caffè**. Popular and
friendly wine bar, just in from the
waterfront, ideal for early evening
drinks. They have a good range of wines
on offer and serve good nibbles. You can
also eat a snack meal here. *Via Principe
Tomaso 1.*

VERBANIA

€€ **Antica Osteria Il Monte Rosso**.
In business since 1854; fusion food
and Mediterranean fish specialities.
In the bay of Suna, where the sculptor
Troubetzkoy spent his summers. *Via
Paolo Troubetzkoy 128. T: 0323 506056,
osteriamonterosso.com.*

€€ **Dei Cigni**. Modern *trattoria*
specialising in fish and seafood.
*Vicolo dell'Arco 1, corner of Viale delle
Magnolie. T: 0323 558842.*

€€ **Il Portale**. Serves delicious seafood;
lakeside terrace (in Pallanza). Closed

Tues and Wed lunch. *Via Sassello 3. T:
0323 505486, ristoranteilportale.it.*
€ **Caffè delle Rose**. Reliable old-
fashioned place on the main pedestrian
street of Pallanza. Good for lunch after
visiting Villa Taranto. *Via Ruga 36. T:
0323 558101.*

LOCAL SPECIALITIES

ANGERA
Angera makes grappa (Acqua d'Angera).
You can visit the distillery at Via Puccini
20 (*rossidangera.it*).

STRESA
The small round crumbly biscuits
called *margheritine* claim to have been
invented in 1868 by the pastry chef
Pietro Antonio Bolongaro, in the shop
(and now café) that bears his name on
Piazza Matteotti, facing the waterfront.
They are said to have been a particular
favourite of Queen Margherita, hence
their name. You can buy them from the
elegant little Chocolaterie des Iles, just
behind the Pasticceria Bolongaro at Via
Cavour 3.

FESTIVALS AND EVENTS

LUINO
The weekly Wednesday market is very
popular.

STRESA
Stresa Festival. International festival of
classical music. July–Sept. *stresafestival.
eu.*

VERBANIA
Festival LetterAltura, focusing
on mountain literature, travel
and adventure, last week of June.
letteraltura.it.

TREMEZZO
Villa Carlotta.

Lake Como
& the Valtellina

Beautiful Lake Como (*Atlas D*), below the alpine foothills, offers perhaps the most dramatic scenery of all the great Italian lakes. High, precipitous mountains fall sheer to the water and villages literally perch on narrow ledges of land. Virgil called it *Lacus Larius*, and the lake is still often known as Lario. Many of the towns on its shores, originally fishing villages, became resorts in the 19th century. The English Romantic poets Shelley and Byron came here, and Wordsworth lived here in 1790. Numerous villas surrounded by lovely gardens were built in the 18th and 19th centuries. The lake is subject to frequent floods and is swept regularly by two winds, the *tivano* (north to south) and the *breva* (south to north).

LAKE COMO HIGHLIGHTS

The most beautiful part of the lake is the centre, where the foreshore is wider and less steep. **Bellagio** (*map p. 227, 3*) is perhaps the loveliest of all the resorts. Fine villas with beautiful gardens can be found here (Villa Melzi; *p. 231*), as well as at **Tremezzo** on the west shore (*map p. 227, 5; p. 229*) and at **Varenna** on the east (*map p. 227, 3; p. 235*). Varenna also offers the dramatic Fiumelatte gorge and a medieval castle.

The town of **Como** (*p. 218*) has impressive examples of Rationalist architecture. For family holidays with simple restaurants and good lake swimming, the northern shore around **Gravedona** is recommended (*map p. 227, 1*). Good walks can be taken from Brunate to **Torno** (*p. 225*), Cadenabbia to **San Martino** (*p. 231*) and to the isolated **abbey of Piona** on its headland (*p. 237*).

COMO TOWN

The town of Como (*map p. 227, 7*) lies in a fine position on the southern lakeshore. Its sprawling industrial outskirts give little hint of the charming town that lies within the old walls, which still preserves its Roman outline. The old centre is particularly attractive, with long, straight, narrow streets. Many of the houses have fine sgraffito façades, Liberty moulding around doors and windows and enticing inner courtyards. The duomo is a splendid building with remarkable sculptures inside and out. Beyond the old centre is an expansive and attractive waterfront. The traditional local industry of silk-weaving survives (*see p. 223*).

HISTORY OF COMO

Originally a town of the Insubrian Gauls—who also founded Milan—Como was captured and colonised by the Romans in the 2nd century BC. The town was a city-state by the 11th century, but in 1127 it was destroyed by the Milanese. Frederick Barbarossa rebuilt it in 1155, and Como secured its future independence by the Peace of Constance (1183). In the power struggles between the Torriani and Visconti families (recorded in fresco in the Rocca Borromeo on Lake Maggiore; *see p. 212*), Como fell to the latter in 1335 and became a fief of Milan. From then on it followed the fortunes of the Lombard capital under the Visconti and Sforza, then falling under Spanish control and finally coming under Austrian rule in 1714. In March 1848, a popular uprising compelled the surrender of the Austrian garrison. The city was liberated by Garibaldi on 27th May 1859.

In more recent times, Como has been associated with Italian Fascism: its corpulent bishop, Alessandro Macchi, was a staunch supporter of the system, and the architect Giuseppe Terragni designed Rationalist buildings in the new spirit.

Among famous natives are two Roman authors, the Elder and the Younger Pliny (AD 23–79 and AD 62–120), uncle and nephew. The Younger Pliny often mentions Como and its surroundings in his *Letters*. He had two villas here. The beauty of the lake is still appreciated by the elite: Hollywood film star George Clooney has a villa at Laglio.

EXPLORING COMO

THE LAKEFRONT
The expansive **Piazza Cavour** (*map opposite, 4*), facing the lake and lined with cafés and restaurants, was created in 1887 by filling in the old harbour. From the foreshore you have a good view: on the right bank you can see the line of the funicular up to Brunate; on the left is the Neoclassical rotunda of the Tempio Voltiano and beyond it the large Villa Olmo. In the distance, the town of Cernobbio climbs the hillside.

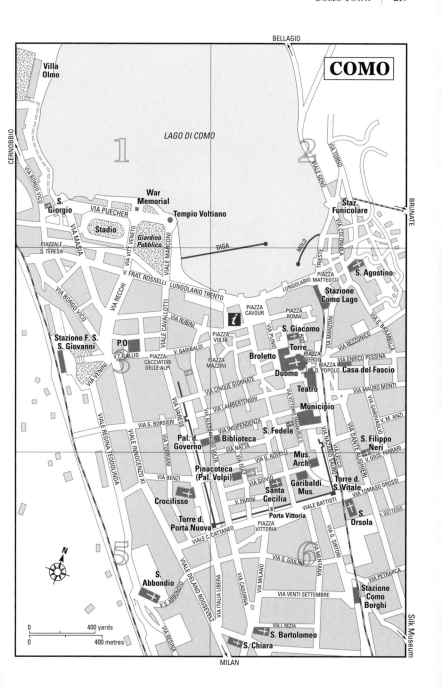

COMO

BELLAGIO

CERNOBBIO

BRUNATE

MILAN

Silk Museum

Villa Olmo

LAGO DI COMO

1

2

VIA BORGO VICO

VIA T. D'ORO

VIALE GENO

War Memorial

Tempio Voltiano

Staz. Funicolare

S. Giorgio

VIA PUECHER

VIA COLONIOLA

Stadio

Giardino Pubblico

VIA MASIA

VIA VITT. VENETO

VIALE MARCONI

TRIESTE

PIAZZALE S. TERESA

V. FRAT. ROSSELLI

DIGA

MOLO

LUNGOLARIO MATTEOTTI

S. Agostino

VIA RECCHI

LUNGOLARIO TRENTO

PIAZZA ROMA

VIA G. B. RAIMONDI

VIA BORGO VICO

VIA CAVALLOTTI

VIA RUBINI

PIAZZA CAVOUR

Stazione Como Lago

VIA MANZONI

PIAZZA VOLTA

S. Giacomo

VIA PLINIO

VIA REZZONICO

Stazione F. S. S. Giovanni

P.O.

V.T. GALLIO

V. GARIBALDI

Torre

PIAZZA VERDI

VIA ENRICO PESSINA

Broletto

PIAZZA D. POPOLO

Casa del Fascio

PIAZZA CACCIATORI DELLE ALPI

PIAZZA MAZZINI

Duomo

VIA VENINI

3

VIA CINQUE GIORNATE

Teatro

VIA MAURO MONTI

VIA LAMBERTENGHI

Municipio

VIA GARDAVALLO

VIA S. VARESE

VIA G. BORSIERI

VIA INDIPENDENZA

VIA VITTORIO EMANUELE

V. M. ANZI

Pal. d. Governo

S. Fedele

S. Filippo Neri

VIALE REGINA TEODOLINDA

VIALE INNOCENZO XI

VIALE ALESSANDRO VOLTA

Biblioteca

VIA NATTA

VIA DIAZ

VIA G. ROVELLI

Mus. Arch.

VIA NAZARIO SAURO

VIALE LECCO

VIA DANTE ALIGHIERI

V. GIUS. FERRARI

Pinacoteca (Pal. Volpi)

VIA BENZI

VIA GIOVIO

Garibaldi Mus.

Torre d. S. Vitale

VIA TOMASO GROSSI

Crocifisso

Santa Cecilia

V. PARINI

VIALE BATTISTI

S. Orsola

V. DOTTESIO

Torre d. Porta Nuova

Porta Vittoria

PIAZZA VITTORIA

4

5

VIALE C. CATTANEO

VIALE DELANO ROOSEVELT

VIA G. GIULINI

6

VIA MENTANA

VIA G. SIRTORI

VIA PETRARCA

VIA ITALIA LIBERA

VIA CADORNA

VIA MILANO

S. Abbondio

V. S. ABBONDIO

Stazione Como Borghi

VIA VENTI SETTEMBRE

VIA REGINA

VIA I. REZIA

S. Bartolomeo

S. Chiara

0   400 yards
0   400 metres

N

MILAN

COMO
War Memorial by Giuseppe Terragni.

The **Tempio Voltiano** (*map p. 219, 3; open Tues–Sun Oct–March 10–4, April–Sept 10–6*) stands at the head of an avenue of tall lime trees. It was erected in 1927 as a memorial to the physicist Alessandro Volta (1745–1827), who was born in Como. In 1799 Volta developed the 'voltaic pile', the precursor of the electric battery. Napoleon created him a count in 1801. Today he is a household name: the volt is named after him. The museum contains his scientific instruments and examples of early piles, charmingly displayed in old-fashioned show cases.

The conspicuous **War Memorial** beyond it was built by Giuseppe Terragni, inspired by drawings of the proto-Futurist architect Antonio Sant'Elia, a native of Como. Sant'Elia was killed in action in 1916. His only constructed work is the Villa Elisi on the hill of Brunate.

Beyond the war memorial are the other buildings of the 1930s waterfront: the **sports stadium** and, opposite it, the rowing club (with a Fascist-spirited slogan in Latin over its entrance: 'Rowing makes the chest stronger') and the yacht club. At the end of the row is the Aero Club with a hangar for sea planes (available for tours; *see p. 246*). Behind the sports stadium on Via Sinigaglia is Terragni's famous **Novocomum** building (1927), which was nicknamed the 'Transatlantico' for its perceived similarity to a streamlined ocean liner.

Beyond the Aero Club, a pleasant lakeside path (*marked by a broken line on the map on p. 219*) continues past private villas, including the Villa Saporiti, with a semicircular Neoclassical rotunda in the centre of its façade. The path ends at **Villa Olmo**, built for the Odescalchi family (1782–95; altered in 1883). It is preceded by an attractive formal garden (*open daily*) with topiary, statues and a charming fountain, and behind are remains of its large park. The villa is used for exhibitions. Beyond Villa Olmo is the bathing lido.

PIAZZA DEL DUOMO

The covered, arcaded **Broletto** (1215; *map p. 219, 4*), the old Town Hall, abuts the duomo's north flank. It is built in alternating courses of black and white marble, with a few red patches. The **Torre del Comune**, of the same period, has been used as a campanile since the addition of the top storey in 1435 (partly rebuilt in 1927). Opposite the duomo, the Bar da Pietro sports the names of famous Como citizens on its stencilled façade: Pliny, Volta and Giovio. Paolo Giovio (1483–1552) was a physician, churchman and historian.

The **duomo** (Santa Maria Maggiore; *open Mon–Fri 9.30–5.30, Sat 10.45–4.30, Sun 1–4.30*), faced entirely in marble, dates mainly from the late 14th century, when it replaced an 11th-century basilica. Its appearance is a curious pastiche, a union of Renaissance and Gothic architectural motifs, with an 18th-century dome. The west front (1460–90) is a good example: the twenty 15th-century statues framing the two large lancet windows are Gothic in conception; the numerous other reliefs and statues from the workshop of the local sculptors Tommaso and Jacopo Rodari, dating from c. 1500, are more Renaissance in style. The two lateral doorways, also decorated by the Rodari, have wonderful detailed carving. Between the doorways are two colossal seated statues of the Elder and Younger Pliny. The north doorway is a fine Renaissance portal (1507), called Porta della Rana from a detail on the carved pier on the left-hand jamb showing a frog (*rana*) catching a large moth.

The work of rebuilding continued through the 16th century (choir) and 17th century (transepts), and ended with completion of the dome in 1770 by Filippo Juvarra. Viewed from behind, in Piazza Verdi, you can see the later additions.

Inside, the aisled nave of five bays is covered with a groin vault and hung with tapestries (1598). In the west wall are brightly coloured stained-glass windows by Giuseppe Bertini (1850). The two stoups supported by a lion and lioness are survivals from the ancient basilica. A graceful little rotunda (1590) serves as a baptistery.

In the south aisle, the altar of Sant'Abbondio is finely decorated with gilded carved wood (1514) and three marble panels below (*for more on Sant'Abbondio, see p. 224*). The next altar has a masterpiece by Bernardino Luini, a *Virgin and Child* with four saints and the donor, Canon Raimondi, with a beautiful angel-musician in front and more on clouds above.

On the fourth north altar is a carved *Deposition* group by Tommaso Rodari (1498) and opposite, hanging in the nave, a painted and embroidered standard of the Confraternity of Sant'Abbondio by Morazzone (1608–10). On either side of the third Neoclassical altar are paintings by Bernardino Luini (*Adoration of the Shepherds*, right) and Gaudenzio Ferrari (*Marriage of the Virgin*, left, with one of his trademark small dogs in the foreground, scratching its ear). By the side door is the sarcophagus of Giovanni degli Avogadri (d. 1293), with primitive carvings. On the second altar, between busts of Innocent XI and Bishop Rovelli, is a lovely carved ancona by Tommaso Rodari.

CASA DEL FASCIO

East of the duomo, past the Teatro Sociale (1811) and across the Nord–Milano railway line, stands the elegant white Casa del Fascio, the former regional headquarters of the Fascist Party, now occupied by the tax police. Built in 1933–6 to a design by Giuseppe Terragni, it is an important example of the architecture of this period. The ground-floor atrium is paved in pale fawn marble. On the left is the former Sacrario, the chapel to the fallen martyrs of the 'Fascist Revolution', with an everlasting lamp. Terragni also built a number of other important buildings in Como, including the Novocomum on Via Sinigaglia (*see p. 221*). Guided tours of the Casa del Fascio and other Rationalist buildings are sometimes given (*see visitcomo.eu*).

PIAZZA SAN FEDELE

In the charming Piazza San Fedele, the former cornmarket (*map p. 219, 4*), are a couple of old houses with wooden eaves and herringbone brickwork, their roofs still partially clad in slabs of stone. The 12th-century church of San Fedele was formerly the cathedral. Opposite it, under the stairs in the Ubik bookshop, you can see the remains of the early Christian baptistery that once served it. The church can be entered either from the piazza or from behind, on Via Vittorio Emanuele II, through an angular doorway with remarkable bas-reliefs showing Byzantine influences. The interior has an unusual plan. It contains a fresco signed by G.A. Magistris (1504; south aisle) and a 17th-century painted and stuccoed vault.

MUSEI CIVICI AND PINACOTECA

At the end of Via Vittorio Emanuele, a former palace houses the **Museo Civico Archeologico** (*map p. 219, 6; open Tues–Sun 10–6*). The rooms are very fine and the collection is well arranged in them. It includes prehistoric material, items pertaining to the Golasecca culture (*see p. 213*) and finds from Roman Como. An adjacent palace is home to the **Museo Garibaldi** (*open Tues–Sun 10–6*), with a Risorgimento collection and material relating to the First and Second World Wars.

Three blocks west, at Via Diaz 84, is the **Pinacoteca Civica** (*open as above*) housed in the modernised Palazzo Volpi (1610–30). The arrangement is chronological, beginning with sculptural fragments and salvaged frescoes from old churches in Como and the surrounding area, including charming scenes from the lives of Sts Liberata and Faustina and an early 14th-century *Young Woman and Death* from the Broletto. Later sections contain many expressive portraits and a powerful *Vulcan* by Pompeo Batoni. The museum also holds the drawings of Antonio Sant'Elia.

PORTA VITTORIA

Facing an arcaded, stuccoed building on the corner of Via Parini is the church of **Santa Cecilia** (*map p. 219, 6*), whose porch incorporates some Roman columns. Despite the Neoclassical exterior, it is an old foundation, rebuilt by a lieutenant of the Spanish garrison in 1644. It served a nunnery, closed by Napoleon, who seized its high altarpiece by Orazio Gentileschi (now in the Brera in Milan). The other 17th-century altarpieces are still *in situ*. Next door is the **Liceo Statale** where Volta taught; beneath it lie the remains of Roman Como's Porta Praetoria (*contact the Musei Civici for guided tours*).

The **Porta Vittoria** (1192) takes the form of a five-tier arcaded tower. It is named in memory of a victory during the Italian struggle for independence: in 1848 the Austrian garrison in the barracks immediately opposite surrendered. Diagonally opposite the church is the house where the architect Sant'Elia lived. On the corner of Via Giovio and Via Cantù is a lovely old pharmacy. At the end of Via Parini is **Via Alessandro Volta**, with the house where the scientist lived and died (no. 62). At no 72–74, near the south end of the same street, is the old Mantero silk mill.

COMO SILK

The Sforza were partial to silk. Galeazzo Maria Sforza (1444–76) is recorded to have ordered 'five mulberry trees to be planted for every perch of land' in his dukedom. Ludovico il Moro continued the policy. A plaque on one of the streets in Como credits the introduction of silk manufacture to Pietro Boldoni, who opened the first recorded mill in 1510. In the Middle Ages, silk manufacture went through several stages, all controlled by different guilds, and there were separate winding, throwing, dyeing, spinning and weaving mills. Production only began to go vertical, with single factories controlling every stage of the process, in the 18th century. By 1870, Como was Italy's main centre for silk production, a position it still enjoys. The interesting **Silk Museum** (Museo Didattico della Seta; *open Tues–Fri 10–6, Sat 10–1, T: 031 303180, museosetacomo.com*), documenting Como's silk industry, is in an old factory on the outskirts of the town, at Via Castelnuovo 9 (*beyond map 6*).

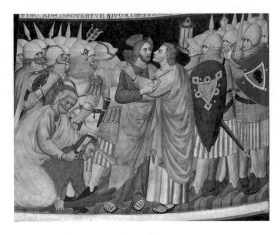

COMO
The Kiss of Judas, detail of the 14th-century apse frescoes in Sant'Abbondio.

SANT'ABBONDIO

Outside Porta Vittoria, beyond a busy road and 500m to the southwest (*map p. 219, 5*), is the fine Romanesque basilica of Sant'Abbondio, beside the railway line. Its twin bell-towers rear magnificently against the draped curtain of wooden mountain behind, vying in height with a neighbouring red-brick factory chimney. On the site of an early Christian building, the present church dates from the 11th century and is dedicated to St Abundius, Bishop of Como and papal legate to the Council of Chalcedon (AD 451), convened to quell the monophysite heresy, which held that Christ's human and divine natures were inseparable. The exterior has two graceful bell-towers and a finely decorated apse. The interior has tall grey columns supporting a clerestory of narrow lancets. The apse is entirely frescoed with scenes from the life of Christ, from the *Annunciation* to the *Entombment*, filled with delightful detail, by mid-14th-century Lombard artists. Under the high altar are the robed remains of St Abundius and two others, with fading notes pinned to them declaring their authenticity, as certified in 1933 by Alessandro Macchi, the Fascist-era Bishop of Como.

BRUNATE

From Piazza Cavour, Lungolario Trieste (*map p. 219, 4*) leads past the once-grand Palace Hotel, the charming, old-fashioned Como Nord Lago railway station and a small port, to the **funicular** station for Brunate (*services every 15 or 30mins, taking 7mins*). Brunate can also be reached from Via Grossi by road or by path. In a fine position overlooking the lake, Brunate (713m) became a resort at the end of the 19th century. From the upper station a 10-min walk leads gently uphill past huge, elaborate

19th- and 20th-century villas and their gardens, beneath an archway to emerge high above the lake. The view is very fine.

At the highest point of the village, near the funicular station (the mechanism of which you can see in the engine room), is the church of **Sant'Andrea**. It has 19th- and 20th-century frescoes inside, as well as a charming 15th-century fresco of a certain St Guglielma, a mysterious saint who according to one tradition was an English princess who married a Hungarian chieftain in the 8th century. Another version makes her the daughter of a 13th-century Hungarian princess and founder of a branch of Christianity which predicted a future for women as leaders of the Church. Her cult has been known in Brunate since before the 15th century.

Steps lead down the other side of the hill, away from the lake to the centre of the village. At **San Maurizio** (871m) is the Faro Voltiano, a monument to Alessandro Volta (1927).

A WALK FROM BRUNATE TO TORNO

This is a good circular excursion. From Torno, north of Como on the east shore (*map p. 227, 7*), there are frequent boats back to Como. The walk is easy except for the final descent of c. 400m. It takes about 2hrs.

At Brunate, find Via Nidrino and the football field. From here the route is signed '**Strada Regia**', the old road from Como to Bellagio. Follow the blue-and-white waymarks downhill right, into the forest. Twenty minutes later you reach a wooden cross and switchback; proceed straight. After 25mins more you come to a farm; follow the arrow for **Montepiatto** (straight, not downhill), which you reach after just 5mins. It is a village that can only be reached on foot. Go right at the fork (yellow tourist sign). After 25mins a group of houses on a hill comes into sight and the trail intersects a stepped path. Proceed downhill left. Twenty minutes (and c. 1,000 steps) later, you come to a tabernacle with the Christ Child and the Archangel Gabriel (?). Turn downhill left. Ten minutes later you come to the first houses of **Torno**, a delightful little village of terraced walkways, on the water. Continue straight downhill, then left (follow the red arrow). Cross the highway and continue down the steps to the waterfront. The landing with the boat back to Como is on your right.

THE COMO ARM OF THE LAKE

The Como arm of the lake is characterised by precipitous mountains on both sides, with rushing torrents entering the lake down deep clefts. Some parts are so steep-sided that at certain times of year they lose the sun early and the whole expanse becomes a kind of sunless sea.

CERNOBBIO

Cernobbio (*map p. 227, 7*) is a resort at the foot of Monte Bisbino (1325m). It has a pleasant waterfront with boats pulled up on the quay and an attractive Liberty-style landing stage. Beyond is the huge white **Villa d'Este hotel**, which occupies a villa built in 1568 by Cardinal Tolomeo Gallio (1527–1607), a native of Cernobbio. It was here, in 1816–17, that Caroline of Brunswick, Princess of Wales, lived in exile after her estrangement from the Prince Regent. She had the park landscaped in the English style and turned the villa into a house of pleasure. Her lewd dress sense and licentious behaviour shocked an entire continent: when George was finally crowned George IV in 1820, Caroline was debarred from the ceremony.

Not to be missed here is the lavish Liberty-style **Villa Bernasconi** (*Largo Campanini 2; villabernasconi.eu*), built for the textiles manufacturer Davide Bernasconi. In a very different style but equally lavish is the nearby neo-Renaissance **Villa Erba**, available for rent for private or corporate functions. Carla Erba was the mother of the film director Luchino Visconti.

VILLA PLINIANA

The yellow Villa Pliniana (1570) stands on a bay on the east bank beyond Torno. In the garden is a famous intermittent spring, described in detail by the Younger Pliny in his *Letters* and later studied by Leonardo da Vinci. The water, abundant when it flows, is channelled from a grotto down the cliff into the lake. Ugo Foscolo, Shelley, Stendhal and Rossini (who composed *Tancredi* here in 1813) were among the illustrious 19th-century visitors to the villa.

MOLTRASIO TO ARGEGNO

'The shore of the lake,' wrote Shelley in 1818, in a letter to Thomas Love Peacock, 'is one continued village.' If that was true then, it is truer still today. Moltrasio, Carate, Urio, Laglio and Torriggia were once separate settlements but today it is difficult to determine where one ends and the next begins. At the Villa Salterio in **Moltrasio**, Bellini composed the opera *Norma* in 1831. He wrote *La Sonnambula* in the 18th-century Villa Passalacqua (available for luxury rentals), which has an Italianate garden.

Laglio (*map p. 227, 7*) is popular with tourists hoping to get a glimpse of George Clooney, whose Villa Oleandra stands on the water here. In the cemetery is a curious tomb in the shape of a pyramid: the burial place of Joseph Frank (1771–1842), a doctor and pupil of Alessandro Volta, renowned for his extravagant parties.

At **Argegno**, where most boats stop, the high mountain ranges northeast of the lake come into view. Argegno lies at the foot of the beautiful, fertile Val d'Intelvi.

ISOLA COMACINA AND OSSUCCIO

Opposite Sala Comacina and Ossuccio is the **Isola Comacina** (*map p. 227, 5*), a pretty little wooded island with a *trattoria* but no permanent residents. The regular boat services call here, and a ferry service operates from Sala Comacina and Ossuccio, using motorised *lucia* boats, the traditional Lake Como craft, with high wooden hoops onto which canvas coverings were draped in wet or scorching weather. A ticket must

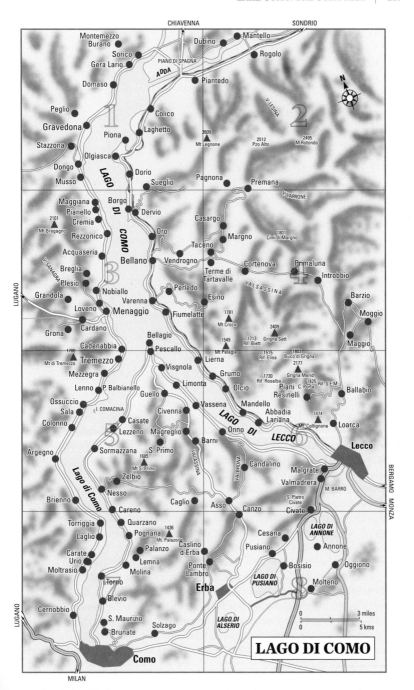

LAGO DI COMO

TREMEZZO
Detail of Canova's *Cupid and Psyche* in Villa Carlotta.

be purchased to visit the island (available at the island landing stage; *the island is open late March–Oct; for times, see isola-comacina.it*). The island was used as a hiding place by political refugees during the disturbed medieval history of Lombardy, and it was captured and raided by Como in 1169. In 1917 it passed by inheritance to Albert, King of the Belgians, but after his death in a climbing accident in the Ardennes it was taken over by the Accademia di Belle Arti of Milan, who commissioned the Rationalist architect Pietro Lingeri to build three houses here as artists' retreats. Paths lead along the shore of the lake and over the top of the island through wild vegetation past the ruins of its many medieval churches.

Finds from the island are on display at the Antiquarium in **Ossuccio** (*open 10–1 & 2–5 except Mon and Thur*), in the picturesque complex of the old hospice of Santa Maria Maddalena, its bell-tower resembling an ornate dovecote. At the top of the village, close to a car park beside the Perlana torrent, is the beginning of the **Sacro Monte**, one of nine 'Holy Mountains' in this part of Italy (*see p. 209*). A path ascends past 14 little chapels containing stucco and terracotta tableaux related to the Mysteries of the Rosary and dating from 1635–1710. At the top is the 16th-century **Santuario della Madonna del Soccorso**.

PUNTA DEL BALBIANELLO

The wooded headland of the Punta del Balbianello (*map p. 227, 5*) was used in the James Bond film *Casino Royale* and also *Star Wars II: Attack of the Clones*. The garden and loggia of the **Villa del Balbianello** can be visited (*open April–Oct Tues and Thur–Sun 10–6; last entry to villa 90mins before closing, to garden 45mins before; fondoambiente.it*). It can be reached by boat (*taxi boats from Lido di Lenno*) or on foot by a signposted path of roughly 800m, which starts from the church square in Lenno. The villa is surrounded by plane trees, magnolias, ilexes and cypresses. It was left to the FAI (Fondo per l'Ambiente Italiano) in 1988 by the explorer Guido Monzino, the first Italian to climb Everest (in 1973) and who reached the North Pole in 1971.

A steep flight of steps lead up from the dock to the villa, built by Cardinal Angelo Maria Durini in 1787 and incorporating the scant remains of a Franciscan convent (the façade of the church and its twin bell-towers survive). In the small formal garden above the villa, with laurel and box hedges, wisteria, azaleas and rhododendrons, is a delightful garden loggia with fine views. It incorporates a library and map room with Monzino's collections relating to the polar regions and mountaineering. The villa contains more of Monzino's collections from his explorations, and 18th- and 19th-century English and French furniture.

LENNO

At Lenno (*map p. 227, 5*) the shore is flatter, at the mouth of the Acquafredda. The parish church of Santo Stefano has an 11th–12th-century crypt and an 11th-century octagonal baptistery opposite. The foreshore here was the site of Pliny's villa 'Comedia' (his other villa, 'Tragedia', was at Bellagio, at the tip of the inlet between the two forks). You can walk along the lakeshore to Villa Balbianello (*see above*). Mussolini and his mistress, Claretta Petacci, were shot by partisans at nearby Giulino di Mezzegra on April 28th 1945, following their capture near Dongo, further up the lake.

THE TREMEZZINA

The attractive Tremezzina, the fertile green shore dotted with villas and gardens, extends along the foot of Monte di Tremezzo from Lenno to just north of Cadenabbia. The shore is flatter and wider here and humanity has had more space to spread out. The old stepped harbours are half covered over, more useful now as car-parking space.

Above the shore at **Tremezzo** (*map p. 227, 5*) looms the vast Grand Hotel, with a floating swimming pool in the lake. On the busy road is the pale pink **Villa Carlotta** (*open mid-March–early Nov 9 or 10–5 or 6; T: 0344 40405, villacarlotta.it*), built at the beginning of the 18th century by Marchese Giorgio Clerici. The interior was altered after 1795 by the Marchese Giambattista Sommariva; the opening scenes of *La Chartreuse de Parme* (1839) recall Stendhal's stay here as Sommariva's guest in 1818. The villa was bought in 1843 by Princess Albrecht of Prussia, who gave it to her daughter Carlotta in 1850, on her marriage to the Crown Prince of Saxe-Meiningen. Carlotta died just five years later, aged 23, and her widower devoted himself to his garden, laying out the magnificent wooded park in the Romantic style. It has beautiful camellias, rhododendrons and azaleas in spring.

In front of the house is a formal Italianate garden with shrubs and a fountain, and a theatrical flight of steps leading up to the house. The interior is interesting for its early 19th-century decorations, including Neoclassical works and Empire-style French furniture, and for its lovely painted ceilings dating from the 18th century. In the main room is Thorvaldsen's frieze of the *Triumphal Entry of Alexander into Babylon*, cast in plaster for Napoleon in 1812 and intended for the throne-room at the Quirinal. Also here are works by Canova (*Cupid and Psyche*, *Penitent Magdalene* and *Palamedes*). This last, and *Mars and Venus* by Luigi Acquisti, have rather comically had fig leaves attached to them. The *piano nobile* (second floor) has good views of the gardens, and in rooms off the long central hall, fine painted-wood 18th-century ceilings and Empire-style French furniture. The park behind the villa is of great botanical interest and is very well cared-for. Behind the villa to the right, the path leads past a rock garden to a plantation of palms and cacti. A valley watered by a stream has a splendid variety of tree ferns. Beyond, a straight path leads past banks of azaleas, and higher up the hillside is a bamboo garden. Behind the villa to the left, a bridge leads across a stream to an area of garden with camellias, a monkey-puzzle tree and Japanese maples. There is a café and picnic area in the lower garden.

Cadenabbia is an attractive resort with a lively waterfront. The first part of Gladys Huntington's 1956 novel *Madame Solario* is set here. From the suburb of Griante, a cobbled path leads to the sanctuary chapel of **San Martino** (*signposted from the landing stage*), perched on a ledge in the cliff and affording splendid views.

THE CENTRO LAGO

The Centro Lago, where the Como and Lecco arms meet, is the most beautiful part of the lake. The younger Pliny's villa 'Tragedia' is thought to have stood here, on the sheltered side of the headland known as Punta Spartivento: 'Wind-splitter Point'. The main resort is the little town of Bellagio, which is surrounded by numerous attractive village enclaves.

BELLAGIO

In a lovely, quiet position on a headland at the division of the lake is the famous resort of Bellagio (*map p. 227, 3*), which retains much of the picturesque aspect of an old Lombard town. It is strung out along two main thoroughfares, the upper Via Garibaldi and the lower road along the lakeshore. Stepped streets link the two, with the doglegging Via Centrale between them. There are surviving local industries of olive-wood carving and horticulture, but the main source of income is tourism.

Opening off the car ferry station is an attractive piazza. Here is the **Hotel Splendid**, with a plaque commemorating Filippo Marinetti, the founder of Futurism, who died here in 1944. Further south, you enter the area of the old medieval walled town, the *borgo*, beyond the broad Salita Serbelloni (with a plaque commemorating Liszt). From the arcaded waterfront (Piazza Mazzini), stepped streets lead up to Via Garibaldi,

CADENABBIA
The chapel of San Martino.

which ends in Piazza della Chiesa, with the 11th–12th-century church of **San Giacomo**. It contains a reconstructed primitive pulpit with symbols of the Evangelists, a painted triptych by the late 15th-century Lombard school (south side), a 19th-century copy of a *Deposition* by Perugino (north side) and, beneath this altar, a 16th-century wooden *Dead Christ* (a Spanish work). In the apse is a gilded tabernacle (16th and 18th centuries).

In the old tower opposite the church is the ticket office for the **Villa Serbelloni**. The entrance gate is behind San Giacomo. The villa and grounds (*shown April–Oct on Tues–Sun, tours last approx. 90mins and are cancelled in the event of rain*) were left to the Rockefeller Foundation in 1959 by Ella Walker Della Torre Tasso to be used as a study centre for students. The younger Pliny's villa 'Tragedia' is thought to have occupied this site. The magnificent park on the spectacular high promontory overlooking the lake was laid out at the end of the 18th century by Alessandro Serbelloni. In front of the villa, which incorporates a Romanesque tower, is a formal garden with topiary and olive, cypress and fruit trees.

Villa Melzi

Between Bellagio and Loppia, with entrance gates at both ends, Villa Melzi (*grounds open March–Oct 9.30–6, giardinidivillamelzi.it*) stands in a fine park with sculpturally pollarded plane trees. It was built in 1808–10 by Giocondo Albertolli as a summer residence for Francesco Melzi d'Eril, Vice President of Napoleon's Italian Republic in 1802 and later one of the architects of the Napoleonic Kingdom of Italy (he was accorded the signal honour of carrying the crown at Napoleon's coronation ceremony). Franz Liszt, the composer and pianist, also stayed here (his daughter Cosima was born in Bellagio in 1837). From the Bellagio entrance, the path takes you past a little **Japanese garden**, a circular pavilion on the lake and, on the slope above, the former orangery, which contains a small and poorly labelled **museum**. The two (rather misshapen) statues in front of the villa, representing Meleager and Apollo, are 16th-century works by Guglielmo della Porta. Beyond the villa at the Loppia end of the gardens is the **chapel**, with particularly fine Neoclassical family tombs.

PESCALLO, LOPPIA AND SAN GIOVANNI

The little fishing village of **Pescallo** faces east, on the Lecco side of the Bellagio peninsula. On the Lecco road just above the village, in the suburb of **Oliverio**, is the **Villa Giulia** with its old olive groves and the wide grassy roadway known as the Vialone, that was cut in the 18th century by the villa's owner, Count Venini, to provide views of both arms of the lake. At the bottom of it you pass, on your left, an elaborate mausoleum built for Giacomo Poldi Pezzoli (*see p. 41*) and then cross the road where steps lead down to the little harbour of **Loppia**, above the half-ruined church of Santa Maria. There is an entrance to Villa Melzi (*see above*) here.

A short way south (left) is **San Giovanni**, a village of cobbled streets, with a waterfront church set back from the steep, stepped harbour. The church contains an altarpiece by Gaudenzio Ferrari (north side). Here also is the **Museo degli Strumenti per la Navigazione**, a small museum of nautical instruments (*open in summer daily 10–1, T: 031 950309, bellagiomuseo.com*).

BELLAGIO TO ASSO

An inland road leads south from Bellagio to Asso via Civenna. Beyond Guello a road on the right climbs to the foot of **Monte San Primo** (1686m). At the edge of the town of **Civenna**, by the cemetery, is a small park with spectacular views of the lake from Gravedona in the north to Lecco in the south. From the small church of **Madonna del Ghisallo** (754m; with votive offerings from champion cyclists), the highest point of the road, there is another excellent view (left) with the two Grigne beyond, and of Bellagio behind. The road descends the steep Vallassina to **Asso** (*map p. 227, 6*), with remains of a medieval castle. Here the graceful 17th-century church of San Giovanni Battista has an elaborate gilded-wood Baroque altar and an *Annunciation* by Giulio Campi. Almost continuous with Asso is **Canzo**, the centre of valley life.

VARENNA

Varenna (*map p. 227, 3*) is an attractive town, very popular in summer as a destination for day trips, with a port connected to the hinterland by narrow, stepped streets. It has a good view across to the promontory of Bellagio. From the main ferry dock, a walkway

VARENNA
Plaster and sacking 'ghost' at the Castello di Vezio.

(built in 1982) leads above the lake (with wonderful sunsets across the water) past a string of cafés overlooking the old port, with its slipway for fishing boats. The old shops on the arcaded waterfront street here are former workshops where the local black marble and green *lumachella*, or shell-marble, from the neighbouring quarries, was prepared for shipping. They house restaurants and boutiques. The walkway brings you out into the main square of old Varenna, with its restaurants, hotels, pollarded plane trees and two churches.

Piazza San Giorgio
At the lakeside end of the square is the 11th-century church of **San Giovanni**, which has remains of 14th–16th-century frescoes (*Adoration of the Magi, St George, Baptism of Christ*). Facing the main road is the church of **San Giorgio**, with a 14th-century fresco of *St Christopher* on its façade. The broad interior contains a pavement and altar made of the local black marble and, above the high altar, a 15th-century polyptych by the local artist Giovan Pietro Brentani. The west wall has traces of a frescoed *Last*

VARENNA
Villa Monastero.

Judgement and in the chapel to the left of the high altar is a fine *Baptism of Christ* signed and dated (1533) by Sigismondo de Magistris (Sigismund of Como).

Just out of the piazza, on the main road to Lecco, is the Information Office and a small **ornithological museum**. Diagonally opposite is the entrance to the **Hotel Villa Cipressi**, which takes its name from its numerous cypresses (60 of which had to be felled after a tornado in 1967). The well-maintained garden, with a venerable wisteria, descends in steep terraces down to the lakeside.

Villa Monastero

Entrance at the beginning of the main road towards Lecco. Gardens generally open daily. House less frequently (check before visiting). T: 0341 295450, villamonastero.eu.

The enormous monastery here, founded in 1208, was closed down in the 16th century by St Charles Borromeo and the villa is now a conference centre. The rooms on show in the interior, decorated with yellow and black marble with richly carved furniture and an extraordinarily elaborate bathroom, mostly date from the late 19th century when improvements were carried out by the German owner.

The lovely garden is laid out on a long, narrow terrace on the lakeside with 19th-century statuary, fine cypresses, palms, roses, hydrangeas and wisteria, and one huge old magnolia tree. There are also numerous citrus trees, including grapefruit. There are beautiful views back towards the Villa Cipressi and Varenna.

Fiumelatte

Beyond the Villa Monastero, the road (signed 'Greenway dei Patriarchi') leads uphill to the town cemetery, from where steps lead to a pretty woodland path (c. 1km) to the spring of Fiumelatte, active from May to October. Like the spring at the Villa Pliniana (*see p. 226*), its flow is intermittent, and though it has been studied by numerous experts (including Leonardo da Vinci), it is still not known why. When in full flow, the waters roll down the hill in a gushing torrent turning the water an opaque, milky white, hence its name: Fiumelatte, 'Milk River'. Another path here, signed 'Baluardo', leads to a wide terrace commanding a panoramic view of the lake.

Castello di Vezio

Behind the main ferry port, signs direct you up a narrow cobbled path (*quite steep, walking time c. 20mins*) to the hamlet and **castle of Vezio**. The precise age and history of the castle (privately owned; *open March–early Nov; castellodivezio.it*) is uncertain, though it is likely to have been built for strategic reasons, possibly during late antiquity. There are legends linking its construction to the Lombard queen Theodolinda (*see p. 130*). Today it offers fine views, a café/bar, a small display of fossils of a Triassic-period reptile known as the Lariosaurus, and a collection of 'ghosts' in the grounds, statues formed of sacking and plaster wrapped around human models and left to dry. When dry, the models extract themselves, leaving the empty husks behind.

A diversion from the path to Vezio takes you to the **Orrido di Vezio**, the pretty gorge of the Esino torrent, with a stone bridge and a house frescoed with a *Madonna and Child*.

THE UPPER LAKE

WEST SHORE: MENAGGIO TO DOMASO

Menaggio (*map p. 227, 3*) is a pleasant town, well served by boats. Beyond the pier and the Grand Hotel, the busy main road can be followed on foot for a few minutes to the pretty piazza on the waterfront. Roads lead uphill behind the church to the narrow cobbled lanes which traverse the area of the castle, with some fine large villas and a 17th-century wall fountain.

Beyond the Sangra river is **Loveno**; the Villa Calabi was the home of the patriot and writer Massimo d'Azeglio (1798–1865). There are several fine walks in the area beneath the beautiful Monte Bregagno (2107m).

Rezzonico, with a castle, was the home of the powerful family which bore its name and numbered Pope Clement XIII among its famous members. The old church of San Vito has a fine *Madonna and Angels* attributed to Bergognone.

The village of **Pianello del Lario** has a 12th-century church and a small museum of lake boats, Museo della Barca Lariana (*Via Regina 1268, museobarcalariana.it*). There is a pleasant swimming beach here and at numerous other places on this northwestern shore. **Musso** is overlooked by the almost impregnable Rocca di Musso, the stronghold in 1525–32 of the piratical *condottiere* Gian Giacomo Medici, who levied tribute from the traders of the lake and the neighbouring valleys. He is buried in state in the Duomo of Milan (*see p. 32*).

Dongo, with Gravedona and Sorico (*map p. 227, 1*), formed the independent Republic of the Three Parishes (*Tre Pievi*), which survived until the Spanish occupation of Lombardy. Mussolini was captured by partisans near Dongo in the spring of 1945, after which he was taken to Mezzegra and shot. The 12th-century church of Santa Maria in the adjacent hamlet of **Martinico** preserves an interesting doorway.

Gravedona is the principal village of the upper lake. The foursquare, turreted Villa Gallio at the north end of the village was built c. 1586 by Pellegrino Tibaldi for Cardinal Tolomeo Gallio. Surrounded by a garden where there is a giant rhododendron, it is now used for exhibitions. Nearer the boat station are the remains of the ivy-covered castle with a clock tower rising above it. **Domaso**, with its two tall bell-towers, is another pleasant resort village.

EAST SHORE: BELLANO TO COLICO

Looking at a map, you see clearly how the steep mountain torrents in the northern part of the lake have pushed silt and debris out into the water forming spits of land onto which human settlement has subsequently clung. **Bellano** (*map p. 227, 3*) is one such town, formerly a place of silk and cotton mills at the mouth of the Pioverna. The deep **Pioverna Gorge** can be viewed from stairs and walkways (*open daily in summer, weekends in winter; see turismobellano.it*). The restored church of Santi Nazaro e Celso is a good example of the 14th-century Lombard style.

Dervio has a ruined castle on a crag above its gorge and an old campanile at the foot of Monte Legnone (2601m). Just beyond Dorio a cobbled road (signposted for Piona)

LECCO
Door handle, basilica of San Nicolò.

diverges left and traverses woods for c. 2km, across a peninsula where the handsome Villa Malpensata faces the water below Olgiasco. At the tip of the peninsula is the Benedictine **Abbey of Piona** (*map p. 227, 1; open 9–12 & 2.30–6; abbaziadipiona.it*), overlooking the main lake as well as a peaceful bay. The simple church has two large stoups borne by Romanesque lions, and behind it is the ruined apse of an earlier church. The irregular cloister has a variety of 12th-century capitals. Monastic products are sold in the shop and vespers are sung every evening in Gregorian chant. There is a ferry station here, open in summer.

Colico, a plain, even ugly town, occupies the flatlands near the mouth of the Adda at the junction of the routes over the Splügen and Stelvio passes. Trains leave from here for the Valtellina (*see p. 239*). A plaque on the main platform commemorates the Hungarian engineer Kálmán Kandó, who in 1903 built the first ever high-voltage three-phase AC electric railway line linking Lecco with Sondrio and Colico with Chiavenna.

LECCO

The town of Lecco (*map p. 227, 6*) has a venerable industrial heritage, thanks to its position beside the Gerenzone torrent, which provided power for the metalworks that grew up here. Lecco's industrial history makes itself felt in its sprawling, rather dilapidated outskirts: but the old centre is very pleasant and much less geared to tourism than other places on the lake.

The heart of town is its pleasant **waterfront**, with a large War Memorial and small boats pulled up on the slipway. To the south is **Ponte Vecchio**, built by Azzone Visconti in 1336–8 and later altered and enlarged. Beyond it, the River Adda flows out of the lake to begin its long descent to the Po. The Palazzo delle Paure contemporary art gallery gives onto the attractive **Piazza XX Settembre**, harmoniously surrounded by three-storey 18th-century buildings, some with Tuscan arcades at street level, with numerous cafés. At no. 3 (south end) is the low, wide, machicolated **Torre Viscontea**, originally built to fortify the city after its conquest by the Visconti in 1296. In the 16th century it was used by a Spanish garrison. The military presence at Lecco continued until the reforms of Emperor Joseph II in 1782.

Just off Piazza XX Settembre to the north, at the top of a wide flight of steps, is the **basilica of San Nicolò** (note the secular door handles), with a wide mid-19th-century Neoclassical interior of elegant *froideur*, the work of the local architect Giuseppe Antonio Bovara. On certain dates between May and Sept it is possible to climb the exceptionally tall (96m), slender bell-tower (*www.campaniledilecco.it*).

From the north end of Piazza XX Settembre, the pretty, cobbled Via Bovara (named after the architect, who was born at no. 39 in 1781) leads uphill. Beyond the roundabout, the road continues north as Via Matteotti. At no. 32 on the right is Palazzo Belgiojoso, home to the **town museums** (*open Tues–Fri 9.30–2, Sat–Sun 10–6*), which are divided into three sections. On the upper floor are the Natural History collections, formed in 1888 around the private collection of Carlo Vercelloni, a local naturalist and taxidermist (d. 1932). Displays include stuffed mammals, reptiles and birds (including a queztal), as well as butterflies, beetles and other insects. The archaeological section is in the basement, with displays of mainly local finds from the Stone Age to the Lombard era, including Golasecca ware from Chiuso, south of Lecco. The ground floor has the local history exhibit, which covers the story of Lecco's industry as well as its role in the Second World War. There are some haunting prints by the artist Giansisto Gasparini on the themes of war, resistance, collaboration and reprisals. The gardens of the *palazzo* are now a public park, also home to a planetarium.

Lecco is known for its associations with the novelist Alessandro Manzoni (*see p. 39*), whose famous novel *I promessi sposi* (*The Betrothed*) is set in and around the town. Beyond the railway is **Villa Manzoni** (*Via Guanella 1; open Tues–Fri 9.30–6, Sat–Sun 10–6, museilecco.org*), a gloomy, austere house, bought by Manzoni's ancestors before 1621 and where Manzoni lived as a boy. It contains a museum of memorabilia and a collection of local paintings.

Beyond the railway bridge is **Pescarenico**, a former fishermen's hamlet, with narrow streets and an attractive piazza on the waterfront (paved in the 17th century). Here you can sometimes see the flat-bottomed, hooped *lucie*, characteristic fishing boats once used all over the lake (named after Lucia in *I promessi sposi*). Across the main road is the church, built by the Spanish in the 16th century and formerly serving a convent of Capuchin friars (dissolved by Napoleon). It has an eccentric triangular campanile and a Neoclassical façade by Giuseppe Bovara. Inside is an ancona with little polychrome scenes of the lives of St Francis and St Clare in *papier mâché* and wax. In front of the church is a tabernacle with friars' skulls, a reminder of the plague.

AROUND LECCO

At **Mandello**, on the lake northwest of Lecco, is the Guzzi museum, housed in the factory where the famous 'Eagle brand' motorbikes are made (*limited opening hours; see motoguzzi.com*). Founded in Genoa in 1921, Guzzi created a wind tunnel in their Mandello plant in 1950, for testing bikes under simulated conditions. It remains the only such wind tunnel in the world.

South of Lecco is **Malgrate**, once, like Como, known for its silk and now a pleasant lakeside resort with good views of Lecco backed by its mountains. Southwest of Malgrate is the Lago d'Annone. From Civate a footpath leads in just over an hour to the picturesque former abbey of **San Pietro al Monte** (630m), with the partly ruined church of San Pietro dating from the 10th century; it has lateral apses, 11th–12th-century mural paintings, and a remarkable baldachin above the main altar.

THE VALTELLINA

The Valtellina, the upper valley of the Adda river, stretches between Bormio (*Atlas C, C1*) and Colico (*Atlas D, C2*), where the Adda empties into Lake Como. The valley floor is scattered with light industry; the steep valley sides are clad in terraces with vines producing the excellent local red wines. The winery names—Grumello, Sassorosso, Negri—are posted up in large letters beside each plot. Above the valley tower high mountain ranges: the Alpi Orobie to the south and to the north the Rhaetian Alps (Alpi Retiche), rising up to form the border with Switzerland. The highest peaks include the glumly-named Monte Disgrazia (3678m) on the Italian side and on the Swiss, the mighty Pizzo Bernina (4049).

HISTORY OF THE VALTELLINA

The valley has had a chequered history. In the 14th century it came under the control of Milan, but in 1512 it was united to the canton of Grisons/Graubünden in Switzerland. The Reformation took a firm hold here, and on 19th July 1620, at the instigation of the Spanish governor of Milan, the Catholic inhabitants of the valley ruthlessly massacred the Protestants (the 'Sacro Macello'). Twenty years of warfare followed, with France and Venice lending support to the Protestants and the Catholic faction aided by the Habsburgs. In 1639, after one of the faction leaders, a rebel former Protestant, converted to Catholicism and was killed by an assailant dressed as a bear (during Carnival), the valley was regained by the Grisons, who held it until Napoleon's partition of 1797, when he added it to his Cisalpine Republic. After Napoleon's fall it came under Austrian control and joined the Kingdom of Piedmont-Sardinia in 1859.

SONDRIO
Piazza Campello.

SONDRIO

Sondrio (*Atlas C, A2*) is the main town of the valley, a pleasant, prosperous, interesting place, well worth a visit. The houses in the old centre are built of the local grey and black stone, with façades rendered in sober pale fawn and cream. The principal square of the old town is **Piazza Garibaldi**, completely pedestrianised and surrounded by a harmonious ensemble of Neoclassical buildings, including the Teatro Sociale, designed by Luigi Canonica and modelled on La Scala in Milan. It opened in 1824, not long after the square itself had been laid out by the Habsburg rulers of Lombardy. Above the rooftops on all sides, tall mountain peaks reach into the sky: this sense of being enfolded in an alpine embrace is everywhere present in Sondrio. To the west of the square, across the main road and spanned by bridges, is the rushing **Mallero torrent**, its waters the pale, limpid grey-blue of melted glacier. On **Via Fracaiolo**, which runs behind Piazza Cavour (the old market square of Sondrio), you can see how the Mallero has been channelled for domestic use: this area was once filled with workshops and the old public laundry survives, with a curious pebble-encrusted nymphaeum beside it, designed by the local architect and painter Gian Pietro Ligari, whose works can also be seen in the Collegiata and MUSA.

From Piazza Cavour a stepped lane, its paving incorporating a slight groove to allow water to flow down one side, leads steeply up between tall houses (including the one where Ligari lived, at no. 2) to the **Castello Masegra**, built on a rocky outcrop ('*crap*' in local dialect). This former stronghold of the lords of Sondrio has frescoed rooms that are sometimes open to the public (*usually on Sat, Sun and holidays from May–Sept; information from the MUSA*). You can descend from Castello Masegra down the picturesque **Via Scarpatetti**, which brings you out into the peaceful Piazza Quadrivio, with its fountain and fine façade of **Palazzo Sertoli**. The interior, which can sometimes be seen, has a particularly fine ballroom.

THE COLLEGIATA

Sondrio's principal church, the Collegiata, is a plain building with a large Diocletian window and detached bell-tower on Piazza Campello, a square named after the cemetery which functioned here until Napoleonic times, when burial within the city walls was forbidden. The Neoclassical façade dates from 1838 while the remainder was built between 1727 and 1797, successor to a medieval predecessor. Grand plans by Pietro Ligari to remodel it further (designs for which are preserved in MUSA) came to nothing for lack of funds.

The interior is dark and solemn, with a dramatically-lit Crucifix at the east end and five paintings by Ligari: the titular saints Gervase and Protase in the sanctuary (both shown in Roman garb; 1725); the *Virgin of the Rosary with Sts Dominic and Stephen* (1738) between the first and second south chapels; the *Mass of St Gregory* between the first and second north chapels; and the *Adoration of the Holy Sacrament* (1727) at the top of the north side. The finely carved choir stalls are by the Venetian master Giovanni Battista Zotti (1705). At the west end (south side) is a work by Antonio Caimi, who was born in Sondrio: *Nicolò Rusca at Prayer* (1852). The urn below it contains relics of Rusca, archpriest and staunch anti-Protestant who was tortured to death in 1618 during the 'Sacro Macello' (*see p. 239*).

MUSA AND MUMIV

Sondrio has two main museums. **MUSA** (Museo Valtellinese di Storia e Arte; *open Tues–Sun 9–12 & 3–6; entrance on Via Lavizzari*) occupies the former palace of the Salis family. It contains archaeological material, period costumes, liturgical objects and paintings of the Lombard school, including works by Pietro Ligari and his descendants. There is a fine (albeit rather preposterous-looking) 18th-century snow sleigh and a charming *Adoration of the Christ Child* attributed to Sigismondo de Magistris. Of particular interest is the *stüa*, which is original to the palace. A *stüa* was traditionally the heart of every Valtellinese home, panelled in wood on walls and ceiling and kept well heated (the word derives from *stufa*, a stove). The *stüa* of the Salis family is lavishly decorated with carved coats of arms and other devices.

Sondrio's mineralogical collection, **MUMIV** (Museo Mineralogico della Valtellina e Valchiavenna; *open Tues–Sun; entrance on Via Dante*) occupies Palazzo Martinengo, the oldest parts of which date from the 16th century.

From the centre of Sondrio, red and white waymarked walks take you up old cobbled mule tracks into the vineyards. One of the paths leads west to the sanctuary church of the **Madonna della Sassella**, which overlooks the Adda river and the valley road, the SS38. There is a restaurant just below the church (Torre della Sassella).

EXCURSIONS FROM SONDRIO

To visit the beautiful **Valmalenco**, the valley of the Mallero torrent north of Sondrio, it is best to start from the small town of **Chiesa in Valmalenco** (*Atlas C, A2; buses leave regularly from Sondrio; see p. 245*). The bus drops you outside the town sports centre (which has a good café/bar), right opposite the cable car station. The cable car, known as the Snow Eagle (the largest in the world; the cabins hold 160 people plus the operator), makes the dramatic 1000m ascent in just four minutes. At the top, depending on the season, you are either in a winter sports paradise or in a land of summer pastures, with wild bilberries, heather, myrtle, gentians and juniper. There are plenty of waymarked walks; a chairlift ascends to the summit of Monte Motta (2336m); alternatively it is a short stroll to the **Lago di Palù**, on the shores of which is a *rifugio* serving meals (accommodation also available; *rifugiopalu.com*). You can hike back to the cablecar past the hamlet of Campolungo, where cows (all with bells) are put out to grass in high summer and where the stone buildings are roofed in the traditional manner, with round slabs of schist.

East of Sondrio at **Tresivio** (*Atlas C, B2*), perched on a rock ledge among vineyards on the north side of the valley, is a sanctuary church known as the Santa Casa Lauretana (*open June–Sept Sat–Sun 10–12 & 3–6; other times by appointment, T: 0342 430118 or 340 474 0388*). Taking the form of a tall cube with a central gable flanked by bellcotes, it dates from the 17th–18th centuries and replaces a much earlier church, which now

TIRANO
Trompe l'oeil spiral stairway in Palazzo Salis.

forms the crypt. In the interior is a lavishly decorated 'Holy House of Loreto' (a shrine built to replicate the house of the Virgin, which, according to legend, was wafted by angels from the Holy Land to Loreto in the Marche). It contains a sculpted Black Madonna. The first north altarpiece is by Pietro Ligari.

After **Teglio**, once the principal place in the valley (to which it gave its name, 'Vallis Tellina'), the road curves northwards to Tirano.

TIRANO

The old district of Tirano (*Atlas C, B2*), on the left bank of the Adda, has historic mansions of the Visconti, Pallavicini and Salis families. The late 16th-century **Palazzo Salis** (*open April–Oct Mon–Sat 10–3.30; last entry 30mins before closing; palazzosalis. com*), still owned by the family, faces a small piazza with three venerable plane trees.

Visitors are allowed up to the *piano nobile*, with its enfilade of frescoed salons, and to the small formal garden at the back. The Sala di Apollo e Aurora has a ceiling fresco of Apollo in his chariot flying across a limpid sky (and around the walls cartoons by the Sondrio-born artist Antonio Caimi for his paintings in the parish church of San Martino). The Camera delle Meravigli is frescoed with the Seven Wonders of the World, plus an eighth, the Colosseum at Rome. The small cabinet known as the Studiolo dell'Olimpo has frescoes of Olympian gods and goddesses in horse-drawn chariots. The chapel is dedicated to St Charles Borromeo. The finest of all the salons, the Saloncello, has a *trompe l'oeil* ceiling depicting an arcaded gallery supporting a balustrade above which rises a lantern open to the sky, in which floats the god Bacchus.

On the other side of the Adda, beyond the railway station to the north, is the pilgrimage church of the **Madonna di Tirano**, begun after 1501 after the Virgin allegedly appeared to a local labourer, commanding him to build a church. The resulting building, broadly in the style of Bramante though with a somewhat top-heavy façade, was consecrated in 1523. The former convent now houses an ethnographic museum, the **Museo Etnografico Tiranese** (*open June–Sept Tues–Sun 10–12.30 & 3.30–6, Oct–May Sat 2.30–5.30; other times on request; museotirano.it*).

The Bernina and Valtellina railways both terminate in Tirano (separate railway stations, adjacent to one another). The **Bernina Express** or Rhaetian Railway (Rhätische Bahn), which links Tirano with St Moritz, Davos and Chur, was constructed in 1910 and has been on the UNESCO list since 2008 (*for information about times and tickets, see rhb.ch*). The smart red trains gently climb several hundred metres to cross the Bernina Pass (2253m), rolling through stunning scenery of craggy peaks and majestic glaciers. The railway is also an extraordinary feat of engineering, making use of very few tunnels but instead implementing a series of curving viaducts (notably the circular Brusio Viaduct and the famous Landwasser Viaduct, on tall arched stilts) to negotiate the steep inclines. Above the tree line at Ospizio Bernina, the railway crosses the watershed between the Adriatic and the Black Sea. Raindrops falling here will either make their way into the Adriatic via the Adda and the Po or into the Black Sea via the Inn and the Danube. The journey affords excellent views of the Pizzo Bernina (4049m) and the largest of the glaciers, the Morteratsch.

GROSIO

Further up the Adda valley is Grosio (*Atlas C, C2*), a large village with 15th–16th-century houses, including a mansion owned by the Venosta (restored as the seat of the Museo Civico). It was the birthplace of Cipriano Valorsa (1515–1604), the 'Raphael of the Valtellina', whose paintings adorn a number of churches in the valley. In the chestnut woods above the road are the ruins of two Venosta castles, one dating from the 12th century with the Romanesque campanile of the church of Santi Faustino e Giovita, and the other from the 14th century with fine battlements. Here in 1966 were discovered thousands of rock carvings (including human figures) dating from the Neolithic period to the Iron Age, the most interesting of which are on the Rupe Magna (*for information on the park and abut guided tours, see parcoincisionigrosio.it*).

CHIAVENNA

From Colico, it is 30mins by train to Chiavenna (*Atlas D, C1*), a mountain village on the Mera river, where the ancient **Collegiata di San Lorenzo**, probably founded in the 5th century, preserves a monolithic 12th-century font in its baptistery, made of local grey *pietra ollare* stone. The church treasury is exceptionally rich.

PRACTICAL INFORMATION

GETTING AROUND

• **By rail:** There is a direct route between Malpensa airport and Como (San Giovanni station). Journey time c. 1hr 40mins.

Como and Lecco are easily reached by frequent train services from Milan, and there is a railway line that skirts the eastern shore of the lake from Lecco to Colico. From Milan Centrale to Como San Giovanni by EuroCity is c.35mins. There are slower trains from Porta Garibaldi station to Como Nord Lago. Also suburban train S11 to Como and S7 or S8 to Lecco (all from Porta Garibaldi). From Milan to Lecco, 50–65mins; to Varenna 1hr 15mins; to Colico 1hr 40mins.

There are trains from Milano Centrale to Sondrio in 2hrs. Trains to Sondrio also leave from Lecco and Colico. Tirano is on the same line. There are trains from Colico to Chiavenna in 30mins.

• **By bus: Como** town and the west side of the lake are served by buses operated by ASF (*asfautolinee.it*). City and regional buses in Como leave from Via Plinio (*map p. 219, 4*). The **Lecco** side of the lake is served by Linee Lecco buses (*lineelecco.it*).

In the Valtellina, buses for **Chiesa in Valmalenco** leave from the bus station in Sondrio (behind the railway station). Take the bus which terminates at Lanzada or Caspoggio and get off at the Vassalini stop in Chiesa, at the far end of the village at the bottom of the hill. Journey time c. 40mins.

• **By boat and hydrofoil:** Services are maintained throughout the year between Como and Colico, calling at numerous places on the way. The timetable changes according to season (*see navigazionelaghi.it*). Tickets valid for 24hrs or for several days can be purchased. Most of the boats run between Como and Bellano (boats in c. 2hrs 30mins, hydrofoils in c. 1hr), while most of the hydrofoils continue to Colico (Como to Colico in c. 1hr 30mins). For the hydrofoil services, a supplementary ticket is required. There is a less frequent service between Bellagio and Lecco in summer (only on holidays for the rest of the year). In the central part of the lake, Varenna, Bellagio and Menaggio are well served. A car ferry runs frequently between Menaggio and Cadenabbia on the west bank to Varenna and Bellagio.

There are companies offering boats for hire all over the lake. There is a

good one operating out of the marina at Ossuccio (*hiringaboat.com, T: 329 214 2280; open March–mid-Nov*).
• **By seaplane:** The Como Aero Club offers trips. For details, see *aeroclubcomo.com*.

INFORMATION OFFICES

Bellagio *Piazza della Chiesa 14* (in the tower opposite the church).
Como IAT. *Piazza Cavour 17* (*map p. 219, 4*). *visitcomo.eu.*
Lecco Infopoint. *Piazza XX Settembre 23.*
Sondrio. *Via Tonale 13* (bus station, behind the railway station). For information on the whole of the Valtellina.
Varenna *Via IV Novembre 7* (just off the main Piazza San Giorgio, in the Lecco direction).

WHERE TO STAY: COMO

BELLAGIO
€€€€ **Grand Hotel Villa Serbelloni**. A grand hotel from the great era of resort tourism. Ideally situated in a former villa of the Serbelloni family, on the headland of Bellagio with stunning views, lakeside pool and excellent restaurant. The lakefront rooms are stunning. Open Easter–Oct. *Via Roma 1. T: 031 950216, www.villaserbelloni.it.*
€€ **Florence**. On the Bellagio lakefront, charming and elegant with a café and restaurant (seating on the water in summer); some rooms have terraces, others overlook the gardens of Villa Serbelloni. Spa. Closed winter. *Piazza Mazzini 46. T: 031 950342, hoterlflorencebellagio.it.*

CERNOBBIO
€€€€ **Villa d'Este**. Historic property on the lake, set in a landmark park. Since 1873 a luxury hotel, now one of the Leading Hotels of the World. Only suites and junior suites have lake views. The swimming pool floats in the lake. Open March–Nov. *Via Regina 40. T: 031 3481, villadeste.com.*

COMO
€€ **Metropole Suisse**. On the waterfront, in a building with alterations made by Terragni. Lake views. *Piazza Cavour 19. T: 031 269444, hotelmetropolesuisse.com.*
€–€€ **Borgo Antico**. Comfortable small hotel. *Via Borgovico 47. T: 031 338 0150, borgoanticohotelcomo.it.*
€ **Le Dame della Cortesella**. Comfortable, centra B&B in an old building. *Via Milano 56. T: 333 792 1883, ledamedellacortesella.com.*

TREMEZZO
€€ **Rusall**. Simple, family-run establishment in a quiet, panoramic location with excellent views. Closed winter. Above the lakeshore towards the San Martino chapel. *Via S. Martino 2. T: 0344 40408, rusallhotel.com.*

VARENNA
€€€ **Royal Victoria**. In a 19th-century villa, with terraced garden, swimming pool and private lake beach. It also has a gourmet restaurant and a more informal grill. *Piazza San Giorgio 5. T: 034 815111, www.royalvictoria.com.*
€€ **Du Lac**. Small and intimate, in a former lake house, with a very pleasant terrace overlooking the water. Open March–Nov. *Via del Prestino 11. T: 0341 830238, www.albergodulac.com.*

WHERE TO STAY: VALTELLINA

SONDRIO
Grand Hotel della Posta. Fine old building, built as a hotel and opened in 1862. Excellent location on Piazza Garibaldi. Spacious, comfortably furnished rooms, small spa/wellness centre, good breakfasts. The helpful staff can give you all the information you need about hiking in the area. *Piazza Garibaldi 19. T: 0342 200397, grandhoteldellaposta.eu.*

WHERE TO EAT: COMO

BELLAGIO
€€€ **Alle Darsene di Loppia**. Fine restaurant in an old ship shed, very close to Villa Melzi. Eat under the pergola in fine weather or indoors when it's cold. Closed Mon. *Via Melzi d'Eril 1. T: 031 952069, ristorantedarsenediloppia.com.*

€€€ **Silvio**. Slow Food restaurant in the hotel of the same name near Villa Melzi. Plenty of lake fish dishes. *Via Carcano 12. T: 031 950322, bellagiosilvio.com.*

€€ **Goletta**. Elegant-informal restaurant attached to the Villa Serbelloni. Specialities from the lake and the land. Good views and good food. *Via Roma 1. T: 031 956426, ristorantegoletta.it.*

€€ **La Pergola**. On the water in Pescallo. A picturesque walk along cobbled lanes from Bellagio. Closed Tues except in Aug. *Piazza del Porto 4. T: 031 950263, lapergolabellagio.it.*

€€ **La Punta**. Restaurant in a fabulous location right on the tip of Punta Spartivento. Classic dishes with some local and lake specialities. *Via Eugenio Vitali 19. T: 031 95188, lapunta.it.*

COMO
€€–€€€ **Ristorante Tennis Como**. Near Villa Olmo, this is the club restaurant, but members of the public are welcome too. Excellent food and good wines. Closed Mon and Sun evening. *Via S. Cantoni 1, T: 031 031 274 1651, tenniscomo.it. Map p. 219, 1.*

€€ **Ristorante Sociale**. Old-established restaurant serving traditional Como cuisine. Brick-vaulted front room with stuccoes and frescoes. Closed Tues. *Via Rodari 6. T: 031 264042. ristorantesociale.it. Map p. 219, 4.*

€€ **Il Solito Posto**. Good *trattoria* with a warm atomsphere and local cooking. *Via Lambertenghi 9. T: 031 271352 ilsolitoposto.net. Map p. 219, 4.*

€€ **Teatro**. Café and restaurant in the same Neoclassical building as the theatre. Right behind the duomo, with tables outside in the square in fine weather and with a garden. *Piazza Verdi 11. T: 031 414 0363. Map p. 219, 6.*

€ **Il Vecchio Borgo**. Grilled fish and meat, also pizza. Very close to the lake and to Como Nord station. Also has rooms. *Piazza Matteotti. ilvecchioborgocomo.it. Map p. 219, 4.*

LECCO
€€ **Corte Fiorina**. *Trattoria* in the secluded cobbled courtyard of Palazzo Bovara. In the old centre, close to Piazza XX Settembre. *Via Bovara 17.*

LENNO
€ **Santo Stefano**. *Trattoria* serving a good mix of classic dishes. Well placed for the Villa Balbianello. Closed Mon and Oct–Nov. *Piazza XI Febbraio 3. T: 034 455434, santostefanolenno.it.*

SALA COMACINA
€€ **La Tirlindana**. On the harbour, tables outside under the spreading tree, or in the vaulted inside room

painted with a mural of the harbour view (of Isola Comacina). Closed Wed in winter. *Piazza Matteotti. T: 0344 56637, tirlindana.lariovalle.com.*

TORNO
€€ **Vapore**. The restaurant of a pleasantly old-fashioned hotel on the old fishing harbour. Local dishes and a sedate atmosphere. *Via Plinio 20. T: 031 419311, hotelvapore.it.*

TREMEZZO
There is no shortage of places to eat on the waterfront at Cadenabbia and Tremezzo. If you are walking to San Martino, €–€€ **Rusall**, a family-managed place in the hotel of the same name, offers good local cuisine. Closed Wed and Jan–March. *Via San Martino 2. T: 0344 40408, rusallhotel.com.*

VARENNA
€€€ **Royal Victoria**. The hotel has two restaurants, a grill and pizzeria (open year-round) facing the main square, and a gourmet restaurant on the waterfront (closed in winter). Both are highly recommended. *Piazza San Giorgio. T: 0341 815111, royalvictoria.com.*

€€ **Al Prato**. Restaurant and wine bar in a secluded cobbled square. No lake view but good food and wine and a convivial atmosphere. *Piazza Al Prato 6. T: 3487 124389.*

€ **Cavallino**. Right on the harbour front near the main ferry dock. Friendly and efficient. Pasta dishes and lake fish. *Piazza Martiri. T: 0341 815219, cavallino-varenna.it.*

WHERE TO EAT: VALTELLINA

SONDRIO
€€ **Olmo**. Popular local *trattoria* in the old market square. The owner

cultivates blueberries and these feature large on the menu. There is even a beer made with them. Otherwise the menu contains local specialities such as *sciatt*, small battered cheese balls. Closed Sun. *Piazza Cavour 13. T: 0342 212210, iolmo. it.*

€ **Locanda dello Zio Peppo**. Relaxed, friendly restaurant and pizzeria in a handsome old building close to Piazza Garibaldi. There are two outdoor terraces, one particularly pleasant, shaded by trees. Local dishes, good wines. Closed Tues. *Via Perego 10. T: 0342 050538.*

For coffee or a drink, there are cafés with outdoor seating in Piazza Garibaldi. **Caffè Liberty** on Via Piazzi, just off Piazza Campello, is also good.

TIRANO
€ **Trattoria Valtellinese**. *Trattoria* in the historic centre, very close to Palazzo Salis. They offer a weekday lunch menu which is very good. Tables outside in summer. *Via Albonico 15. T: 0342 701147.*

LOCAL SPECIALITIES

LAKE COMO
Como is famous for its silk, which is widely available. A. Picci (*Via Vittorio Emanuele II 56; map p. 219, 4*) is a historic shop, in business since 1919. The Mantero silk manufacturer has been in business since 1902: they are still known for their beautiful scarves.

Bellagio is known for its woodwork (including olive wood) from Mario Tacchi's shop and workshop (founded in 1855) at Via Garibaldi 18. The offering is fairly touristic but there are some nice items.

Found in restaurants all around the lake, and often added to pasta sauces, *missoltini* are a speciality: a kind of cured kipper. The fish are known elswhere in Italy as *agoni*.

VALTELLINA AND VALCHIAVENNA

Chiavenna is famous for its *crotti*, traditional cellars used to mature cheese, wine and other local products, with a room above, heated by a stove, for eating, drinking and conviviality.

The thing to eat in Chiavenna are *gnochetti*. The **bresaola** is also very typical, both of the Valchiavenna and Valtellina.

Wild bilberries (*mirtilli*) are a speciality of the Valmalenco. The Valtellina is known for its **cheeses** (Bitto and Valtellina casera) and for apples (Golden Delicious, Red Delicious and Gala). Traditional dishes are *taroz* (pron. 'tarOTS'), a mash of potatoes and green beans; and *sciatt* (pron. 'shat'), little cheese balls. Buckwheat flour is much used in the Valtelltina to make pasta, particularly the long, flat ribbons known as *pizzoccheri*.

The Valtellina is also known for its rustic **red wines**: Francia, Grumello, Inferno, Sassella and Valgella. The strong Sfursat (or Sfurzat), made from dried grapes, is drunk as a dessert wine.

Also typical of the Valtellina and Valchiavenna is the smooth grey stone known as *pietra ollare*. It is used to make both decorative and functional objects.

FESTIVALS AND EVENTS

CHIAVENNA

The **Sagra dei Crotti** festival of the traditional cellars takes place in Sept (*sagradeicrotti.it*).

COMO

In summer, around the feast of St John the Baptist (24 June), the **Sagra di San Giovanni** is held at various places around the lake, with fireworks displays.

The **Palio del Baradello**, a re-enaction of an event in 1159 when Frederick Barbarossa came to Como to recruit troops for his assault on Milan, takes place in Como town in Sept. It involves parades in historic costume, a tug of war, a boat race in traditional *lucie* boats and other entertainment and feasting (*paliodelbaradello.it*).

VALTELLINA

This is one of the few parts of continental Europe where **rugby** is played (there is a rugby pitch at Sondrio, for example). If you come at the right time of year, you might catch a match.

Cantine aperte, when winemakers open their cellars and offer tastings, are held at several times throughout the year: last Sun in May, around the time of the grape harvest in autumn and around St Martin's Day (11 Nov).

The **Sondrio Festival**, chiefly dedicated to natural parks, is held annually in October, with films and other events (*sondriofestival.it*).

BERGAMO
Viewed from the heights of San Vigilio.

Bergamo

Bergamo (*Atlas C, A3–A4*) is one of the most visited cities in Lombardy. Its airport, only a few kilometres outside town, is the third busiest in Italy (after Milan and Rome), served by many low-cost airlines. This popularity, however, is entirely justified. Bergamo stands just below the first foothills of the Alps, between the valleys of the Brembo and the Serio, and is dramatically divided into two sharply distinguished parts. The beautiful and peaceful Città Alta, with a lovely tall skyline on its steep green hill enclosed by mighty Venetian walls, is almost always

visible from the Città Bassa, the lower town on the plain below. A road and cobbled lanes lead up the hill and the two districts are connected by funicular.

HISTORY OF BERGAMO

Bergamo has been split in two since Roman times: the *civitas* stood on the hill, with the *suburbia* beneath it. The centre of a Lombard duchy in the early Middle Ages and seat of a bishop in the 10th century, it emerged as a free commune in the 12th century. In the 14th century the Visconti and the Torriani families disputed possession of the city. Visconti rule ended in 1428, when Venice took the town. Bergamo remained a Venetian possession until the fall of the Venetian Republic to Napoleon in 1797. From the Congress of Vienna (1815) until 1859 it was part of the Austrian empire. The Bergamasques played a prominent part in the Risorgimento and contributed the largest contingent to Garibaldi's 'Thousand', which set sail for Sicily from Genoa in 1860. In the 20th century Bergamo was one of the richest towns in Italy, with a booming economy (clothes manufactories, metal works etc.) and much new building took place on the outskirts. The town has its own newspaper and symphony orchestra. Famous natives include the composer Donizetti (1797–1848) and the painter Giovanni Battista Moroni (c. 1525–78; *see p. 269*).

BERGAMO HIGHLIGHTS

The bustling lower town (*map opposite*) is distinguished by its spacious layout, the work of **Marcello Piacentini** (*see below and p. 254*). There are three churches with **altarpieces by Lorenzo Lotto** (*p. 254*).

The **Accademia Carrara** (*map opposite, 2; p. 272*) is one of Italy's most important small picture galleries, a good place to see portraits by the Bergamo-born Giovanni Battista Moroni as well as an early work by Raphael. Another Bergamo artist is the sculptor Giacomo Manzù. There are a number of works by his hand around town, including in the **GAMeC** (*p. 275*), the excellent modern art gallery.

In the upper town (*map p. 261*) is the wonderful church of **Santa Maria Maggiore** (*p. 260*) and the famous **Colleoni Chapel** (*p. 264*). Opera lovers will want to visit the **Donizetti Museum** (*p. 268*; his grave is also here, in Santa Maria Maggiore). The **Archaeological Museum** (*p. 267*) has a good collection. The circuit of **city walls and gates** (*p. 270*) is a fine sight. You can also take a funicular to the pretty hamlet of **San Vigilio** (*p. 267*), for lunch and fine views.

BERGAMO: THE LOWER TOWN

The Città Bassa grew up in the area between the medieval *borghi*, successors of the Roman *suburbia*. In the centre, the broad avenues and pleasant squares were laid out in 1927 by the architect Marcello Piacentini. He also designed the eclectic buildings for banks and public offices with arcades and the clock tower, all very different from the works he designed only a few years later during the Fascist regime. His buildings fit well with Bergamo's earlier Neoclassical monuments, including the two little Doric 'temples' at Porta Nuova, opened in 1837 as an entrance to the town.

From this handsome district there is a panoramic view of the towers of Città Alta on the skyline and the green fields and gardens which stretch up to its 16th-century walls (with the gate of San Giacomo conspicuous to the left). A sequence of straight avenues, dating from the 19th century (Viale Papa Giovanni, Viale Roma and Viale Vittorio Emanuele II), lead all the way from the railway station to the foot of the hill.

AROUND PORTA NUOVA

Just inside Porta Nuova is **Piazza Matteotti** (*map opposite, 6*), really a park with well-kept flower beds and various monuments, the most striking of which (and the closest to Porta Nuova) is by the Bergamo-born Giacomo Manzù and dedicated to the Partisans who fought against Mussolini's regime in WWII. A murdered partisan is shown

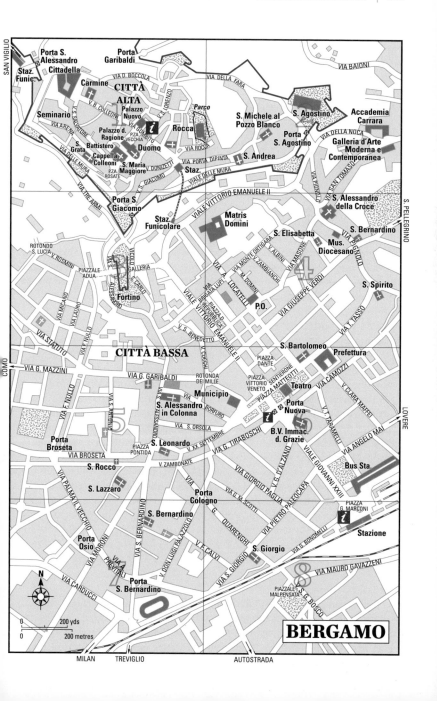

BERGAMO

hanging by his feet, approached by a mourning woman. The sculpture commemorates a mass shooting of partisans by the Fascists in Piazza Loreto in Milan on 10th August 1944. Manzù almost certainly witnessed the scene: he describes it vividly on the back of the statue: 'Partisan, I saw you hanging immobile. Only the hair on your forehead stirred, as the evening breeze crept softly through the silence, to touch you as I should have liked to do.' It was Piazzale Loreto that was then chosen as the place to expose Mussolini's own dead body a few months later (*see p. 113*).

The large building which houses the **Town Hall** was built by the Brescian architect Rodolfo Vantini in 1854; the smaller mayor's office is across the way in a building with Corinthian pilasters, dating from 1840. In front is a tall monument (1933, by the little-known architect Pino Pizzigoni) to the four Calvi brothers, who died in WWI. Topped by a flagstaff, it has bronze statuettes and marble reliefs designed by Manzù, who was a friend of the architect. Almost all the other large buildings are occupied by banks, including one of 1909 which was decorated by Luca Beltrami. In a clump of ilexes is a monument to Cavour. (*For the district of Sant'Alessandro, entered here, see p. 258.*)

The dead-straight **Sentierone**, which crosses the main road, was opened and paved in 1762 as the town's principal promenade. It is still a place where people gather. The **Teatro Donizetti** was given its façade in 1897, when it was named after the great composer, born in Bergamo, whose statue stands in the gardens.

PIAZZA VITTORIO VENETO

Adjoining Piazza Matteotti to the north is an area once occupied by a marketplace, where a famous annual fair was held from the 9th century onwards. When the importance of the fair declined, the decision was taken to redesign the area and in the 1920s Marcello Piacentini laid out the arcaded **Piazza Vittorio Veneto** (*map p. 253, 6*) and the surrounding *piazze* on a particularly successful open grid plan. He designed the **Torre dei Caduti** (*open Fri–Sun 10–1 & 3–6; museodellestorie.bergamo.it, T: 035 226332*) as a 'Victory Tower' but it was inaugurated (in the presence of Mussolini) in 1924 as a memorial to the fallen of the First World War. It is built in the same sandstone which was used in the towers of the upper town, and has a clock and bell. You can climb the stairs to see the view from the top and on the way up are memorials to the First World War and (on the third floor) a small **exhibition dedicated to the work of Piacentini**. An obelisk outside is dedicated to Napoleon 'Buonaparte l'Italico' and dated 1797.

VIA TASSO AND BORGO PIGNOLO
(THREE CHURCHES WITH WORKS BY LORENZO LOTTO)

VIA TASSO

The Dominican church of **San Bartolomeo** (Santi Bartolomeo e Stefano; *map p. 253, 4–6*) has a high altarpiece of the *Virgin and Child*, the Pala Martinengo (*coin-operated light on the left of the presbytery*), by Lorenzo Lotto. Saints crowd around the throne, which has clawed feet which the two little cherubs seem anxious to cover with a heavy brown carpet (the artist's signature and the date, 1516, are clearly visible on the

PIAZZA MATTEOTTI
Detail of Giacomo Manzù's Partisan Monument (1972).

cartouche here). The scene is set beneath a barrel vault in a domed 'church' reminiscent of Bramante's architecture, which gives the painting a remarkable sense of space. Two angels lean over the parapet, busy directing operations and hanging up symbols. But it is the two marvellously graceful angels in blue hovering over the Virgin, with her crown in their hands, that are the focal point of this painting. It was commissioned by Alessandro Martinengo Colleoni (adopted son of the *condottiere* Bartolomeo Colleoni; *see p. 264*) in 1513 and is the earliest work by Lotto painted for a church in Bergamo. The church is also interesting for its intarsia stalls by the Dominican friar Damiano Zambelli (1520), and the frescoes in the nave and sanctuary by Gaspare Diziani (1751).

On the opposite side of Via Tasso is the **Palazzo della Prefettura e Provincia** (1870), which has works by Manzù in the garden, including his *Homage to Caravaggio* with its beautifully-worked basket of fruit, evoking the famous painting in the Ambrosiana library in Milan (*see p. 79*).

Beyond the **Pasticceria Salvi** (no. 48), recommended for coffee and a pastry, Via Tasso ends at the church of **Santo Spirito** (*closed 12–3*), with a good interior of 1521 (and a curious sculpture on the exterior, a 1971 attempt to render the Holy Spirit in metal). The fourth south chapel has an exuberantly colourful *Madonna Enthroned with Saints* by Lorenzo Lotto (*coin-operated light*). St Sebastian is shown in the act of plucking an arrow from his shoulder. The young St John the Baptist is strenuously hugging the mystic Lamb at the foot of the throne, which is decorated with a Persian carpet. The circular choir of angels above is painted with extraordinary skill. In the next (fifth) chapel is a beautiful polyptych by the skilled native painter Andrea Previtali. Another work by him can be seen on the first north altar: the *Baptist and Four Saints*, with a river and cascades in the background. The second north altarpiece is a good polyptych by Bergognone (*see p. 168*), Previtali's near contemporary.

LORENZO LOTTO IN BERGAMO

Lotto (1480–1556) is a late Renaissance painter known for his perceptive portraits and mystical interpretations of religious subjects. He was born in Venice, and although Giorgio Vasari says he trained with Giorgione and Titian in the workshop of Giovanni Bellini, he always remained somewhat apart from the main Venetian tradition. All the same, he is known to have been a friend of Titian and was certainly influenced by him. He travelled widely in Italy and, as well as Venice, he worked in the Marche, where he chose to spend his last years. He was a very prolific painter but was much less famous than his contemporaries. There is a wit and individualism to his work that makes him one of the most interesting painters of his time.

Lotto spent some of his happiest years in Bergamo (from 1518–28) and the town has proudly preserved the paintings he carried out here. Three high altarpieces commissioned from him for its churches (San Bartolomeo, Santo Spirito and San Bernardino) are still *in situ*. His *Trinity*, painted for the high altar of the church of the same name, is now in the Museo Diocesano. The *Mystical Marriage of St Catherine* painted for Niccolò Bonghi (who is present in the painting), in lieu of one year's rent for the painter's lodgings in Bergamo, is in the Accademia Carrara, together with the portrait of Lucina Brembati, a noblewoman of Bergamo, which was purchased from a private collection. Also in the Accademia Carrara is the predella for the Martinengo altarpiece in San Bartolomeo. Lotto's mastery of fresco painting can be appreciated in the little church of San Michele al Pozzo Bianco. His mysticism and extraordinary powers of interpreting the scriptures, as well as his narrative skills, are summed up in the extremely well-preserved intarsia works in Bergamo's most important church, Santa Maria Maggiore. While staying in Bergamo, Lotto also painted some works for churches just outside the town (*see pp. 279, 280 and 283*).

BORGO PIGNOLO

The aspect of the town changes abruptly in Borgo Pignolo. Via Pignolo (*map p. 253, 4*), at first a pedestrian precinct with a few art galleries and a lute-maker's shop, leads up to cross the busy Via Verdi and Via San Giovanni, on the corner of which is San Bernardino (*described below*). The street, now with herring-bone porphyry paving, is lined with some noble houses. Palazzo Bassi-Rathgeb, built for the Cassotti family in the early 16th century, houses the **Museo Diocesano Adriano Bernareggi** (*Via*

SANTO SPIRITO
Detail of Lorenzo Lotto's altarpiece, showing the Virgin and Child
with Sts Sebastian and Anthony Abbot.

Pignolo 76; open Tues–Sun 3–6.30, fondazionebernareggi.it, T: 035 244492). It houses a collection put together by Adriano Bernareggi when Bishop of Bergamo from 1932–53, and is now run by a foundation. The most important work is an extraordinary *Holy Trinity* (with a good landscape) painted by Lorenzo Lotto (1519/21) for the (destroyed) church of the Trinità. The museum has some gilded wood altarpieces and works by Moroni, Daniele Crespi and Marco d'Oggiono (the *Redeemer*).

The foundation has the key to the small church of **San Bernardino** (*on the corner of Via San Giovanni; opened on request*), which contains a particularly beautiful altarpiece of the *Madonna Enthroned* by Lorenzo Lotto, painted in 1521. Again it is the angels which are the most attractive elements. One, dressed in brown at the foot of the throne, has been busy writing down the Madonna's words (Lotto's signature can be seen amidst the flower petals on the step here). Above, a group of angels protect the Madonna by holding up a large green cloth, providing the painter with the opportunity to show his amazing skill in portraying the human figure from many different angles. The Virgin, dressed in Lotto's typical crimson colour, provides a strong contrast to the intense black cloak of St Anthony Abbot, and yellows and blues are also prominent. The sky, with the sun setting, is wonderfully painted. The fresco of the *Madonna and Child* on the second south altar is by Andrea Previtali.

Other **palaces on Via Pignolo** include no. 80, which once belonged to Tasso's family and, opposite, **Palazzo Daina** (no. 69), which has diamond-shaped decorations around its doors and windows. **Palazzo Agliardi** (no. 86; privately owned: but see *bergamogiardiniedimore.it/en/palazzo-agliardi*) has a *salone* frescoed in the 18th century by Carlo Carlone.

The church of **Sant'Alessandro della Croce** (*closed 12–3*) has a *Coronation of the Virgin* by Giovanni Battista Moroni flanked by two works by Andrea Schiavone on the west wall. There are small paintings in the sacristy (*opened on request*) by Moroni, Andrea Previtali and Lorenzo Costa (a particularly lovely *Christ Carrying the Cross*).

BORGO SANT'ALESSANDRO

Via XX Settembre (*map p. 253, 5–6*) is entered from Piazza Matteotti between two marble columns set up to commemorate a fair which took place in this area from 1620–1882. This peaceful shopping street is now largely pedestrian and is paved in porphyry. It curves round to the **Piazza Pontida**, with its cafés and a large bookshop, and from here the interesting old **Via Sant'Alessandro** runs uphill to the north. The house at no. 13, with a small courtyard and the Vecchio Tagliere restaurant, was the birthplace of the sculptor Giacomo Manzù in 1900 (many of his works can be seen in the town). A column erected in 1618, made up from Roman fragments, stands outside the church of **Sant'Alessandro in Colonna**. The paintings in the interior include (in the south transept) a successful work by the local artist Giovan Paolo Cavagna, showing St Peter rising heavenwards on a cloud, below which the air clears to reveal the city of Bergamo. Cavagna also painted the fourth north altarpiece showing a miracle of St Alexander, and the *Madonna in Glory with Saints* on the fourth south altar. Another work by him can be seen nearby in the church of **San Rocco** in Via Broseta (*map p. 253, 5*): here St Roch reveals his plague sores to the kneeling members of a confraternity.

Via Sant'Alessandro continues to wind northwards around an old fort before entering the upper town through the Porta San Giacomo.

BERGAMO: THE UPPER TOWN

The upper town of Bergamo (Città Alta) is extremely picturesque, with its towers and domes starkly beautiful against the prealpine sky. In the early morning and late at night its streets, many of them paved with herringbone porphyry, are still and tranquil. By day it is thronged with tourist groups who come to see its monuments (chief of these the Colleoni Chapel) and to climb its towers.

Approaches from the lower town
By funicular: At the point where Viale Vittorio Emanuele II (the main avenue coming up from the lower town) bends sharply east is the lower station of the funicular (*map p. 253, 3*), which tunnels up through the Venetian walls into the centre of the town. It makes the short journey in a couple of minutes and is still the most convenient and pleasantest approach (*for details of the service, see p. 277*). The old-fashioned stations have been carefully preserved and the tracks are lined with plants and flower beds. The upper station is particularly attractive.
By road (and bus): The only approach by road from the lower town is Viale

Vittorio Emanuele II, which enters the Porta Sant'Agostino and then follows the Viale delle Mura at the top of the southern walls as far as Colle Aperto. This is the route followed by bus no. 1 from the airport via the railway station and Viale Papa Giovanni, Viale Roma and Viale Vittorio Emanuele II. It is a frequent service, about every 7mins.

On foot: There are several choices: through Porta Sant'Agostino by Via Pignolo, or by Via della Noca, a picturesque green lane with wide steps which ascends from the piazza in front of the Accademia Carrara; or through the Porta San Giacomo by Via Sant'Alessandro and the pretty Vicolo San Carlo (joined also by the steps called Via Salita di Scaletta, up from the lower station of the funicular).

NB: Churches and museums (and even shops) in the upper town usually close for a couple of hours around lunchtime.

VIA GOMBITO AND PIAZZA VECCHIA

In the little **Piazza Mercato delle Scarpe** (Shoemarket Square; *map p. 261, 5*), the upper funicular station is discreetly hidden behind a doorway. Its 19th-century appearance has been preserved, together with its delightful café which has a terrace overlooking the lower town. In the little piazza, where seven narrow old roads meet, the fountain covers a cistern built in 1486. From here **Via Gombito**, the main street of the upper town—and always the most crowded—with some pretty old-style shopfronts (there are clothes shops as well as places to eat along the way), climbs up past a little piazza with a 16th-century fountain. The church of **San Pancrazio** has a Gothic portal decorated with 14th-century statues and a 15th-century fresco. Beyond is the 12th-century **Torre del Gombito** (52m high). It can be climbed in spring–late autumn (*advance booking only; T: 035 242226, comune.bergamo.it/turismo*).

Via Gombito ends at **Piazza Vecchia** (*map p. 261, 2*), the centre of the old town and its largest square. There is a fountain of 1780 in its centre and a welcoming café at either end. The bright white portico of **Palazzo Nuovo** (the Biblioteca Civica), was designed by Palladio's follower Vincenzo Scamozzi in 1611 but modified before it was finished in the 20th century: today its monumental marble aspect is rather overpowering. To the right is **Palazzo del Podestà** with its tower (*both described below*), connected by outside stairs to **Palazzo della Ragione**, rebuilt in 1538–43, bearing a Lion of St Mark and with a meridian of 1789 beneath its wide portico. Beyond the portico is the much smaller Piazza del Duomo.

PIAZZA DEL DUOMO

The upper town's most important buildings are crowded together in this small space (*map p. 261, 2–5*). The façade of the duomo is to the left, while the entrance to the north porch of the church of Santa Maria Maggiore (which has no façade) is straight ahead, with the Colleoni Chapel squeezed in next to it. Its little baptistery stands on its own to the right.

SANTA MARIA MAGGIORE

Open Mon–Thur 9–12.30 & 2.30–5, Fri–Sun 9–6. The four intarsia panels of biblical scenes by Lorenzo Lotto on the choir screen are only visible on Sundays (when the symbolic covers, also designed by Lotto, are removed). To see Lotto's famous intarsia panels in the choir, you need to book in advance at fondazionemia.it, T: 035 211355. The Treasury is open Mon–Sat 10.30–12 & 2.30–5.30, Sun 2.30–5.30.

This Romanesque basilica, the most important monument in Bergamo, recognised as the 'city's chapel', has been administered by the Congregazione della Misericordia Maggiore (MIA) since the mid-15th century. At that time, the city government passed from the Church to the *comune*, and Santa Maria came to be recognised also for its civic role. It was begun by a certain Maestro Fredo in 1137, and although without a façade, it has a beautiful Romanesque exterior, and is entered by the **north porch** (1353), the work of Giovanni da Campione. Above the delightful arch, delicately decorated with animals, and borne by two red marble lions, is a tabernacle with three statues of saints, including an equestrian statue of St Alexander. Above is another tabernacle with the *Madonna and Child and Saints* sculpted by Andreolo de' Bianchi (1398). The door itself is surrounded by more intricate carving on its various columns.

The vault of the centrally-planned **interior** was covered in the 16th–17th century with splendid stuccoes, frescoes and paintings (those in the octagonal dome are by Giovan Paolo Cavagna, 1615). The huge **paintings in elaborate frames** in the two transepts and high up at the west end are by Antonio Zanchi (*Moses Striking Water from the Rock*, 1669), Pietro Liberi (*The Flood*, 1661; restored in 2015), and Luca Giordano (*Crossing the Red Sea*, 1681).

Some 14th-century **frescoes from the Romanesque church** survive on the walls, including a *Last Supper* and a scene of St Eligius and his smithy, as well as an extremely interesting *Tree of Life* of 1347 (the upper part of it is covered by Liberi's huge canvas). It follows the famous text of St Bonaventura and his meditation on the life of Christ, and is one of the largest representations of this subject in Italy. Other walls are covered with **tapestries** commissioned to add to the sumptuous atmosphere, and rarely seen in a church. Designed by the Florentine painter Alessandro Allori, they were woven in the Medici manufactory in Florence from 1583–6 and depict the life of the Virgin. Most of them are now very faded: the Flemish tapestry of the *Crucifixion* (1696–8) is much better preserved, as are the smaller ones, also from Antwerp, hung in other parts of the church.

The **tomb of Donizetti** (d. 1848) is by Vincenzo Vela, author of many 19th-century commemorative sculptures in Italy, and nearby is the tomb of Donizetti's master Simone Mayr (1763–1845): both monuments date from the 1850s.

The confessional carved by the local master craftsman Andrea Fantoni in 1704 is a Baroque masterpiece. The funerary monument of Cardinal Longo is attributed to Ugo da Campione (1330). The altarpiece (*Christ in Glory*) in the chapel to the right of the choir is a good work by the little-known Antonio Boselli (1514), and on the altar nearby is the *Last Supper*, one of Francesco Bassano's best works (1585).

Above the entrance to the sanctuary hangs a gruesome Crucifix carved in northern Europe in the mid-14th century (the emaciated figure of Christ has signs of the

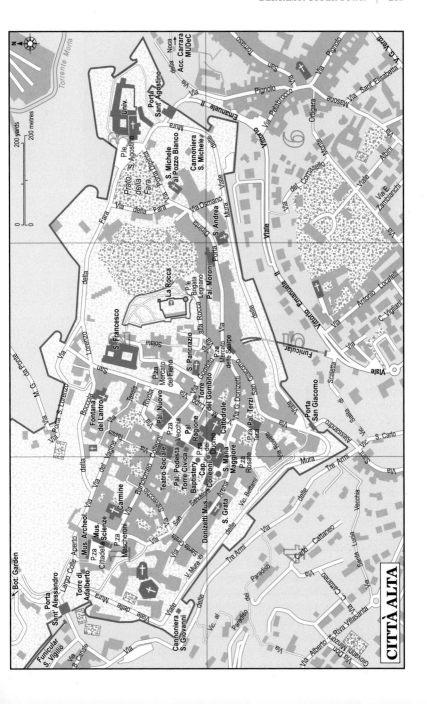

SANTA MARIA MAGGIORE
Servant boy eyeing Judas' money bag. Detail of Francesco Bassano's *Last Supper* (1585).

plague). The pulpits, decorated with Flemish tapestries, have remarkable bronze handrails dating from 1603. Tapestries also cover the organ lofts. The large painting of the *Assumption* by Camillo Procaccini (1594) fits the curve of the apse.

The intarsia panels on the choir screen and stalls

The choir screen, carved by Bernardino Zenale, has four large intarsia panels designed by Lorenzo Lotto with symbolic symbols which relate to the four panels behind them showing the *Crossing of the Red Sea*, the *Flood, Judith and Holofernes* and *David and Goliath*. The covers are removed on Sundays and religious festivals so that you can see these remarkable biblical scenes.

Lotto also designed the choir, with a magnificent double set of intarsia panels: each pair consists of a symbolic scene on the cover which protects the biblical scene behind. The covers can be unlocked (all with the same key) and removed to reveal the scenes behind (*only shown by previous appointment, see above*). The rectangular choir stalls were designed for the clergy and the semicircular choir behind for the laity.

Lotto received the commission in 1524 and painted 70 canvases which were then used by Gianfrancesco Capoferri to produce the inlay for the 70 intarsia panels. Lotto supplied most of the designs from a distance, as he left Bergamo for Venice in 1525, never to return. However, it is known that he also intervened directly to engrave some of the scenes. Together he and Capoferri developed a new method of producing intricate intarsia: in some instances the wood was burnt or treated to produce certain colours. They are justly considered a masterpiece, not only for the intricacy of the carving (some 15 different woods were used to produce the tonal effects) but also for the esoteric interpretation given by the artist to the significance of each narrative scene. Lotto combines ideas of Neoplatonism, pagan philosophy and alchemy with Christian and Hebrew iconography to mirror the biblical scenes behind. The panels have been interpreted as a 'Theatre of Memory'. These are the only works Capoferri produced (he died in 1533, the year the choir was finished). The arrangement of the panels was altered when they were finally installed here in 1574.

The Treasury

The entrance is near the door out to the south porch (*for admission times, see above*). Stairs wind up round the Romanesque apse (hidden when the Baroque decorations were carried out), allowing you to see the 14th-century frescoes (note the one with the Child playing with flowers, and the Child being washed). At the top is a vaulted matroneum (the windows which opened onto the nave of the church have been blocked up), which also survives from the Romanesque church and where the Treasury is exhibited. The six gilded silver discs come from a precious processional Cross by Andreolo de' Bianchi (1392): the silver *Agnus Dei* is especially beautiful. Protected with cloth covers (which you can remove), are two 15th-century illuminated choirbooks by Iacopo da Balsemo. The tapestry illustrating the *Visitation* belongs to the 16th-century series which hangs in the church. The large detached fresco (in parts only sketched) of St Alexander on horseback dates from 1336; and another fresco shows the Madonna and St Elizabeth nursing their babies side by side. The seven small copper reliefs made in 1525 were probably designed by Lotto. Giovanni da Campione is thought to have made the five damaged statuettes of angels.

OUTSIDE SANTA MARIA MAGGIORE

It is worth exploring the exterior of the Romanesque building. To the left you can see the exterior of the apses, the Gothic sacristy door (northeast, also by Campione), and the exterior of the polygonal new sacristy (1485–91, built after the old one was demolished to make room for the Colleoni chapel).

The isolated building behind the apse, above a fountain, was adapted in the early 19th century as the seat of the Ateneo, a scientific and literary institute founded in 1768. From here you can see the cupola and bell-tower (1360, Giovanni da Campione, finished in the 15th century and given its little copper dome in 1591).

Behind is **Piazza Rosate** where the south porch can be seen, with a pair of white marble lions protecting their cubs and a terracotta frieze, also by Giovanni da

Campione (the Gothic spire was added in 1403). The door beside it is kept open and the church is often used as a short cut between Via Arena and Piazza Vecchia. A gate by an old fountain here leads into a small garden, in the centre of which is the little 11th-century **Cappella di Santa Croce**. An iron walkway continues into the **Aula Picta della Curia**, with a huge arch and remains of 13th-century frescoes also in the walled-up two-light window (the bronze statue commemorates Pope John XXIII, born nearby; *see below*). From here, steps lead past the exterior of the church back down to Piazza del Duomo and the charming little **Baptistery**, by Giovanni da Campione (1340). It originally stood inside Santa Maria Maggiore, but the clerics of the Duomo ordered it to be moved outside so that they could register baptisms. It is kept locked behind a gate, but the interior is illuminated. Behind is a little garden.

CAPPELLA COLLEONI
Map p. 261, 1–4. Open 9.30–12.30 & 2–6.30. Nov–Feb 9.30–12.30 & 2–4.30.
Incredibly enough, at the end of the 15th century part of the north wall of Santa Maria Maggiore, right beside its main entrance through the north door, was allowed to be demolished in order that the *condottiere* Bartolomeo Colleoni could build his funerary chapel on this site. To make space it was necessary to eliminate the church sacristy as well, so a new one was built at the east end in 1485. Four years before his death, in 1472, Colleoni commissioned the most famous sculptor of his time, Giovanni Antonio Amadeo, to build the chapel as his burial place.

> ### BARTOLOMEO COLLEONI
> This great mercenary captain-general (c. 1400–75), born in Bergamo, served both the Venetian Republic and the Visconti at different periods. He lived in the castle of Malpaga south of Bergamo (its interesting interior with frescoes illustrating its owner's achievements, can be visited; *see p. 283*), and he died there at the age of 80. Because of his resounding successes in battle he accumulated great wealth during his lifetime and commissioned Amadeo to design the Cappella Colleoni as his burial place. The great captain also left a legacy to the Venetian Republic in order that a statue be set up to him in a public square: his idealised equestrian monument by Verrocchio in Campo di Santi Giovanni e Paolo in Venice is one of the great bronze masterpieces of the Renaissance.
>
> But Colleoni also chose to dedicate part of his wealth to a good cause, to ensure his safe journey to Heaven. To this end, he founded the Luogo Pio Colleoni in Bergamo Alto in 1466, which is still in operation as a charity. Its headquarters (*Via Bartolomeo Colleoni 9; sadly not open to visitors*) preserves some detached 15th-century frescoes showing Colleoni as well as his portrait by Giovanni Battista Moroni.

Although it is rather overpowering in this small space, and too close to the lovely Romanesque portal of Santa Maria Maggiore, the chapel is considered one of the finest High Renaissance works in Lombardy. The over-lavish decorations on the exterior seem unconnected with the architectural forms. The elaborate carving celebrates the life of Colleoni by means of complicated allegories combining Classical and biblical allusions. In the rose window and two eccentric lateral windows are copies of cannon shafts which Colleoni used for the first time in pitched battle. The chapel is protected by a railing set up here in 1912.

The interior is even more difficult to appreciate since decorations were added in the 18th century and as a result the elaborate marble tomb carving by Amadeo makes less of an impact. There are two sarcophagi: Colleoni was buried in the lower one, surmounted by an equestrian statue in gilded wood (added in 1493). The tomb of his daughter Medea, who predeceased him by six years, is simpler and has a beautifully serene effigy, also by Amadeo. Three statues by the stonemason Pietro Lombardo (1490) stand on the Baroque high altar. The remaining decoration is good 18th-century work, including marquetry seats, ceiling frescoes of the *Martyrdom of St Bartholomew* and *St John the Baptist* by Tiepolo (1732–3), and a *Holy Family* by Angelica Kauffmann (in the sanctuary). The black-white-and pink marble floor is well preserved.

THE CATTEDRALE

Map p. 261, 5. Open 7.30–12.30 & 3–6.30. Weekends 7–7. cattedraledibergamo.it. See also the programme of organ concerts and choir recitals.

The cathedral of Bergamo was begun in 1459 by Filarete, finished in 1689 by Carlo Fontana and given a new façade in 1880.

It has an attractive light interior. The first south altarpiece, *St Benedict between Sts Jerome and Louis of Toulouse*, is a good work by Andrea Previtali (1524; restored in 2018). In the predella are three episodes connected to the lifting of the interdict which Pope John XXII had inflicted on the town. The influence of both Giovanni Bellini and Lorenzo Lotto is apparent, and the white robes of the bishops are most striking. In the **south transept**, the altar is by Filippo Juvarra and on the right at the top is a painting by Sebastiano Ricci of *Sts Firmus, Rusticus and Proculus*. On the right wall of the south transept is a painting of saints by Sebastiano Ricci (1704).

The 18th-century paintings in the **apse** include one (middle left) by Tiepolo, a dramatic scene of the *Martyrdom of Bishop Giovanni of Bergamo* (1743–5): the great Venetian painter had also been called to Bergamo ten years earlier to fresco the ceiling of the Colleoni Chapel with other martyrdoms.

Under the sanctuary is the solemn **crypt**, designed in 1979 and containing the tombs of the bishops of Bergamo since 1914. The chapel on the right of the sanctuary has **relics of Pope John XXIII** ('Papa Giovanni'), born near Bergamo in 1881 and canonised in 2014. These include the simple wood coffin in which he was first buried in St Peter's (from 1963–2000). The huge bronze statue of him dates from 1989.

The 18th-century altar in the north transept has two huge barley-sugar columns in green Varallo marble. At the entrance to the second north chapel is a statue of St Charles Borromeo by Giacomo Manzù. The altarpiece on the first north altar is by Giovanni Battista Moroni.

The Cathedral Treasury

Piazza Duomo. Entrance below the cathedral entrance steps. Open Tues–Fri 9.30–1 & 2.30–6, weekends 10–1 & 2.30–6. T: 035 248772, fondazionebernareggi.it.

The display includes finds from a Roman domus on this site and excavations of the early Christian basilica of St Vincent. Frescoes from the basilica include a scene of members of a charitable foundation of the Misericordia giving alms to a pauper. There is also a reliquary Cross dating from 1386, an early 15th-century processional Cross, 15th-century vestments and reliquaries. The most precious object is the lovely silver 'Cross of St Proculus', thought to date from as early as the 9th or 10th century.

PALAZZO DEL PODESTÀ AND THE TORRE CIVICA

The **Palazzo del Podestà** (*Piazza Vecchia 8; open Oct–May Tues–Sun 9.30–1 & 2.30–6; June–Sept Tues–Fri 10–1 & 2.30–6, Sat–Sun and holidays 10–7; T: 035 247116, museodellestorie.bergamo.it*) houses an excellent interactive museum, part of the Museo delle Storie di Bergamo. It tells the story of Bergamo in the 16th century, although on the ground floor there are Roman excavations. Off the upper floor of a little courtyard, with remains of frescoes, there are various exhibits and videos related to life in Bergamo in the golden years of the Venetian period. The route taken by travellers along the old post-road between Venice and Bergamo is recreated on a moving screen (the stops are the same as the exits on today's *autostrada*).

The massive 12th-century **Torre Civica** or Campanone can be climbed (*lift or stairs; open Nov–March Tues–Fri 9.30–1 & 2.30–6, Sat–Sun and holidays 9.30–6; April–Oct Tues–Fri 10–6, Sat–Sun and holidays 10–8; T: 035 247116, museodellestorie.bergamo. it*). Hanging at the top are the three bells, which ring every half hour. The *campanone* itself (1655) is the largest. There are spectacular views taking in the green fields within the walls with an old ammunition store, the hill of San Vigilio and, nearer at hand, the Cappella Colleoni, Santa Maria Maggiore and the cathedral, crowned in 1851 with a gilded statue of the patron of Bergamo, St Alexander. Information panels tell you what you are looking at.

VIA BARTOLOMEO COLLEONI TO COLLE APERTO

From Piazza Vecchia, Via Bartolomeo Colleoni, as a continuation of Via Gombito, is an important thoroughfare, with attractive shops and cafés. It passes (left) the **Teatro Sociale**, designed in wood by Leopold Pollack in 1803–7. Beside a little garden at no. 9 is the Luogo Pio Colleoni (*only open on special occasions*), bequeathed by the *condottiere* (*see above*) to a charitable institution.

The church of the **Carmine** (*map p. 261, 1*) was rebuilt in the 15th century and again in 1730. It contains a finely-carved wooden ancona of the *Immaculate Conception*, with numerous saints, painted and gilded. Since its restoration in 2015 it has been attributed to the little-known Venetian Jacopino Scipioni, who is documented at work in the town in the early 16th-century.

Via Colleoni ends in the pleasant Piazza Mascheroni. The clock tower gives access to Piazza della Cittadella, with a 14th-century portico and two museums. The **Museo Civico di Scienze Naturali Enrico Caffi** (*map p. 261, 1; Piazza della Cittadella 10; open April–Sept Tues–Fri 9–12.30 & 2.30–6, Sat, Sun and holidays 10–1 & 2.30–6.30;*

Oct–March Tues–Sun 9–12.30 & 2.30–5.30; Sat, Sun and holidays 10–12.30 & 2.30–5.30; T. 035 286011, museoscienzebergamo.it; combined ticket with the Museo Archeologico), contains a well-arranged collection including an ethnographical section devoted to the explorer Costantino Beltrami, born in Bergamo (1779–1855), who discovered the source of the Mississippi in 1823.

The **Civico Museo Archeologico** (*Piazza della Cittadella 9; open April–Sept Tues–Fri 9–12.30 & 2.30–6, Sat–Sun 10–1 & 2.30–6.30; Oct–March Tues–Sun 9–12.30 & 2.30–5.30, Sat–Sun 10–12.30 & 2.30–5.30; T: 035 286070, museoarcheologicobergamo. it; combined ticket with the Museo di Scienze Naturali*), which originated in a collection formed by the town council in 1561, is small and nicely arranged and has locally-found material from prehistoric times to the early Christian and Lombard eras. The Roman section includes epigraphs, funerary monuments, statues, mosaics and frescoes from a domus in Via Arena (a particularly fine detail of a sparrow). There are also Carolingian and Venetian coins.

COLLE APERTO & SAN VIGILIO

Beyond Piazza della Cittadella (go through the iron gate) is the **Torre di Adalberto** (*map p. 261, 1*), a tower probably dating from the 12th century, opposite a little walled public garden. Outside the gateway is **Largo Colle Aperto**, usually busy with cars and buses, with an esplanade overlooking fields that stretch to the northwest corner of the walled city (the powder store was built in the 16th century by the Venetians). Here is the well-preserved **Porta Sant'Alessandro**.

On the hillside above (signposted off the main road which continues uphill) are the steps which lead up through the **Botanical Garden** (*Scaletta Colle Aperto, off Via Beltrami; usually open 10–12 & 2–6; ortobonicodibergamo.it, T: 035 286060*), inaugurated in 1972 and containing examples of an estimated 1200 species (a greenhouse protects succulents).

On the hillside outside Porta Sant'Alessandro is **Donizetti's birthplace** (*Via Borgo Canale 14; open weekends 10–13 & 3–6; by appointment during the week; T: 035 244483, donizetti.org*).

SAN VIGILIO

Just beside Porta Sant'Alessandro is the station of the funicular railway for the little suburb village of San Vigilio (*runs daily 10–8, every 15mins, taking 3mins; longer hours in summer; atb.bergamo.it*). Opened in 1912, it runs along the walls of the Forte di San Marco.

San Vigilio (461m) is a quiet little resort with several restaurants and a hotel. On a sunny day it is well worth making the trip here. On the right of the upper station a cobbled lane (with a view of the Città Alta) leads uphill: by an Art Nouveau house, steps continue up left to a little public garden on the site of the castle (*open 9 or 10–dusk*) with remains of a 16th–17th-century Venetian fortress on a mound with stunning views on every side. A number of pleasant walks can be taken in the surrounding hills (Monte Bastia and San Sebastiano).

The most pleasant (and peaceful) return to the centre of the upper town from Colle Aperto follows Via San Salvatore out of Piazza Mascheroni (*map p. 261, 1*), climbing up past high walls and gardens. Turn right into the pretty cobbled Via Arena, which leads downhill from the huge seminary building (1965) named after Pope John XXIII, who was a student here (there is yet another statue of this greatly-loved pontiff) past the interesting monastery wall of **Santa Grata** (with traces of frescoes). The Benedictine nuns sing lauds here at 7.30am and on holidays celebrate Mass at 8am. (*see monasterobenedettinesantagrata.it*). Its eccentric portal is opposite the huge 17th-century Palazzo della Misericordia (no. 9), which houses the Istituto Musicale Donizetti (founded in 1805) and the **Donizetti Museum** (*map p. 261, 1–4; Via Arena 9; open Tues–Fri 10–1, Sat, Sun and holidays 10–1 & 3–6; T: 035 247116, museodellestorie. bergamo.it*), first opened to the public in 1906 and retaining its arrangement from that time. A grand staircase leads up to the *piano nobile*, where a large hall decorated in 1802 exhibits manuscripts, documents, wind instruments, portraits, mementoes etc., while a recording plays Donizetti's music. His master Giovanni Simone Mayr (d. 1845) is also commemorated here. You can see the piano at which the composer worked.

Via Arena ends on the south side of Santa Maria Maggiore, but it is worth going up right through Piazza Rosate (where a large Neoclassical building, complete with columned pronaos, houses a school) and into the little piazza on the left to see the exterior of **Palazzo Terzi** (*map p. 261, 5; privately owned; for admission, see palazzoterzi.it*), considered the most attractive private residence in the upper town, dating from the 16th century but with later additions.

THE ROCCA AND THE EASTERN EDGE OF THE HILL

From Piazza Mercato delle Scarpe, Via Rocca climbs up to the park of the **Rocca** (*map p. 261, 2; open April–Sept 9–8, Oct–March 10–6, Nov–Feb 10–5.30*) with conifers, cypresses and a few palm trees, laid out as a War Memorial with weaponry used in WWI. The old castle, originally built by the Visconti in 1331 and reinforced by the Venetians in the 15th century, was restored in 1925. It contains the **Museo dell'Ottocento** (*Piazzale Brigata Legnano, open Oct–May Tues–Sun 9.30–1 & 2.30–6; June–Sept Tues– Fri 10–1 & 2.30–6, Sat, Sun and holidays 10–7; T: 035 247116, museodellestorie.bergamo. it*), covering the years 1797 to 1870, from Napoleon to the unification of Rome with Italy, including the Risorgimento. It incorporates the little church of Sant'Eufemia, documented from 1006. In the well-kept little garden, with benches, you can go up the steps (its railing intertwined with an ancient wisteria) to follow the walkway and climb the tower. The view takes in Santa Caterina and the lower town and a hillside with the orchard and terraced gardens of Palazzo Moroni, while to the west there is a splendid panorama of the upper city, with its towers and domes.

Via Solata leads to the triangular Piazza Mercato del Fieno (Haymarket), with two medieval towers and the former convent of **San Francesco** (*map p. 261, 2; open Oct–May Tues–Sun 9.30–1 & 2.30–6; June–Sept Tues–Fri 10–1 & 2.30–6, Sat, Sun and holidays 10–7; T: 035 247116, museodellestorie.bergamo.it*), dating from the end of the 13th century, with two dilapidated cloisters and remains of 14th-century frescoes.

Suppressed by Napoleon, it became a hospital, a prison and then a school. From the first cloister a ramp leads down to the second cloister, which is open to the valley and affords good views of the hills and mountains.

On the far side of the steep Via San Lorenzo, on Via Boccola, is the **Fontana del Lantro** (*map p. 261, 2; open in spring and summer; enquire at the information office*). This 16th-century cistern, fed by two springs, was built at the same time as the city walls. The water source was already known by the year 928, and the name is thought to come either from atrium or from *later*, referring to the milky colour of the water as it gushes out of the spring. There is a walkway with a view of the cistern with its 16th-century vault pierced by holes through which buckets were drawn up. A second cistern dates from the 17th century.

VIA PORTA DIPINTA TO PORTA SANT'AGOSTINO

Via Porta Dipinta (for centuries the main approach to the town) descends from Piazza Mercato delle Scarpe. **Palazzo Moroni** (*map p. 261, 5; Via Porta Dipinta 12; admission to the piano nobile and to the garden readily granted, but only by previous appointment: see fondazionepalazzomoroni.it*), with good windows and a handsome portal and a grotto in the courtyard, was built in 1636 by Francesco Moroni. Moroni employed Gian Giacomo Barbelli, a painter from Crema, to fresco the grand staircase and the ceilings of the *piano nobile* (one illustrating the *Fall of the Giants*, and another with impressive *trompe l'oeil*). Alterations were carried out in the 19th century when the terrazzo floors were laid. The furnished rooms have paintings, including three very important works by Giovanni Battista Moroni: the *Knight in Pink* (considered his masterpiece), portrait of Isotta Brembati, and *Old Lady in Black*. There is also a family group attributed to Andrea Previtali; *St Catherine* attributed to Luini; and *Mary Magdalene* by another Leonardesque painter, Giampietrino. The palace has been run by a foundation since the death of the last count here in 2009. The very large garden behind covers about a twelfth of the entire area of the Città Alta.

GIOVANNI BATTISTA MORONI

Moroni (c. 1525–78), born in the Valle Seriana outside Bergamo and a pupil of Moretto (*see p. 302*), who had studied under Titian, is known above all for his quiet, dignified portraits. These very particular works—he was one of the few Italian Renaissance artists to make portraiture his speciality—combine the realism of German painters like Holbein with a Venetian sense of light, such as seen in the portraits of Titian, who personally commended Moroni's work. The strength of Moroni's style lies in the unforced poses of his sitters, the strong sense of composition, and a restrained treatment of texture and colour. Moroni's portraits are mostly of the minor aristocracy and merchant middle class of Bergamo. There are works in the city's churches and museums, of course, but also in major public collections around the world. One of his best-known works is *The Tailor* (c. 1571), now in the National Gallery, London. Milan's Pinacoteca Ambrosiana holds another exceptional portrait, as does the Brera.

The church of **Sant'Andrea** (*map p. 261, 6; open 8–6*), designed in 1841 by Ferdinando Crivelli, is interesting for its Neoclassical architecture with columns in the nave and apse. At the end of the north side, above the confessional, the *Mourning over the Dead Christ with Sts Peter and Andrew* is a very good late work (1525, in good condition) by Andrea Previtali. The second south altarpiece, the *Madonna and Child with Saints* (1536), is a particularly good work by Moretto. The Child is struggling to get off the Madonna's lap and the broken column in the background is reminiscent of works by Veronese. There is a lovely bowl of apples on the ground in front of the throne.

In a quiet corner of town a short way further on is the simple church of **San Michele al Pozzo Bianco** (*map p. 261, 3; open 9–5 or 6; coin-operated lights in the porch outside the main door*), visited for its frescoes of 1525 by Lorenzo Lotto in the little chapel to the left of the sanctuary. These include the *Visitation* above the entrance arch and the three lunettes inside illustrating the *Birth of the Virgin, Annunciation, Marriage of the Virgin* and *Presentation in the Temple*. Lotto seems to have enjoyed making use of the colour white (suited to the name of the church). In the *Visitation*, the Madonna wears white beneath a striped golden stole, and in the birth scene the white pillows and sheets are conspicuous, as is the apron and veil of the seated lady reading. The dome and pendentives with the four Evangelists are also by Lotto. The life of the Virgin cycle was completed in 1577, with the *Flight into Egypt, Adoration of the Shepherds* and *Adoration of the Magi* on the lower walls, by another painter (otherwise little known), who also frescoed the main chapel and the one on the right. The nave has remains of 14th-century frescoes, and those in the crypt are even earlier.

The road skirts the **Prato della Fara**, a pleasant green with an attractive row of houses. At the end is the Gothic façade of the ex-church of Sant'Agostino, which now serves as the Aula Magna of the **University of Bergamo**, established in the town in 1968 and which has its headquarters in the former convent here. A gate leads into the public park which encircles the bastion of the walls around some of the abandoned conventual buildings as far as Porta Sant'Agostino.

THE CITY GATES AND WALLS

The mighty walls which encircle the upper town were built in 1561–88 by the Venetians but were never needed to defend Bergamo. Today on their summit is the **Viale delle Mura** (*map p. 261, 1–3*), a busy avenue where the numerous bastions are planted with plane trees. At their foot are fields or gardens.

The main gate is the **Porta Sant'Agostino** (*map p. 261, 3*), opened in 1574 (guarded by the Venetian Lion of St Mark on its outer face), near a little public garden beside the church of Sant'Agostino. There is a good view of the walls from here. Just outside the gate, approached from Via Vittorio Emanuele II, is the entrance to the **Cannoniera di San Michele** (*open April–Sept on Sun 10–12, 2–6; commune.bergamo.it/turismo*). One of about 27 such defences in the walls, this one protected Porta Sant'Agostino. A tunnel leads down to a hall, used by the soldiers, which still contains cannon balls. You can see the two holes (now blocked) used for positioning the cannon, as well as a

SAN MICHELE AL POZZO BIANCO
St Ambrose peers at the wounds of Christ through *pince-nez*. Detail of the
crypt fresco of Christ in a mandorla surrounded by Doctors of the Church.

passageway—high enough for a horse—which leads outside the walls. The limestone has formed into stalactites.

Viale delle Mura is open to traffic but also has paths and small gardens on the bastions. It has views over the lower town and, just below the walls, well-kept private gardens. It passes the cobbled Via Osmano, one of the approaches to the upper town, and then runs behind the green domes of the church of Sant'Andrea. Don't miss the topiary swan on the wall beneath a garden with an ancient wisteria. After the avenue crosses over the funicular, it soon reaches **Palazzo Medolago** (1791), an elegant building with columns and sculpted roundels just inside the **Porta San Giacomo** (*map p. 261, 5*), the grandest 16th-century gateway (also decorated with a Venetian lion) and well-preserved. Outside, it is approached by a stone bridge built in 1780, where Via Sant'Alessandro (here cobbled and closed to traffic) enters the town. You are directly above Viale Vittorio Emanuele II here, so there is a good view of the lower town, and at the foot of the walls there is a well-kept garden which has palm trees. The Viale now winds round the 16th-century Palazzo Brembati, with little statues on the balustrade of its hanging garden. Some way further on, past a few stretches of the medieval walls and the old cobbled lane which leads up to the Monastery of Santa Grata, the Viale turns sharply right at the grass-grown **Baluardo di San Giovanni** (*map p. 261, 1*; the Cannoniera, where the cannon were kept and the arms stored, is usually open from April–Sept; *see commune.bergamo.it/turismo*) and soon reaches Colle Aperto with Porta Sant'Alessandro where there is a particularly good view of the walls with the fields below.

ACCADEMIA CARRARA

Map p. 253, 2. Piazza Carrara. Open 10–6 except Tues. T: 035 234 396035 or 234 39964, lacarrara.it.

Somewhat out on a limb, Bergamo's important art gallery is best reached on foot from the upper town by the path which descends from Viale Vittorio Emanuele II and Via Pignolo, just outside Porta Sant'Agostino. Called Via della Noca, this is a peaceful path with steps which ends in front of the gallery. From the lower town it is a walk of about 20mins from Porta Nuova via Via Tasso and Borgo Pignolo. You can also take bus no. 6 or 9 from Porta Nuova (map p. 253, 6) to Piazza Oberdan (just beyond map 2).

The Accademia Carrara picture gallery is housed in the impressive Neoclassical building which was purchased by Count Giacomo Carrara for his gallery and academy, both founded in 1780, and enlarged in 1807–10 by Simone Elia. The collection was augmented in the 19th century by important paintings donated by Guglielmo Lochis and the art historian Giovanni Morelli. The Venetian school is particularly well represented. The gallery was reopened in a new (chronological) arrangement in 2015. There are seats in every room and good labelling, also in English.

FIRST FLOOR

Room 1 (Earliest works): The small portrait of Leonello d'Este in profile is one of only two painted portraits to have survived by the famous Renaissance court artist Pisanello (*see p. 350*). Leonello was a patron of Pisanello and is also recorded by him in no fewer than six portrait medals in bronze. This portrait dates from around 1441 and is sadly very damaged. It shows the ruler, with his long nose and receding brow, against a background of roses. Also here are small Madonnas by Carlo Crivelli (with decorative fruits) and Andrea Mantegna (a work painted on canvas rather than panel, hence its subdued colours). Another work by this great

artist, a *Resurrection*, was identified in the gallery deposits in 2018 (and is to be restored): it seems to have been the upper part of a *Descent into Limbo* now in a private collection.

The narrative scenes displayed here are by the Venetian painters Antonio Vivarini and Giovanni d'Alemagna. The *Three Crucifixes*, signed and dated 1456 by Vincenzo Foppa, shows Christ on the Cross between the two thieves beyond a Roman arch which opens onto a landscape in which the city of Jerusalem is depicted. This is the first documented work by this influential Lombard painter. Discovered in 1764 by Giacomo Carrara, it was beautifully restored in

2018, when a layer of yellow varnish was removed. The painting of *St Jerome* is another early work signed by Foppa.

Room 2 (Venetian painters): One entire wall is hung with five works by Giovanni Bellini or his workshop. The two *Madonnas* are amongst the most famous works of this, his favourite subject, and both are signed: the *Lochis Madonna* has a beautiful classical Madonna and a restless Child. The window sill is in veined red Verona marble. The *Morelli Madonna*, restored in 2008, is one of the masterpieces of Bellini's maturity. It was probably commissioned for private devotion c. 1484 by Alessio Agliardi, a native of Bergamo who was an engineer and friend of Bartolomeo Colleoni. It later found its way to the provincial church of Alzano outside the town. It has a beautiful landscape in the background and a pear on the parapet. The *Dead Christ between the Virgin and St John the Evangelist* (also very well restored in 2008) is the first of at least twelve other paintings of this subject by Bellini. It has an air of intense compassion, with the face of the Madonna worn out with tears and John's open mouth depicting his despair.

Here also are hung works by Bartolomeo Vivarini, Vittore Carpaccio and Francesco di Simone da Santacroce, all contemporaries of Bellini. The *Madonna and Child* is the only work known signed by Jacopo, son of Antonello da Messina (note the beautiful glass cup). Antonello visited Venice, where he had an important influence on the painters of his time.

Room 3 (donor portraits): Some of the most important collectors who were donors to the gallery include Count Giacomo Carrara (by Fra' Galgario, c. 1737) and Count Guglielmo Lochis (by Piccio, 1835).

Room 4 (the Renaissance in Florence and the Marche): Botticelli painted the small panel with various episodes from the story of Virginia: having refused the advances of a Roman consul, she was finally killed by her own father to save her honour. It was probably painted for a room in the Vespucci residence in Florence. The portrait of Giuliano de' Medici in profile is one of several portraits of Giuliano by Botticelli; this version is probably a replica of one in the National Gallery of Washington.

One of the masterpieces of the Gallery is **Raphael's *St Sebastian***. Shown fully dressed, the identification as St Sebastian rests on the fact that he holds an arrow as a symbol of his martyrdom (Sebastian is traditionally portrayed nude with his body pierced with arrows). The panel was painted in 1502 or 1503, when Raphael was under 20, and the influence of Perugino, the most celebrated painter in Italy at that time, is particularly evident. It was beautifully restored in 2018 and the wonderful details, also of the landscape, are now fully visible.

Room 5 (Tuscany and Flanders): The works here illustrate the close ties between these two states in the Renaissance. There is also a display of part of a pack of Tarot cards illustrated by Bonifacio Bembo for the Duke of Milan c. 1440 (35 of them are in the Morgan Library in New York).

Rooms 6–8 (School of Bellini): Marco Basaiti represents the school with several good male portraits, and there is an exquisite *Judgement of Paris* by Carpaccio, a tiny work with a pond in a clearing in a wood. In Room 7 the *Madonna and Saints* by Andrea Previtali shows what this painter from Bergamo learnt from Bellini when he trained under him in Venice. In Room 8 there are three small works by Giovan Francesco Caroto (1527) and a very unusual painting of a man in prayer before Christ on the Cross, signed by Vittore Belliniano, one of the rare works by this mysterious painter who adopted his master's name. It was painted in 1518, two years after Bellini's death, and has a beautiful landscape and a well-painted figure of Christ.

Room 10 (Milan and Lombardy): Bergognone (*see p. 168*) is particularly well represented (note especially the very small *Meeting between the*

Emperor Theodosius and St Ambrose, interesting also for the street scene in the background which seems to depict Milan with the campanile of San Gottardo). St Ambrose is also portrayed by the painter known as the Master of the Pala Sforzesca (*see p. 50*). The *Madonna Nursing the Child* is by Bernardino Zenale.

Room 11 (Leonardeschi): Works by painters who were close followers of Leonardo da Vinci include a portrait by Ambrogio de Predis and Andrea Solario's *Ecce Homo*.

Room 12 (16th-century Piedmont): There are paintings here by Gaudenzio Ferrari (*see p. 138*) and Defendente Ferrari (no relation).

Room 13 (Ferrara): There are some good works by Lorenzo Costa.

SECOND FLOOR

Room 14 (the Renaissance in Europe): There is a very fine portrait of Louis de Clèves by Jean Clouet, and Dürer's *Way to Calvary*.

Room 15 (Lorenzo Lotto): The *Holy Family with St Catherine* is a typically unusual scene taking place in a green bower with a landscape in the distance: Joseph lifts a white muslin sheet to show the saint the drowsy Child lying on a green cloth, while the Madonna asks them not to disturb her tranquillity. Catherine is again one of the protagonists in the *Mystical Marriage of St Catherine*, signed and dated 1523. Here the Virgin is superbly painted, and the colours red, yellow and blue

predominate. The donor Niccolò Bonghi is an awkward presence: presumably he insisted that he should be portrayed full on. The landscape at the top of the painting was quite simply cut out of it by a French soldier while serving in Bergamo.

The portrait of Lucina Brembati is one of Lotto's best portraits: the extremely self-satisfied sitter is shown bedecked in jewels with the moon in the night sky in the background. There are also three smaller works by Lotto here, including the *Story of St Stephen*, with a beautifully painted wood. Lotto's contemporary from Bergamo, Cariani, painted the portrait of Giovanni Battista Caravaggi (c. 1520).

Room 16 (early 16th-century Venetian painting): The *Madonna and Sts John the Baptist and Mary Magdalene* was painted c. 1513 by Palma il Vecchio (*see p. 281*) shortly after he arrived in Venice, where he is known to have frequented the painter Andrea Previtali, pupil of Giovanni Bellini. Appropriately enough, Previtali is also represented here (in particular with his *Madonna* of c. 1523, featuring the donors Paolo Cassotti and Agnese Avinatri).

Room 17 (Giovanni Battista Moroni): Portraits include Crisostomo Zanchi and a small one of a very young girl from the Redetti family wearing a ruff, one of his most delightful works.

Rooms 18–19 (later 16th century): Room 18 has a *Madonna and Child with the Young St John* by Jacopo Bassano. In Room 19 are works by Guercino, Sassoferrato and Matthias Stomer.

Room 20 (17th-century Dutch art): Jan Brueghel the Elder is represented with a still life and genre scenes. *St Domitilla* is by Rubens.

Room 21 (portraits by Lombard painters): These include Carlo Ceresa (from Bergamo) and Fra' Galgario (Count Giovanni Secco Suardo).

Rooms 22 and 23 (18th-century Venice): Pietro Longhi, Giovanni Battista Tiepolo, Francesco Guardi and Bellotto.

Room 24 (sculpture from the Federico Zeri collection): Donated in 1998, the works reflect the eccentricity of the donor. They cover various periods and include a damaged *Andromeda* by Pietro Bernini, father of Gian Lorenzo.

Rooms 25–28: The last rooms have early 18th-century sculptures in terracotta and wood by the Fantoni family; portraits by Il Piccio; an historical scene by Francesco Hayez (1842); and a good portrait of Santina Negri by Giuseppe Pellizza da Volpedo (1889).

The important collection of prints and drawings, especially representative for the Lombard and Venetian schools, is open to scholars by special request.

GALLERIA D'ARTE MODERNA E CONTEMPORANEA

Map p. 253, 2. Piazza Carrara. Open 9–1 & 3–6 except Tues. T: 035 270 272, gamec.it.

Across the road from the Accademia Carrara, a 14th-century monastery has been well restored by Vittorio Gregotti as an exhibition centre. Part of the ground floor houses the Galleria d'Arte Moderna e Contemporanea (the GAMeC). It displays a small collection of 20th-century works including: *Eggs on a Book*, a superb still life by Felice Casorati (1949); the portrait of his spaniel called Betty, an untypical Boccioni (1909); a battle scene by Aligi Sassu (1936); and works by De Chirico and his younger brother Alberto Savinio. There is also a representative small group of sculptures by Manzù, donated by the artist himself: *Portrait Bust of Pio* (in which his son appears to be 'protected' in a straight-jacket); *Japanese Lady*; a statuette of a cardinal; *Lovers*; and a bas-relief of Oedipus. Manzù's self-portrait (in monochrome tempera) shows him drawing a female nude model (dating from around 1953). In the courtyard is a version of his well-known sculpture of his children Giulia and Milato playing on a carriage. Manzù was born in Bergamo and the town preserves a number of his works.

MUSEO DEL MONASTERO DI MATRIS DOMINI

Map p. 253, 4. Via Antonio Locatelli 77 (just across Via Vittorio Emanuele II from the lower station of the funicular). Open Thur 9–11.30, Sat 3.30–5.30, Sun 9–11 or by appointment; T: 035 3884811, matrisdomini.org.

This is a very interesting little museum in a convent of Dominican nuns, the only convent in Lombardy which managed to reopen after its suppression by Napoleon (albeit 40 years later, in 1835). Nine nuns live here today. In the charming little cloister is the entrance to the museum, opened in 2000 to preserve remains of the Romanesque frescoes of the first church here (consecrated in 1273), which were discovered and detached in the 1970s. The 14th-century scenes include St Peter with his two keys beside a cupboard with two locks on its shelves (the door of Paradise must once have been depicted close by); a charming *Visitation*; a fragment which seems to depict Mary and Joseph searching for Jesus in the Temple; and the story of St Dominic resuscitating a boy who has fallen from his horse. In the former refectory are remains of mid-13th-century frescoes (*Last Supper, Crucifix*, fragments of a *Last Judgement*). Five stained glass tondi from the rose window of the earlier church date from 1308 and are thought to be the earliest to have survived in all Lombardy. Also interesting is part of the roof of the old church, moved here to protect its frescoed terracotta tiles.

In the church, which is open all day, the most interesting painting is the 17th-century *Massacre of the Innocents* in the choir by Pietro Ricchi. The high altar with its elaborate marble intarsia by the Manni family is dated 1691.

PRACTICAL INFORMATION

GETTING AROUND

• **By air:** Orio al Serio airport is just 5km from the town centre. A shuttle bus (no. 1) takes 30mins from the Città Alta and 15mins from the railway station (*see orioaeroporto.it*).

• **By car:** Parking in Bergamo can be difficult. You are advised to leave your car in the lower town and make use of the excellent funicular (or no. 1 bus) to the Città Alta. There are many pay car parks but they can get full. The huge free park at Piazzale della Malpensata (*map p. 253, 8*) is usually a good bet (except on Mon, market day). There is free parking also in Via Statuto and adjacent streets just to the west of Borgo Sant'Alessandro, convenient if you choose to walk up one of the medieval stepped lanes to the upper town. In the centre of the upper town (except on Sun from 10–12 & 2–7, and in spring and summer also on Fri and Sat evenings from 9–1am, when the upper town is totally closed to cars) there is limited space in Piazza Mercato del Fieno (*map p. 261, 2*).

• **By rail:** Trains link Bergamo with Milan Centrale, Porta Garibaldi or Lambrate stations (journey time 1hr). Branch lines go to Lecco (40mins) and Brescia (1hr).

By bus: From the railway station, bus no. 1 runs along Viale Papa Giovanni XXIII through Piazza Matteotti (the centre of the lower town), Viale Roma and Viale Vittorio Emanuele II to the funicular station for the upper town (same ticket). Bus no. 1A continues to the upper town all the way to Colle Aperto.

By funicular: Runs 7am to quarter past midnight (slightly later on Sat) every 7mins or so. Used by residents as well as visitors. Tickets can be bought at the offices in the upper and lower stations. For timetables, see *atb.bergamo.it*.

INFORMATION OFFICES

Lower town Piazzale Marconi, outside the railway station (*map p. 253, 8*). *T: 035 210204, comune.bergamo.it/turismo*.
Upper town At the time of writing, scheduled to move to the Teatro Sociale on Via Colleoni (*map p. 261, 1–2*). For more information see *visitbergamo. net*.

There is a **24hr ticket** which allows entrance to all six of Bergamo's history museums (Palazzo del Podestà, Campanone, Donizetti Museum, San Francesco, Torre dei Caduti, Rocca). For details, see *museodellestorie.bergamo.it*.

WHERE TO STAY

LOWER TOWN

€€€ **Excelsior San Marco**. In a characterless large modern block also used for conferences, but with a roof garden restaurant (closed Sun). Only a short way from the funicular to the upper town. Efficient service and sometimes with advantageous special offers. *Piazza Repubblica 6. T: 035 366111, hotelsanmarco.com. Map p. 253, 4*.

€€ **Arli**. Some 60 rooms of all types, simple but comfortable. *Largo Porta Nuova 12. T: 035 322014, arli.net. Map p. 253, 6*.

UPPER TOWN

€€€ **Relais San Lorenzo**. A fairly new luxury hotel with a roof terrace and spa, one of the few in the upper town and at its peaceful end near Colle Aperto. The restaurant (Hosteria, closed Mon and Tues lunch) incorporates excavations of the medieval town. *Piazza Mascheroni 9/a. T: 035 237383, relaisanlorenzo.com. Map p. 261, 1*.

WHERE TO EAT

LOWER TOWN

€ **Vecchio Tagliere**. Lively place serving solid Bergamasque food. Also has rooms. *Piazzetta Manzù (off Via Sant'Alessandro 13). T: 035 244725, www.alvecchiotagliere.it. Map p. 253, 5*.

UPPER TOWN

€€€ **Casual Ristorante**. Next to the funicular station for San Vigilio.

Recently opened by the chef Enrico Bartolini, it specialises in fish dishes. Closed Tues. *Via San Vigilio 1. T: 035 260944, casualristorante.it. Just beyond map p. 261, 1.*

€€ **Da Ornella**. Boasts a 100 year-old tradition of serving good food from the Valle Brembana. The *polenta taragna* with local cheeses is a speciality. Closed Thur. *Via Gombito 15. T: 035 232736, trattoriadaornella.it. Map p. 261, 2.*

€€ **Taverna Colleoni dell'Angelo**. In an historic building in the main piazza of the upper town, right next to its most famous buildings. Serves regional dishes. Closed Mon. *Piazza Vecchia 7. T: 035 232596, colleonidellangelo.com. Map p. 261, 2.*

€€ **Antica Trattoria della Colombina**. Traditional *trattoria* which has been in operation for many decades, with a Liberty-style dining room and summer seating outside. Closed Mon. *Via Borgo Canale 12. T: 035 261402, trattorialacolombina.it. Map p. 261, 1.*

€€ **Donizetti**. Right on the main street where you can also have a plate of pasta, or delicious *hors d'oeuvres*: convenient but not cheap. In warm weather there are tables outside under an old loggia. Frequented by local residents as a wine bar. Closed Tues. *Via Gombito 17/a. T: 035242661, donizetti.it. Map p. 261, 2.*

SAN VIGILIO

Baretto di San Vigilio. Right by the top funicular station, with a lime-shaded outdoor terrace overlooking Città Alta and the plain. Good food and wine, wonderful atmosphere. Open every day except in deep snow. *Via al Castello 1. T: 035 253191, baretto.it.*

CAFÉS

Caffè del Tasso in the upper town (*Piazza Vecchia 3; map p. 261, 2*) is good for coffee or aperitifs. The lower town has some grand old-established cafés, including **Balzer** (*Portici Sentierone 41, balzer.it; map p. 253, 6*) and **Pasticceria Jean Paul** (Closed Mon; *Via Moroni 361, pasticceriajeanpaul.it; map p. 253, 7*).

LOCAL SPECIALITIES

Cheeses of the region include Taleggio, Formai de Mut ('cheese from the mountains') and Bitto. These are usually available in restaurants and grocery stores (try **Ol Formager** at Piazzale Oberdan 2; end of Via San Tomaso; *beyond map p. 253, 2*).

Polenta is the staple main dish of Bergamo. *Casoncelli* (similar to ravioli) have a rich sweet and sour filling. The ubiquitous desert, also to be found in *pasticcerie*, is *polenta e osei*, a delicious sponge cake (which comes in all sizes) with a chocolate and nut filling and iced with marzipan and sugar. It mimics a traditional Brescian savoury dish of polenta topped with roasted songbirds. The Torta Donizetti is a sponge studded with dried apricots and pineapple.

FESTIVALS AND EVENTS

The **International Piano Festival** of Brescia and Bergamo is held from April to June (see *festivalpianistico. it*). The **Donizetti Festival** is held every autumn (*donizetti.org*). A **dance festival** is held in May and June (*festivaldanzaestate.it*).

The Bergamasco

The Bergamasco, the traditional territory of Bergamo, consists of two main valleys, the Valle Brembana and the Valle Seriana, in the mountains north of Bergamo. The lower reaches of the valleys are industrial, but the higher regions are prettier with small ski resorts. There are interesting churches (with hidden treasures such as frescoes and altarpieces by Lorenzo Lotto, and two paintings by Palma il Vecchio). On the plain south of Bergamo is Bartolomeo Colleoni's castle of Malpaga, the pleasant town of Treviglio, and Caravaggio, probable birthplace of the great artist of that name.

THE VALLE BREMBANA

The lower part of the verdant valley of the River Brembo, north of Bergamo, runs through the west part of the Parco Regionale dei Colli di Bergamo, where the village of **Ponteranica** (*Atlas C, A3*) has a parish church containing a polyptych, signed and dated 1525, by Lorenzo Lotto (*see p. 256*). It shows the *Redeemer, Annunciation* and *St John the Baptist between Sts Peter and Paul.*

ALMENNO SAN BARTOLOMEO AND ALMENNO SAN SALVATORE

These two neighbouring municipalities on the west bank of the river (*Atlas C, A3*) are interesting for their churches in isolated positions. The **Pieve di San Salvatore** (or Madonna del Castello: *only open before Mass on weekdays at 5.30, and at 9am and 7pm on Sun*) is marked by a tall campanile above the river (in which you can see a few remains of a large Roman bridge destroyed in a flood). This is the oldest church in Almenno, thought to have been founded c. 755. The interior was altered in the 12th century when the beautiful pulpit in sandstone with the symbols of the Evangelists was installed, and the sanctuary, with its Ionic capitals, was frescoed. The ancient columns in the crypt date from before the 11th century. The adjoining Santuario was opened in 1590 with its delightful ciborium over the high altar, with paintings of sibyls attributed to Andrea Previtali, and an altarpiece of *St Charles Borromeo between Sts Roch and Pantalon* by Giovan Paolo Cavagna.

Close by (5-min walk) is the large 12th-century **Basilica di San Giorgio** (*May–Oct weekdays 2.30–5.30; weekends also 10–12; in other periods on request, T: 035 553205*), with a good exterior. The whale bone hanging in the nave, dating from the Pliocene epoch, was found nearby. The most interesting frescoes are those high up—and difficult to see—on the inside of the nave arches (on the right): they date from the late 13th or early 14th century.

Also outside Almenno San Salvatore is the church of **San Nicola** (or Santa Maria della Consolazione; *open as for San Giorgio*), next to the former Augustinian convent, founded in 1486. It has an attractive interior, with stone vaulting supporting a painted wood roof, and side chapels beneath a matroneum. It contains 16th-century frescoes by Antonio Boselli, and an altarpiece of the *Trinity* by his contemporary Andrea Previtali.

Outside Almenno San Bartolomeo is the little circular church of **San Tomé**, one of the best Romanesque buildings in Lombardy (*open Tues–Sun 10–12 & 2.30–4.30 or 5.30*). Excavations have revealed remains of tombs dating from the 1st and the 9th centuries. The church is now generally thought to be an 11th-century building, although the apse and presbytery may have been added later. The nuns' door connected it to a fortified convent. The beautiful interior has an ambulatory and above it a matroneum (which can be reached by stairs) beneath a delightful cupola and lantern lit by four windows. The capitals are decorated with sirens, eagles and other creatures.

In Almenno Sant Bartolomeo is the **Museo del Falegname** (*museotinosana.it*), a private museum dedicated to carpentry, with a collection of tools (from the 17th century), reconstructed artisans' workshops, bicycles and puppets.

CELANA AND SOTTO IL MONTE

Northwest of Pontida (with the Benedictine abbey of San Giacomo Maggiore), the tiny hamlet of **Celana** (*Atlas D, C4*) is worth visiting for the altarpiece in its church by Lorenzo Lotto (signed and dated 1527). On the other side of Monte Canto, **Sotto il Monte Giovanni XXIII** has named itself after Pope John XXIII, the regnal name of Angelo Roncalli, born here in 1881 and pope from 1958–63. He was canonised in 2014. You can visit his birthplace in the village, as well as the church where he was baptised. There is now a pilgrims' reception centre here (which shows a film of his life) with a café and bookshop (*papagiovannisottoilmonte.org*).

SEDRINA, ZOGNO AND SERINA

In **Sedrina** (*Atlas C, A3*), the church of San Giacomo Maggiore has an altarpiece of the *Madonna in Glory above Sts Joseph, Gerome, Francis and John the Baptist* signed and dated 1542 by Lorenzo Lotto. It includes a view of the Valle Brembana. It was commissioned for the church by three local wine merchants who met Lotto in Venice and has remained *in situ* ever since. **Zogno**, further north, is the chief place in the lower Valle Brembana. The museum of San Lorenzo (*opened on request; T: 0345 91083*) has an *Adoration of the Shepherds* by Palma il Vecchio (*see below*).

Beyond Zogno, the road forks. To the right, up a side valley, is **Serina**, the birthplace of Palma il Vecchio c. 1480. There is a polyptych of the *Presentation of the Virgin* by him in the sacristy of the church (*open all day 8–5.30*), probably painted when the artist was in his 30s.

PALMA IL VECCHIO

Little is known about this painter's life apart from the dates (c. 1480–1528) and his original name, Jacopo Negretti. He adopted the name of Palma and became known as Palma il Vecchio to distinguish him from his great-nephew Palma Giovane, born c. 1548. Palma il Vecchio specialised in the type of contemplative religious picture known as the *sacra conversazione* (a group of sacred personages painted together), a format first introduced by Alvise Vivarini and Giovanni Bellini and which often served for private devotional paintings. Palma's female figures seem to be modelled on a type of fulsome blonde beauty that clearly shows the influence of Titian. At times his work shows similarities with that of his contemporary and friend Lorenzo Lotto. You can see important works by him in Lombardy (Milan, Bergamo) as well as in Venice, but most of his artistic production is now outside Italy.

Although he left the Bergamasque valleys for Venice, probably before 1510, to train under Andrea Previtali, pupil of Bellini, he kept his ties to his birthplace and painted altarpieces for some of the churches in these valleys. Today you can see three of these: in Zogno, Serina and Alzano Lombardo. He died in Venice in 1528.

SAN PELLEGRINO AND THE UPPER VALLE BREMBANA

San Pellegrino Terme (*Atlas C, A3*) is famous for its mineral water springs (which produce the San Pellegrino water, widely available all over Italy and beyond). The elegant spa town was laid out at the beginning of the 20th century with grand Art Nouveau buildings including the Palazzo della Fonte and the former Casinò Municipale. QC Terme, at Viale della Vittoria 53, is the thermal bathing complex (*qcterme.com*).

The **Val Taleggio**, branching west, has given its name to the well-known Italian cheese produced here. The picturesque medieval village of **Cornello** (*Atals C, A3*) is the historic home of the Tasso family. In the 16th century the villagers are said to have run a postal service across the Alps. **Piazza Brembana** is a summer resort and a base for climbs in the mountains.

THE VALLE SERIANA

This is the principal valley in the Bergamesque Alps (Alpi Orobie). The lower part is mainly industrial but the upper reaches are unspoilt. The churches have some good works by the Fantoni family of sculptors and carvers (*see p. 283*).

Alzano Lombardo (*Atlas C, A3*) has a tradition of wool working. The basilica of San Martino (*open 8–11.30 & 3.30–7*) was rebuilt in 1670 and has a splendid interior with coupled marble columns and stuccoes designed by Girolamo, member of the Quadrio family of architects (and who also worked on Milan's Duomo). The church has a pulpit by Andrea Fantoni and an 18th-century painting by Andrea Appiani. The three sacristies have superb carvings and intarsia work. The first has Baroque walnut cupboards carved by Grazioso Fantoni (1679–80), while the second (1691–3) has even better carving in walnut and boxwood by his son Andrea, assisted by his three brothers. Above are statuettes showing the martyrdom of saints and apostles, and in the ovals the story of Moses and scenes from the New Testament. The seated statues represent the Virtues; the *prie-dieu* has a *Deposition*, also by Fantoni; and the stuccoes are by Girolamo Sala. The intarsia (1700–17) in the third sacristy is partly by Giovanni Battista Caniana; the barrel vault has more stuccoes by Sala. In the museum (*open Wed–Fri 8.30–10, Sun 3–7; T:035 516579, museosanmartino.org*) are works by Palma il Vecchio (*Martyrdom of St Peter Martyr*) and Jacopo Tintoretto. There are also interesting paintings by Giovan Paolo Cavagna and late 17th-century portraits by Fra' Galgario. The sculptures are by the Fantoni and by Caniana.

At **Olera**, up a side road to the west, the parish church (*only open Sun 11–5; T: 334 612 4186*) contains a polyptych by another great Venetian, Cima da Conegliano.

The industrial village of **Albino** is worth visiting for its church of San Giuliano (*open 8–12 & 4–6*), which has a *Crucifixion* by Giovanni Battista Moroni (*see p. 269*), who was born at nearby Bondo Petello.

GANDINO

As you go further into the mountains, the valley becomes distinctly pretty. Gandino (*Atlas C, B3*), an ancient little town noted for its carpets, was the birthplace c. 1400 of the sculptor Bartolomeo Bon the Elder, who worked mainly in Venice. The basilica of **Santa Maria Assunta** (*open 7.30–12 & 3–6*) was rebuilt in 1623–30 and has a very fine interior on an interesting central plan. The dome was finished in 1640 and the *trompe l'oeil* fresco added in 1680. The bronze balustrade dates from 1590. Giacomo Ceruti painted the spandrels above the arches, and the organ was built by Adeodato Bossi in 1868 (in an earlier case by Andrea Fantoni). Outside the church is a little baptistery of 1967 and beside it the **Museo della Basilica** (*open Sat–Sun 2.30–7 or on request; T: 035 746115 or 035 745425*). It contains two series of Flemish tapestries (1580), a silver altar (begun in 1609 and finished in the 19th century), a 16th-century German sculpture of Christ on the Cross (with movable arms) and ancient textiles.

CLUSONE

The small resort of Clusone (*Atlas C, B3*) has a medieval **Town Hall** with a remarkable astronomical clock made by Pietro Fanzago in 1583, and numerous remains of frescoes. Above is the grand basilica of **Santa Maria Assunta** (*open 8–5.30*), built in 1688–1716 by Giovanni Battista Quadrio, preceded by an impressive terrace with statues added at the end of the 19th century. The high altar has sculptures by Andrea Fantoni (who also designed the pulpit) and an *Assumption* by Sebastiano Ricci. There is a 16th-century altarpiece by Giovan Paolo Cavagna. To the left is the **Oratorio dei Disciplini** with a fresco on the exterior depicting the *Dance and Triumph of Death* (1485), fascinating for its iconography. Inside (*open 10–12 & 3–6*) are well-preserved frescoes of 1480 showing small, colourful scenes of the Passion. Over the choir arch is a fresco of the *Crucifixion* (1471). The life-size polychrome wood group of the *Deposition* is attributed to the school of Fantoni. Further downhill are the grand **Palazzo Fogaccia** (*only open for special events*), built in the early 18th century by Giovanni Battista Quadrio, with a garden; and the church of **Sant'Anna** (*open 8–5.30*), with 15th- and 16th-century frescoes inside and out and a fine altarpiece by the little-known Domenico Carpinoni, in a lovely frame.

Just outside Clusone is **Rovetta**, where the house and workshop of the Fantoni family of sculptors, who originated here, is now a little museum (*open mid-June–mid-Sept Tues–Sun 3.30–5.30; at other times, T: 034 673523*). In the church of the Ognissanti (*open 7–6.30*) the *Madonna in Glory Venerated by the Apostles and Saints* (1734) is the first major altarpiece painted by Tiepolo. He had come to Bergamo to fresco the ceiling of the Colleoni Chapel (*see p. 264*).

ON THE PLAIN

TRESCORE BALNEARIO AND MALPAGA

East of Bergamo, on the plain of the River Serio, is **Trescore Balneario** (*Atlas C, A4*), a small spa with sulphur and mud baths. A chapel in the park of the Villa Suardi, south of the Via Nazionale (SS42), contains interesting frescoes (1524) by Lorenzo Lotto, commissioned by Giovan Battista Suardi and illustrating the lives of St Barbara and St Brigid (*open by appointment at the Tourist Office; T: 035 944777 or 335 750 7917*).

South of Bergamo, the castle at **Malpaga** (*Atlas C, A4; open for guided tours on holidays 2.30–dusk; otherwise by appointment, T: 035 840003*) is approached by a road bordered on either side by narrow canals regulated by locks connected to the Serio river. It is set in the centre of an agricultural estate, surrounded by farm buildings with double loggias. The 14th-century castle, on the extreme western limit of the territory controlled by the Venetian Republic, was bought as a residence by Bartolomeo Colleoni (*see p. 264*) in 1456, the year after he became captain of the Venetian army. He heightened the castle in order to protect it against firearms (you can see the castellations of the first castle in the walls) and built the pretty loggias. The castle is particularly interesting for its frescoes. Those in the courtyard were commissioned by Colleoni's grandchildren in the early 16th century to illustrate his achievements in battle: the siege of Bergamo in 1437 includes a good view of the Città Alta, and under the loggia is a scene of the great soldier's last battle in 1497 (Colleoni is shown in a red hat). The Sala dei Banchetti contains more 16th-century frescoes, here showing the visit of King Christian I of Denmark to the castle in 1474 on his way to Rome (the soldiers in white-and-red uniform are those of Colleoni). The reception room upstairs retains the original 15th-century frescoes from Colleoni's own lifetime (recently restored), with courtly scenes in the International Gothic style. Colleoni died (at the age of 80) in the bedroom with the 15th-century *Madonna and Child with Saints* in a niche.

TREVIGLIO

Treviglio (*Atlas C, A4*) is an agricultural and industrial centre, home to SDF, a large manufacturer of tractors and other farm machinery. In the pleasant old centre, in Piazza Manara, the Gothic church of **San Martino** contains a beautiful polyptych by Bernardino Zenale and Bernardino Butinone (1485) at the head of the south aisle. Extremely well preserved and painted on a gold ground, it is one of the most important late-Gothic paintings produced in Lombardy. At the base are charming portraits of the four Evangelists in the guise of Doctors of the Church. The church bell-tower can be climbed on Sundays (*www.treviglio.18tickets.it*).

Opposite the church's west entrance is the **Caffè Milano**, founded in 1896 and retaining some original furnishings in the interior. Hermann Hesse came here in 1913 and liked it. The *Turta de Treì* cake was invented here. Set into the façade of the building is a relief known as *La Gatta* (it actually shows a horse), a symbol of a medieval feud between Treviglio and nearby Caravaggio. Today the two towns play one another at bowls.

From Piazza Manara, Via Galliari leads to the **Santuario della Madonna delle Lacrime** (*closed indefinitely for restoration*), begun in 1619 and with another triptych by Butinone. Behind it, encased behind a Liberty façade, is an 11th-century Augustinian cloister with an old well-head at its centre.

On Via Bicetti Butinone is the town's **museum**, named after Ernesto and Teresa della Torre and formed around the collection of a local neurosurgeon, left to the city in 1961. It has since been amalgamated with other collections, for example of works by the local painter Giovanni Battista dell'Era (d. 1798). The museum also shows contemporary works, winners of Treviglio's painting and sculpture prize.

CARAVAGGIO

Caravaggio (*Atlas C, A4*) was the probable birthplace of the painter Michelangelo Merisi (1571–1610), known to the world as Caravaggio. It has been suggested that as a young man he must have been influenced by the school of local painters from Brescia, namely Moretto, Giovan Girolamo Savoldo and Girolomo Romanino, who produced religious subjects often concentrating on naturalistic details, and intimate settings, and some night scenes. However Caravaggio soon left Lombardy for Rome, where he became Italy's most famous painter of the 17th century.

An avenue leads to a large sanctuary (Santa Maria del Fonte) dedicated to the Madonna, who is said to have appeared to a peasant woman here in 1432 on the site of a miraculous spring. The domed church was enlarged by Pellegrino Tibaldi in 1575 and is visited by thousands of pilgrims every year (festival on 26 May). There is a little Museo Navale (*open Sat 3–6 except Aug; T: 0363 356211*). At the time of writing, a huge Amazon warehouse was under construction nearby.

ROMANO DI LOMBARDIA

Tn the east of the Serio river is Romano di Lombardia (*Atlas C, A4*), with an interesting urban plan. The church of Santa Maria Assunta (*open by appointment, T: 0363 910633, romano@diocesibg.it*), reconstructed in the 18th century by Giovanni Battista Caniana, contains a *Last Supper* by Giovanni Battista Moroni. It has been suggested that the marvellous figure of the butler holding a flask of wine is a self-portrait. Above the Neoclassical Palazzo Rubini (*open Sun 10–12*) is the 13th-century Visconti castle (*open by appointment: cultura@comune.romano.bg.it, T: 0363 982341*).

PRACTICAL INFORMATION

GETTING AROUND

• **By rail: Treviglio** is well served by trains from Milan (Centrale and Porta Garibaldi). The suburban line S5 also goes from Porta Garibaldi and Porta Venezia. Journey time to Treviglio is c. 45mins, to **Caravaggio** c. 50mins. The line continues to Crema. Treviglio is also on a direct train line from Bergamo (journey time 30mins). There are services between Treviglio and **Romano di Lombardia** in 8–15mins.

• **By bus:** The towns and villages of the Valle Brembana and Valle Seriana, as well as Trescore Balneario and Malpaga on the plain, are difficult to reach by public transport. There are local buses but services can be erratic. From Bergamo, they leave from the bus station in Piazza Marconi in front of the railway station. For timetables, see *bergamotrasporti.it*.

INFORMATION OFFICES

Trescore Balneario. Pro Loco office at Via Suardi 20. *T: 035 944777, prolocotrescore.it.*

The *visitbergamo.net* website is a good source of information.

WHERE TO EAT

ALMENO SAN BARTOLOMEO
€– €€ **Ristorante Collina**. On the byroad up to Roncole in woods above the town. In an unattractive modern building but family-run and there is usually fish from Lake Como on the menu as well as regional specialities. *Via Capaler 5. T: 035 642570, ristorantecollina.it.*

ALMENO SAN SALVATORE
€ **Ristorante La Frasca**. In an old convent. Also a pizzeria. *Via Convento 3. T: 035 642548, ristorantelafrasca.com.*

BRUSAPORTO
€€€ **Da Vittorio**. Famous Michelin-starred restaurant founded by Vittorio and Bruna Cerea in the 1960s. Two of their sons, Enrico and Roberto, are now the chefs. The short menu changes seasonally and always includes a great variety of seafood. Closed Wed lunch and for three weeks in Aug. It also has a small hotel with 10 rooms (La Dimora). *Via Cantalupa 17. T: 035 681024, davittorio.com.*

TRESCORE BALNEARIO
€€ **Della Torre**. Restaurant with rooms, serving regional specialities. *Piazza Cavour 26. T: 035 941365, albergotorre. it.*

TREVIGLIO
€ **Osteria Zio Nino Terra**. In a columned courtyard behind the cathedral. Local meats, *costoletta alla milanese*, polenta. Good value lunch menu. *Via Roma 9/Via Bicetti de' Butinoni. T: 0363 273787.*

LOCAL SPECIALITIES

In **Treviglio**, the *Turta de Treì*, half cake-half pie, is the speciality of the long-established Caffè Milano in the cathedral square.

BRESCIA
Looking towards Piazza Paolo VI,
with the Torre del Popolo
and Duomo Nuovo on the left.

Brescia

The second largest town in Lombardy after Milan, Brescia (*Atlas C, B4*) appears to be thriving. Lying at the foot of the Cidneo (the ancient Cydnean) hill, it has numerous attractions for the visitor, including the most important Roman remains yet discovered in northern Italy. Its three main *piazze* are particularly pleasant. Brescia has an excellent museum and art gallery and the great number of churches in town have paintings by local 16th- and 17th-century artists, the most interesting of whom is Moretto.

HISTORY OF BRESCIA

Brescia, probably founded by Gaulish Celts, had come under Roman influence by the 3rd century BC and you can still see traces of the criss-cross Roman street plan in the old city centre. The town of Brixia was designated a colony by Augustus and it flourished under the emperors, when the main monuments still visible today were built. Reduced to rubble by Goths and Visigoths, Brescia re-emerged to prominence under the 8th-century Lombard king Desiderius, who was born in the neighbourhood. Brescia was a member of the Lombard League and then, in 1258, was captured by the tyrant Ezzelino da Romano. Later it was contested by a number of powerful families: the Milanese Torriani and Visconti, the Veronese Scaligeri and Pandolfo Malatesta; but from 1426 to 1797 it prospered under Venetian suzerainty. Between 1509 and 1516 it was twice captured by the French under Gaston de Foix. After 1814, it came under Austrian rule, during which time it acquired its nickname the *Leonessa* (she-lion), for a spirited ten-day rebellion in 1849, the *Dieci Giornate*, quelled by the ruthless Austrian general, Baron von Haynau (in turn nicknamed the 'hyena of Brescia').

At the mouth of the Val Trompia, along which the Romans had built an aqueduct, Brescia has always enjoyed an abundance of water, and many fountains (some of them permanently running) can still be seen in its public squares as well as in palace courtyards. The town expanded to the south in the 1970s when its economy, based on the service industries, was flourishing, and Brescia Due is connected via the old city centre to the northern suburbs by a (driverless) metro, which opened in 2013. The town is still known for its production of arms (the Beretta arms manufactory, family-owned since 1526, operates at Gardone Val Trompia some 18km north of town; *Atlas C, B4*).

Brescia has received a notable number of immigrants in recent years: in 2016 it bestowed Italian citizenship on 9,376 new inhabitants, a number second only to Milan. This multi-ethnic presence is very evident today.

BRESCIA HIGHLIGHTS

There are three squares very close together in the heart of the town, all lined with cafés, which make a good place to begin a visit. **Piazza Paolo VI** (*map 1; see below*) has buildings from all periods, including a remarkable circular Romanesque duomo. **Piazza della Loggia** (*map 1; p. 292*) is dominated by a fine Palladian Town Hall. **Piazza della Vittoria** (*map 3; p. 294*) is a creation of the Fascist era, surrounded by functional Rationalist buildings embodying that era's vision of a model city.

The superb **Museo di Santa Giulia** (*map 2; p. 297*) has beautifully displayed material from the Roman, Lombard and medieval eras. The **Pinacoteca Tosio Martinengo** (*map 4; p. 300*) reopened in 2018 with a stunning display of its paintings, including many by the native artist Moretto.

On Via dei Musei are the remains of **Roman Brescia** (*map 2; p. 294*), including a temple and theatre.

The church of Santi Nazaro e Celso (*map 3; p. 309*) has an **altarpiece by Titian**.

PIAZZA PAOLO VI

This piazza (*map 1*), named after Pope Paul VI, who was from Brescia and who was canonised in 2018, was the heart of the post-Roman settlement. In summer, it is the coolest place in town due to the breeze which comes down from the castle hill (just visible to the north). In winter, the winds here can be bitter. Two cathedrals stand here, successors to the summer and winter cathedrals built by the 4th-century bishop Philastrius. Today the massive **Duomo Nuovo**, built in the local white botticino

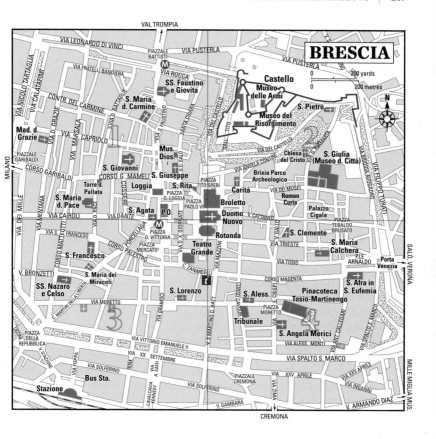

stone and with a green cupola, stands between the remarkable circular building of the ancient **Duomo Vecchio** and the **Broletto**, the Lombard Town Hall, both dating from the 11th century. Two fountains adorn the square, which has an attractive row of buildings, with pavement cafés, lining its east side.

THE ROTONDA OR DUOMO VECCHIO

The Romanesque Rotonda (*open Tues–Sat 9–12 & 3–6, Sun 9–10.40*) stands on the site of the old winter cathedral of Santa Maria de Dom. It is an extremely interesting building of the 9th–11th centuries, arguably the most important structure of its kind in Lombardy. Its beautifully stone-dressed exterior is very well preserved. The entrance (through a portal added in the 16th century) is on an upper level, so that inside you look down into the ancient interior, an unexpected and very moving sight. The circular ambulatory, supported by eight pillars, has 16 little bays with alternating cross vaults and barrel vaults. In the polygonal lantern above, probably dating from after 1095, a coronet of windows provides the light.

In front of the entrance is the red Verona marble **sarcophagus of Bishop Bernardo Maggi**, with beautifully carved reliefs. Moved here from another part of the church in 1896, it is placed at eye level so that you can see all the details. On one side is the scene of the bishop acting as mediator between the Guelphs and Ghibellines and taking an oath at an altar (even the altar cloth is carefully carved) to enact a peace settlement. The bishop's left arm is one of the few parts of the monument which has been damaged. On the other side is the effigy of the bishop, the first *signore* of the city, bearing the date of his death (1308) and showing a procession of clerics at his funeral, holding candles and swinging censers. At his head and feet are the four symbols of the Evangelists: amusingly, the animal heads have been given human bodies (so that they can all hold their books in their hands). At one end of the sarcophagus is a relief of *St George and the Dragon*. Facing the sarcophagus, at either side of the entrance, are the stairs which once led up to the campanile (which collapsed in 1708).

A short flight of steps takes you down to the ambulatory. On either side of the entrance to the sanctuary, sarcophagi are mounted on the wall: on the right is the **tomb of Bishop Balduino Lambertini**, with reliefs by Bonino da Campione (1349) of the Madonna and Child enthroned with seven saints and the bishop himself. This is one of only three signed works by this sculptor (*see p. 133*). On the left is the **tomb of Domenico de Dominici** (d. 1478). The long inscription records that he was sent on a diplomatic mission to the Court of Matthias Corvinus, King of Hungary, to reconcile him with the Holy Roman Emperor Frederick III and with Louis of Bavaria.

Beneath the sanctuary is the ancient **Crypt of St Philastrius**. Philastrius (Filastrio), founder of the two original cathedrals, was an early bishop of Brescia, appointed in 379. His relics were brought here in 838. This crypt predates the Rotonda by some centuries: it is all that remains of Philastrius' original basilica of Santa Maria de Dom.

The **sanctuary** itself, preceded by a transept, was added in the 15th–16th centuries. In the transept on the right is a delightful painting (1656) by Francesco Maffei of the *Translation of the Patron Saints*, from the castle to the duomo in 1581, with St Charles Borromeo (*see p. 201*) in the procession. Glass panels in the pavement show remains of the presbytery of the earlier church, and traces of Roman structures, including pillars of a hypocaust, hollow bricks for heating walls, and a mosaic with sheep and the name of a deacon, Syrus, with the letters HLTCS (*hunc locum tesselavit cum suis*), indicating that he paid for the pavement out of his own pocket. The high altarpiece is an *Assumption of the Virgin* (1526) by Brescia's most famous painter Moretto (*see p. 302*). Also in the sanctuary is a marble bust of Pope Alexander VIII (who began his ecclesiastical career as Bishop of Brescia) by Orazio Marinali. Kept locked away here in a chapel is the Treasury, with some very precious Crosses dating from the 11th century (usually only shown on the last Friday of March and on 14th Sept). The organ was built by Gian Giacomo Antegnati, a native of Brescia, in 1536 (still a very fine instrument although subsequently restored).

Modern iron steps lead down to the lowest part of the Rotonda. At the west end is a capacious alcove, the original entrance to the church, and now used as the **baptistery**, with a huge 15th-century font. On either side of the alcove are fragments of the original mosaic pavement.

BRESCIA, DUOMO VECCHIO
Detail of the tomb of Bishop Bernardo Maggi (14th century).

THE DUOMO NUOVO

The new cathedral was designed in 1604 by the local architect Giovanni Battista
Lantana (his only known work, although later modified) on the site of the old summer
cathedral of San Pietro de Dom. The façade dates from the 18th century and the
Neoclassical dome (82m high) was only built in 1825 by Luigi Cagnola. It is said to be
the largest in Italy after St Peter's in Rome and the Duomo of Florence. The elaborate
interior, on a rectangular plan, finally consecrated in 1914, is in the shining white
botticino marble of the exterior and has mostly 18th- and 19th-century works of art
(apart from a Mannerist chapel at the top of the north aisle). Also in the north aisle is
the conspicuous bronze monument (1984) to the Brescia-born Pope Paul VI (canonised
in 2018). The bas-reliefs record episodes in his life, including the Vatican Council; the
renunciation of his tiara (with which he was the last pope to be crowned, in 1963); the
encyclicals he issued; his meeting with the Patriarch Athenagoras I, which ended the
excommunication of the Orthodox Church pronounced some 900 years earlier; and
his address to the UN Assembly. He is also remembered particularly for his reform
of the Roman rite. He decreed that cardinals over the age of 80 should no longer be
admitted to conclaves. He left word in his will that he wished for no monument. At the
top of the south aisle is the tomb of St Apollonius, the best-known work attributed to
the local sculptor Maffeo Olivieri (1504), with beautiful carving. It was made to house
the 4th-century bishop's relics. In front of it, in a small casket, are relics of St Benedict.

Behind the Duomo Nuovo is the **Biblioteca Queriniana** (*Via Mazzini 1, corner of
Via Cattaneo; map 2; open Tues–Fri 8.45–6, Sat 8.30–12.30*), founded by Cardinal
Querini in 1747, with a beautiful reading room. Among its treasures are a 6th-century
Evangelistary with silver letters on purple vellum, and a Concordance of the Gospels
by Eusebius (11th century).

THE BROLETTO

The Broletto, the old Lombard Town Hall, , built in 1187–1230, stands at the north end of Piazza Paolo VI. At its south end it incorporates the **Torre del Popolo**, formerly the tower-house of the Poncaroli family, one of many that once stood in the early medieval town, built by warring factions as expressions of power and status. The Broletto has been greatly altered over the centuries. The exterior preserves its medieval appearance, with four-light windows in the handsome stone facing. A Baroque portal, incorporating two ancient Roman columns, leads into the grand **courtyard**, with a fountain, and a Baroque loggia on one side. Today the building houses the offices of the Province and Prefecture but erased inscriptions on the façades testify to its time as the seat of the Venetian governor. Each governor, on leaving office, would put up a fulsome inscription. The Broletto adjoins the **ex-church of Sant'Agostino**, the west front of which has early 15th-century terracotta ornamentation and two huge lion's heads above.

PIAZZA DELLA LOGGIA

This is a beautiful piazza (*map 1*), with a distinctly Venetian flavour, reminding us of the happy relationship Brescia enjoyed with the more powerful city throughout her history.

Coming from Piazza del Duomo, you emerge beneath the clock tower (**Orologio**), erected in 1547, which has a lovely clock face and two figures at the top, known as Tone and Batesta, who strike the hours on a bell (a great deal smaller but similar to those on the Torre dell'Orologio in Piazza San Marco in Venice). The pretty arcade along this side of the piazza was the scene of a brutal political murder in 1974: eight people lost their lives and over a hundred were injured in a bomb blast. The memorial here is by Carlo Scarpa. You will find numerous circular plaques in the pavement of the roads nearby (near Piazza Tito Speri and along some of the lanes leading up from there to the Castle Hill), commemorating those who have lost their lives in subsequent tragic massacres. Above the arcades can be seen the top of the **Porta Bruciata**, a fragment of the oldest city wall.

The **statue of *Bella Italia*** was set up in 1864 as a memorial to the 'Ten Days' (*Dieci Giornate*) in 1849 when the town rebelled against the Austrians. It takes the place of a column surmounted by a Venetian lion, which was pulled down and smashed by Napoleonic troops in 1797.

The piazza is dominated by the **Loggia**, the Town Hall (*it can be visited Mon–Fri 9–12.30 & 2–7, Sat 9–12–30*), a beautiful Renaissance building with exquisite classical sculptural detail. The ground floor, with a spacious portico beyond three wide arches, was begun in 1492 and was completed before the end of the century. The construction of the upper floor was halted until the mid-16th century, when the great Venetian architects Jacopo Sansovino and Andrea Palladio were both consulted (and the present windows were designed according to Palladio's drawings). The building was devastated by fire in 1575 and again in 1908, but it was carefully reconstructed and its appearance remains more or less as it was in the 16th century. The **Palazzo Notarile** (note its very fine doorway) beside the Loggia, begun in the same style, was never finished.

TITIAN AND PALLADIO IN BRESCIA

Titian's polyptych of the *Resurrection*, commissioned by Altobello Averoldi for the high altar of the church of Santi Nazaro e Celso (*see p. 309*) came close to being re-directed to the Este court. Before it reached the town, the panel with St Sebastian was seen in Titian's studio in Venice by Jacopo Tebaldi, ambassador to the court of Alfonso I in Ferrara, and letters survive in which he writes to the duke suggesting he should acquire it (and have it replaced by a copy for Brescia). But since Bishop Averoldi was papal nuncio at the court of Venice, Duke Alfonso decided not to antagonise him by such a gesture, even though he fully appreciated Titian's extraordinary talent since the artist was already at work for him in Ferrara. Both the bishop and the artist are thought to have been present when the work was delivered to the church in 1522.

Years later, Titian, already in his 80s, returned to Brescia to paint three large canvases for the ceiling of the assembly room in the Loggia: the subject of the central panel was the Apotheosis of Brescia and the other panels personified the age-old activity of the manufacture of arms (*see p. 313*), with Vulcan in his forge, and the agricultural traditions of the surrounding countryside, with Ceres. They were installed in 1568 but destroyed only six years later by fire.

Palladio, who is recorded in Brescia in 1550, 1562, 1567 and 1575, managed to see Titian's panels *in situ* before they were lost. He recorded his admiration for them, suggesting they were among the most beautiful works to be seen in all Europe. Today they are only recorded in engravings.

Venice is again recalled in the lovely **Palazzo Monte di Pietà** to the left of the Loggia, which has a little 'loggetta' with two high arches and a balcony below an upper loggia. The decision to incorporate numerous ancient Roman inscriptions (and even some carved Classical festoons) in the local stonework was made in 1485, and they are most interestingly actually part of the structure (so you need to look carefully to find them all). The move to present them in this way may have been inspired by the pronouncement in favour of the protection of Roman remains made by pope Pius II in 1462 and by Pope Sixtus IV's donation of some ancient bronzes to the people of Rome in 1471 (the origin of the Capitoline Museums). This Brescia open-air lapidarium can perhaps be taken to be the first public archaeological display in Europe.

VIA MAMELI

This street leads west out of the piazza, passing, on the corner of Via delle Cossere, the ***Mostasù***, a sculpture of a face without a nose, testimony to a Guelph-Ghibelline squabble in 1311 when the Holy Roman Emperor had the noses cut off all the city's statues. Opposite, the Contrada San Giovanni leads to the church of the same name (*see p. 306*) At the end of the street is the **Torre della Pallata**, built in 1248 on Roman foundations and used during the Middle Ages as a warehouse and prison.

PIAZZA DELLA VITTORIA

This piazza (*map 3*) was designed by Marcello Piacentini and is an interesting example of the kind of rhetorical Modernism that was dear to the Fascist regime. Built in grey marble and white stone, it survives intact more or less as it was when Mussolini came here in 1932, to inaugurate it from the red marble **Arengario**, a rostrum with bas-reliefs by Antonio Maraini celebrating Brescia as the 'lioness of Italy' during the *Dieci Giornate* (Tito Speri is one of the figures on the rostrum; *see p. 310*). Bishop Maggi (*see p. 290*) also features, as do the painters Moretto and Romanino. On one side of the square, a brick 'skyscraper' rises beside a marble insurance building with the Café Impero in the portico below. The contenders on the opposite side are a clock-tower and, in a building with a similarly tall arcade, the Republic café-lounge. The daringly vertical, horizontally striped **Post Office** has a bold, foursquare design with no roof visible. The piazza's atmosphere of false grandeur is palpable (the clock at the time of writing told the wrong time), but this pedestrian space today is nevertheless quite lively—though with nothing like the throngs that filled it for the start of the Mille Miglia car race in its heyday (*see p. 313*).

Left of the Post Office is a **First World War memorial**, also set up by the Fascist regime—with a large chunk of granite from the mountain battlefields. It abuts the church of Sant'Agata (*see p. 304*).

VIA DELLE X GIORNATE

The pleasant long raised arcade which lines Via delle X Giornate continues all the way to Corso Zanardelli, where it becomes a double arcade flanking one side of a wide pedestrian street of shops. These arcades, the **Portici**, follow the line of the ancient Roman city walls. There are benches to rest here—and don't miss the home-made cake shop for dogs next to the **Teatro Grande**, Brescia's most important theatre. Its façade dates from 1782 and the interior from 1811, and it still has a Rococo foyer of 1769.

ROMAN BRESCIA

Via dei Musei (*map 2*) follows the line of the Roman decumanus maximus. It leads to the archaeological area of Roman Brixia.

BRIXIA: PARCO ARCHEOLOGICO

Map 2. Via dei Musei 55. Open Tues–Sun Oct–mid-June 9.30–5; other months 10.30–7. Combined ticket available with the Museo di Santa Giulia. T: 0302 977833, bresciamusei. com. If there are a lot of visitors, you will be given a time slot for the Republican Sanctuary. It is below ground (you are accompanied by a custodian) and visitors are limited in order to ensure the preservation of the frescoes.

BRESCIA, PIAZZA DELLA VITTORIA
The Post Office building, which stands at one end of the square designed
by Marcello Piacentini and formally opened by Mussolini in 1932.

THE REPUBLICAN SANCTUARY

While you wait to go in, a video is shown, showing the history of the sanctuary. Once inside you can see the remains, which are dated to the 1st century BC and include the original red *opus caementicium* pavement of the pronaos and, in the inner chamber, a floor of tiny uncoloured tesserae (with a raised pavement in black-and-white mosaic where the columns were). The head of an acrolithic female cult statue was found here. The walls of the inner chamber are decorated with faux marble panels framed in vermilion and with *trompe l'oeil* columns. But the most interesting painted decoration is the depiction of a fringed wall hanging attached with rings to a curtain rail, with a pretty border and ribbons. The frescoes have been dated 89–75 BC. Two huge Corinthian capitals with acanthus leaves exhibited here are of the same period.

THE CAPITOLIUM (IMPERIAL-ERA TEMPLE) AND THEATRE

The **Capitolium**, erected by Vespasian in AD 73 at the north end of what was the forum, is today the most imposing monument of Roman Brixia. It stands on a high stylobate approached by steps, 15 of which are original, and has a hexastyle pronaos

BRESCIA, REPUBLICAN SANCTUARY
Detail of the *trompe l'oeil* wall decoration (1st century BC).

of reconstructed Corinthian columns with, behind, a colonnade of three columns on each side. The one column to have survived, complete with its capital, stands apart. It was protruding from the ground (in the palace garden on this site) in 1823 and was the reason why excavations were begun just here. Over a hundred years later in 1939, the Fascist regime ordered a hasty part-reconstruction of the temple in brick (only completed in 1950). The temple had three cellae dedicated to the Capitoline Triad: Jupiter (central cella), Juno and Minerva (the smaller lateral cellae).

You can go in to the cellae, which still reflect the atmosphere of the 1930s, when the original pavement in yellow and white marble, blotched with blue (giallo antico and pavonazzetto) was restored. Here are exhibited two Classical heads of Minerva and one of Silenus. On the walls of the central cella is a lapidary collection of Roman inscriptions in the local botticino marble.

Beyond a turnstile you can explore the **Roman Theatre**. Palazzo Gambara, which used to cover it, has been partly dismantled to reveal its shape. Although it has lost its seats, its outline is still clearly visible, built into the slope of the Cidneo hill.

PIAZZA DEL FORO

The cobbled rectangular square on the other side of Via dei Musei (the old decumanus maximus) is called Piazza del Foro after the Roman Forum, whose site it occupies. The church of **San Zeno al Foro** (*only open for services*) is enclosed by a little Baroque forecourt (note the dolphins with their tails entwined). The Tourist Office housed in the 18th-century **Palazzo Martinengo** has archaeological excavations beneath it (*entered at Via dei Musei 30 beyond a little garden; opened by volunteers usually Tues–Sun 10–6; ask at the Tourist Office*) revealing further remains of the Roman city. These include fragments of wall paintings which are thought to have belonged to baths built just to the west of the forum at the end of the 1st century AD and an earlier domus of the Augustan period below. In another area you can see the holes made for the poles of Iron Age huts: people at this period built their dwellings within the tumbledown Roman mansions, and even lit their fires directly on the mosaic floors. An excellent plan illustrates the excavation levels from the prehistoric period to the Lombard era. A video reconstructs the visible ruins. Other remains found during the same excavations are to be opened in two more underground rooms of the palace.

More **remains of the forum** can be seen behind railings on the east side of the piazza, now well below the level of the pavement. One column stands, complete with its Corinthian capital. At the south end of the forum stood a **basilica**, fragments of which lie below Piazza Labus, reached from here by Via Gallo. Some of its pilasters are incorporated into the façade of a house and there are plans to reopen these excavations to the public (*for information, sabap-bs.archeologia@beniculturali.it*).

MUSEO DI SANTA GIULIA: MUSEO DELLA CITTÀ

Map 2. Via dei Musei 81. Generally open Tues–Sun 9 or 10 until 5 or 6. Late opening some evenings. Combined ticket with Brixia Parco Archeologico. T: 0302 977833, bresciamusei.com. Throughout the museum there are multi-media supports and exhibits for the visually impaired.

The former Benedictine convent of Santa Giulia comprised a group of buildings with three cloisters and several churches. Formerly called San Salvatore, it was founded in 753 on land belonging to Desiderius, King of Brescia (and later King of the Lombards). Ermengarde, the daughter of Lothair I, and many other royal and noble ladies were sisters in the original nunnery, which survived until it was suppressed by Napoleon in 1798. The land here is at the heart of old Roman Brescia. Formerly plentifully supplied with water, it had subsided into marsh but was reclaimed when the Lombards repaired the western arm of the Roman aqueduct.

The Museo della Città is arranged in the old convent complex in chronological order from the prehistoric era to the time of the Venetian Republic (15th century). There is an excellent section on Roman Brescia and a separate part of the museum dedicated to the history of the convent. All sections are well labelled, also in English. The order of the visit is clearly marked; only the highlights are given below. It is not possible to do justice to the museum without spending many hours here.

HISTORY OF THE CONVENT EXHIBITION

You are welcomed by the surprising 17th-century **sculpture of the crucified St Julia**, in Carrara marble by Giovanni Carra. The next gallery documents the Lombard period, including some of the original columns and capitals from the crypt of San Salvatore (*see below*). Accessed off a small cloister is the square undercroft below Santa Maria in Solario (with a Roman cippus for a central column supporting the

Romanesque vault). Here is displayed an exquisite little **4th-century ivory coffer** with scriptural scenes from the Old and New Testament in relief. Very well preserved, it has fascinating details and is clearly Classical in inspiration. The miniature Cross with gold and pearls is a touching survival from the 10th or 11th century.

Narrow old stairs ascend to the upper church, also dating from the 12th century, which is covered with early 16th-century frescoes by Floriano Ferramola and his workshop. Here is displayed the so-called **Cross of Desiderius**, thought to date from the late 8th century. An extremely precious work, it is made of wood overlaid with silver gilt and set with over 200 gems (dating from the Roman period to the 9th century). It incorporates cameos and miniatures and, on the lower arm, a remarkable triple portrait painted on gilded glass in the 4th century.

A modern staircase leads down to a larger cloister with a pretty double loggia and where the exterior of Santa Giulia and its campanile can be seen.

MUSEO DELLA CITTÀ

Prehistory: The finds are mostly from Brescia and its province, although one of the most striking exhibits is a helmet of a type worn by soldiers fighting in the Alps from the 4th–1st centuries BC, found at Daone in Trentino-Alto Adige. Perfectly preserved, it was purchased for the museum in 1886. The Gaulish silver horse-trappings date from the 3rd century BC.

Exhibits from the Roman-era: Finds from the Roman period are numerous: epigraphs, glass and a Greek amphora (c. 510 BC). There is a section of Roman road (the cardo maximus), with cart ruts, and remains of a Roman domus which fronted it. Note the holes in the simple mosaic pavement made by the poles of the wooden huts erected by the Lombards a few centuries later.

The section on Roman finds continues upstairs, in rooms around the third (and largest) cloister. A large stone head of a female deity is possibly that of the acrolithic cult statue in the Republican Sanctuary (see p. 295). The most remarkable exhibits are a group of bronzes discovered together in 1826 (it is thought they may have been hidden away for safety, perhaps at the end of the 4th century AD). There are six **Flavian-era gilded bronze portrait heads** (five male and one female) and, displayed in a room on its own, the treasure of treasures, the **Winged Victory**, a splendid bronze statue nearly 2m high, probably the chief figure of a chariot group from the roof of the Capitolium. It appears to be a Venus of the Augustan age (of the Venus of Capua type) remodelled as a Victory under Vespasian. The statue is unforgettable. Victory stands with her foot raised: beneath it would have been the helmet of Mars, which she proudly tramples to the ground. A shield would have rested on her bent leg. The tunic (or chiton), fastened at the shoulders, falls right to the ground while the heavier cloak (himation) on top of it is wrapped around the legs.

Beyond a room of finds from the Roman theatre and forum, on the right is an area of excavations under the monastery kitchen garden, where

BRESCIA, MUSEO DI SANTA GIULIA
Head of a monk (14th century) from the former Benedictine abbey of Leno,
founded by the Lombard king Desiderius in 758 and dismantled by the Venetians.

two Roman houses, the **Domus dell'Ortaglia**, came to light in 2003. They were inhabited for some four centuries and the finds are also exhibited here. One of the rooms has a mosaic floor with a central emblema of Dionysus serving wine to his panther from a rhyton.

The itinerary around the large cloister continues with Roman small bronzes, fragments of opus sectile marble floors, and, at the end, an amphora with Hercules and the Nemean lion. Another section has huge mosaics displayed upright on the walls and finds from the necropoleis of the Roman town.

Early Christian, Lombard, Carolingian and medieval exhibits:

The fragment of a rare **sarcophagus in African onyx** dating from the 4th century and carved with scenes from the Old and New Testament introduces the section devoted to the Christian era. The end room has **precious ivories**, including two dating from the 5th century: the consular diptych of Boethius, and the so-called Querini diptych, with pairs of lovers on each leaf, Hippolytus and Phaedra and perhaps Endymion and Selene.

The section on the Lombard and Carolingian period has grave goods in bronze and gold found all over Brescian territory, and including a hoard of gold Crosses and textiles dated to between the 8th and 10th centuries. A charming **weather vane** in the form of a gilded metal cockerel is dated AD 820.

Steps lead up to a room of later exhibits (up to 1426). Frescoes and a delightful group of four very unusual telamones carved in the local stone and all similarly dressed come from the Broletto and are dated to the end of the 13th century.

The church of San Salvatore: The itinerary leads up to the **nuns' choir**, built in the early 16th century when it was frescoed by Floriano Ferramola. Here is the tomb of Francesco Martinengo (d. 1515), an elaborate work in various types of marble and stone with bronze reliefs. At the other end of the room, a window grille overlooks the **church of San Salvatore**. Founded c. 753, this is the only building which has survived from the original convent. The nave has 13 Roman columns, all with beautiful capitals (only some of them Roman; the others, with basket-work, date from the 8th century) and traces

of Carolingian frescoes above the nave arches. The soffits were originally clad in lovely fretwork masonry, traces of which survive. The southwest chapel has frescoes by Girolamo Romanino. The best piece of Lombard carving in the museum is the peacock, one of a pair which probably used to decorate an ambo. Below is the **crypt**, dating from 760–3 (enlarged in the 12th century), with 42 columns of varying origins and capitals by the school of Antelami.

Steps lead down to a gallery of sculptural fragments in marble and terracotta. A 15th-century relief (in Greek marble from the island of Thasos) shows the town's patron saints, the brothers Faustinus and Jovita, martyred c. AD 126 and Bishop Honorius. The marble statues of Christ between Faith and Charity, from a funerary monument, are by the famous 16th-century sculptor who worked mostly in Venice, Alessandro Vittoria.

PINACOTECA TOSIO MARTINENGO

Map 4. Piazza Moretto 4. Open Oct–May Tues–Fri 9–5, Sat 10–9, Sun 10–6, June–Sept Tues–Sun 10.30–7. bresciamusei.com. The gallery was reopened in 2018 after eleven years of closure, fully renovated and with the paintings rehung. At the time of writing, work was still in progress in the garden and courtyard. A café was planned.

Piazza Moretto, a pleasant little cobbled square with two cedar trees, has a bronze statue of Brescia's most famous painter, Moretto (*see p. 302*), with his palette and a female allegory of Painting, set up in 1898 by Domenico Ghidoni. The late 16th-century Palazzo Martinengo da Barco houses the Pinacoteca Tosio Martinengo, first opened to the public in 1908 to display the two collections of Paolo Tosio (1851) and Francesco Leopardo Martinengo (1884). The two benefactors are recorded in portraits at the top of the stairs. The collection is beautifully arranged chronologically and is well-labelled, also in English. The walls of the various rooms are hung in velvet, in rich colours.

Room I. Early works: The four panels of magnificently dressed saints against a gold ground are by the Venetian master Paolo Veneziano. The panels from a polyptych by a certain Maestro Paroto (only known through a tiny number of works) are dated 1447. They are beautiful Gothic works, all with the same background of dark green foliage. They were purchased at a Sotheby's sale in 2012. The charming *St George and the Dragon,* with details highlighted in gilded relief, has a fairytale background against a golden sky. The bronze medals here include examples commemorating Gianfrancesco Gonzaga I (Marquis of Mantua), Novello Malatesta and Ludovico Gonzaga, all signed by Pisanello on the reverse. Other cases display ivories and Limoges enamels.

Room II. Early Renaissance in Lombardy: Detached frescoes by Floriano Ferramola include a falconry hunting scene with birds and a shaggy dog. The important Brescia-born painter **Vincenzo Foppa** is easily recognised, as he rendered the faces of his subjects in typically silvery grey tones and experimented with the effects of light. His Standard of Orzinuovi was borne in a procession against the plague in 1514 and is his last documented work. The cases contain late 15th-century enamelled plates and coloured glass made in Venice.

Room III: The *Head of the Redeemer* is attributed to Andrea Previtali.

Room IV. Treasures of the Tosio collection: Displayed against midnight blue velvet walls is **Raphael's *Redeemer*** (1505/6). It shows the young Saviour (just sprouting a beard) in the act of blessing, wearing a crimson cloak (note the perfect details of the blood beneath the Crown of Thorns and in the wounds made by the Cross). The fragment of the bust of an angel, also by Raphael, was painted when he was 17 years old for an altarpiece at Città di Castello (destroyed by earthquake in the 18th century). Painted on wood, it was later transferred to canvas. Also here is an extremely refined early 16th-century copy of Raphael's *Madonna of the Pinks* (the original, in the collection of the Duke of Northumberland, was acquired in 2004 for the National Gallery of London). This is one of many early copies made of this painting. The Madonna's blue dress is exquisitely painted and the exchange of little bunches of carnations (which seem to have been freshly picked) between the Mother and Child is a particularly memorable detail.

Also here are two paintings by **Moretto**. The *Portrait of a Lady as Salome* (c. 1557) shows the sitter in a magnificent fur cape and with her hair decorated with pearls.

Rooms V–VI. Moretto and Lotto: More early works by **Moretto** are exhibited here. The Venetian artist **Lorenzo Lotto**, who was a friend of Moretto, painted the splendid *Adoration of the Shepherds* in Room VI. Although a favourite subject for painters of his time, Lotto typically produces here a unique iconography: the Child is playing with a sheep which has stepped right into the crib (the Babe's golden curls matching the sheep's wool), while two shepherds (portraits of the donors) try to prevent the animal from actually stepping on the Child. The two angels with their huge wings seem unaware of the humans. Painted in 1530, it puts firmly in the shade the painting of the same subject by Lotto's contemporary Giovan Girolamo Savoldo, exhibited close by. Moretto's *Supper at Emmaus* here also shows the influence of Lotto.

MORETTO DA BRESCIA

Alessandro Bonvicino, always known as Moretto (c. 1498–1554), was born in Brescia and was almost exclusively active in and around his native city. He was clearly influenced by the Venetian school and Titian, but also by his friend Lorenzo Lotto. Amongst his pupils were Callisto Piazza from Lodi and Giovanni Battista Moroni from Bergamo. He is famous for his portraits, and it is thought that he might have been the first Italian painter to produce full-length portraits of a single sitter—a custom that had developed in Germany, especially with Cranach, but which was untried in Italy. In the 19th century, he was considered the 'Brescian Raphael'. He was particularly skilled at—and seems particularly to have enjoyed—painting rich fabrics. In Brescia his works can be seen in the Pinacoteca as well as in numerous churches including San Giovanni, San Francesco, San Nazaro, Santa Maria Calchera, the Duomo Vecchio, San Giovanni and San Clemente, where he is buried.

Room VII: Savoldo is beautifully represented here by his small *Rest on the Flight into Egypt* (on loan from the Bank of Brescia since 2018), which has a lovely landscape. *Christ and the Adulteress* by Polidoro da Lanciano shows how strongly the Venetian school influenced this group of painters.

Room VIII displays large altarpieces by **Girolamo Romanino and Moretto** (*Madonna and Child with Four Saints*, with a particularly lovely St Euphemia). Moretto's *Passion of Christ* is a very unusual painting, almost monochrome, with an angel holding a silver-coloured cloak. Romanino's *Supper in the House of Simon* is a fine detached fresco. The lectern with intarsia dates from 1520.

Room IX has interesting fresco fragments by Lattanzio Gambara (1555) and two small paintings by Alessandro Maganza (a banquet scene) and Pietro Marone (the Queen of Sheba on a journey by camel). In the case are small bronzes, armour, majolica and even a double bass.

Room X. Portraits: These include works by the three contemporaries born in Brescia: Moretto, Girolamo Romanino and Giovan Girolamo Savoldo. Savoldo's *Boy with a Flute* (c. 1525) shows the influence of the more famous painter Lorenzo Lotto (note the musical score pinned on the wall). There is also a very fine portrait by Moroni.

Room XII: The display is devoted to **Pitocchetto**, with nine of his delightful genre paintings of cobblers, a washerwoman, a lady spinning, beggars with a stray cat, and a strange scene in a wood (with one of the figures hiding his or her face from the viewer).

Room XIII, with its Neoclassical decoration, provides a fitting setting for a splendid display of 16th–18th-century

BRESCIA, PINACOTECA TOSIO MARTINENGO
Supper in the House of Simon by Girolamo Romanino. The memorable figure of the 'sinful woman' on her knees under the table occurs again in his work, in the church of San Giovanni (*see p. 307*).

Venetian glass, reflected in the two mirrors.

Rooms XIV–XIX. Genre scenes and allegory: Works by local 17th-century painters include a *Four Seasons* in the style of Arcimboldo. The paintings by the little-known Antonio Cifrondi, who died in Brescia in 1730, are particularly interesting. Another local painter (and contemporary of Cifrondi), Faustino Bocchi, is known for the funny little people he paints in his ironic '*bambocciate*'.

Rooms XX–XXI. Neoclassicism: Angelica Kauffmann's *Birth of St John the Baptist* (1806) features Martinengo, who commissioned the work. Andrea Appiani and Thorvaldsen are also represented in this room. The black-figure amphora is an original ancient Greek work. Tosio commissioned **Canova** to make the ideal portrait bust of Eleonora d'Este (1819), and Luigi Ferrari to sculpt a marble version of the *Laocoön*. The huge *Meeting of Jacob and Esau* is by the famous 19th-century painter **Francesco Hayez**, as is the

Flight from Parga (a scene of Greek refugees from Ottoman occupation, a subtle allusion to the unpopular Austrian occupation of Lombardy).

The gallery owns an important **collection of drawings** (*shown only with permission*): outstanding among them is a *Deposition* by Giovanni Bellini.

A short way north, in Via Tosio, the **Ateneo** can sometimes be visited. This was a Neoclassical palace owned by Count Paolo Tosio, now restored and open as a house museum (*for information, see ateneo.brescia.it*).

THE CHURCHES OF BRESCIA

Brescia has an extraordinary number of churches, nearly all of them still open for worship, with frescoes and altarpieces by Brescia's most famous painter, Moretto, and his contemporary Girolamo Romanino, also born here. Together with Giovan Girolamo Savoldo, also from Brescia, the three painters constitute an impressive artistic school, active in the first half of the 16th century. The churches are listed here in alphabetical order.

NB: Most of the churches are closed between 11.30 or 12 and 3 or 4. For an up-to-date list of opening times see www.comune.brescia.it.

Sant'Afra in Santa Eufemia (*map 4*). The church has a martyrdom of the titular saint by **Paolo Veronese**.

In the pleasant **Piazzale Arnaldo**, with the large Neoclassical Corn Exchange (1823) along the entire length of one side, a monument commemorates the friar Arnaldo da Brescia, who preached against the corruption of the clergy, was accused of heresy and burned at the stake in 1155. This area has many cafés and restaurants popular with young people in the evenings.

Sant'Agata (*map 1*). Built c. 1438–72. The interior has Baroque frescoes in the nave and in the raised sanctuary, the apse lunette has a fresco of the *Crucifixion* (1475) above the high altarpiece of the *Martyrdom of St Agatha* (on the Cross), dating from 1522. By the

side door is a 15th-century sculpture of the *Pietà* and an early 16th-century *Madonna and Child*. The last altar on the north side has more good 16th-century paintings.

Sant'Alessandro (*map 4*). The church stands in pretty little piazza with a fountain. The first south altar has a beautiful diptych (1444) of the *Annunciation* by the Venetian artist **Jacopo Bellini**, father of Giovanni. Gold dominates the painting, both in the garments and in the wall tapestry behind. The predella is by a pupil. The second altar on this side is a *Deposition* (1504) by Vincenzo Civerchio, and the fourth a small *Ecce Homo* by Lattanzio Gambara (1563). The first north altar has a 15th-century wood Crucifix.

Sant'Angela Merici (*map 4*). This sanctuary stands on the site of the church of Sant'Afra, destroyed in 1945. Inside, stairs lead up to the nave, rebuilt in the 1950s. The church is interesting for its paintings by artists belonging to the late 16th-century Venetian school: in the apse is a *Transfiguration* by the most famous of these, **Jacopo Tintoretto** (with the help of his son Domenico). The second south altarpiece, *St Apollonius Baptising St Aphra*, is by Francesco Bassano, who died two years before Tintoretto, and the first north altar has a *Martyrdom of St Aphra* by the workshop of Paolo Veronese. The lunette of the *Adoration of the Shepherds* in this aisle is one of the few works signed by Veronese's son, Carletto Caliari. The second south altar has an *Assumption of the Virgin* by Bartolomeo Passarotti and the third altar a *Madonna and Saints* by Giulio Cesare Procaccini, both of them 16th-century artists from Bologna. The polyptych of the *Deposition and Saints* in a handsome frame in the south aisle is an earlier work.

San Clemente (*map 4; only open for services*). The painter **Moretto**, who lived nearby, is buried here (fine tomb on the left side). Many of the altarpieces are by his hand, including the high altarpiece of the *Madonna Enthroned*, with St Clement and other saints. The first south chapel has a *Resurrection* by **Romanino** (like the Titian in San Nazaro, also a night scene) and the *Annunciation* scenes on either side of the chancel arch are by Moretto's pupil Callisto Piazza.

Santissimo Corpo di Cristo (*map 2*): Always known simply (but almost irreverently) as San Cristo, the church is approached by steps from a lane off Via dei Musei and has a simple façade with a good carved portal. The entrance is through one of the three cloisters of the monastery on the left. There are 16th-century frescoes inside and more (damaged) in the circular chapel off the south aisle.

San Faustino in Riposo (*see Santa Rita*).

Santi Faustino e Giovita (*map 1; only open 7.30–11*). Via San Faustino is a lively street, with numerous immigrant-run shops—greengrocers, butchers, tailors, snack bars and food markets—as well as *pizzerie* and small ethnic restaurants that are popular in the evenings. The economics department of Brescia University has its headquarters here. The church of Santi Faustino e Giovita has an old square campanile and a pretty little 17th-century interior with pairs of columns supporting the arches in the nave and a *trompe l'oeil* ceiling. On the side walls of the presbytery are frescoes devoted to the titular saints (1749) by the great Venetian painter Gian Domenico Tiepolo, who here shows his independence from his more famous father, Giovanni Battista, with whom he collaborated all his life. The *Adoration of the Child* on the south side of the church is by Lattanzio Gambara.

San Francesco (*map 3*). Built in 1254–65, the attractive church has a large rose window in the façade typical of Umbrian Franciscan churches. The columned interior has numerous works of art of interest. In the north aisle is a painted Crucifix (1310–20) on a gold ground attributed to the Maestro di San Francesco. The larger Cappella dell'Immacolata, with a dome, was decorated in the 1730s. It has a Baroque balustrade and intarsia stalls dating from the mid-16th century. The last chapel on this side has detached frescoes, one by the 14th-century Paduan school. **Girolamo Romanino** painted the beautiful high altarpiece of the *Madonna and Saints* (c. 1516) in the polygonal apse (in a lovely carved wood frame). It is considered one of the most important works by this painter. The high altar has good early 16th-century carvings by a local sculptor. On the right side of the triumphal arch is a 17th-century Crucifix and in the chapel on the right of the sanctuary, over the altar, there is a very striking fresco of *St Peter*, probably dating from the end of the 13th century. Off a corridor here can be seen an ancient little Gothic chapel where a saintly friar who died in 1967 was buried in 1994 (he is still greatly revered). In the south aisle are some good 15th-century frescoes. The fifth south altar has an image of St Francis, difficult to date, which was framed in the 18th century. The fourth south altarpiece is a fresco of the *Descent of the Holy Spirit* by Romanino. Between the fourth and second altars are more interesting 14th-century frescoes including an *Entombment* dated to around 1320, which shows many affinities with Giotto. The group of Franciscan monks is thought to represent a theological school, and above it are row upon row of heads of angels and saints. The second altarpiece shows St Michael Archangel sending the devil to Hell, painted in the late 16th century by an imaginative local painter

called Pietro Rosa. The first south altar has a beautiful altarpiece of *St Margaret of Antioch between St Francis of Assisi and St Jerome* by Moretto (c. 1530), showing the evident influence of the Venetian school. In the lunette above is a fresco by a follower of Moretto.

Be sure to visit the lovely 14th-century **cloister**, entered on the right of the façade. Above one side rises the flank of the church and convent (where twelve friars still live) and the old campanile. The church owns a precious 16th-century Cross only shown on special religious festivals.

San Giorgio (*map 1; only open at weekends*). The 16th-century façade of the church, now used as a concert hall, is approached by a flight of steps. Remains of a medieval rectory were found here during restoration work in 2009. It contains 13th and 14th-century votive frescoes, as well as 16th-century frescoed decoration.

San Giovanni Evangelista (*map 1*). From Via Mameli, a lane (Contrada S. Giovanni) leads past a palace (no. 31) with a grotto with lions in its courtyard, to San Giovanni Evangelista, with its striped façade in brick and stone. This is an important church, where many of the late 16th-century and 17th-century altarpieces by local painters have been restored in recent years.

The third south altarpiece of the *Massacre of the Innocents* (in a lovely gilded frame) is by **Moretto**. The fourth altar on this side has a 17th-century reliquary with skulls and bones, relics said to have been brought back from the Holy Land by St Gaudentius, Bishop of Brescia, born c. 360 (his own bones are

BRESCIA, SAN GIOVANNI EVANGELISTA
Detail of Moretto's *Gathering Manna in the Desert* (1521–4).

also thought to be among them).

At the end of the north aisle is a door into a chapel with frescoes dated 1486. The last little domed chapel on this side, the **Corpus Domini Chapel**, was completely decorated in 1521 with very good paintings in the lunettes and on the walls by Moretto and **Girolamo Romanino** (including Romanino's memorable *Supper in the House of Simon*, with the 'sinful woman' on her knees under the table; and *Gathering Manna in the Desert* by Moretto). The

small *Deposition* over the altar here is an earlier work by Bernardino Zenale.

The fourth north altar has a *Madonna and Child with Saints*, also by Romanino. At the beginning of this aisle, the baptistery has a *Trinity and Saints* by Il Francia (Francesco Raibolini), born in 1460 Bologna, where most of his works are to be found today, and a *Marriage of the Virgin*, another work by Romanino (1515). Above the entrance to the baptistery is a panel painting celebrating the work and ministry of Pope St Paul VI.

San Giuseppe (*map 1*). Founded by the Franciscans in 1519. Inside there is a barrel-vaulted nave and a raised chancel. Below the altar in the crypt are little bundles of bones and other relics. The organ was built by the Antegnati family in the 16th century. In 1739 the Venetian composer Benedetto Marcello, who had moved to Brescia the previous year, was buried here. The cloisters of the huge adjoining convent survive and the largest of them, entered from Via Gasparo da Salò 13, is now the premises of the **Museo Diocesano** (*open daily except Wed 10–12 & 3–6*). It has paintings and vestments from churches in and around Brescia, including two scenes from the life of St Simon Magus, and Sts Peter and Paul 'supporting' the Church, all three tempera paintings by **Moretto**. The very striking panel painting of *Christ Blessing* from the Duomo Nuovo has recently been attributed to Moretto and dated around 1513: it has had many different attributions in the past, including Titian, and it is a very fine work. The charming gold-ground triptych of *St Ursula*, with her maidens (all with their stoles), and flanked by Sts Peter and Paul is by the Venetian painter Antonio Vivarini and dates from the mid-15th century.

San Lorenzo (*map 3*). Via Moretto, named after the prolific local painter, is an attractive residential street, pedestrianised in the section between Via Gramsci and the little court in front of San Lorenzo. Built in 1751–63, the church still preserves its late Baroque interior, which has a particularly successful plan with a vestibule at the west end and a dome and is decorated with 18th-century altarpieces, including the high altarpiece of the *Martyrdom of St Lawrence*, commissioned from Giambettino Cignaroli, the eldest of a family of artists from Verona. The central chapel on the north side was beautifully decorated in honour of the charming little fresco (?15th-century) of the Madonna and standing Child, discovered here during the construction of the church. In the vestibule are some of the earliest works, a *Way to Calvary* dated 1616, and a monument to a bishop who died in 1538.

Santa Maria della Carità (*map 2*). The façade has two ancient columns and frescoes in grisaille. The plan is circular with a dome and it was frescoed all over in the 18th century when the marble pavement was laid. The high altar in *pietre dure*, built to protect a miraculous 15th-century image of the *Madonna and Child*, is also notable. Attached to the church is a copy of the sanctuary of Loreto.

Santa Maria in Calchera (*map 4*). In a little piazza with a garden of ilex and box, a fountain and a monument (1918) to the mathematician Nicolò Tartaglia, this small church (*open for services*) has a *Visitation* (1525) on the high altar by Callisto Piazza. The first altarpiece on the left, *Christ in the House of Simon*, is by **Moretto** (c. 1550). This seems to have been a favourite subject for Brescian painters, who memorably depict the 'sinful woman' anointing Christ's feet on her hands and knees (recalling Romanino's two works of the same subject; *see pp. 303 and 307*). This is one of Moretto's best paintings and has recently been restored.

Santa Maria del Carmine (*map 1; often closed*). This 15th-century church, with a brick façade crowned with numerous pinnacles and a wide double portal, contains paintings by **Vincenzo Foppa** and a wood *Pietà* attributed to Guido Mazzoni. The precious organ was built by the Antegnati family in 1633.

Santa Maria delle Grazie (*map 1; open mornings only*). Built in 1522. The delightful Rococo interior (1617) has an exuberance of gilded stucco reliefs in the central barrel vault and in the side aisles. In the chapel to the right of the sanctuary is a *Madonna and Child and Three Saints* by **Moretto**. The Santuario, built around a fresco of the *Nativity* attributed to Andrea Bembo and said to be miraculous, is much visited by worshippers. It is approached through a cloister dating from 1951, hung with numerous ex-votos. The sanctuary itself was built and decorated in the 1880s.

Santa Maria dei Miracoli (*map 3*). The elaborately carved Renaissance façade of 1488–1500 includes a very unusual projecting central tribune, and the design of the rectangular interior is also bizarre, with a dome at the west end. The four paintings in the presbytery were commissioned in the last decade of the 16th century from (otherwise little known) local artists.

Santa Maria della Pace (*map 1; only open 9–11*). This large, façadeless church was designed by the Venetian architect Giorgio Massari in the early 18th century, when Pompeo Batoni painted the *Presentation in the Temple* for the high altar. This painter, who died in Rome in 1787, also provided the painting of *St John of Nepomuk* for the second north altar. It is surprising to find works by Batoni here: he is more readily associated with portraits, of Austrian archdukes or English 'milords' on the Grand Tour. The third north altar has a painting of *St Charles Borromeo* by the Venetian painter Giovanni Battista Pittoni, dating from the same time.

Santi Nazaro e Celso (*map 3*). This 18th-century church has many altarpieces by **Moretto**. It also has a superb early work by **Titian**, commissioned by Bishop Altobello Averoldi for the high altar and dated by the artist, 1522. If services are not in progress you are allowed to go right up to it behind the altar. In the form of a polyptych, it has a central *Resurrection of Christ* in a night scene, which also pervades the two rectangular panels of the *Annunciation* (the Annunciatory Angel is particularly beautiful). In the other two side panels the donor is shown kneeling with saints (St Sebastian is tied to a tree). This last is a remarkable study of human anatomy and the intrinsic drama of the nude figure shows the influence of Michelangelo's *Slaves* as well as the Hellenistic statue of the *Laocoön*, discovered in Rome just at this time. The *Resurrection* is not a subject the great artist returned to often in his exceptionally long career. (*For more on Titian in Brescia, see p. 293.*) The custodian will also take you to see the charming **Chapter House**, frescoed with a design of vine leaves and with portraits of prelates (including Averoldi).

Santa Rita (*map 1*). Officially San Faustino in Riposo, this tiny circular church is always known as Santa Rita by the locals, who come here frequently to pray to her (her statue is draped with necklaces offered by the faithful). Mementoes of the popular saint, born in Umbria in 1381 (and patron of the unlucky) are sold inside. When you leave the church, don't miss the view of its quaint little exterior in the lane behind: its conical steep terracotta roof is topped by a bell-tower.

CASTLE HILL

The castle stands on the Cidneo (the 'Cydnean Hill'), an eminence first mentioned by Catullus. Sources suggest that this was a sacred area on a route which lead along the hills between Bergamo and Verona. Today there are several ways to approach it: by Via Piamarta, which leads gently uphill past the church of San Cristo, along a deserted old cobbled street between high walls and then through public gardens; along Via Gabriele Rosa; or from **Piazza Tito Speri** (*map 1–2*), where the signposted way leads steeply uphill by steps in about 15mins. This little secluded square, on Via dei Musei, is named after the hero of the 'Ten Days' resistance in 1849 against the Austrians (he was put to death two years later). The statue (1888, Domenico Ghidoni) depicts Speri in fighting form with a feather in his cap.

The castle was rebuilt by the Visconti in the 14th century and again by the Venetians in the 16th century. Its extensive walls now enclose gardens, museums and an observatory. The entrance (*open 8am–8pm*), in botticino marble, was possibly designed by the Venetian architect Michele Sanmicheli and bears the Lion of St Mark, emblem of the Republic of Venice. Above the entrance, the coat of arms surmounted by the *cornu* hat of the Doge of Venice, was defaced by Napoleon's troops.

On the wide terrace known as **Piazzale della Locomotiva** (from the steam engine, built in 1906, that served the Brescia–Iseo–Edolo line) is a building that served as the headquarters of Julius Jacob von Haynau, the Austrian general who put down the *Dieci Giornate* rebellion. At the highest point of the hill is the **Museo delle Armi Luigi Marzoli** (*open June–Sept Tues–Sun 10–5, Oct–May Tues–Sun 9.30–1 & 2.30–5*), designed in the 20th century by Carlo Scarpa. In some of the rooms are remains of 14th-century frescoes. Many of the arms and firearms were made in Brescia, which was (and still is) renowned for its weapons production. The armour used for protecting a horse's flank, in the form of circular shields, is particularly interesting. In one room you can look down at the remains of the wide steps of a 1st-century AD Roman temple which once dominated the Cydnean Hill.

Downhill to the right is the **Museo del Risorgimento** (*closed at the time of writing*), founded in 1887 and arranged on two floors of a large 16th-century grain store. The collection illustrates Italian history from the last years of the 18th century up to Unification.

The limestone of Castle Hill, locally known as *médolo*, is home to a small beetle that lives only here: the tiny (2mm), blind *Boldoria ghidinii*.

PRACTICAL INFORMATION

GETTING AROUND

• **By air:** If you arrive at Bergamo's Orio al Serio airport, there are shuttle buses to Brescia (*autostradale.it*).

• **By car:** The most central car park is beneath Piazza Vittoria (*map 3*). Otherwise there is parking outside the castle walls (*map 2*) or near Piazzale Arnaldo (*map 4*). The car park at Fossa Bagni is close to the metro station of San Faustino (*map 1*), not far north of the centre, which you can reach in a few minutes on foot or take the metro for one stop to Piazza Vittoria.

• **By rail:** Brescia can be reached by direct Trenord services from Milan (40mins), Cremona (60mins), Lecco (1hr 45mins) and Bergamo (55mins). Brescia's railway station, incidentally, is the oldest in Italy, opened in 1854. It is a fine Austro-Hungarian building.

• **By bus:** There are two bus stations in Brescia close together: one in Via Solferino and the other at the railway station (*map 3*). For city bus routes and timetables, see *bresciamobilita.it*. For places in the province, there are country buses run by Arriva (*arriva.it*).

• **By metro:** Brescia's driverless underground railway opened in 2013. Some 13km long, it serves the satellite town of Brescia Due to the south and the hospital and suburbs to the north. It has stops in the centre at the railway station, Piazza Vittoria and San Faustino. You need to be equipped with a Travel Card in order to use it, but since distances in the historic centre are minimal and everywhere of interest can easily be reached on foot, you might find that you do not need it.

• **By bicycle:** Bikes can be hired with a Brescia Mobilità ticket through the Infopoint tourist offices (*see below*).

INFORMATION OFFICES

Brescia has three excellent tourist offices open all day every day. They are all called Infopoint: **Infopoint Centro** at Via Trieste 1 (*corner of Piazza Paolo VI; T: 030 240 0357; map 1*) and **Infopoint Stazione** in Piazzale Stazione (*T: 030 306 1240; map 3*). The third Infopoint is in **Palazzo Martinengo** (*Piazza del Foro 6, by the Parco Archeologico; T: 030 374 9916, provincia.brescia.it/turismo; map 2*). Good general websites are *bresciatuourism.it* and *comune.brescia.it*.

WHERE TO STAY

€€€ **Vittoria**. Elegant, comfortable late Liberty-style hotel, built in the Fascist era in 1931. A little bit run down, but atmospherically so, with original furnishings. *Via X Giornate 20. T: 030 280061, www.hotelvittoria.com. Map 3*.

€€ **Igea**. Opened in 2016, a very pleasant modern hotel a few metres from the railway station and within easy walking distance of the historic centre. Ask for a room on the inner courtyard as the rooms on the front are on a busy road. Very reasonable rates. Excellent breakfast, and restaurant with a good lunch menu. *Via Stazione 15. T: 030 44221, hoteligea.it. Map 3*.

€ **Albergo Orologio**. Boasting a tradition of hospitality since 1893,

this little hotel with 18 rooms is in an attractive old house in a pedestrian precinct in a lane just ten metres from Piazza Paolo VI. Numerous restaurants close by. *Via C. Beccaria 17. T: 030 375 5411, www.albergoorologio.it. Map 1.*
€ **Ca' del Gando**. B&B with just three very simple rooms on this peaceful street in an excellent position halfway between the archaeological area and Museo di Santa Giulia. *Via dei Musei 75. T: 340 675 3630, cadelgando.it. Map 2.*

WHERE TO EAT

€€€ **Raffa**. A large restaurant serving international cuisine, but also local dishes such as kid and rabbit. Closed Sun. *Corso Magenta 15. T: 030 49037. Map 4.*
€€ **Al Frate**. Historic *trattoria* which has recently had a makeover. The walls are covered with old advertising posters which looks a bit gimmicky, but the food is good . Closed Mon lunch. *Via dei Musei 25. T: 030 377 0550, alfrate.com. Map 2.*
€€€ **La Sosta**. One of the best known restaurants in Brescia, in a historic building with garden. Closed Sun evening and Mon. *Via San Martino della Battaglia 20. T: 030 295603. lasosta.it. Map 4.*
€€ **Al Fontanone**. Cosy *trattoria* close to the Museo Santa Giulia. Small and snug, popular for Sunday lunch. Local specialities and good wines. Closed Sun evening and Mon. *Via dei Musei 47/a. T: 030 40554. Map 2.*
€€ **La Dispensa del Gusto**. Lively restaurant behind Piazza Paolo VI. Salads, cold meats, pasta dishes and good wine. *Via Beccaria 11. T: 030 503 6188. Map 1.*

€€ **I Nazareni**. Palestinian restaurant, very popular with students and groups of young people. Delicious tabbouleh, humus, falafel. Either order single dishes or combine several as mezes. *Via Gasparo da Salò 22. T: 030 523 2676, inazareni.it. Map 1.*
€€ **Osteria al Bianchi**. Founded in 1881, this is very well known, serving all the local specialities. Closed Tues and Wed. *Via Gasparo da Salò 32. T: 030 292328, osteriaalbainchi.it. Map 1.*
€€ **La Vineria**. Formerly a wine bar, hence the excellent wine list, this is now a good restaurant with an interesting menu. Closed Sun and Tues evening and all day Mon. *Via X Giornate 4. T: 030 280543, lavineriabrescia.it. Map 3.*

Simple restaurants and *pizzerie* can be found around Piazzale Arnaldo (*map 4*) and in the area of the Carmine and Via San Faustino (*map 1*).

CAFÉS AND BARS

The **Agora Caffè**, or Bottega del Buon Panino, is a tiny place with only 4 or 5 tables but handy for a quick plate of pasta or a sandwich. Closed Mon. *Via dei Musei 75/a; T: 3276779536; map 2.* The **Panificio Maurizio Sarioli** (closed Sun; *Via dei Musei 18/Piazza Tito Speri; map 2*) has delicious snacks, both savoury and sweet. A renowned place for coffee and cake is the **Pasticceria San Carlo** (*Via XX Settembre 28/Via Romanino; map 3*). **Caffè Incavalla** on Via Mameli (*map 1*) is popular for morning coffee. **Bar Chinotto**, at Corso Palestro 41, is deservedly popular with locals for a quick lunch of cold cuts and salad, and in the early evening for aperitifs (*map 3*).

FESTIVALS AND EVENTS

Piano Festival (with Bergamo), April–June. **Teatro Grande** opera season Sept–Nov, concerts Oct–March. The **Mille Miglia** veteran car race is held in May (the three-day course of 1,000 miles—1,600km—runs from Brescia via Ferrara to Rome and back to Brescia). The **Museo Mille Miglia** (*open 10–6, T: 030 336 5631, museomillemiglia.it*) at Viale Bornata 123, east of town (bus 3 or 12 from the railway station or bus 11 from Via Mazzini, bus stop on the corner of Via dei Musei) records the history of the famous original race, which took place between 1927 and 1957 (won by Stirling Moss in 1955). It has vintage cars of the types that took part in the race (some of them in magnificent condition), as well as films and audio-visuals, and a shop. The museum is housed in the restored Monastero di Santa Eufemia. There is a restaurant attached, the Taverna del Museo Mille Miglia (*T: 030 336 5680, tavernamuseomillemiglia.it*).

LOCAL SPECIALITIES

A typical **local cheese is** Bagòss. A good place to find it, together with locally produced salami, is at the Saturday street market in Piazza Vittoria and Piazza della Loggia. You can also get it at the delicatessens at Via Cattaneo 12 and Via Cattaneo 5 (*map 2*).

Sweet delicacies include *Brossolà*, a round, cone-shaped sponge cake, and *Persicata*, like quince cheese but made with peaches.

At Via Cattaneo 26 (*map 2*) there is an interesting old shop (**G. Pedersini**) where men's hats are made and sold.

Brescia's traditional aperitif is the **Pirlo**, a Spritz made with white wine, soda and Campari.

Brescia was once known for its **cutlery** and you can still buy good knives at the old-fashioned Coltelleria V. Morocutti (*Via X Giornate, under the arcade on the corner of Piazza della Loggia*).

BRESCIAN FIREARMS

When the diarist John Evelyn visited Brescia in 1646, he reported: 'that city consists most in artists, every shop abounding in guns, swords, armores', and proceeded to buy himelf a fine carabine made by Lazzarino Cominazzo. Brescia had long been known for its metalworkers. There was a whole community of grinders, filers and polishers of quality swords by the mills on the river Mella. Some even supplied the French court and were ennobled for their efforts. Firearms too were produced in specialised workshops along the Val Trompia and Val Camonica and then sent to Brescia for assembling, chasing, engraving and personalising. The Cominazzo family in particular enjoyed a high reputation, which explains why Evelyn was so pleased with his purchase. Firearms attributed to the best-known member of the family, Lazzarino, can be found in the Tower of London and the Metropolitan Museum in New York. By the 17th century, Brescia had become a mass producer of arms for the Venetian Republic. Beretta, now a household name in the field, were merchants at that stage. They later moved into the manufacture of top-quality guns.

DARFO BOARIO TERME
Pavilion of the Antica Fonte thermal water spring.

Lago d'Iseo
& the Valle Camonica

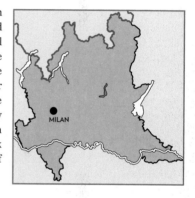

The pretty Lago d'Iseo, in the northern hinterland of Brescia, makes a good day trip from that city. As you travel between the two (either by car or train; there are good rail links), you pass through the Franciacorta wine region, known chiefly for its sparkling white wines. To the north of the lake is the Valle Camonica, the steep valley of the River Oglio, famous for its thermal spa at Boario Terme and for the prehistoric rock carvings which can be seen in a number of localities.

LAGO D'ISEO

Lago d'Iseo (*Atlas C, B3–B4*), an expansion of the Oglio river, surrounded by mountains, was the *Lacus Sebinus* of the Romans. It is still often referred to by the name Sebino. Its shores are sprinkled with small resorts and in the centre rises Monte Isola, an island popular for boat trips (in 2016 it was linked to the mainland by a system of yellow plastic floating piers, a site-specific artwork by Christo and Jeanne-Claude which attracted large numbers of visitors). The road around the lake makes its journey through a series of long tunnels: it is easy to understand why in ancient times, the main route went through the mountains. The old Strada Valeriana, which linked Brescia with the Valle Camonica, has been revived in part as a hiking trail.

THE WESTERN SHORE

At the very western tip of the lake, on the Oglio's west bank, is **Credaro**, where the church of San Giorgio (*usually open Sat–Sun 8–5 or later; T: 034 935 1110 or 349 294 1599*) has a chapel with frescoes by Lorenzo Lotto, carried out in 1525. Here too, beneath the barren slopes of Monte Bronzone (1333m), is **Sarnico**, at the outflow of the Oglio, well known to motor-boat racing enthusiasts. It was here, in 1842, that Pietro Riva first set up the boatyard that became famous for its sleek, wooden-hulled motor boats. Riva still makes boats here; it was bought by the Ferretti group in 2000. Sarnico also has a number of Art Nouveau villas built at the beginning of the 20th century by Giuseppe Sommaruga.

The lakeside road takes you on through the picturesque **Riva di Solto**, with palm trees and banana trees. The bays have unusual rock strata and the hills here were quarried for their black marble (there are some columns in St Mark's in Venice made from the local stone). From the foreshore there are fine views of the opposite bank and the Piramidi di Zone (*see below*).

The road winds on, partly through tunnels and under archways in the rock, to the principal resort on this Bergamo side of the lake: **Lovere** (pron: Lóvere). On the lakeshore is the arcaded, pedimented Neoclassical **Accademia di Belle Arti Tadini** (*open May–Oct Tues–Sat 3–7, Sun and holidays 10–12 & 3–7; accademiatadini.it*), built by Luigi Tadini to house his collection, which he opened to the public in 1828. It includes works by Jacopo Bellini, Magnasco and Vincenzo Civerchio, as well as porcelain, arms and bronzes. In the garden, the cenotaph of Tadini's son Faustino, who died in 1799, is by the collector's friend, the great sculptor Antonio Canova. Further north, turn up Via XX Settembre away from the lake for the church of **Santa Maria in Valvendra** (1473–83), which contains organ-shutters decorated outside by Floriano Ferramola and inside by Moretto (1518). Also on the waterfront is a small **Natural History Museum** (Museo Civico di Scienze Naturale; *Via Marconi 9, open Tues–Sun 3–6, T: 035 960032, museoscienzelovere.it*).

There is a path above the town to the Altopiano di Lovere (990m), with some attractive country villas, and to Bossico, among meadows and pine woods.

THE EASTERN SHORE

Opposite Lovere, beyond the inflow of the Oglio, is **Pisogne**, with a spacious waterfront. The church of Santa Maria della Neve contains splendid frescoes of the *Passion of Christ* by Romanino (1532–4). **Marone** is a large village beneath Monte Guglielmo (1949m), the highest point in the mountain range between the lake and the Val Trompia. A road winds up to an area of chestnut woods, of geological interest for the well-known **Piramidi di Zone**, great pyramids of rock surmounted by granite boulders, caused by the erosion of the moraine deposits. A walking trail here follows the Strada Valeriana, once the main trade route between Brescia and the Valle Camonica.

Sale Marasino, a port for Monte Isola, has a conspicuous 18th-century church overlooking the water and the 16th-century Villa Martinengo. **Sulzano** is a sailing centre and also a port for Monte Isola.

MONTE ISOLA

The wooded island of Monte Isola (or Montisola), 3.2km long and rising steeply to a craggy peak, surmounted by a white sanctuary church, is the largest lake island in Europe. It is closed to private cars (except for those of the mayor, the doctor and the

LAGO D'ISEO
View of Peschiera Maraglio on Monte Isola, with the ferry to Sulzano.

priest). Motor vehicles are generally limited to delivery vans and agricultural trucks. Transport is either by public bus, by bicycle or on foot (you can tour the whole island on foot in about 3hrs). The main port, clinging to the eastern foreshore opposite Sulzano, is the pretty and well-preserved fishing village of **Peschiera Maraglio**, which has a good choice of places to eat. You can walk out along the lakefront, with good views of the Isola di San Paolo and the Rocca Martinengo above the village of Sensole. At one point the waterfront is lined with a stand of taxodium trees, a tropical cypress whose roots grow out of the water. Olives grow on the lower slopes of the mountain: they are harvested in late autumn and olive oil is one of the main products of the island.

In **Siviano**, the Museo della Rete has displays on fishing and net-making, for which the island is traditionally known. From Cure, above Senzano, a road winds up to the sanctuary of the **Madonna della Ceriola**, with 16th-century frescoes.

Two small privately-owned islets lie off Monte Isola, both of which once had convents on them. To the north is the island of Loreto and to the south, the picturesque **Isola di San Paolo**. The old conventual complex is now a villa, surrounded by fine trees.

THE SOUTH SHORE

The little town of **Iseo** is a pleasant resort centred around two main squares, which adjoin each other behind the harbour of Porto Gabriele Rosa. The arcaded Piazza Garibaldi and Piazza Statuto were both laid out during the period of Venetian rule. The Palazzo d'Arsenale on Piazza Statuto, now an exhibition space, was the armoury and warehouse during the Venetian period. West of Piazza Statuto is the warren-like old medieval quarter of Contrada del Sombrico. Streets from here lead inland to the duomo of Sant'Andrea, whose tower was built by Count Giacomo Oldofredi (1325). His tomb is built into the façade. Inside the church is a painting of *St Michael* by Francesco Hayez. At the top of the town, the Castello Oldofredi, built in the 12th–13th centuries, was a monastery from the 16th century until dissolution by Napoleon. It now houses the Museo della Guerra (*open weekends 9–12 & 3–6*), with displays on both world wars.

On the southern edge of the lake is a marshy area known as the **Torbiere del Sebino**, a large peat bog surrounded by reeds, and an important wildlife habitat. Waterlilies grow here in abundance and it is a sanctuary for aquatic birds. Traces of Bronze Age pile-dwellings were found here. The visitor centre is in Provaglio (*torbieresebino.it*).

THE FRANCIACORTA

The fertile, vine-clad foothills between Brescia and the Lago d'Iseo are known as the Franciacorta (*Atlas C, B4*), a region with a number of villas built by noble Brescian families in the 18th century and where today vineyards compete for space with the multiple warehouses and workshops of light industry. The area has long been known for its excellent red and white wines, particularly for its sparkling white, produced largely from Chardonnay, with some Pinot Bianco and Pinot Nero. Numerous cellars in the area welcome visitors.

THE WINES OF FRANCIACORTA

Franciacorta is a tiny wine district at the tip of the Lago d'Iseo. Geography has played an important role here. Scree, silt and sand brought down from the mountains by glaciers have created ideal terrain for grape-growing. In the 13th century Franciacorta wine already enjoyed a considerable reputation. In a document dated 1570 a certain Conforto, a doctor from Brescia, makes mention of the health-promoting properties of the bright and bubbly elixir. Today the region's wines are still known for their bubbles. Franciacorta's DOCG sparkling white wine is probably Italy's finest *metodo classico*, some of which (for instance wines from the Ca' del Bosco winery; *cadelbosco. com*) rivals champagne in quality. Other well-known wineries are Bellavista, west of Torbiato (*bellavistawine.it*), and Bredasole in Paratico (*bredasole.it*). Franciacorta wines come in many guises. The Satèn, always a *blanc de blancs*, is delightfully dry but the bubbles are more subdued, allowing the creamy, buttery quality of the Chardonnay to come through and making it instantly approachable to drink.

At the Villa Evelina in **Capriolo** there is a private agricultural museum with displays on wine and winemaking (visits by appointment; *riccicurbastro.it/museo*). At **Rodengo Saiano** is the Abbazia di San Nicola (*church open 9–11.30 & 3.30–7; T: 030 610182, abbaziasannicola.it*), a Cluniac foundation, inhabited by Olivetan monks since 1446. It contains three cloisters, frescoes by Romanino and Lattanzio Gambara, a painting by Moretto, and fine intarsia stalls (1480).

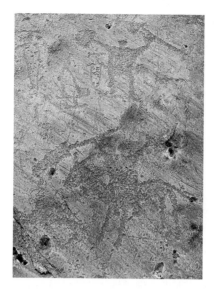

VALLE CAMONICA
Rock carving of two warriors in the Parco di Luine.

THE VALLE CAMONICA

The steep, wooded and fertile Valle Camonica is the upper course of the Oglio as it flows down from the Bergamasque alps into Lago d'Iseo. It is famous for its remarkable prehistoric rock carvings, which you can see throughout the valley, especially in the two parks at Capo di Ponte and Darfo Boario Terme, and at Cimbergo, Ossimo and Sellero. The chestnut woods were once an important source of wealth, as both nuts and timber were exported. The inhabitants of the valley (and especially of Boario) were traditionally excellent woodcarvers. Ironworks were established here in the Middle Ages and the valley has hydroelectric power stations. The cheeses and salt meats locally produced are of excellent quality. The extreme upper end, below the Tonale Pass, was the scene of many dramatic battles in the First World War.

DARFO BOARIO TERME
The main town in the valley is Darfo Boario Terme (*Atlas C, B3*), traditionally known for its cabinetmakers. The parish church of Darfo, **Santi Faustino e Giovita**, with a Neoclassical façade and stone bell-tower, has an *Entombment* attributed to Palma Giovane. The well-known **Terme di Boario spa** (*termediboario.it*), where you can bathe in and also drink the curative water, is important medically for inhalation and thermal mud treatments and is home to the European Parkinson's Therapy Centre.

Visitors are welcome to sample the water: ask for a tasting cup at the desk at the bottom of the steps that lead down into the park. There are three fountains: Antica Fonte (the water tastes strongly of iron); Igea (the water emerges warm) and Boario.

Over 10,000 rock carvings (*incisioni rupestri*) may be seen here in the beautifully kept **Parco di Luine** (*open April–Sept Tues–Sun 9–12 & 2–6, Oct–Nov 9–12 & 1–5; www.vallecamonicaunesco.it; turn left past the spa and follow signs to Gorzone and Terme di Angolo; before Gorzone, turn left at a brown sign for Luine*). Here large boulders of the local purplish rock rear out of the landscape, many of them scratched with a multiplicity of designs. Most of the incisions date from 2200–1800 BC and those which date from even earlier are the oldest so far found in the valley. Some of them have human figures of warriors, sometimes mounted, and armed with swords and spears. There are also numerous examples of the amoeba-like 'Camunian rose', a four-lobed shape which was chosen as the logo of the region of Lombardy.

You can see the rock known as **Corni Freschi**, with its rock carvings, just west of the main SS42 at Località Gottardo, at the point where the Oglio describes a sharp loop.

South of Boario, a road ascends the Valle di Scalve past **Gorzone**, dominated by a castle of the Federici first built in the 12th century (*privately owned*), through **Angolo Terme**, a small spa with a very fine view of the triple-peaked Pizzo della Presolana. Further on the road enters the gorge of the Dezzo, a narrow chasm with overhanging cliffs. Unfortunately, the torrent and its falls were almost completely dried up by hydroelectric works many decades ago.

Just north of Boario is **Erbanno**, unusual for its plan consisting of parallel straight streets along the hillside and a piazza on two levels.

ESINE AND BRENO

At **Esine** (*Atlas C, B3–C3*), the church of Santa Maria Assunta contains frescoes (1491–3) by a local painter called Giovan Pietro, from Cemmo in this valley. **Cividate Camuno**, further north, is the site of *Civitas Camunnorum*, the ancient Roman capital of the valley. It preserves a few ancient remains and a much more conspicuous medieval tower. Roman finds are displayed in the Museo Archeologico della Valle Camonica, housed in an unassuming modern building on a roundabout (*Via Roma 29, museoarcheologico.valcamonicaromana.beniculturali.it*).

A winding road ascends west via **Ossimo** (where prehistoric statue-stelae dating from 3200–2000 BC have been found) to **Borno**, a resort among pinewoods in the valley of the Trobiolo torrent, beneath the Corna di San Fermo (2326m). The Santuario dell'Annunciata, with a fine view of the valley, has two 15th-century cloisters.

Between Cividate and Breno, in the hamlet known as Spinera, and accessed off the pretty, narrow Via Spinera, are the roofed remains of a Roman **sanctuary of Minerva** (*open March–Oct Sat–Sun 10–12.30 & 2–6; other times by appointment, T: 0364 344301*). **Breno** itself is dominated by the ruins of its medieval castle (9th century and later). The parish church has a granite campanile and frescoes by Giovan Pietro da Cemmo and Romanino. **Bienno**, to the southeast, is a medieval village, with fine 17th- and 18th-century palaces. It was once home to numerous forges, operated by channelled mountain water, where the smiths traditionally made pots and pans.

Today the picturesque quaintness of the village has made it the haunt of artists. There is a forge museum and a water mill museum, and the church of Santa Maria degli Orti has frescoes by Romanino.

CAPO DI PONTE

Above Breno the dolomitic peaks of the Concarena (2549m) rise on the left and the Pizzo Badile (2435m) on the right. The villages are mostly high up on the slopes of the foothills on either side, and include **Cerveno**, with a remarkable 18th-century *Via Crucis* that has nearly 200 life-size statues.

Capo di Ponte (*Atlas C, C2*) came to prominence with the discovery in the Permian sandstone of tens of thousands of rock engravings dating from Neolithic to Roman times, a span of some 8,000 years. These are the feature of the **Parco Nazionale delle Incisioni Rupestri di Naquane** (*for opening times see vallecamonicaunesco.it/parco-naquane*), one of the best prehistoric sites in the world. So far some 180,000 engravings made by the Camuni, a remarkable Alpine civilisation, depicting hunting scenes, everyday life, religious symbols, etc., have been catalogued here. The largest rock has 900 figures carved in the Iron Age. Other prehistoric carvings have been found in the localities of Ceto, Cimbergo and Paspardo, on a secondary road to the south, and above Sellero to the north. There is a research centre (the Centro Camuno di Studi Preistorici) at Capo di Ponte.

Just outside Capo di Ponte, in woods to the north, is **San Salvatore**, a Lombard church of the early 12th century. Across the river in **Cemmo**, birthplace of the local artist Giovan Pietro, is the church of San Siro, dating from the 11th century, probably on the site of a Lombard church. The road continues to **Pescarzo**, a pretty little village with interesting peasant houses.

THE UPPER VALLE CAMONICA

Cedegolo (*Atlas C, C2*), with a church entirely frescoed by a certain Antonio Cappello (1669–1741), stands at the foot of the lovely Val di Saviore, below Mt Adamello (3555m). **Edolo**, surrounded by beautiful scenery, is the main place in the upper Valle Camonica. **Ponte di Legno** (1260m) sits in a wide-open basin beneath the Adamello and Presanella mountains. To the north a precipitous road (the SS29), one of the highest in Europe, ascends the **Val di Pezzo** and crosses the Passo Gavia (2621m) to Bormio at the head of the Valtellina. The Tonale Pass (1884m), in the Presanella foothills, is on the former Austro-Italian frontier, separating Lombardy from Trentino.

LAGO D'IDRO & MONTIRONE

The Lago d'Idro (*Atlas C, C3*), the Roman *Lacus Eridius*, 9.5km long and 2km wide, is surrounded by steep, rugged mountains. Its waters are used for hydroelectric power and it is renowned for its trout. On the west bank are **Anfo**, with an old castle founded by the Venetians in 1486 but largely rebuilt, and **Sant'Antonio**, where the church has a 15th-century fresco cycle. **Bagolino** is a mountain village in a good position on the Caffaro (visited by skiers and famous for its carnival). **Ponte Caffaro**, beyond the head of the lake, marks the old international frontier.

To the south of Brescia is **Montirone** (*Atlas A, B1*), where the beautiful Palazzo Lechi (*see palazzolechi.wordpress.com*), built in 1738–46 by the little-known Antonio Turbino, is very well preserved and has magnificent stables. It contains paintings by Carlo Carloni or Carlone (his best work), and was visited by Mozart in 1773 and Napoleon in 1805.

PRACTICAL INFORMATION

GETTING AROUND

• **By rail:** Trains run from Brescia up the east side of Lago d'Iseo and into the Valle Camonica to Edolo (a very scenic route). Trains stop at Iseo (c. 30mins), Provaglio-Timoline (for the Torbiere del Sebino wetlands; c. 30mins), Sulzano (for boats to Monte Isola; 30–40mins), Sale Marasino (35–45mins), Marone-Zone (for the 'Piramidi'; 40–50mins) and Pisogne (50mins–1hr). In the Valle Camonica, trains from Brescia stop at all the main centres, including Capo di Ponte for the rock carvings (1hr 35mins).

• **By bus:** A network of local buses run by SAB-Arriva serves Iseo, Sarnico, Lovere, Boario Terme and other localities. For timetables, see *arriva.it*. A network of buses links the villages on Monte Isola, with plenty leaving from Peschiera Maraglio. For timetables, see *dati.comuniweb.voli.bs.it*.

• **By boat:** Ferries for Monte Isola leave from Sulzano and Sale Marasino, with some services from Iseo and Tavernola Bergamasca. The main ports on the island are Peschiera Maraglio,

Siviano and Carzano. During school term time there are also boats between Lovere and Pisogne. For timetables, see *navigazionelagoiseo.it*. You can take bicycles on the ferry to Monte Isola but not motorbikes (only residents' motorcycles are allowed).

• **By bicycle:** Bikes can be hired on Monte Isola, in Peschiera Maraglio.

INFORMATION OFFICES

Boario Terme *Piazza Einaudi 2. T: 030 374 8751.*
Iseo *Lungolago Marconi 2c. T: 030 374 8733.*
Monte Isola On the waterfront at Peschiera Maraglio.

General websites for the area are *bresciatourism.it* and *visitlakeiseo.info*.

WHERE TO EAT

DARFO BOARIO TERME
€€ **Osteria Landò**. Here you can choose to eat *à la carte*, to take the daily menu, or simply opt for one of their 'gourmet pizzas'. Between Darfo Boario Terme

and Erbanno. *Via Stazione 1. T: 0364 529187, ristorantelando.com.*

ISEO

€–€€ **Osteria del Vicoletto**. A good place to stop for lunch. In a narrow street behind the Town Hall, close to the port. *Vicolo Portelle 14. T: 030 984 0730.*

MONTE ISOLA

€ **Tre Archi**. In Peschiera Maraglio, on the waterfront. A good restaurant and pizzeria with friendly service and plenty of dishes using local ingredients. Spacious outdoor terrace. *Via Peschiera Maraglio 170. T: 348 170 7760.*

LOCAL SPECIALITIES

Monte Isola is known for its dried lake fish, often used in pasta sauce. The locally produced olive oil is also good, as is the salami. *Migole* is a dish of local meat or salami served on polenta.
Franciacorta wines are widely served throughout the region. If you want wine without bubbles, ask for *vino fermo*.

FESTIVALS AND EVENTS

Sulzano holds a wild boar festival (*Sagra del Cinghiale*) in Oct. The *Sua Maestà* salami festival is held annually on **Monte Isola** in April. To find out more about the **Franciacorta** wineries that welcome visitors, and for times of open cellar days and other events, *see franciacorta.net.*

TORRE DEL BENACO
Limonaia, hothouse for citrus cultivation, with the tower
and battlements of the castle behind it.

Lake Garda

Lake Garda (*map p. 471, E2–E3*) is the largest of the northern Italian lakes, famed for its scenery, its good sailing winds and its mild climate, which permits the cultivation of olives and lemons. Some of the grand hotels on the mild west shore were built at the end of the 19th century for Austrian and German visitors but most of the resorts were developed in the 1920s and 1930s. The inspiring beauty of the lake has made it traditionally popular with writers. Goethe visited Garda at the start of his Italian journey in 1786 and saw his first olive trees here.

Byron stayed at Desenzano in 1816, and Tennyson visited in 1880. D.H. Lawrence lived on its shores in 1912 and 1913, and he describes the lemon gardens in *Twilight in Italy*. The Latin name for the Lake Garda was *Lacus Benacus* and today it is still sometimes referred to as Benaco. It is particularly well furnished with good restaurants.

LAKE GARDA HIGHLIGHTS

Sirmione (*map 7; p. 326*), in a spectacular position on a narrow peninsula, has the remains of a Roman villa as well as a castle. There is another Roman villa at **Desenzano** (*map 7; p. 328*).

Citrus cultivation around the lake dates from at least the 16th century. This was the northernmost locality in the world where citrus fruits could be grown commercially, in special hothouses known as *limonaie*. These shelters are unique to Garda and a few still survive. You can visit one at **Torri del Benaco** (*map 5; p. 336*), a pleasant town and a good base from which to explore.

Salò and **Gardone Riviera** (*map 5; pp. 330–1*) are attractive resorts with interesting histories. They also make good bases from which to explore.

There is spectacular **walking** in the mountains on both sides of the lake.

THE SOUTHERN SHORE

SIRMIONE

Sirmione (*map 7*) stands at the tip of a narrow promontory, 3.5km long and in places only 119m wide, in the centre of the southern lakeshore. It was a Roman station on the Via Gallica, halfway between Brescia and Verona. The Latin name for Garda, *Lacus Benacus*, derives from a Celtic word meaning 'horned', perhaps a reference to this peninsula. Sirmione, today as then, is a famous resort. It can be very crowded in season (though deserted in winter). There are enjoyable walks on the peninsula, as well as the remains of a Roman villa. You can swim in the lake on the east side.

THE TOWN CENTRE

The picturesque 13th-century **Rocca Scaligera** (*open 8.30–7.30; closed Sun afternoon and all day Mon*), where Dante is said to have stayed, marks the entrance to the town. Completely surrounded by water (copper-headed Pochard ducks inhabit its moat), it was a stronghold of the Della Scala family, lords of Verona. The massive central tower, 29m high, has a good view.

Via Vittorio Emanuele (closed to cars) leads north from the castle through the scenic little town towards the ruins of Catullus' vast villa at the end of the peninsula. A road on the right leads to the 15th-century church of **Santa Maria Maggiore** (or Santa Maria della Neve), which preserves some antique columns in its porch, one of the outermost ones being a Roman milestone. There are traces of frescoes in the interior, including a lion of St Mark with drawn sword. At the end of Via Vittorio Emanuele is a spa with a hotel that uses warm sulphur springs rising in the lake.

Via Catullo continues, passing close to **San Pietro in Mavino**, a Romanesque church of 8th-century foundation with early frescoes.

THE ROMAN VILLA

The peninsula tip is covered with the sprawling remains of a vast Roman villa, thought to have belonged to the poet Catullus and known as the Grotte di Catullo (*open March–Oct Tues–Sat 8.30–7.30, Sun and holidays 9.30–6.30; Nov–Feb 8.30–5, until 2 on Sun and holidays; www.grottedicatullo.beniculturali.it*). The name '*grotte*' derives from that fact that before excavation, the villa's vaulted substructures seemed like natural grottoes. The extensive ruins are set amid olive groves on the end of the headland, with splendid views out over the lake and of the rocks beneath the clear shallow water. A succession of country houses stood here between the 1st century BC and the late 3rd century AD, when the site was abandoned. It is conceivable that the villa may have belonged to the family of the Valerii Catulli. Many wealthy Romans came to Sirmione for the summer, and Catullus—who is known to have had a villa here—speaks of '*Paene peninsularum, Sirmio, insularumque ocelle*' ('Sirmione, gem of all peninsulas and islands'). The site was only properly investigated in the 19th and beginning of the 20th centuries. Near the entrance is a small antiquarium, with pottery and exquisite

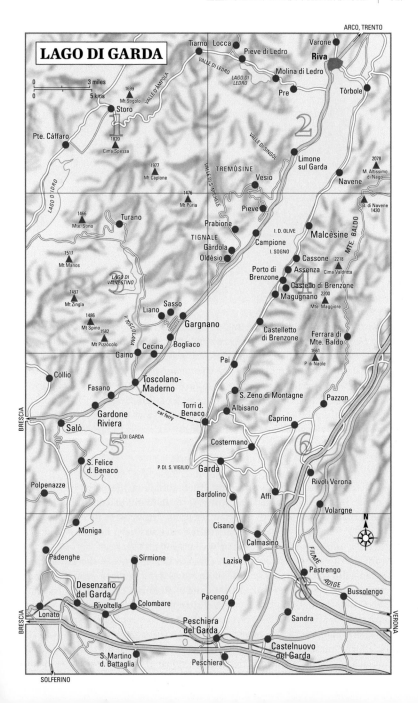

DESENZANO
Fishing putto. Detail of a floor mosaic in the 4th-century Roman villa.

fragments of frescoes dating from the 1st century BC. Of the villa itself, little that is readily comprehensible remains, as it was plundered for building material over the centuries and its site is now covered by an olive grove. The most conspicuous survivals are the vast substructures and vaults (the eponymous *grotte*), built to sustain the main upper floor, which occupied an area over 160m long and 100m wide. There are also a number of huge cisterns, as well as a baths complex and the ruins of what would once have been long, graceful terraces looking out over the water, with a covered walkway (cryptoporticus) below the western colonnade.

DESENZANO

Desenzano del Garda (*map 7*) is a pleasant little resort. From the quay, a bridge crosses the entrance to a picturesque harbour with cafés, restaurants and the **Galleria Civica**. Behind is the main piazza, with pretty arcades and a monument to St Angela Merici (1474–1540), foundress of the Ursuline Order, who was born here. Just out of the piazza is the **duomo**, with a *Last Supper* by Giambattista Tiepolo.

Nearby to the northwest, on Via Crocefisso, is the entrance to the excavations of a **Roman villa** (*open Tues–Sun 8.30–dusk; closes Sun afternoon in winter*), mostly dating from the 4th century AD but on the site of an earlier edifice of the 1st century AD. It is the most important late Roman villa in northern Italy, of great interest for its colourful 4th-century mosaics. The grand reception rooms of the main villa include an octagonal hall, a peristyle, an atrium with two apses and a triclinium with three apses, all with mosaics. Other, less grand rooms to the south may have been baths. An antiquarium (beneath which the Roman edifice of the 1st century AD, with an underfloor heating system, was discovered) has finds from the site, including remains of wall paintings. Separate excavations to the north have revealed a residential area, with part of an apsidal hall and baths, to the east. The villa was discovered in 1921, and excavations have continued, even though the site is in the centre of the town.

THE BATTLEFIELDS OF SAN MARTINO AND SOLFERINO

The low moraine hills south of the lake, formed by the ancient glacier of the Adige, have been the theatre of many battles: during Prince Eugene's campaign in the War of the Spanish Succession (1701–06); during Napoleon's enterprises (1796–1814); and during the Wars of Italian Independence (1848–9, 1859 and 1866). From Rivoltella, halfway between Sirmione and Desenzano, a by-road leads away from the lake up to the tower (74m high) of **San Martino della Battaglia** (*map 7*), which commemorates Vittorio Emanuele II's victory over the right flank of the Austrian army on 24th June 1859. The interior (*open mid-March–mid-Oct Mon–Sat 9–12.30 & 2.30–7, Sun and holidays 9–7; mid-Oct–mid-March Tues–Sun 9–12.30 & 2–5.30; solferinoesanmartino. it*) contains sculptures and paintings relating to the campaign.

At nearby **Solferino** (*Atlas A, C1*), Napoleon III, in alliance with Vittorio Emanuele, defeated the rest of the Austrian army on the same day. The Austrians were under the personal command of the 29-year-old emperor Franz Joseph, the last time he ever led his troops into battle. An ossuary chapel in the little town (follow Via Ossario) displays the skulls of the 7,000 dead, collected from the battlefield and placed in grisly formation here, completely covering the sanctuary walls. The Swiss businessman Henry Dunant was an eyewitness of the conflict and was so appalled by the suffering of the wounded soldiers, abandoned and left to die uncomforted, that he personally organised aid and relief work to tend them, regardless of which side they were on (the altarcloth in the chapel is embroidered with the words '*Omnes Fratres; Tutti Fratelli; Alle Brüder; Tous Frères*'). Dunant's *A Memory of Solferino* was the inspiration for the foundation of the International Red Cross. The museum on the square in front of the ossuary chapel has mementoes of the battle (*open mid-March–mid-Oct Tues–Sun 9–12.30 & 2.30–7; Oct–Feb by appointment; T: 030 991 0370, solferinoesanmartino.it*). The little Albergo 'Alla Vittoria' offers coffee. It is also possible to climb the square Rocca, known as the 'Conning Tower of Italy' (*La Spia d'Italia*), from where there are fine views of the lovely countryside that hosted these two most sanguinary encounters.

CASTIGLIONE DELLE STIVERE
In Castiglione delle Stivere (*Atlas A, C1*) is the **Museum of the Red Cross** (Museo Internazionale della Croce Rossa; *open April–Oct 9–12 & 3–6; Oct–March 9–12 & 2–5; closed Mon; T: 0376 638505, micr.it*). Also here, in the Nobile Collegio delle Vergini di Gesù, is the **Museo Storico Aloisiano** (*open in the afternoon at weekends, T: 0376 638062*) with mementoes of St Aloysius Gonzaga, who was born here in 1568 and of whose family the town was once a fief. The museum has paintings by Francesco Bassano, Federico Barocci, Giulio Carpioni and Giambettino Cignaroli; a Flemish clock of 1567, and collections of glass, ironwork and furniture.

THE LOMBARD SHORE

SALÒ

Salò (*map 5*), the Roman *Salodium*, is an appealing town on a deep bay, with a slightly old-fashioned atmosphere and a lovely historic centre. It was the birthplace of Gaspare Bertolotti (also known as Gaspare da Salò, 1540–1609), generally considered to be the inventor of the violin. There is a statue of him on the waterfront. In more recent times, Salò was notorious for being the centre of Mussolini's short-lived puppet republic (*see below*).

THE REPUBLIC OF SALÒ

The Republic of Salò or Italian Socialist Republic (*Repubblica Sociale Italiana* or RSI) was formed in September 1943 as a puppet state of Nazi Germany, set up by Hitler in a last attempt to re-establish the Fascist government of Italy.

In 1943, four days after the Armistice, the Germans brought Mussolini to Salò, having released him from prison. Lake Garda was an ideal place to govern from, as the borders of the German Reich had reached Limone, only 20km north, with the annexation of the Trentino-Alto Adige.

Germany and Japan were the only countries to recognise the Republic, which carried out brutal policing activities throughout Italy. It was brought to and end with the Liberation of Italy by the Allies in 1945 and Mussolini's subsequent capture (and execution) by partisans a few days later, as he fled northwards towards the Alps.

For the 19 months of its existence, the Republic commandeered numerous grand villas on the shores of Lake Garda, for use as ministries, administrative offices, hospitals and residences, including for Mussolini himself (at Gargnano) and for his mistress Clara Petacci (at Gardone Riviera). Many of those buildings are now hotels. Signboards have been placed outside the buildings today, with a map showing the extent of the Republic, the number of properties taken under its control, and detailing who and what they were used for. The huge Villa Alba at Gardone, for example, built in 1910 for a wealthy businessman from Magdeburg, served as a military communications and radio control centre. The Hotel Bellariva at Fasano housed officials from the German Embassy and was linked to the embassy building itself by an underground tunnel. At Maderno, the Hotel Golfo was the seat of the Fascist Party of the Republic and headquarters of the Black Brigades.

THE OLD TOWN

Salò's long harbour front, lined with restaurants and cafés, has a system of raised walkways linking the various quays, so that you can walk its entire length. There are fine views of the lake and of the little town itself, backed by wooded mountains. On the central waterfront is a handsome arcaded building, the **Palazzo della Magnifica Patria**, which until the extinction of the Venetian Republic was the seat of the local government known as the Comunità di Riviera. During the Republic of Salò it was used as offices for interpreters. Today it is the Town Hall (the ticket office for boats is also here). Set some way back from the waterfront is the **duomo**, a fine building in a late-Gothic style built at the end of the 15th century, with a good Renaissance portal (1509). It contains an altarpiece of *St Anthony* and a donor dated 1529 by the prolific Brescian painter Girolamo Romanino, who often produced particularly colourful and original works. Close by on Via Fantoni is **Palazzo Fantoni**, seat of the Biblioteca Ateneo, which has its origins in the Accademia degli Unanimi, founded by Giuseppe Milio in 1564. The Unanimi were a group of around 20 well-born young men of Salò who got together to discuss ethics and other questions: probably much like the Academy of the Olympians in Vicenza, whom Goethe describes as convening to argue about whether invention or imitation had contributed more to the fine arts. Milio was a poet and a writer on horticultural subjects, and was apparently keen on bee-keeping. The emblem of the Unanimi was a beehive. Today the library has over 25,000 volumes, many of great historical interest.

Occupying an old church and convent on the main street above the old centre is **MuSa**, Salò's museum and art gallery (*Via Brunati 9, museodisalo.it*), with a small permanent collection of paintings, archaeological finds and scientific instruments relating to the seismic observatory here. It also hosts good temporary exhibitions.

GARDONE RIVIERA

Gardone Riviera (*map 5*), in a sheltered position with parks and gardens planted with rare trees, was once famous as a winter resort. On the lakefront and in the hills behind rise grand villas, now hotels. On the waterfront, by the boat landing, is a short *lungolago* with hotels, bars and pizzerias. **Villa Fiordaliso** was the home of Claretta Petacci, Mussolini's mistress, during the Republic of Salò (*see above*). It is now a hotel and restaurant. The huge, Neoclassical **Villa Alba** (1904–10), on the landward side of the main road, is now a conference centre and a popular venue for weddings. It was built for a German businessman, Richard Langensiepen, who had large holdings of land on the lake which he used for the commercial cultivation of flowers.

Above the main road, at Via Roma 1, is the **Heller Garden**, a botanical garden belonging to the André Heller Foundation (*open March–Oct daily 9–7, hellergarden. com*). The gardens were originally laid out by the doctor, dentist and botanist Arturo Hruska over a long period between 1910 and 1971. Since their acquisition by Heller they have been planted with works of contemporary sculpture and turned into a 'garden of ecological awareness', filled with Tibetan prayer flags, palm trees with their trunks painted in rainbow peace colours, Buddha statues, a Torii gate rising above smoking undergrowth (the smoke being produced by nozzles which emit water vapour), pools stocked with large koi carp and staff in tie-dye shirts. Hruska's botany is somewhat overwhelmed. The statuary includes works by Heller himself (spitting heads), Miró, Keith Haring, Roy Lichtenstein and Mimmo Paladino. When you buy your ticket you will be given a handlist and a map.

Via Roma continues to wind uphill to **Gardone Sopra**, a very pretty little enclave of narrow streets and clustering houses with a few cafés and restaurants. Also here is the Vittoriale, built by Gabriele d'Annunzio (*see below*). Pleasant walks along marked trails can be taken in the hills behind Gardone and Salò.

VITTORIALE DEGLI ITALIANI

Via del Vittoriale 12. Open 8.30–7, Oct–March 9–5. vittoriale.it.

The Vittoriale degli Italiani, the famous last residence of Gabriele d'Annunzio, was created for him by a local and otherwise unknown architect called Giancarlo Maroni, who lived here from 1922 until his death in 1952. Evidently the eccentric martial poet worked in close collaboration with his architect and together they created the villa's elaborate and gloomy décor as well as the garden surrounding it.

GABRIELE D'ANNUNZIO

Gabriele d'Annunzio (1863–1938) was born Francesco Rapagnetta, the son of a well-to-do and politically prominent landowner. He married the daughter of a duke but was not a model husband—among his mistresses was Eleonora Duse, for whom he wrote a number of plays. Marcel Proust, who was at the opening night of one of his theatrical works, set to music by Debussy, said that the best thing about it was the lead actress's legs.

D'Annunzio began his career as a poet: his first verses, *In Early Spring*, were published when the author was just 16; they were closely followed by *New Song* (1882), which established his fame. His best-known poetic work is the anthology *In Praise of Sky, Sea, Earth and Heroes* (1899). His novels raised eyebrows because of their self-seeking, amoral Nietzschean-superman protagonists and the characters endlessly over-indulging in aesthetic rapture, but his command of language is astonishing and produced many imitations (as well as parodies). Today he is considered a key figure of Italian Decadentism and his writings, together with his lifestyle, embody the cultural climate which bred Fascism.

Outside Italy D'Annunzio is much better known for his military exploits. In 1914–16 he called for Italy to enter the First World War on the side of Britain and France, rather than honour the Triple Alliance, the secret agreement between Germany, Austria-Hungary and Italy formed in 1882. He volunteered for dangerous duty in several branches of service, notably the air corps, and lost an eye in action. When Italy lost Istria at the Treaty of Versailles, he and a few hundred supporters occupied the port city of Fiume and held it for 18 months, until forced to withdraw by the Italian navy. His legions were the first to wear the black shirt that became emblematic of the Fascists and he made peace with Mussolini. He spent his last years writing here on Lake Garda. Though he never held an important government position, he was given a state funeral.

Near the entrance (you will be given a map of the complex with your ticket) is the **Museo d'Annunzio Segreto**, highly recommended, with film and stills documenting d'Annunzio's life (unfortunately there is nowhere to sit while you watch) and exhibits including his huge collection of shoes. Beyond this stretch the gardens and villa itself, the **Prioria** (*shown on a 30-min tour*), which has been preserved as a museum. The interior, including an Art Deco dining room, is crammed with a jumble of Art Nouveau *objets d'art*, chinoiserie, mementoes, sacred objects, Indian works of art, and even an organ. Off the dark hallway is a reception room with an inscription that D'Annunzio made Mussolini read on his visit here: 'Remember that you are made of glass and I of steel.' The garden in front of the villa harbours odd statuary and columns surmounted by projectiles. A path descends through the pretty woods of the Acquapazza valley towards the main road. The gardens also include a **dog cemetery** (D'Annunzio was famously fond of dogs).

Opposite the villa, the **Auditorium** houses the biplane from which D'Annunzio dropped leaflets on Vienna announcing Italian victory in 1918. Viale di Aligi leads past a fountain filled with small dogfish to a building that houses the **motorboat MAS 96**, in which D'Annunzio took part in the assault on Fiume. The 'MAS' of the boat's name stands for *Memento Audere Semper*: Remember Always to Dare.

Beyond, at the top of the hill, lies D'Annunzio's grand **mausoleum**, where he and his architect are buried. The mausoleum is circular, in imitation of the imperial mausolea of Hadrian and Augustus in Rome or of Theodoric in Ravenna. At the top are ten sarcophagi containing the remains of ten heroes of Fiume, which D'Annunzio claimed for Italy and was unwilling to relinquish when it was declared a free buffer state at the end of the First World War. Concrete sculptures of dogs loll on the mausoleum roof. In the interior is a huge bronze Crucifix by Leonardo Bistolfi (1926). From here, a path leads through woods to the prow of the ship *Puglia*, donated to D'Annunzio by the Italian Navy and reconstructed here as a monument.

TOSCOLANO-MADERNO

Toscolano-Maderno (*map 5*) is a lively resort, formed of two small settlements, each with its own port, at the two sides of a peninsula formed by deposits brought down by the Gaino stream. Up until recently the peninsula was covered in olive plantations. Today it has holiday villas and bungalows and a large working paper mill.

As you approach from Gardone, you come into **Maderno**, with a bustling main square on the waterfront and very narrow streets behind (not recommended for cars). On the waterfront square is the 12th-century church of **Sant'Andrea**, which shows remains of Roman and Byzantine architecture, especially in the decoration of the pillar capitals, doors and windows: an older church seems to have been incorporated in the building. The interior has remnants of frescoes and, in the sanctuary (on the left), a painting of the *Virgin and Child* by Veronese. Another painting by Veronese, of the bishop Herculanus (Ercolano), is in the 18th-century parish church which stands across the square from Sant'Andrea.

To reach **Toscolano**, you cross the Gaino. Signed from the old hump-backed bridge is the **Museo della Carta**, arranged in a pretty old paper mill, one of many that operated in this valley from the 15th century until the mid-20th (*open March–early Oct daily 10–6, mid–end Oct weekends only 10–6, www.valledellecartiere.it; café*). The short, easy walk to the museum, up the narrow, gorge-like valley, is interesting, lined with information boards about the paper mills and hydroelectric station.

On the north side of the promontory, in Toscolano, where Isabella Gonzaga of Mantua came to spend time in the summer, is the church of **Santi Pietro e Paolo**, with paintings by Andrea Celesti, a Venetian artist who was much in favour in the Serenissima until, for reasons unclear, he fell foul of Doge Alvise Contarini (legend has it that he painted a likeness of the doge with ass's ears). By 1688 he was at work in Toscolano. The **Santuario della Madonna di Benaco**, behind Santi Pietro e Paolo on the lake, has a barrel vault and numerous 15th-century frescoes. Four Roman columns stand in front of the church. Nearby, entered from the car park in front of the modern paper mill, is an enclosure with scant remains of a **Roman villa**, occupied from the 1st–5th centuries AD, with remnants of mosaic, a baths complex and nymphaeum. Only a small part of the villa survives. In its heyday it must have been magnificent indeed, opening out directly onto the water. Toscolano, called Benacum, was the chief Roman settlement on the west shore of the lake. The villa has been identified as belonging to the family of the Nonii Arrii, specifically to a certain Marcus Nonius Macrinus, a 2nd-century consul from a patrician family of Brescia (he was buried in Rome, on the Via Flaminia). At the time of writing, opening times were subject to change (*for information, ask at the Tourist Office in Toscolano-Maderno*).

GARGNANO AND LIMONE

Gargnano (*map 3*) is a very attractive little port. Several large stone pavilions where lemon trees were once cultivated can be seen on the terraced hillside. San Francesco is a 13th-century church with a cloister. An inland road from Gargnano to Limone has spectacular views: it passes the hill sanctuary of Madonna di Monte Castello, which has the finest view of the whole lake. Mussolini lived here, at Villa Feltrinelli, from 1943 until three days before his death.

Limone sul Garda (*map 2*) takes its name from its lemon groves, said to be the first in Europe. Up until the beginning of the 20th century it was surrounded by terraced lemon and citron gardens. Limone was accessible only by boat before the road along the shore from Gargnano was built in 1931, and its numerous hotels date from its development as a resort in the 1950s and 1960s. In previous centuries it was a very romantic spot, possibly the inspiration for one of Goethe's best-known lyrics: *Kennst du das Land, wo die Zitronen blühn* ('Do you know the land where the lemon trees blossom; where golden oranges gleam amidst dark foliage…?'). Goethe had sailed down from Torbole past Limone, where he admired the lemon gardens.

THE NORTH END OF THE LAKE

The breezy upper part of the lake, where the water is deepest, is much used for sailing and windsurfing. The predominant winds (which can swell into violent storms) are the *sover* (or *soar* or *sora*), from the north, and the *ora*, from the south. The northern end of the lake is in the region of Trentino-Alto Adige and has a distinctly alpine feel.

RIVA DEL GARDA

Riva del Garda (*map 2*), the Roman *Ripa*, is a lively town, sheltered by Monte Rochetta to the west. It became a fashionable winter resort at the turn of the 20th century—Thomas Mann and Franz Kafka both came to take the waters here—and remained in Austrian territory until 1918. The old centre is **Piazza III Novembre**, overlooking the port. Here are the 13th-century Torre Apponale, the 14th-century Palazzo Pretorio, the 15th-century Palazzo Comunale and some medieval porticoes. The **Rocca**, a 14th-century castle encircled by water, has been heavily restored over the centuries and now houses the **Museo Civico** (*open Easter–Oct Tues–Sun 10–12.30 & 1.30–6; July–Sept daily same times*). It has two main sections: a Pinacoteca with local painting and sculpture from the 14th–19th centuries, including works by the Neoclassical painter Giuseppe Craffonara (born in Riva in 1790) and a *Last Supper* by Pietro Ricchi, a pupil of Guido Reni known for his candlelit night scenes. The *Last Supper* was painted for the refectory of the Inviolata (*see below*) c. 1645. The second section has archaeological finds from the north Garda region, including a display of extraordinary stone stelae from Arco (4th–3rd millennia BC), of suggestively human form and decorated with incised daggers, spears and talismanic objects. North of the waterfront, on Largo Marconi (between Via Negrelli and Viale dei Tigli) is the church of the **Inviolata**, with a fine Baroque interior and paintings by Pietro Ricchi (*see above*).

At the mouth of the Vale di Ledro, a valley of great botanical interest, is the **Lago di Ledro**, nearly 3km long, with the little resort of Pieve di Ledro. When the water is low, on the east side of the lake near Molina, you can see some of the c. 15,000 larchwood stakes from lake dwellings of the early Bronze Age, discovered in 1929. There is a fascinating museum here (Museo delle Palafitte; *open March–June and Sept–Nov daily 9–5; July–Aug daily 10–6, palafitteledro.it*), and a clutch of Bronze Age huts has been reconstructed on a wooden platform above the water.

Torbole sul Garda (*map 2*), a summer resort on the lake's northeastern tip, played a part in the war of 1439 between the Visconti and the Venetians, when fleets of warships were dragged overland by teams of oxen and launched into the lake here (the '*Galeas per montes*' expedition). Goethe stayed at Torbole in 1786.

THE VENETO SHORE

The east side of Lake Garda is bounded by a high cliff (2078m), the northern peak of Monte Baldo, the ridge which lines the shore as far as Torri del Benaco. A region of great interest for its flora and fauna, part of it is a protected area once known as *Hortus europae* from its remarkable vegetation, which varies from lemon trees and olives on its lower slopes to beechwoods and Alpine flowers on the summit. The highest peaks are Cima Valdritta (2218m) and Monte Maggiore (2200m). There are marked hiking trails on the slopes (*maps and walking guides are available from bookshops locally*).

MALCESINE AND CASSONE

Malcesine (*map 4*) is a likeable resort with a little port. It was the seat of the Veronese Captains of the Lake in the 16th–17th centuries, and their old palace is now the Town Hall. The little garden on the lake is open to the public. Narrow roads lead up to the castle, of Lombard origin but in the hands of the Della Scala from 1277. It was restored by Venice in the 17th century and later used as an Austrian defence post. It is open to the public (*mid-March–Oct*) and contains a museum of Natural History, illustrating the flora and fauna of the lake and of Monte Baldo. There is also a room dedicated to Goethe, who had been forced by unfavourable winds to land for a night at Malcesine, and while sketching the castle was almost arrested as an Austrian spy. The next day he docked at Bardolino, where he mounted a mule to cross into the Adige Valley for Verona. There is a fine view from the top of the tower. Concerts are often held in the castle. A cableway runs to the top of Monte Baldo, and there are pleasant walks in the area.

To the south, the coast becomes less wild. At **Cassone** (a suburb of Malcesine) there is a small Museo del Lago (*open Tues–Sun 10–12 & 3–6; Sun only in winter*) in a building on the waterfront that was once a fish incubating plant.

Further on, the road passes a cemetery and the early 12th-century church of San Zeno. At **Pai** (*map 6*) there is a magnificent view of the opposite shore of the lake. The coast here is known as the Riviera degli Olivi, from its many olive trees.

TORRI DEL BENACO

Torri del Benaco (*map 5*), the Roman *Castrum Turrium*, was the chief town of the Gardesana during the years of Venetian rule. The Gardesana federation comprised ten towns between Malcesine and Lazise, headed by a Capitano del Lago. Today Torri has a pretty horseshoe-shaped port and the town itself is lively and attractive. In places you can still see stretches of its fortifying walls. At one end of the terrace outside the Gardesana hotel (once the headquarters of the Gardesana's ruling council) is a monument to Domizio Calderini, a Humanist scholar born in Torri in 1444. The Latin epitaph is by his friend, the great Tuscan poet Poliziano. Behind it, the **Oratory of the Holy Trinity**, now a War Memorial chapel, has 15th-century frescoes, including a *Last Supper* with fish a prominent feature of the meal. Looming above the port are the swallowtail battlements of the impressive **Castello Scaligero**, a castle of the Della Scala dating from 1383 (*museodelcastelloditorridelbenaco.it*). It contains a museum illustrating the history of fishing on the lake and the production of olive oil. There is a also a section dedicated to the rock carvings found in the district, the oldest supposedly dating from 1500 BC (*see below*). A splendid *limonaia* of 1760, which protects a plantation of huge old lemon trees—as well as citrons, mandarins and oranges—against its south wall, can also be visited: the scent of blossom is delicious in spring. These structures were built of tall stone struts roofed over with wooden slats in winter, and protected by glass panes in front. Lemons were once cultivated in great abundance on Garda, but this is one of very few *limonaie* to survive. Unfortunately it backs onto a field where boys play football, and at the time of writing most of the glass panes had fallen victim to their over-enthusiastic kicks.

TORRI DEL BENACO
View of the harbour from the castle ramparts.

PUNTA SAN VIGILIO TO GARDA

The headland of **Punta di San Vigilio** (*map 5; parking on the main road*) is a romantic and secluded place, now occupied by a hotel with a fine restaurant. The hotel complex includes a walled lemon garden and a café-bar on the waterfront, with tables out on the harbour mole. From here it is possible to walk all the way along the foreshore to the town of Garda (*about 30mins*).

In the hills behind San Vigilio, a path leads to the **rock carvings** of the Roccia de la Griselle. A short way towards Garda, on the left, you will see the path (marked 'Graffiti'). It leads uphill and then forks right into woodland. Follow the 'Graffiti' signs. A narrow path takes you to a flat rock (the second one you come to) covered with incised images of ships and weapons.

The resort of **Garda** (*map 6*) was developed after the Second World War at the head of a deep bay. It was famous in the Roman and Lombard periods, and was later a fortified town; it still retains some fine old houses and a string of agreeable cafés. A very simple market is held on the waterfront.

BARDOLINO, LAZISE AND PESCHIERA

The hills become lower and the landscape duller as the broad basin at the foot of the lake opens out. **Bardolino** (*map 6*), an ancient place retaining some commercial importance, is well known for its wine: not great wine, but fresh and fruity and easy to drink. In 2013 the Cantina Guerrieri Rizzardi opened a new cellar here (*guerrieririzzardi.it*). A tower and two gates remain from an old castle of the Scaligeri. In a little courtyard, is the tiny Carolingian church of San Zeno, which retains its

9th-century form with a tower above the crossing and ancient paving stones. It has four old capitals and fragments of frescoes. The 12th-century church of San Severo has contemporary frescoes.

Lazise (*map 8*), with a very pretty waterfront, retains part of its medieval wall and a castle of the Scaligeri, with Venetian additions. The 16th-century double-arched Venetian customs house on the lakefront attests to its former importance. San Nicolò is a 12th-century church with 16th-century additions and 14th-century frescoes.

Peschiera del Garda (*map 8*), which stands at the outflow of the River Mincio, has an ancient fortress, one of the four corners of the Austrian 'quadrilateral', a system of four defensive fortresses developed by the Austrians after they were awarded this north Italian territory following the fall of Napoleon. The other three forts were Verona, Mantua and Legnago). The impressive fortifications at Peschiera, begun by the Venetians in 1553, were strengthened by Napoleon and again by the Austrians.

Close by is Italy's most famous theme park for young children, called **Gardaland**, which was based on Disneyland when it opened in 1975. Today it receives around 3 million visitors a year (and is especially popular with children under ten).

PRACTICAL INFORMATION

GETTING AROUND

• **By rail:** The Venice–Milan line serves Peschiera, Desenzano–Sirmione and Lonato. Regional trains connect the lake stations to Verona or Brescia in less than 30mins; fast trains stop at Desenzano–Sirmione only.

• **By bus:** Bus services run several times daily by the roads on the west and east banks from Peschiera and Desenzano to Riva. Frequent service from Verona via Lazise and Garda to Riva, and from Brescia to Desenzano, Sirmione, Peschiera and Verona, and between Salò and Desenzano, and Desenzano, Salò and Riva. Run by ATV, see *www.atv. verona.it.*

• **By boat: Public boat services** (including two modernised paddle-steamers built in 1902 and 1903) are run by Navigazione Laghi (*navigazionelaghi.*

it). These operate from around mid-March–early Nov (the timetable changes three times a year). Printed timetables are available from tickets offices, information offices and hotel lobbies. A daily boat service runs between Desenzano and Riva in 4hrs, calling at various ports en route—but not all services follow the same route. Check the website for details. Hydrofoils run twice daily in 2hrs 40mins (with fewer stops). All year round a car ferry operates between Maderno and Torri di Benaco in 30mins (every 30mins, but less frequently in winter) and there is a summer ferry from Limone to Malcesine in 20mins (hourly). Tickets are available allowing free travel on the lake services for a day. Tours of the lake in the afternoons in summer are also organised.

Boats for rent are available from Garda Yachting Charter on Lungolago

Zanardelli in Maderno (*www.gyc.it, T: 0365 548347*). The northern tip of the lake around Riva is reserved for sailing boats. **Boat trips to Isola del Garda** can also be made at certain times from April to Oct. The island is privately owned by the Borghese Cavazza family, who offer guided tours of their neo-Venetian mansion and its grounds. Booking is required (*for information, times, departure ports and prices, see www.isoladelgarda.com, or T: 328 612 6943*).

• **By cablecar:** For details of the cablecar (*funivia*) service from Malcesine to Monte Baldo, see *funiviedelbaldo.it.*

• **By bicycle:** A new cycle lane 2km long and suspended from the rockface some 50 above the lake was opened in 2018 from Limone to Capo Reamol (mostly parallel to the road). It is also open to walkers.

INFORMATION OFFICES

General websites are *visitgarda.com* and *lagodigarda.it.* Tourist offices include the following (more are open in summer):
Desenzano *Via Porto Vecchio 34. T: 030 374 8726.*
Salò *Piazza Sant'Antonio. T: 0365 21423.*
Sirmione *Viale Marconi 2. T: 030 916114.*
Toscolano-Maderno *Via Garibaldi 24, T: 0365 644298, prolocotoscolanomaderno.com.*

WHERE TO STAY

NB: Most of the places on Lake Garda are open during the summer season only, April/May–Oct.

GARDA
€€–€€€ **Hotel La Vittoria**. Plainly elegant, comfortable rooms in a renovated harbourfront villa. Restaurant and coffee terrace. *Lungolago Regina Adelaide 57. T: 045 627 0473, hotellavittoria.it.*

FASANO
€€–€€€ **Bella Riva**. Family-friendly hotel right on the lake at Fasano, between Gardone and Maderno. In an old villa used for German embassy staff during the Republic of Salò, renovated with modern décor. Pleasant gardens right on the lakefront, with swimming pool. *Via Podini Mario 1–2. T: 0365 540773, bellarivagardone.it.*
€€€ **Grand Hotel Fasano e Villa Principe**. A former hunting lodge of the emperors of Austria set in a lovely park with garden terrace overlooking the lake. *Corso Zanardelli 190. T: 0365 290220, ghf.it.*

GARDONE RIVIERA
€€€ **Villa Fiordaliso**. *See Where to Eat, below.*
€€€ **Villa del Sogno**. The former villa of a German industrialist, used as a convalescence home by German officers during the Republic of Salò. Set in a beautiful garden with swimming pool and tennis court, the hotel is gracious and old-fashioned, impeccably run, with a vast and ample terrace overlooking the water, divided into a variety of sitting areas, for breakfast, pre-dinner cocktails, or dinner in the candlelit gazebo. *Via Zanardelli 107. T: 0365 290181, villadelsogno.it.*

GARGNANO
€€€€ **Villa Feltrinelli**. Mussolini's home during the Republic of Salò, a magnificent villa with frescoed rooms, is now a very grand hotel, set in a lakeside

park. *Via Rimembranza 38–40. T: 0365 798000, villafeltrinelli.com.*

€€€ **Villa Giulia**. Lakeside villa with lovely garden and a Michelin-starred restaurant. *Viale Rimembranza 20. T: 0365 71022, villagiulia.it.*

MALCESINE

€–€€ **Hotel Castello Lake Front**. An excellent summer hotel. Modern and airy, no clutter, large windows with lake views, and its own beach. Right in the heart of the old town. *Via Paina 21. T: 045 740 0233, h-c.it.*

RIVA DEL GARDA

€€ **Grand Hotel di Riva**. A classic resort hotel with a quiet park, frequented also for its roof-garden restaurant. *Piazza Garibaldi 10. T: 0464 521800, grandhotelriva.it.*

SALÒ

€ **Vigna**. Simple, family-run, three-star hotel. Friendly and comfortable. *Lungolago Zanardelli 62. T: 0365 520144, hotelvignasalo.it.*

SAN VIGILIO

€€€€ **Locanda San Vigilio**. Well-appointed rooms in a 15th-century house and its outbuildings right on the lake. Rooms vary a great deal; the nicest ones are in the house itself. Excellent restaurant attached. *T: 045 725 6688, locanda-sanvigilio.it.*

SIRMIONE

€€€ **Palace Hotel Villa Cortine**. Luxury accommodation in a 19th-century villa with large park, on the lakeshore. *Via Grotte 6. T: 030 990 5890, hotelvillacortine.com.*

TORRI DEL BENACO

€–€€ **Albergo Gardesana**. Comfortable, friendly hotel overlooking the harbour and castle. Very good value. Restaurant. Parking. *Piazza Calderini 5. T: 045 722 5411, gardesana.eu.*

WHERE TO EAT

DESENZANO

€€€ **Esplanade.** Fresh seasonal cuisine with a garden overlooking the lake. This has been a good place to eat for many years. Closed Wed. *Via Lario 10. T: 030 914 3361. ristorante-esplanade.com.*

€ **Cavallino**. A well established restaurant, good for fish. Closed Mon. *Via Murachette 29. T: 030 912 0217, ristorantecavallino.it.*

€ **Ristorante-Pizzeria Garda.** Unpretentious, reliable place. Friendly service. A good lunch spot—it is very close to the Roman villa, on the waterfront. *Lungolago Cesare Battisti 21. T: 030 914 1714.*

GARDONE RIVIERA

€€ **Villa Fiordaliso**. In business since 1890, in an old villa in a small park (this is also a Relais & Châteaux hotel; rooms vary greatly) with summer seating on a terrace above the lake. Closed Mon, midday Tues. *Corso Zanardelli 150. T: 0365 20158, villafiordaliso.it.*

€ **Wimmer**. Cheerful pizzeria on the waterfront, named after Luigi Wimmer, an entrepreneur of Austrian descent who built the first lodging house in Gardone and who rose to become its mayor. Closed Mon. *Piazza Wimmer 5. T: 0365 20631.*

GARDONE SOPRA

€ **Accadueocafé**. Pleasant place where you can sit out under a vine trellis with a glass of good house white wine and a sandwich or bruschetta, looking out at the lake below, which shimmers through the trees. *Via Carera.*

GARGNANO

€€€ **La Tortuga.** A gourmet's delight, known for fine food and excellent selection of regional, Italian, and imported wines. Closed Tues. By the harbour. *Via XXIV Maggio 5. T: 0365 71251, ristorantelatortuga.it.*

€€€ **Villa Giulia**. *See Where to Stay, above.*

MALCESINE

€€ **Vecchia Malcesine**. Lake fish, quail, white chocolate 'soup': a high-quality Michelin-starred offering just south of the harbour. *Via Pisort 6. T: 045 740 0469, vecchiamalcesine.com.*

€ **Osteria Santo Cielo**. Very close to the park that surrounds the Town Hall, south of the port, a snug vaulted tavern serving salads, platters of cold meat and cheese and other snacks, to be washed down with a beaker of house wine. *Piazza Turazza 11. T: 045 740 0469, osteriasantocielo.com.*

SALÒ

€–€€ **Il Cantinone**. Historic wine cellar now a restaurant, in a secluded square behind the harbour. Good local dishes, lake fish, home-made desserts. Closed Thur. *Piazza San Antonio 19. T: 0365 20234.*

SAN VIGILIO

€€€ **Locanda San Vigilio**. Superb restaurant with an excellent wine list. In a lovely secluded spot. Eat either in the narrow loggia overlooking the water or in the old living room (with an open fire in chilly weather). *T: 045 725 6688, locanda-sanvigilio.it.*

SIRMIONE

€€€ **La Rucola**. Acclaimed restaurant very close to the castle. Open at midday upon reservation only; advisable also to book evenings. *Vicolo Strentelle 3. T: 030 916326, ristorantelarucola.it.*

€€€ **Osteria del Vecchio Fossato**. Inventive menu featuring local specialities and influences from further afield. A restaurant with a contented following. *Via Antiche Mura 16. T: 030 919331, osteriadelvecchiofossato.it.*

€ **Pizzeria Scaligeri's**. Simple, unfussy, reliable pizza place right by the castle. Ideal as a no-frills lunch stop. *Via Dante 5, T: 030 916581, scaligeri.info.*

TORRI DEL BENACO

€€ **Agli Olivi**. *Trattoria* with a wide terrace commanding lovely views of the lake. In the olive groves of Albisano, just above Torri (can be reached on foot, a pleasant half-hour walk; or by car). Fillets of lake perch, fish ravioli, delicious desserts (the chocolate salami is particularly good). *Via Valmagra 7. T: 045 722 5483, agliolivi.com.*

€€ **Bell'Arrivo**. Cosy *trattoria* with inner garden. Right on the harbour. *Piazza Calderini 10. T: 0456 299028, galvanihotels.com.*

LOCAL SPECIALITIES

The **wines** of Lake Garda are the white Lugana, fresh and fruity and the red Gropello, rustic and full-bodied. Plenty of restaurants serve **lake fish**. The *carpione* (*Salmo carpio*), a kind of large trout, is found only in Garda. Menus often feature *lavarello* (*Coregonus lavaretus*), freshwater whitefish (also known as *coregone*).

FESTIVALS AND EVENTS

Riva del Garda *Intervela*, international sailing week, July; *Flicorno d'Oro*, international band competition, Aug. *Mostra Internazionale di Musica Leggera Vela d'Oro*, pop festival, Sept. **Salò** Music festival, July.
Torri del Benaco *Festa dell'Olio*, with food fair, market of local products and folk music, Jan.

MANTUA, PALAZZO TE
The Chariot of the Moon driving away the Chariot of the Sun.

Mantua

Mantua (in Italian Mántova; *Atlas A, C2–D2*) is famous for its associations with the Gonzaga, under whose rule it flourished in the 15th and 16th centuries. The focus of modern-day life remains in the historic centre, with the vast Palazzo Ducale and its famous fresco by Mantegna. The old centre also has a special atmosphere since it is surrounded on three sides by the sluggish waters of the Mincio, which form lakes, so that the city is approached from the north and east by causeways. Historically Mantua enjoyed a prominent position, on good a line of communication, but since the early 20th century it has been a difficult place to reach by public transport and this contributes to its special feeling of isolation. Although in Lombardy, it has much (if not more) in common with its close neighbours in the Veneto and Emilia Romagna.

HISTORY OF MANTUA

Virgil was born a short way southeast of Mantua, at *Andes* on the Mincio (traditionally identified with Pietole) in c. 70 BC and some of Mantua's earliest recorded history is due to the poet's interest in his birthplace. The origins of the town itself are thought to be connected to an Etruscan settlement on the Mincio at Forcello (*Atlas A, D2*). Matilda of Canossa (*see p. 388*) is known to have been active in the city government, supporting the Pope against the Emperor. Some ten years after her death in 1115, Mantua became a free commune and remained so until 1273, when the Bonacolsi became *signori*.

Under Gonzaga rule from 1328, the town was famous as a centre of art and learning, especially during the reigns of Ludovico II (1444–78), Francesco II (1484–1519) and his consort Isabella d'Este, the greatest patron of her time, and their son Federico II (1519–40). The dynasty was admired for its enlightened patronage and civilised way of life and for several centuries brought a welcome stability for the inhabitants.

When the Gonzaga fortunes began to wane, many of their finest paintings and sculptures were sold to Charles I of England (in 1627–9). Two years later a war broke out over the heirs to the Gonzaga, and Mantua was sacked by troops of the Holy Roman Emperor. At this time it is estimated that nearly three quarters of the population were wiped out by plague. The duchy was extinguished in 1708 by the Austrians, who confiscated it from the last duke after he had supported the Bourbon over the Habsburg claim to the throne of Spain and then fled to Venice in panic, abandoning Mantua. The Austrians fortified the town as the southwest corner of their 'quadrilateral' (*see p. 338*). It held out against Napoleon for eight months in 1796–7, and was retaken by the French in 1799. The town was again under Austrian rule from 1814–66. When Verdi wrote his *Rigoletto* in 1851, in order to make it safe from censorship, he chose to set it not in France but in Mantua, a city whose ducal line was long extinct and whose days of glory were behind it.

In the 1950s an important petrochemical industry was established here (the refinery stands out on the skyline across the Lago Inferiore). In 2008 Mantua, together with the little Gonzaga town of Sabbioneta (some 34km southwest), was placed on the UNESCO World Heritage list. Mantua was slightly damaged by earthquake in 2012 but only Palazzo della Ragione and the Broletto were still under scaffolding at the time of writing. The *Gazzetta di Mantova*, founded in 1664, boasts of being the oldest daily newspaper in Italy.

MANTUA HIGHLIGHTS

The vast Gonzaga palace, **Palazzo Ducale** (*map 4*), is celebrated above all for the Camera degli Sposi, frescoed by Mantegna (*p. 357*). Mantegna's former home, the **Casa del Mantegna**, can also be visited (*map 5; p. 371*).

At the southern tip of town is the Gonzaga dukes' former summer villa, **Palazzo Te** (*map 7; p. 366*), the masterpiece of Giulio Romano.

The basilica of **Sant'Andrea** (*map 4; p. 363*) is the most complete architectural work by the great architect and theorist Leon Battista Alberti. The **Museo Diocesano** is also well worth a visit (*map 4; p. 373*).

To appreciate Mantua's extraordinary aquatic setting, it is fun to take a **boat trip on one of the lakes** (*p. 377*).

NB: The lovely, large red and grey cobblestones of central Mantua's squares can be hard on the feet unless you wear stout-soled shoes.

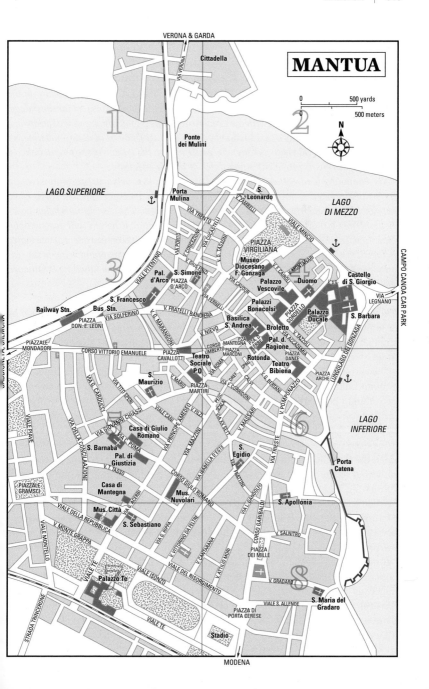

PALAZZO DUCALE

Map 4. Open Tues–Sun 8.15–7.15, last entry 6.20. T: 0376 224832, mantovaducale. beniculturali.it. To book, T: 041 241 1897. The ticket office is on Piazza Sordello (to the left of the main entrance). At the time of writing, you could buy tickets just for the palace, or for the palace and Castello with the Camera degli Sposi (for which you will be given a timed entrance, since only a certain number of people are allowed in at any one time, up to a maximum of 1,500 visitors a day). Free entrance on the 1st Sun of the month (when a 'dog-sitting' service is provided). Annual tickets are also available.

NB: The palace is vast (there are some 700 rooms and 15 courtyards) and only a certain number of the apartments are open at any one time. The visit takes place along prescribed routes, which are clearly indicated by arrows in each room. The descriptions below cover the highlights but are not intended as a guided tour, as any itinerary will depend upon what is open at the time of your visit. Numerous parts of the palace are being opened up to visitors; it is worth checking the excellent website before you visit. Numbering in the text corresponds to the rooms in situ and the plan on pp. 348–9. All the labelling is provided also in English.

The whole of the upper side of the expansive, cobbled Piazza Sordello is occupied by the famous Palazzo Ducale, a huge fortress-palace that remains a fitting emblem of the grandeur and ambition of the Gonzaga princes. The Gothic façade gives no idea of the extent of what lies behind.

The vast rambling palace is divided into three main parts, each with various suites of rooms built by successive generations of the ruling dynasties and all connected to each other by corridors and courtyards—similar to the sprawling Residenz in Munich. The first palace, known as the Corte Vecchia and facing Piazza Sordello, was built by the Bonacolsi, lords of Mantua in the 13th–early 14th century. The palace was adapted by the Gonzaga after they seized control of the city in 1328. Later in that century they added the Castello di San Giorgio to defend the approach from the lake (it was once connected to the palace by drawbridges only); in the 16th century came the Corte Nuova wing, mainly planned by Giulio Romano.

Architects who worked on the palace included the Tuscan Luca Fancelli in the 15th century and, in the 16th and early 17th centuries, Giulio Romano and Antonio Maria Viani. Decorations in the Neoclassical style, by Paolo Pozzo, were added by the Austrians.

No furnishings remain in the palace today, which is visited chiefly for its famous Camera degli Sposi painted by Mantegna. But the carved and painted ceilings of numerous rooms are spectacular, and there is a particularly good collection of Classical statuary brought from Sabbioneta and other Gonzaga residences near Mantua. Most of the great Gonzaga art collections begun by Isabella d'Este, wife of Francesco II, and enriched in the 16th century, have been dispersed (they included works by Michelangelo, Titian, Veronese, Tintoretto, Rubens and Caravaggio).

ART AT THE COURT OF THE GONZAGA

In 1490 the 16-year-old Isabella d'Este, daughter of the Duke of Ferrara and sister of the Duchess of Milan, married Francesco Gonzaga of Mantua. Together they gathered around them artists, writers and musicians to create a court of high culture and discriminating taste. Isabella was an extremely cultivated and independent lady who established her own respected position at court: she was one of the first women to be admired in her own right and not just seen as an appendage to a rich and powerful husband. Among the famous artists who flourished under the Gonzaga's enlightened patronage were Pisanello and Leon Battista Alberti. Andrea Mantegna was court artist from 1460 until his death in 1506. Giulio Romano, both architect and painter, was called to Mantua in 1524 by Isabella's son Federico II, and worked there until his death in 1546. Besides his work on the Corte Nuova of the Palazzo Ducale, he also designed many of the ceilings in the *palazzo* and provided the dukes with a summer villa, the Palazzo Te, his most important architectural work. Titian made frequent visits to the city and painted Isabella d'Este's portrait twice, as well as that of her son Federico II with his dog (that painting is now in the Prado). Pier Jacopo Alari Bonacolsi, nicknamed 'L'Antico', was born in Mantua and was commissioned by the Gonzaga to make bronze copies of Classical works, for which Isabella d'Este nurtured a particular passion.

CORTE VECCHIA

The Corte Vecchia, or ducal palace proper, overlooking Piazza Sordello, consists of the Domus Magna, founded by Guido Bonacolsi c. 1290, and the taller, swallowtail-crenellated Palazzo del Capitano, built a few years later by the Bonacolsi at the city's expense. The Austrians altered the windows of the façade in the Gothic style (you can clearly see in the brickwork where this was done) and it was restored to its original 15th-century appearance at the beginning of the 20th century, funded by the Samuel Kress Foundation. The entrance to the palace is through this façade. You will be directed up Antonio Maria Viani's 17th-century Scalone delle Duchesse.

1: Sala del Morone. Named after the little-known Domenico Morone, who in 1494 painted the interesting panel displayed here of the *Expulsion of the Bonacolsi*, which took place in the piazza outside in 1328. The Gonzaga were victorious since they had the support of the troops of Cangrande della Scala from Verona. The front of Palazzo Ducale is very clearly depicted (it proved a useful source during 20th-century restoration work and the Duomo still had its Gothic façade (pulled down in 1761). Berenson commented: 'Refined cavaliers on deftly-groomed horses are making elegant thrusts at one another'.

2: Appartamento Guastalla. Named after the wife of the last duke, Ferdinando Carlo Nevers, who commissioned the portrait medallions here of the entire Gonzaga dynasty (including himself) in 1701. The windows look on to the huge Piazza Lega Lombarda.

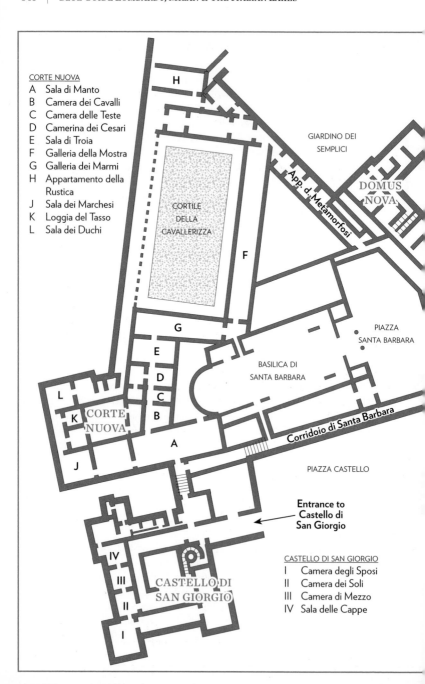

CORTE NUOVA
A   Sala di Manto
B   Camera dei Cavalli
C   Camera delle Teste
D   Camerina dei Cesari
E   Sala di Troia
F   Galleria della Mostra
G   Galleria dei Marmi
H   Appartamento della Rustica
J   Sala dei Marchesi
K   Loggia del Tasso
L   Sala dei Duchi

GIARDINO DEI SEMPLICI

App. di Metamorfosi

DOMUS NOVA

CORTILE DELLA CAVALLERIZZA

PIAZZA SANTA BARBARA

BASILICA DI SANTA BARBARA

Corridoio di Santa Barbara

CORTE NUOVA

PIAZZA CASTELLO

Entrance to Castello di San Giorgio

CASTELLO DI SAN GIORGIO
I   Camera degli Sposi
II   Camera dei Soli
III   Camera di Mezzo
IV   Sala delle Cappe

CASTELLO DI SAN GIORGIO

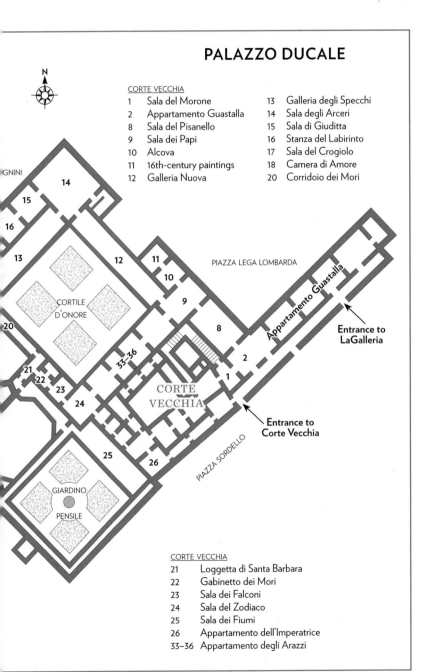

PALAZZO DUCALE

CORTE VECCHIA

1	Sala del Morone	13	Galleria degli Specchi
2	Appartamento Guastalla	14	Sala degli Arceri
8	Sala del Pisanello	15	Sala di Giuditta
9	Sala dei Papi	16	Stanza del Labirinto
10	Alcova	17	Sala del Crogiolo
11	16th-century paintings	18	Camera di Amore
12	Galleria Nuova	20	Corridoio dei Mori

PIAZZA LEGA LOMBARDA

Appartamento Guastalla

Entrance to
LaGalleria

CORTILE
D'ONORE

CORTE
VECCHIA

Entrance to
Corte Vecchia

PIAZZA SORDELLO

GIARDINO
PENSILE

CORTE VECCHIA

21	Loggetta di Santa Barbara
22	Gabinetto dei Mori
23	Sala dei Falconi
24	Sala del Zodiaco
25	Sala dei Fiumi
26	Appartamento dell'Imperatrice
33–36	Appartamento degli Arazzi

8: Sala del Pisanello. This room contains a fragment of a mural painting showing a battle tournament, an unfinished but vivacious composition showing a mounted mêlée, considered one of the masterpieces of Pisanello. Forming a border along the top of the painting is a beautiful frieze incorporating the Lancastrian 'SS' collar entwined with marigold flowers, one of the emblems of the Gonzaga—it was Henry VI of England who granted the Gonzaga the concession to use the heraldic crest of the House of Lancaster.

On the other wall are sinopie of Arthurian scenes, also by Pisanello.

9: Sala dei Papi. The sinopia of Pisanello's tournament scene in the previous room is displayed here. Careful study shows that the artist made modifications to his original design in the final fresco.

10: Alcova. Contains paintings, including two late 15th-century panels of the bishop saints Ignatius and Augustine dressed in splendid golden robes, by a painter from Verona.

PISANELLO, THE COURTLY ARTIST

Antonio di Puccio (1377–1455) is always, for reasons unknown, called Pisanello (his only connection with Pisa seems to have been that his father was born there). He was famous in his day and is still a very well-known Renaissance artist. This is all the more astonishing since only four of his panel paintings have survived and just three of his murals (none of them in good condition) can be seen today in northern Italy. But some 400 of his exquisite autograph drawings still exist, including a book of them which came to light in the early 19th century and was later purchased by the Louvre. These include portrait sketches, as well as detailed studies of plants and animals.

Many of the commemorative medals he cast in bronze or lead, with portraits of his patrons and contemporaries (in imitation of antique coins or ancient Roman medallions), are preserved in museums all over the world. In Lombardy you can see examples here in Mantua and in Brescia (*p. 301*). Pisanello became a very sought-after court artist and although he worked mainly for the Gonzaga in Mantua and for the Este in Ferrara, he also received commissions from the Duke of Milan and the King of Naples and from the Church. The chivalric cycle which at once gave its name to the Sala del Pisanello in the Palazzo Ducale has an extraordinary composition with crowds of knights in armour some on horseback, some fallen to the ground, all involved in a tournament given at the castle of King Brangoire as recounted in the Arthurian romance. The action is not always easy to make out but the depiction of horses seen from every angle with their riders in equally odd positions, is memorable. Other works for the Gonzaga are documented but no longer survive (chapels in the castle here and at Marmirolo).

Pisanello's style has much in common with that of Gentile da Fabriano, whom he apparently knew when in Venice. One of the four paintings which survive (now preserved in the Louvre) is a beautiful portrait in profile thought to be Ludovico II's sister Margherita Gonzaga (1418–39) who married Leonello d'Este.

MANTUA, PALAZZO DUCALE
Detail of Pisanello's battle mural.

11: Amongst the 16th century paintings here is a large *Way to Calvary* by a Ferrarese painter which has an interesting street scene, and the *Conversion of St Paul* by the little-known Girolamo Mazzola Bedoli.

12: Galleria Nuova. Built by Giuseppe Piermarini in 1771 to link the Appartamento Guastalla with the Appartamento Ducale, this displays 16th- and 17th-century altarpieces including dramatic works by Carlo Bononi and Antonio Maria Viani.

APPARTAMENTO DUCALE

13: Galleria degli Specchi. Originally an open loggia on the Cortile d'Onore, built and decorated under the supervision of Antonio Maria Viani for Vincenzo I shortly after 1600. The lunettes at either end by Karl Santner and Viani, as well as the three huge paintings in the barrel vault and the seven lunettes of the Virtues by pupils of Guido Reni, including Giovanni Giacomo Sementi, all survive from the loggia before it was enclosed and turned into this huge Neoclassical hall by

Giocondo Albertolli in 1773. Above the mirrors is a frieze of putti against a gold ground.

14: Sala degli Arceri. This monumental hall, with a high ceiling, has monstrous carved harpies between charming frescoes of horses, just their legs glimpsed behind curtains blowing in the breeze. Here are displayed some of the most important paintings in the palace, all of them dating from the first two decades of the 17th century. *The*

Gonzaga Family in Adoration of the Trinity, painted for Duke Vincenzo in 1605 by Rubens, was cut into pieces during the French occupation; the central part has been pieced back together as far as possible and shows the magnificently robed Vincenzo Gonzaga with his wife Eleonora de' Medici and his (deceased) parents duke William and Eleanor of Habsburg. The family kneel below the Holy Trinity. God the Father is depicted as a somewhat languid individual but he holds a wonderful glass globe. Three other fragments of the work, which was originally a great deal larger and included all five of the duke's children, are exhibited beside it, including a charming little white dog. Other pieces of it found their way to London, Vienna and Parma.

Don't miss the other fascinating little work by Rubens here, painted around the same time for a convent in Mantua, a *bozzetto* for an altarpiece (which was never executed) showing the *Martyrdom of St Ursula and the 11,000 Virgins*.

There is also a very fine painting of the *Virgin Presenting St Margaret to the Trinity* by Antonio Maria Viani. He served as architect to Vincenzo I and in fact the blue monochrome lunette by Domenico Fetti here shows Viani presenting a model of the church of Sant'Orsola to Margherita Gonzaga d'Este (sister of Vincenzo I). The huge lunette of the *Miracle of the Loaves and Fishes* (note the ghostly crowd approaching on the right) and the delightful small *Presentation of the Virgin* are also by Fetti.

15: Sala di Giuditta. Named after the four large nocturnal scenes telling the story of Judith by the Neapolitan painter Pietro Mango, who was at work in Mantua in the 1650s. The paintings below of Christ and the Apostles are by Domenico Fetti. The beautiful blue, gold and red ceiling (brought here together with those in the following two rooms by Vincenzo I from Francesco II's Palazzo di San Sebastiano; *see p. 370*) features one of the Gonzagas' many symbolic emblems, the crucible (*see Room 17*). Other family devices included the muzzle (discretion), Mt Olympus (pre-eminence), the girdle (chastity), the gauntlet (military prowess), the tower (resilience) and the dog (fidelity). They often appear as part of the decorative scheme in the Gonzaga palaces.

16: Stanza del Labirinto. Named after the maze (impossible to take a wrong turning in) carved in the ceiling with the motto *Forse che si, forse che no* ('Maybe, maybe not'). The four painted panels on the upper part of the walls are by Sante Peranda and Palma Giovane. The outer band around the ceiling is carved with a rather vainglorious inscription lauding Vincenzo's part in the failed Siege of Nagykanizsa, a battle on Hungarian soil against the Ottomans in 1601.

17: Sala del Crogiolo. Has the remainder of the crucible ceiling from Palazzo di San Sebastiano. Gold bars are being lowered into the flames to test their mettle. This was the favoured emblem of Francesco II, who used it to symbolise his probity after he had been accused of temporising between Venice and Milan. The frieze of putti is by Lorenzo Costa the Younger (c. 1580). The portraits of the Pico family from Mirandola were painted by Sante Peranda.

GONZAGA RULERS OF MANTUA

CAPTAINS OF MANTUA

Luigi 1328

Guido 1360–9
Friend of Petrarch

Ludovico I 1369–82
Patron of Serafino Serafini

Francesco I 1382–1407
Beheads his first wife, Agnese Visconti,
for adultery; m. Margherita Malatesta;
builds Castello di San Giorgio

MARQUISES OF MANTUA

Gianfrancesco 1407–44
m. Paola Malatesta; created Marquis
by the Holy Roman Emperor
Sigismund in 1433; patron of Pisanello

Ludovico II 1444–78
m. Barbara of Brandenburg; patron of
Alberti, Luca Fancelli and Mantegna;
commissions the Camera degli Sposi

Federico I 1478–84
m. Margaret of Bavaria; patron of
Mantegna and Luca Fancelli; builds
the Domus Nova

Francesco II 1484–1519
m. Isabella d'Este, great patroness

DUKES OF MANTUA

Federico II 1519–40
Created Duke in 1530; patron of

Giulio Romano, Titian and Correggio;
commissions Palazzo Te

Francesco III 1540–50
m. Catherine of Austria

Guglielmo I 1550–87
Brother of Francesco III; m. Eleanora
of Habsburg; commissions Santa
Barbara and unifies the disparate parts
of Palazzo Ducale; patron of Palestrina

Vincenzo I 1587–1612
m. Eleonora de' Medici; patron of
Rubens, Antonio Maria Viani, and
Monteverdi

Francesco IV 1612

Ferdinando I 1612–26
Brother of Francesco IV

Vincenzo II 1626–7
Brother of Francesco IV

Carlo I 1627–37
Uncle of Vincenzo II; sells the family's
most precious works of art to Charles I
of England

Carlo II 1637–65
Grandson of Carlo I

Ferdinando Carlo Nevers 1665–1708
m. Anna Isabella of Guastalla; his
titles are appropriated by Joseph I of
Austria in retaliation for his support of
the French in the War of the Spanish
Succession.

18: Camera di Amore e Psiche. Named after the painting on canvas in the tondo of 1813 in the centre of the lovely wood ceiling. More paintings by Sante Peranda and Palma Giovane are hung here.

Beyond a little room with a pretty red, white and black marble floor, you emerge in the lovely **Corridoio dei Mori (20)**, described below.

THE GONZAGA SALE TO CHARLES I OF ENGLAND

The extraordinary story of the sale of the best part of the immense Gonzaga art collection to Charles I of England in 1627–9 needs to be told. An inventory drawn up in 1627 of the Gonzaga possessions listed some 2,000 paintings. The idea of a purchase was first mooted by the Countess of Arundel, wife of the famous connoisseur Thomas Howard, Earl of Arundel, who understood the significance of the collection and the attraction of a sale to the Gonzaga, who at the time were in dire financial straits. The King needed little persuasion since he was a great connoisseur himself: he was painted by Velázquez and Van Dyck; Bernini carved his bust; Rubens also worked for him and he acquired two of the first Rembrandts to leave the Netherlands. He also purchased the Raphael cartoons for the Vatican tapestries (now in the V&A).

The secret negotiations for the collection were fraught with difficulty, involving dishonest dealers from both countries. The works were sent to Venice, from where they were finally transported in two sea voyages (in the first of which a storm caused terrible damage), while a group of more delicate pieces was entrusted to the Ambassador to Venice, Sir Isaac Wake, who took them to England over land. The result was that England acquired the most important Italian art collection of its time and the rulers of Europe were agog. Among the treasures were the eleven Roman Emperors (the *Caesars*), the *Entombment*, and *Madonna and Child with St Catherine* (and a rabbit), now in the Louvre, all by Titian; the *Madonna della Perla* by Raphael (now in the Prado); and paintings by Andrea del Sarto and Correggio. Contemporary artists included Annibale Carracci and Caravaggio (although the *Death of the Virgin* by Caravaggio ended up in the Louvre). Added to these were great numbers of valuable antique statues and busts. But the most celebrated works to leave Mantua for England were Mantegna's *Triumphs of Caesar* (still in England, at Hampton Court).

Despite this coup, it is sad to reflect that a far greater number of artworks which had belonged to the great dynasty were either lost or destroyed (and just weeks after the execution of Charles I in 1649, many of the works he had purchased from the Gonzaga were dispersed and left England in the Commonwealth Sale).

CORTE NUOVA

A: Sala di Manto. This huge room, with its beautiful coffered ceiling and classical reliefs around the upper wall, is dedicated to the mythical origins of Mantua. Manto, daughter of the blind soothsayer Tiresias, is said to have come to Italy and borne a son, Ocnus, who founded the city. The (damaged) cycle of panels around the walls, by Lorenzo Costa the Younger and other artists, tells the story. Here are displayed three very fine Classical statues, Roman copies of

Greek masterpieces, including one of the caryatids from the southern portico of the Erechtheion in Athens.

The area of the Corte Nuova known as the **Appartamento di Troia** was built and decorated by Giulio Romano and his assistants in 1536 for Federico II, and the painted and stuccoed ceilings are exquisite. Some masterpieces of Classical sculpture are beautifully arranged here. The Gonzaga collection of Greek and Roman works comes from their palace in Sabbioneta and country villas near Mantua.

The **Camera dei Cavalli (B)** is named after the paintings of horses by Giulio Romano's assistant Rinaldo Mantovano, which formerly hung here but which have been lost. It has an exquisitely decorated ceiling with a *Fall of Icarus* in the centre. Remains of wall frescoes show the Gonzaga device of Mount Olympus amid the mazy waters, an allegory of Mantua's position on the Mincio lakes. The window overlooks a charming little garden with a loggia. The very fine ancient Greek sculpture displayed here includes a female head and the head of an athlete, both dating from the 5th century BC, and a funerary stele of Parian marble (4th century BC).

In the **Camera delle Teste (C)** is exquisite painted and stucco decoration with circular niches. The *Jupiter* in the centre of the ceiling was painted by Rinaldo Mantovano. A sarcophagus is displayed here depicting the myth of

Endymion. There is also a statue of a Roman youth in a toga and a relief of a dancing maenad (1st century BC).

The **Camerina dei Cesari (D)** was created by Giulio Romano to provide a setting for Titian's *Caesars*, a series of eleven portraits of the first Roman emperors, the most important commission the great artist received from Duke Federico II. Twelve Caesars were planned, but the last, Domitian, had to be omitted since the wall space was insufficient. The paintings at once became famous and copies were made even in Titian's own lifetime: the copies here today were made in the 17th century. Giulio's very fine frescoed decoration and stuccowork frames survive. The originals were sold to Charles I in 1627 and then destroyed in a fire when they were in Madrid in 1734. The bust of one of the Dioscuri is a Roman work of the 2nd century BC.

The final room is the splendid **Sala di Troia (E)**, entirely frescoed with scenes of the Trojan War by Giulio Romano and his pupils, with the gods of the Olympian pantheon on the ceiling. Federico II used this room as a council chamber. Together with the striking head of a Roman soldier in profile, sporting a splendid helmet, the ancient sculpture here consists of very fine and well-preserved sarcophagus fronts carved with illustrations of the legend of Medea, the battle between the Greeks and Amazons, the Sack of Troy and the Labours of Hercules.

CORTE VECCHIA (CONTINUED)

The narrow **Corridoio dei Mori (20)** has a lovely vault frescoed in the early 17th century with grotesques and a

sequence of a great variety of trees. From the windows there is a view of the top of the façade of Santa Barbara and its delightful campanile, and in the other direction you can look down on the lovely Cortile d'Onore with the columns of the *piano nobile* set into the walls.

At the end is the **Loggetta di Santa Barbara (21)**, with a vault painted in 1580 with a great variety of putti. The **Gabinetto dei Mori (22)** has another exquisite gilded ceiling, with Venus and cherubs in the centre (1657) and a frieze of carved Moors. A beautiful painting of the *Madonna and Child with the Young St John* and a landscape with a river in the background has been hung here.

The following suite of rooms was decorated for Duke Guglielmo (r. 1550–87). The **Sala dei Falconi (23)** has a vault painted with falcons by Lorenzo Costa the Younger, and 16th-century family portraits on the walls. Costa also painted (this time in oil) the vault with the night sky of the **Sala del Zodiaco (24)**, which shows the constellations happily aligned to bring fortune to Duke Guglielmo, his wife Eleanor of Austria and their son Vincenzo. The walls and reliefs above the doors date from the Napoleonic period (1813).

The light loggia known as the **Sala dei Fiumi (25)** was originally Duke Guglielmo's dining room. Under the Austrians in 1775 it was turned into a Rococo pergola, with allegories of Mantuan rivers and two stucco 'grottoes'. It overlooks the Giardino Pensile (Hanging Garden), constructed some 14m above ground level in 1579 for Duke Guglielmo. Its delightful Kaffeehaus was added in the 18th century.

26: Appartamento dell'Imperatrice. Named after Empress Marie Louise, Napoleon's second wife, this was created in 1778 by Paolo Pozzo and was used by Beatrice d'Este, wife of Ferdinand of Austria. The bedroom (26) dates from the renovations made in 1811. The Empire-style bed was brought here by Eugène de Beauharnais when he was Viceroy of Italy.

33–36: Appartamento degli Arazzi. Dating from 1783, this overlooks the Cortile d'Onore (formerly part of Duke Guglielmo's apartment). The four rooms are hung with nine superb Brussels tapestries designed after Raphael's *Acts of the Apostles* cartoons (now in the V&A, London). Woven c. 1510, these are the most important replica of the famous Vatican series, and in amazingly good condition. They were acquired by Cardinal Ercole Gonzaga in 1559 to decorate the church of Santa Barbara and under the Austrians were taken to Vienna to adorn the private suite of the emperor Franz Joseph. After WWI they were returned to Mantua. The **chapel (34)**, with a barrel vault, has false painted 'tapestries'. The last room, the **Sala degli Imperatori (36)**, with the remaining three Raphael tapestries, has Neoclassical decorations by Paolo Pozzo.

CASTELLO DI SAN GIORGIO (AND CAMERA DEGLI SPOSI)

Separate ticket and separate entrance; see p. 346 and plan on p. 348.

The Castello di San Giorgio, built for Francesco I in 1395–1406 (the exterior was formerly covered with frescoes), is a keep which constituted the main defence of the city from the north at the end of the bridge across the lakes. In the mid-15th century Ludovico II decided to come and live here and commissioned the Camera Picta (Camera degli Sposi) from Mantegna (who probably also painted a chapel for him which no longer exists). Luca Fancelli was appointed to add the portico to the courtyard. At the end of the 15th century Isabella d'Este, Francesco's II's wife, used some of the small rooms in the castle for her treasures. When Francesco III married Catherine of Austria in 1545, a suite of rooms was decorated for them and they gave the name ('*sposi*': the bridal couple) to Mantegna's painted room.

You are directed through the splendid Piazza Castello, with its double columns, across the moat into the castle with its 15th-century courtyard. Opposite the Scalone di Enea (a spiral ramp), the Scala dei Cavalli, leads up to the Camera degli Sposi.

Camera degli Sposi

The magnificent paintings by Mantegna (1465–74) were commissioned by Ludovico, the second Marquis of Mantua. The work was immediately recognised as a masterpiece and was of fundamental importance to later Renaissance artists. The room appears to have been used by Ludovico as a bedroom as well as an office and as a place for receiving visiting dignitaries.

On the north wall, above the fireplace, Ludovico and his wife, Barbara of Brandenburg, are shown seated, surrounded by their family, courtiers and messengers. Between the husband and wife is their son Gianfrancesco with his hands on the shoulders of his younger brother, Ludovico, and a sister, Paola, shown holding an apple. Rodolfo stands behind his mother, and to the right is his sister Barbara, with her nurse behind. The dwarf is particularly memorable since she is the only participant looking straight at us. Ludovico turns to receive a messenger (apparently bearing news which arrived in Mantua on 1st January 1462 about the Duke of Milan being taken ill). Beneath Ludovico's chair is his old dog Rubino, who died in 1467. On the right is a group of courtiers dressed in the Gonzaga livery.

On the west wall are three scenes presumed to represent the 1462 meeting between the Marquis, on his way to Milan, and his son Francesco, the first member of the Gonzaga family to be nominated Cardinal, travelling back from Milan. The first full figure in profile is the Marquis, dressed in grey with a sword at his side, talking to Francesco, in cardinal's robes; the children are also members of the Gonzaga family and are accompanied by a large woolly dog. The group to the right is thought to include the Holy Roman Emperor Frederick III (in profile) and, dressed in red in the background, Christian I of Denmark. On the left are servants in the Gonzaga livery with magnificent hounds and a splendid grey charger—a reminder that the Gonzaga were famous horse breeders and dog lovers. Above the door is a dedicatory inscription (now illegible), supported by charming putti with butterfly wings, signed and dated 1474, by Mantegna. The landscape in the background of all three scenes is particularly beautiful (and reminiscent of ancient Roman painted gardens) and includes Classical monuments (derived from buildings in Rome and Verona) and an imaginary city, and extraordinary rock formations. Hidden in the frieze on the pilaster to the right of the door is Mantegna's self-portrait.

The vaulted ceiling has a *trompe l'oeil* oculus in the centre, one of the first examples of aerial perspective in painting. The curious, inventive scene shows a circular stone balustrade on which winged putti are playing; and peering over the top of it are five court ladies, a peacock and more putti, and balanced on the edge is a plant in a tub. The illusionistic vault, with a background of painted mosaic, is divided by *trompe l'oeil* ribs into eight sections with white and gold medallions in fictive relief containing the portraits of the first eight Roman emperors and, below (damaged) mythological scenes.

The last two walls were decorated with painted gold damask (now very damaged), and the lower part of the walls has painted marble intarsia.

The adjoining suite of three rooms was decorated in 1549 for Francesco III. The **Camera dei Soli** is painted in pretty pastel shades with vine tendrils against a white ground. The fireplace by Luca Fancelli survives from the 15th century. Here is a temporary arrangement of the Romano Freddi collection of paintings, sculpture and ceramics (on long-term loan to the palace). Put together from the 1970s onwards, it includes a pair of bronze gridirons by Niccolò Roccatagliata and a curious reliquary bust in polychrome majolica. The **Camera di Mezzo** has another painted vault, and in the **Sala delle Cappe**, with a barrel vault, are very fine grotesques and stucco and shell decoration.

The upper floor has prisons (*sometimes open for special tours*), and a Risorgimento Museum is planned here.

AREAS OF THE PALACE TEMPORARILY CLOSED

Corte Nuova: The splendid **Cortile della Cavallerizza**, where the columns are teased into outlandish corkscrew forms, was designed by Giulio Romano with the help of Giovanni Battista Bertani. Formerly known as the Cortile della Mostra, it was renamed in the early 18th century, when it was used as a riding school. On one of the long sides is the **Galleria della Mostra (F)**, begun by Bertani in the 1570s for the display of the most important part of the ducal collection. The short end, the **Galleria dei Marmi (G)** (or dei Mesi), was built as a loggia by Giulio Romano and was enlarged for Duke Guglielmo. At the other end of the courtyard is the **Appartamento della Rustica (H)**, also laid out by Giulio Romano in 1539 for Federico II. A Museum of Alchemy is to be opened here.

The Corte Nuova also includes the **Sala dei Marchesi (J)**, with a painted wood ceiling and fine stucco work. Beyond is the **Loggia del Tasso (K)**, where the Gonzaga are said to have received Torquato Tasso on his flight from Ferrara. In July 1586 Vincenzo Gonzaga negotiated Tasso's release from hospital in Ferrara, where he had been confined since 1579 for mental disorders. At the Mantuan court he enjoyed a brief moment of creative fervour, completing his tragedy *Galealto*, retitled *Re Torrismondo* (1587), but then relapsed into his state of inquietude and fled from Mantua and took to wandering in the area between Naples and Rome.

The **Sala dei Duchi (L)** is the pendant to the Sala dei Marchesi, again glorifying the achievements of Mantua's rulers, in this case Federico II. Four canvases bruiting his exploits, by Tintoretto and his *bottega*, which formerly hung here, ended up in Munich.

Corte Vecchia: On the ground floor is the **Appartamento di Isabella d'Este**, which the marchioness had laid out for herself after the death of her husband, Francesco II. For her Studiolo she commissioned paintings from Mantegna, Perugino, Lorenzo Costa (all now in the Louvre), and two paintings by Correggio were added later to complete the series. Leading off it is her Grotta, which contains exquisite intarsia cupboard doors by the Della Mola brothers. Both rooms have fine gilded wood ceilings. The door frame leading from the Grotta back to the Studiolo is by Gian Cristoforo Romano (c. 1505). There is also a secret garden here.

CLAUDIO MONTEVERDI

When Monteverdi, who was born in Cremona in 1567, arrived in Mantua at the age of 23, Vincenzo I Gonzaga took him on at court to play the viola and as a singer. Monteverdi accompanied Vincenzo to Hungary in 1595 and to Flanders in 1599. In the same year he married the singer Claudia Cattaneo, who also performed for Vincenzo, and they had three children. Her tragic early death in 1607 prompted Monteverdi's famous *Lamento d'Arianna*. From 1601 to 1612 he was the Duke's *maestro e de la Camera e de la Chiesa sopra la musica*. The success of his *Orfeo* here in 1607 was the first landmark in the history of opera. His *Vespers*, composed in 1610, are thought to have been written for the church of Santa Barbara, and it is known that they were sung in the church of Sant'Andrea in 1611. During his two decades in Mantua he published various books of his famous madrigals. The year after Vincenzo's death in 1612, Monteverdi left for Venice where he was immediately appointed Maestro di Cappella at San Marco, a position he held until his death in 1643 (he was buried in the Frari). Today the State Archive in Mantua preserves nearly all his letters.

Giardino dei Semplici: This **medicinal herb garden** was laid out in the early 17th century for Duke Vincenzo I and is to be restored. It is overlooked by the **Appartamento delle Metamorfosi**, named after the scenes from Ovid's *Metamorphoses* (many now lost) which adorn it. Its other name, Galleria del Passerino, comes from Rinaldo Bonacolsi, 'il Passerino' (the Sparrow), who was killed by the Gonzaga in the battle depicted in Room 1, when they seized control of Mantua in 1328. His mummified body, mounted on a stuffed hippo, was kept displayed here until the early 18th century, when presumably the Austrians, victors in their turn, disposed of the grisly keepsake.

Domus Nova: In the Domus Nova, a remarkable work built by Luca Fancelli for Federico I, are the **Appartamento di Eleonora de' Medici**, wife of Vincenzo I, designed by Viani. On a mezzanine floor, the so-called **Appartamento dei Nani** (so named when it was thought to have been built for the court dwarves), is in fact a miniature reproduction of the

Scala Santa in Rome made by Viani for Ferdinando Gonzaga c. 1620, and used for religious functions, and probably to house precious relics. There are plans to use it as a childrens' museum.

Basilica of Santa Barbara: This huge palace chapel, built in 1572 in the very centre of the ducal complex, is today a parish church (*sometimes open at weekends*). It is a beautiful building, the most important work of the local architect Giovanni Battista Bertani. In 2017 the passageway or 'Passetto', used by the Gonzaga to attend services unobserved, was reopened so that visitors can see it from above.

The long Corridoio di Santa Barbara links the Corte Vecchia with Corte Nuova and the Castello di San Giorgio.

THE *PIAZZE* AND MUSEO ARCHEOLOGICO

There is a separate entrance on Piazza Sordello into a wing of Palazzo del Capitano which houses the **LaGalleria contemporary art exhibition space**. You can also explore some of the courtyards (*no ticket required*), including the huge **Piazza Lega Lombarda** (formerly called the Giardino del Pallone) and (when open) the **Giardino dei Semplici**, and from Piazza Paccagnini down through an archway into **Piazza Santa Barbara**, in front of the basilica and out into the beautiful **Piazza Castello**. It is also worth walking out to the lakefront to see the exterior of the palace from that side. Overlooking Piazza Castello is the **Museo Archeologico** (*open April–Oct Tues, Thur and Sat 2–7, Wed, Fri and Sun 8.30–1.30; other periods Tues–Sun 8.30–1.30; polomuseale.lombardia.it*), arranged in a 19th-century market building on the site of a palace theatre built by the Gonzaga. Since 2018 the museum has been under the direction of Palazzo Ducale and is being rearranged. Prehistoric finds from the territory include the so-called 'lovers of Valdaro'—their skeletons found together, with arms entwined—and there is a good collection from the Roman period.

PIAZZA SORDELLO

Piazza Sordello (*map 4*) was named in 1866 after Sordello da Goito, an early 13th-century minstrel, poet and troubadour, still famous in Dante's time since he appears in the *Divine Comedy* (*Purgatorio VI:74*). On the side of Piazza Sordello opposite Palazzo Ducale are two battlemented brick **Bonacolsi palaces**, once belonging to the family who ruled Mantua before the Gonzaga. Above the left-hand palace rises the **Torre della Gabbia**, from which protrudes an iron cage (or *gabbia*; seen from Via Cavour) where condemned prisoners were exposed. The second, Palazzo Castiglioni, dates from the 13th century. You can see its lovely garden beyond the entranceway. The Rococo **Palazzo Bianchi**, with statues on the roof and two giant caryatids flanking its portal, is now the Bishop's Palace.

At the lower end of the piazza, ingeniously protected behind a low pink wall, are the excavations of a Roman domus dating from the early 3rd century AD.

THE DUOMO

At the far end of Piazza Sordello is Mantua's duomo (*map 4; open 7–12 & 3–7*), with an unsuccessful façade of 1756, built to replace the Gothic front which was lost when the building burned down in 1545. Part of the striking brick south side survives from the earlier building, as well as the mighty rectangular Romanesque campanile which towers above the east end.

The architecture of the interior, designed by Giulio Romano after 1545 for Cardinal Ercole Gonzaga, is particularly remarkable. It is a superb imitation of an early Christian basilica, with a double row of classical columns beneath a carved architrave, and richly ornamented barrel vaults in the inner aisles. The walls are covered with exquisite stucco decoration, and the red and white marble pavement beneath the gilded coffered ceiling add to its dignity. The nave is unusually light since it has large windows between the pilasters and carved niches.

South aisle: The first altarpiece dates from the 17th century and shows St Eligius replacing a horse's shoe: the saint, known locally as St Alò, is a favourite in Mantua, where horses have always been of importance. The huge 6th-century Christian sarcophagus, complete with its lid, has damaged carvings of the Nativity and the Apostles. The second altar has a 14th-century marble altarpiece.

The **Baptistery** (*coin-operated light*), entered through an elegant portal, has a beautifully proportioned red marble font sitting on a black marble pedestal and decorated with reliefs. The remains of 14th- and 15th-century frescoes here are very damaged.

Transepts, cupola and presbytery: There is another coin-operated light for these areas of the duomo. The **transepts** are covered with frescoes commissioned from Ippolito Andreasi and other little-known painters by the Venerable Annibale (Francesco) Gonzaga, whose tomb is in the presbytery. In the south transept, the 17th-century altarpieces in handsome marble frames are by Antonio Maria Viani and the Bolognese painter Domenico Canuti (*Guardian Angel*). The north transept is the burial place of the Blessed Osanna Andreasi: she is displayed in an elaborate silver urn. She was a mystic and councillor to Isabella d'Este, who was present at her death in 1505 and was instrumental in ensuring her beatification less than a decade later. Today her house in Via Frattini (*map 6*), owned by the Dominicans and interesting for its 15th- and 16th-century ceilings, can be visited.

The **dome and apse** were frescoed in the first years of the 17th century (it is thought that Viani was responsible for the *Apotheosis of the Redemption*, 1605). Beneath the high altar Anselm II, Bishop of Lucca, is buried. He was born in Mantua and died here in 1086 and is Mantua's patron saint (feast day 18th March). A learned churchman, he was interested in canon law and gave his support to Pope St Gregory and Matilda of Canossa (*see p. 388*).

There are five 18th-century paintings in the **presbytery**, but only the two late 16th-century paintings by Girolamo Mazzola Bedoli (*Vision of the*

Apocalypse, and *Prayer in the Garden*), closest to the crossing, can be seen.

Cappella del Santissimo Sacramento: From the left transept, steps lead up to this lovely little octagonal domed chapel, possibly on a design by Giulio Romano. The decorations, from various periods, include delicately sculpted pilasters in the style of the great Venetian masters Pietro and Tullio Lombardo, and (later) 16th-century paintings by Brusasorci (*St Margaret*) and Paolo Farinati (*St Martin*), and late 18th-century stucco tondi. Above the 18th-century altar, the *Calling of St Peter and St Andrew* is a copy by Felice Campi of an original painted by Fermo Ghisoni (which in turn was a copy of a work by his master Giulio Romano). Ghisoni's painting was stolen by the French in the 19th century.

North aisle: The fifth chapel, with a little dome, has a painting of *St Jerome* by Felice Campi. A corridor leads through an atrium where there is a funerary monument to Antonio Cavriani, who as Cardinal Ercole Gonzaga's doctor accompanied him to the Council of Trent. He is recorded here in an expressive bust. Beyond, up steps, is the **Santuario dell'Incoronata**, which is in fact a separate church built by Luca Fancelli in the style of Alberti. Here is a fresco of the *Madonna and Child and St Leonard* dated 1482 and, opposite, the burial place of the Blessed Giovanni Bono, born in Mantua in 1168. To the left, with a bust but no inscription, is the tomb of Battista Spagnoli (1448–1516), known as 'il Mantovano', a poet whom Erasmus called 'a Christian Virgil', and the 'good old Mantuan' of Shakespeare's *Love's Labour Lost*. Above the main altar here is a fresco of the *Madonna and Child* in a large wood ancona erected in 1840. Beneath the fresco of the *Death of the Virgin* (and on the left of a locked door), don't miss the tombstone with Gothic lettering of Bonifacio, Matilda of Canossa's father. Opposite, you can look through a glass door into the early 14th-century Gothic **sacristy** (*coin-operated light*), beautifully decorated in 1482 by a follower of Mantegna.

PIAZZA BROLETTO & PIAZZA DELLE ERBE

An archway leads out of Piazza Sordello into the beautiful old historic centre of Mantua, with its cobbled *piazze* and arcaded streets superimposed on the old Roman town. Piazza del Broletto (*map 4*) is dominated by the building of the old municipal assembly, the **Palazzo del Podestà** (1227), with its tall corner tower. On its façade is a quaint figure of Virgil sculpted in the 13th century, showing the poet at a rostrum wearing his doctor's hat. The great poet was born near Mantua and has always been particularly revered here. The *palazzo* was damaged by earthquake in 2012 and restoration was still in progress at the time of writing. One of the town's few fountains stands here, with the tail fins of three dolphins elegantly entwined. It is well worth visiting the restaurant beneath an archway (Masseria), which occupies a Gonzaga office, since here you can see a very interesting early 14th-century **fresco of the city**, and giant marigolds (the arms of Gianfrancesco, the first Marquis) frescoed on the ceiling. On the opposite side of the piazza is **Palazzo Andreasi**, built in the early 16th century with a handsome row of arcades on its ground floor.

The **Arco dell'Arengario**, with its loggia above two pretty Gothic windows, survives from the 13th century and leads into the adjoining **Piazza delle Erbe**, a square with arcades down the two long sides and a delightful row of houses closing the far end. Here is **Palazzo della Ragione**, dating partly from the early 13th century but with 14th–15th-century additions. It has swallow-tail crenellations. The splendid **clock-tower** was erected in 1473 by Luca Fancelli (possibly on a design by Leon Battista Alberti) for Marquis Ludovico Gonzaga. The extraordinary astrological clock was supplied by the clock-maker Bartolomeo Manfredi and is still in perfect working order. Beneath it is an early 17th-century statue of the Madonna (the balcony beneath dates from the following century). There is a little drinking fountain beside the entrance.

The **Rotonda di San Lorenzo** is a small round church probably founded in the 11th century (possibly by Matilda of Canossa) and documented from 1151. Today its beautiful simple Romanesque exterior is a remarkable sight, memorable also because it is now well below ground level. Extraordinarily enough it had all but disappeared by the late 16th century, incorporated in later buildings, but it was isolated in 1908, carefully restored and subsequently saved from the threat of demolition. It now looks as if it has always stood here and you can visit the venerable domed interior (*open 10–1 & 3–6; Sat–Sun 10–6*), which has two orders of columns and a matroneum.

The medley of houses at this end of the piazza is particularly pretty, and at the end of the row is the well-preserved **Casa del Mercante**, built in 1455 with Gothic blind arcades and handsome windows and four columns at pavement level. There is a miscellany of simple houses on the last side of the piazza, some with balconies and some with little terraces, and above them the huge dome of Sant'Andrea is well seen.

THE BASILICA OF SANT'ANDREA

Piazza Mantegna. Map 4. Open 7–12 & 3–7.

Ludovico II Gonzaga commissioned this Renaissance building from Leon Battista Alberti in 1470, as a fit setting to display the relic of the Holy Blood. Although it was built by Luca Fancelli between 1472 and 1494 (after Alberti's death), then enlarged in 1530 under Giulio Romano, and has a dome added by Filippo Juvarra in 1732, it still remains Alberti's most complete architectural work and is thus of the greatest interest.

The remarkable façade, with giant pilasters, is entirely Classical in inspiration. At the top is a huge arched vault, a very unusual addition much discussed by architectural historians. The painting and gilding perhaps detract from the majesty of the architecture, which is totally devoid of figurative sculpture except for the nine little seraphim beneath the pediment, all with different expressions. The pilasters have

BASILICA OF SANT'ANDREA

unusual carved decorations and basket-work motifs and at the bottom is a horizontal frieze of acorns and acanthus leaves.

Under the barrel-vaulted porch, a beautiful marble frieze with animals and birds surrounds the west door. The brick campanile of 1413 is a survival from the 11th-century monastery on this site.

The huge wide interior, on a longitudinal plan, has a spacious barrel-vaulted nave without columns or aisles. The rectangular side chapels, also with barrel vaults, are preceded by giant paired pilasters raised on pedestals. Between them, behind grilles, are small, lower domed chapels. The transepts, with the same proportions, are also rectangular. The feeling of spaciousness and light is unforgettable despite the fact that every wall surface is covered with painted decoration and *trompe-l'oeil* work carried out under the direction of Paolo Pozzo in 1780 (when all the pilasters were also painted with monochrome candelabra against a yellow ground).

The decoration of the nave chapels survives from the 16th century, partly the work of pupils of Giulio Romano.

South side: Begin your visit here. You can appreciate Alberti's architecture in the first little chapel (the baptistery), whose walls are bare. The third chapel (of St Sebastian) is frescoed by Rinaldo Mantovano (1534). The sixth chapel (of St Longinus) has a fine altarpiece, a 16th-century copy of the original by

Giulio Romano (now in the Louvre), while the frescoes, designed by Romano, were also executed by Rinaldo Mantovano. The one on the left shows the discovery of the Holy Blood.

Dome and crossing: The frescoes in the dome and apse are late 18th-century. On the left of the high altar is a kneeling statue in marble of the hunch-backed Duke Guglielmo Gonzaga at prayer (1572: he was known to have been extremely devout). Beneath the dome is an octagonal balustrade marking the centre of the crypt, where the precious **reliquary of the Holy Blood** is kept (it is carried in solemn procession, the *Sacri Vasi*, on Good Friday). The crypt is opened on request.

In the north transept is a door that leads out to a piazza, from where you can see the exterior of the church and one walk of the Gothic cloister of the monastery that stood on this site. The transept chapel contains 16th- and 17th-century funerary monuments, including that of Pietro Strozzi, an ingenious work of 1529 with four caryatids, designed by Giulio Romano.

LEON BATTISTA ALBERTI

Leon Battista Alberti (1402–72) is one of the most important figures of the Italian Renaissance, not only for the buildings he designed as architect but also for his treatises: *De Pictura*, *De Statua* and *De Re Aedificatoria*. In these he expounded new codes of aesthetics and ethics which greatly influenced the work produced by the humanist painters, sculptors and architects of his day. He examined the idea of beauty based on theories of *misura*, or proportion, and explored the mathematical intricacies of linear perspective. His architectural works often have elements of ancient Roman buildings, such as barrel vaults, entablatures and polychrome marbles.

When he arrived in Mantua in 1459, he had already designed the Palazzo Rucellai in Florence and had begun to transform the church of San Francesco in Rimini into the Tempio Malatestiano, a monument to Sigismondo Malatesta, so that his reputation was well established. It was Ludovico II who commissioned him to design the huge church of Sant'Andrea in the centre of Mantua, which remains his most important completed architectural work. The centrally planned church of San Sebastiano, also by Alberti (*map 7*), was never finished. It is known that Ludovico and Alberti became friends (numerous letters survive) and the architect's passionate interest in ancient Rome was shared by Mantegna, who was at work for the Gonzaga in the same period.

North side: The sixth chapel has a strikingly simple painting of the Crucifix by Fermo Ghisoni. The fourth chapel has a wood ancona dating from 1616 by Antonio Maria Viani and two huge paintings by Lorenzo Costa the Younger. In the second chapel there is a beautiful altarpiece of 1525 by the more famous Lorenzo Costa.

The first little chapel, the Cappella del Mantegna (*kept locked but there is a coin-operated light*), is the **burial place of Mantegna**, chosen by the artist in 1504. It contains his tomb with his bust in bronze, possibly his self-portrait, in a roundel of porphyry and Istrian stone. The charming panel of the *Holy Family and the Family of St John the*

Baptist is almost certainly by Mantegna. Above is his coat of arms. The terracotta decoration and frescoes on the walls and dome, including the symbols of the Evangelists, were designed by Mantegna and probably executed by his son Francesco. The painting of the *Baptism of Christ*, probably also to a design by Mantegna, is also the work of Francesco.

PALAZZO TE

Map 7. Open Mon 1–6, Tues–Sun 9–6. Combined ticket with Museo della Città in Palazzo San Sebastiano. T: 0376 323266, palazzote.it and museicivici.mn.it. There is a café and bookshop at the garden exit.

Palazzo Te, the summer villa of the Gonzaga dukes, stands on the southern outskirts of the town in an area that was once countryside, originally surrounded by water. It is entered by an isolated old gate with two eagles on the gate posts. One of the most important secular buildings in Italy, it was built for Federico II Gonzaga by Giulio Romano, on the site of the Gonzaga stables. Begun in 1525, the bold rustication and giant orders of pilasters give the façades a monumental appearance, although it is in fact built of brick and stucco since no building stone was available locally. Spaciously laid out around a courtyard with symmetrical loggias, it is Giulio Romano's most famous work, inspired by the great villas of Rome, and a masterpiece of Mannerist architecture. The rooms of the palace, bare of furniture, are of great interest for their extraordinary painted and stuccoed decoration, in particular on the ceilings. They were all designed by Giulio Romano, although he was helped in their execution from 1526 to 1535 by some of his many pupils, including Francesco Primaticcio and Rinaldo Mantovano. In theme the decoration is almost entirely secular, with its references to the Classical world: it was in this palace that Federico held his splendid entertainments and in 1530, when Emperor Charles V granted him the Dukedom of Mantua, Federico received his powerful imperial benefactor here. Its unusual name remains a mystery but is thought to have been derived from the name of the locality.

TOUR OF THE PALACE

The first room past the ticket office contains a model of the building and a portrait of Giulio Romano by Titian, his contemporary: Titian first came into contact with the architect during his frequent visits to the city. The two artists employed to collaborate on the decoration of Palazzo Ducale at the time this portrait was painted, around 1536, just after Palazzo Te had been completed inside and out. Titian's portrait was only rediscovered in the mid-20th century, when it was acquired by the province of Mantua and the Lombard Region. Historians have found the drawing for a centrally-planned building which the architect holds in his hand difficult to identify, so it may have been for a project never executed.

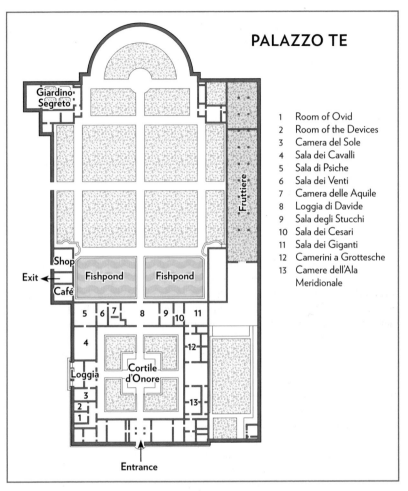

PALAZZO TE

1 Room of Ovid
2 Room of the Devices
3 Camera del Sole
4 Sala dei Cavalli
5 Sala di Psiche
6 Sala dei Venti
7 Camera delle Aquile
8 Loggia di Davide
9 Sala degli Stucchi
10 Sala dei Cesari
11 Sala dei Giganti
12 Camerini a Grottesche
13 Camere dell'Ala
   Meridionale

From here you pass through the small **Room of Ovid (1)** and **Room of the Devices (2)** (thought to have been part of the private apartment of Federico's mistress, Isabella Boschetti), with painted friezes, landscapes, and red marble fireplaces, to the **Camera del Sole (3)** with its lovely ceiling painting traditionally attributed to Francesco Primaticcio, Giulio Romano's most famous pupil: the chariot of the Moon with Diana is seen just arriving to drive away that of the Sun with Apollo. Seen from below, no part of either the horses' or Apollo's anatomy is left to the imagination. This ceiling, which also has lozenges against a blue ground with white stucco reliefs inspired by Classical coins and gems, is just the first of many other splendidly decorated rooms.

From here you can go out to the loggia on the wide **Cortile d'Onore** to see the way Giulio Romano has played with the rules of Classical architecture, designing sections of the entablature to look as though they were slipping out of place and pediment cornices that don't quite meet. Next is the **Sala dei Cavalli (4)** with frescoes of (named) horses with their bridles on, as if they had just been led out of the Gonzaga stables to pose for Rinaldo Mantovano to paint their portraits (they must have been the favourite steeds out of some 650 known to have been kept by the marquises). Above the horses are scenes of the Labours of Hercules in red monochrome, and around the top of the walls a charming frieze of putti. The Gonzaga emblems of the green lizard and Mount Olympus feature in the ceiling.

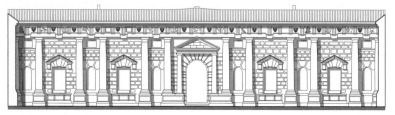

PALAZZO TE: CORTILE D'ONORE

The **Sala di Psiche (5)** has some of the most extraordinary frescoes in the palace. All by Giulio Romano's own hand, they illustrate the story of Psyche as told by Apuleius, and reflect Federico's own particular tastes. A frieze bears the legend *'Honesto ocio post labores ad reparandam virt quieti construi mandavit Federicus Gonzaga II'*. Here, in other words, the duke planned to come to regain his strength in quietude after his labours. Quietude is not precisely what the frescoes promise: Zeus lustily seducing Olympias, a river god with water gushing from between his thighs, putti sucking greedily from the teats of goats all seem to celebrate sybaritic excess. The giant Polyphemus appears above the fireplace. Apuleius's text can be read on a touch screen.

The next room, the **Sala dei Venti (6)** (the heads of the various winds appear in the tondi of the vault), was Federico's study. It has a ceiling with signs of the Zodiac and tondi illustrating horoscopes, together with a fine stucco frieze and fireplace. The **Camera delle Aquile (7)**, the Duke's bedroom, has a fresco of the *Fall of Phaëthon* in the centre and stuccoes including four eagles.

The lovely **Loggia di Davide (8)**, with biblical frescoes, opens onto a fishpond under a bridge with the gardens beyond. The first room in the further wing of the palace, the **Sala degli Stucchi (9)**, was the last work executed by Primaticcio before his departure for France (where he was to produce his finest decorations). The two Classical friezes, in imitation of a Roman triumphal column, are thought to have been executed in honour of Charles V's visit. The **Sala dei Cesari (10)** has an exceptionally successful *trompe l'oeil* frieze of putti and Roman historical scenes in the vault.

The famous **Sala dei Giganti (11)**, in which painting and architecture are united in a theatrical *trompe l'oeil*, is the work of Rinaldo Mantovano and others, but still to designs by Giulio Romano. It represents the Fall of the Giants, crushed by the thunderbolts of Jupiter hurled from Mount Olympus (probably not coincidentally making use of this

MANTUA, PALAZZO TE
Detail of the decoration in the Sala di Psiche, by Giulio Romano.
The atmosphere of debauched revelry reflects the tastes of Duke Federico II.

favourite Gonzaga emblem). The pavement was originally concave and was made up of large stones in imitation of a river bed. The room has strange acoustic properties, and its relatively large size is made to feel smaller and even oppressive by the vast scale of the turmoil depicted on the walls, a masterpiece of illusionism.

Three little rooms follow, the **Camerini a Grottesche (12)**, with elegant grotesques in the vault. The **Camere dell'Ala Meridionale (13)**, with coffered ceilings and friezes, have Neoclassical stuccoes on the lower part of the walls.

UPPER FLOOR

The upper floor of the palace contains collections from the Museo Civico, some of them well arranged in the attic, where the brick vaulting of the chambers below is very well seen. The contents include paintings by Federico Zandomeneghi (d. 1917) and Armando Spadini (d. 1925); an Egyptian collection left to the city in 1840 by Giuseppe Acerbi from Mantua (he lived in Egypt from 1826–34); and the Gonzaga collection of weights and measures. The numismatic collection has portrait medals of the Gonzaga, including Gianfrancesco and Ludovico II (both by Pisanello), Elisabetta, Duchess of Urbino (a speaker in Castiglione's *Courtier*), Federico II and Isabella d'Este.

THE GARDEN

Beyond the fishponds is the garden, closed at the end by an exedra added c. 1651. Looking back you can see the magnificent façade of the palace which was designed as its main entrance. The huge **Fruttiere** is used as an exhibition space. In one corner is the delightful little **Giardino Segreto**, a 'secret' garden entered through a very pretty octagonal vestibule decorated with grotesques. The portico, with its barrel vault, has pebble mosaics and a fresco of men and animals at rest, as well as a tiny loggia. Giulio Romano also provided this little retreat for his patron Federico II in 1531. The garden itself has plaster niches with illustrations of Aesop's Fables in stucco. Don't miss the relief in the central niche above the loggia which has a portrait of one of the Duke's favourite dogs sitting on a sarcophagus (which was used as the dog's tomb). The grotto was added in the 1590s by Vincenzo I, complete with sponge stone and shells.

GIULIO ROMANO

The architect and painter Giulio Romano (?1499–1546) is mentioned by Shakespeare in *The Winter's Tale*: '…that rare Italian master, Julio Romano, who, had he himself eternity and could put breath into his work, would beguile Nature of her custom, so perfectly he is her ape'. He was a distinguished Renaissance painter and architect and one of the creators of Mannerism. Born Giulio di Pietro di Filippo de' Gianuzzi, his birth date is a matter of some dispute (1492/99), but his birthplace was definitely Rome. The chief assistant and principal heir of Raphael, he completed several of his master's unfinished works, notably the *Transfiguration* and the frescoes in the Vatican. In his own work he developed a highly personal, anti-Classical style of painting. In 1524, at the invitation of the Gonzaga, Giulio left Rome for Mantua, where he remained until his death, completely dominating the artistic affairs of the duchy. The most important of all his works is the Palazzo Te, built and decorated entirely by him and his pupils. It had an important influence on later Italian architecture.

MUSEO DELLA CITTÀ & SAN SEBASTIANO

Map 7. Open Tues–Sun 9–6, Mon 1–6. Combined ticket with Palazzo Te. T: 0376 367087, museodellacitta.mn.it. Every half-hour visitors are taken to see the nearby church of San Sebastiano, which is otherwise kept locked.

The old, rather forbidding-looking Palazzo di San Sebastiano was built by Francesco II Gonzaga in 1506–8, and it became his favourite residence. Some of its best ceilings were removed in the early 17th century to decorate Palazzo Ducale, where they can still be seen (*see p. 352*). The building fell into disrepair after the Gonzaga era and was subsequently used as an isolation hospital and then a school. The present restoration dates from 2005. It now houses the Museo della Città.

On the ground floor you can see the loggia (now with 18th-century statues) and some rooms which still have the Gonzaga emblems on the ceilings, but the most interesting exhibits are on the upper floor. These include a remarkable statue of *Virgil Enthroned*, in Verona marble with traces of polychrome made in the early 13th century for the roof terrace of Palazzo della Ragione; five life-size terracotta statues from a palace façade; and three colossal early 16th-century terracotta busts (very well preserved) of Virgil, Francesco II Gonzaga and the Blessed Battista Spagnoli (a Carmelite Humanist, poet and philosopher). A room with an umbrella vault has some marble sculpture from various Gonzaga residences including two ancient Roman sphinxes, and a venerable marble seat known as 'Virgil's throne'. In another room with a pretty vault are Classical sculptures, both Roman and 16th century, and a bronze candelabrum by L'Antico. The carved plutei are the originals from the façade of the church of San Sebastiano (*see below*). There is an interesting tempera painting of Rome dated sometime after 1538, and a bust of Pope Julius II in terracotta, probably by a collaborator of Tullio Lombardo. Other terracottas include a relief of St Francis and St Bernardino (15th century), a half figure of Spagnoli (painted black), and a remarkable terracotta bust of Francesco II Gonzaga in armour by Gian Cristoforo Romano, one of the best-known portraits of this marquis.

Mantegna's famous painted frieze of the *Triumphs of Caesar* (now in Hampton Court palace), designed for the Gonzaga, was documented in this palace in 1507. Here it is recorded in good copies of the scenes executed in the 17th century and found by chance in a private residence in the town in 1926: they were detached and mounted on canvas ten years later.

On the top floor is a collection of paintings and frescoes from the 15th and 16th centuries. A *Madonna and Child* attributed to Antonio da Pavia is interesting as it is just one of very few paintings by this follower of Mantegna who is known to have been at work in Mantua around 1528. The *Way to Calvary* is by Francesco Bonsignori, and dated c. 1510.

SAN SEBASTIANO

The church of San Sebastiano (*map 7; for admission, see above*) was commissioned from the famous Renaissance architect Leon Battista Alberti in 1460. It was intended as a mausoleum for the Gonzaga but was left unfinished. After it was deconsecrated in 1848 it was used as a munitions store and ended up as a memorial to the fallen in the two World Wars. The façade, with its double entrances, has three carved plutei (copies of the originals now in the Palazzo di San Sebastiano), carved on both sides in stone from Vicenza and attributed to Luca Fancelli. The two flights of steps at each side, which provide access to the beautiful raised vestibule, were modified in 1925. The bare brick interior preserves its perfect proportions on a Greek cross plan, but has lost all its atmosphere. It now provides space for a wood model of how the finished church might have looked, as well as models of Alberti's other famous buildings. The crypt at ground level also survives, adapted as a War Memorial.

CASA DEL MANTEGNA

The Casa del Mantegna (*map 5; open Tues–Sun 10–7.30; T: 0376 360506, www.casadelmantegna.it*), restored in 1940, now houses a gallery for modern art exhibitions, the Centro d'Arte Moderna e Contemporanea. Mantegna, as the most important artist at the Gonzaga court, was given this plot of land by Marquis Ludovico and here, in 1466–74, he built a house-museum for himself. Here he arranged his collection of ancient art and Lorenzo the Magnificent travelled from Florence in 1483 to visit it. Mantegna lived in the house until 1502, when he donated it to Francesco II Gonzaga. Today its interest lies solely in the remarkable circular pebbled **courtyard** with four brick and terracotta doorways and a surviving legend over one of them: '*Ab Olympo*'— an illusion, perhaps, to Mantegna's Gonzaga benefactors, who used Mt Olympus as one of their emblems.

MANTEGNA

By the time Mantegna (1431–1506) arrived in Mantua from Padua in 1460, he was already famous. In fact the Gonzaga had been trying for some years to entice him to their town, and once here he took up residence and remained for the rest of his life. His most famous work, the Camera Picta (Camera degli Sposi) in the Castello di San Giorgio remains the greatest attraction to visitors to Mantua today. Unfortunately some of the other works he carried out for the Gonzaga, including a chapel he painted apparently in the same Castello di San Giorgio, and the work he did at their country residence at Marmirolo, have not survived. The series of nine panels showing the Triumphs of Caesar painted for the Gonzaga and considered one of the finest achievements in Italian Renaissance art, are now in Hampton Court in the UK. It is known that copies of them were produced by other artists even in his own lifetime (Mantua has a series painted in the 17th century; *see p. 355*). The two paintings he did for Isabella d'Este's *studiolo* in the Palazzo Ducale are now in the Louvre.

Mantegna was deeply impressed by the art of ancient Rome and Classical elements appear in almost all his works (he lived in Rome between 1488 and 1490, when he was at work for Pope Innocent III). Mantegna married Nicolosia, daughter of Jacopo Bellini (and sister of the famous painters Gentile and Giovanni) so was clearly influenced by the Venetian school. In Mantua not only was he given the land on which to build himself a house-museum but the Gonzaga also allowed him to possess a chapel in Sant'Andrea, which he decorated as his own burial place (*see p. 365*).

ON & AROUND PIAZZA MARTIRI DI BELFIORE

The busy **Piazza Martiri di Belfiore** is named after the so-called 'Martyrs of Belfiore', a group of patriots including natives of Mantua who supported Mazzini in the Italian Risorgimento against the Habsburgs, and who were hanged in 1852–3 at Belfiore, a few kilometres west of the centre. The piazza is dominated by a huge public building built during the Fascist regime: the other monumental buildings here date from earlier in the 20th century and include the Post Office and a bank building. (Another building from the same period which rivals these for its sheer eccentricity, but in another part of town, is the Camera di Commercio on the corner of Via Calvi and Via Spagnoli (*map*

6) with its plethora of columns and capitals of all shape and sizes. It is the work of the local architect Aldo Andreani and dates from 1913.)

Just off the square beside a little park (site of a Saturday-morning produce market), a bridge crosses the canal which links the two lakes on either side of the old town. It is called simply the **Rio** and here you can see the rusticated portico on the waterfront of the old **fish market**, built by Giulio Romano in 1546. The canal, roughly a kilometre long, was dug in 1190 and served as a defence at the southern limit of the old city and later mills grew up along its banks. One of the best places to see it (since it has been partly covered over) is from the bridge (*map 3*), restored in 1496, close to the church of San Francesco, where the houses which line the waterfront are reminiscent of Venice.

VIA MAZZINI AND THE CASA DI GIULIO ROMANO

The peaceful, residential, cobbled **Via Mazzini** (*map 5*), with some fine palaces with courtyards and gardens, leads south and on the corner of Via Giulio Romano is the **Museo Tazio Nuvolari** (*open Tues–Fri 3–6, Sat–Sun 11–6*), dedicated to the Mantua-born motor-racing champion. Nuvolari (1892–1953) was twice winner of the Mille Miglia car race (*see p. 313*).

At no. 18 Via Poma (the continuation of Via Giulio Romano to the west), you can see the very interesting façade of the **Casa di Giulio Romano**. The great architect and painter purchased the property in 1538 when it was on the outskirts of the town, and transformed it in the 1540s. Vasari was his guest here in 1541. Although the house was enlarged in the 19th century, its splendid façade survives. Today it is privately owned, so sadly not open to the public. Opposite it to the left is the **Palazzo della Giustizia**, formerly Guerrieri, with bizarre monster caryatids attributed to Viani.

MUSEO DIOCESANO FRANCESCO GONZAGA

The huge **Piazza Virgiliana** (*map 4*), fronting Lago di Mezzo and with lovely trees, was laid out in the Napoleonic period. The grandiose **monument to Virgil**, erected in 1927 by Luca Beltrami, has marble allegories of heroic and pastoral poetry.

MUSEO DIOCESANO

The Museo Diocesano (*Piazza Virgiliana 55; open Wed–Sun 9.30–12 & 3–5.30; T: 0376 320602, museodiocesanomantova.it*), which contains some fine treasures, is housed in the 15th-century monastery of Sant'Agnese, where Emperor Charles V stayed on his two visits to the city in the 16th century. It was suppressed in the 18th century and the building was given its Neoclassical façade by Paolo Pozzo in 1795. The museum is named after Francesco Gonzaga, Bishop of Mantua from 1593 to his death in 1620, who acquired many of the beautiful works of art now preserved here.

The entrance is through the cloister and the works are arranged in its four upper walks in an excellent chronological display, tracing the history of Mantua and its diocese from Roman times.

The first walk exhibits Roman and Lombard sculptures and a 14th-century marble statuette of the *Virgin Annunciate*. In a parallel gallery is the Pinacoteca, with a number of works by Giovanni Baglione and a *Madonna and Child with Sts Anselm and Charles Borromeo* (which includes a view of Mantua) by Domenico Fetti. The striking (posthumous) **portrait of Matilda of Canossa** (*see p. 388*) is a copy of a lost original by Parmigianino. There is a series of very fine **bronze heads** (some inlaid with silver), two of Caesar, one of Augustus and one of Antoninus Pius, all by L'Antico. On the walls are three damaged painted tondi of the Birth, Death and Resurrection of Christ from the atrium of the church of Sant'Andrea, designed by Mantegna but two are early works by Correggio who had come here to study the works of the great master.

Three rooms display three different private collections: the beautiful **ivories** include Byzantine and Arab coffers from the 11th and 12th centuries; a *Good Shepherd* from Goa; and a French Gothic *Madonna and Child* made from a particularly large tusk. The numismatic collection includes Greek and Byzantine **coins**. The spectacular Limoges **enamels** date mostly from the 16th and 19th centuries.

Two rooms contain all that survives from the fabulous **Treasury of the Gonzaga**, works that were saved from dispersal because they had been donated either to the duomo or to the church of Santa Barbara. Here you can see the incredibly elaborate reliquary urn of Santa Barbara in ebony, quartz and gold, made in Venice in the late 16th century; and three delightful millefleurs tapestries woven in France around 1520 (probably used as carpets in Santa Barbara; it is known that the Gonzaga owned upwards of 100 tapestries). The statue of *St George and the Dragon* is by the Venetian brothers Jacobello and Pier Paolo Dalle Masegne (who were in Mantua at the end of the 15th century).

Also preserved here is the celebrated **missal of Barbara of Brandenburg** (wife of Marquis Ludovico II and portrayed with him in the Camera degli Sposi), now usually displayed in an anastatic copy printed in 2016. This is one of the most important works to survive by the famous illuminator Belbello da Pavia (other pages are attributed to Girolamo da Cremona). It was made for the marchioness in 1461 and a touch screen enables you to study all the illuminations.

Other treasures include a statuette of the *Madonna and Child* (c. 1370); two Gonzaga documents with seals designed by Benvenuto Cellini (1552) and Andrea Mantegna (1471); six gold plaquettes by the circle of Mantegna; a precious reliquary Cross which incorporates 10th-century enamels but which dates from 1573; and an elaborate jewelled pendant with the monogram of the Name of Jesus and set with diamonds, rubies, opals and pearls, made in Germany for Duke Guglielmo Gonzaga.

A section of the museum is devoted to the splendid **suits of armour** (some of them 15th-century) which were found on the life-size ex-voto statues in the sanctuary of Santa Maria delle Grazie (*see p. 389*). They represent the most important collection of this kind in Italy. Well displayed against a blown-up reproduction of a 19th-century print of the interior of the church, they are also accompanied by a stuffed crocodile: a fellow crocodile still hangs in Santa Maria delle Grazie (where it symbolises the devil).

A spiral stair leads up to a small section dedicated to 14th–19th-century **ceramics** produced on Mantuan territory for use in private houses and monasteries. Another side room has six **tapestries** made in Paris in 1598 for Bishop Francesco Gonzaga. There is also a representative collection of 18th-century works by the Manutan-born artist Giuseppe Bazzani.

PALAZZO D'ARCO

Map 3. Piazza d'Arco. Open 9.30–1 & 2.30–6. Guided tours in Italian every half-hour. Tours last about 1hr. T: 0376 322242, museodarcomantova.it.

This interesting house museum is in the former home of a noble family from Trento who renovated the 16th-century *palazzo* in 1784. It was left to the city by Countess Giovanna d'Arco on her death in 1973 (her bedroom on the ground floor can be visited). An Austrian cousin of the family, Count Giorgio d'Arco, wrote to Count Francesco Eugenio d'Arco in 1769, recommending to him the *maestro di cappella* Leopold Mozart, who was on his way to Mantua with his son Wolfgang Amadeus, who was to give a concert here (*see p. 376*). Father and son stayed with the Arco on that occasion (and the letter is preserved here).

On the *piano nobile* are a large number of rooms with 18th- and 19th-century furniture and a miscellany of objects including late 18th-century Meissen porcelain, musical instruments (a rare theorbo made in Venice in 1647 and a fortepiano made in Mantua in 1819), costumes, Murano chandeliers and late medieval statuettes. The numerous portraits include a small painting of a blind lady recently attributed to Annibale Carracci. Amongst the other paintings are a *Christ Triumphant* by Lorenzo Lotto, *Christ on the Cross* by Van Dyck, a *Madonna and Child* by Bernardino Luini, and a series of seven large canvases illustrating the life of Alexander the Great by the local 18th-century painter Giuseppe Bazzani. The library of some 20,000 precious volumes has been catalogued online. A room dedicated to Andreas Hofer, the Tyrolean patriot who was tried by a Napoleonic court here before being shot outside the walls in 1810, is decorated with *papiers peints* of 1823 with grisaille views of Italy. The kitchen with its copper pans is also shown.

In the garden are the remains of a 15th-century palace (acquired by the Arco family in 1884), where (on the upper floor approached by a very steep flight of stairs) the **Sala dello Zodiaco** has remarkable painted decoration attributed to the painter and architect Giovanni Maria Falconetto (c. 1520), based on a lost Roman cycle by Pinturicchio. The very beautiful frieze around the top of the walls, the background decorated with gilded wax roundels (to catch the light), illustrates Classical myths. Below are twelve lunettes with the signs of the Zodiac above elaborate representations of Classical myths against landscapes with Roman or Byzantine buildings (derived from monuments in Rome, Ravenna and Verona). Below each scene is a panel in grisaille. Beside the figure of Hercules, in the panel dedicated to Cancer, there is a man dressed in black holding a bunch of keys, thought to be a self-portrait of the artist or the (unknown) person who commissioned the decoration of this extraordinary room.

In a small building in the garden two rooms on the first floor preserve the Natural History collection of Luigi d'Arco (d. 1872).

SAN FRANCESCO

Close to Palazzo dell'Arco is the Gothic church of San Francesco (*map 3*; 1304; well rebuilt in 1954 after war damage), an important foundation greatly patronised by the early Gonzaga, who used the large chapel on the south side as their burial place. The chapel is closed indefinitely for restoration but some very interesting sculptural fragments have been removed and temporarily displayed in the first chapel on the south side (including a *Nativity* and four symbols of the Evangelists dating from 1304). It is a strange fact that hardly any tombs of the Gonzaga dynasty can be seen today.

The church still has some frescoes (fine but very worn) by Serafino Serafini showing scenes from the life of St Louis of Toulouse. In 1526 the Florentine *condottiere* Giovanni dalle Bande Nere, father of Cosimo I de' Medici, was buried here in full armour. He had died after a battle wound shattered his leg, which became gangrenous and had to be amputated below the knee (apparently with ten men holding him down while the surgeon sawed). He died soon afterwards of septicaemia. His remains were later taken to the Medici Chapel in Florence. The deconsecrated church of San Maurizio further south (*map 5*) contains the lid of his original tomb.

EIGHTEENTH-CENTURY MANTUA

On Piazza Dante (*map 6*) is the Accademia Nazionale Virgiliana, a Neoclassical building by Giuseppe Piermarini (1775). It incorporates the **Teatro Bibiena** (or Teatro Scientifico; *open Tues–Fri 10–1 & 3–6; weekends 10-5.30, still sometimes used for concerts*). It was built in 1767–9 by Antonio Galli Bibiena, member of a famous family of theatre and set designers. He died in Mantua just three years after Mozart had given the inaugural concert here in 1770 at the age of 13, during his first visit to Italy.

In the parallel Via Ardigò is the **Palazzo degli Studi** with the Biblioteca Teresiana by Paolo Pozzo, inaugurated in 1780, and the study collections of Giuseppe Acerbi (d. 1846). The Liceo Classico 'Virgilio' here has a Natural History collection.

Just to the south on Via Pomponazzo is the huge **Palazzo Sordi**, built in 1680 by the Flemish architect Frans Geffels (1624–94), who worked mainly in Mantua. The elaborate façade includes a stucco tondo of the *Madonna and Child* and, on the corner, the bust of the owner in his wig. Geffels also worked on the huge Palazzo Valenti Gonzaga at Via Frattini 7 (*map 6*), where you can see its splendid courtyard with remains of stuccowork and frescoes (the interior, with frescoes by Geffels, is sometimes open to the public by the FAI (*T: 0376 364524; see valentigonzaga.com*). This is also a place where you can stay.

The **Teatro Sociale** (*map 5*), built in 1818–22 by Luigi Canonica with funds raised by subscription, dominates the unattractive and very busy Piazza Cavallotti. The theatre has an imposing Ionic portico, and is still very active.

THE LAKES

You should go and see at least one of the lakes which surround the northern tip of the town. They are formed by the River Mincio, a tributary of the Po, which widens out to form a lake of three reaches known as Lago Superiore, Lago di Mezzo and Lago Inferiore. Pleasant parks with trees and benches line their shores at most points.

The presence of so much water, which cools the air more in winter, it would seem, than in summer, gives the town its rather chill atmosphere. In winter, in fact, Mantua can feel like one of the coldest spots on earth, due to its high relative humidity and the biting wind that blows down the river. In recent years naturalists have taken an interest in the birdlife and flora of the marshlands and lakes, where lotus flowers introduced from China in 1921 grow in abundance. (*For more information on the nature reserves on the Mincio, Oglio and Po rivers, see p. 389.*) Boat trips operate except in winter (*see p. 378*).

PRACTICAL INFORMATION

GETTING AROUND

• **By car:** The best place to park is at Campo Canoa, just 1km from the centre at the far end of Ponte San Giorgio (*beyond map 4*). It is free and there is a free shuttle bus to Piazza Sordello every 10mins (7am–9pm).

• **By rail:** There are rail links to Milan (journey time 2hrs–2hrs 30mins via Codogno, where a change is sometimes necessary). You can reach Cremona in 1hr via Piadena, where the line is met by trains from Brescia and Parma. The Parma stretch also serves Castelmaggiore, from where there are buses to (5km) Sabbioneta.

• **By bus:** Mantua's feeling of isolation is emphasised by the practical difficulties of reaching it by public transport. Buses run by APAM (*apam.it*) link Mantua with Sabbioneta, Brescia, Sirmione (Lake Garda), San Benedetto Po and Ostiglia, from Piazza Don Leoni outside the railway station (*map 3*).

• **By bicycle:** The tourist information offices supply excellent maps and descriptions of the routes for cyclists in Mantuan territory. The most traffic-free route for cycling between Mantua and Sabbioneta (47km) has been mapped. There is also a 2- or 3-day cycle tour mapped in the regions associated with Matilda of Canossa.

There is also a cycle route that takes you north through the Parco Regionale del Mincio as far as Peschiera del Garda (*Atlas A, C1*). A cycle path traverses the Parco del Mincio southeast of Mantua as far as the Po (*see parcodelmincio.it and terredelmincio.it*).

Free bike sharing is available with the Mantova Card (login details at the tourist offices or Apam Infopoint; *Piazza Cavallotti 10, map 5*). Cycles can be rented for the day from La Rigola (*Via

Trieste 5, T: 0376 366677; map 6), and Mantua Bike (*Viale Piave 22/b, T: 0376 220909; map 5*).

• **By boat:** There are three companies which in the summer months provide boat trips on the lakes and in the Parco Naturale del Mincio (*see p. 389*). Motonavi Andes Negrini, from the landing-stages at the foot of the two bridges across the lakes (*Via San Giorgio 2, map 4, motonaviandes.it*). Naviandes, from the landing stage at the end of Ponte San Giorgio, also organise longer trips (which include lunch on board) down the Mincio via the Leonardo lock to the river Po (*Piazza Sordello 48, map 4, naviandes.com*). I Barcaioli del Mincio run boat trips in the Mincio nature reserve and on Lago Superiore during the flowering of the lotuses (*fiumemincio.it*).

INFORMATION OFFICES

Mantua *Piazza Mantegna 6, map 4, www.turismo.mantova.it*. Open all day. Infopoint in the Casa di Rigoletto (*Piazza Sordello 23, map 4*).

The **Mantova Card**, valid 72hrs, allows you free entrance to 17 museums in Mantua and Sabbioneta (there are also family cards). It can be purchased at the tourist offices, Palazzo Ducale and Palazzo Te. It also gives you free bus transport including the no. 17 and 17S between Mantua and Sabbioneta, as well as free bike sharing. See *mantovacard.it*.

WHERE TO STAY

€€ **Hotel dei Gonzaga**. In a superb position overlooking Piazza Sordello. Good bedrooms with wooden floors

and bright lighting (some of them not sufficiently insulated from noise from the neighbouring rooms). Modern bathrooms. Very welcoming staff, and a bowl of fruit and piece of cake and fruit juice always available in the hall. Room prices don't include breakfast. The hotel also runs the Residenza Accademia, Ca' degli Uberti and Ca' Tazzoli. *Piazza Sordello 52. T: 0376 321533, hoteldeigonzagamantova.it. Map 4.*

€€€ **Palazzo Castiglioni**. Luxury suites very well furnished, mostly on the second floor of this historic palace on Piazza Sordello, opposite the Palazzo Ducale. The suite in the tower is particularly attractive, with frescoes preserved on the walls. There is also a garden, and the *piano nobile* of the palace still has its historic furnishings. *Piazza Sordello 12. T: 0376 367032, palazzocastiglionemantova.com. Map 4.*

€€€ **Palazzo Valenti Gonzaga**. Privately-owned palace with frescoes in the bedrooms and public spaces. An individualistic, but grand and fun place to stay. *Via Frattini 7. T: 0376 364524, www. valentigonzaga.com. Map 6.*

€€ **Casa San Domenico**. Elegant and refined, with genuine antiques and a rooftop terrace with views over the city. Just to the south of the Rio canal. *Vicolo Scala 8. T: 335 259292. Map 6.*

€ **Residenza Bibiena**. B&B in two separate buildings opposite each other close to the Lago Inferiore (and only a few steps from the historic centre). Rather disturbed by traffic on the Lungo Lago dei Gonzaga. The accommodation is very simple. *Piazza Arche 5 and 8. T: 0376 355699, residenzabibiena.it. Map 6.*

Mantua has a great many B&Bs. You can find the details from the Tourist Office.

WHERE TO EAT

€€ **Masseria**. Restaurant and pizzeria with tables outside in good weather. The back room is decorated with an interesting 15th-century mural of Mantua (*see p. 363*). Good desserts. Closed Thur. *Piazza Broletto 8. T: 0376 365303, ristorantemasseria.it. Map 4.*

€€ **Bistrot Retròbottega**. Pleasantly modern light décor and an interesting menu. Good central place for a quick lunch. You are greeted with an excellent quote from Virginia Woolf. *Via G.B. Spagnoli 6/8. T: 0376 366224. Map 6.*

€–€€ **Osteria dell'Oca**. Successor to a famous local *osteria*, and still serving some of the signature dishes: it announces that it provides '*cucina dei principi e di popolo*'. The Mantuan risotto is very good and the *grana padana* cheese with quince *mostarda* is excellent. *Via Trieste 37. T: 0376 327171. Map 6.*

€ **Antica Osteria ai Ranari**. A good old-fashioned local place. Home cooking, Mantuan cuisine. Closed Mon. *Via Trieste 11. T: 0376 328431, ranari.it. Map 6.*

CAFÉS AND SNACKS

Good coffee and cakes at the old-fashioned **Caffè Caravatti** on Piazza delle Erbe (*map 4*). For an aperitif there are lively cafés on Piazza Marconi (**Caffè Diemme** is recommended; *map 6*). For ice cream, go to **Giavazzi**, near the old fish market (and next to a fish shop) on the corner of Via XX Settembre (*map 6*). **Caffè Roberta** next door is also a good place for coffee and a pastry.

For a piece of excellent pizza or a delicious sandwich, try the **Forneria delle Erbe** right in the old centre (*Portici Broletto 28*). The **Panificio Freddi** in Piazza Cavallotti (*www. panificiofreddi.it; map 5*) is famous for its bread and Mantuan pastas, and you can always find something for a good snack here. For a fine selection of cheeses, cold meats, *culatello* and *mostarda*, try the wonderful old-fashioned **Salumeria** at Via Orefici 16 (*map 6*).

LOCAL SPECIALITIES

Mantua is famous for its *tortelli di zucca* (pumpkin ravioli), *salame mantovano* (salami with pepper and fresh garlic) and *torta sbrisolona* (round crisp shortbread cake with almonds). You will also see shops selling *mostarda*, a compote of fruit (typically quince, but other chopped-up fruits are also used) in a clear, mustard-flavoured syrup. It goes extremely well with *Grana padana* cheese. *Torta mantovana* is a very simple sponge cake made with butter.

The weekly **market** is on Thur in the streets and adjoining *piazze* of the old centre. An antiques market is held on the 3rd Sun of the month in Piazza Sordello. There is a local farmer's market in Piazza Martiri di Belfiore (*map 5–6*) every Sat morning.

FESTIVALS AND EVENTS

Numerous concerts are held throughout the year, and an excellent literary festival has been held in early Sept since 1996. It takes place in numerous locations all over town (*festivaletteratura.it*). The relic of the Holy Blood is processed around town on Good Friday.

Sabbioneta & the Province of Mantua

Sabbioneta, about 34km southwest of Mantua (*Atlas A, C3*), was planned in 1556 as an Ideal City, and today is one of the most delightful places to visit in all Lombardy, a UNESCO World Heritage site, linked to Mantua. Its creator was Vespasiano Gonzaga (1531–91), member of a cadet branch of the famous Gonzaga family of Mantua. Sabbioneta was made a dukedom by the Holy Roman Emperor Rudolph II in 1577.

Today the tiny fortified town, with fields reaching right up to its hexagonal walls, preserves the beautiful buildings built in the 1570s and 1580s by Vespasiano, all of them reflecting his deep admiration for the Classical world of Rome. Recently restored, the two palaces, gallery and theatre can all be visited. Vespasiano's creation however failed to take on a permanent character of grandeur and importance. The quietness in some seasons in the regular streets, with simple little two-storey houses and a number of walled gardens, amounts to a kind of desolation. At its height the town probably had a population of some 2,000. There are just a few very discreet signs for visitors.

Tips for visiting Sabbioneta

You can park in Piazza d'Armi (see map overleaf) and for a limited time in Piazza Ducale. Otherwise there are other car parks on the outskirts, from where the walk into the centre is very quick. To visit the various monuments (Palazzo Giardino and the Galleria, the Theatre, Palazzo Ducale, the Incoronata and the Synagogue) you need to buy a ticket from the Information Office in Palazzo Giardino. If you have the Mantova Card (see p 378), it is also valid here. The opening times are more or less standard: April–Oct Tues–Sun 9.30–1 & 2.30–6, with closing time at 5pm in Nov–March. T: 0375 52039, www.iatsabbioneta.org and coopculture.it.

PIAZZA D'ARMI AND PALAZZO GIARDINO

This huge open space (*map 3*), which today is at the entrance to town, occupies the site of a 14th-century castle (only the foundations of two towers remain), which stood here until it was demolished at the end of the 18th century. Four brick arches survive (with pretty decoration) which led from the castle and ammunitions store. On the green, with a few benches, stands a Roman Corinthian column which supports a Roman **statue of Athena**, set up here by Duke Vespasiano. The west side of the square is occupied by a huge school built in 1930. But the most beautiful building here is Vespasiano's incredibly long brick **Galleria all'Antica**, linked to Palazzo Giardino, his garden palace. The arcaded passageway beneath it provides a magnificent approach to the Information Office (where you can buy a ticket for all the monuments).

PALAZZO GIARDINO

This was Vespasiano's summer villa, built in 1578–88 as a retreat where he could study, read and entertain friends. It remains today, together with the Galleria all'Antica, the most interesting building in the town. The exterior has a remarkable oak cornice, but is otherwise plain.

Ground floor: The decoration of the interior was carried out by Bernardino Campi (*see p. 402*) and his collaborators, almost certainly to the Duke's specifications. The **atrium** has, in the key of the umbrella vault, the Duke's coat of arms with the Imperial double eagle, the motto '*Libertas*' and the insignia of the Golden Fleece. The barrel vault of the **Camerino di Venere** is decorated with grotesques and stucco lunettes. The Tourist Office occupies the **Sala dei Venti**, its vault painted with huffing and puffing putti and with birds. It has a lovely red Verona marble fireplace. From here you can see the remains of the walled garden with three nymphaea. The most interesting decorations on this floor are in the **Camera di Alessandro Magno e Giulio Cesare**, with its painted ceiling and stucco tondi.

First floor: A delightful series of rooms has stuccoes and frescoes by Campi and his pupils, including Carlo Urbino. They depict the Circus Maximus and Circus of Flaminius in Rome, as well as scenes from Greek mythology. One room illustrates four tales of human vanity in the face of divine might—the Fall of Phaëthon, Fall of Icarus, Apollo and Marsyas and Minerva and Arachne—together with Gonzaga personal devices such as the muzzle. The original polychrome marble floors are preserved. A corridor with illustrations from the story of Orpheus, including exotic animals such as a rhino (some of them probably seen by Vespasiano on his travels in Africa), leads to the **Studiolo**, a centrally planned room with a beautifully decorated dome and scenes from the *Aeneid*. Another room, the **Sala degli Specchi** (so called because it was once decorated with Venetian mirrors), has painted landscapes. Off this room is the lovely little **Gabinetto delle Grazie**, with grotesques on the walls and stucco decoration on the ceiling.

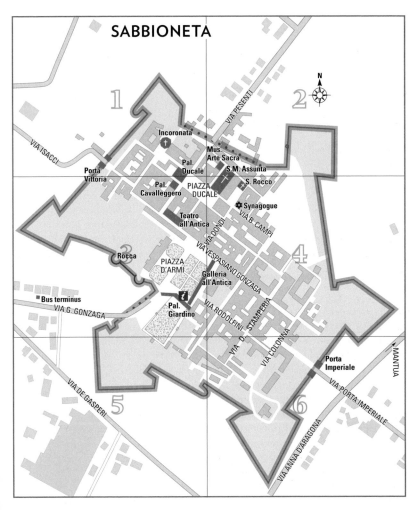

SABBIONETA

The remarkable **Galleria degli Antichi**, 96m long, was built in 1584–6. Extremely well lit from its numerous windows on both of the long walls, it was commissioned by Vespasiano for the display of his superb collection of Classical busts, statues and bas-reliefs (most of them now in Palazzo Ducale in Mantua, but nine busts remain here in oval niches). Its walls are decorated with frescoes, including sumptuous gilded vases holding a great variety of plants and flowers and, at either end, *trompe l'oeil* perspectives executed by two Tuscan-born artists who had trained in Rome, Alessandro Alberti and his brother Giovanni. Be sure to take a good look at these scenes. Surrounding the entrance door you will see two mischievous putti, one of them urinating, the other breaking wind as he performs a handstand. At the far end you are given the illusion that there is a door out to another part of the 'palace' but in fact there is just a window here.

> ## VESPASIANO GONZAGA
>
> Vespasiano (1531–91), member of a cadet branch of the Gonzaga family of Mantua, was great-grandson of Gianfranceso Gonzaga (1446–96), who was a brother of Federico I. When still a child, Vespasiano acted as page at the Imperial court of Charles V. He was a cultivated man and had a military career as a *condottiere*. He spent many years at the court of Philip II of Spain, who came to value his counsel and in 1585 conferred on him the Order of the Golden Fleece (preserved in the Museo d'Arte Sacra). Some years previously, in 1577, he had been made Duke of Sabbioneta by the Holy Roman Emperor. After a successful operation on his brain to relieve his migraines (the hole in his head was discovered when his tomb was opened; *see p. 386*) he decided to devote the last years of his life to beautifying this remarkable little town. Although he married several times, his son died as a boy and only a daughter survived him. The year after his death, the dukedom was taken over by Mantua.

TEATRO ALL'ANTICA

On the corner of Via Vespasiano Gonzaga and Via Teatro is the Teatro all'Antica (*map 3*), the last building erected for the duke (1588–90), designed by the famous Venetian architect Vincenzo Scamozzi. Though clearly derived from Scamozzi's great theatre at Vicenza, this is the first example of a theatre built as an independent structure (i.e. not within a larger building) and is provided with a foyer, separate entrances for the public, for performers and for members of the court, as well as with dressing rooms, etc. It has a handsome exterior with an inscription honouring Rome (ROMA QUANTA FUIT IPSA RUINA DOCET: 'Rome's very ruins tell how great she was'), and a charming interior (which can hold an audience of 200). The auditorium has a peristyle with stucco statues of Greek gods and monochrome painted figures of Roman emperors. Above is a frescoed loggia with a painted frieze of spectators and musicians, by a Venetian artist, inspired by Veronese's frescoes at Maser. On the two side walls are large frescoes of the Capitoline Hill and Hadrian's mausoleum in Rome. The fixed backdrop, which represented a piazza and streets, was destroyed in the 18th century (what you see today, a street of houses in perspective, beautifully constructed in wood, dates from 1996). The ceiling, which is lower than the original ship's keel roof, also dates from the 18th century.

PIAZZA DUCALE

The cobbled Piazza Ducale (*map 3–4*), with porticoes on three sides, has a number of fine buildings, chief of which is the **Palazzo Ducale** (*see below*). To the left of it is the handsome 16th-century **Palazzo del Cavalleggero**, of brick with stone dressings, now owned by the Italian state. Also in the piazza is the church of **Santa Maria Assunta**,

SABBIONETA

The decoration of Palazzo Giardino reflects the earthy tastes of the Gonzaga, also well seen at Mantua in Palazzo Te. Here a putto-atlas figure supports an entablature (while spraying visitors below).

with a red and white chequered façade (*open for services on holidays*), built in 1582 and equipped with a wonderful peal of bells. The little Chapel of the Holy Sacrament was added by Antonio Bibiena in 1768 and has a green dome (and separate entrance on the piazza). Inside it has a delightful double perforated dome in stucco and wood and two marble reliquary 'cupboards'. Behind the church, on Via Assunta, the **Museo d'Arte Sacra** (*map 2; opening hours are erratic; T: 0375 52035 or ask at the Information Office*) has two paintings by Bernardino Campi. The *Teson d'Oro* (Golden Fleece) was the gold medal presented to Vespasiano in 1585 by Philip II of Spain when he was made a Knight of the Order; it was found in his tomb in the Incoronata (*see overleaf*) in 1988.

PALAZZO DUCALE

Rebuilt by Vespasiano in 1561 as his official residence, the palace has a handsome exterior with a portico on the ground floor and busts above the windows. Sadly today, the inside is bare and since 'restoration' in the 1960s it has had a very neglected feel, but the ceilings are very fine and the equestrian statues well worth seeing.

Ground floor: The **Sala della Gran Guardia** has a good wooden ceiling, and the small room off it has a frescoed barrel vault. The **Saletta delle Stagioni** has allegorical figures representing the Seasons. The large **Sala di Diana** (the central panel of Diana by Bernardino Campi is very ruined) is decorated with grotesques and painted lunettes.

Piano nobile: The **Salone delle Aquile** is frescoed with festoons of fruit and large eagles. Here are displayed four delightful wooden equestrian statues representing Vespasiano himself, two of his ancestors, and a captain. They were made in 1589, in willow and poplar wood, by a Venetian sculptor (the polychrome was repainted in the 18th century) and were part of a group of ten (the other six perished in a fire in the early 19th century, except for the five busts exhibited here). The **Sala degli Imperatori** has a panelled oak ceiling and a frieze of fruit and vegetables, including peppers and maize (both of which Vespasiano must have seen in Spain, as neither was grown in Italy in the 16th century). In the frieze at the top of the walls are good copies by Bernardino Campi of Titian's eleven *Caesars* painted for the Palazzo Ducale in Mantua, including the missing twelfth emperor, Domitian (*see p. 355*). In the central **Galleria degli Antenati**, probably used as a studio and with a balcony overlooking the piazza, there are splendid reliefs in stucco of Vespasiano's ancestors by Alberto Cavalli, and a barrel-vaulted ceiling with more very fine stuccowork and paintings. The adjoining room has a painted (but damaged) frieze of elephants around the top of the walls. Off the Sala delle Aquile, the **Sala dei Leoni** has a good carved wood ceiling, and a room with four windows is frescoed with views of Constantinople and Genoa.

Three steps lead down to the **Sala dell'Angelo** and the **Sala degli Ottagoni**, both with lovely carved and coffered ceilings of cedar wood.

Just off Piazza Ducale, beyond the Oratory of San Rocco (*closed*) in Via Bernardino Campi, is the **Synagogue** (*map 4; skull caps must be worn; they are provided at the door*), on the top floor of a house. It has an interesting interior by a local architect Carlo Visioli (1824). There was a Jewish community in the town from 1436.

THE INCORONATA

The Convent of the Servi di Maria incorporates the octagonal church of the Beata Vergine Incoronata (*map 1*), built in 1586–8 and modelled on the Incoronata of Lodi (*see p. 146*). It was beautifully decorated with frescoes in the 18th century. The late 17th-century **mechanical organ** has its original pipes (concerts are given here in Sept). On the left of the high altar the **monument to Duke Vespasiano**, with its sarcophagus of rare pink and grey marble, was erected by Giovanni Battista della Porta in 1592. The Duke's helmet placed on top of the sarcophagus (with the visor closed) produces a dramatic effect. The splendid bronze **statue** of him, shown seated in the guise of a Roman emperor, was made in 1579 (well before his death) by Leone Leoni, who had already made portraits of Charles V and Philip II, which the Duke may well have seen and appreciated when he was at their courts. In 1588 it was set up in the piazza outside (and only moved here in 1656). Vespasiano is buried in the crypt below (in a side corridor, photographs and sketches show what was found in his tomb when it was opened in 1988).

THE WALLS AND GATES

The **Porta Vittoria** (1567; *map 1*) was one of the main gates, and on the opposite side of the town, **Porta Imperiale** (1579; *map 6*) has a dedicatory inscription on the travertine outer face to the Emperor Rudolph II, two years after he had conferred the Dukedom of Sabbioneta on Vespasiano. There is a good view of the splendid and very well-preserved walls from here and the little moat (inhabited by herons). There is a delightful walk which you can take along a grassy path at the foot of the walls to the south, along the edge of fields between these two fortified gates, interrupted only by the road which enters the town beside the **ruins of the Rocca**.

Just outside Sabbioneta in **Villa Pasquali** is the church of Sant'Antonio Abate (*for opening times, ask at the Information Office*), built in 1765–84 by Antonio Bibiena. The second tower on the handsome brick façade was never completed. The interior is especially remarkable for the beautiful perforated double ceiling of the dome and three apses in terracotta. The various treasures of the church are carefully preserved.

SAN BENEDETTO PO

San Benedetto Po (*Atlas A, D3*) is the most interesting place in the province of Mantua after Sabbioneta. On the right bank of the Po, it grew up round the important Benedictine abbey, founded in 1007 and protected by Countess Matilda of Canossa (*see p. 388*), who was buried here. United to the Abbey of Cluny until the 13th century, it flourished in the 15th century when it had a famous library, and survived up until its suppression by Napoleon in 1797.

THE ABBEY

The extensive buildings, mostly dating from the 15th century, are in the large central piazza of the little town. The beautiful church, **San Benedetto in Polirone**, was partly rebuilt and restored by Giulio Romano in 1540–4 for Cardinal Ercole Gonzaga. The famous architect retained some of the Romanesque and Gothic elements but transformed it into a splendid Mannerist work and had it frescoed throughout. It is considered one of Giulio's best buildings. Since no local stone was available, he had to use brick and stucco. Some of the altarpieces are by his pupil, Fermo Ghisoni. The 33 terracotta statues in various parts of the church are by Antonio Begarelli, an early 16th-century sculptor who was particularly skilled in this medium. The church also has a 15th-century altarpiece by Francesco Bonsignori, good 18th-century wrought-iron work, a Neoclassical altarpiece by Giovanni Battista Bottani (born in Cremona), and an 18th-century organ.

Off the ambulatory, with its elaborate stalls carved in 1550, is the Romanesque church of **Santa Maria**, with a pretty interior. The mosaic pavement of 1151, with figures of animals, the Cardinal Virtues, etc., is well preserved at the east end (and there is another fragment in the nave). The altarpiece is by Fermo Ghisoni. In the sacristy, with frescoes by the school of Giulio Romano and fine wooden cupboards, is an equestrian portrait of Matilda of Canossa by Orazio Farinati: her empty tomb is just outside. Her remains were sold by the abbot to Pope Urban VIII in 1633, when Bernini was commissioned to provide a monument in St Peter's. She was the first woman—and indeed the first person who was neither pope nor saint—to be buried in the Vatican.

MATILDA OF CANOSSA

Matilda (1046–1115) was one of the most famous women rulers in history. Her father Bonifacio administered vast territories in the Italian peninsula on behalf of the German emperor: when he was killed, his wife Beatrice assumed his power, together with their daughter Matilda (then only aged six). Since by feudal law women were not allowed to inherit, this naturally led to disputes but Matilda nevertheless managed to hold onto the land after her mother's death. She allied herself with the pope and encouraged his independence from the emperor. She used Justinian law (which had been long forgotten) to uphold her claim, since that great Roman emperor had established that female heirs had the same rights as male. Matilda also employed distinguished jurists to study Justinian's *Digest* concerning civil laws (which he laid out in just 27 brief and memorable sentences), including the fundamental concept that 'all men are equal'. Matilda spent her life founding or restoring cathedrals and churches on Italian territory (she is credited with some 100 such works) and facilitating travel between them. She was tireless in her efforts on behalf of the papacy, labouring to diminish imperial secular power, and supported Pope Gregory VII in his reforms. As a young woman she often travelled with the pope through Italian territory (her detractors suggested she was his concubine) and she promptly abandoned not one but two husbands when they took refuge with the emperor. In 1077 Matilda proudly received Emperor Henry IV in her castle of Canossa (which survives in ruins near the Certosa di Parma; see *Blue Guide Emilia Romagna*) after he had waited outside the walls barefoot in the snow, in bitter winter weather, to ask her to intercede on his behalf with her ally Pope Gregory VII to lift his excommunication. An expression in Italian, '*andare a Canossa*', is still sometimes used to signify an action which involves great humiliation. By the time Matilda died at the age of 69, the history of the free Italian communes had begun. She was at first buried in the monastery of San Benedetto Po. Many centuries later, Parmigianino painted an idealised portrait of this great lady. Although the original work has been lost, there is a good copy in the Museo Diocesano Francesco Gonzaga in Mantua (*see p. 374*).

To the right of the church is the entrance to a cloister, off which a Baroque staircase by Giovanni Battista Barberini (1674) leads up to the **Museo Civico Polironiano** (*open summer Mon 9–12.30, Tues–Fri 9–12.30 & 2.30–6.30, Sat–Sun 9–12.30 & 3–7; by appointment in winter; T: 037 662 3036*), a large ethnographic museum of the region. Displays are arranged around the upper floor of the cloister of San Simeone, in the grand abbot's apartments and the simpler monks' cells, and in the late 18th-century library, a Neoclassical space designed by Giovanni Battista Marconi. The lower walk of the 15th-century cloister of San Simeone has 16th-century frescoes and a garden that has been replanted following its 16th-century design.

Across the piazza, on the other side of the church, is the former **refectory** (*open as above*), built in 1478, with a museum of sculptural fragments and ceramics, and a *Madonna* by Antonio Begarelli. The very fine huge fresco, only discovered in 1984 and attributed as an early work (1514) to Correggio, provided the architectural setting for a *Last Supper* by Girolamo Bonsignori, now in the Museo Civico of Badia Polesine and replaced here by a photograph. Two sides of the 15th-century cloister of St Benedict survive in the piazza, and the huge 16th-century infirmary behind the refectory.

NATURE RESERVES ALONG THE MINCIO, OGLIO & PO

In recent years numerous well-signed cycle routes have been instituted in these areas, one of them (42km) all the way from Mantua to Peschiera del Garda (*Atlas A, C1*). There are also cycle routes along country roads from Mantua to Sabbioneta (47km), and through the Mincio park from Mantua south to the Po (28km). Maps and printed guides are readily available at the Tourist Office in Mantua, and there is also an app. Bicycles can be hired for free (*www.sipom.eu and www.oltrepomantovano.eu.*). There are also numerous rural villas (known as *Corte*) in the area, most of them now abandoned, which were built by the Gonzaga in their heyday.

PARCO NATURALE REGIONALE DEL MINCIO

Between the Lake Garda and the River Po, the valley of the Mincio extends to the north and south of Mantua. These wetlands support a fascinating range of birdlife, including herons, grebes, bitterns and kingfishers, and waterlilies, hibiscus and lotus flowers bloom here in summer. The marshes with their reeds are now a protected area. There is a Visitor Centre at **Rivalta** (*Atlas A, C2; terredelmincio.it; T: 0376 653340*), with a little ethnographical museum recording the fishermens' life on the river. Professional boatmen (I Barcaioli del Mincio; *T: 0376 349292, fiumemincio.it*) offer river trips from March to Oct from the little port of **Grazie di Curtatone**.

Close by to the south is the sanctuary of **Santa Maria delle Grazie**, a pilgrimage church (*open 7.30–12 & 3–6.30*) founded by Francesco I Gonzaga in 1399. The church is well-known for its two tiers of life-size statues in various materials set up as ex-votos—an astonishing sight. Some of the figures were clad in the 15th-century armour now exhibited in the Museo Diocesano Francesco Gonzaga in Mantua (*see p. 374*). Baldassare Castiglione, who was born at Casatico about 7km west of here in 1478, was buried in the church when he died in 1529 and his tomb is probably by Giulio Romano (with an epigraph by Pietro Bembo). Castiglione is the author of *The Courtier*, the famous chronicle of court life considered a treatise on manners. His mother was a Gonzaga and so it was natural that he became a member of the court of Marquis Francesco II Gonzaga (he was also a diplomat and afterwards frequented the dukes of Urbino and was sent by Clement VII as papal nuncio to Spain). A typical Renaissance man, he was a close friend of Raphael's (whom he mentions in his book and who painted a wonderful portrait of him, now in the Louvre).

On the opposite bank of the Mincio is **Soave di Porto Mantovano**, still within the nature reserve, with rare aquatic plants, and on the cycle route between Mantua and Peschiera del Garda.

Downstream from Mantua, also still in the protected area, is **Pietole** (*Atlas A, D2*), a village thought to be on the site of *Andes*, where Virgil was born. West of the motorway just before Bagnolo San Vito, is the archeological site of **Forcello**, the first Etruscan settlement (5th century BC) discovered north of the Po and the most ancient site so far discovered in Lombardy (*T: 0376 413317, parcoarcheologicoforcello.it*).

PARCO REGIONALE OGLIO

Canneto sull'Oglio (*Atlas A, B2*) preserves a massive tower belonging to its former castle. The Museo Civico (*open Sun 10–12.30 & 2.30–6 or 3–7; March–Oct also Sat 2–6 or 3–7*) is dedicated to life on the River Oglio and also has a collection of dolls, which have been manufactured in the town since 1870. To the north is **Asola**, which preserves its old walls, and to the southeast **Bozzolo** (*Atlas A, C2*), with a 14th-century tower and a Gonzaga palace.

ALONG THE PO

Downstream from the confluence of the Po with the Oglio is **Borgoforte** (*Atlas A, C3*), with an 18th-century castle and a parish church containing works by Giuseppe Bazzani. On the south bank of the river at **Motteggiana** is the Ghirardina, a 15th-century fortified villa of the Gonzaga attributed to Luca Fancelli. Southeast of here, reached via Suzzara, with its high tower which survives from a castle of 1372, is **Gonzaga** (*Atlas A, C3–D3*), a pretty little town in farming country which was the ancestral home of the famous ducal family.

Downstream from the confluence of the Po with the Mincio, at **Ostiglia** (*Atlas A, D2*), the marshes are protected as a bird sanctuary. A short distance further downriver is the **Isola Boschina**, its woods a rare survival of the vegetation that was once typical of the Po landscape.

On the south bank of the river is **Revere** (*Atlas A, D3*), where there is a palace of Ludovico Gonzaga (his first architectural undertaking), with a charming courtyard and portal by Luca Fancelli. Here the Museo del Po has archaeological and historical material. The 18th-century parish church has paintings by Giuseppe Bazzani.

PRACTICAL INFORMATION

GETTING AROUND

• **By bus:** For Sabbioneta, buses run by APAM (*www.apam.it*) every day from outside the railway station in Mantua in c. 1hr. There is free bus travel with the Mantova Card (*mantovacard.it*). Buses terminate in Via Giulia Gonzaga, less than 5mins' walk from Piazza d'Armi.

• **By bicycle:** Tourist Information offices supply excellent maps and descriptions of the routes for cyclists in Mantuan territory. The most traffic-free route for cycling between Mantua and Sabbioneta (47km) has been mapped. There is also a 2- or 3-day cycle tour mapped in the regions associated with Matilda of Canossa.

INFORMATION OFFICES

Sabbioneta *Piazza d'Armi 1. T: 0375 52039, iatsabbioneta.org.*
San Benedetto Po *Piazza Matilda di Canossa. T: 0376 623036, turimosanbenettopo.it* and *oltrepomantova.it.*
Parco del Mincio *parcodelmincio.it* and *terredelmincio.it.* For cycle routes: *cicloturismo.turismo.mantova.it.*

WHERE TO STAY

SABBIONETA
€ **Al Duca**. In a very pleasant secluded position with a garden across the road, in the same street as the Carmine church. With a restaurant. *Via della Stamperia. T: 0375 52474. al.duca@tin.it. Map 4.*

€ **Luna Residence House**. In a nice position, with just five rooms. *Via Colonna (corner of Via della Zecca). T: 0375 201421, lunaresidencehotel.it. Map 6.*

SAN BENEDETTO PO
There are a number of B&Bs here. The most central is € **A Casa dell'Antiquario**, in Via Cesare Battista.

WHERE TO EAT

SABBIONETA
Everything in Sabbioneta closes down for a few hours at midday so you will probably want to take time over your lunch. There are nice places to picnic at the foot of the walls. € **Osteria La Dispensa** on Via Galleria degli Antichi (entered from under the portico beneath the Galleria; *map 3*) offers a lunchtime menu (*T: 0375 221107*). € **Zanetti**, opposite Palazzo Ducale (*Piazza Ducale 8; map 4*), has fresh sandwiches, simple refreshments and cordial service. A very good *pasticceria* is **Atena** at Via Vespasiano Gonzaga 41, opposite Piazza d'Armi (closed Mon; *map 3*).

SAN BENEDETTO PO
There are restaurants and *pizzerie* on or near Piazza Canossa and Piazza Folengo, and others along the banks of the Po.

FESTIVALS AND EVENTS

At **Sabbioneta**, concerts are held in May–June in the theatre; organ recitals take place in Sept in the Incoronata.

CREMA
Sanctuary church of
Santa Maria della Croce.

Cremona & its Province

C remona (*Atlas A, A2*), a peaceful city set in a wide, flat landscape of cornfields at the very rim of Lombardy, has a world-wide reputation for its stringed instrument makers and restorers. In the 16th–18th centuries it was home to the most famous violin-makers of all time, including Antonio Stradivari (some of whose precious instruments are preserved here). In fact, music is present wherever you go, and it is rare to enter the beautiful duomo without the accompanying sound of the organ or singing. Violin-makers' shops are also a common sight.

Cremona's churches are particularly noteworthy for their 16th-century frescoes and altarpieces, many of them by the Campi brothers, a gifted local family of painters. The trio of extremely fine brick buildings on Piazza del Comune, the duomo, bell-tower and baptistery, are important survivals from the age of the Lombard city-states.

HISTORY OF CREMONA

Founded by the Romans as a colony in 218 BC, Cremona became an important fortress and road junction on the Via Postumia (built in 148 BC between Genoa and Aquileia). The town prospered in the Augustan age, when new public buildings were erected. Its decline after a siege and sacking by Vespasian in AD 69 ended in destruction by the Lombards in 603. Cremona re-emerged as a free commune in 1098, at war with its neighbours, Milan, Brescia and Piacenza. In 1334 it was taken by Azzone Visconti of Milan, and from then on remained under Milanese domination. It enjoyed a century of patronage and prosperity after it was given in dowry to Bianca Maria Visconti on her marriage to Francesco Sforza in 1441.

Cremona is an important agricultural market for southern Lombardy. In recent years it seems that the town has suffered from a feeling of isolation and restlessness amongst its younger inhabitants, and the poor public transport connecting it to its more important neighbours may have contributed to this.

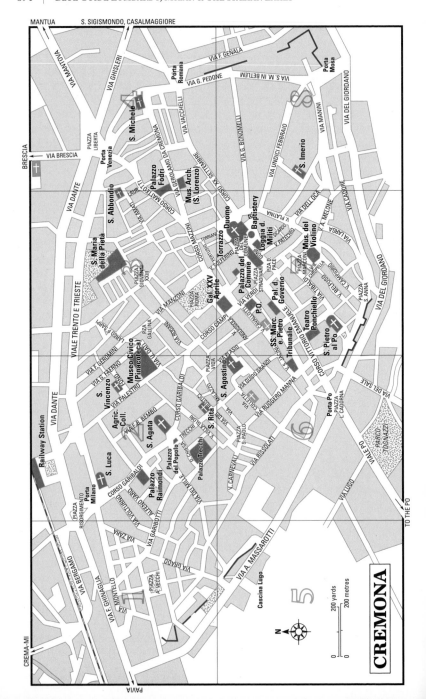

CREMONA

CREMONA HIGHLIGHTS

Piazza del Comune (*map 7*), at the highest and central point of the old town, has the most important buildings. The **duomo** (*described below*) occupies almost all of one side with its majestic exterior and sea of pinnacles, while the incredibly high bell-tower, the **Torrazzo** (*p. 398*), reaches far up into the sky, on winter days its summit invisible in the clouds. Together with the magnificent **baptistery** (*p. 398*), which stands beside the duomo, these are the most important sights.

One of the main streets of old Cremona is the pedestrianised **Corso Campi** (*map 3–7*), named after the local family of painters. At the intersection with Via Sofonisba Anguissola (named after another artist born in Cremona) is the **Galleria XXV Aprile** shopping arcade, a good example of Fascist architecture built in 1933 by the engineer Nino Mori, who also built the Chamber of Commerce building on **Piazza Stradivari** (*map 7*). The pleasant park in **Piazza Roma** has a statue of Amilcare Ponchielli (1834–86), composer of the opera *La Gioconda*, with its famous 'Dance of the Hours', who was born near Cremona. There is also a monument to Stradivarius, who was buried in the church of San Domenico on this site (demolished in 1878; Stradivarius' tombstone is now in the Museo del Violino). The house where he lived can also be visited (*p. 401*).

Cremona's museums include a superb new one dedicated to the violin (**Museo del Violino**; *map 7; p. 400*); a fine **archaeological museum** (*map 4; p. 401*) and the **Pinacoteca (Museo Civico)** (*map 2; p. 401*).

Many of Cremona's churches preserve interesting artworks. **Sant'Agostino** (*p. 403*) contains a painting by Perugino.

THE DUOMO

Cremona's duomo (*map 7; open 7.30–12 & 3.30–7*), a very interesting Romanesque basilica, was begun in 1107 (the foundation stone is preserved). It was consecrated in 1190 but finished considerably later. Numerous (sung) services take place throughout the day, and the organ can often be heard here. The exterior is beautifully lit at night.

Exterior of the duomo

The lovely main façade, begun in 1274, has a rose window above a porch with a tabernacle which protects three large statues of the Madonna and Child and the patron saints Himerius and Homobonus. These beautiful but unusual works, influenced by the great Sienese and Pisan school of sculptors as well as by the French Gothic style, are thought to be by Marco Romano, a Sienese sculptor who, in the first two decades of the 14th century, was also at work in Tuscany and Venice (where his only signed and

CREMONA
Façade of the duomo, an extraordinary pastiche, with a 13th-century
rose window and arcades and 17th-century upper section.

dated work can be seen in San Simeone Grande). The frieze directly below dates from 1220–30, and depicts the Labours of the Months (interrupted by a statue of a bishop in the centre). These reliefs are by the workshop of Wiligelmus, who was also at work on Modena cathedral (founded just eight years earlier than this church). The panel should be read from right to left, beginning with Spring and ending with February. The lions which support the porch were made in 1285. On the door jambs are four amazing bearded figures of prophets, which are also attributed to the workshop of Wiligelmus. The façade is further decorated with two rows of numerous narrow blind arcades. The part above the rose window, with its volutes incorporating sculpted roundels, was added in 1606 and bears the arms of Gregory XIV, who became Bishop of Cremona in 1560 and was pope from 1590–1.

The transepts also have splendid façades, this time in brick. The north transept (left) dates from 1288, with another beautiful lion-borne porch: the *Annunciation* statues on either side are thought to be by the hand of Wiligelmus himself, and the frieze of Christ and the Apostles, dating from the same century, shows Christ as Pantocrator in a roundel, squeezed into his throne holding the Book and blessing. The supporting lions are huge and they entrap an eagle and a lamb beneath their paws.

The beautiful apse, faced in marble and decorated with charming blind arcades, fills the piazza behind. From the roof rise pairs of brick turrets with green conical roofs. The brick façade of the south transept dates from the late 14th century and has three more turrets.

Interior of the duomo

The huge interior, usually kept very dark (even the pillars were painted darker in the 18th century), is remarkable especially for the frescoes on the walls of the nave and apse—though unfortunately they are extremely difficult to see without strong light. They were carried out from 1506 to 1529 by Boccaccio Boccaccino, Gian Francesco Bembo, Altobello Melone, Girolamo Romanino, Pordenone and Bernardino Gatti.

North transept: The Chapel of the Madonna del Popolo is beautifully decorated with stuccoes and has lovely paintings (1570) by Bernardino Campi and Giulio Campi (*for the Campi family, see p. 402*), as well as Malosso, who was a pupil of Bernardino's. The splendid silver Cross, nearly 2m high, with numerous tabernacles and statuettes decorated with enamels and gold, was made in 1478 and signed by two goldsmiths named Ambrogio Pozzi and Agostino Sacchi (about whom little is known). The base was added in 1774. It is one of the most amazing works ever produced of its kind. It faces the altarpiece of *St Michael Archangel* by Giulio Campi (behind it some interesting earlier frescoes have been discovered, shown here in reproductions). Next to it is a very fine *Deposition* (1566) by Antonio Campi (Giulio's brother). To the right of the side door onto the street are four marble rectangular panels signed by Giovanni Antonio Amadeo (1474; more reliefs by this very skilled sculptor—*see p. 163*—can be seen incorporated into the two pulpits in the nave, which were reconstructed in 1820). Also in this transept is an ancona in gilded wood which houses nine little stories of St Roch by Genovesino.

Sanctuary: The high altarpiece of the *Assumption* is by Bernardino Gatti (1573). The intarsia choir stalls dating from the 1480s by Giovanni Maria Platina cannot unfortunately be seen from a distance. The fresco of *Christ with the Patron Saints* in the apse is by Boccaccio Boccaccino. The *Annunciation*, high up over the triumphal arch (*usually lit*), also by Boccaccino, was the first fresco to be painted, in 1506.

Nave frescoes: A cycle illustrating the lives of the Virgin and Christ begins at the first north arch. The scenes are painted in pairs, divided by painted pilasters. On the north side in the sanctuary, *Christ Disputing with the Doctors* is Boccaccino's last important work (1518). On the south side the scenes are by Melone and Romanino, except for the first three which were painted by Pordenone, the most famous painter of this group, in 1520: these break out of the cycle by abandoning the scheme of twin subjects divided by pilasters and introduce a quite new form of painting, portraying particularly violent Passion scenes. In the first scene, of Christ being nailed to the Cross, the cross seems to extend out from the fresco and into the church. The grain of the wood and the pre-drilled hole for the nail are particularly well rendered.

West end: On the west wall (*always lit*) is a *Deposition* beneath a *Crucifixion*, both rather disturbing frescoes by Pordenone (the deposed Christ again seemingly extends outwards from the painting as if on an apron stage, and the scene includes a peacock in the painted mosaic apse).

South aisle: In the south aisle, the first altarpiece is also by Pordenone and is particularly beautiful—and striking for its contrasting atmosphere of calm. It shows St Philip presenting the donor, Canon Schizzi, to the Virgin, accompanied by an angel plucking at a stringed instrument.

In the south transept (high up, looking back towards the nave) is a huge painting of the *Triumph of Mordechai*

(1567) by Giulio Campi. In the cross-vaults of this transept are some very unusual late Gothic Old Testament scenes dating from 1430, accompanied by long inscriptions.

Outside the 17th-century Cappella del Sacramento, stairs lead down to the 17th-century crypt, with the delicately carved tomb of Sts Peter and Marcellius (1506) at the altar. On a nave pillar by the crypt steps is a marble triptych of 1495 and (protected by glass) a beautiful high relief depicting the *Charity of St Himerius* (1482), with remarkable perspective by the famous Lombard sculptor Giovanni Antonio Amadeo.

At the time of writing, work was in progress at the Palazzo Vescovile next to the duomo, as well as in the 16th- century Camposanto dei Canonici (which has some 11th-century mosaics) to create a Diocesan Museum. Excavations were carried out beneath the cathedral in 2000.

THE BERTAZZOLA AND TORRAZZO

Joining the duomo to its Romanesque bell-tower is a handsome portico, affectionately known as the **Bertazzola**, dating from the early 16th century (although the statues on the top were added in 1739). The bell-tower, known as the **Torrazzo** (*open Tues–Sun 10–1 & 2.30–6; combined ticket with the baptistery*), is one of the highest medieval towers in Europe (112m). It was completed in 1250–67 and crowned with a Gothic lantern in 1287–1300, probably by the local sculptor Francesco Pecorari. A total of 502 steps lead up past a room with an astronomical clock, made in 1583 by the Divizioli, still with its original mechanism (it is wound by hand every day). At the time of writing there were plans to open a museum here. In the courtyard there is a statue of a legendary figure called Giovanni Baldesio (or Baldes), dating from the 13th century.

THE BAPTISTERY

The octagonal baptistery (*open 10–12.30 & 2.30–5.30; closed Mon in Dec and Jan; combined ticket with the Torrazzo*) is a plain Lombard building dating from 1167 and partially faced with marble in 1558. It was only isolated from the surrounding buildings in the early 20th century. Once again its entrance is protected by a columned porch with supporting lions. The vertiginous brick cupola in the interior provides a splendid sight above two rows of little galleries, and lit by twin lancet windows as well as by the central lantern with a carved and painted dove of the Holy Spirit. Interesting sculptures are exhibited here. The original bronze angel from the lantern (replaced *in situ* by a copy) was made in the 12th or 13th century, with hinged, moveable wings in

CREMONA, BAPTISTERY
Siren stoup attributed to the
workshop of Wiligelmus (13th century).

order to rebuff the winds. The Cross was added in 1369. A stoup decorated with sirens is attributed to the workshop of Wiligelmus. The delightful marble ox, symbol of St Luke, dates from the same time. It is thought to have been part of an exterior pulpit on the Bertazzola (the lion symbol of St Mark is still *in situ* there). The Greek marble telamon and caryatid known respectively as Baldes and Berta (thought to depict legendary figures or perhaps Adam and Eve) are particularly striking sculptures, again attributed to the workshop of Wiligelmus. Also here is a cast of the duomo's foundation stone (1107), the inscription held up by the prophets Enoch and Elijah (the original is preserved in the Sagrestia dei Canonici in the duomo).

PALAZZO COMUNALE

The **Loggia dei Militi**, opposite the duomo to the left, is a Gothic Lombard building of 1292 (with handsome three-light windows), restored as a War Memorial. Next to it is the **Palazzo Comunale**, a castellated 13th-century brick building with a spacious loggia below. It still serves as the Town Hall and its historic rooms can be visited (*entrance from the rear, through the Spazio Comunale on Piazza Stradivari; lift or stairs to the second floor; open 9 or 10–6 or 7*). A finely carved portal gives access to the Council Chamber, which has two interesting paintings by Genovesino: a huge *Multiplication of the Loaves and Fishes* (1647) and a smaller *Last Supper*, unusual in its vertical format. There is an excellent view of the duomo from the window of the adjoining room.

MUSEO DEL VIOLINO

Map 7. Open Tues–Sun 10–6. T: 0372 080809, museodelviolino.org. There are numerous multimedia installations with musical recordings, and instruments can be 'played' on touch screens. Professional violinists come here regularly to keep the historic instruments in tune. Excellent labelling, also in English. Café and restaurant.

The superb Museo del Violino is approached from Piazza Marconi, which has benches above its underground car park (the Roman finds from excavations here can be seen in the Museo Archeologico). The museum is beautifully arranged in the large Palazzo dell'Arte, built in a pleasing Rationalist style in 1943, using brick and wood rather than the cold marble typical of the Fascist era. It provides space not only for a museum but also for a concert hall, with exceptional acoustics.

The history of the violin from the fiddle onwards is documented, and the origin of the word 'viola' explained (from the Latin *vidula*, or young widow). There is an iconographical section with paintings featuring musical instruments. The violinmaker's workshop is usually occupied by an artisan at work on making an instrument. A map shows how the violin spread from Europe all over the world. Recordings of famous 20th-century violinists can be heard in a specially-designed space.

CREMONA AND VIOLIN-MAKING

Cremona is famous for the violins and violas that were made here in the 16th–18th centuries by the Amati family and their pupils, the Guarneri and Antonio Stradivari. Stradivari (in Latin, Stradivarius, 1644–1737) was born and died in Cremona. Today the town is still famous throughout the world for its violins.

The Consorzio Liutai 'A. Stradivari' is at Piazza Stradivari 1 (*open Tues–Fri 11–1 & 4–6.30, T: 0372 463503, cremonaviolins.com*). This is a consortium of private violinmakers, founded in 1996, and which today represents some 60 workshops in Cremona and its province. Their hallmark guarantees that an instrument is handmade in Cremona and certifies its authenticity and origin. The showroom has some of these instruments for sale and they can be played by appointment. The Consortium also organises (again by appointment) fascinating visits to workshops to see an instrument being made, and they run a summer festival for children up to the age of 18, with master-classes and concerts all over town.

In the 16th century, Andrea Amati founded the school of stringed-instrument makers at Via Palestro 17. His grandson Nicolò Amati (1596–1684) was his most famous follower. The school (Scuola Internazionale di Liuteria) is still renowned and is now at Via Colletta 5 (*map 6*). The Stanze della Musica, with an historic collection of plucked string instruments, is displayed in the Museo Civico (*map 2*). The Musicology Department of Pavia University has its seat at Corso Garibaldi 178.

The five most famous Cremona violins owned by the city are displayed together. The one by Andrea Amati is thought to have been commissioned by Charles IX of France in 1566; the Hammerle of 1658 is by Nicolò Amati, Andrea's grandson. The others are a violin made by Giuseppe Guarneri in 1689, the 'Cremonese' made in 1715 by Antonio Stradivari, and the 'Guarneri del Gesù' (1734) by Guarneri's son Giuseppe Guarneri del Gesù. There is also a fine collection of other stringed instruments (17th–20th centuries).

A room is dedicated to **Stradivarius**, with the models he made in wood and paper, his tools, drawings, etc. A charming painting dated 1886 illustrates his workshop. His tombstone, salvaged from the demolished church of San Domenico (*see p. 395*), is also preserved here. The simple house at Corso Garibaldi 57 (*map 2*), where he lived from 1667–80, can be visited. It is signalled on the street by a bench with a seated statue of the great violinmaker. To visit, apply at the shop indicated on the noticeboard.

MUSEO ARCHEOLOGICO

Map 3–4. Open Tues–Sun 10–5. Via San Lorenzo 4. T: 0372 407775.

Superbly arranged in the 13th-century interior of the ex-church of San Lorenzo (deconsecrated in the 18th century), this is one of the best-displayed museums of its kind in northern Italy. It has excellent labelling, also in English (and special exhibits for the blind). The church itself, with a basilican plan with ancient columns and palmette capitals, has been the subject of excavations in the apse, where Palaeochristian walls have been unearthed. It also provides ample space for finds from all over Cremona: these finds include **mosaic pavements** (exhibited in the nave); examples from a cache of at least 650 **amphorae** found in the town centre in 1993, in an area once probably part of the Roman port on the Po; and artefacts found in digs during the 19th century. From the most recent excavations in Piazza Marconi (ended in 2008) come pavements from a Roman domus with exquisite vermilion wall-paintings and a nymphaeum (reconstructed here from the fragments). Also in the centre of the nave are two 2nd-century BC mosaic floors discovered in Via Colletta in 2014. The mosaic with a small labyrinth framing a scene of Theseus killing the Minotaur gave its name to another domus discovered in the last century. Special exhibits cover brick stamps, work tools (including a woven basket of willow, oak and elm which survives from the 2nd century BC), cults and superstitions, games, cooking utensils, perfume phials and more. At the west end are stone and terracotta **architectural fragments** from public buildings. In a vaulted side chapel (the 15th-century **Cappella Meli**, with a lovely pink-veined pavement and remains of a fresco of the *Madonna and Child with Two Saints* attributed to Bonifacio Bembo) are finds from burial sites all over town. Don't miss the Roman ***Winged Victory*** statue, displayed on its own in another side room.

THE PINACOTECA (MUSEO CIVICO)

Map 2–3. Via Ugolani Dati 4. Open Tues–Sun 9–6, Sun and holidays 10–6. T: 0372 407770.

The museum is housed in the huge Palazzo Affaitati, built in 1561 by Francesco Dattaro and with a monumental staircase by Antonio Arrighi (1769). The nucleus of the large collection is that of Count Sigismondo Ala Ponzone, left to the city in 1842.

The two most important works in the collection are *Scherzo con Ortaggi* by Arcimboldo and **St Francis in Meditation** by **Caravaggio**. The latter was restored in 2016 so that the details in this typically dark painting can now be appreciated, including the Crucifix laid at an angle on the book, and even a few trees of the woods in the background. The saint is shown just before he received the stigmata: scholars have recognised Caravaggio's self-portrait in his face. It is in its original dark frame, which bears the arms of Monsignor Benedetto Ala, who befriended the artist in 1606.

The three brothers of the **Campi family** (*see below*) are well represented, as well as their pupil Bernardino. The fresco of the Roman hero Curtius riding his horse into the abyss, detached from a palace façade, is a particularly good work by Giulio. The *Portrait of a Man and Boy* is by Lavinia Fontana, a contemporary of the Campi.

THE CAMPI FAMILY

Not a particularly talented painter himself, Galeazzo Campi (1477–1536) nevertheless left the world three gifted sons: Antonio (1524–87), Vincenzo (1536–91) and the most famous, Giulio (c. 1508–73). Antonio and Vincenzo are both noted for a use of chiaroscuro that foreshadows Caravaggio (the great artist is known to have been influenced by their work). Vincenzo was also particularly drawn to genre painting, producing bawdy scenes of working-class life. Here in Cremona, Giulio's work can be seen in the churches of Sant'Abbondio, Sant'Agata, Santa Margherita, San Sigismondo and in the duomo. Works by Antonio hang in the Museo Civico. But the brothers' work also spread further afield. Both Giulio and Antonio worked for Habsburg patrons, Giulio for Charles V, and Antonio for Philip II. Bernardino Campi (1521–91), son of a goldsmith called Pietro Campi (probably no relation), was a pupil of Giulio. He came into his own at the court of Vespasiano Gonzaga in Sabbioneta (*see p. 382*), where he carried out a large-scale programme of decoration, probably to his patron's specifications. One of the main streets of Sabbioneta is named after him.

Il Genovesino, who was the most important painter at work in Cremona in the mid-17th century, is represented by some small works as well as a portrait of Sigismondo Ponzone, the collector, with his dog. Beyond rooms with 18th–19th-century portraits by Giuseppe Diotti and Il Piccio, are rooms with Chinese and Japanese porcelain, nine carved wood reliefs by the local sculptor Giacomo Bertesi, Limoges enamels, and ivories (including an 11th-century diptych).

The Sala di Platina on an upper floor is named after the intarsia sacristy cupboards (1477) by Giovanni Maria Platina. The *Coronation of Christ and the Virgin by God the Father*, with very unusual iconography, is by Bonifacio Bembo and other works here are attributed to him. A *Madonna and Child* by a Ferrarese painter, with the subjects both laughing, is painted on both sides by Altobello Melone of the 15th-century Cremona school.

Another section of the museum, Le Stanze per la Musica, exhibits the Carlo Alberto Cerutti collection of some 50 historic plucked string instruments (and there is a little music room for concerts here). A separate room reached from the entrance staircase exhibits Ponzone's collection of antiquities, including a 4th-century BC red-figure krater and some Roman busts.

THE CHURCHES OF CREMONA

The main churches of interest in Cremona are described here in alphabetical order.

Sant'Abbondio (*map 3–4*). Corso Matteottti is a street with many fine old mansions, such as **Palazzo Fodri** (no. 17), dating from c. 1500, decorated with a terracotta frieze above its small marble portal and, above the windows, roundels with busts. **Palazzo Pallavicino** at no. 19 is a huge Neoclassical building. To the left, the narrow Vicolo Lauretano (spanned by a *Madonna and Child* and two angels in beaten metal) leads to the church of **Sant'Abbondio**, in a quiet spot. It has an interesting 16th-century interior frescoed by the otherwise little-known Bolognese artist Orazio Samacchini. The high altarpiece of the *Madonna and Child*, with two male saints (and nude putti playing with their armour) is by Giulio Campi (1527), who also frescoed the apse above, with the help of Malosso. In the vestibule is the *Madonna in Glory* surrounded by angel musicians by Giulio Campi's father, Galeazzo. The Loreto Chapel, entered from here, dates from 1624. From a door in the piazza you can see the Renaissance cloister.

Sant'Agata (*map 2; open for services*). The Neoclassical façade of **Sant'Agata** was built in 1848 by Luigi Voghera. Inside, on the right, is the Trecchi tomb by Gian Cristoforo Romano (1502–5), with beautifully carved bas-reliefs. The painting of the *Life of St Agatha* (painted on both sides) is by a northern Italian master of the 13th century. The handsome frescoes on the sanctuary walls are by Giulio Campi (1536).

Opposite the church is the old **Palazzo del Popolo** or Palazzo Cittanova (1256), with a ground-floor arcade. It was the headquarters of the popular—or Guelph—party in the days of the free city-state of Cremona. Behind it on Via Trecchi is **Palazzo Trecchi**, first built in the 15th century but altered in later centuries, which has a very pleasant café in the courtyard (and in the garden in summer). Opposite at no. 19 is **Villa Sartori**, which has early frescoes in the interior (but is privately owned).

Sant'Agostino (*map 6*). A 14th-century church with a handsome tower and terracotta ornamentation on the façade. In the interior on the south side are frescoes by Bonifacio Bembo in the vault of the third chapel; a stoup with reliefs by Bonino da Campione (1357); and an *Annunciation* by Antonio Campi. The *Madonna with Sts John the Evangelist and Augustine* is signed and dated 1494 (on the throne) by the great painter **Perugino** (it was commissioned for an altar in the church by a local nobleman, Eliseo Roncadelli). It repeats a composition used in other works by the artist (including one in the Uffizi), but for all that is very beautifully painted and its autography has never been questioned. It is particularly interesting since no

CREMONA, SANTA RITA
Christ Disputing with the Doctors, by Giulio Campi (1547).

other complete works by Perugino can be seen in northern Italy today.

San Luca (*map 2; often closed*). The 15th-century façade of **San Luca**, adorned with the terracotta ornament typical of Cremona, is in poor repair. Adjoining it is the little octagonal Renaissance chapel of **Cristo Risorto** (1503), attributed to Bernardino de Lera. Also by Bernardino de Lera is **Palazzo Raimondi** (1496), at Corso Garibaldi 178. It has damaged frescoes on its curved cornice.

Santi Marcellino e Pietro (*map 7*). This church, rather in need of restoration, has elaborate marble and stucco decorations in the interior (1602–20). It owns two good works painted by Genovesino in his maturity (*Presentation of the Virgin in the Temple* and *Martyrdom and Glory of St Ursula*, 1652).

San Michele (*map 4*). The church stands at the end of Via Gerolamo da Cremona, near remains of the old city walls. Lombard in origin (7th century), it is the oldest church in Cremona. It was reconstructed in the 11th and 12th centuries and the exterior of the apse, decorated with brickwork, dates from this time. In the interior are 12th-century columns in the nave with lovely leafy capitals and a raised sanctuary. The second south altarpiece, the *Nativity*, is by Bernardino Campi (the detached fresco fragment of the *Madonna and Child* is attributed to Benedetto Bembo). The third altarpiece, of *Christ on the Cross*, with saints (and the kneeling donor dressed as a Knight of Malta), is by Giulio Campi. At the

end of this side are two panels of the *Annunciation* (organ doors of 1508) by the little-known Alessandro Pampurino. The third north altar has a *Pietà* also by Pampurino, surrounded by six small rectangular paintings of the life of Christ (1606). On the first altar there is popular statue of *St Anne*, with the Madonna reading, and (behind glass) a fresco fragment of the Madonna waiting to give birth (with Joseph helpfully holding up a towel).

San Pietro al Po (*map 7*). The name of this monastic church is a reminder that it once stood on the banks of the Po (the little piazza in front of it slopes steeply down to a street which follows the former course of the river). The interior is sumptuously decorated with 16th-century paintings and stuccoes. At the east end of the two sides are reliquary cupboards. The fourth north altarpiece of the *Madonna and Saints* (1524) is signed by Gian Francesco Bembo; the third altarpiece of the *Madonna and Saints* is signed and dated 1567 by Antonio Campi (with a fresco of the *Circumcision* above by his brother Giulio Campi) and the second altarpiece of the *Nativity* is considered the best work of Bernardino Gatti (1555). The first altarpiece (in the baptistery) of the *Madonna and Child* is by Malosso.

Santa Rita (officially Santa Margherita; *map 2; open 10–12.30 & 2.30 or 3–4.30 or 5, except Sun afternoon*). This little church, recently restored, dates from 1547, when the six frescoes of **scenes from the life of Christ by Giulio Campi** (considered his best work) were painted (now detached). There is a fine scene of the *Sermon on the Mount* and of *Christ Disputing with the Doctors.* Giulio also made the statuettes of the twelve Apostles in terracotta (darkened to look like bronze). Not far away, at **Via Milazzo 16**, is a remarkable Art Nouveau house façade with stucco motifs of campsis flowers.

San Vincenzo (*map 2*). The Baroque façade of 1629 is deceptive, concealing a much older brick church with apses and a bell-tower at the back. In the interior are works by Francesco Boccaccino and Gervasio Gatti.

THE PO

Corso Vittorio Emanuele, with the Teatro Amilcare Ponchielli by Luigi Canonica (1808), leads to Piazza Cadorna (*map 6*). Viale Po, an avenue some 2km long which starts here, the site of the old Porta Po, has a cycle lane and pavements on either side. At no. 15 there is a pleasant café, Km0. If you are on foot, it is perhaps pleasanter to diverge left after this (along a path alongside Parco Tognazzi), to take the narrower Via del Sale. It is about a 20min walk to the Parco Lungo Po Europa, on the banks of the great river Po, where boat trips can be taken in summer.

SAN SIGISMONDO

On the eastern outskirts of the town (on the Casalmaggiore road, beyond map 4), over 2km from Piazza Libertà (Porta Venezia). To get there, take the infrequent bus no. 2 for the hospital (otherwise it is a rather unpleasant walk of about 45mins along a main road). You can get a bus back to the centre of town (Piazza Roma) from outside the hospital on the other side of the main road. The church is usually open, but if closed, ring at the closed order of Dominican nuns on the right.

This important Lombard Renaissance church was where Francesco Sforza was married to Bianca Visconti in 1441, with the town of Cremona as the bride's dowry. The present building was started in 1463 in celebration of the event. The interior contains splendid painted decoration carried out between 1535 and 1570, much of it by the local artists Camillo Boccaccino and Bernardino Gatti. This is also a good place to see works by the Campi family.

On the south side, the first chapel contains a niche (difficult to see) in which two glass carafes are preserved; these were found in 1963 on a brick dated 1492 at the base of the façade (they were filled with oil and wine to commemorate the beginning of this church's construction). The foundation stone is preserved here.

The high altarpiece, which includes portraits of Francesco and Bianca Sforza, is by Giulio Campi (signed and dated 1540) and preserves its beautiful contemporary frame. The presbytery and apse have fine frescoes by Camillo Boccaccino.

The barrel vault of the nave was decorated by Bernardino and Giulio Campi and Bernardino Gatti. On the west wall, on either side of the rose window, is an *Annunciation* by Giulio Campi. Another work by Giulio Campi can be seen in the fifth south chapel (altarpiece), while the vault here was decorated by Bernardino Campi, who also produced the altarpiece in the next (sixth) chapel and the fresco of *Paradise* in the 'dome'. The transept vaults were painted by Giulio Campi. On the north side, the fifth chapel is entirely decorated with paintings, frescoes and stuccoes by Antonio Campi, while the third chapel has more fine works by Bernardino Campi.

AROUND CREMONA

The small province of Cremona is chiefly bordered by rivers, and Cremona itself is only just north of the Po. The rich alluvial soil makes it ideal for farming, and in fact the area's agricultural vocation can be seen and felt everywhere. The countryside is studded with huge *cascinali* (rural building complexes in which hay barns, stables, granaries and old farm workers' housing rise side by side), many of which are now abandoned. Most of the towns and villages still bear the imprint of the country market centre, with lovely central squares often surrounded by arcaded walks.

CREMA

Crema (*Atlas A, A1*), on the west bank of the Serio, is the most important town in the province after Cremona. It was under Venetian rule from 1454 to 1797 and was the birthplace of the composer Francesco Cavalli (1600–76). Arriving by train from the west, you enter the town along the course of the Vacchelli canal, which flows gently through flat fields, with a towpath alongside it, popular with fishermen and sunbathers. The centre of town is on the west bank of the Serio and south of the Vacchelli. Remains of the old walls are visible in a park by the banks of the Serio, pierced by the Neoclassical **Arco di Porta Serio** (1805), beyond which is Piazza Garibaldi. A short way up to the left, Via Dante leads south to Piazzetta Winifred Terni de Gregorj, with the 17th–18th-century **Palazzo Terni**, in brick with Baroque stone facings, statuary and other ornament. Here too is the **Museo Civico**, in an early 15th-century ex-Augustinian convent (*open Tues 2.30–5.30, Wed–Fri 10–12 & 2.30–5.30, Sat–Sun 10–12 & 3.30–6.30; free; café*). The two cloisters have lapidary fragments and the main collections on the upper floor include coins, ceramics, arms and armour, applied arts, musical instruments and paintings from the 16th century to the present.

Piazza Duomo, with numerous cafés under Tuscan arcades, lies to the west. The **duomo** (1284–1341), built in the medieval style of the stone carvers and masons from the Campione region, contains a painting of *Christ Appearing to St Mark in Prison* (fourth bay on the south side), one of the last works of the great Bolognese painter Guido Reni, left unfinished at his death in 1642. As you leave the duomo by the north door, look right to see the 16th-century **Palazzo Pretorio**, adorned with a Lion of St Mark, relic of Venetian rule here. Its archway leads to the main thoroughfare, Via Matteotti, with *pasticcerie* selling local specialities.

North of the railway line, approached up a tree-shaded road (*15mins on foot*) is the sanctuary church of **Santa Maria della Croce**, a handsome, brick-built, centrally-planned church in the style of Bramante by Giovanni Battagio (1490–1500). It stands

CREMA, MUSEO CIVICO
Tombstone of Aaron Moses, son of Jacob Levi (1490).
The Jewish community in Crema began to flourish after the mid-15th century,
when the Duke of Milan permitted them to set up money-lending businesses.

on the site where the Virgin is said to have appeared in 1490 to a woman stabbed by her husband and close to death, promising that she would not die of her wounds before receiving the Holy Sacrament. And so, according to the story, it proved. The site of the apparition is now a chapel (known as the Scurolo) reserved for prayer. In the main body of the church are four late 16th-century altarpieces: two by Bernardino Campi (*Adoration of the Magi, Deposition*), one by Antonio Campi (*Nativity*) and the fourth (*Road to Calvary*) by Carlo Urbino. The sanctuary is an important pilgrimage destination.

PIZZIGHETTONE

Pizzighettone (*Atlas A, A2*) is an old town divided in two by the Adda. Significant remains of its fortifications are preserved, including the circuit of walls (last strengthened in 1585); and the **Torre del Guado**, on the banks of the Adda, where François I was imprisoned after the Battle of Pavia in 1525 (*see p. 153*). The main church of **San Bassiano** has a frescoed *Crucifixion* by Bernardino Campi.

SONCINO

East of Crema is Soncino (*Atlas A, A1*), an attractive town once known for its water mills (several survive). The tyrant Ezzelino da Romano, ally of Emperor Frederick II, died here after his defeat by the Guelphs in the battle of Cassano d'Adda.

The historic centre is surrounded by splendid **town walls** (13th–15th century), nearly 2km in circumference. The **Rocca Sforzesca** castle (*closed Mon; soncino.org*) was rebuilt by Galeazzo Maria Sforza and is among the best preserved in Lombardy.

It was restored in 1886 by Luca Beltrami. Close to the castle, in an old silk mill, is the **Museo della Seta**, with displays on the silk industry.

The main street of the old town, Via IV Novembre, begins from the site of the south gate. On the right is the 15th-century **Palazzo Azzanelli**, with terracotta decoration. The street leads into the main square. Before it, on the right, is the church of **San Giacomo**, which has a curious seven-sided tower (1350) and a cloister. It contains two stained-glass windows by a certain Ambrogio da Tormoli (1490) and a late 15th-century terracotta *Pietà*. In the main square (Piazza Garibaldi) is the 11th-century **Torre Civica**. Nearby at Via Lanfranco 6–8 is the **Museo della Stampa** (*closed Mon; museostampasoncino.it*) in a medieval tower house thought to be on the site of the first printing works founded in the town in 1480. The press was set up by the Jewish Nathan family, who were allowed by the Sforza (in return for cash loans) to take up residence here, having been forced to leave Germany. They adopted the name of the town for their press and, in the decade in which they lived and worked here, they printed their first book (in 1483) and the first complete Hebrew Bible (in 1488). A reproduction press is still in operation.

On the southern outskirts, on Via Francesco Galantino, is the church of **Santa Maria delle Grazie** (*ring for admission at the convent*), begun in 1492 and consecrated in 1528, splendidly decorated with terracotta friezes and frescoes, many of them attributed to Giulio Campi (including those on the triumphal arch and sanctuary vault).

East of Soncino is **Orzinuovi** (*Atlas A, A1*), with imposing remains of Venetian ramparts. From here the road descends to **Verolanuova** (*Atlas A, B1*), where the church of San Lorenzo contains two large paintings by the great Venetian painter Giovanni Battista Tiepolo, in excellent condition.

PRACTICAL INFORMATION

GETTING AROUND

• **By rail:** Services run by Trenord link Cremona to Milan (1hr 15mins), Bergamo (1hr 15mins) and Brescia (1hr). Crema can be reached by train from Milan Porta Garibaldi (1hr 5mins) or Lambrate (45mins). There are also trains from Cremona to Pizzighettone (journey time c. 25mins).

• **By bus:** The network of local buses serving Cremona is quite sparse.

From Crema there are buses roughly hourly to Soncino and Orzinuovi, and a few services a day from Orzinuovi to Verolanuova.

• **By bicycle:** For bicycle hire, enquire at the Infopoint in Cremona.

• **By car:** There is a free car park in Piazza della Libertà in Cremona (*map 4*) and in a courtyard off Via Villa Glori (*map 2*). The underground car park in Piazza Marconi (*map 7*) is a pay park.

INFORMATION OFFICES

Cremona Infopoint is at Piazza del Comune 5 (*map 7; T: 0372 23233, turismocremona.it*). For information on the museums, *musei.comune.cremona.it*. **Crema** Pro Loco office at Piazza Duomo 22 (*prolococrema.it*). **Soncino**. In the Rocca Sforzesca ticket office. Closed Mon.

WHERE TO STAY

CREMONA

€€ Impero. In a solid, Fascist-era building. Well located; some rooms have views of the duomo. *Piazza della Pace 21, T: 0372 413013, hotelimpero.cr.it. Map 7.*

€€ Locanda Torriani, a small hotel with just 10 rooms round a courtyard in the shadow of the Torrazzo. With restaurant. *Via Torriani 7. T: 0372 30017, locandatorriani.it. Map 3.*

€ Duomo. A simple small hotel just 10mins from the duomo. Also a pizzeria. *Via Gonfalonieri 13. T: 0372 35242, hotelduomocremona.com. Map 7.*

CREMA

€–€€ Relais Vimercati. Just six comfortably furnished rooms and suites in the historic Palazzo Donati. *Via Vimercati 13. T: 331 167 9168, relaisvimercati.it.*

WHERE TO EAT

CREMONA

€€€ Il Violino. Local cuisine and fish. *Via Sicardo 3. T: 0372 461010, ilviolino. it. Map 7.*

€€ Ristorante Cerri. Bar and restaurant offering typical Cremonese dishes. Closed Tues and Wed. *Piazza Giovanni XXIII 3. T: 0372 22796. Map 3.*

€€ Hosteria 700. In Palazzo Barbò. They make their own *mostarda*. Cremonese *marubini* (similar to tortellini) with butter and sage or in broth. Closed Mon evening and Tues. *Piazza Gallina 1. T: 0372 36175, hosteria700.com. Map 3.*

€€ La Sosta. Modern décor and old-fashioned Cremonese cuisine in a 15th-century building. Closed Sun evening and Mon. *Via Sicardo 9. T: 0372 456656, osterialasosta.it. Map 7.*

€€ Locanda Torriani. Restaurant and guest house. Offers a contemporary take on traditional local cuisine. Closed Sun evening and Mon. *Via Torriani 7. T: 0372 30017, locandatorriani.it. Map 3.*

€ Chiave di Bacco. Calling itself a lounge bar/bistro, the restaurant of the Museo del Violino. *Piazza Marconi. T: 0372 808850. Map 7.*

€ Duomo. A pizzeria. Always open. *Via Gonfalonieri 13. T: 0372 35296. Map 7.*

€ Osteria Pane e Salame. As the name suggests, a place you can come for just a plate of ham and salami. But the menu is wider than that, with pasta dishes and a good choice of simple main courses. Always open. *Via Platina 32. T: 0372 438125. Map 7.*

CREMA

€€ Botero. Fine dining: a fusion between traditional local and contemporary international. Good wine list. Closed Sun evening and Mon. *Via Verdi 7. T: 0373 87911, ristorantebotero.it.*

€ Caffè Vienna. Coffee, cakes and simple lunches, and with a *menù del giorno*. *Via Mazzini 84 (corner of Via Dante).*

SONCINO

€€ Molino San Giuseppe. Restaurant in an old water mill, specialising in meat dishes. Closed Mon and Tues.

Via Borgo Sotto 4. T: 0374 83060, ristorantemolinosangiuseppe.net.

CAFÉS AND CAKE SHOPS

CREMONA
Cremona is absolutely brimming with cafés and pastry shops. Directly opposite the Torrazza, next to the duomo at the **Pasticceria Duomo** (*Via Boccaccino 6; closed Tues*), you can sip cappuccino, sample delightful cakes and pastries and admire the finest brickwork in Lombardy, all at once. **Ai Portici**, under the arches of Palazzo Comunale, is a very pleasant café and wine bar.

Pasticceria Milanese Ebbli has a pretty interior (*Via Cavallotti 5; open 7–1 & 5.30–9 except Tues afternoon; map 7*).

On the square in front of the railway station is **Dondeo** (*Via Dante 18; map 2*), one of the favourite cafés of the Cremonese.

For snacks try the **Panificio Generali** at Corso Mazzini 79 (*map 3*).

CREMA
Crema has a number of speciality cakes: Torta Bertolina (traditionally an autumn delicacy, made with grapes); a sweet loaf known as Mattonella del Duomo; and Torta Helvetia (almond meringue, sponge and hazelnut cream with rum). *Spongarda* is a cake made with dried and candied fruits and spices. All can be found at **Pasticceria Radaelli** (*Via Matteotti 9*).

LOCAL SPECIALITIES

CREMONA
Cremona is known for its *mostarda* (pickled candied fruit in a mustard-flavoured syrup, giving it a sweet and sour flavour), as an accompaniment to meat dishes such as the Gran Bollito Cremonese (traditionally prepared with at least five different stewed meats), or with salami or cheese.

Specialities of the region include salami and matured cheeses. **Nougat** (*torrone*) is also made here.

Among the best places to find all these in Cremona are: **Enogastronomia Mazzini** (*Corso XX Settembre 49, enogastronomiamazzini.com; map 4*); **Formaggi d'Italia** (*Via Mercatello, corner of Piazza del Comune; open all day at weekends; map 7*); and **Gastronomia Zilli** (*corner of Piazza Marconi and Via Bella Chiopella; map 7*).

CREMA
The culinary speciality of Crema are *tortelli cremaschi*, a sort of hand-made ravioli with a sweet and sour filling, typically served with melted butter and sage.

FESTIVALS AND EVENTS

Cremona is best known for its classical music festivals: the **Festival di Cremona Claudio Monteverdi** in May and June and the **Festival Stradivari** in Sept and Oct. The Consorzio Liutai 'A. Stradivari' runs the Cremona **Summer Festival** for children and young adults (*see cremonaviolins.com*). The Teatro Ponchiello has a **concert season** from Jan to April and opera from Oct to Dec.

A **street market** is held in the centre of Cremona twice a week (on Wed and Sat mornings) in Piazza Duomo, Piazza Stradivari and Piazza della Pace. Cremona also hosts a festival celebrating its famous nougat, the **Festa del Torrone**, in late Nov (*festadeltorrone.com*).

Practical Information

PLANNING YOUR TRIP

CLIMATE

The nicest months in Lombardy are May–June and Sept–Oct. Early spring and late autumn can be wet and chilly, with strong blustery winds. In Milan and the main cities of the Po valley, high summer is extremely hot—not ideal for sightseeing. The upper Alpine valleys, however, are at their best, with a profusion of wild flowers. The lakes are crowded from mid-June to early Sept; before and after this season, the waterfronts can be practically deserted. In August, Italians are on holiday, so that smaller shops and businesses close, as local life moves from the towns to the holiday resorts.

MAPS

Detailed maps of the region, as well as plans of many cities, are included in this guide, with grid references to the text. If you want a larger, fold-out map, the Touring Club Italiano (TCI; *see p. 95*) publishes several sets of excellent maps, including one of the Lombardy region. They are widely available from many booksellers, as well as from the TCI's own shop in Milan.

DISABLED TRAVELLERS

All new public buildings are obliged to provide facilities for the disabled. Historic buildings are more difficult to convert, and access difficulties still exist. Hotels that cater for the disabled are indicated in tourist board lists. Airports and railway stations provide assistance, and certain trains are equipped to transport wheelchairs. Access to town centres is allowed for cars with disabled drivers or passengers, and special parking places are reserved for them.

GETTING AROUND

BY CAR

Despite the persistent clichés about chaotic driving, Italians are usually considerate and patient when behind the wheel, ever alert for other road users changing lanes without warning and able to weave in and out of gridlock jams or to tolerate long waits behind delivery vans in the narrow streets of their historic towns. Motorways are busy and the lanes can seem alarmingly narrow. And as 80 percent of goods transported travel by road, there are large numbers of lorries.

Certain customs differ from those of the UK or America. Unless otherwise indicated, cars entering a road from the right are given precedence. Trams and trains always have right of way. If an oncoming driver flashes his headlights, it means he is proceeding and not giving you precedence. Drivers tend to ignore pedestrian crossings.

Roads in Italy

Italy's motorways (*autostrade*; for information: www.autostrade.it) are indicated by green signs or, near the entrance ramps, by large boards of overhead lights. All are toll-roads. Choose the lanes with cash or bank card booths, not TelePass unless you have that system set up. At the entrance to motorways, the two directions are indicated by the name of the most important town (not by the nearest town), which can be momentarily confusing. Dual-carriageways are called *superstrade* (also indicated by green signs). Secondary highways (*strade statali, regionali* or *provinciali*) are indicated by blue signs marked SS, SR or SP and then the road number.

Parking

Many city centres are closed to traffic (except for residents). Access is allowed to hotels and for the disabled. It is always advisable to leave your car in a guarded car park, though with a bit of effort it is almost always possible to find a place to park free of charge, away from the town centre. Always lock your car when parked, and of course, never leave anything of value inside it. Convenient car parks have been listed in the text.

BY RAIL

Information on rail links is given in individual chapters. Lombardy is served by trains run by Trenitalia (*trenitalia.it*), Italo (*italotreno.it*), and Trenord (*trenord.it*). The latter only operates local trains. You can buy tickets online but there are still manned ticket offices, as well as ticket machines, in most of the larger railway stations. The smaller ones have ticket machines only. There is a large ticket office and information office in Milan's Stazione Centrale and at Milan Cadorna. The trains themselves vary: high-speed services between the main towns are clean and well appointed while many of the local trains (which are a great deal cheaper) are quite run-down. Nevertheless, the network is extensive, prices are very reasonable and the service is mostly efficient.

On all high-speed trains you have a seat reservation when you purchase your ticket. For the local services you can't reserve and you have to validate your ticket at a machine in the station before you board the train. Machines for this are placed by platform entrances. You can be fined if you forget to do it. Larger stations have left-luggage offices and there is also an App (Bag BnB) which allows you (for a small fee) to leave luggage in the nearest place convenient to you.

BY BUS

Information on regional bus services is given in each individual chapter. There are many different companies serving different local areas and services vary considerably. Some are very frequent; others are sparse and timetabled to be convenient for local users, commuters or school children. In the case of city buses, you normally need to buy your ticket in advance, at a newspaper kiosk or tobacconist. There is usually a ticket office in the bus station for regional buses, but these also tend to operate a system of paying the driver..

BY BICYCLE

In most provincial Lombard towns, bicycle is the way people get around. Bikes are available for hire from stands in the centre of some towns or at their railway stations. Many cycle lanes have been introduced as well as extensive cycle routes in the countryside. Local tourist offices can help you with details.

TAXIS

These are hired from ranks or by telephone; there are no cruising cabs. From Milan Malpensa airport to the city centre, there is a fixed fare. Otherwise, before beginning a journey, always make sure the cab has a meter that is switched on and in working order. Fares vary from city to city. No tip is expected. Supplements are charged for late-night journeys and for luggage.

LANGUAGE

In all the main tourist areas, in hotels, restaurants, museums etc., English is spoken. In remoter places, this is not always the case and even a few words of Italian are a great advantage (and will be greatly appreciated). There is a Lombard dialect, but everybody can speak and understand Italian. Letters of the alphabet are pronounced roughly as in English with the following exceptions:

c and **cc**	before e and i have the sound of **ch** in chess
ch	before e and i has the sound of **k**
g and **gg**	before e and i are always soft, like **j** in jelly
gh	always hard, like **g** in get
gl	nearly always like **lli** in million (there are a few exceptions, for example, *negligere*, where it is pronounced as in English)
gn	like **ny** in lanyard
gu and **qu**	always like **gw** and **kw**
j	like **y** in you
s	like **s** in six, except when it occurs between two vowels, when it is pronounced like the English **z** or the s in rose
sc	before e and i is pronounced like **sh** in ship

ss	always voiceless
z and **zz**	usually pronounced like **ts**, but occasionally, before a long vowel, have the sound of **dz**

ACCOMMODATION

A small selection of hotels and B&Bs, chosen on the basis of charm and location (corresponding to the places covered in the guide), is given at the end of each chapter. The listings use the following price categories per double room per night:

€€€€	€500–900 and above
€€€	€300–400
€€	around €200
€	around €100

A per-night tourist tax will be added to the room rate. By law breakfast is an optional extra, although a lot of hotels include it in the room price. When booking, always specify if you want breakfast or not. If you are staying in a hotel in a town, it is often more fun to go round the corner to a café for breakfast. Hotels are obliged to issue an official tax receipt. You can be fined if you leave the premises without one.

FOOD & DRINK

Italian food is delicious and one of the many reasons to come to Italy. A selection of restaurants is given at the end of each chapter. It used to be the case that eating establishments ranged from the elegant (*ristorante*) to rough and ready (*osteria*), with the *trattoria* (small restaurant) category somewhere in between. Today those classifications are far less rigid and a restaurant's name gives little away about its pretensions. Even places calling themselves a café or bar often offer excellent simple full meals. It is best to check the menu, which most places have posted up outside, to get an idea of what is on offer. A service charge is almost always automatically added to the bill; tipping is therefore not strictly necessary but a few euro are appreciated.

The listings at the end of each chapter in this guide use the following price categories for dinner per person (wine excluded):

€€€€	over €125
€€€	€80–€125
€€	€30–€80
€	under €30

BARS AND CAFÉS

Bars and cafés are open from early morning to late at night. The tradition of popping into a café for a quick espresso, which is usually taken standing up, is still widespread everywhere. The traditional system, still adhered to in many places, is to pay the cashier first, then give your receipt (*scontrino*) to the barman in order to get served. If you sit at a table the charge is usually higher, and you will be given waiter service (so don't pay first). However, some simple bars have a few tables that can be used with no extra charge, and it is always best to ask, before ordering, whether there is waiter service or not. Choose a *pasticceria* if you want something good to eat to accompany your coffee. The best ice cream normally comes from a *gelateria*. At a crowded café counter, a certain amount of self-assertion is needed, since queues are not the general rule. It is incumbent on you the customer to make yourself heard.

REGIONAL CUISINE

This book takes in two other regions of Italy beside Lombardy itself: the west side of Lake Maggiore in Piedmont and the east bank of Lake Garda in the Veneto. The cuisines have important local variations.

Lombardy is prime agricultural land, and its cuisine is characterised by abundant meat and cheese, and by the use of butter rather than olive oil. The signature cheese of the region is Grana Padano, a hard cheese made in the Po valley. In appearance it is similar to Parmesan, but is mellower and less tangy. There are plenty of other local cheeses too, such as Bagòss from Brescia, Taleggio, Robiola and Quartirolo, and Bitto and Formai de Mut from the mountain regions.

A ubiquitous first course is ravioli, typical of Bergamo and Brescia, known as *casonei* (or *capunsei* or *casoncelli*). It comes with a variety of fillings and sauces; the simplest is with melted butter and fresh sage leaves. *Tortelli di zucca* are also popular: pasta pockets filled with pumpkin. The Valtellina is proud of its *bresaola* (salted, air-dried beef). Also common here are *pizzoccheri* (buckwheat pasta ribbons) and *sciatt* (cheese balls: the word, in dialect, means 'toad').

Traditional main courses are the *costoletta alla milanese*, a breaded veal cutlet fried in butter, and *osso buco*, sliced veal shin cooked slowly in tomato sauce. The Lombard lakes all serve good fish: *lavarello* (a white fish) and *missoltini* (dried and salted, like a kipper). The fish to look out for in Lake Garda is the *coregone*. The signature dish of Pavia is *rane in umido*, frogs cooked in a sauce of tomatoes and leeks.

Rice is grown in Lombardy as well as in Piedmont, and many places in these regions, as well as in Milan, specialise in risotto. The staple of Bergamo is polenta.

An interesting local relish (traditionally served with boiled meat but also excellent with hard cheese) is *mostarda* (a fruit compote made with honey and white wine and seasoned with mustard and other spices). The *mostarda* of Cremona is particularly famous.

Good Lombard desserts include the Milanese Christmas cake *panettone*; Bergamasque *polenta dolce* (cornflour cooked with milk, egg yolks, amaretti, butter and cinnamon); and Mantuan *torta sbrisolona* (wheat and cornflour, sugar, egg yolks, chopped almonds, baked until dry then crumbled rather than sliced).

The famous appetiser of Piedmont is *vitello tonnato* (*vitel tonné* in dialect, made with boiled spiced veal sliced thin and smothered in a sauce of tuna, anchovies and capers), has its origin here. Ravioli is once again popular, and here it is known as *agnolotti*. It comes either filled with meat or with spinach and cheese. Main courses include *bagna cauda* (a hot spicy sauce with garlic and anchovies used as a dip for raw vegetables) and *brasato al Barolo* (beef marinated in a Barolo wine sauce with lard, carrots and spices, then slowly braised in the marinade together with meat broth and tomatoes).

All across the region you will encounter shops, cafés and snack bars offering *piadine*, circular flatbreads. Served with all kinds of fillings, both savoury and sweet, they make an excellent quick and easy meal.

WINE

Most Italian wines take their names from the geographical area in which they are produced or the grapes from which they are made. The finer wines are indentified by the estate on which the grapes were grown. The best are marked DOC (*di origine controllata*). This is Italy's *appellation controlée*, which specifies maximum yields per vine, geographical boundaries within which grapes must be grown, permitted grape varieties and production techniques. Superior even to DOC is the DOCG (*di origine controllata e garantita*). This is not to say that DOCG wines are automatically better than any other. Regulations are rigid, and winemakers wanting to experiment with alternative grape varieties or vinification techniques sometimes find themselves barred from the DOC or DOCG classifications and have to label their wines IGT (*vino da tavola con indicazione geografica tipica*), in other words a *vin de pays*. Simple *vino da tavola* is table wine. It can be excellent, but the quality is not guaranteed.

Red wines are *vini rossi* on the wine list; white wines, *vini bianchi*; rosés, *chiaretti* or *rosati*. Dry wines are *secchi*; sweet wines, *amabili* or *dolci*. *Moscato* and *passito* is wine made from grapes that have been left on the vine or dried before pressing. In Lombardy, many white wines are *spumante*, meaning fizzy. If you do not want wine with bubbles, ask for something *fermo*.

Wines of Piedmont (Lake Maggiore)

Piedmont is one of the finest wine-growing areas in Italy, home to the famous **Barolo** and **Barbaresco** wines, superb expressions of the Nebbiolo grape. **Dolcetto** is a lighter red. Grown throughout Piedmont, Dolcetto grapes are low in acid and high in tannin, which accounts for the wine's bittersweet mixture of softness and astringency. **Barbera** is another grape used for single-varietal reds. Light and tart when young, its high-acidity gives it excellent maturing potential.

Cortese is a single-varietal white. Sometimes made with small percentages of other non-aromatic whites, it is perfect with appetisers, delicate pasta and rice dishes. **Gavi**, probably the most famous Piedmontese white, is the best expression of the Cortese grape. It is good with fish and seafood.

Wines of Lombardy

Lombardy produces a famous DOCG wine, **Franciacorta**, famous for its *metodo classico* sparkling wines (*see p. 318*). Some interesting rustic red wines come from the **Valtellina**, made from Nebbiolo, here called Chiavennasca, by small boutique growers. The DOCs Valtellina and Valtellina Superiore are divided into four sub-appellations: Grumello, Inferno, Sassella and Valgella, all delicious with the famous bresaola of the region. Late-pressed grapes make the rich, strong **Sfurzat**, the Amarone of the Valtellina, made with the same raisining technique as the better-known Valpolicella wine.

Wines of Lake Garda

The Lake Garda wine-growing region includes the Soave district, Valpolicella and Bardolino. **Soave** makes an excellent dry white, while the **Valpolicella** region makes well-known reds. **Amarone** is made from grapes that have been dried like raisins. The wine is dry, but very rich and full-bodied. **Recioto** is the sweet version, where the grapes have not fermented to complete dryness. Another excellent white from the region is **Lugana**, made from the Trebbiano di Lugana grape, grown on the southern shores of Garda below Desenzano and Sirmione. Refreshing and fruity, the wine is widely available as a house white in restaurants and goes extremely well with light food. A simple red is **Gropello**, from the southwestern shores of Garda.

ADDITIONAL INFORMATION

BANKS AND CASH MACHINES

All banks now have ATM machines outside, but if you need to go into a bank they usually only have cash desks open in the morning on weekdays 8.30–1.30, even though they also open for an hour or so in the afternoons (usually 2.30–3.30).

CHURCHES AND CHURCH DESCRIPTIONS

Some churches ask that sightseers do not enter during a service, but if you are on your own, not in a group, you can normally do so, provided you are silent and do not approach the altar in use. Make sure that you are decorously dressed, with legs and shoulders covered. Coin-operated lights illuminating altarpieces take €1 or 50c coins. In Holy Week most of the sacred images are covered and are on no account shown. In many churches there is a sacristan who will open chapels for you (a small tip will be appreciated). In the descriptions of churches, the terms 'north' and 'south' refer not to compass north and south but to the liturgical north (left-hand side) and south (right-hand side), taking the high altar as being at the east end.

CRIME AND PERSONAL SECURITY

Pickpocketing can be a problem in all towns. Be alert on buses and metro trains, in crowded markets and railway stations. Thefts should be reported at once to the

Polizia di Stato or Carabinieri. A statement has to be given in order to get a document confirming loss or damage (essential for insurance claims). Interpreters are provided. Italian law requires everyone to carry some form of photo ID: it is therefore best to keep your passport with you. The Carabinieri (and standard European) emergency number is 112. The Italian state police respond to 113.

OPENING TIMES

Where possible these have been given in the text, but they should be taken as an approximate guide since they are always subject to change, and less-visited places often have erratic hours because of staff shortages. Some monuments are kept open by volunteers (*see for example touringclub.it/i-luoghi-aperti-per-voi*). If a website is provided in our text, do take the precaution of checking for updates before you visit, or check at the local tourist office. For the most famous places (except in deep winter) it is always wise to book in advance on line, and note that in Milan you can only visit Leonardo's *Last Supper* by pre-booking (*see p. 66*).

As a general rule, state-run museums are closed on Mon (unless it is a public holiday). Some museums are closed on the main public holidays: 1 Jan, Easter, 1 May, 15 Aug and 25 Dec. Some specialist museums are open by appointment only.

Churches tend to open early in the morning for the first Mass and then close for a few hours during the middle of the day, typically from noon until 4 or 5pm. Some larger churches, especially those which have become major visitor destinations, are open all day. Parks, gardens and archaeological sites tend to close at dusk.

Shops used to be open Mon–Sat 8.30/9–1 and 3.30/4–7.30/8. In larger towns and cities it is now normal for shops to stay open all day and in larger cities there are convenience stores open round the clock. In smaller places where there is still a high proportion of owner-managed shops, you will find that they close for lunch. August is the great holiday month in Italy and many smaller shops, restaurants and other businesses close altogether for a fortnight or so.

PHARMACIES

Pharmacies (*farmacie*) are usually open Mon–Fri 9–1 & 4–7.30 or 8. A few are open also on weekends and holidays (listed on the door of every pharmacy). In all towns there is also at least one pharmacy open at night (also shown on the door of every pharmacy). For emergencies and to call an ambulance, T. 118.

PUBLIC HOLIDAYS

Italian national holidays are as follows:

1 Jan	New Year's Day
6 Jan	Epiphany
Easter Sun and Easter Mon	
25 April	Liberation Day
1 May	Labour Day
2 June	Anniversary of the Republic

15 Aug	Assumption
1 Nov	All Saints' Day
8 Dec	Immaculate Conception
25 Dec	Christmas Day
26 Dec	St Stephen

Each town keeps its patron saint's day and colourful celebrations are often held.

TELEPHONES AND THE INTERNET

A large number of hotels now offer free wifi, as do many cafés and bars and in some towns there are now wifi open zones in *piazze* etc. The country dialling code for Italy is +39. The city code for Milan is 02. When making calls, even from one Milan number to another, for example, you should not drop the zero.

TIPPING

Most prices in hotels and restaurants include a service charge, so tipping is far less widespread in Italy than it is in North America. Even taxi drivers rarely expect more than a euro or two added to the charge (which officially includes service). In restaurants, it will be appreciated if you round up the bill and leave a little extra. Hotel porters also expect a small gratuity.

Glossary of Terms

Acrolith, extremity of a statue (hand, foot, head) made of stone, while the body of the statue would have been of wood or other perishable material

Aedicule, in a building, small niche or opening, framed by columns at the sides and with a pediment (*qv*) above

Ambo (pl. ambones), pulpit in a Christian basilica; two pulpits on opposite sides of the nave from which the Gospel and Epistle were read

Ambulatory, section of a church, usually with chapels, that curves round and behind the high altar and choir

Amorino (pl. amorini), in painting and sculpture, an infant cupid

Amphora, antique vase, usually of large dimensions, for oil and other liquids

Ancona, an altarpiece, usually carved, though it can also consist of painted panels inserted into a single frame

Annunciation, the appearance of the Angel Gabriel to Mary to tell her that she will bear the Son of God; an image of the 'Virgin Annunciate' shows her receiving the news

Apostles, those who spread the Christian word, traditionally twelve in number, being the disciples (excluding Judas but with his replacement Matthias) and later including St Paul and his followers

Apse, vaulted semicircular end wall of the chancel of a church or chapel

Architrave, in Classical architecture, the horizontal beam or lintel running across a row of columns

Arianism, a branch of early Christianity that did not accept the equal divinity of Christ and the Father. It was professed by the Goths and early Lombards. St Ambrose devoted most of his life to opposing it and claiming Milan and its people for orthodox Nicene Christianity

Assumption, the ascension of the Virgin to Heaven, 'assumed' by the power of God

Atlas (pl. atlantes), male figures used as supporing columns. Also known as telamones

Attic, topmost storey of a Classical building, hiding the spring of the roof; in art, it refers to a style from Attica in Greece

Baldacchino, canopy supported by columns, usually over an altar

Basilica, originally a Roman hall used for public administration; in Christian architecture, an aisled church with a clerestory and apse and no transepts

Bas-relief, sculpture in low relief

Biforium, an aperture divided into two lights or openings

Black-figure ware, ancient Greek pottery style of the 7th–5th centuries BC where the figures appear black against a clay-coloured ground

Borgo, a suburb; a street leading away from the centre of a town

Bottega, the studio or workshop of an artist; the pupils who worked under his direction

Bozzetto (pl. bozzetti), sketch, often used to describe a small model for a piece of sculpture

Broletto, a seat of city government, derived from the word *brolo*, meaning a walled field, often later a market place, the medieval eqivalent of the Roman forum, where municipal affairs were dealt with

Cage cup, type of very delicate Roman glass cup consisting of an inner beaker encased in a patterned 'cage' of appliqué glass in contrasting colours, either spelling out a motto or forming a design. Specimens of the genre date from the 4th century. Two can be seen in Lombardy, in Milan and Varese

Campionese, denoting a school of medieval sculptors from the region of Campione d'Italia on Lake Lugano. They were active in Italy and Switzerland up until the end of the 14th century, and are often documented at sites where work was already underway but required completion

Canopic jar (or vase), ancient Egyptian funerary urn used to preserve the internal organs

Cantoria (pl. cantorie), singing-gallery in a church

Capitolium, ancient Roman temple dedicated to the trio of gods worshipped on the Capitoline Hill at Rome: Jupiter, Juno and Minerva

Cappella (pl. cappelle), a chapel

Cardo, main north–south street of a Roman town, at right-angles to the decumanus (*qv*)

Cartoon, from *cartone*, meaning a large sheet of paper—a full-size preparatory drawing for a painting, fresco or tapestry

Caryatid, female figure used as a supporting column

Cassone, a marriage chest, designed to hold items of the bride's trousseau

Cavea, the part of a theatre or amphitheatre occupied by the rows of seats

Cella, the sanctuary of a temple, where the cult statue would have been placed

Cenacolo (pl. cenacoli), a scene of the Last Supper (in the refectory of a religious house)

Chiaroscuro, distribution of light and shade in a painting

Ciborium, casket or tabernacle containing the Host (Communion bread)

Cinquecento, Italian term for the 'fifteen-hundreds' i.e. the 16th century

Cippus (pl. *cippae*), sepulchral monument in the form of an altar

Cisalpine Republic, Napoleonic republic of northern Italy, which lasted between 1797 and 1802. It was succeeded by the Italian Republic, of which Napoleon was President

Clerestory, upper part of the nave wall of a church, taller than the side aisles and pierced with windows

Cloisonné, type of enamel decoration where areas of colour are partitioned by narrow strips of metal

Comune, a town or municipality with its own governing body

Confessio, crypt beneath the high altar and raised sanctuary of a church, usually containing the relics of a saint

Corbel, a projecting block, usually of stone

Corinthian, ancient Greek and Roman order of architecture characterised by column capitals decorated with acanthus leaves

Cornice, topmost part of a temple entablature (*qv*); any projecting ornamental moulding at the top of a building beneath the roof or ceiling

Crenellations, battlements, specifically the indented parts

Crocket, curving element of moulded foliage decorating the ribs of a spire

Crossing, in cruciform churches, the point where the four arms—nave, chancel and transepts—meet. It is often surmounted by a dome

Cryptoporticus, vaulted subterranean corridor

Cupola, dome

Decastyle, having ten columns

Decumanus, major east–west street of an ancient Roman town

Deposition, the taking down from the Cross of the dead body of Christ

Diocletian window, large window in the shape of a demi-lune. It takes its name from apertures of the same shape in the Baths of Diocletian in Rome

Dioscuri, Castor and Pollux, according to mythology the sons of Zeus by Leda, brothers of Helen of Troy

Diptych, painting or ivory tablet in two wings or sections

Doctors of the Church, traditionally the four fathers of the early Christian Church, Sts Ambrose, Augustine, Jerome and Gregory

Domus, an ancient Roman well-to-do town house

Doric, one of the ancient orders of architecture, characterised by plain column capitals and stout fluted columns standing directly on the platform, with no base (cf. Tuscan Doric)

Dormition, the death of the Virgin Mary, traditionally represented as a 'falling asleep'

Dossal, a cloth hung behind the altar or at the sides of the chancel; sometimes the term is used to describe a painted altarpiece

Duomo, cathedral

Emblema (pl. emblemata), in an ancient mosaic floor, the central panel, usually showing a scene from mythology. An emblema was usually lively, detailed, figurative and colourful while its surround was much simpler, often geometric, and sometimes monochrome

Engaged column, column that is not free-standing but which partially retreats into the wall

Entablature, typically, the horizontal section of a building façade or porch, above a row of columns, consisting of the architrave (*qv*), the frieze and the cornice

Evangelistary, a book of excerpts from the Gospels, intended to be used as readings during church services

Evangelists, the authors of the four Gospels, Matthew, Mark, Luke and John, often denoted in art by their symbols, respectively a man/angel, a lion, a bull and an eagle

Exedra, semicircular recess

Ex-voto, tablet, small painting or other gift offered in gratitude to a saint

Fresco (in Italian, *affresco*), painting executed on wet plaster (*intonaco*). On the rough plaster (*arriccio*) beneath, the artist made a sketch (or sinopia, *qv*) which was covered little by little as work on the fresco proceeded. Since the *intonaco* had to be wet during this work, it was applied each day only to that part of the wall on which the artist was sure that he could complete the fresco (these areas, which can now often be detected by restorers, are known as *giornate*). From the 16th century onwards cartoons (*cartoni*) were used to help the artist with the over-all design: the *cartone* was transferred on to the *intonaco* either by pricking the outline with small holes over which a powder was dusted, or by means of a stylus which left an incised line on the wet plaster. In the 1960s and 1970s, many frescoes were detached from the walls on which they were executed and so the sinopie beneath were discovered (and sometimes also detached)

Ghibelline, in Italian medieval history, member of a faction that supported the power claims of the Holy Roman Emperor over those of the pope. Their opponents were the Guelphs. The Visconti were prominent Lombard Ghibellines

Giant order, column or pilaster (*qv*) with a vertical span of two or more storeys on a façade

Gonfalon, in Italian *gonfalone*, the banner of a medieval commune or guild

Golasecca culture, Bronze and Iron Age civilisation that flourished from the 9th–4th centuries BC, centred to the southeast of Lake Maggiore

Graffiti, design on a wall made with an iron tool on a prepared surface, the design showing in white. Also used loosely to describe scratched designs or words on walls

Greek cross, church plan based on a cross with arms of equal length

Grisaille, painting in various tones of grey

Grottesche (or grottesques), painting or stucco designs used by the ancient Romans and discovered in the 1490s in the Domus Aurea in Rome (then underground, hence its name, from 'grotto'). The delicate ornamental decoration, normally on a light background, is characterised by fantastical motifs with intricate patterns of volutes, festoons, garlands and borders of twisted vegetation and flowers interspersed with small winged human or animal figures, birds, masks, griffins and sphinxes. This type of decoration became very fashionable and was widely copied by late Renaissance artists

Guelph, in Italian medieval history, member of a faction that supported the power claims of the papacy over those of the Holy Roman Emperor. Their opponents were the Ghibellines (*qv*)

Hemicycle, a semicircular structure or space projecting from a room, a public square, etc.

Herm (pl. hermae), quadrangular pillar decreasing in girth towards the ground, surmounted by a head

Hexastyle, having six columns

Historiated, embellished with a design intended to convey a message rather than be purely decorative

Hypocaust, ancient Roman heating system in which hot air circulated under the floor and between double walls

Incunabulum (pl. incunabula), any book printed before 1500

Intarsia, a decorative inlay made from wood, marble or metal

Intrados, underside or soffit of an arch

Ionic, order of Classical architecture identified by its column capitals with two volutes (*qv*)

Krater, a large, wide-mouthed vessel used for mixing wines, especially in ancient Greece

Lancet, narrow, blade-shaped window aperture, typical of Gothic architecture

Lantern, a small circular or polygonal turret with windows all round, crowning a roof or a dome

Latin cross, a cross where the vertical arm is longer than the transverse arm, as opposed to the Greek cross, where both arms are of equal length

Lavabo, hand basin usually outside a refectory or in a sacristy

Lavatorium, the Latin name for a room outside a convent or monastery refectory, with a large hand basin (*lavabo*) in stone or marble where the rites of purification were carried out before a meal

Liberty, Italian Art Nouveau

Loggia, covered gallery or balcony, usually preceding a larger building

Lunette, semicircular space in a vault or

ceiling, or above a door or window, often decorated with a painting or relief

Machicolated, of a parapet, having holes in the floor through which missiles, boiling oil etc. could be dropped on attackers

Maenad, female companion of Dionysus (Bacchus), god of wine, in his revels

Majolica (or Maiolica), a type of earthenware glazed with bright metallic oxides that was originally imported to Italy from Majorca and was extensively made in Italy during the Renaissance

Mandorla, tapered, almond-shaped aura around a holy figure (usually Christ or the Virgin)

Mannerist, in art, denotes the style that emerged in the late Renaissance (early 16th century) and pre-dated the Baroque. It is characterised by dramatic compositions, bright, even garish colours and often anatomically unnatural poses contributing to an atmosphere of unreality and drama rather than serenity or calm

Matroneum, upper gallery in a church or other place of worship, reserved for women

Medallion, large medal; loosely, a circular ornament; a roundel

Millefleurs, literally, 'a thousand flowers', a tapestry style where figures appear against a grassy background spangled with multiple small blooms

Monochrome, painting or drawing in one colour only

Monolithic, usually of a column, made of a single block of stone

Municipio, A Town Hall

Narthex, entrance vestibule across the west front of an early Christian basilica

Necropolis (pl. necropoleis), literally (in Greek), a 'city of the dead', in other words a cemetery

Nymphaeum, a summer house in the gardens of baths and palaces, originally a temple of the Nymphs, decorated with statues and often containing a fountain; in a Roman villa, a room decorated with fountains and statues of water gods and nymphs

Oculus, round window or other aperture

Opus caementicium, Roman building material made of an aggregate or mortar filled with pieces of broken brick, tile and stone rubble

Opus sectile, mosaic or paving of thin strips of coloured marble or other stone cut into shapes and pieced together to form a pattern or figurative design

Pala, large altarpiece

Palaeochristian, early Christian, from the origins of the faith until around the early 6th century

Palazzo (pl. palazzi), palace, any dignified and important building

Pantocrator, literally 'He who Controls All', representation of Christ in Majesty traditionally featured in the main apse of an early Christian basilica

Papal States, the territories, mainly in central Italy, that were under the rule of the popes

Passion, the Crucifixion, suffering and death of Christ

Patera, a Greek or Roman dish for libations to the gods; in art, a circular ornamental disc, usually with a carved design

Pediment, angular or rounded gable above the portico of a Classical building, or above a doorway or window aperture

Pendentive, concave spandrel beneath a dome

Piano nobile, the main floor of a palace

Pietà, representation of the Virgin mourning the dead Christ (sometimes with other figures)

Pietre dure, hard or semi-precious stones, often used in the form of mosaics to decorate furniture such as cabinets and table-tops

Pilaster, a shallow pier or rectangular column projecting only slightly from the wall

Pinacoteca, a picture gallery

Pluteus (pl. plutei), marble panel, usually decorated; a series of them used to form a parapet to precede the altar of a church

Podestà, chief magistrate who ruled a medieval city with the help of a council and representatives from the corporations

Polychrome, many-coloured

Polyptych, painting or panel in more than three sections

Predella, small painting or panel, usually in sections, attached below a large altarpiece, illustrating scenes of a story such as the life of a saint

Pronaos, vestibule or anteroom in front of the cella (*qv*) of a temple

Putto (pl. putti), sculpted or painted figure, usually nude, of a chubby male child, with or without wings

Quadriga, a two-wheeled chariot drawn by four horses abreast

Quattrocento, Italian term for the 'fourteen hundreds' i.e. the 15th century

Red-figure, ancient Greek pottery style of the 6th–4th centuries BC where the figures appear in red against a black ground

Reliquary, receptacle for the relics of a saint

Reredos, wood or stone screen or partition, often elaborately carved, behind an altar

Risorgimento, the 19th-century nationalist political movement that resulted in the Italian wars of independence and ultimate unification of the country under Vittorio Emanuele II

Rococo, frothy, highly ornamented design style of the 18th century, a development of the Baroque, characterised by sinuous foliate forms

Romanesque, architecture of the Western (not Byzantine) Empire of the 7th–12th centuries, preceding the Gothic and typified by sturdy columns and round arches

Rustication, in architecture, the system of cutting grooves between the joints of masonry cladding (ashlar) on the exterior of grand buildings, to make them appear more massive

Rhyton, ancient Greek or Roman drinking horn

Sanctuary, in a church, the area at the liturgical east end, often kept closed by a railing

Scagliola, imitation marble or *pietre dure* (*qv*) made from selenite

Seicento, the 'six hundreds', in art terms, denoting the 17th century

Sgraffito, decorative technique whereby a surface is coated in two layers of contrasting colour and a design is scratched into the surface, revealing the colour of the layer underneath

Sibyl, in the ancient world, a female soothsayer, adopted in Christian iconography as a forerunner of the prophets who foretold the coming of the Messiah

Sinopia (pl. sinopie), large sketch for a fresco made on the rough wall in a red earth pigment called sinopia (because it originally came from Sinope, a town on the Black Sea). When a fresco is detached for restoration, it is possible to see the sinopia beneath, which can also be separated from the wall

Situla, water bucket for ritual use

Soffit, of an arch, the underside

Spandrel, surface between two arches in an arcade or the triangular space on either side of an arch

Spolia, architectural elements from an earlier building recycled in a newer one

Stamnos, big-bellied ancient Greek or Roman vase with two small handles at the sides

Stele (pl. stelae), upright stone bearing a commemorative inscription

Stoup, vessel for Holy Water, usually near the west door of a church

Stucco (pl. stucchi), decorative plaster-work

Stylobate, in Classical architecture, the platform on which the columns of a temple stand

Telamon (pl. telamones), a sculpted male figure used as a supporting column; the same as an atlas

Tempera, a painting medium of powdered pigment bound together, in its simplest form, by a mixture of egg yolk and water

Tessera, small cube of marble, stone or glass used in mosaic work

Thermae, originally simply Roman baths, later elaborate buildings fitted with libraries, assembly rooms, gymnasia and circuses

Tondo (pl. tondi), round painting or relief

Transenna, open grille or screen, usually of marble, in an early Christian church

Transept, the 'arm' of a cruciform church, extending laterally from the top of the nave

Triptych, painting or tablet in three sections

Triton, river god

Trompe l'œil, literally, a 'deception of the eye'; used to describe illusionist decoration and painted architectural perspectives

Tuscan Doric, variant of the Doric order (*qv*) whereby the columns stand on a simple base and the shaft is unfluted

Tympanum, the area between the horizontal top of a doorway and an archway above it; also the triangular or segmental space enclosed by the mouldings of a pediment

Viale (pl. *viali*), wide avenue

Villa, country house with its garden

Virtues, the Theological Virtues are Faith, Hope and Charity; the Cardinal Virtues are Prudence, Fortitude, Temperance and Justice

Volute, scroll-like decoration at the corners of an Ionic capital; also typically present console-style on the façades of Baroque churches

Zoömorphic, in art and sculpture, a figurative element in the form of an animal

Glossary of Artists

Mainly Lombard artists are listed here, as well as important figures from elsewhere who were active in Lombardy or had an influence on its art.

Alberti, Leon Battista (1404–72). Influential Renaissance architect and architectural theorist. *See p. 365.*

Albertolli, Giocondo (1742–1839). Architect and stuccoist who taught at the Accademia di Brera from its foundation year. His works can be seen in Milan and Monza.

Alessi, Galeazzo (1512–72). Umbrian architect influenced by Antonio da Sangallo. He built palaces and churches in Milan in the 1550s, introducing the Baroque idiom, with equal importance given to complicated structural and decorative elements.

Amadeo, Giovanni Antonio (1447–1522). Son-in-law of Guiniforte Solari. Trained as a sculptor, Amadeo's architectural works often had elaborate sculptural ornamentation (*see also p. 163*).

Anguissola, Sofonisba (c. 1535–1625). Painter who enjoyed a successful international career. Born in Cremona, she spent much time at the court of Madrid. She died in Palermo.

Antegnati, Gian Giacomo (active between 1515 and 1550). Born in Brescia, the founder of a famous dynasty of organ makers. Many of their organs survive in Lombard churches.

Antico, Il (Pier Jacopo Alari Bonacolsi, c. 1460–1528). Sculptor, born in Mantua. He was particularly skilled in producing works in the style of the ancient Romans as well as restoring antique works. He also produced numerous exquisite bronze statuettes and vases, now preserved in museums throughout Europe.

Appiani, Andrea (1754–1817). Famous as Napoleon's favourite painter. Also a good portraitist. Born in Milan, most of his surviving works (including frescoes in the Neoclassical style) are there.

Arcimboldo, Giuseppe (1527–93). Painter who worked in Milan and Monza and was also court artist in Prague. Though he produced a fine allegorical fresco in the duomo of Monza, he is best known for his paintings using fruit and vegetables and even little animals to form human portraits, a bizarre idea which he alone perfected.

Aulenti, Gae (1927–2012). One of the most important Italian architects of the 20th century. Aulenti made her name in Paris, when she created the Musée d'Orsay in a disused railway station in 1985. Her home was in Milan, where a new urban district is named after her. She is also remembered as a successful designer.

Baglione, Giovanni (1566–1644). Painter. He worked mostly in Rome, where he wrote a life of his contemporary, Caravaggio.

Balla, Giacomo (1871–1958). Painter, sculptor, set designer and writer, one of the principal exponents of the Futurist movement.

Bambaia, Il (Agostino Busti, 1483–1548). Marble sculptor born in Busto Arsizio, known for his beautiful sepulchral monuments. He was active mostly in Milan, where in 1537 he headed the 'Fabbrica' of the Duomo. He continued the classical style of Amadeo and Briosco.

Barbiano di Belgiojoso, Lodovico. *See Studio BBPR.*

Barocci, Federico (Federico Fiori, 1535–1612). Painter, born in Urbino, a great admirer of Raphael. His paintings are characterised by a luminous quality and joyous use of colour.

Bassi, Martino (1546–91). Milanese architect who worked on a number of churches in the city.

Barzaghi, Francesco (1839–92). Milanese sculptor who studied at the Accademia di Brera. He erected a number of commemorative statues in the city.

Bassano, Jacopo (Jacopo da Ponte, c. 1510–92). The most famous member of a family of painters from Bassano del Grappa in the Veneto, known for his landscapes and also as a pioneer of the genre scene, being one of the first artists to be interested in peasants and animals. He often worked with his son **Francesco Bassano** (1549–92), who was also a gifted painter but whose life ended in tragedy when he threw himself to his death from a top-floor window. Many works by the family can be seen in churches and museums.

Batoni, Pompeo (1708–87). Artist in the Neoclassical spirit, famous for the numerous portraits he painted of wealthy British aristocrats on their Grand Tour, often with masterpieces of Classical sculpture in the background. He was much in favour with the Habsburgs (and also painted their portraits) but also produced some fine altarpieces.

Battagio, Giovanni (fl. 1465–93). Architect, born in Lodi, where some of his work can be seen (he was also active in Crema). From 1481 he was in Milan, where he came into contact with Bramante, whose style greatly influenced his work.

Bazzani, Giuseppe (1690–1768). Mantuan painter whose works can be seen almost exclusively in that town or close by, even though he was clearly influenced by European painters of his time, including Watteau and Fragonard.

Bellini, Giovanni (c. 1433–1516). Painter, great master of the Venetian Renaissance. Together with his brother **Gentile Bellini** (c. 1429–1507), he learned his art in the atelier of their father, **Jacopo Bellini** (c. 1433–1516). One of the first painters to use oils, he was innovative in his use of colour. He is particularly known for his many devotional images of the Madonna and Child. His sister married Mantegna.

Bellotto, Bernardo (1721–80). Painter, nephew and pupil of Canaletto. Like his uncle, he may have used a camera obscura as an aid to accuracy. He was court painter at Dresden for a time and also worked for Maria Theresa, producing views of Vienna.

Beltrami, Luca (1854–1933). Eclectic architect born in Milan and known also for his excellent restoration work, based largely on historical documents. In the 1890s in Milan he restored the Castello Sforzesco and the church of Santa Maria delle Grazie. He died in Rome, where he designed a monument in St Peter's to Benedict XV.

Bembo, Bonifacio (b. c. 1420). Probably born in Brescia and known to have worked for Francesco Sforza in Pavia. He also frescoed a chapel in the Castello Sforzesco in Milan. Today he is perhaps best known for the delightful set of Tarot cards he illustrated (some of which can be seen in the Accademia Carrara in Bergamo). **Benedetto Bembo** was his brother. The painter **Gian Francesco Bembo** (early 16C), active in Cremona and whose work shows the influence of Giulio Romano, may have been a grandson.

Bergognone (Ambrogio da Fossano, c. 1455–1523). Painter, Foppa's most important follower, who worked in both fresco and oils. Works by him can be seen in Milan and elsewhere in Lombardy (*see p. 168*). His brother **Bernardino da Fossano** was also a painter.

Bertani, Giovanni Battista (c. 1516–76). Mantuan painter, architect and sculptor who collaborated with Giulio Romano in Mantua.

Bertini, Giovanni Battista (1799–1849). From a family specialised in painting stained glass, he produced neo-Gothic windows for the Duomo of Milan, introducing a revival of the use of stained glass which had great success in other cathedrals in Europe and also in America. He was sometimes helped by his sons **Pompeo Bertini** and **Giuseppe Bertini**. The latter (1825–98) was a fresco painter who taught at the Brera and who worked in Como. One of his pupils was Lodovico Pogliaghi.

Bevilacqua, Ambrogio (Il Liberale, fl. 1480–1503). Milanese painter known for a few works he produced in mixed media, deriving from his artisan's interest in materials. His style otherwise shows the influence of Bergognone. A room is named after him in the Museo Bagatti Valsecchi in Milan.

Bianchi, Andreolo de' (fl. 1389–98). Born in Bergamo, this little-known sculptor and goldsmith seems only to have produced works for his native city.

Bibiena, Antonio Galli (Il Bibiena, 1700–74). Theatre designer from a family of architects known for their skill in this field. His father, Ferdinando Galli Bibiena (1657–1743), devised a new theory of spatial relationships for stage performances in the theatre, which he put into practice for the dukes of Parma and for the court in Vienna. Antonio was born in Parma and also worked in Vienna from 1721 until around 1740. He later built theatres in Rome, Hungary, Florence and Bologna, and at the end of his life was in Mantua, where he died.

Boccaccino, Boccaccio (before 1466–1525). Painter, born in Ferrara. He lived in Cremona, where some of his best works can be seen in the duomo. He was much influenced by the Venetian school and skilled in frescoed decorations. His son **Camillo Boccaccino** (1504–46) also worked mostly in Cremona.

Boccioni, Umberto (1882–1916). Painter and sculptor. Boccioni went to Paris in 1906 with Gino Severini and the following year took up residence in Milan, where he met Filippo Tommaso Marinetti and joined the Futurist movement. His *Rissa in Galleria* (*Violence in the Galleria*) depicts a fight which broke out in the Galleria Vittorio Emanuele II, demonstrating the social tensions of his time.

Boeri, Stefano (b.1956). Architect and city planner who teaches at the Politecnico in Milan. He is famous for his promotion of forestation in urban contexts, which he has put into practice in Milan, where he has his studio. In 2018 he organised the first World Forum on Urban Forests (in Mantua). For more, see *stefanoboeriarchitetti.net*.

Boltraffio, Giovanni Antonio (c. 1467–1516). One of the Leonardeschi (*see p. 50*), a close follower of Leonardo. He is known to have worked with Marco d'Oggiono (their *Resurrection and Saints* is now in Berlin) and it is sometimes difficult to distinguish the difference between the works of these two painters.

Bonino da Campione (d. 1397). *See p. 133.*

Bonsignori, Girolamo (Fra' Girolamo Bonsignori, c. 1472–1529). Painter who worked in the Veneto as well as in Lombardy. His brother **Francesco Bonsignori** (c. 1460–1519) was a better-known painter.

Bordone, Paris (or Paris Bordon, 1500–71). Painter from the Veneto who studied under Titian and worked for a time at the French court. He often included architectural backgrounds in his paintings and is also known for his portraits, which can be seen in many galleries in Italy.

Boselli, Antonio (16C). Painter and wood carver active in Bergamo, where he carried out a number of commissions for churches. He is thought to have been a friend of Lorenzo Lotto; the two possibly even discussed designs.

Bossi, Giovanni Battista (1864–1924). Little-known architect born in Novara but who worked almost exclusively in Milan, erecting buildings in the Art Nouveau style.

Botta, Mario (b. 1943). Internationally-known Swiss architect and designer who studied in Venice under Carlo Scarpa. He has built residences influenced by the rural architecture of the Ticino as well as numerous important public buildings (San Francisco, Buenos Aires). *See botta.ch.*

Bovara, Giuseppe Antonio (1781–1873). Architect. Born in Lecco, where he was a friend of the author Alessandro Manzoni. Though he worked elsewhere in Lombardy, notably Bergamo, he is closely associated with his native town, where

he spent most of his long life, redesigning its centre and providing it with buildings that fulfilled his ideal of pure and sombre Neoclassicism.

Bramante, Donato (1444–1514). *See p. 80.*

Bramantino (c. 1455–c. 1530). Bartolomeo Suardi was always known as Bramantino as he was apparently much influenced by the classical outlook of Donato Bramante (but he is also thought to have studied under Bernardino Butinone). He lived in Milan, where Francesco II Sforza nominated him court architect and painter. His works display great originality.

Briosco, Benedetto (c. 1460–after 1514). A sculptor who was one of the best followers of Amadeo, whom he succeeded as *capomaestro* at the Certosa di Pavia. His sepulchral monuments can be seen in churches in Milan, Pavia and Cremona.

Bugatti, Carlo (1855–1940). Cabinet maker who worked in a range of styles, following fashions of his day, both Art Nouveau and Orientalising.

Butinone, Bernardino (b. c. 1450). Painter, born in the Bergamasco. He often collaborated with Bernardino Zenale.

Buzzi, Carlo (d. 1659). Architect, a follower of Pellegrino Tibaldi, working in a Baroque style and known for his work on churches (particularly the Duomo of Milan).

Buzzi, Lelio (1553–1608). Architect, no relation of Carlo. He was commissioned by the Church to undertake many projects, in Milan, Pavia and Saronno.

Buzzi, Tomaso (1900–81). Architect, well-known in Milan, which he left in 1957 to create 'La Scarzuola', a folly in Umbria.

Cagnola, Luigi (1762–1833). The most important Neoclassical architect in the Napoleonic period in Lombardy. Born in Milan, he worked mostly in that city.

Caimi, Antonio (1811–78). Painter. Born in Sondrio, he studied at the Brera in

Milan and enjoyed a career as a successful portrait painter. He was also active in his native Valtellina, where his sister Maria had married a local noble. He produced paintings for the church of San Martino in Tirano. He was also a keen antiquarian and received numerous commissions for the restoration of monuments.

Campi family. Painters. *See p. 402.*

Campionese. A term loosely used to describe stonemasons and sculptors from the environs of Campione d'Italia on Lake Lugano, who were at work in northern Italy in the Middle Ages. The most famous of these were **Matteo and Bonino da Campione** (*see p. 133*). **Giovanni da Campione** was active in Bergamo in the mid-14th century. **Ugo da Campione**, also known from works in Bergamo, was Giovanni's father.

Canaletto (Giovanni Antonio Canal, 1697–1768). Painter best known for his views of Venice, which were influenced by the imaginary scenes or *capricci* of Luca Carlevaris. He was particularly successful in London, where he also worked for ten years.

Caniana, Giovanni Battista (1671–1754). Little-known architect and woodcarver who carried out intarsia work for churches in the Bergamasco.

Canonica, Luigi (1762–1844). Neoclassical architect in Milan during the Napoleonic period.

Canova, Antonio (1757–1813). Neoclassical sculptor who enjoyed a high reputation in his own lifetime and was instrumental in negotiating the return of many Italian artworks purloined by Napoleon.

Caravaggio (Michelangelo Merisi, 1571–1610). The most important Italian painter of the 17th century. Although born in Lombardy (*see p. 284*), only two works by him are preserved in Milan, his *Basket of Fruit* at the Ambrosiana and the *Supper at Emmaus* in the Brera.

Cariani, Giovanni (Giovanni Busi, 1485/90–after 1547). Painter at first greatly influenced by the Venetian school and then active in Bergamo, where he came into contact with the works of Lorenzo Lotto and the Lombard school.

Carlone, Carlo (1686–1775). Originally trained as a stucco artist but followed his vocation as a painter. He trained in Venice and was later taken up by ecclesiastical patrons in Austria, where he came to the notice of Eugene of Savoy, who employed him to produce a fresco for the Belvedere. Many of the frescoes in the duomo of Monza are by his hand. His best work in Italy is in Montirone, south of Brescia.

Carpioni, Giulio (1613–78). Venetian painter who studied under Padovanino, and most of whose works are to be seen in the Veneto.

Carrà, Carlo (1881–1966). Painter, one of the founders of the Futurist movement. After serving in the First World War in 1917 he was hospitalised in Ferrara, where he came into contact with De Chirico and the Metaphysical school. He later adhered to the group connected to the art magazine *Valori Plastici*, attracted by the *rappel à l'ordre*, in opposition to the avant-garde movements of the time. His works can be seen in all the most important collections of modern art in Italy.

Cavagna, Giovan Paolo (c. 1550–1627). Painter from Bergamo, known largely for his altarpieces, though he also painted portraits. He was influenced by the Venetian school. His works are known for their realism and for the inclusion of landscape details.

Cerano, Il (Giovanni Battista Crespi, 1573–1632). Painter, architect and sculptor named after the town where he came to prominence. An exponent of the transitional style between Mannerism and the Baroque, he was much appreciated by the promulgators of the Counter-Reformation and his works are to be seen in many towns in the region. Cardinal Federico Borromeo appointed him director of the Accademia Ambrosiana.

Ceruti, Giacomo (Il Pitocchetto, 1698–1767). Milanese painter who worked in Brescia and Bergamo and is today particularly well represented in the Pinacoteca of Brescia, where nine of his genre paintings (for which he is best known) are displayed. These include domestic scenes (a spinner, a washerwoman, a cobbler), as well as children and barefoot beggars (hence his nickname, from *pitocchio*, vagabond). The subjects are often looking directly out of the paintings but always succeed in avoiding the pathetic.

Cerva, Giovanni Battista della (fl. c. 1540–8). Painter who produced only a few works (to be seen in Novara and Milan).

Cesare da Sesto (1477–1523). One of the so-called Leonardeschi painters (*see p. 50*). He also worked in Rome and southern Italy.

Cesariano, Cesare. (1476/78–1543). Milanese architect and painter who worked almost exclusively in his native city. A pupil of Bramante, he was responsible for the first printed edition (1521) of the treatise on architecture by Vitruvius, for which he supplied a commentary and illustrations.

Chirico, Giorgio de (1888–1978). One of the most important European painters of the early 20th century, the inventor of the Metaphysical style of painting before WWI. His works are often characterised by enigmatic human forms and unreal fictive spaces sometimes with Classical elements, but deserted and with an atmosphere of mystery. He also produced numerous good still lifes, portraits and scenes dominated by horses with long flowing manes and tails. He lived most of his life in Rome (although he was at work in Milan from 1932–5). His brother Andrea, also a painter, used the name **Alberto Savinio** (1891–1952). De Chirico was also a sculptor and set designer, a writer and theorist.

Cignaroli, Giambettino (1706–70), Painter, born in Verona, and from a family of artists who worked in the Veneto and Piedmont.

Cima da Conegliano (Giovanni Battista Cima, c. 1459–1518). Painter, born in Conegliano in the Veneto. He is known for his altarpieces, many of them large in size, produced for churches in Venice and her territory.

Civerchio, Vincenzo (c. 1470–1544). Painter from Crema, where some of his works can be seen in the cathedral and in several other churches. His paintings are also to be found in other Lombard towns.

Correggio (Antonio Allegri, c. 1489–1534). Painter, born near Modena and always known after the name of the town of his birth. He seems to have studied with Mantegna and was greatly influenced by Raphael and Michelangelo, whose works he saw on a visit to Rome. Otherwise his life is poorly documented. He worked mainly in Parma and is especially known for his dome frescoes, where a daring use of foreshortening creates a dizzying illusion of suspension in space; and also for subtly erotic mythological scenes, popular with young aristocratic patrons.

Costa, Lorenzo. There were two artists of this name active in Lombardy. **Lorenzo Costa the Elder** (c. 1460–1535) was born in Ferrara and worked for the Bentivoglio in Bologna before becoming court painter in Mantua in 1507, after the death of

Mantegna. His paintings often include lovely landscapes. **Lorenzo Costa the Younger** (c. 1537–83) was a painter from Mantua who trained in Rome before returning to his home town to work in the Palazzo Ducale. He is not the son of 'the Elder', and only possibly the grandson.

Crespi, Daniele (1598–1630). Painter, pupil of **Giovanni Battista Crespi** (*see Cerano*). He worked only in Lombardy, an important exponent of the early Baroque. He was a victim of the great plague of 1630–1.

Crivelli, Carlo (c. 1430–95). Born in Venice, Crivelli is a master easily recognisable for his extremely decorative works against a gold ground, usually including delightful and intricate details of fruit and flowers. His figures are always elegant, with long thin hands. He uses colour with great sensitivity. There are often eccentric elements in his altarpieces, many of which were painted for the Franciscans. He trained in Venice under Jacopo Bellini and Vivarini, and was clearly influenced by Flemish painting. He was famous in his lifetime, working mostly in the Marche (where many of his works can still be seen). He was a conservative painter who ignored the classicism adopted by many of his contemporaries, including Mantegna. One of the few important painters not to be mentioned by Vasari, Crivelli came to the attention of collectors in the 19th century, when many of his works were bought by English enthusiasts (the National Gallery of London has the best collection of his works in Europe). The paintings in the Brera were seized by Napoleon in 1811 from churches in the Marche.

De Lucchi, Michele (b. 1951). Architect and designer born in Ferrara. Apart from his work in Milan (reconstruction of Palazzo Triennale) and Monza, he has worked in Germany and Japan and constructed the Bridge of Peace in Tbilisi in Georgia. He is especially influenced by Ettore Sottsass and prefers wood to all other materials.

Diziani, Gaspare (1689–1767). Painter who as a young man joined the circle of Sebastiano Ricci in Venice, and after a time in both Munich and Dresden, returned to Venice where he left frescoes and altarpieces and stucco decoration in palaces and churches. His work is also to be found in a few churches in Lombardy.

Dolcebuono, Gian Giacomo (c. 1440–c. 1506). Milanese architect and sculptor, who was very active in the design and decoration of the Duomo of Milan and the Certosa di Pavia.

Embriachi, Baldassare degli (fl. c. 1390–1409). The most important member of a family from northern Italy who carved caskets and other decorative objects in bone (and sometimes also in ivory).

Fancelli, Luca (c. 1430–after 1494). Architect, born near Florence. In 1460 he arrived in Mantua, where he received commissions from the Gonzaga marquises Federico I and Ludovico III. While there he also carried out Leon Battista Alberti's projects for two famous churches. Interestingly enough, his name is linked to another great artist, Brunelleschi, since he apparently worked on Palazzo Pitti in Florence following Brunelleschi's death.

Fantoni, Andrea (1659–1734). The best-known member of a family of skilled wood workers from the Valle Seriana. **Grazioso Fantoni** had several sons, all talented carvers. Andrea is the best known.

Ferramola, Floriano (1480–1528). Painter from Brescia, where some of his works can be seen today in the Pinacoteca and Santa Giulia. He was also skilled in fresco and sometimes collaborated with Moretto.

Ferrari, Bernardino (1490–c. 1524). Painter, born in Vigevano, where some of his works can still be seen. He is otherwise little known, though he also worked in Milan. Scholars have been uncertain in attributing his paintings, since his style bears similarities to other artists working under the influence of Leonardo. He is thought to have died of plague.

Ferrari, Gaudenzio (c. 1470–1546). *See p. 138.*

Fetti, Domenico (c. 1589–1624). Painter close to the Venetian school. He was born in Rome, where he worked in the studio of Ludovico Cigoli, and he was in Mantua from 1613–22 at the court of Duke Ferdinando Gonzaga. He spent the last years of his life in Venice painting small mythological and genre scenes.

Filarete (Antonio di Pietro Averlino, c. 1400–69). The most important architect at work in Milan in the first half of the 15th century. He wrote a treatise on architecture and was also a sculptor.

Filippino degli Organi (d. 1450). Master mason from Modena, in charge of the early design of Milan's Duomo.

Fondulis, Agostino de' (also Fondutis or Fondulo, 1483–1522). Architect and sculptor known particularly for his works in terracotta (statues and friezes). From a family of sculptors, he worked with Bramante in Milan and was responsible for spreading that great architect's ideas in the rest of Lombardy.

Fontana, Annibale (1540–87). Sculptor from Milan who is remembered especially for his works in Santa Maria presso San Celso in that city.

Fontana, Carlo (1634–1714). Architect. Born near Como, but his greatest works are in Rome, where he succeeded Bernini as papal architect. He is a great exponent of the Baroque style, known chiefly for his churches and church façades as well as for commemorative monuments.

Fontana, Lucio (1899–1968). Painter, sculptor and ceramist born in Argentina. At the Accademia di Brera he studied under Adolfo Wildt, and his exhibition at the Galleria del Milione in 1930 was heralded as the first time non-figurative sculpture was shown in Italy. He invented Spatialism and is famous above all for his slashed white canvases.

Foppa, Vincenzo (1425–1515). *See p. 91.*

Funi, Achille (1890–1972). Painter, trained at the Brera. He was influenced by De Chirico and became a leading member of the Novecento group. He produced a number of works to decorate public buildings.

Galgario, Fra' (Vittore Ghislandi, 1655–1743). Portrait painter from Bergamo, where he was a friar in the convent of Galgario. He worked in Sebastiano Bombelli's studio in Venice from around 1689 to 1702. His portraits can be seen in his native city as well as in the Ambrosiana in Milan.

Galli, Francesco (c. 1470–1501). Painter, nicknamed Napoletano, who is known to have worked in Leonardo's studio in Milan and who died in Venice in 1501.

Gambara, Lattanzio (1530–74). Lombard painter from Brescia, where a few of his works can be seen today. He worked in Cremona under Giulio Campi, and he married Girolamo Romanino's daughter. He also carried out important frescoes for the Duomo of Parma towards the end of his life.

Gardella, Ignazio (1905–99). Born in Milan, he became one of Italy's most important architects, working all over the country.

Gatti, Bernardino (c. 1495–1576). Painter born in Pavia but who worked mostly in the churches of Cremona, where he died.

Sofonisba Anguissola was his pupil from 1549.

Gatti, Gervasio (1549–1631). Little-known painter active in Piacenza as well as Cremona.

Genovesino, Il (Luigi Miradori; 1605/10–56). An interesting painter presumably from Genoa but who worked mostly in Cremona, where he died.

Genovesino, Il (Bartolomeo Roverio, c. 1577–c. 1630). Lombard painter about whom very little is known.

Ghidoni, Domenico (c. 1860–1920/21). Little-known sculptor born near Brescia, whose monuments can be seen in several *piazze* in that town.

Ghisoni, Fermo (Fermo da Caravaggio, c. 1505–75). A little-known painter born in Caravaggio near Bergamo. A few of his works can be seen in Mantua (where he was a pupil of Giulio Romano).

Giampietrino (Giovanni Pietro Rizzoli, c. 1485–1549). Painter from Milan. Usually regarded as one of the Leonardeschi (*see p. 50*), he became known for his Madonnas.

Giordano, Luca (1634–1705). Painter, such a fast worker that he was nicknamed '*Luca fa presto*' (Luca works fast) by his contemporaries. He completed over 3,000 paintings in the course of his career. He was apprenticed to Jusepe de Ribera for nine years and frequented the atelier of Pietro da Cortona, before going to Parma to see the works of Correggio and Veronese.

Giovanni d'Alemagna (mid-15C). Painter originally from Germany, active in the territory of Venice, where he collaborated with his brother-in-law Antonio Vivarini.

Giovanni di Balduccio (fl. 1330s). Sculptor, born in Pisa, where he was influenced by the work of Giovanni Pisano. He was at work in Milan in the 1330s and introduced Gothic elements from the Pisan school of sculpture to the city.

Giovanni della Chiesa (fl. 1494–1512). Painter, active in Lodi and at the Certosa di Pavia.

Giovanni da Milano (b. c. 1320). The earliest important painter to have been born in Lombardy (in a small town near Como). He was one of the best and most sophisticated followers of Giotto: although he always signed his works 'Giovanni di Milano', he lived and worked in Florence, where he acquired citizenship in 1366 and where today a few of his panel paintings and his only known fresco cycle can be seen. His attention to detail is typical of artists who also produced illuminated manuscripts. Towards the end of his life he was at work in the Vatican.

Giovenone, Girolamo (c. 1490–1555). Painter, born in Vercelli. He was close to Gaudenzio Ferrari, with whom he is known to have exchanged ideas and models.

Guardi, Francesco (1712–93). Painter, born in Venice and famous for his views of his native city, celebrating its landscapes, seascapes and pageantry. His sister married Giovanni Battista Tiepolo.

Guercino (Giovanni Francesco Barbieri, 1591–1666). Painter, important exponent of the Bolognese school. He had a pronounced squint (which is what his nickname refers to), a fact which probably enhanced his work. Certainly chromatic effects were more important than perspective for him. In the course of his career, he painted more than 100 altarpieces.

Guttuso, Renato (1912–87). Committed Communist and controversial painter noted for his bold brush strokes and use of colour as well as for his daring realism. A native of Sicily, he spent many years living and working in Varese.

Hayez, Francesco (1791–1882). Born in Venice, Hayez studied there and in Rome but from 1822, when he was first appointed as a teacher at the Brera Academy, he lived mostly in Milan, where he died in 1882. In 1850 he became professor of painting at the Brera and five years later was its director. He specialised in historical paintings, often displaying an 'irritating perfection', but it is perhaps in his portraits of the Milanese aristocracy that he excels. He is arguably the most celebrated Italian painter of the 19th century.

Induno, Gerolamo (1825–90). Painter of historical and genre scenes, very popular during the Risorgimento period. Born in Milan, he studied at the Brera. His elder brother **Domenico Induno** (1815–78), also a painter, was also a student at the Brera, under Francesco Hayez.

Jacopino da Tradate (15C). Sculptor. Born at Tradate, outside Milan, he is known to have worked on the Duomo in that city. He later went to Mantua to work for the Gonzaga.

Juvarra, Filippo (1678–1736). Architect and stage designer. His master was Carlo Fontana in Rome. He is most famous for his work in the city of Turin, where he enjoyed royal patronage. His style typifies the transition between the Baroque and the Rococo.

Lanino, Bernardino (c. 1509–82/83). Painter from Piedmont, a pupil of Gaudenzio Ferrari. His son **Gerolamo Lanino** (b. 1555) worked in his *bottega*.

Lanzani, Bernardino (Bernardino da San Colombano, fl. 1490–1526). Painter who carried out a number of frescoes in Pavia.

Legnanino, Il (Stefano Maria Legnani, 1661–1713). Born in Milan, he was one of the best late 17th-century Lombard artists.

Leonardo da Vinci (1452–1519). *See p. 66.*

Leoni, Leone (1509–92). Sculptor. He had a successful career at the courts of Europe, supplying them with bronzes. His only work to be seen in Milan today is the Medici monument in the Duomo.

Ligari, Gian Pietro (1686–1752). Architect and painter, born near Sondrio. He studied in Rome and Milan but is chiefly associated with his native Valtellina. A versatile artist, he produced frescoes for private houses, paintings for churches and private devotion, as well as architectural designs, including for the cathedral of Sondrio. The Roman classical Renaissance and the Baroque remained his chief influences. His children **Vittoria Ligari** (1713–83) and **Cesare Ligari** (1716–70) were also painters.

Lomazzo, Giovanni Paolo (1538–1600). Milanese painter and theorist, known for his treatises on Mannerist-era art and artists, including Leonardo. He turned to writing after losing his sight, while still only in this 30s.

Lombardi, Cristoforo (also Cristoforo Lombardo, d. 1555). Sculptor and architect, Renaissance and classical in style, in charge of works at Milan's Duomo from 1526. He had previously collaborated with Bambaia (for example on the tomb of Gaston de Foix). He was active in other parts of Lombardy, for example Cremona and Saronno. The Stampa family were important patrons.

Lombardo, Pietro (c. 1438–1515). Sculptor, born in Lombardy, but who is mainly associated with Venice, where he carried out numerous sculptural commissions. His work is of fundamental importance to the development of the Venetian Renaissance, revealing the influence of Tuscan masters and resulting in works characterised by a clear Classicism.

Longhi, Pietro (1701–85). Painter, born

in Venice and famed above all for his charming small genre paintings detailing contemporary life in his native city.

Lotto, Lorenzo (1480–1556). *See p. 256.*

Luini, Bernardino (c. 1480–1532). Painter. He is known to have used cartoons by Leonardo da Vinci for some of his paintings. *See p. 50.* He was succeeded by a number of sons, also artists: **Aurelio Luini**, **Giovan Pietro Luini** and **Evangelista Luini**.

Maffei, Francesco (1605–60). Interesting and original painter from the Veneto, who worked in Vicenza and Rovigo. One of his works can be seen today in Brescia. His best works are religious or allegorical, particularly those that show the apotheosis or glorification of local dignitaries. His rapid, nervous brushstrokes and unpredictable use of colour invest his works with a bizarre, other-worldly atmosphere. He died of plague in Padua.

Magistris, Sigismondo de (16C). Painter, active in the Como area but otherwise little known. He was probably related to **Giovanni Andrea de Magistris**, who was active around the same time and in the same area.

Magnasco, Alessandro (1667–1749). A painter from Genoa, but who lived and worked in Milan. He produced numerous dark, melodramatic scenes, in landscapes which usually include small human figures.

Malosso (Giovanni Battista Trotti, 1555–1619). Painter and architect born in Cremona, where he studied under Bernardino Campi and where he carried out most of his altarpieces and frescoes (sometimes in collaboration with Giulio Campi).

Mantegazza (15C). Family of sculptors. The brothers **Cristoforo** and **Antonio** worked on the Certosa di Pavia.

Mantegna, Andrea (1431–1506). *See p. 372.*

Mantovano, Rinaldo (fl. 1528–64). Painter who was assistant to Giulio Romano in Mantua in both the Palazzo Ducale and Palazzo Te. He was the artist chosen to make portraits of the Gonzaga horses. Those in Palazzo Te survive and it was he who frescoed the Sala dei Giganti, the most famous room in that palace, following Giulio Romano's design.

Manzoni, Piero (1933–63). Painter born in Lombardy who was influenced by the work of Lucio Fontana. One of his most provocative works is *Merda d'artista*, a tin of his own excrement. Considered a forerunner of Arte Povera and Conceptual Art, he died in Milan.

Manzù, Giacomo (Giacomo Manzoni; 1908–91). Sculptor, born in Bergamo, where some of his best bronzes can still be seen. He also worked for the Church and was commissioned in 1963 to produce bronze panels from one of the doors of St Peter's (and he is well-known for his series of statues of cardinals, now in various museums). He lived much of his life in Ardea, south of Rome, where there is a museum dedicated to his works.

Maraini, Antonio (1886–1993). Sculptor and art critic. His work was much admired by the Fascist authorities and he received support along with numerous commissions and official posts in arts administration.

Marco d'Oggiono (fl. 1487–1524). Painter of the group known as the Leonardeschi (*see p. 50*). He is known to have collaborated with Boltraffio.

Marinali, Orazio (1643–1720). Sculptor, mainly active in the Veneto and known chiefly for his garden statuary, depicting stock characters from traditional theatre.

Marini, Marino (1901–80). Sculptor,

influenced and inspired by Etruscan art and known especially for his many equestrian sculptures, exploring the relationship between horse and rider.

Martini, Arturo (1889–1947). Arguably Italy's most important 20th-century sculptor, whose memorably dramatic monumental works can be seen in numerous museums all over the country. He often used terracotta, clay or stone for his statues, but he also produced small bronzes.

Matteo da Campione (d. 1396). *See p. 133.*

Mazzola Bedoli, Girolamo (1500–69). Painter, a follower and pupil of Parmigianino.

Melone, Altobello (1490/1–1543). Painter, born in Cremona, where he took over from Boccaccio Boccaccino in the task of frescoing the duomo. He was influenced by Girolamo Romanino. His style is Mannerist or 'anticlassical'.

Mengoni, Giuseppe (1829–77). Architect, known chiefly for his Galleria Vittorio Emanuele II in Milan and for the tragic accident which led to his death, falling from its roof.

Messina, Francesco (1900–95). Sculptor. Born in Sicily but who lived and worked in Milan, where he was Director of the Brera from 1936–44. His studio is now a museum. Despite this, very few of his works are to be seen today in Lombardy.

Michelino da Besozzo (c. 1370–1455). Painter and miniaturist, active in Lombardy and the Veneto. He had important patrons and was an exponent of the International Gothic style.

Moncalvo, Il (Guglielmo Caccia, 1568–1625). Painter nicknamed after his birthplace in Piedmont. Collaborated with Bernardino Lanino. He worked mostly in Piedmont and Lombardy.

Montagna, Bartolomeo (c. 1450–1523). Lombard painter much influenced by the Venetian school. He worked mostly in Vicenza.

Montorfano Giovanni Donato (c. 1460–1502). An artist from Lombardy, known only for his works in Milan. He is not considered a painter of the first rank but it is interesting to compare the survival of his (fragmentary) *Crucifixion* in the refectory of Santa Maria delle Grazie with Leonardo's *Last Supper*, which is not true fresco and has survived less well.

Morandi, Giorgio (1890–1964). Painter, born in Bologna, where he lived and worked. He was one of the most famous painters of the Novecento movement and one of the few who is well known outside Italy. He produced landscapes and Metaphysical works but is much the best known for his still lifes of bottles.

Morazzone, Il (Pier Francesco Mazzuchelli, 1573–1625/6). Painter named after his birthplace in the province of Varese, influenced by Cerano and Gaudenzio Ferrari. Most of his works are still to be seen in Lombardy (Varese, Como). Early in his career he also carried out some frescoes in churches in Rome.

Moretto (Alessandro Bonvicino, c. 1498–1554). *See p. 302.*

Moroni, Giovanni Battista (c. 1525–78). *See p. 269.*

Mottis, Agostino de (fl. 1450–75). Painter, member of a family of Lombard Renaissance artists at work in the 15th century. His father, **Cristoforo de' Mottis** worked on the Milan Duomo.

Muzio, Giovanni (1893–1982) Milanese architect and city planner. He collaborated on some projects with Giò Ponti. Amongst his best-known works are the Università Cattolica (1919–34) and Palazzo dell'Arte, built in 1933 for the Triennale exhibitions, both in Milan.

Nervi, Pier Luigi (1891–1971). Architect. Born in Sondrio, he became Professor of Architecture in Rome. A great advocate of reinforced concrete, he designed many buildings making daring and innovative use of it.

Niccolò da Varallo (1420–89). Painter who also produced beautiful, simple historiated stained glass for the Duomo of Milan.

Nuvolone, Carlo Francesco (1609–62) Milanese painter from a family of artists active from the 16th–18th centuries. A pupil of Cerano, he became the most important painter at work in Lombardy in the mid-17th century. He and his brother **Giuseppe Nuvolone** also worked in Milan.

Olivieri, Maffeo (1484–1543). Sculptor, born in Brescia and known for both religious and secular works in wood, stone and bronze, often in an elegant classical style.

Ottone, Casimiro (1856–1942). Painter from Vigevano. He studied at the Brera and produced works in many genres, turning to still lifes of flowers in old age.

Pagano, Giuseppe (1896–1945). Architect, one of the protagonists of the Novecento. Arrested as an anti-Fascist in 1943, he was deported to Mauthausen where he died two years later.

Palma il Vecchio (Jacopo Negretti, c. 1480–1528). *See p. 281.* **Palma Giovane** (Giacomo Negretti, 1548–1628), well-known artist of the Venetian school, was his great-nephew.

Pecorari, Francesco (fl. 1330–6). Architect and sculptor from Cremona who is recorded in Lombardy just for two beautiful church towers (the Torrazzo in his native city and San Gottardo in Milan).

Pellizza da Volpedo, Giuseppe (1868–1907). Painter, an exponent of Divisionism. Born into a family of agricultural labourers, he studied at the Accademia di Belle Arti in Florence under Giovanni Fattori. His most famous work, *Il Quarto Stato*, was little recognised at the time. The artist committed suicide in 1907 at the age of 39, a few months after his wife's death in childbirth.

Peranda, Sante (1566–1638). Painter, active in Venice, influenced by Palma Giovane, with whom he collaborated in Mantua. One of his best portraits is that of Giulia d'Este, today preserved in Palazzo Ducale in Mantua. He also produced canvases of historical subjects.

Peressutti, Enrico. *See Studio BBPR.*

Perugino (Pietro di Cristoforo Vannucci; c. 1450–1523). The first great Umbrian painter, called Perugino by his contemporaries, although he may not have visited Perugia until 1475. His formative years were spent in Florence in the workshop of Verrocchio with Leonardo da Vinci. Well-known in his lifetime, his elegant, graceful figures and spacious, luminous landscapes greatly influenced his famous pupil Raphael.

Piacentini, Marcello (1881–1960). Architect and urban designer well known for his work on the layout of the lower town of Bergamo in 1927. He also designed buildings during the Fascist era, including one of Brescia's central *piazze*, but he worked all over Italy and was involved with the plan for EUR in Rome. His style exhibits a severely Rationalist, stripped Classicism, stark and monumental.

Piazza family. Dynasty of painters from Lodi, mainly active in the 16th century, consisting of the brothers **Martino** (b. 1475/80) and **Alberto** (b. c. 1490, known also as Albertino), who often worked together; Martino's sons **Cesare**, **Callisto** and **Scipione**; and his grandson **Fulvio**. They were prolific and their work can be seen all across the region.

Piccio, Il (Giovanni Carnovali, 1804–73). Painter, trained at the Accademia Carrara in Bergamo and known for his mythological and biblical scenes, landscapes and portraits. His style reveals an interesting tension between the antique and the modern.

Piermarini, Giuseppe (1734–1808). The most important Neoclassical architect of his time. In Milan he also acted as city planner and held the chair of Architecture at the Accademia di Brera from 1776 for many years. He also worked in Umbria.

Pisanello (Antonio di Puccio, 1377–1455). *See p. 350.*

Pisis, Filippo de (1896–1956). Painter, born in Ferrara, one of the great Italian artists of the 20th century, recognisable for the light, sketchy style of his cityscapes and still lifes.

Pitocchetto. *See Ceruti, Giacomo.*

Platina, Giovanni Maria (c. 1455–1500). Little-known woodcarver who produced beautiful intarsia choir stalls for the cathedral of Cremona.

Pogliaghi, Lodovico (1857–1950). Lombard painter, sculptor and stage designer. He also worked on monuments in Rome.

Pollack, Leopold (1751–1806). Architect, born in Austria but active in Italy, where he was a pupil of Giuseppe Piermarini and continued his master's Neoclassical style.

Ponti, Giò (1891–1979). Milanese designer and architect. He founded the periodical *Domus* in 1928 and was its director until the end of his life. His creativity ranged from ceramics and furniture to bathroom fittings and the decorative arts. He designed objects for mass production, influencing the taste of his time. As an architect he is remembered for his contribution to the construction of the Pirelli Tower in the 1950s.

Pordenone (Giovanni Antonio de' Sacchis, c. 1483–1539). Painter, according to Vasari, self-taught. His early works reveal a style closely influenced by Giorgione and Titian. Later, he fell under the spell of Michelangelo and his works become more sculptural, with highly mannered gesture and an unsettling, barely suppressed violence, filled with writhing figures that seem to invade the viewer's space. He enjoyed depicting costume and appears to have been fascinated by the more gruesome aspects of martyrdom.

Portaluppi, Piero (1888–1967). Milanese architect and interior designer. Some of the residences he built for clients in Milan can be visited as museums. His style is easily recognisable for its Art Deco overtones. He was particularly careful about details, including lighting and flooring.

Pozzo, Paolo (1741–1803). Little-known architect who built some Neoclassical works in Mantua.

Predis, Ambrogio de (b. 1455). Painter, one of the so-called Leonardeschi (*see p. 50*).

Previtali, Andrea (c. 1480–1528). Renaissance-era painter from Bergamo, where he has left some lovely altarpieces. He was a pupil of Giovanni Bellini in Venice and on his return to Bergamo, came under the influence of Lorenzo Lotto, with whom he also collaborated.

Primaticcio, Francesco (1504–70). Painter and sculptor, a pupil of Giulio Romano in Mantua and a follower of his anticlassical style. He later left Italy for France, where he worked for the royal court.

Procaccini, Giulio Cesare (1574–1625). Painter and sculptor, born in Bologna but who spent much of his career working in Milan, to commissions from Charles Borromeo. His works reveal a transition from Mannerism to the Baroque. His elder brothers **Camillo Procaccini** (1551–1629) and **Carlo Procaccini** (1571–?1630) were also painters, active alongside him.

Quadrio, Girolamo (1625–79). Architect, a pupil of Carlo Buzzi. He worked in Milan (on the Duomo and other churches), in Saronno, in Como and in the area around Bergamo. In Milan he also took over some projects after the death of Francesco Maria Richini. His son, **Giovanni Battista Quadrio** (1659–1722) was also an architect and also worked on the Duomo of Milan.

Raphael (Raffaello Sanzio, 1483–1520). One of the most admired of all Italian painters, a native of Urbino and whose greatest patrons were in Rome, but who has nevertheless left some works in Lombardy, notably in the Brera (*see p. 53*). He died at 37 and is buried in the Pantheon in Rome.

Reni, Guido (1575–1642). Painter of the Bolognese school, hugely admired in the 19th century. His work has two principal moods: either restrained, scholarly and classicising, even sentimental at times; or imbued with a naturalism that is almost Caravaggesque.

Ricchi, Pietro (Il Lucchese, 1605–75). Painter born in Lucca, who studied in the *bottega* of Guido Reni in Bologna. From 1634 he was in Milan and then Brescia, and towards the end of his life was at work in the Veneto.

Ricci, Sebastiano (1659–1734). Painter of the Venetian school, its greatest 18th-century master. His works are characterised by vivid colour and a lightness of touch. Ricci's life was busy (his art was sought-after and he received many commissions, both in Italy and beyond) and complicated (he was once imprisoned after a plot to poison a mistress was foiled). He suffered from gallstones and died on the operating table.

Richini, Francesco Maria (1584–1658). Architect, deservingly hailed as the greatest exponent of the Milanese Baroque. His influence was not confined to his native city; in fact all across Central Europe there are churches inspired by his designs. His most successful surviving buildings in Milan are the courtyard of the Brera and the church of San Giuseppe. He also built the crypt in the Duomo (1606) which houses the remains of St Charles Borromeo.

Rizzoli, Giovanni Pietro. *See Giampietrino*.

Rodari, Tommaso (1484–1526). Sculptor, best known for his northern Renaissance sculpture and altarpieces in Como. He spent some time in the workshop of Amadeo. His brother **Jacopo Rodari** was also a sculptor.

Rogers, Ernesto N. *See Studio BBPR*.

Romanino, Girolamo (c. 1484–1566). Painter, born in Brescia but who also worked in Venice. He was clearly influenced by his great contemporary, Titian, though his works have an originality all his own, veering towards Mannerism, and he was a great lover of colour.

Romano, Gian Cristoforo (1456–1612). Sculptor and medallist, born in Rome and active at the Este court in Ferrara. Isabella d'Este was an admirer of his work and brought him to Mantua. On the marriage of Isabella's sister Beatrice to Ludovico il Moro, he was summoned to Milan, where he remained until the dynasty fell.

Romano, Giulio (?1499–1546). *See p. 370*.

Rosa, Ercole (1846–93). Sculptor, born in Rome, known for his heroic commemorative monuments.

Rosa da Tivoli (Philipp Peter Roos, 1657–1706). From a German family of painters, he specialised in animals. He came to Italy in 1677 and lived for the rest of his life in Tivoli, where he kept a menagerie so that he could draw his subjects from life.

Rosso, Medardo (1858–1928). Sculptor. He spent his youth in Milan but lived for 30 years in Paris, where he was influenced by Rodin. He had a special skill in modelling wax. His original style is immediately recognisable: he seems to produce a fusion of the figure with the atmosphere in an attempt to abolish borders.

Roverio, Bartolomeo. *See Genovesino.*

Rusnati, Giuseppe (c. 1560–1713). Baroque-era sculptor or religious statues and statue groups, in charge of stone carving at Milan's Duomo from 1693. He also worked at the Certosa di Pavia and at the Sacro Monte in Varese.

Salaì (Gian Giacomo Caprotti, 1480–1524). Painter, a disciple of Leonardo who also produced copies and imitations of the master's works.

Sant'Elia, Antonio (1888–1916). Futurist architect, known mainly for his visionary designs and sketches, which had a great influence on the new generation. He was killed in battle in WWI.

Sassu, Aligi (1912–2000). Painter and sculptor, born in Milan. He was influenced by French art (Delacroix, Van Gogh) and by the art and colours of Spain, where he spent the second half of his life, on Majorca.

Savinio, Alberto. *See Chirico.*

Savoldo, Giovan Girolamo (1480/5–after 1548). Painter, a native of Brescia and a contemporary of Moretto and Romanino. A number of his works can still be seen in Brescia today, though he worked mainly in Parma, Florence and Venice. His works show Venetian influence, particularly in the use of light.

Scarpa, Carlo (1906–78). Architect and designer, born in Venice, who specialised in designing museum and exhibition spaces. He is remembered for great sensitivity in the choice of materials (he often favoured wood) and his ingenuity in methods of display. Some of his best museum designs can be seen in the Veneto (Palazzo Querini Stampalia and Gallerie dell'Accademia in Venice, and the Museo di Castelvecchio in Verona). In Lombardy he designed the museum on the castle hill of Brescia.

Schiavo, Paolo (Paolo di Stefano Badaloni, 1397–1478). Painter, born in Florence. A follower of Masolino, with whom he went to Castiglione Olona to work for Branda Castiglioni.

Schiavone, Andrea (Antonio Meldolla, d. 1563). Painter, said to have taught himself the art by copying works by Parmigianino. Throughout his career, his art remained derivative, modelled on that of great masters such as Tintoretto and Giorgione.

Serafini, Serafino de' (1323–93). Painter, mainly active in Modena, though he also enjoyed Gonzaga patronage and left some works in Mantua.

Sironi, Mario (1885–1961). Painter who at first adhered to the Futurist movement. When Mussolini took power in 1923, he declared that he did not wish to encourage a style of official state art. Sironi, who believed wholeheartedly in Fascism, nevertheless decided to produce frescoes and friezes for public buildings which he felt communicated Fascist 'values'. His works, as well as being rhetorical, are often gloomy. They can be seen in many of the most important galleries of 20th century painting in Italy.

Solari, Cristoforo (1468/70–1524). Milanese architect and sculptor who worked for Ludovico il Moro at the Duomo in Milan and the Certosa di Pavia. His architectural works can also be seen in Lombardy.

Solari, Giovanni (c. 1410–80). Member of a family of stonemasons who came originally from the Campione d'Italia region of Lake Lugano. The first member of the dynasty active in Milan was **Giorgio Solari**. As masons and sculptors, they were important in Milan at the time of the construction of the Duomo. **Guiniforte Solari** (1429–81), who worked with Filarete, was his son, very active in Milan and Pavia. Guiniforte's son **Pietro Solari** (c. 1445–93) worked with his father until he was called to Moscow by Ivan III. He worked on construction of the Kremlin.

Solario, Andrea (1460–1524). Painter, one of the Leonardeschi (*see p. 50*). He spent some time in France.

Sommaruga, Giuseppe (1867–1917). Architect, born in Milan. He studied at the Brera and was influenced by the Viennese Seccessionist master Otto Wagner. He went on to become one of the great exponents of the Liberty (Art Nouveau) style in Italy.

Spadini, Armando (1883–1925). Painter, born near Florence, and who died in Rome. Intimate family scenes of everyday life are characteristic of his works, and he was clearly influenced by the Impressionists.

Starnina, Gherardo (c. 1354–1413). Painter born in Florence but who also worked in Milan and in Spain.

Stauris, Rinaldo de (15C). Sculptor from Cremona known for his building ornaments in terracotta

Studio BBPR. Studio of architects whose name is made up from the initials of its four members: **Gian Luigi Banfi** (who died at Mauthausen in 1945), **Ludovico Barbiano di Belgiojoso**, **Enrico Peressutti**, and **Ernesto Nathan Rogers**. They started their practice in Milan in 1932 and carried out important works all over Italy. A number of their designs can be seen in Milan: Torre Velasca and Castello Sforzesco are two examples. The studio was famous for its urban architecture until the 1970s.

Terragni, Giuseppe (1904–43). Architect. Terragni was active in CIAM, the main forum for propagating the ideas of International Modernism. A committed Rationalist and dedicated Fascist. There are good examples of his work in Como.

Thorvaldsen, Bertel (c. 1770–1844). Danish sculptor and restorer who from 1797 was Canova's main rival in Rome, where he became president of the Accademia di San Luca and where he restored a number of Classical statues in the Vatican collections. He also worked for Napoleon in Lombardy and Piedmont. His Neoclassical works often include plaster or stucco friezes and bas-reliefs. He made a bust of Lord Byron, and Goethe asked him to carve a funerary portrait of his son.

Tibaldi, Pellegrino (1527–96). Sculptor and architect, the son of a stonemason. He worked for many years in Rome, where he enjoyed important patronage. He met Charles Borromeo in 1561 and from that time on was employed to restore, rebuild and enlarge a great number of churches and other buildings, in his characteristic sober, elegant style.

Tiepolo, Giovanni Battista (1696–1770). The most important fresco painter in Venice in the 18th century. He received many commissions from aristocratic patrons and from the Church. He was a follower of Veronese, and his Rococo decorative style, with many charming details, was particularly well suited to ceilings. His son, **Gian Domenico Tiepolo** (1727–1804) worked with him but later developed his own style, more interested in scenes of contemporary social life.

Tintoretto, Jacopo (Jacopo Robusti, c. 1519–94). Painter, born in Venice. He was a prolific and daring painter, creating religious scenes of drama and fervour, made intense by a wonderful use of light and with intense contrasts produced between the illuminated areas and those in shadow. He had a large *bottega* and also passed on his skills to his son **Domenico Tintoretto** (c. 1560–1635).

Titian (Tiziano Vecellio, c. 1485–1576). Successor to Giovanni Bellini as the most important painter in Venice. He was painting when the Serenissima was at the height of her power and received numerous commissions, both for devotional images and for portraits, a genre at which he excelled. He revolutionised painting in his adoption of the canvas (as opposed to wooden) support. Titian was in demand not only at home but in most of the Italian courts of the day and his patrons included the papacy, Habsburg emperors and Philip II of Spain.

Urbino, Carlo (c. 1525–85). Painter, born in Crema. He left behind numerous Renaissance altarpieces. He is frequently to be found working alongside the Campi brothers.

Vermiglio, Giuseppe (1587–after 1635). Painter, born in Piedmont. He studied in Rome, where he was greatly inspired by the work of Caravaggio. He worked mainly in his native Piedmont and in Lombardy.

Veronese (Paolo Caliari, 1528–88). Painter, born in Verona, hence his nickname, although he worked and achieved fame in Venice and its territory. Although a devout Catholic, he was also interested in secular subjects and his elegant, colourful figures are often sumptuously dressed. He frequently included painted architectural elements in his works. He had a great influence on succeeding generations, including Tiepolo.

Vespino, Il (Andrea Bianchi, 16–17C). Painter and imitator of Leonardo da Vinci, of whose paintings he made some direct copies.

Viani, Antonio Maria (c. 1555–1635). Painter and architect from Cremona, where he studied under Giulio Campi. After a period working at the court in Bavaria, where he absorbed Mannerist ideas, he returned to Lombardy in 1591 and soon established an important position at the Mantuan court of Vincenzo I Gonzaga.

Vivarini, Antonio (c. 1415–84). Venetian painter, a contemporary of Giovanni Bellini. He was the master of his brother, **Bartolomeo Vivarini** (1450–99) and brother-in-law of Giovanni d'Alemagna. The brothers are known for their altarpieces and other devotional images.

Wiligelmus (12C). Sculptor known only from his name carved on the exterior of Modena cathedral but recognised as an early medieval master.

Zavattari family. At least four generations of painters and stained-glass workers belonged to this family, all of whom worked in the area of Milan and Pavia. The founder of the dynasty was **Cristoforo** (whose presence is recorded in the late 14th century in the work site of the Duomo of Milan). His son **Franceschino** (who was in Monza also earlier, in 1420) is referred to as *dominus magister* in the contract for the work in the Chapel of Theodolinda the duomo there, in which his sons **Gregorio** and **Giovanni** must have collaborated.

Zenale, Bernardino (c. 1450–1526). Painter, also known as Bernardo Zenale. Born in Treviglio, where there is a polyptych by his hand in the duomo. He often collaborated with Bernardino Butinone.

Lombardy Chronology

c. 400 BC Arrival of the Insubres, Gaulish Celts, in the Lombardy region

218 BC The Romans found Cremona

220 BC The Romans found *Ticinum* (modern Pavia)

222 BC Milan (*Mediolanum*) comes under Roman control

c. 70 BC Virgil is born near Mantua

49 BC *Laus Pompeia* (Lodi Vecchio) becomes a Roman town

AD 286 Diocletian divides his empire into four, making Milan one of its capitals

313 Constantine's Edict of Milan puts an end to the persecution of Christians

374 St Ambrose becomes bishop of Milan

388 St Ambrose writes a letter comparing the towns of northern Italy to 'crumbling corpses'

401 Invasion of Visigoths leads the emperor Honorius to move his seat of administration from Milan to Ravenna

452 Milan sacked by the Huns

476 Fall of the Western Roman Empire. Power is assumed by the Ostrogoths under Odoacer

489 Theodoric wrests power from Odoacer in Lombardy and makes Pavia his capital

524 Boethius, the Roman statesman and poet, is brutally killed at Pavia by order of Theodoric

568 Arrival of the Lombards in Italy. They capture Milan the following year

572 The Lombards make Pavia their capital

595–602 The Lombard queen Theodolinda and her husband Agilulf renounce Arianism for Nicene Christianity

603 The Lombards destroy Cremona

724 The Lombard king Liutprand brings the relics of St Augustine to Pavia

774 Charlemagne, King of the Franks, defeats the last Lombard king, Desiderius

800 Charlemagne is crowned Holy Roman Empire and asserts authority over the whole region

10th–12th centuries Gradual assertion of autonomy by city states, often at war with one another, often either siding with the Holy Roman Emperor or opposing him

1111 Milan destroys Lodi

1127 Milan destroys Como

1176 Frederick Barbarossa is defeated by the Lombard League and forced to recognise the independence of Lombard cities

1260 Milan comes under the rule of the Guelph Torriani

1273 The Bonacolsi become lords of Mantua

1277 Milan is taken from the Torriani by the Ghibelline Visconti

1296 The Visconti conquer Lecco

1302–11 The Torriani briefly regain power in Milan

1311–95 The Visconti once more emerge as rulers of Milan

1328 The Gonzaga take Mantua from the Bonacolsi

1334 Cremona falls to the Visconti

1335 Como falls to the Visconti

1359 The Visconti conquer Pavia

1361 The Law School of Pavia receives University status

1395 Gian Galeazzo Visconti becomes the first Duke of Milan. He founds the Certosa di Pavia the following year

1402 Giovanni Maria Visconti is Duke of Milan

1412 Filippo Maria Visconti succeeds to the Dukedom of Milan

1417 The Visconti die out in the male line and power struggles ensue

1425 Branda Castiglioni sets Masolino to work in his home town, Castiglione Olona

1426 Brescia comes under Venetian rule

1428 Venice takes Bergamo from the Visconti

1433 The Holy Roman Emperor Sigismund of Luxembourg makes Gianfrancesco Sforza Marquis of Mantua

1438–40 Battles between Milan and Venice for control of Lake Garda end with Venetian victory

1441 Francesco Sforza marries Bianca Maria Visconti outside Cremona, thus assuring his claim to the Duchy of Milan

1450 Francesco Sforza becomes Duke of Milan

1454 Crema comes under Venetian control; the Peace of Lodi is signed between Milan and Venice, halting further Venetian encroachments

1466 The unpopular Galeazzo Maria Sforza is Duke of Milan

1476 Galeazzo Maria Sforza is assassinated. His son, Gian Galeazzo, succeeds to the Dukedom

1482 Gian Galeazzo Sforza is said to have introduced rice as a crop

1490 Isabella d'Este becomes Marchioness of Mantua. She is the greatest art patron of her day

1494–9 Rule of Ludovico il Moro in Milan. Bramante and Leonardo are at work in Lombardy

1499 The French king claims Milan. Ludovico il Moro is taken into captivity

1499–1535 Power in Milan alternates between France and the Sforza

1509, 1516 The French, under Gaston de Foix, capture Brescia

1510 The first recorded silk mill is opened in Como

1525 Battle of Pavia. French defeat

1530 Federico II Gonzaga is created Duke of Mantua

1535 Death of the last Sforza

1540 The Spanish take control of Milan and its territories, which they retain until 1700. Gaspare da Salò, inventor of the violin, is born on Lake Garda

1556 Vespasiano Gonzaga begins work on his new planned city of Sabbioneta

1567 Monteverdi is born in Cremona

1609 Cardinal Federico Borromeo founds the Biblioteca Ambrosiana

1620 The Sacro Macello of the Valtellina, in which the Catholic townsfolk massacre the Protestants, leads to 20 years of sectarian religious strife

1621 Foundation of the Ambrosiana art academy in Milan

1627–9 Priceless artworks from the Gonzaga collection are sold to Charles I of England

1630–1 Milan suffers a devastating outbreak of plague

1644 Birth of Antonio Stradivari in Cremona

1664 Foundation of the *Gazzetta di Mantova*, Italy's first daily newspaper

1700 War of the Spanish Succession. The Bourbons take control of Milan

1708 The Austrians abolish the Duchy of Mantua

1713 The Treaty of Utrecht awards Lombardy to Austria

1748 Maria Theresa comes to the throne. Her reign sees a period of prosperity and agricultural reform, leading to the expansion of the silk industry

1778 First performance at La Scala

1796 Battle of Lodi, a victory for Napoleon, after which he begins to take possession of Lombardy, incorporating it into his Cisalpine Republic

1797 Donizetti is born in Bergamo

1799 Alessandro Volta, born in Como, develops the 'voltaic pile', an early form of battery

1802 Napoleon forms the Italian Republic, with Milan as its capital

1805 Napoleon crowns himself King of Italy in Milan

1809 Napoleon officially opens the Brera gallery in Milan

1814 Fall of Napoleon

1815 Congress of Vienna. Lombardy is awarded to Austria, who incorporate it into their empire as Lombardy-Venetia

1827 Publication of Manzoni's great novel *I promessi sposi*

1840 Opening of the Milan–Monza railway line, the second in Italy (after Naples–Portici)

1848 *Cinque Giornate* uprising in Milan against Austrian rule. First Italian War of Independence

1849 Brescia mounts its *Dieci Giornate*, a ten-day rebellion against Austrian rule. The Austrians defeat the Italians and usher in another decade of rule

1859 Battles of Magenta and Solferino. Austria suffers heavy losses and loses Milan. Many parts of Lombardy join the Kingdom of Piedmont-Sardinia

1860 Garibaldi's 'Thousand' sets sail for Sicily. The largest contingent is from Bergamo

1861 The Kingdom of Italy is formed under Vittorio Emanuele II

1864 Founding of the Banca Popolare di Lodi, the first co-operative bank in Italy

1866 Mantua joins the Kingdom of Italy

1870s Beginning of an era of rapid industrialisation in and around Milan

1898 Working-class unrest. Low wages and high food prices lead to riots in Milan

1900 Assassination of King Umberto I at Monza

1906 International Exposition in Milan, showcasing the city's industrial prowess

1918 End of WWI. Italy makes important territorial gains from the ruins of Austria-Hungary

1919 Mussolini founds the Fascist movement in Milan

1922 Milan is the starting point for Mussolini's march on Rome

1930 The Design Biennale (precursor of the Triennale) moves from Monza to Milan

1935 A conference on Isola Bella (Lake Maggiore) leads to the brief uniting of Italy with France and Britain against rising Nazi Germany

1939 Signature of the 'Pact of Steel' between Germany and Italy

1943 Air raids cause widespread destruction in Milan. Italy surrenders to the Allies. Germany forms the puppet Republic of Salò on Lake Garda

1945 Mussolini is captured on Lake Como in April and executed

1946 Italy votes to become a republic

1958 The first Milan Fashion Week is held

1969 A terrorist bomb claims many lives in Milan

1974 Another terrorist bomb claims more lives in Brescia

1996 Closure of the last of Milan's steelworks

2011 Milan's Unicredit Tower (231m) becomes the tallest building in Italy

2015 Milan holds the World Expo

2018 Opening of the Prada 'Torre' in Milan

Index

Page references which lead to a more detailed description, or or to the location of an artist's best or most famous work, are given in bold. Numbers in italics are picture references. For fuller entries on many of the artists, architects and sculptors who feature in this guide, refer to the Glossary of Artists on p. 428.

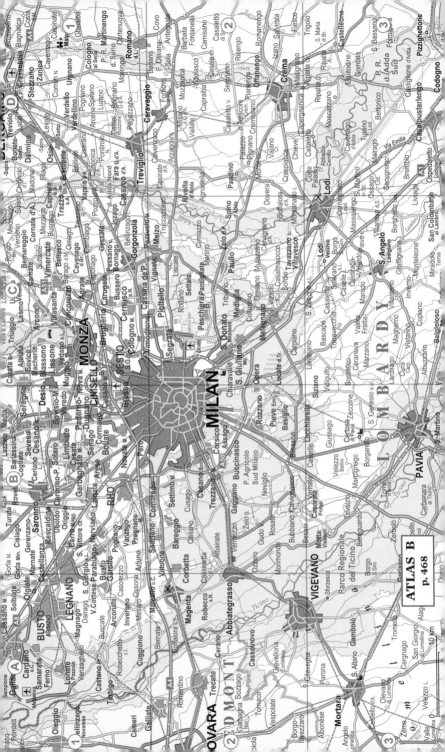

ATLAS A
p. 469

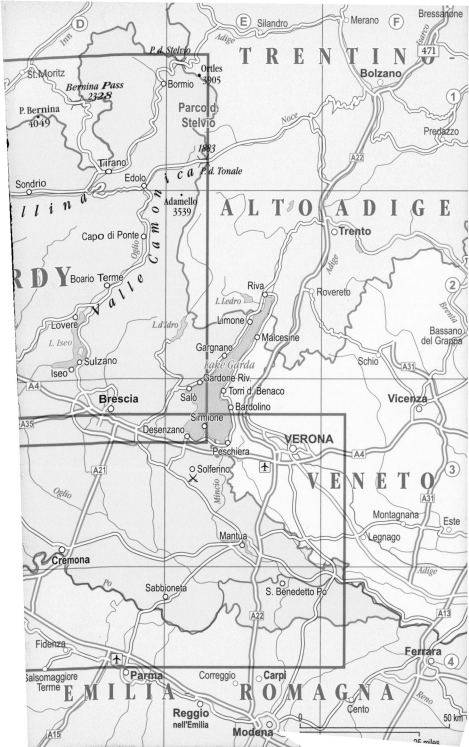